The Online Journalism Handbook

The Online Journalism Handbook has established itself globally as the leading guide to the fast-moving world of digital journalism, showcasing the multiple possibilities for researching, writing and storytelling offered to journalists through new technologies.

In this new edition, Paul Bradshaw presents an engaging mix of technological expertise with real world practical guidance to illustrate how those training and working as journalists can improve the development, presentation and global reach of their story through web-based technologies.

The new edition is thoroughly revised and updated, featuring:

- a significantly expanded section on the history of online journalism business models;
- a new focus on the shift to mobile-first methods of consumption and production;
- a brand new chapter on online media law written by Professor Tim Crook of Goldsmiths, University of London, UK;
- a redeveloped section on interactivity, with an introduction to coding for journalists;
- advice on the journalistic uses of vertical video, live video, 360 and VR.

The Online Journalism Handbook is a guide for all journalism students and professional journalists, as well as being of key interest to digital media practitioners.

Paul Bradshaw established and leads the MA in Data Journalism and the MA in Multiplatform and Mobile Journalism at Birmingham City University, UK and works with the BBC England data unit. He publishes the Online Journalism Blog, founded the investigative crowdsourcing site Help Me Investigate, and is recognised worldwide as one of the leading lights in online journalism, data journalism and social media. His other books include *Finding Stories in Spreadsheets* (2016), *Snapchat for Journalists* (2016), *The Data Journalism Heist* (2015) and *Scraping for Journalists* (2017).

Tim Crook is Professor of Media and Communication, Head of Media Law and Ethics and Radio at Goldsmiths, University of London. He is also Visiting Professor of Broadcast Journalism to Birmingham City University. He has worked professionally in radio, theatre, television and film as a journalist, producer, playwright, director and sound designer for more than 40 years. Throughout this period he has taught media law and ethics to professional journalists and students at all levels.

The Online Journalism Handbook

Skills to Survive and Thrive in the Digital Age

Second edition

Paul Bradshaw

Routledge
Taylor & Francis Group

LONDON AND NEW YORK

Second edition published 2018
by Routledge
2 Park Square, Milton Park, Abingdon, Oxon OX14 4RN

and by Routledge
711 Third Avenue, New York, NY 10017

Routledge is an imprint of the Taylor & Francis Group, an informa business

First edition published by Pearson 2011

British Library Cataloguing-in-Publication Data
A catalogue record for this book is available from the British Library

Library of Congress Cataloging-in-Publication Data
Names: Bradshaw, Paul (Data journalist) author.
Title: The online journalism handbook : skills to survive and thrive in the
digital age / Paul Bradshaw.
Description: Second edition. | London ; New York : Routledge, 2017. |
Includes bibliographical references and index.
Identifiers: LCCN 2017002113 | ISBN 9781138791572 (hardback : alk.
paper) | ISBN 9781138791565 (pbk. : alk. paper) | ISBN 9781315761428
(ebook)
Subjects: LCSH: Online journalism.
Classification: LCC PN4784.O62 B73 2017 | DDC 070.4—dc24
LC record available at https://lccn.loc.gov/2017002113

ISBN: 978-1-138-79157-2 (hbk)
ISBN: 978-1-138-79156-5 (pbk)
ISBN: 978-1-315-76142-8 (ebk)

Typeset in ITC Stone Serif
by Keystroke, Neville Lodge, Tettenhall, Wolverhampton
Printed and bound by CPI Group (UK) Ltd, Croydon, CR0 4YY

Contents

Illustrations

Figures

Table

Acknowledgements

I would like to thank my family for their support and love while writing this book (and because they're cool), as well as the following people who have all had a part to play in its creation: Franzi Baehrle, Robyn Bateman, Martin Belam, Fergus Bell, Crina Boros, Andy Boyle, Malcolm Coles, Sam Coley, Maria Crosas Batista, Matt Burgess, Chase Davis, Laurence Dodds, Pamela Duncan, Amanda Farnsworth, Antia Geada, Alastair Good, Jonny Greatrex, Leila Haddou, Rob Hammond, Ross Hawkes, Jon Hickman, David Holmes, Bella Hurrell, Alessandro Iacovangelo, Kitty Imbert, Brent Jones, Nicolas Kayser Bril, Niall Kennedy, Hedy Korbee, Paul Lashmar, Neil MacDonald, Gurpreet Mann, Barbara Maseda, Christian McDonald, Lisa McLeod, Richard Millington, Robb Montgomery, Nick Moreton, Glen Mulcahy, David Neal, Dan Nguyen, Anna Noble, Joe Norman, Donna Papacosta, Carla Pedret, Meg Pickard, Stephen Quinn, Liisa Rohumaa, Patrick Scott, Michael Smith, Mariah Stewart, Cleland Thom, Einar Thorsen, Joe Tidy, Adam Tinworth, Tom Warren, Thomas Wilburn, Tom Wills and Josh Wilwohl, as well as colleagues past and present at Birmingham City University, and the many students who have inspired me over the years.

1 Introduction to the second edition

What an exciting time. This is a period of enormous creativity and change, a time when young journalists (and many older ones) have a unique opportunity to try new things, learn and grow quickly and innovate in a completely new form of storytelling.

Every year brings new challenges to get to grips with: new technologies to experiment with, new ways of finding and reporting the newsworthy and new debates about our craft to engage in. Online journalism is such an exciting subject – and there is little sign of things settling down anytime soon.

When Alan Rusbridger left the *Guardian* in 2015 after 20 years as editor of the publication, he noted how those two decades had been characterised by ongoing change: 'Twenty years later, we swim in unknown unknowns', he said. Words were 'as likely to be in the form of live blogs as stories'; images were as likely to be still as moving. Audio, interactives, data, graphics and 'any combination of the above' might be needed to tell the story most effectively (Rusbridger 2015).

Since the first edition of *The Online Journalism Handbook*, the 'online' in online journalism has become ever more varied and distributed. 'Online' could mean publishing on the web, or on chat apps. It could mean email newsletters or social media; it could mean getting your stories onto someone's watch, or into their connected speaker or car.

The 'online' in online journalism has also become almost invisible – part of the fabric of *all journalism*. Broadcasters, newspaper reporters and magazine correspondents are all required to engage with audiences through multiple platforms, and to create content for the web and social media. More journalists now work online in the UK than in any other medium – the proportion doubling in just three years between 2012 and 2015 (Thurman et al. 2016).

It is an industry reinventing itself. Thousands of traditional jobs in the industry have disappeared over the last decade – but thousands of roles that didn't exist before have been created too, from data units and video teams to social media managers and community curators. On the surface these organisations may look the same, but in their internal organisation they are unrecognisable from a decade ago: web- and mobile-first, multimedia and multiplatform, data-driven and code-savvy; and converging technically while diverging commercially.

Then there are the new faces: hundreds of online-only startups from BuzzFeed and Vox to Mumsnet and ProPublica have set the pace in exploring new models for publishing and establishing new ways of engaging and serving communities. And increasing numbers of journalists are going outside traditional news organisations to reach a community and raise funding for their reporting directly.

Journalists across the industry have become much more entrepreneurial than was once the case; they are expected to take on many of the responsibilities that a publisher once did. They must make decisions about when and where to publish, take an active role in expanding the distribution of their content and monitor how effective that is. These demands require not just technical and editorial skills around storytelling, but also strategic and project management skills.

Online publishing has brought a global audience to our doorstep, and allowed them to connect with each other and publish themselves, but it has also fragmented them across multiple devices and platforms. News organisations increasingly have to manage relationships with technology companies such as Facebook and Snapchat, while constantly monitoring changes in the algorithms of search engines and social platforms, and experimenting in publishing on new connected devices.

A much wider range of organisations now employ individuals within publishing roles. From football clubs and fashion brands to technology platforms and non-profit organisations, the ability to communicate directly with a community and serve their information needs is raising new questions about the role of traditional journalists, and raising the bar for what we expect of professional communicators.

Changes in the second edition

When the first edition of *The Online Journalism Handbook* was published, expectations of journalism online were at their peak. Interactive publishing promised to allow ordinary people to share and check information; to circumvent the information powerbrokers, newspaper proprietors, network executives, media moguls and journalists. By sharing information, it was hoped, people could challenge received wisdom and publish their own version of events; anyone could broadcast 24/7 to the world; share and exchange information in real time, and even defy censorship.

Those expectations have since been tempered by a realism about the threats that the same technologies can help to create: fake news, fake social media accounts and fake commenters; domination by a new breed of media monopoly; widespread surveillance; and threats to the privacy of journalists, readers and sources (challenges which are addressed in the opening chapter on the history of online journalism).

This second edition of *The Online Journalism Handbook* represents an almost complete rewrite from the first edition. The proliferation of social platforms in particular has been recognised in two new chapters: one dedicated to writing for social media platforms, and a second on community and social media management. Liveblogging and mobile journalism now also warrant a separate chapter, and there's an increased focus on techniques for finding and verifying information online.

The chapter on online video now includes specific exploration of live and vertical formats, and the role of drones, virtual reality and 360-degree filming, while the chapter on audio covers a number of new formats. The chapter on interactivity has been expanded significantly to address the increasing number of formats being used in the media to engage readers, from quizzes to chatbots, while also exploring the growing demand for journalists who can code.

Journalism's role in a networked age

Throughout the book I attempt to address the question of what journalism is for, in an age when anyone can publish directly to an audience; and when information is free and abundant. In particular, it focuses on four roles of journalism that have seen increased importance in a networked age.

The first is journalism's role in giving a *voice to the voiceless*: with such abundance of information it is easier than ever to overlook those who do not have the ability or access to publish their stories online. In fact, there is a term for this tendency: *nodocentrism*. As Ulises Mejias describes it: 'If something is available in the network, it is perceived as part of reality, but if it is not available it might as well not exist' (Mejias 2010, p.612). Mobile journalism, covered in Chapter 6, makes it easier than ever for journalists to get out into the physical world and digitise the stories that exist there. In a networked world there is no reason for the journalist to be restricted to a desk.

A second and related need is to *make the hidden findable*. Not everything online is easy to find: as Chapter 3 explains, there are parts of the web which are hidden to search engines, stories which are scattered across hundreds of pages, or which only come into focus when gathered from a range of sources and combined. Journalists have the ability to shine a spotlight on these corners, and make it easier for others to dig deeper into them. Data journalism and interactivity, each of which is given its own chapter, now make it easier to identify problems which affect communities, and personalise a user's experience to highlight how it affects them.

The third role of the networked journalist is *to connect communities*. The algorithms of search engines and social media make it easier than ever to search for – and find – information which confirms our own biases (what is called 'confirmation bias'). Journalists have always acted as go-betweens, carrying messages between those exercising power and those who are subject to it, or reporting on trends and innovations to those who need to know about them. This is recognised in the increasing role of community management, covered in Chapter 12, and video and audio, which can help bring us closer to communities we are separated from. If there is a risk that communities become more isolated in their own 'filter bubbles', it is vital that journalists remember that their role is to stand outside those bubbles – and poke holes in them.

The fourth role centres on *verification and debunking*. The proliferation of propaganda, hoaxes and 'fake news' represents one of the challenges of our time. Under pressure to react and report in real time, it is easier than ever to pass on false information without realising it. But it is also easier than ever to check and debunk the same falsehoods. Some key techniques for this are outlined in Chapters 3 and 6.

I hope that this book gives you the tools, techniques and inspiration you need as you grow as a journalist online. This is your time, and the challenges and opportunities are yours to take on and make the most of. Good luck, and enjoy it.

Bibliography

The access date for web material is 20 February 2017 unless otherwise given.

Mejias, Ulises. The limits of networks as models for organizing the social, *New Media & Society* 12(4), 2010: 603–619, http://journals.sagepub.com/doi/abs/10.1177/1461444809341392?rss=1&

Rusbridger, Alan. 'Farewell, readers': Alan Rusbridger on leaving the Guardian after two decades at the helm, *Guardian*, 29 May 2015, www.theguardian.com/media/2015/may/29/farewell-readers-alan-rusbridger-on-leaving-the-guardian accessed 6 June 2015

Thurman, Neil, Cornia, Alessio and Kunert, Jessica. *Journalists in the UK*, Reuters Institute for the Study of Journalism, 2016, http://reutersinstitute.politics.ox.ac.uk/publication/journalists-uk

2 Histories, futures and the changing business and technologies of journalism

Chapter objectives

This chapter will cover:

- How key events in the history of online journalism have shaped journalism today
- The shift from desktop to mobile
- The rise of 'platform publishing' – and concerns over the power of those platforms
- Sensor journalism
- Automation and 'robot journalism'
- Debates over the business model that might support journalism online
- The increasing role of analytics in journalism – and the debate over metrics
- Information security: how journalists can protect their stories and sources
- Future developments in journalism and their potential effect.

Introduction

> History doesn't repeat itself – but it does rhyme.

It is fair to say that 'internet time' operates at a different speed to developments elsewhere. Companies rise and fall, trends come and go and the focus is forever on the imminent, pressing, near future: 'What's next?'

Surrounded by this change it can be tempting to ignore the past. But understanding the past is one of the best ways to understand where we are right now – and what is most likely to happen next.

If you are one of those people who asks, 'What technologies should we be looking out for next?' then this chapter is for you. The path to that future has already started: not just histories of technologies, but the history of cultural change, commercial change and legal change.

It is often said that 'The future is already here – it is just unevenly distributed'. Many of the features of our future are already here – if you know where to look. And so, much of the 'history' of online journalism explored in this chapter has actually yet to take place in every part of the media industry, with the same lessons being learned over and over again in different publications. The newspaper sector, for example, has often been the first to experience the impacts of technological change – and also among the first to innovate in response. Many magazines and broadcast organisations are only now beginning to adapt to similar, albeit delayed, effects. And in different countries and at different speeds, similar transformations are repeating themselves.

You may find yourself in an organisation that decides to experiment with a paywall, or crowdfunding. You may be hired as part of a new data journalism or wearable tech unit; or join a newsroom which is going mobile-first or platform publishing. You will find useful stories about all these in this chapter.

How did we get here?

While the technology of mass communication advanced after the Second World War the tools of the trade remained the same right up to the 1980s: a notebook, a pen, a typewriter, two sheets of paper, a 'black' (photocopy paper) and a metal spike.

A typed report went to the printers where experts in movable type (of the kind pioneered by 15th century publisher Johannes Gutenberg) would ensure it rolled out on huge printing presses before being distributed by air, rail, ship, lorry and newspaper boy. Corrections were done on the 'stone' where demarcation of duties meant journalists had to ask printers to literally move lumps of hot metal typesetting under extreme pressure of deadlines and financial penalties. Of course, if the story wasn't good enough the editor had his own archive system – the spike.

Now, the tools of the trade have changed: a story can be published and distributed online instantaneously from a laptop computer or phone. And the word 'spike' seems as antiquated as the metal em rulers once used by sub-editors to lay out pages.

When journalists were first given personal access to the internet the response was positive. Email allowed them to be good at something they liked to do: talk to each other. In the early 1990s most journalists got their first introduction to the internet via email, intranets, newsletters and basic information sites. Few could have predicted how this new medium, characterised by global reach and interactivity, would provide exciting new opportunities while at the same time helping to undermine the industries in which they worked.

Big media was confident. Newspapers had survived new technological innovations previously, adapting in response to the spread of radio and television. Journalists and proprietors were still in charge of content and distribution. The business model for print media had stayed the same for over a century. The choice for the consumer was clear: you bought a paper or magazine, switched on the TV or tuned in to a radio station. And yet those at the centre of news or the millions affected by it had little voice, just the slim chance of being quoted by a reporter or having an opinion broadcast as a soundbite.

Some journalists, many of them savvy technology specialists, were aware that this was just the start. Tim Berners-Lee, at the European Centre for Nuclear Research (CERN), was developing a computer language and address system that would lead to the launch in 1991 of what would be called the World Wide Web, later just 'the web'. The web allowed *links* between documents using *hypertext*, and the two – linking and documents – would form the foundation of publishing online.

Soon 'the web' and 'the internet' would be used interchangeably, but the internet, of course, was a much older technology. Developed using technologies which had their origin in the space race of the late 1950s and early 1960s, the internet was a 'network of networks' which allowed computers to speak to each other. Email, which had been around since the 1970s, used the internet, and later some mobile apps would connect directly to the internet; but webpages and websites used the web (confusingly, this included services such as Hotmail, that provided a web interface for email).

By 1993 the web had taken off with the introduction of Mosaic, the first web browser that could display text as well as graphics, and within a few years journalists were using the web for work, media outlets were experimenting with the medium and some individuals were starting to set up their own websites. The US took the lead and the White House was one of the first information portals. It was also one of the web addresses that gave journalists their first taste of the vagaries of the net. A simple search often led them not to the government site but to one of the new upstart sites from the area that was to make the most money from the internet – the porn industry.

Early adopters

The first incarnation of online journalism came in the form of bulletin boards, electronic newsletters and paid-for information services. Early pioneers worked for outlets such as OnLine Today and The Source.

However, mainstream media was still slow to embrace the web and appeared to have a 'you go first' policy. A notable exception in the UK was the *Daily Telegraph*, which launched what it called the *Electronic Telegraph* in 1994. A year earlier a team at the University of Florida's journalism school laid claim to the launch of the first journalism site (at the same time the US allowed commercial traffic on the internet) but it was left to other industries to demonstrate the capabilities and potential of the internet. In 1995 search engine Yahoo! opened for business as did the bookseller Amazon and the ads site Craigslist. This year also signalled the start of online shopping and the auction site eBay.

Some of that entrepreneurial zeal rubbed off on a self-styled libertarian called Matt Drudge who founded an email newsletter which he would later transform into one of the most influential and notorious news aggregation sites. Detractors criticised him for his mix of news and gossip. But Drudge was more concerned by the practicalities of web journalism. He told Sky News in 2007 the secret of his website was 'To keep it going'. Today, drudgereport.com, which broke one of web journalism's first scoops – the news of Bill Clinton's affair with Monica Lewinsky – still attracts millions of visitors.

Dotcom boom and bust

By the late 1990s most journalists were adept at getting their information online even if they were not working on a website. Newspapers, magazines, TV and radio organizations had websites run by small teams and presented them as a showcase for their brand. The majority of articles were cut-and-paste content from the parent organisation, creating an impression that online journalism was just 'shovelware'.

BBC Online, launched in 1997, was a natural destination for many but there were other webzines and sites (many with a technology or business bent) such as The Register, The Street, Slashdot, Salon and Slate, making innovations in news delivery and allowing readers a say in forums.

Salon, in particular, staffed by former journalists of the *San Francisco Examiner*, demonstrated that print journalists could reinvent themselves. During a strike in 1994 a few of them had taught themselves HTML and launched an online newspaper marketed as a 'smart tabloid'. Its conversational tone and forums pointed to a new relationship between the journalist and reader, a sense of community.

The success of these start-ups undoubtedly helped to galvanise newspapers' online strategies and persuade them to invest more in terms of technology and staff. Several nationals in the UK including the *Guardian* and the *Financial Times* invested millions in their online 'product'.

However, there were other key factors behind this confidence:

- Sites could make money through adverts and subscriptions
- Search engines such as Google contributed to a surge in traffic and new, untapped markets
- Papers started to see classified adverts migrate to the web
- Open source technology allowed people to create content such as blogs cheaply
- Market confidence in e-commerce spurred stock prices
- Venture capitalists backed online projects hoping for the next Amazon.

But this speculative bubble was to burst. By 2001 many enterprises had spent too much, produced no profits and gone bust. Revenue from the net was minuscule in comparison to that delivered by newspapers.

Web 2.0 and the rise of participatory media

Online journalism's next big change would be cultural, not merely technological. The web was entering a phase of mass adoption and a raft of new websites were making it increasingly easy for users to publish themselves. Blogger, Wikipedia, MySpace and Flickr were among the new platforms that characterised a phase summed up in the term 'Web 2.0'. Facebook and YouTube followed soon after.

The terrorist attacks on New York in September 2001 provided one of the earliest demonstrations of this shift: as news websites crashed under demand from users, people turned instead to blogs which passed on information about survivors. The Iraq War in 2003, the Asian tsunami in 2004 and the London Underground bombings in 2005 further demonstrated the appetite for information on the web and the agility of the medium to respond in real time. In 2004 Dan Gillmor documented the changes in his book *We the Media*: 'Via emails, mailing lists, chat groups, personal web journals – all nonstandard news sources – we received valuable context that the major American media couldn't, or wouldn't, provide', he wrote (Gillmor 2004, p.x).

Journalists began to blog themselves and track what was happening on the blogosphere using sites such as Technorati. Where once they kept up with the news by reading what other journalists had to say they now had to also keep up with news, analysis, opinion and agendas created by people within their field or community who maintained blogs. And where once they might respond to breaking news events by chasing official sources, they increasingly looked to user-generated content such as social media updates, images, audio and video.

Blogging's impact on online journalism

Blogging had such a significant impact on journalism that it is worth exploring it separately. There are various candidates for the 'first blogger' (including some who pre-date the World Wide Web) and the first 'blog', but the key change came in 1999 when the first blogging services emerged that allowed anyone to create a blog without knowledge of HTML.

Up to that point most blogs were simply lists of links to other useful sites – a feature which remains central to blogging to this day. As well as linking frequently within individual blog posts many blogs feature a static 'blogroll' in their design: a list of links to other blogs the author finds useful, typically displayed in the outside column.

However, as blogs developed in sophistication as a content management system and distribution network, and the medium attracted publicity, people with more professional objectives – including freelance journalists, academics, marketers, activists and independent publishers – started to see the potential of the medium, and it took another direction.

Commercially run blogs, and blog networks, were launched. Some – such as Boing Boing, Perez Hilton and the *Huffington Post* – quickly reached readerships larger than most news websites. Others acted as showcases for their authors' careers in public speaking and consultancy, columns and book deals. Figures such as author Robert Scoble, cartoonist Hugh MacLeod and marketer Seth Godin found a global audience for their work thanks to the distribution networks of the web.

At the same time, the practice of 'blogging' started to outgrow the blog platform itself, becoming embedded in almost every social media platform, from the status updates of Facebook to the microblogging of Twitter. Even Instagram, Tumblr, YouTube and Snapchat are built on the ideas of photoblogging and video blogging. Now 'blogging' is used routinely by celebrities, sportspeople and politicians as a way of communicating directly with audiences, a development which has had significant implications for the journalists who previously acted as middlemen in that process.

The road to convergence

One of the most damaging barriers to progress was the seeming ambivalence of newspapers to their dotcom operations, creating an artificial 'us' and 'them' culture between print journalists and their dotcom colleagues. In the 1990s it was not unusual for web journalists to be given separate contracts, moved to another floor or even another building. (The *New York Times* only moved journalists into the same building in 2007. It was later seen as a model of convergence.) The resulting breakdown in communication, duplication of content and roles impaired the quality of web journalism.

The integrated approach of the last decade, in which journalists worked together, was fashioned out of financial expediency, improvements in technology and the success of sites in generating traffic, new audiences and advertising. Rupert Murdoch's speech in 2005 to the American Society of Newspaper editors warning of complacency is frequently cited as the tipping point for newspapers and attitudes to change in the digital era. He portrayed himself as a 'digital immigrant' and identified the challenge of creating a presence online that people would make their homepage (the first page that opened on their browser every day). Instead of people reading their morning newspaper over a coffee, 'In the future, our hope should be that for those who start their day online, it will be with coffee and our website' (quoted in the *Guardian* 2005).

His speech spurred a change in the working practices of his newspapers and more investment in the *Sun* and *Times* online. Other newspaper groups responded and online journalists welcomed the renewed impetus and momentum to the 'new newsroom'. In 2006 the *Telegraph* and the *Financial Times* rolled out integrated newsrooms with journalists producing content for both platforms.

Cultural convergence

Physical changes in the newsroom were only the first step towards a truly converged strategy. Domingo et al. (2007) identified three more: multiskilled professionals; multi-platform delivery; and active audience. Similarly Garcia-Aviles et al. (2009) identified project scope, newsroom management and journalistic practices as key factors to consider alongside the organisation of the journalists themselves. Regardless of where they sat, many journalists still saw themselves as 'print', 'broadcast' or 'web', and pre-existing production practices driven by the deadlines of the printing press or broadcasting schedule still dominated. Some journalists were reluctant to embrace integration, and few were given training on new ways of producing news. As Rob Minto, interactive editor at the *Financial Times* from 2005–2011, noted: 'The battle was not with the readers, who took data-driven graphics, podcasts and videos as part of the mix. It was with our colleagues, who were already pushed for time' (Minto 2013).

The global financial crisis of 2008, however, was to transform newsrooms further. In that year alone the regional newspaper publisher Northcliffe announced it would cut 1000 jobs from editorial, advertising, printing and distribution staff. MEN Media announced it would cut 150 jobs and closed its weekly editorial offices. On the nationals 65 editorial jobs went from News International titles, 80 from the *Financial Times* and 100 from the *Independent* (*Telegraph* 2008).

As more jobs went, news organisations increasingly created new multiplatform and digital roles to replace them. Future's announcement of 100 job losses in 2011 was described as 'a move favouring digital over print' (Halls 2011). Two years later when they cut a further 55 jobs they explained: 'As Future becomes an increasingly digital business, we need to reduce costs and staff levels devoted to print products' (Smith, P. 2013).

In 2013 *Trinity Mirror* cut 92 posts but created 52 new ones, including 12 'community content curators', and 8 regional digital roles. The *Telegraph* cut 80 editorial staff but also announced it would create 50 'new digitally focused jobs'. The following year it created a further 40 roles, focusing on investigative, data, interactive and video, and with a new breaking news team.

In broadcast the BBC got rid of 415 staff but created 195 new posts as part of plans to be 'at the forefront of producing news for the digital age using new technologies' (BBC 2014). And in magazines *Immediate Media* was up front about its desire to encourage 'naysayers' to leave as it cut around 150 staff, but hired 300. 'The focus has been on building a new generation of tech-savvy staff', it said, 'chiefly in the areas of digital, technology, e-commerce and database marketing' (Reynolds and Sweney 2014).

The trend was clear: as customers and advertising moved into digital, publishers wanted to be there too. Time Inc.'s senior vice president of digital went as far as to say 'We are not a magazine company. We are a media company with a portfolio. We want to build the next LinkedIn' (Cardew 2014).

Despite these changes, by 2016 surveys in converged newsrooms in six European countries suggested that full convergence was still some way away: there was a clear imbalance in time spent on serving different platforms and although a shift had taken place from print to convergence culture, 'Investing time to produce content that makes use of the digital channels' interactivity and innovative formats does not find its way into the standard repertoire of daily work' (Menke et al. 2016, p.14).

The impact of web-only publishers

At the same time as traditional publishers were getting to grips with the early stages of convergence, a new wave of online-only news outlets was launching without the baggage of expensive printing or broadcasting legacies.

Gawker Media, the *Huffington Post* and BuzzFeed launched in the US in 2003, 2005 and 2006 respectively and were to have a massive impact on the wider industry, including on employment practices and pay. In 2008, for example, Gawker announced that it was launching a payment system based on the frequency and popularity of writers' posts. A specific number of posts was set each month for 'base' pay, with further bonuses based on target pageviews (Boutin 2008).

The *Huffington Post* launched with dozens of celebrity contributors, but soon invited unpaid contributors to publish blog posts on its platform, too. When in 2011 the company was sold to AOL for $315 million many bloggers felt that their contribution had been exploited. They launched the Facebook group 'Hey Arianna, Can You Spare a Dime?' to campaign for founder Arianna Huffington to share some of the windfall, while the journalists' union America's Newspaper Guild demanded that some of the money be invested in paid journalism. A lawsuit was brought on behalf of thousands of uncompensated bloggers, but dismissed the following year. BuzzFeed also invited users to contribute content to its site, without payment, providing community guidelines and tools to help users create quizzes and checklists.

Traditional publishers began to follow suit. The *Guardian* was quick to imitate the *Huffington Post* in launching the contributor-driven Comment is Free section in 2006, and in 2009 regional publisher Northcliffe Media sought to build 40 websites driven by user content with the launch of its hyperlocal LocalPeople network. By 2012 the chief executive of the regional newspaper publisher Johnston Press was announcing that he was aiming for half of the content of their titles to be created by 'citizen contributors' by 2020, by which time he expected 'few daily print products' to still be publishing (Pugh 2012).

The magazine world was also quick to see the opportunity to get free content in exchange for 'prestige' and 'exposure'. Forbes launched a 'contributor platform', which paid contributors based on the number of people reading their work. 'The bigger their loyal audience the more they make', chief product officer Lewis D'Vorkin explained in 2013. 'Others find reward in association with the Forbes brand' (Smith, C. 2013). But 60 per cent of contributors weren't paid (Bilton 2014), and in 2016 Forbes was forced to launch an investigation after suggestions were made that one contributor had asked a PR company for £300 in order to write about their client. Other publications launching platforms for contributors (with only some getting paid) included *Entertainment Weekly* and *Condé Nast Traveler,* and a new term was being coined to refer to them: *platishers* (Glick 2014): 'platform publishers'.

Analytics-driven publishing also led to new pressures on reporters. In 2015 Trinity Mirror tried to introduce web traffic targets for individual journalists as part of new job descriptions, but later shelved the plans in the face of possible industrial action. There were two strong arguments against the move: first, that reporters would end up writing easier but less important stories rather than stories which might be more important but take more time to report, or which might not have such broad appeal. Second, there were concerns that a story's traffic could be influenced by a number of factors, many of which were not within the reporter's control.

Community-driven

Also relying heavily on volunteer contributions was the growing number of *hyperlocal* news websites, catering for a smaller audience than traditional regional publishers, and often built around blogging technology. For these contributors, however, it was not necessarily exposure or prestige that motivated them to report, but rather the 'different kinds of direct and indirect reciprocal exchange' (Harte et al. 2016) that allowed them to contribute to their local community, and vice versa. Likewise the majority of publishers did not earn a living from their publication, but rather saw it as a form of community participation or active citizenship (Radcliffe 2015).

In the UK over 400 hyperlocal websites had been counted by 2015, compared to 1045 local newspapers, and one in ten people were using these services on a weekly basis (Radcliffe 2015).

In addition to hyperlocal news operations there were many special interest publications adopting a similar user-driven approach. Mumsnet was perhaps the best-known example of this: launched as a basic forum for parents to exchange information and tips in 2000, it built such an enormous audience that by 2009 the leaders of UK political parties were lining up to be interviewed in webchats, and the site has since launched a number of high-profile campaigns. In the US the forum reddit had followed a similar trajectory, being acquired by magazine publisher Condé Nast in 2006.

What many of these new sites had in common was a desire to serve a specific community by providing a platform for that community to speak to itself. Instead of hiring journalists to fill pages of content, they instead hired community managers who could stimulate discussion, recruit contributors – and create content too (see Chapter 12 for more). Those who didn't convince people to contribute, failed: LocalPeople sites set out to attract 75 per cent of the local online audience, but only managed between 0.7 per cent and 4.6 per cent (Thurman et al. 2012), and many sites were closed. In the US hyperlocal network Patch.com was sold to AOL in 2009 which expanded it from 46 to 900 sites in the space of a few years. But reader posts were minimal as the network showed a 'lack of clear engagement with their wider communities [and] an overreliance on official sources' (St John III et al. 2013). By 2013 it had cut staff from 540 to 98, and hundreds of sites had been closed. A controlling stake in the network was sold to Hale Global in 2014.

The rise of data-driven journalism

As computing power, storage capacity and access to databases increased, data became an increasingly important source of stories for journalists. A watershed moment came in 2010, as the year was dominated by stories based on WikiLeaks's data from conflicts in Afghanistan and Iraq, and diplomatic communications.

That data – hundreds of thousands of documents – could now be stored on a memory stick smaller than your finger. And thanks to network connectivity, hundreds of thousands of personnel now had access to such material. The two factors combined to make it much more likely that large collections of data and documents would be leaked to journalists. The datasets behind the 2014 and 2015 'Luxembourg Leaks' and 'Swiss Leaks' stories about tax evasion and avoidance were based on datasets twice as large as WikiLeaks's Cablegate stories. 'Offshore Leaks' in 2013 was 150 times bigger. And the data behind the Panama Papers stories in 2016 was larger than all of those combined.

But it wasn't just leaks, or investigative journalists working on data. New Freedom of Information laws and a growing *open data* movement made it much easier for journalists to access data on everything from politics and the environment to education and culture – or for citizens to get hold of it and highlight stories that journalists should be digging into. The growing availability of structured information online also made it easier for people to turn that data into stories about sport, music and film.

The US, where Freedom of Information laws had existed since the 1960s, had a well-established history of 'computer-assisted reporting' (CAR) – using spreadsheets and databases to find stories in data. But this new internet-based practice of creating stories from data needed a new name. The term 'data journalism' was popularised in part by the *Guardian*'s launch of a 'datablog' in 2009, and in the US by the political data journalism site FiveThirtyEight, founded a year earlier. Data journalism's distinctiveness from CAR lay in the way that it often connected to data directly on the internet; the growth of 'data visualisation', often abbreviated to 'datavis'; and the way that user interactions and interactivity could be built into the storytelling.

A significant amount of data journalism was being created by non-journalists, including designers, developers and statisticians. News organisations and magazines realised they needed to do better when reporting on and using this increasingly important source of stories.

Many news organisations established dedicated data units, and most started recruiting journalists with data journalism skills, particularly at broadsheets including the *Guardian*, *The Times*, *Telegraph* and *Financial Times*, as well as newswires including Reuters and the Press Association. In Northern Ireland data and investigations site The Detail was established in 2011. Two years later Trinity Mirror established a regional newspaper data unit, recognising the work already being done by journalists such as Claire Miller in Cardiff, while at a national level it created the standalone site Ampp3d, which would later be incorporated into the *Mirror* website. Archant created its investigations unit in 2015, and Johnston Press the following year.

The magazine sector soon followed suit, seeing data journalism as a way to distinguish itself from the growing numbers of blogs competing for their audience, with some, such as RBI, selling data services to high-paying customers. The BBC's visual journalism unit created data journalism and interactives for the BBC News site, while BBC England's data unit, based in Birmingham, was established in 2015, and a new data lab to support the regional press and hyperlocal journalism followed soon after. Hyperlocal sites were also innovating around data-driven reporting, with Love Wapping's Mark Baynes scrutinising local spending, and Talk About Local winning funding from Google to build its data-driven Local News Engine tool in 2016.

Sensor journalism and drones

By 2013, a new source of data was making waves in the industry: sensors. *Sensor journalism* projects included a *Sun Sentinel* story about speeding police cars (based on toll-gate sensor data) and the radio station WNYC sending sensors to listeners to help them track cicadas.

One of the biggest opportunities for sensor journalism lay in the pockets of every reader and journalist: mobile phones now contained dozens of sensors recording everything from geolocation and movement to light and background noise.

But other types of sensors were also becoming smaller and cheaper: in sport for example, North America's National Football League announced it would be placing sensors under players' shoulder pads during matches, and *drones* were adding another way of gathering information from hard-to-reach locations using sensors.

Robot journalism and augmented journalism

It wasn't long before companies saw an opportunity to generate stories automatically from the data being generated by certain sources. Automated journalism, or *robot journalism*, relied on predictable sources of data in fields where stories could be written routinely at a scale or speed that human journalists could not match. Early examples included lower league sports matches, crime reports, weather and company financial reports: Reuters had published computer-generated headlines based on the American Petroleum Institute's weekly report as early as 2001 (Stray 2016) while Adrian Holovaty's automated crime map chicagocrime.org in 2005 was a seminal development in data journalism. But in 2013 two companies – Narrative Science and Automated Insights – made particular efforts to introduce the technology into news organisations.

The *LA Times* began using the technology to generate reports on earthquakes based on authoritative sources such as the US Geological Survey, often more quickly than anyone else. Associated Press (AP) used it to generate earnings reports. From 300 corporate earnings stories per quarter the numbers rose to around 4440. Automated Insights' James Kotecki pointed out: '4,100 of these stories would not exist without [robot journalism]' (Lee 2014). In 2016 the Press Association announced that it would use robot reporters to cover sports, football and elections.

In addition to adding increased *scale* to reporting, robot reporting was typically more *accurate*: around 7 per cent of human-written company earning reports at AP contained errors (such as transposed digits) compared to 'only about one percent' (Graefe 2016) when generated automatically.

The technology had its limitations, however. Data could be incomplete, biased or contain errors. Likewise the algorithms used to interpret it might also be subject to problems: one robot reporting on a project in Norway generated a headline which '[celebrated] the poor guy scoring a late own goal as the hero of the game' (Waldal 2016). A report into automated journalism noted that '[a]lgorithms cannot ask questions, explain new phenomena, or establish causality' (Graefe 2016). Journalists would still be needed to observe non-quantified events, and help form public opinion.

The hope was that automated journalism would lead to *augmented journalism*, performing repetitive tasks in order to enable journalists to perform analysis or see patterns that might not be possible without automation. In 2014, for example, Reuters started a project called News Tracer to detect and verify breaking news on Twitter, before creating algorithms to surface trends in polling data in 2015, and an 'automation for insights' system alerting journalists to 'interesting events in financial data' (Stray 2016). One research project explored how a 'data-driven' approach to investigations could provide an alternative to the traditional 'hypothesis-driven' approach, allowing computers to highlight unusual patterns in data rather than relying solely on journalists to decide on the 'story' that they were expecting to find (Broussard 2014).

By 2016 the French newspaper *Libération* was using artificial intelligence to successfully write, schedule and publish updates optimised for social media, and *Le Monde*'s fact-checking team was developing a way to automate the identification of false news. The *Telegraph*'s 'Rob_oblogger' was automating the generation of graphics for football and rugby liveblogs. Two startups Wochit and Wibbitz – were creating hundreds of automatically generated videos every day for customers ranging from Hearst magazines and Gannett newspapers to the Weather Channel, Time Inc., CBS Interactive and the *Huffington Post*. Publishers could choose to let the technology do most of the work or give their human reporter a more active role with some automated suggestions for footage or script based on an original text article.

Automated journalism threw up new ethical challenges. One piece of research by Montal and Reich (2016), for example, highlighted the lack of clear authorship in some pieces, while an analysis of social media 'trend' detection software showed 'biases towards those who are vocal and have an audience, many of whom are men in the media' (Thurman et al. 2016) as well as biases around particular topics and times.

Dorr and Hollnbuchner (2016) outlined an ethical framework around 'algorithmic journalism', suggesting that news organisations and journalists consider issues of accuracy and objectivity, and how it might be possible to exercise transparency and disclosure around the inputs and other elements involved.

The move to mobile-first

Producing for print and web, or broadcast and web, led to newsroom restructures across the industry. But then things were complicated further by the rapid rise of a third platform: mobile.

Commentators had for some time been predicting that mobile would become the dominant way that people consumed news at some point, but the speed with which it happened still took the industry by surprise. In mid-2013 the BBC was noting that at weekends the number of visitors to its website coming from mobiles had overtaken those on their desktops for the first time. Within 12 months most newspaper and magazine publishers were reporting that mobile had become the dominant source of traffic, every day. Another 12 months later, the *Mail Online*, *Express* and *London Evening Standard* were all reporting that mobile users outnumbered desktop users two to one; the *Mirror*'s mobile traffic was more than three times as high as desktop (Ponsford 2015a).

Very quickly, many news organisations decided that they needed to adopt 'mobile-first' publishing strategies. But what did that really mean?

The first challenge was that the term 'mobile' disguised a wide range of devices being used both at home and on the move: from mobile phones and tablets, to 'mini' tablets and larger screen phones sometimes called 'phablets'.

Of course 'mobile' was still 'online', but two factors in particular made mobile-first a different thing altogether to the idea of 'web-first'. The first was screen size and orientation: mobile devices are much smaller than desktop monitors, and are typically viewed vertically (portrait), rather than horizontally (landscape). The second is bandwidth: mobile users, when not using a wifi connection, do not have the luxury of broadband-speed internet connections and are likely to give up if pages load too slowly.

The problem was that publishers had started to rely on users having fast internet connections, and over the years webpages had become more and more bloated as more and more code was added to serve advertisements and trackers, and collect information on user behaviour. One commentator noted, for example, that it took the *Guardian* 55 pages of code to create just one 800-word page of text (Filloux 2016).

This was also a problem – and an opportunity – for internet giants such as Facebook and Google that relied on users being able to access news content on their sites quickly.

In 2015 Facebook launched Instant Articles, a mobile-optimised format which promised to load up to ten times faster than standard web articles. Google followed quickly with its Accelerated Mobile Pages (AMP) format, supported by Twitter, and in the meantime Apple had also joined the game with its mobile-optimised Apple News format.

The major advantage for these companies was that the formats not only improved user experience, but kept users within their own websites and services, and gave them control over new avenues of advertising sales. Both Facebook and Apple initially took 30 per cent of any advertising it sold on stories using the format (publishers were allowed to keep 100 per cent if they sold it themselves); Google didn't take any cut, but required publishers to use one of Google's official partner ad networks.

But gaining access to potentially bigger audiences on Facebook and Apple came with a number of drawbacks. One was data on users: now it had to be shared, and in some cases publishers would have access to less user data than before. Another was functionality: the sort of interactivity enabled by JavaScript, for example (see Chapter 11 for more), was disabled within these formats. But the biggest is simply control: all the formats come with limitations that the publishers have little control over. For example, Facebook limited the number of ads that could be sold based on the number of words. And there was always the possibility that terms would be changed by these platforms later on.

The tension was summed up by grouping the likes of Facebook, Apple and Google under the term 'frenemy': a portmanteau of the words 'friend' and 'enemy'. In other words, these were organisations that might be seen as a potential competitor, but that publishers might still decide to be 'friendly' with – for now. Launch partners for Facebook's Instant Articles, then, included BuzzFeed, the *New York Times*, *National Geographic*, *NBC News*, the *Guardian*, BBC News, *Bild* and *Spiegel Online*. They might not trust the social media giant, but they were prepared to work with it if it meant having an input into the decisions being made.

In the meantime, having a mobile-first strategy meant assuming that a typical reader would be accessing your stories on a mobile device. News website content management systems (CMS) were increasingly designed to be *responsive*: in other words, to 'respond' to the device being used, and display content accordingly. That might mean, for example, that on a mobile device you only see the story whereas someone on a laptop computer might see extra sidebars and related stories; or that fewer images were shown or, typically, images of a smaller size and resolution that load more quickly.

Publishers also focused more on *web performance optimisation* (WPO): making sure pages loaded as quickly as possible. After working with Google on AMP, the *Washington Post* went further by launching a 'progressive web app' to significantly improve its load times.

But mobile-first also meant acknowledging that for a large proportion of readers, the mobile web was the social web: journalists would have to do more to take their content to readers on social platforms like Facebook, Twitter, Instagram and Snapchat.

The rise of platform publishing and distributed content

During an interview for the podcast *Re/code Decode* in 2015 the founder of BuzzFeed, Jonah Peretti, revealed some illuminating statistics. Less than a quarter of BuzzFeed's traffic, he said, came direct to the website or its apps, and only 8 per cent came through Google or Facebook. Of the rest:

- 27 per cent of traffic was views of Facebook-native video
- 21 per cent of traffic involved Snapchat content
- 14 per cent of traffic was views on YouTube
- 4 per cent of views were of images on Facebook
- 3 per cent of views came on other platforms.

This approach has been called 'platform publishing' or 'distributed content': a strategy whereby multiple platforms are used in order to publish directly to audiences. While not the first to adopt such a strategy, BuzzFeed made it a talking point when it announced in 2014 that it would hire 20 new staff to create original content 'solely for platforms like Tumblr, Imgur, Instagram, Snapchat, Vine and messaging apps' as part of a new 'BuzzFeed Distributed' division (BuzzFeed 2014).

An increasing number of publishers were also deciding to do away with a website altogether: the video news company NowThis scrapped its website in 2015 in favour of publishing entirely on social platforms; and when First Look Media launched its social justice news project Reportedly, it did so on Medium, Twitter, Facebook and reddit. 'We don't try to send people away from their favorite online communities just to rack up pageviews', they explained in an announcement (Carvin 2014).

Part of the reason for the shift was that 'native content' (content which was published directly on social media platforms) appeared to perform much better when compared to attempts to get users to follow links to watch or read it on their sites instead. This was partly due to platforms favouring their own content: Facebook, for example, was more likely to show users videos uploaded directly to the site than when users shared YouTube video links instead (Csutoras 2015); native videos were more attractively displayed; and for users it was simply easier to view a native video than to click a link and wait for another site to load. The advantages were not so clear in all situations however: one study of Instant Articles suggested that the format had had little impact on engagement with news content (Hoffman 2015).

Condé Nast International, Vox Media and CNN were among those creating new roles 'to help coordinate and deepen [their] relationships with social media and video platforms, messaging apps and even hardware manufacturers' (Marshall 2016). But managing those relationships and working across multiple platforms involved trade-offs. Brian Fitzgerald, co-founder and president of Evolve Media, told Digiday that shorter form content had become a priority, for example. 'By doing more platform publishing, we have had to sacrifice budget for longer-form content published directly to our site' (Moses 2016).

In a special report on the distributed content landscape, the World Association of Newspapers and News Publishers (WAN-IFRA) compared the rush to the early days of the web, 'when suddenly publishers realised that the internet was about to become a vehicle for content, and raced to provide their information for free' (Pfeiffer 2015a). The report recommended that publishers consider the corporate goals of each platform they are considering publishing on, and how that might impact on their own objectives, as well as each platform's core audience and their information consumption profiles. But it also warned publishers against locking themselves in to Facebook, a related loss of branding and context, and relying too much on superficial metrics (Pfeiffer 2015b).

Platforms become publishers too

While publishers took moves to publish directly on social media platforms, the platforms themselves also began to act more like publishers, hiring journalists, commissioning content and attracting criticism for controversial editorial decisions.

YouTube began as a platform for people to upload videos, but started to behave like a media company within a year of its launch: in 2006 it was making deals with TV companies, in 2007 it was helping users to sell advertising; by 2008 it was partnering with film companies; and it introduced online film rentals in 2010. By 2015 it was 'setting up TV-style production deals with some of its most popular creators' and commissioning four original series (Cooper 2015).

Snapchat was equally quick to enter the media production game: launching, closing, then relaunching channels and stories on its platform in 2015, and joining with the Tribeca Film Festival to sponsor a competition in 2016 for filmmakers to use Snapchat (the best work was published on Snapchat itself later that year). It also launched an online technology magazine, *Real Life*. Perhaps most interesting was the company's reported desire to move away from allowing publishers to sell their own advertising and instead to pay them a flat licence fee up front. 'It's the same model that TV networks use when they buy programming', noted one report (Kafka 2016).

The blog hosting platform Medium was acquiring and commissioning content from the time of its launch in 2013, when it acquired the longform reporting site Matter while still in closed beta. In 2014 it hired tech writer Steven Levy; in 2015 it commissioned its first video series and partnered with *Esquire* magazine to create a sponsored publication; and in 2016 it began courting publishers with custom tools and 'two new ways that publishers can opt in to earn revenue on Medium' (Medium 2016): promoted stories; and membership.

Other social networks decided to buy content in other ways: Twitter paid $10 million in April 2016 for the rights to stream ten National Football League games; and two months later Facebook, Instagram and NBC announced a deal to show Olympics highlights on the platforms.

A number of stories about Facebook, in particular in 2016, highlighted how it was moving into traditional publishing territory. The first was the revelation that Facebook was employing journalists to curate its Trending Topics section, rather than leaving it to algorithms. The reports led to claims of bias, and Facebook moved quickly to fire the team (this in turn led to a new 'fake news' problem – see p.38). But perhaps a more significant story was that the company was commissioning over $50 million of content for its site from dozens of media companies and celebrities, as it tried to increase the volume of video on the site.

Wearable tech, glance journalism and the Internet of Things

While publishers focused on an increasing number of social platforms, new frontiers were being opened outside the web, in the sphere broadly referred to as the *Internet of Things* (IoT).

Wearable technology (referred to as 'wearable tech') had been around for years before the launch of Google Glass and the Apple Watch in 2013 and 2015 respectively, but the involvement of the two technology giants made publishers take notice. VICE's Tim Pool used Google Glass to report on protests in Turkey in 2013, while Voice of America created a series of special reports using it to report live from events including concerts, and the *Manchester Evening News*'s Alex Hibbert used it to report from a supermarket on Black Friday. The *Guardian* and Cable News Network (CNN) were among those launching apps that users could install on the device.

Although the technology failed to take off, soon the idea was being resurrected by Snapchat when it launched its 'Spectacles' three years later, while the Oculus Rift virtual reality headset – bought by Facebook – introduced a different type of wearable technology for news organisations to get to grips with.

Apple's smartwatch, meanwhile, saw the coining of a new phrase: *glance journalism*, named after the 'glance' feature that allowed Apple Watch users to skim through notifications. The *Financial Times* had already launched a 24-hour news app on the Samsung Gear S smartwatch in 2014 and ESPN had created a sports alert app for the fitness bracelet Jawbone, but news organisations launching apps specifically designed for the Apple device included the *Wall Street Journal*, *New York Times*, *Time* magazine and the *Guardian*, which called its watch app 'Moments'. Design focused on the *glance-optimised headline* (GOH), made to be consumed in the small amount of text that might be taken in with a glance at your watch, as well as the ability to move content to the user's phone, and vice versa.

The next platform to open up was the *connected home*. This time it was Amazon leading the way for publishers, with its connected speaker Echo, launched in the US in 2014. Powered by its voice recognition technology Alexa, the speaker was able to recognise users' commands and, among other things, provide information in return – including audio news updates using its Flash Briefings feature, and narrated responses to questions using the Skills feature.

It was a couple of years before Echo began to attract significant interest from the news industry, but the turning point came in 2016: the *Guardian* was a launch partner as the device was launched in the UK, making its podcasts available on the device, as well as news, opinion and reviews. The *Washington Post* created features to answer questions around politics and that year's Olympics; the *Daily Mail* and BBC were among other news organisations to make news available on the device. Google launched its own competitor Google Home the same year, with the *Huffington Post*, Lonely Planet, Product Hunt, *Wall Street Journal* and CNBC among media organisations working on the platform.

With the workplace long since connected through desktop computers, mobile phones and wearable technology connecting people on the move, and connected speakers listening at home, there was only one place left: the car.

Like wearable tech, connected cars had been around for years, initially with limited applications for news media and connectivity largely limited to navigation, diagnostics and, later, entertainment. But by 2011 cars were being quietly referred to as 'the fifth screen' (the first four being cinema, TV, computers and phones) and media organisations were starting to pay attention. As with the connected home, the biggest opportunity appeared to be in the untapped field of online audio. David Callaway, editor-in-chief of

USA Today, noted that the publishers expected a new form of cars to emerge 'with radically different audio systems and more interactive experience. They will need a lot of content' (Huang 2015).

And as with the connected home, and the development of Apple's Siri and the artificial intelligence (AI) technologies underpinning all of these, a broader development was becoming clear, too: alongside the keyboard, mouse and touch, 'voice' was going to become one of the major ways that users interacted with the news.

TIMELINE OF WEB JOURNALISM

- 1991: Tim Berners-Lee releases World Wide Web browser and server software
- 1994: *Daily Telegraph* launches Electronic Telegraph
- 1994: Launch of Drudge Report. Founder Matt Drudge breaks first big online scoop in 1998 with Monica Lewinsky story
- 1997: Launch of BBC Online
- 1999: Pyra Labs creates Blogger, free software that allows anyone to set up their own blog
- 2001: Readers flood websites for news following terrorist attacks of September 11
- 2001: The *Guardian* publishes minute-by-minute coverage of sports events, a process which would later be described as 'liveblogging'
- 2002: US Senate Republican Leader Trent Lott stands down after bloggers pick up remarks ignored by mainstream press
- 2003: Invasion of Iraq: Salam Pax, the 'Baghdad Blogger', posts updates from the city as it is bombed, providing a particular contrast to war reporters 'embedded' with the armed forces and demonstrating the importance of non-journalist bloggers
- 2003: Christopher Allbritton raises $15,000 through his blog Back-to-Iraq 3.0, to send him to report independently from the war, demonstrating the ability of blogs to financially support independent journalism (called the 'tip-jar model')
- 2004: Rathergate/Memogate: CBS anchorman Dan Rather resigns after bloggers raise questions about accuracy of CBS report on George W. Bush's National Guard service
- 2004: Asian tsunami on Boxing Day demonstrates reach of web from inaccessible areas as images and video are published to web from mobile phones
- 2005: Podcasts take off as iTunes adds them to its jukebox
- 2005: Rupert Murdoch tells newspaper industry that it has been slow to respond to digital developments. Buys social networking site MySpace
- 2005: July 7 Bombings, London: mobile phone image of passengers walking along a Tube tunnel posted on MoBlog and the *Sun*, and goes global from there. A significant moment in moblogging
- 2007: Talking Points Memo blog breaks story of US attorneys being fired across the country, demonstrating the power of 'crowdsourcing': involving readers in an investigation, and carrying it out in public

- 2007: Mainstream media reports Virginia Tech massacre using information from Facebook and other social networking sites
- 2007: Myanmar protests are tracked via blogs and social networking sites as journalists blocked entry
- 2008: News of a Chinese earthquake spreads via Twitter
- 2008: Journalists look to Twitter as a tool after terrorist attacks in Mumbai, India are reported in real time by the microblogging service
- 2010: Citizen journalism site iReport is used to track and connect relatives after the Haiti earthquake
- 2010: WikiLeaks works with news organisations on a series of major stories. The Iraq and Afghanistan war logs and Cablegate dominate the year and contribute to a broader interest in data journalism
- 2010: Online news consumption and advertising surpasses print for the first time in the US
- 2011: Amazon launches the Kindle Singles format, kickstarting interest in e-publishing 'longform' journalism of a greater length than traditional feature articles
- 2012: The *New York Times* 'immersive' story Snow Fall is published, marking a broader move online towards longform journalism aimed at tablet users
- 2013: Edward Snowden leaks information about global surveillance operations to the *Guardian*, triggering a debate about information security and highlighting the difficulty of protecting sources and whistleblowers
- 2013: Google Glass is launched, leading to increased experimentation in both newsgathering and apps on wearable technology
- 2014: The podcast *Serial* becomes the fastest podcast to reach 5 million downloads and streams on iTunes, stimulating new interest in the format
- 2014: A Metropolitan Police report reveals that authorities are using the RIPA Act to monitor journalists' communications with sources, triggering the 'Save Our Sources' campaign
- 2014: The *New York Times*'s internal Innovation Report is leaked, providing a rare – and highly critical – insight into the cultural challenges facing traditional news organisations trying to adapt to the internet age
- 2014: Information hacked from the film studio Sony Pictures is leaked, for suspected political reasons. The information is widely reported in the entertainment and business press, but also stimulates ethical debate around the use of hacked data
- 2015: Live video app Meerkat launches, quickly followed by Twitter's Periscope and Facebook Live. Live video becomes an essential element in publishing strategy.
- 2015: The Apple Watch is launched, kickstarting interest in 'glance journalism'
- 2015: Chat app Telegram opens up its bot store to developers, and news organisations begin building chatbots to help users interact with their content
- 2015: Facebook Instant Articles and Apple News launch, followed by Google's Accelerated Mobile Pages in 2016, marking the start of a battle over mobile news

- 2016: The *Independent* newspaper in the UK goes online-only
- 2016: An attempted coup in Turkey is livestreamed on Facebook Live and Periscope. As the media is seized by the military, the president also uses Apple FaceTime to broadcast live
- 2016: Facebook accused of censorship after it deletes posts featuring the Vietnam War photo The Terror of War. Norwegian newspaper editor, Espen Egil Hansen, sees his open letter to Mark Zuckerberg on the subject go viral
- 2016: Amazon Echo launches in the UK and Google Home launches in the US, opening up new opportunities for publishing in the connected home
- 2016: Mark Zuckerberg announces Facebook will introduce new measures to tackle 'fake news' and work with fact-checking organisations amid suggestions other countries used propaganda to influence the US election.
- 2016: Citizens caught within a siege in Aleppo post harrowing goodbye messages using social media, connecting with a global audience in the absence of journalists on the ground. But communication is confused by a proliferation of automated accounts intended to discredit the reports

The decline of print – and the spread of journalism

For more than a decade almost every story about print was a bad news story. One presentation to the Leveson Inquiry into press regulation in 2011 made particularly depressing reading: between 2005 and 2010 regional newspaper group Newsquest had lost more than half of its revenue, and Trinity Mirror was not far behind. Northcliffe lost 43 per cent and Johnston Press almost a quarter. Print circulations had plummeted by almost a quarter at regional newspapers and quality national newspapers, and by 17 per cent in consumer magazines and popular national newspapers (Enders Analysis 2011).

By 2014 it was reported that around 40 per cent of jobs in the industry had gone in five years (Harding 2014) and a quarter of local government areas now had no daily newspaper (Media Reform Coalition 2014), and by 2016 one study calculated that the number of local newspaper titles had dropped 35 per cent in 30 years (Ramsay and Moore 2016). The true drop was even larger, as many titles had shifted from daily to weekly production. Between 2010 and 2015 advertising spending on national newspapers fell by a third (Mance 2016).

The picture was just as bad in the US: 'Few industries have been affected by the digital or information age as much as newspapers and other traditional publishing industries', the Bureau of Labor Statistics (2016) reported. Since 1990 the newspaper publishing industry had lost almost 60 per cent of its workers. The magazine industry and radio broadcasting weren't affected until 2007, but lost a third and a fifth of their workforces respectively after that point.

The headline figures masked a more complicated story. From 1990 to 2015 in the US, employment in internet publishing and broadcasting had risen from about 30,000 to nearly 198,000. And as commercial organisations used the web to publish directly to consumers that sector was increasingly hiring journalists too: one survey of communication graduates noted that 'Many of those producing what they consider journalism do not work for news organizations' (Sonderman et al. 2015): 17 per cent of graduates employed by commercial brands, 19 per cent of those in politics, government and think tanks and 20 per cent of those who worked for technology companies saw themselves as journalists. Notably, many were creating their own enterprises: a third of communication graduates described themselves as entrepreneurs and journalists.

In the UK the Labour Force Survey recorded increasing numbers of people describing themselves as journalists or newspaper and periodical editors: between 2015 and 2016 the figure increased from 64,000 to 84,000; the highest total recorded since the survey began in 2001 (Office for National Statistics 2016; Cox 2016), largely due to those working in a self-employed capacity.

While print circulation was declining, online readership was going in the opposite direction. Between 2014 and 2015 online readership of local newspaper websites in the UK increased by over 32 per cent (Ponsford 2015b). By 2014 the *Guardian*, *Telegraph* and *Independent* already had more readers online than in print, and within two years they were joined by all the national newspapers apart from two behind paywalls: *The Times* and the *Sun*.

Inevitably, many publications began to drop their expensive print editions. In 2013 the world's oldest newspaper, *Lloyds List*, stopped printing after 279 years: 97 per cent of readers had said they preferred to use it online. In 2014 the *Reading Post* went digital-only after 49 years in print, and women's magazine *Company* did the same after 36 years, one of dozens of magazines to explore a post-print existence online. In 2016 the *Independent* became the first national UK newspaper to stop printing.

What had happened? There were certainly lots of theories.

The 'original sin' myth

A recurring argument within the news industry has centred around whether publishers made a mistake in giving away their content for free in the early days of the web. This is sometimes referred to as the 'original sin' myth: the suggestion that if news organisations had charged for their content from the start, they would not now be struggling to survive commercially.

There are a number of weaknesses to this argument. One is the fact that many publishers actually *did* attempt to charge for their content, but failed to persuade consumers to pay. The second and broader weakness is that online newspapers were not the only organisations able to publish news: they were not in the same position to charge for content as they had been in print.

Many newspapers launched websites as a defensive strategy against online-only competitors such as AOL, Yahoo! and MSN. Had newspapers decided not to publish online at all, those organisations, with lower costs and greater economies of scale, might well have come to dominate online news while print publishing advertisers transferred their activity to the web. Indeed, Martin Nisenholtz, who helped launch the *New York Times* website, said that giving away content was a necessity to compete and build the significant market share that they came to enjoy (Jarvis 2014) while at a regional level at least one analysis concludes that news aggregators have come to dominate regardless, and that print publishers may have been better to avoid the web altogether (Chyi and Tenenboim 2016).

One of the counter-arguments to the 'original sin' theory is that news organisations were actually not aggressive enough when they launched their websites. Steve Buttry, who worked in news organisations at the time, argued that the industry's biggest mistake was 'responding to digital challenges and opportunities with defensive measures intended to protect newspapers, and timid experiments with posting print-first content online, rather than truly exploring and pursuing digital possibilities' (Buttry 2016).

Many anecdotes about the history of online news overlook the role of advertising in the business models of publishing, and the way that the internet affected the advertising market. Throughout the 20th century the majority of news content was either subsidised by, or entirely funded through, advertising. Most news consumers got their news for free through broadcast channels or paid a small proportion of the overall cost of production to get it printed on paper.

But advertisers were following their target audiences online. In 2010 regular consumption of news online in the US surpassed consumption of news in print, and for the first time less money was spent on print advertising than on advertising online (Pew Research Centre 2011). By 2016 in Europe online advertising was overtaking TV advertising too (Fennah 2016).

The internet provided advertisers with a new way to reach audiences. In order to try to keep advertisers as clients, most news organisations launched websites and sold advertising on those as well. But the competition online was much fiercer, and this had an impact on news organisations in three particular ways:

1 Many news organisations dominated local advertising markets, allowing them to keep advertising rates artificially high. Competition online reduced advertising rates.
2 Online-only competitors did not have the same costs as print and broadcast news organisations (including debts on loans taken out to acquire competing titles). This allowed them to charge much less for advertising and still make a profit.
3 Some online services competed not just on price, but on the quality of service that they offered to advertisers.

One of the earliest examples of this competition was Craigslist: instead of paying to place a classified ad in your local paper, people could place the same classified ad online for free. Online marketplaces like eBay also helped people find buyers for small items easily. As people began to use online classifieds sites instead of local newspapers, revenue plummeted: from a high of $19.6 billion for US newspapers in 2000 to less than half that within eight years (Jones 2009). One study estimated that Craigslist alone 'cost' local newspapers $5 billion in lost advertising revenue, which in turn was correlated with increased subscription prices and decreasing circulation and display advertising rates. In contrast to the 'original sin' argument the authors found evidence that '[a]ffected newspapers [were] less likely to make their content available online' (Seamans and Zhu 2013).

The same story was repeated with classified advertising for jobs, cars and houses as websites like Monster.com, Realtor.com and Cars.com began offering the same service on a bigger scale, at a lower cost and more convenience for users. Some media organisations eventually launched, invested in or bought, specialist online classifieds services: when *Daily Mail* publisher DMGT acquired Jobrapido in 2012, for example, it already owned property and car classified services, as well as Jobsite, OilCareers and Broadbean.

Advertising: the half that worked

Display advertising – larger adverts that tended to be placed alongside articles – would suffer a similar fate. It had often been said that half of the money spent on advertising was wasted, but the trouble was that no one knew which half. The major advantage of online advertising was being able to measure precisely *which* advertising worked, and increasingly to only pay *when* it worked.

Early online advertising adopted the model of print advertising, was displayed next to editorial content and sold on the basis of the numbers of people who would be 'exposed' to it. The rate of payment was often called *CPM* (cost per thousand): if an advert had a CPM of £1, and 120,000 people saw that page, the advertiser would pay £120 (£1 for every thousand viewers).

Like print advertising, it was impossible to know whether your advertising worked for those thousands of users, and it became increasingly clear that banner advertising in particular was not very effective: a term was even coined to describe the way that people ignored advertising on websites: 'banner blindness'.

Partly in response to this, websites began to charge only when an advert had a measurable impact: *CPC* (cost per click) meant advertisers were only charged every time a person *clicked* on the advert; *CPI* (cost per installation) rates were based on the numbers of times an app was installed as a result of the ad. *CPA* (sometimes cost per action, sometimes cost per acquisition) charged every time someone completed a certain *action* (for example calling a number, ordering a brochure or subscribing to something) which might be considered *acquiring* a customer. *CPL* (cost per lead) was a similar metric where payment was given for every customer lead acquired.

Google was one of the web services using these metrics, but it also had another advantage: it could target users much more accurately based on their behaviour. Publishers had historically sold advertising based on market research: for example that their readership of people aged 20–45 in Merseyside might see your advert. But search engines could allow you to target your advertising much more specifically: to someone searching for 'Toy shops', for example. In his book *The Search*, John Battelle called this the 'database of intentions' (Battelle 2005): whereas publishers might target people who belonged to broad demographics, Google was able to target individual users who were specifically intending to do things (based on their search terms at least).

Google also introduced an auction system whereby advertisers bid against each other on search terms. Instead of having a fixed rate for advertising, like publishers, it used technology to automate the process of fixing prices. Terms like "insurance" or "loans" could earn more money because competition was higher, and advertisers were prepared to pay more to gain customers.

While search engines like Google were able to sell advertising based on users' intentions, social networks were able to sell advertising audiences that were very specifically defined. When people signed up for a service like Facebook, they provided information about their location, age, education, gender, relationship status and even sexual orientation. As they used the service more and more, further information was added about the books, films, music and pages that they liked.

Advertisers using Facebook, then, could specify that they only wanted their ads to be seen by 'single women aged 65 and above, living within 20 miles of Oxford, with an interest in surfing', or any other combination of characteristics.

Facebook and Google reinforced their dominance further through providing services to publishers that collected data on users even when they weren't on Facebook or Google itself. Google's AdSense, for example, allowed hundreds of thousands of websites to sell advertising, but it also allowed Google to track users of those sites. If you've ever been followed around the web by advertising for a particular product, this is probably why. Google's Chrome browser, and mobile operating system Android, allowed Google to track user activity even on sites which did not use Google ads.

Facebook's 'like' buttons could be installed on any site to make it easier for people to share content – but they also gave the social media giant the ability to track user behaviour in the same way. With its acquisition of the ad platform Atlas in 2014 it looked to repeat what Google had done with AdSense.

News organisations tried to compete by focusing more on video, where advertising could be sold at much higher rates, and by selling *programmatic advertising*: an automated process whereby advertisers use software to set the triggers under which advertising might be purchased. One form of this was *real-time bidding* (RTB) whereby ads were auctioned to automatic bidders as they were being loaded onto the page.

But by 2015 advertising-based websites had another problem. The Reuters Institute Digital News Report 2015 was just one of a number of reports noting 'significant consumer dissatisfaction with online advertising, expressed through the rapid take up of ad blockers' (Newman et al. 2015). Apple's iOS 9, rolled out that year, extended support for ad blockers to the web browser on the iPhone. But ads were not blocked on Apple News or on Facebook, handing further control to those companies.

Publishers were struggling to compete in this market; but they did not command the scale of audiences or control over platforms that Google, Facebook and other internet giants boasted. By 2016, 85 cents of every *new* dollar spent on advertising online was going to Google or Facebook (Herrman 2016), with Microsoft, Yahoo and Twitter taking up a large chunk of the rest. In the UK they accounted for over half of display advertising.

It was clear that the advertising-based model of 20th century print and broadcast was not always going to work in a 21st century digital world, for many traditional publishers at least. Advertising might be part of the business model going forward, but it would not be enough on its own.

The rise of native advertising

Without the scale or technological power of Google and Facebook, publishers looked to play to their strengths in other areas. One area which appeared to hold particular promise was 'native advertising' or 'branded content'. Online reinventions of the 'advertorial' concept (an advert which appears to look like editorial content), native advertising was typically produced by the media organisation itself, rather than being created by the advertiser. One of the most striking examples of the format was the *Wall Street Journal*'s 'Cocainenomics', an in-depth investigation into the cocaine trade which doubled as a promotion for a new Netflix TV series; other examples used familiar editorial formats such as listicles or sponsored discussions.

Promising higher effectiveness for advertisers, and a format which could not be replicated by Google or Facebook, it led to heavy investment from a range of publishers. In 2013 Trinity Mirror attempted to fund its new *Sunday People* website entirely through native advertising, while the *New York Times* set up a dedicated branded content unit in 2014 and the *Atlantic*, the *Telegraph*, News UK and the *Guardian* were among dozens of publishers doing the same.

The blurring of editorial and advertising created obvious ethical issues, particularly when editorial staff were used to create 'branded content'. One study, which found 68 per cent of magazine publishers to be using staff in this way, also reported that 45 per cent believed the biggest threat to native advertising was the 'lack of separation of the editorial and the commercial side' (Waldman 2016).

Research by Poutanen, Luoma-Aho and Suhanko (2016) based on interviews with lifestyle magazine editors and news editors explored these ethical issues in more detail. It identified four particular ethical dilemmas facing the 'hybrid editors' who had to make decisions relating to native advertising and similar formats:

1 Balancing the editorial role and promoting a media brand;
2 Balancing journalistic integrity and advertisers' desires;
3 Balancing commercial and journalistic content production; and
4 Balancing disclosure and attractiveness of new forms of online advertisement.

(Poutanen et al. 2016)

They concluded that what had been common practice in lifestyle journalism would soon become common practice in news media too, but that news media lacked sufficient guidelines to negotiate those challenges.

In addition to its ethical challenges, native advertising brought other problems too. It was expensive to create, and by 2016 there were suggestions that renewal rates were low as advertisers appeared uncertain that they were getting enough return for the expensive campaigns. In the same year BuzzFeed was censured by the Advertising Standards Authority for failing to clearly label its article '14 laundry fails we've all experienced' as being paid for by the fabric dye manufacturer Dylon. Like so many previous 'magic bullets' for publishing's commercial problems, it seemed that native advertising might not be the only solution after all.

Diverging revenue streams

Beyond advertising, publishers had been exploring a range of other revenue streams, including events, webinars, training, analysis, data services, book publishing, promotional services, merchandise and e-commerce.

The NME was one of the best examples of a traditional publisher which reinvented its business model online, and later in print. One of the first to launch online, in 1996, the music magazine built revenue around ticket sales and merchandise rather than advertising or subscriptions, but it also explored a range of other avenues including events, festival partnerships and even a radio station. In 2010 it announced a deal to provide content to MSN, and the same year it launched a t-shirt range based on classic magazine covers. In 2015, with its paid circulation at an all-time low of 15,000, it took the decision to become a free magazine, and expanded distribution to 300,000.

Another music publication, Pitchfork, started off as a website but expanded its business into a Pitchfork Festival, a video site and eventually a quarterly printed journal. When Condé Nast bought Pitchfork in 2015 it was notable that the CEO Bob Sauerberg described it not as a magazine but as a 'digital property' with 'an enthusiastic and young audience, a growing video platform and a thriving events business' (Flanagan 2015).

Some publishers used the work of their writers as a way to move into book and ebook publishing. Amazon's launch of the 'Kindle single' format in 2011 for works between 5000 and 30,000 words played a major role. In the UK the *Guardian* launched 'Guardian Shorts' with the short ebook *Phone Hacking: How the Guardian Broke the Story*, the same year as *Vanity Fair* magazine published its on the same topic, while in Canada the *Toronto Star*, *The Globe and Mail*, the *National Post* and the *Edmonton Journal* all experimented with the format.

Events had always been a part of the magazine industry, but the number of events increased noticeably in that field as print revenues dropped. Future Publishing created a division specifically dedicated to events in 2012; magazine publisher UBM acquired numerous exhibitions companies in Asia, and Time Inc. acquired *UK Cycling Events* to complement its cycling publications. By 2015 EMAP noted that their events business was accounting for 40 per cent of turnover.

News organisations started to explore the same opportunities too: the *Texas Tribune* was generating one fifth of its revenue from events by 2013, while the *New York Times*'s conference business was described as 'a potential $20 million enterprise' by the public editor (Sullivan 2015), who highlighted the potential ethical issues arising from using journalists on conference panels in sponsored events: sponsors 'have no control or role in determining the content of the conferences', she emphasised. In the UK both the *Guardian* and *The Times* used events as part of their premium membership and subscription strategy.

E-commerce was another unfamiliar business that publishers had to get to grips with. Again, magazines were early to experiment, examples ranging from *House and Garden* partnering to launch the retail site Spirit-Boutique.com in 2011, to *Harper's Bazaar*'s ShopBazaar – and newspapers including the *Daily Mail* and *Telegraph*, and websites including reddit and BuzzFeed, also began to sell items to readers. Many more chose to use *affiliate schemes*: this involved including a link which users might follow to buy products on sites such as Amazon or eBay. Any purchases made by readers then generated a small commission for the publisher. Hearst magazines, for example, displayed affiliate links beneath product reviews on Goodhousekeeping.com, while in 2015 Gawker claimed it had driven around $150 million worth of e-commerce transactions using similar links.

Many media startups used flagship publications as a way to attract clients for other parts of their business. The creative agency Church of London, for example, publishes the film magazine *Little White Lies* – but also magazines for clients including Google, Honda, Stella

Artois, the British Film Institute and Sony PlayStation (Rowlands 2013). Some hyperlocal sites supported themselves in a similar way, using their online profile to attract work in areas such as social media consultancy, web design and editorial training.

From hard paywalls to meters

Alongside these experiments in new revenue streams, publishers also continued to attempt to persuade users to pay directly for content. *Paywalls* – barriers that forced users to pay before they could access content – were always a trade-off: any income generated by the minority of readers who are willing to pay has to be set off against the extra costs involved in acquiring and retaining subscribers, the impact on search engine rankings and the loss in advertising revenue through having much smaller audiences. One newspaper said that it took down its paywall because 'We traded every dollar in advertising we lost for a nickel in online subscription revenue' (Marsh 2014).

Financial newspapers like the *Wall Street Journal* and *Financial Times* were among the first to introduce paywalls, in 1997 and 2001 respectively. With content that had financial value to an affluent readership whose employers often paid for their subscriptions, it was a relatively straightforward proposition. But when mass market newspapers tried the same approach, it didn't go so smoothly. The *LA Times* and *New York Times* launched paywalls in 2003 and 2005 respectively, both dropping them after two years, while many other publishers struggled to make them work. By 2009 Arianna Huffington was stating that 'The paywall is history' (Huffington 2009).

But it wasn't. Publishers regrouped and rethought, and a significant innovation came in 2011 when the *New York Times* launched a *metered paywall*. Instead of requiring all users to pay before viewing any content, a metered or 'soft' paywall allowed a certain number of free articles per month, before users were asked to pay to see any more. This addressed two major problems: how to allow readers to 'sample' the product before buying it; and the need to maintain large audiences when only small sections of your readership were heavy enough readers to be willing to pay.

In the same year Google launched its OnePass initiative to help publishers sell subscriptions, and a year later the Slovakian startup Piano Media appeared to offer similar hope when it created a 'national paywall' covering nine publishers in the country. Similar paywalls were set up in neighbouring Slovenia and Poland, and by 2014 Piano Media was being used on over 100 sites across Germany, the US, the UK and Spain.

Suddenly paywalls were everywhere. One study found almost three-quarters of newspaper companies surveyed were charging readers; it also reported much higher retention rates for the metered paywalls (Marsh 2014). Metered paywalls allowed news organisations to experiment to find the 'sweet spot' which allowed for the best combination of paying customers and casual readers who made up the numbers that could be pitched to advertisers. Some allowed users to view articles for free if they came from social media (to encourage sharing); others, like the *Independent*, provided articles for free if the user lived in the UK but charged for those visiting from other countries.

But many did not last. In the UK paywalls at the *Sun* and the *Independent* only lasted two years before both were dropped in 2015, while Johnston Press's attempt to introduce paywalls to local newspapers was abandoned after just a year in 2010. Wolverhampton's

Express and Star scrapped its paywall after just nine months. Google One Pass was shut down in 2012. Piano Media's Slovenian paywall failed too, although it continued to operate in other countries.

The *Telegraph*'s metered paywall lasted three years before being replaced in 2016 with a separate paywalled content section called Telegraph Premium, an approach sometimes called a *two-tier* or *freemium system*. Only *The Times*, which introduced its paywall in 2010, and DC Thomson in Scotland, since 2014, stayed the game.

Getting readers to pay – a history of 'golden bullets'

Paywalls weren't the only way of allowing readers to fund journalism directly. Crowdfunding, micropayments, apps and the 'tip-jar' model were all used in different ways to fund journalistic projects.

2008 was a major year for apps, with the launch of Apple's app store on iPhones coinciding with paywalls failing to deliver. By 2009 dozens of publications had apps in the store, including the *Independent*, *Guardian* and *Telegraph* and the *Manchester Evening News*. The CEO of Associated Northcliffe announced that he would launch 15 apps over the following year, covering regional newspaper titles as well as *Mail Online* and *Metro*.

The launch of the iPad in 2010, and then Apple Newsstand and in-app subscriptions in 2011, only encouraged more to jump on the app bandwagon. With its magazine-like appearance and use in the home, publishers became hugely optimistic that they could return to the old days of selling 'editions', as well as old-fashioned, full page advertising alongside it. When *Wired* magazine launched its app, it sold 100,000 copies of the first edition – more than it normally sold in print. But the second edition only sold 31,000, and sales declined further after that (Benkoil 2010). Magazines including *Men's Health*, *People* and *Glamour* could only attract iPad readerships equivalent to less than 1 per cent of their print audience (Ives 2010).

Apps had been heralded by some as a 'golden bullet': one technology that could solve publishers' problems and turn back the clock to a time when they dominated media consumption. But the problem was that people seemed reluctant to pay for news apps, and even when they downloaded them, did not renew them, or use them very often.

What was often overlooked was that phones and tablets were not a replication of the old-fashioned newsstand: there was a lot more competition. The app used more often than any other on a phone or tablet was the web browser, and it already provided access to endless free sources of news. Social networking apps such as Facebook and Twitter, where an increasing number of users were encountering news content, also dominated. What reason, then, was there for users to use yet another app for news? Especially an app which only provided access to one publisher's reporting?

A further problem was quality: many news and magazine apps merely reproduced pages from print editions rather than thinking about how they might play to the strengths of the new medium, and customers were frustrated by performance issues including slow loading and frequent crashes. Some publishers, particularly in the magazine sector, realised it might be more fruitful to look at apps as a separate product entirely. *Men's Fitness* and *Women's Fitness*, for example, both launched specific workout apps, while *Golf Monthly* created an app called Short Game Tips. *What Car?* magazine created an app to help people put a value on used cars; *Uncut* magazine launched separate apps about David Bowie, Bruce Springsteen and The Rolling Stones. In news media *The Economist*'s Espresso app focused on the essentials; BuzzFeed's app was video-driven; and Quartz's app mimicked the behaviour of a text message chat.

Fragmentation and saturation were the next challenge: by 2012 Google's mobile operating system Android (and Google Play Store) rose quickly to become a serious competitor to Apple, meaning that many news organisations now had to create and maintain two versions of their apps. Apple's app store was becoming increasingly crowded, and publishers sometimes had to wait weeks for changes to an app to be approved. In 2013 Apple's iOS7 update sidelined the Newsstand app, making it harder for people to find publications. At the same time, due to improvements in browser technology, it was now possible to create the same experiences with web apps (see Chapter 11 for more) using HTML5, so many publishers decided to take control, reduce costs and do that instead.

By 2015 people were installing far fewer new apps than before, and only using a handful regularly. Apps were still being developed, particularly at larger publications, but elsewhere attention had begun to turn to platform publishing (see above) and bots that could live *inside* the most popular chat apps (see Chapter 11).

Print dollars, digital dimes: micropayments

Many publishers looked towards *micropayments* as another way to get people to pay for content. Unlike paywalls – which required the user to pay a regular fee in order to access all content behind the paywall – micropayments allowed users to pay much smaller amounts for individual pieces of content. The most commonly cited example of a micropayment is paying for individual songs on iTunes, rather than having to buy entire albums (or having to subscribe for unlimited access); another example would be the tiny payments made by advertisers to publishers every time someone clicks on an online ad.

But when it came to paying for content, micropayments have been notoriously unsuccessful. DigiCash, for example, launched its digital payment system in 1990, but closed it in 1998. CyberCash launched in 1994 and went bankrupt in 2001, the same year that micropayments company Peppercoin launched. It was bought for its assets by another company six years later.

Part of the problem was the cost of processing payments, which often exceeded the payments themselves. Another was convenience: many users were unwilling to pay even small amounts for content if they could get the same content more conveniently for free elsewhere, especially when most news content had nothing like the shelf life, or distinctiveness, of music.

But that didn't stop new companies launching. Two of the best-known experiments in journalism were TinyPass and Blendle. Google also tried to enter the game in 2014 with Contributor. All allowed customers to add credit to their account which would then be used to pay for articles that they viewed on partner sites as they moved around the web.

Launched in 2011, TinyPass's innovation was that it could be installed as a WordPress plugin, and many bloggers used it as a way to make money from their work. But as paywalls increased in popularity (see above) it began to work with publishers more, and eventually merged with Piano Media in 2015. Blendle launched in 2014 having partnered with over a dozen Dutch news websites. It allowed users to request a refund if they weren't satisfied with an article, while users could also follow the best and most popular articles, which were curated on its site. Within a year of its launch Blendle had agreements with over 100 publishers including *Die Zeit, Focus, Wired, GQ, Der Spiegel, Süddeutsche Zeitung, Frankfurter Allgemeine Zeitung* and *Zeit Magazin*.

Some of the longer-lived experiments in micropayments were closer to the tip-jar model of payments: instead of being required to make a small payment in order to see content, the tip-jar model allowed readers to give money as a sign of appreciation of the content that they were already reading. Flattr, launched in 2010, allowed publishers to display a special button which users could click to donate money from their Flattr account to the publisher. TinyPass's 'Applause' tool worked in a similar way.

Going direct: the rise of crowdfunding

Crowdfunding started in cultural fields like music where as early as 2000 the ArtistShare platform allowed musicians to raise donations directly from their fans, but the same techniques were also being used in the charity sector on donation platforms like GoFundMe. Journalism fell somewhere in the middle: users might donate because they believed in a good cause, or because they wanted to back a great reporter.

One of the earliest dedicated journalism crowdfunding projects was Spot.Us, which received funding in 2008 from the Knight Foundation to launch a platform where readers would nominate, and donate to, investigations. In the years that followed several similar projects were launched: in 2011 Emphas.is (for crowdfunding photojournalism); in 2013 Beacon Reader, Vourno (for video journalism) and Indie Voices (for journalism in the developing world); and in 2014 the Guardian Media Group launched its own project, Contributoria.

By 2016 all had closed, but that did not mean that crowdfunding in general wasn't working for journalists. One study of projects on Kickstarter, for example, found that the amount of money donated to journalism projects had risen to over $1.7 million per year by 2015, with media organisations increasingly using the platform too (Vogt and Mitchell 2016). And journalism projects had also been successfully funded on other crowdfunding sites including IndieGoGo and Patreon, and on donation sites including Donar Online. Examples ranged from supporting hyperlocal journalists and fact-checking projects to investigations, podcasts, books and magazines.

In many cases the lines between donation, membership and subscription were blurred: donations to crowdfunding projects typically came with different levels of rewards, which included free access to content, merchandise and access to events or other opportunities. The founders of Dutch startup De Correspondent, for example, raised $1.7 million to launch its publication, but 19,000 donors also became subscribers in the process, while donors to projects on crowdfunding platform Beacon were rewarded with access to content from *all* projects on the site.

The rise of philanthropy and public funding

The decline in the numbers of traditional news organisations led to increasing calls for journalism to be treated as a public good worthy of philanthropic funding. Between 2000 and 2011 the number of non-profit news operations outside the US more than quadrupled to over 50 (Kaplan 2013), while there were 70 in the US and Canada alone.

The most prominent of these was ProPublica, founded in 2007 with funding from the Sandler Foundation. In 2010 it became the first online organisation to win a Pulitzer Prize for Investigative Reporting, and the following year it became the first non-print organisation to win the Pulitzer Prize for National Reporting. In the UK the Bureau of Investigative Journalism, founded in 2010, followed a similar model, funded by the Potter Foundation. It won the Amnesty Media Awards two years running for its work on the Iraq War logs and deaths in police custody.

Many of those who made millions from new media also decided to use their money to support old media: Facebook co-founder Chris Hughes was 28 when he bought the *New Republic*. After reportedly spending over $20 million to try to reinvent the publication, he sold it four years later. In 2013 Amazon's Jeff Bezos expressed a similar ambition when he bought the *Washington Post* for $250 million, while eBay founder Pierre Omidyar put his money into an entirely new venture, First Look Media, hiring the people who broke the Edward Snowden story. His investment firm Omidyar Network also backed a number of non-profit organisations including News Trust and the Sunlight Foundation. Google established the Digital News Initiative fund in 2015 with tens of millions of euros to support innovative technology projects around journalism. Notably, it was focused on European news organisations, where the technology giant was facing most pressure from regulators over its dominance. In the US a similar role had been played by the Knight Foundation since the establishment of its News Challenge fund in 2007. But an ongoing problem for news organisations and journalists was the lack of charitable status, which denied news organisations tax exempt status and prevented them from applying for a range of funds.

THE GROWING IMPORTANCE OF ANALYTICS IN ONLINE JOURNALISM

Analytics is a broad term used in the media industry to refer to the *process* of measuring user behaviour and using those measurements to try to improve the performance of the organisation. This can include:

- Using analytics to improve journalism
- Using analytics to improve advertising
- Using analytics to improve the product (e.g. the website or app)
- Using analytics to improve marketing (e.g. increase subscriptions or reduce the number of people cancelling subscriptions).

What is measured is normally called *metrics*. For example, you might measure how many people view a story, whether they scroll down the page, or how long they spend on it; whether they clicked on something or posted a comment, or shared that story on social media or elsewhere. Each of those measurements is a different metric.

Metrics can also be used to measure commercial performance: for example you might measure how many people responded to an ad in some way, or from which pages on your site people tend to leave it, or what sort of behaviour characterises someone who tends to cancel their subscription. *The Times* newspaper, for example, now uses a sophisticated analytics system to identify users who are most likely to take out a subscription, the sorts of content most likely to encourage them to do so and the patterns of behaviour that might indicate they may cancel.

Analytics is full of jargon. Here are some of the key terms explained:

Pageviews refers to the number of pages that were viewed over the specified period. You might hear people use the term *hits* – but this term can be confusing, because it can also mean how many items were loaded by visitors (image, HTML, etc.). Avoid this term if you can, and make sure you understand whether the person is talking about pageviews or something else.

Unique users is a measurement of how many separate users are using your site. For example, if you have 100 unique users and 200 pageviews, that means on average each user is viewing two pages. However, unique users are not always so 'unique': identification is normally done by each different *device* accessing a webpage. If the same person accesses your site on their phone, laptop and tablet, they could be counted as three separate users, unless they are logged in with a user account or identified in some other way. Likewise, if someone accesses your site on Chrome, Firefox and Safari, or deletes cookies or other form of tracking.

Bounce rate refers to the percentage of users who leave after viewing just one page: in other words they 'bounce' out of the site. This is generally quite high, but gives you a benchmark against which to test various strategies to try to keep users on your site: if they are working, the bounce rate should go down.

Dwell time or *visit duration* refers to the amount of time a user spends on your page. Dwell time is often used alongside bounce rate: an engaged reader who spent a long time on a page before 'bouncing' out of the site is clearly different from the frustrated browser who only spent a couple of seconds before bouncing out. Publishers try to increase dwell time by using formats known to do well on this front, such as longform, liveblogs, data journalism, interactivity and visual journalism.

These four terms give you the basic information about your audience: how many people visit your site, how many pages they tend to read, for how long, and how many fail to read more than one page. The most basic publishing strategy seeks to increase the audience, the number of pages each visitor reads and the amount of time they spend there.

There are many more metrics that are likely to play a role in any publishing strategy. Analytics can also tell you about whether users are new or returning; what type of device they are using; what country they are in; and in some cases demographic information such as gender, age and so on. Analytics tools also tell you about *acquisition* (whether they have come from search engines, social media, direct to the site or through other avenues like email).

Engagement might be measured through a range of metrics, including the time spent per visit or how far down the page they scrolled, through to the proportion of users sharing an article, or actions such as posting comments and voting. The more *engaged* the average user is, the more a publisher can normally charge for advertising.

Analytics tools

There are a number of tools that you can use to measure the analytics of your own site or content. The best-known free analytics service is *Google Analytics* (analytics. google.com): once signed up to the site, you will be given a piece of code to copy and paste into your website which will then start to measure what happens as people use your site. Paid-for analytics services include *Chartbeat*, which focuses on the real-time analytics that are often displayed on a screen in newsrooms so journalists can see which stories are performing best.

Many platforms have some sort of analytics built in: *WordPress*, for example, gives you basic metrics on the numbers of people who have visited your site each day, with a breakdown by story. *Medium* tells you how many people read your article, how long they spent reading and how many 'liked' it. *Twitter's* analytics dashboard (analytics. twitter.com) shows you your best performing recent tweets, and allows you to download a spreadsheet so you can perform your own analysis on metrics including link or hashtag clicks, favourites, retweets, follows and media views. You can also download data from *Facebook* pages' 'Insights' view, or use the dashboard to look at the updates which had the most interaction.

Third party analytics tools like *Bitly* (bit.ly) and *Buffer* (bufferapp.com) will give you a special URL for any link you want to share, and then track when people click on that link. This allows you to test what times most people click on your link, which social media platforms the links tend to perform best on or what accompanying text is most effective in getting users to click. Buffer in particular allows you to schedule social media updates to try to maximise their impact.

New threats to journalism online

In January 2013 an anonymous individual contacted the documentary maker Laura Poitras, with a request that they exchange encrypted messages. The individual was Edward Snowden, and that contact with Poitras would not only transform the public's understanding of state surveillance, but highlight the challenges facing journalists who wanted to protect their stories and sources in an ever more connected and networked world.

The first stories from that exchange were published in June that year. At first they revolved around the US's National Security Agency (NSA), its collection of millions of phone call records and its claims that they had direct access to user data held on the computers of Apple, Google and Facebook. Later the focus would move to the UK intelligence agency GCHQ, as it was revealed that it had access to the same communications, including users' email contacts and web search history, as well as images from video chats.

Around the world governments were passing laws to make it easier to monitor citizens. Between 2013 and 2014, 19 countries out of 65 studied by Freedom House passed new legislation that increased surveillance or restricted user anonymity (Freedom House 2014).

The revelations had major significance for journalists: 'metadata' about phones and internet communication revealed very detailed information about the movements of individuals, what webpages they visited and who they communicated with. Data was collected even when phones were switched off. This made it possible to identify who journalists were making contact with, not only at the time but retrospectively too. And it wasn't just the security services who had access to this information.

In early 2014 this fact was brought home to UK journalists when it was revealed that a police force had used the Regulation of Investigatory Powers Act (RIPA) to obtain the phone records of reporters and editors at the *Sun* newspaper. The police looked at all calls made to the political editor's mobile telephone or to the news desk and then looked for connections with the police force. 'One number was identified as the switchboard number for Hinchingbrooke Hospital', an official report noted. 'It was established that Officer 15 DPG's wife Member of Public 3, was employed at that hospital' (Metropolitan Police 2014, p.34).

Soon journalists realised that other public bodies had done the same: Suffolk Police had used RIPA to identify an *Ipswich Star* reporter's source. Kent Police had accessed the landline and mobile phone records of a *Daily Mail* reporter. And when a Derby City Council employee arranged to meet a local journalist the council used RIPA to visibly spy on the meeting, leading to the employee ending communications. In total 19 police forces had accessed journalists' communications data in three years, spying on hundreds of sources including police officers and staff, prison officers, hospital staff, military staff and those in central and local government. It was not known how many other public bodies had done the same: HM Revenue and Customs, the Home Office, the Royal Mail Group, the Department of Transport, the Department of Work and Pensions, the Charity Commission and local authorities also had access to the same surveillance powers, and most had used them in some capacity.

Journalists were worried. In 2015 research among investigative journalists found that concerns over surveillance had prevented 14 per cent from pursuing a story or reaching out to a particular source, while 2 per cent had considered leaving the profession entirely (Holcomb et al. 2015). The same year *Press Gazette* launched its 'Save Our Sources' campaign in the UK: it helped lead to some amendments to the law, but by the end of 2016 a new law was about to give public bodies even more powers.

The Investigatory Powers Act required internet service providers to keep details of all webpages visited by users throughout the year, gave authorities access to phone records and allowed them to conduct mass interception of communications of targeted groups of people, Although there was some requirement for authorities to get permission to access journalistic sources, there would be no opportunity for news organisations to argue their case against this, and journalists would not be aware that their communications had been compromised.

The importance of journalists being security-conscious in their communications was now paramount: the traditional legal defence was becoming something of the past. What's more, the increasing use of wearable technology, connected home and car technology, workplace surveillance and the rise of smart cities would only make it more difficult to avoid movements being tracked.

Hackers targeting hacks

Journalists and media organisations were not just being targeted by state authorities. In 2013 the entertainment website E! Online and Associated Press both had social media accounts hacked by the Syrian Electronic Army. The *New York Times* admitted its computers had been attacked in order to obtain data and *New York Magazine* was reportedly hacked over a story about women claiming to have been raped by Bill Cosby. The *New York Times*, *Global Post*, CNN and Forbes were all targeted by 'spear phishing': highly targeted emails designed to fool people into passing on their login credentials (Freedom House 2014).

Reporters might be hacked for a number of reasons. In some cases social media accounts were hacked in order to spread misinformation or propaganda; sometimes they were used as attacks against the news organisation itself; in other cases attacks were designed to collect information from within the news organisation. In many cases journalists and publishers might be hacked without realising it: journalists' computers at Al Jazeera were remotely accessed without anyone at the organisation finding out until years later. More broadly, data breaches at social media platforms including Twitter, Tumblr, LinkedIn and Yahoo! compromised the security of millions of users, including journalists.

Commercial organisations were caught at it too: the Leveson Inquiry into phone hacking in journalism said that the same practices were being used by blue chip companies. In 2014 Microsoft accessed a blogger's email to identify the source of a story about the company; and in 2015 Vodafone Australia admitted that one of its employees accessed a journalist's phone records in an attempt to uncover her sources.

And news organisations might be aiding hacking without realising it: in 2009 a malicious link was inserted in an email sent by Reporters Without Borders to its supporters, infecting the computers of those who clicked on it. The Investigatory Powers Act also gave security services similar powers not only to hack into computers and other devices, but to compel organisations to assist them in doing so.

Information wars: fake news, sockpuppetry and propaganda

With information becoming increasingly digital, the potential to manipulate that information increased too. When organisations or individuals created fake profiles and posted comments or reviews to push a particular agenda, this was given its own name: 'sockpuppetry'. Examples ranged from posting favourable reviews of your own book, to attacking commercial rivals, attempting to undermine critical scientific reports or spreading propaganda.

In some cases people were paid to post – in 2013 Yelp deemed 20 per cent of its reviews 'suspicious' and Wikipedia banned 250 accounts it suspected of the practice – but increasingly, sockpuppets were being automatically created and managed, including by government agencies (Bakir 2015) and in political campaigns. 'Astroturfing' was used to describe a similar technique: PR and lobbying companies creating the appearance of fake 'grassroots' campaigns to manipulate the media.

In 2016 the US election drew attention to a third problem: 'fake news'. Some fake news sites were simply propaganda: created to generate anger that might influence the election in a particular direction. Others were motivated by the commercial gains to be had by driving large amounts of traffic generated by those same emotions: in Macedonia a small cottage industry appeared to have sprung up based on using fake news sites to generate advertising revenue from Facebook and advertising widgets.

Most of the criticism over fake news was aimed at Facebook. Their decision earlier that year to fire the human editors overseeing its 'Trending Topics' section had led to fake stories appearing in that section within days. Other commentators highlighted its decision to give less weight to publishers and brands in its news feed algorithm. One BuzzFeed investigation into over 1000 posts on 'hyperpartisan' Facebook pages found that 'the least accurate pages generated some of the highest numbers of shares, reactions, and comments on Facebook', and more engagement than mainstream news pages (Silverman et al. 2016). By November Mark Zuckerberg was forced to announce plans to tackle fake news through improved reporting systems and detection systems.

The decade up until that point had seen a significant increase in the numbers of sites and sections devoted to factchecking and verification. Between 2008 and 2012 the number of factchecking stories in the US increased by more than 300 per cent (Graves et al. 2015) while the number of factchecking sites globally tripled over the same period (Lowrey 2015). Many established news organisations supplemented their normal coverage with dedicated sections: Channel 4 News led the way during the 2005 election with its Fact Check blog, then made it a regular feature from 2010. The *Guardian*'s Reality Check blog followed a year later (Graves and Cherubini 2016) and a BBC section of the same name in 2016. The 2015 UK election saw factchecking text blocks integrated into debate coverage at the BBC, *Telegraph*, ITV and other news organisations.

Outside news organisations there was also an increase in independent factchecking sites, such as FullFact, a UK charity which was founded in 2010 and included journalists among its trustees. Many of these sites successfully used crowdfunding around specific elections to fund their work.

At the same time as Facebook was being asked to take a more active editorial role in blocking fake news stories, it was also being accused of censorship. In September 2016 the social network became embroiled in controversy after it removed a post by a Norwegian journalist featuring the Pulitzer prize-winning Vietnam War 'napalm girl' photograph. The editor-in-chief of the Norwegian newspaper *Aftenposten*, Espen Egil Hansen, wrote a front-page open letter to Mark Zuckerberg. In it he acknowledged that Facebook's editorial control superseded his own, and accused Zuckerberg of abusing his power. 'I am worried that the world's most important medium is limiting freedom instead of trying to extend it, and that this occasionally happens in an authoritarian way', he wrote (Hansen 2016).

The same year Facebook complied with a police request to deactivate a live video stream from a user engaged in a standoff with officers, suspended live footage from protests and disabled Palestinian journalists' accounts. In most cases the social network was responding to a legal request, but where a traditional publisher might mount a legal defence there was little reason for Facebook or other technology companies to do so. Journalists and news organisations were realising that they had ceded at least some editorial independence to the platforms that they published on.

PROTECTING SOURCES AND STORIES ONLINE

Information security ('infosec') is important to every journalist, whatever field they work in. Not only are communications and movement data now stored routinely and accessible to public bodies, but workplace communications and movements are also increasingly monitored. Anyone with a large audience can be a target. Below are some simple initial steps to take to protect your colleagues, your sources and your stories online.

1   Create a threat model
    The first step to addressing your security online is to identify why you need to *think* about security online. If you're an entertainment reporter or you only edit other reporters' material, it can be easy to assume that you are not at risk. But that's not necessarily the case.

    A *threat model* evaluates the security risks in your work. It involves answering four simple questions:

    1   What information do you not want other people to know? (This can be anything from passwords to contacts' details, data and documents, but can also include colleagues' details or details of your organisation's passwords)
    2   Why might someone want that information? Who?
    3   What can they do to get it?
    4   What might happen if they do?

    Two key pieces of information which are likely to be of interest to others are the passwords of your social media accounts and those of your publication or programme; and information held by colleagues in other roles. 'Phishing' attacks, for example, often work by infiltrating minor employees' accounts first, and then using those to send emails to the 'true' target. So even if you think your information doesn't matter, you may still be a target.

    If you are working on sensitive stories—anything involving protestors or activists, but also fields like health, crime and finance—then you will need to consider the possible threats to your security, and what steps you might need to take to protect that.

2   Use multiple passwords, make them strong and use two-factor authentication wherever possible
    One very basic security practice is to make sure that you use strong passwords, and don't use the same password for different accounts (companies including LinkedIn, Tumblr and Twitter have all had their computers hacked and customer details leaked).

    A strong password is normally very long and uses a combination of upper and lower case letters, digits and special characters such as the pound sign. One way to create such a password is to use a 'pass phrase' instead, which uses a combination of words together. If you find it difficult to remember multiple passwords for multiple accounts, consider using a *password manager*.

Many services, including Gmail, Twitter and WordPress, now also offer *two-factor authentication*. This means that a second proof of identity is normally required as well as your password (typically this means a code is also sent to your mobile phone). Find out how to turn on two-factor authentication on any platforms that offer it.

3   Have a place on your site explaining how sources can contact you securely
News organisations now increasingly offer information on their 'contact us' pages which explain how to share documents or contact journalists securely. The open source secure platform SecureDrop, for example, is maintained by the non-profit Freedom of the Press Foundation to help sources avoid tracking, and has been used by a range of news organisations. Typically each organisation's SecureDrop platform is hosted on a separate server to their main site, meaning that it does not use cookies or store activity logs.

Contact pages also include links to 'encryption keys' to contact the news desk and individual journalists. These allow people to send emails or documents which can only be opened by that specific individual (see below).

4   Consider encrypting communications and information
Encryption is the process of 'encoding' something so that people cannot read it unless they have the 'key' to decode it. You can encrypt an email, a message or a document, so that if it is intercepted it can still not be decoded and read.

At the most basic level it is worth considering communication tools that are encrypted by default. The text messaging app Signal, for example, makes it harder for people to intercept and read your text messages, and the chat app Telegram is based on similar principles. You can also use OTR (Off the Record) tools for encrypted instant messaging, or specific encrypted email services. Make sure you read around to find out any concerns that people have over those tools' vulnerability to attack.

Most encryption used by journalists involves PGP (Pretty Good Privacy). This can be set up on email software such as Thunderbird, and involves sharing a 'public key' that others can use to send you messages. Once someone has sent you a message encrypted with your public key, only you can decode (decrypt) it. Likewise, if you want to send someone else an encrypted message, you can use their public key to encrypt it for their eyes only.

There are a number of weaknesses to consider with regard to encryption: the first is that only the *contents* of messages are encoded: it will still be possible to see who is contacting who, when and (in emails) with what subject line, without having a decryption key. Second, if someone has hacked your device they can still monitor you composing the message or receiving the message. Finally, it is worth noting that while platforms like WhatsApp are encrypted, the keys are still stored securely and might be accessed by government agencies.

5   <u>Understand what information is collected about you and your sources</u>

One of the most enduring myths in journalism is the idea of the 'secret meeting'. Some journalists mistakenly neglect information security in the belief that meeting in person offers protection against widespread surveillance. However, it is only when you explore how much is recorded about everyday activities that you can realistically assess the chances of meetings being 'secret'.

Our mobile phones are the most obvious aspect of this: as long as you or your source is carrying a mobile phone (even when switched off), the movement of that phone and its owner is being recorded. Attempts to prevent recording of information can be just as important: if two people remove the batteries of their phones around the same time, then that is also an indication of some sort of meeting or relationship between the two.

Remember that your car can be used to identify you, too: in the UK there are hundreds of ANPR (Automatic Number Plate Recognition) CCTV cameras which track the movements of cars and, by extension, their owners. Increasing numbers of other CCTV cameras also feature facial recognition technology that allows them to track people from one camera to another. 'Gait' recognition further promises to identify individuals regardless of whether their face is showing, by their unique way of moving.

It is likely that your source's workplace keeps a log of all the webpages that they visit on their computer and any work-owned mobile phone, as well as all emails sent and documents printed. They may have to swipe in and out of the building, as may visitors. Any contacts should be made on personal devices.

This is in addition, of course, to the legally required storage of all the webpages that you visit, the searches that you make and who you are emailing and calling, on your computer and phone (you can use browsers like Tor to browse privately).

Of course your threat model should help you make an informed judgement about whether someone with access to all of that information is likely to be a threat. With stories involving protestors and activists, it may well be. With stories involving potential whistleblowers, you might focus more on the information their employer would have access to.

For more guidance on information security you can download the free ebook *Information Security for Journalists* from www.tcij.org/resources/handbooks/infosec

Summary

As online journalism entered its third decade it seemed like the pace of change was not slowing down – if anything, the industry and the way that people consumed information was changing faster than ever.

Online journalism's early days based around adding links and images to text already look quaint when compared to the multimedia, multiplatform, mobile-optimised reporting that is now standard. But it is not just the form of storytelling that has changed. The business of journalism in the 21st century is very different to the way that it operated for a century before that. There are fewer certainties – advertising and charging readers are no longer the obvious models that they once were – but there are also now more opportunities available to those who wish to build a business around an audience, from events and crowdfunding to merchandising and ecommerce.

The economics and ethics of publishing now require more thought. Most journalists agree that involving users improves their journalism, but by inviting your community to publish on your platform are you helping to connect and amplify them – or exploiting their free labour? Do new revenue streams such as native advertising and affiliate links also bring new potential conflicts of interest that need to be addressed?

It is clear that the bar has been raised in terms of what is expected of individual journalists. It is no longer enough simply to relay information from one part of society to another; journalists are expected to be expert curators and verifiers, data journalists or multimedia producers. Our ability to protect our sources now relies not on institutional support, but on technological savviness.

As new opportunities continue to open up to publishers, the one skill above all that journalists will need is *adaptabilty*. To tell the most important stories to the right audience, on the best platforms and in the best ways – that is what journalists do. But it is also about using the experience of the newsroom – and an awareness of history – to learn from those mistakes that have been made, and avoid repeating them.

Activities

1   Chart the development of a major news site such as nytimes.com by using the web to go back in time.

   a   Go to the WaybackMachine site at www.archive.org which stores 150 billion pages.
   b   Using the search engine field type in the web address of your site.
   c   By clicking on the years displayed you will build up a picture of how many pages, multimedia features and designs the site has had.
   d   What multimedia features did it use to report big new stories such as the 9/11 attacks in New York?
   e   Answer the following questions: in which year did it launch interactive features, forums, blogs, podcasts, video, user-generated content, data journalism, liveblogs?
   f   Now use the search engine again to track the history and development of the WaybackMachine site!

2   Identify a story that has recently been covered by a number of news organisations, and explore how they treat it differently on different platforms.

   a   Look at how they have reported it on their website.
   b   Look at how they have reported the same story on their social media platforms: are they doing it in a 'native' way, different to their website version? Or is it merely 'promoting' or republishing the same story?

    c   Repeat the process for chat platforms such as Snapchat.

    d   Has any coverage been produced, or commissioned, by the platforms themselves?

    e   How might you report a story 'natively' on platforms other than a website?

3   Pick a publication that interests you and explore how it is funded. Ask the following questions:

    a   Does it charge users to access content, for example through a paywall?

    b   What sort of advertising does it sell? Does it sell native advertising? Look for their media pack online: this normally includes information such as advertising rates and formats. Also search for industry coverage of that publication's initiatives in advertising using publications such as InPublishing, Journalism.co.uk and MediaBriefing.

    c   Does the publication sell merchandise or have an ecommerce facility?

    d   Does the publication use affiliate links so that it earns money whenever someone clicks on a product on another site and buys it?

    e   Has the publisher ever used crowdfunding, or been awarded funds from projects like the Google Digital News Initiative? (Again, try searching the industry press for mentions of the organisation and those terms.)

4   Explore what makes a successful or unsuccessful crowdfunding project. Look for journalistic projects that are using, or have used, a crowdfunding platform like Kickstarter. Answer the following questions:

    a   What makes for a compelling project – and which ones don't work very well?

    b   Find articles about and by people who have managed crowdfunded journalism projects. What are the potential problems and pitfalls they identify? Can you think of any others?

    c   What would make you donate to a project? And why would you choose not to?

    d   If you were to plan a crowdfunded journalism project, what sort of project would have the best chance of success? Put together a 'pitch' for your crowdfunding page.

5   Publish the same piece of content on Medium, WordPress and Blogger. Find out how to set up Google Analytics on Blogger. Use a URL shortening tool like Bitly to get special shortened links that you can share on different social media platforms. Then share those links (to all three versions) across different social media, email and chat apps.

    Now compare the metrics that you get for the different versions: how does Medium's metrics differ from WordPress and how does that differ from Google Analytics? What extra context does Bitly give you? What information is missing – and how might you find it?

    Now, ask yourself: what is your objective as a journalist? Why? And how might you measure how successful you have been in achieving your objective? What issues, dangers or problems might there be in that approach?

Further reading

Allan, Stuart and Thorsen, Einar (2014) *Citizen Journalism, Volume 2: Global Perspectives* (Global Crises and the Media), New York: Peter Lang

Boczkowski, Pablo, J. (2010) *News at Work*, Chicago: University of Chicago Press

Bruns, Axel (2005) *Gatewatching: Collaborative Online News Production*, New York: Peter Lang

Carlo, Silkie and Kamphuis, Arjen. *Information Security for Journalists*, Logan Handbook Series, available free at www.tcij.org/resources/handbooks/infosec

Craig, David A. (2011) *Excellence in Online Journalism*, London: Sage

Graefe, Andrew. *Guide to Automated Journalism*, Tow Center for Digital Journalism, 2016, http://towcenter.org/research/guide-to-automated-journalism

Jones, Janet and Lee, Salter (2011) *Digital Journalism*, London: Sage

New York Times Innovation Report 2014, https://www.scribd.com/doc/224332847/NYT-Innovation-Report-2014

Petre, Caitlin. *The Traffic Factories: Metrics at Chartbeat, Gawker Media, and The New York Times*, Tow Center for Digital Journalism, 7 May 2015, http://towcenter.org/research/traffic-factories

Pfeiffer, Andreas. The distributed content landscape: an overview for publishers, WAN-IFRA, 26 October 2015, http://blog.wan-ifra.org/2015/10/26/the-distributed-content-landscape-an-overview-for-publishers-part-1

Pitt, Fergus. *Sensors and Journalism*, Tow Center for Digital Journalism, 2014, http://towcenter.org/research/sensors-and-journalism/http://towcenter.org/research/sensors-and-journalism

Zion, Lawrie and Craig, David (2015) *Ethics for Digital Journalists*, New York: Routledge

Online resources

Accelerated Mobile Pages (AMP) Project: https://www.ampproject.org
Facebook Instant Articles: https://instantarticles.fb.com

Bibliography

The access date for web material is 20 February 2017 unless otherwise given.

Bakir, Vian. News, agenda building and intelligence agencies: a systematic review of the field from the discipline of journalism, media and communications, *International Journal of Press/Politics* 20(2), 2015: 131–144

Battelle, John (2005) *The Search: How Google and Its Rivals Rewrote the Rules of Business and Transformed Our Culture*, London: Portfolio

BBC. BBC News to cut a further 415 jobs, BBC News, 17 July 2014, www.bbc.co.uk/news/entertainment-arts-28342929

Benkoil, Dorian. Are magazine iPad apps profitable in the long haul? *MediaShift*, November 2010, http://mediashift.org/2010/11/are-magazine-ipad-apps-profitable-in-the-long-haul321

Bilton, Ricardo. How publishers-turned-platforms pay their amateur contributors, Digiday, 9 April 2014, http://digiday.com/publishers/publishing-platforms-pay-contributors

Boutin, Paul. Denton to pay bloggers based on traffic, Gawker, 1 January 2008, http://gawker.com/339271/denton-to-pay-bloggers-based-on-traffic

Broussard, Meredith. Artificial intelligence for investigative reporting, *Digital Journalism* 3(6), 28 November 2014: 814–831, DOI: http://dx.doi.org/10.1080/21670811.2014.985497

Bureau of Labor Statistics, U.S. Department of Labor. Employment trends in newspaper publishing and other media, 1990–2016 on the internet, *The Economics Daily*, 2 June 2016, www.bls.gov/opub/ted/2016/employment-trends-in-newspaper-publishing-and-other-media-1990-2016.htm

Buttry, Steve. The newspaper industry's colossal mistake was a defensive digital strategy, The Buttry Diary, 18 October 2016, https://stevebuttry.wordpress.com/2016/10/18/the-newspaper-industrys-colossal-mistake-was-a-defensive-digital-strategy

BuzzFeed. BuzzFeed announces major expansion across all business lines, BuzzFeedPress, 11 August 2014, https://www.buzzfeed.com/buzzfeedpress/buzzfeed-announces-major-expansion-across-all-business-lines

Cardew, Ben. Time Inc.'s M Scott Havens: 'We want to build the next LinkedIn or Facebook', *Guardian*, 29 June 2014, https://www.theguardian.com/media/2014/jun/29/time-inc-scott-havens-digital-linkedin

Carvin, Andy. Welcome to reported.ly! Reportedly, 8 December 2014, https://medium.com/reportedly/welcome-to-reported-ly-3363a5fb7ea5

Chyi, Hsiang Iris and Tenenboim, Ori. Reality check: multiplatform newspaper readership in the United States, 2007–2015, *Journalism Practice*, 27 July 2016: 1–22, DOI: http://dx.doi.org/10.1080/17512786.2016.1208056

Cooper, Daniel. YouTube's making 'TV' series and movies with its most popular creators, Engadget, 28 April 2015, https://www.engadget.com/2015/04/28/youtube-awesomeness-tv-deal

Cox, Jasper. Record 84,000 journalists in the UK in 2016 according to Labour Force Survey (up 20,000 in a year), *Press Gazette*, 12 December 2016, www.pressgazette.co.uk/record-84000-journalists-in-the-uk-in-2016-according-to-labour-force-survey-up-20000-in-a-year

Csutoras, Brent. Videos on Facebook: Native vs YouTube. Which wins? *Search Engine Journal*, 29 June 2015, https://www.searchenginejournal.com/videos-facebook-native-vs-youtube-wins/134389

Domingo, David, Salaverría, Ramón, Aguado, Juan Miguel and Giménez Toledo, Elea. 'Four dimensions of journalistic convergence: a preliminary approach to current media trends at Spain'. Paper for the 8th International Symposium of Online Journalism. University of Texas at Austin, 2007, https://online.journalism.utexas.edu/2007/papers/Domingo.pdf

Dorr, Konstantin Nicholas and Hollnbuchner, Katharina. Ethical challenges of algorithmic journalism, *Digital Journalism*, 19 April 2016, DOI: http://dx.doi.org/10.1080/21670811.2016.1167612

Enders Analysis. 'Competitive pressures on the press', presentation to the Leveson Inquiry, 6 October 2011, https://www.kcl.ac.uk/sspp/policy-institute/CMCP/local-news.pdf

Fennah, Alison. European online advertising surpasses TV to record annual spend of €36.4bn, Interactive Advertising Bureau, 11 May 2016, www.iabeurope.eu/research-thought-leadership/press-release-european-online-advertising-surpasses-tv-to-record-annual-spend-of-e36-2bn

Filloux, Frederic. Bloated HTML, the best and the worse, Monday Note, 15 August 2016, https://mondaynote.com/bloated-html-the-best-and-the-worse-cac6eb06496d

Flanagan, Andrew. Pitchfork acquired by Condé Nast, Billboard, 13 October 2015, www.billboard.com/biz/articles/6729354/pitchfork-acquired-by-condé -nast

Freedom House. Freedom on the net 2014, Freedom House, 2014, https://freedomhouse.org/sites/default/files/FOTN_2014_Full_Report_compressedv2_0.pdf

Garcia-Aviles, Jose A., Meier, Klaus, Kaltenbrunner, Andy, Carvajal, Miguel and Kraus, Daniel. Newsroom integration in Austria, Spain and Germany, *Journalism Practice* 3(3), 2009: 285–303, DOI: http://dx.doi.org/10.1080/17512780902798638

Gillmor, Dan (2004) *We the Media*, Sebastopol, CA: O'Reilly

Glick, Jonathan. Rise of the platishers, Recode, 7 February 2014, www.recode.net/2014/2/7/11623214/rise-of-the-platishers

Graefe, Andrew. Guide to automated journalism, Tow Center for Digital Journalism, 2016, http://towcenter.org/research/guide-to-automated-journalism

Graves, Lucas, Nyhan, Brendan and Reifler, Jason. The diffusion of fact-checking, American Press Institute, 22 April 2015, www.americanpressinstitute.org/wp-content/uploads/2015/04/The-Growth-of-Fact-Checking.pdf

Graves, Lucas and Cherubini, Federica. The rise of fact-checking sites in Europe, Reuters Institute for the Study of Journalism, November 2016, http://reutersinstitute.politics.ox.ac.uk/sites/default/files/The%20Rise%20of%20Fact-Checking%20Sites%20in%20Europe.pdf

Guardian. Murdoch's speech: full text, *Guardian*, 14 April 2005, https://www.theguardian.com/media/2005/apr/14/citynews.newmedia

Halls, Andy. Voluntary redundancies as Future Publishing focuses on digital, Journalism.co.uk, 19 July 2011, https://blogs.journalism.co.uk/2011/07/19/voluntary-redundancies-as-future-publishing-focuses-on-digital

Hansen, Espen Egil. Dear Mark. I am writing this to inform you that I shall not comply with your requirement to remove this picture, Aftenposten, 9 September 2016, www.aftenposten.no/meninger/kommentar/Dear-Mark-I-am-writing-this-to-inform-you-that-I-shall-not-comply-with-your-requirement-to-remove-this-picture-604156b.html

Harding, James, James Harding: journalism today, BBC Media Centre, 13 January 2014, www.bbc.co.uk/mediacentre/speeches/2014/james-harding-wt-stead.html

Harte, Dave, Williams, Andy and Turner, Jerome. Reciprocity and the hyperlocal journalist, *Journalism Practice*, 31 August 2016, DOI: http://dx.doi.org/10.1080/17512786.2016.1219963

Herrman, John. Media websites battle faltering ad revenue and traffic, *New York Times*, 17 April 2016, www.nytimes.com/2016/04/18/business/media-websites-battle-falteringad-revenue-and-traffic.html

Hoffman, Martin. Datenanalyse: Facebooks Instant Articles sing nicht so erfolgreich, wie du glaubst, MRTNH.DE, 6 November 2015, http://mrtnh.de/datenanalyse-facebooks-instant-articles-sind-nicht-so-erfolgreich-wie-du-glaubst/#comment-26531

Huang, Chia Lun. Get your podcasts ready for a new, seat-belted audience, WAN-IFRA, 2 December 2015, http://blog.wan-ifra.org/2015/12/02/get-your-podcasts-ready-for-a-new-seat-belted-audience

Huffington, Arianna. The paywall is history, *Guardian*, 11 May 2009, https://www.theguardian.com/commentisfree/2009/may/11/newspapers-web-media-pay-wall

Ives, Nat. Making sense of early sales for magazines' iPad editions, *Advertising Age*, 22 October 2010, http://adage.com/article/media/making-sense-early-sales-magazines-ipad-editions/146640

Jarvis, Jeff (2014) *Geeks Bearing Gifts: Imagining New Futures for News*, New York: CUNY Journalism Press

Jones, Sydney. Online classifieds, Pew Internet and American Life Project, May 2009, www.pewinternet.org/~/media//Files/Reports/2009/PIP%20-%20Online%20Classifieds.pdf

Kafka, Peter. Snapchat wants to stop sharing ad revenue with its media partners, Recode, 18 October 2016, www.recode.net/2016/10/18/13326196/snapchat-discover-ad-sales-plan-changes

Kaplan, David. *Global Investigative Journalism: Strategies for Support*, Center for International Media Assistance, 2007, https://www.scribd.com/document/99636874/CIMA-Investigative-Journalism-Report

Kaplan, David. *Global Investigative Journalism: Strategies for Support*, 2nd edn, Center for International Media Assistance, 2013, www.cima.ned.org/wp-content/uploads/2015/01/CIMA-Investigative-Journalism-Dave-Kaplan.pdf

Knight, Megan. Data journalism in the UK, *Journal of Media Practice* 16(1), 2015, www.tandfonline.com/doi/abs/10.1080/14682753.2015.1015801

Kulwin, Noah. This week on 'Re/code Decode': CEO Jonah Peretti explains how BuzzFeed won the internet (Updated), Recode, 16 September 2015, www.recode.net/2015/9/16/11618618/this-week-on-recode-decode-ceo-jonah-peretti-explains-how-buzzfeed

Lee, Matthew. Rise of the robot journalist, Delayed Gratification, 15 August 2014, www.slow-journalism.com/rise-of-the-robot-journalist

Lichterman, Joseph. The Winnipeg Free Press' bet on micropayments will generate about $100,000 in revenue this year, NiemanLab, 13 April 2016, www.niemanlab.org/2016/04/the-winnipeg-free-press-bet-on-micropayments-will-generate-about-100000-in-revenue-this-year

Lowrey, Wilson. The emergence and development of news fact-checking sites, *Journalism Studies*, 28 July 2015, DOI: http://dx.doi.org/10.1080/1461670X.2015.1052537

Mance, Henry. UK newspapers: rewriting the story, *Financial Times*, 9 February 2016, https://www.ft.com/content/0aa8beac-c44f-11e5-808f-8231cd71622e

Marsh, Peter. The state of paid content: for free, for a fee, or somewhere in between, International News Media Association, 4 November 2014, www.inma.org/blogs/ahead-of-the-curve/post.cfm/the-state-of-paid-content-for-free-for-a-fee-or-somewhere-in-between

Marshall, Jack. The rise of the publishing platform specialist, *Wall Street Journal*, 25 March 2016, www.wsj.com/articles/the-rise-of-the-publishing-platform-specialist-1458896683

Media Reform Coalition. The elephant in the room: a survey of media ownership and plurality in the United Kingdom, April 2014, www.mediareform.org.uk/wp-content/uploads/2014/04/ElephantintheroomFinalfinal.pdf

Medium. Making medium more powerful for publishers, 3 Min Read, 5 April 2016, https://blog.medium.com/making-medium-more-powerful-for-publishers-39663413a904

Menke, M., Kinnebrock, S., Kretzschmar, S., Aichinger, I., Broersma, M., Hummel, R., Kirchhoff, S., Prandner, D., Ribeiro, N. and Salaverriá, R. Convergence culture in European newsrooms. Comparing editorial strategies for cross-media news production in six countries. *Journalism Studies*, 11 October 2016, DOI: 10.1080/1461670X.2016.1232175

Metropolitan Police. Operation Alice: Closing Report, Metropolitan Police, September 2014, www.iocco-uk.info/docs/Met%20Operation%20Alice%20Closing%20Report.pdf

Minto, Scott. Untitled, *Financial Times* Tumblr, 2013, http://financialtimes.tumblr.com/post/43643107894/rob-minto-interactive-editor-2005-11-when-i

Montal, Tal and Reich, Zvi. I, robot. You, journalist. Who is the author? *Digital Journalism*, 5 August 2016, DOI: http://dx.doi.org/10.1080/21670811.2016.1209083

Moses, Lucia. The hidden (and not so hidden) costs of platform publishing, Digiday, 9 February 2016, http://digiday.com/publishers/hidden-not-hidden-costs-platform-publishing

Newman, Nic, Levy, David A. L. and Kleis Nielsen, Rasmus. Reuters Digital News Report 2015, Reuters Institute for the Study of Journalism, 2015, http://reutersinstitute.politics.ox.ac.uk/publication/digital-news-report-2015

Office for National Statistics. EMP04: employment by occupation, Office for National Statistics, 17 August 2016, https://www.ons.gov.uk/employmentandlabourmarket/peopleinwork/employmentandemployeetypes/datasets/employmentbyoccupationemp04

Holcomb, Jesse, Mitchell, Amy and Purcell, Kristen. Investigative journalists and digital security, Pew Research Center in association with Columbia University's Tow Center for Digital Journalism, 5 February 2015, www.journalism.org/2015/02/05/investigative-journalists-and-digital-security

Pfeiffer, Andreas. The distributed content landscape: an overview for publishers – Part 1, WAN-IFRA, 26 October 2015a, http://blog.wan-ifra.org/2015/10/26/the-distributed-content-landscape-an-overview-for-publishers-part-1

Pfeiffer, Andreas. Far from home: the distributed content landscape – Part 2, WAN-IFRA, 9 November 2015b, http://blog.wan-ifra.org/2015/11/09/far-from-home-the-distributed-content-landscape-part-2

Ponsford, Dominic. NRS: UK monthly readership of Sun falls behind Independent amid mobile traffic surge, *Press Gazette*, 3 June 2015a, www.pressgazette.co.uk/nrs-uk-monthly-readership-sun-falls-behind-independent-amid-mobile-traffic-surge

Ponsford, Dominic. Regional press digital growth outstrips print decline as Manchester Evening News tops website table, *Press Gazette*, 26 August 2015b, www.pressgazette.co.uk/regional-press-digital-growth-outstrips-print-decline-manchester-evening-news-tops-website-table

Poutanen, Petro, Luoma-Aho, Vilma and Suhanko, Elina. Ethical challenges of hybrid editors, *International Journal on Media Management* 18(2), 30 March 2016: 99–116, DOI: http://dx.doi.org/10.1080/14241277.2016.1157805

Pugh, Andrew. Johnston Press predicts 'few daily print titles' by 2020, *Press Gazette*, 25 April 2012, www.pressgazette.co.uk/johnston-press-predicts-few-daily-print-titles-by-2020

Radcliffe, Damian. Where are we now? UK hyperlocal media and community journalism in 2015, Centre for Community Journalism, October 2015, https://www.communityjournalism.co.uk/wp-content/uploads/2015/09/C4CJ-Report-for-Screen.pdf

Ramsay, Gordon and Moore, Martin. Monopolising local news: is there an emerging democratic deficit in the UK due to the decline of local newspapers? London: King's College London, Centre for the Study of Media, Communication and Power, May 2016, https://www.kcl.ac.uk/sspp/policy-institute/CMCP/local-news.pdf

Reynolds, John and Sweney, Mark. Magazine chiefs urge industry change from burning platform to growth, *Guardian*, 25 May 2014, https://www.theguardian.com/media/2014/may/25/magazine-change-digital-job-cuts

Rowlands, Barbara. The fall and rise of magazines from print to digital, *Guardian*, 7 March 2013, https://www.theguardian.com/media-network/media-network-blog/2013/mar/07/fall-rise-magazines-print-digital

Seamans, Robert and Zhu, Feng. *Responses to Entry in Multi-Sided Markets: The Impact of Craigslist on Local Newspapers*, 28 May 2013. NET Institute Working Paper No. 10–11. DOI: http://dx.doi.org/10.2139/ssrn.1694622

Silverman, Craig, Strapagiel, Lauren, Shaban, Hamza, Hall, Ellie and Singer-Vine, Jeremy. Hyperpartisan Facebook pages are publishing false and misleading information at an alarming rate, BuzzFeed, 20 October 2016, https://www.buzzfeed.com/craigsilverman/partisan-fb-pages-analysis

Smith, Chris. Redesigning Forbes for the digital age – Q&A with Lewis D'Vorkin, *Guardian*, 29 January 2013, https://www.theguardian.com/media-network/2013/jan/29/forbes-digital-lewis-dvorkin

Smith, Patrick. Future hit by revenue slowdown and cost challenges as 55 jobs go, MediaBriefing, 3 September 2013, https://www.themediabriefing.com/article/future-hit-by-revenue-slowdown-and-cost-challenges-as-55-jobs-go

Sonderman, Jeff, Loker, Kevin, Yaeger, Katie, Ivancin, Maria, Lacy, Stephen and Rosenstiel, Tom. Facing change: the needs, attitudes and experiences of people in media, American Press

Institute, 6 August 2015, https://www.americanpressinstitute.org/publications/reports/survey-research/api-journalists-survey

St John III, Burton, Johnson, Kirsten and Nah, Seungahn. Patch.com: the challenge of connective community journalism in the digital sphere, *Journalism Practice* 8(2), 2014: 197–212, DOI: http://dx.doi.org/10.1080/17512786.2013.859835

Stray, Jonathan. The age of the cyborg, *Columbia Journalism Review*, Fall/Winter 2016, www.cjr.org/analysis/cyborg_virtual_reality_reuters_tracer.php

Sullivan, Margaret. As print fades, Part 1: 'live journalism' at The Times, *New York Times*: Public Editor's Journal, 10 August 2015, http://publiceditor.blogs.nytimes.com/2015/08/10/as-print-fades-part-1-live-journalism-at-the-times

Telegraph. Financial crisis: UK job losses, 3 December 2008, www.telegraph.co.uk/finance/financialcrisis/3542572/Financial-crisis-UK-job-losses.html

Thurman, Neil, Pascal, Jean-Christophe and Bradshaw, Paul (2012) Can big media do 'big society'?: A critical case study of commercial, convergent hyperlocal news. *International Journal of Media and Cultural Politics* 8(2–3), DOI: 10.1386/macp.8.2-3.269_1

Thurman, Neil, Schifferes, Steve, Fletcher, Richard, Newman, Nic, Hunt, Stephen and Schapals, Aljosha Karim. Giving computers a nose for news, *Digital Journalism* 4(7), 23 February 2016: 838–848, DOI: http://dx.doi.org/10.1080/21670811.2016.1149436

Vogt, Nancy and Mitchell, Amy. Crowdfunded journalism: a small but growing addition to publicly driven journalism, Pew Research Centre, 20 January 2016, www.journalism.org/2016/01/20/crowdfunded-journalism

Waldal, Espen. Building a robot journalist, Bakken & Baeck, 18 November 2016, https://medium.com/bakken-b%C3%A6ck/building-a-robot-journalist-171554a68fa8

Waldman, Noah. Study: 68% of publishers use editorial staff to create native ads, Contently, 16 August 2016, https://contently.com/strategist/2016/08/16/study-68-of-publishers-use-editorial-staff-to-create-native-ads

3 Finding leads and sources online

Chapter objectives

This chapter will cover:

- The importance of strong search skills for speed and depth in reporting
- How to keep up to date with your field – and get leads to come to you
- Setting up your dashboards to monitor key sources
- Advanced search techniques for finding key authoritative information
- Finding experts online
- Finding sources on social media
- Finding people on the ground: advanced search on Twitter
- Human interest stories: identifying newsworthy Facebook pages and forums.

Introduction

Journalism combines two core skills: information gathering and production. There was a time when journalists could rely on their organisation's infrastructure for much of the information. Not any longer.

Newswires, press releases, the news diary and readers or listeners calling in once helped supply many of the leads that would eventually fill that day's bulletin or paper. Now, however, most of that information is already available online: the sports fan can read statements on their team's official website; the fashion fan can follow major brands on Instagram and Snapchat; while local parents might be following their children's school's Facebook page, and receiving updates from the local police force, council and train operators on Twitter. In some cases non-news organisations will actively compete with news organisations to 'scoop' them in being the first to their own story (Sherwood et al. 2016).

Contrasting with this easy availability of information to the public is a parallel opening up of research-based knowledge and experts. In a study of journalists' sourcing habits,

John Wihby notes: 'At a time when journalism moves with ever-greater speed, it is not trivial that studies are just a click away, without barriers; more research is now unrestricted and "open access"' (Wihbey 2016), while the authors of such research are also more accessible through the academic blogosphere.

In that context, editors are now asking journalists to do more: just repeating what everybody already knows is no longer enough: now reporters need to dig a little deeper.

Setting up useful alerts and feeds

The first step in covering any subject is to set up your personal news feeds. This is the same process whether you are covering a geographical area, reporting on a particular topic or even devoting time to one ongoing story.

Your personal news feeds are just that: personal. They are different to newswires such as Reuters and Associated Press (AP) that are used by newsrooms around the world, but the principle is much the same: to bring developments straight to you so you can judge whether to follow up.

There are two main technologies that are used for a personal news feed: email alerts, and RSS feeds. Email alerts are relatively straightforward: you receive an email every time something new happens in a field of interest. RSS is a way to bring a number of news feeds into one or more pages which you can check at a glance.

Email has the advantage of being very simple to set up, but the disadvantage of requiring you to open and check each email separately. RSS feeds require you to use a tool called an RSS reader, and can take a bit of getting used to. But once set up it is much easier and quicker to check everything that's going on.

Setting up email alerts

The most commonly used tool for setting up email alerts is Google Alerts (Google.co.uk/alerts), although there also alternatives like Talkwalker. They work much the same as a search engine, with this key difference: once you type in a search you can then choose to be alerted as soon as *new* results are found.

For this reason it is useful for setting up alerts for phrases that are likely to indicate newsworthy information. These include:

- Crimes and emergencies, such as 'fire', 'robbery' or 'crash'
- 'Report' or 'research'
- 'Anniversary'
- 'Launch'
- 'Protest'
- 'Campaign'
- 'Fundraising'.

You will need to add extra keywords to limit results to those relevant to your location or field. For example, if you are reporting on fashion you might add an alert for 'fashion research' while a reporter for a newspaper in Birmingham might set up alerts for 'Birmingham fire' or, better still, particular areas in the city such as 'Jewellery Quarter fire'.

You might also set up alerts for key individuals, organisations, terms and places that you report on: a motoring reporter might have alerts for terms like 'Jaguar Land Rover' and 'Hyundai', for example.

It is important to highlight that many of the results that you get will not be newsworthy: many of the results, for example, will come from news organisations themselves. When setting up the alert you can limit it so that it does not include results from Google News, or focuses only on blogs, or 'discussions' (forums). This can be useful depending on what you want to be alerted to. Even if you do include Google News results it will allow you to keep up to date with what is happening in your field.

Google Alerts can be particularly powerful, however, if you combine it with the advanced search operators detailed below: asking to be alerted when a new PDF appears on the local council website mentioning a key term or place, for example. But don't assume that Google will always know when this has been done (and remember that a large proportion of information is not indexed by Google at all – see the section on the 'invisible web', p.66).

Beyond Google you can also set up email alerts whenever a webpage is changed. This can be particularly useful for pages where organisations publish new information: for example sports teams' results pages, public bodies' meeting listings and Freedom of Information (FOI) disclosure logs (see Chapter 10 for more on FOI). These tools are broadly referred to as 'change detection' and the most widely used site for this is changedetection. com (alternatives include Versionista.com and IsItUpdated.com). However, bear in mind that these alerts can be patchy, so it is still worth checking manually every so often.

Needless to say some of those organisations might provide an email update facility or RSS feed themselves. If so, consider subscribing.

Using RSS feeds and RSS readers

RSS – which stands for rich site summary or, more appropriately, relatively simple syndication – is a technology which allows you to receive a 'feed' of information from a specific source. You can find RSS feeds for all sorts of sources, from news and magazine websites to individual journalists, blogs, press offices, government bodies, sports results, data releases, campaigning tools, events listings and even search engines.

On their own these feeds are no different to an email alert, but it is the ability to combine those feeds on a single screen that makes them especially powerful. It works just as Twitter does in this respect (with some key differences – see p.54) and is done in an 'RSS reader'. An RSS reader provides a dashboard which shows you the latest updates from *all* the RSS feeds you are following.

Two of the most widely used RSS readers by journalists are Netvibes (netvibes.com) and Feedly (feedly.com). Each has its advantages: Netvibes works best on desktop and you can share dashboards publicly so colleagues can use them as well. Feedly works well on mobile. You can also subscribe to RSS feeds using services like Flipboard (Flipboard.com) which allows you to 'curate' individual items into Flipboard magazines that you can then share.

After creating an account with the service most RSS readers work in a similar way: there is a search bar where you can search for feeds, or paste the web address of a site you want to follow.

If you paste the address the service will try to detect any RSS feeds and give you the option of subscribing to them. In many cases it may find more than one feed: typically there will be different feeds for the latest posts, and for the latest comments. You should subscribe to the posts feed. (If it does not find the feed, try the following: paste a different URL on the same site, or look on the webpage itself for an RSS icon, or use a search engine to search 'RSS feeds' on that site.)

Some sites offer a range of different RSS feeds across the site. The BBC, for example, offers different feeds for news in different regions, for different subjects like business, politics or education, for sections like the magazine and Have Your Say and for media such as video. You can also get a different RSS feed for every single football team covered in its sport section. On the *Guardian* website you can follow individual journalists through RSS feeds (just paste the URL of their profile page), and its system also provides RSS feeds for specific topics such as 'tax' or the 'budget deficit': when you paste an article's URL into an RSS reader, it will show you the various options.

The most useful RSS feeds are not on news sites but on sites that allow you to follow newsworthy information *at its source*, before it has been reported by other journalists. Civic sites like WhatDoTheyKnow (for following FOI requests) and TheyWorkForYou (follow what happens in parliament) provide customisable RSS feeds that allow you to receive updates when a particular MP speaks or a particular term is used, or an FOI request is received by a particular body or uses a particular keyword.

Once you start to follow a lot of feeds you can also organise these into folders (each will have its own screen, or dashboard) along different themes. For example, you might have a folder for feeds related to health stories, another for sport, another for arts and culture, and so on. Or you might have a folder for each part of a city you are covering. You might have a folder for following competing news sources, and one for leads. Or you might have a folder for your most important feeds, and then others for less important ones.

CLOSER LOOK
RSS IS DEAD? USING SOCIAL MEDIA INSTEAD

The rise of social networks like Twitter led many commentators to argue that RSS was 'dead'. After all, Twitter performs a very similar function to an RSS reader: you can follow many different accounts (feeds) and see updates all on one screen. So why do we need an RSS reader when we can follow updates on Twitter instead?

There are two very good reasons why RSS is not dead – at least for journalists. The first is that Twitter is a very *ephemeral* tool for following developments: you are unlikely to see an update unless you happen to be using Twitter at the time that it is sent up. This makes it hard to catch up with important developments, which is what an RSS reader allows you to do much better.

The second reason is that RSS readers allow you to follow very *specific and comprehensive* updates that may never appear on Twitter: search-based RSS feeds from WhatDoTheyKnow or TheyWorkForYou are customised to you and are unlikely to be tweeted; likewise, news organisations' social media accounts do not tweet every story, so if you want to make sure that you get an update when a *Guardian* article about tax evasion is published, you can never be sure that the organisation will tweet that. There are also many updates which organisations have to publish online (and in RSS feeds) but which they do not wish to publish – and so draw attention to – on social media.

Put another way, you do not have enough control over Twitter updates to be able to ensure that you always see the right ones. Twitter is designed as a *real-time* update system: what is happening *now*. That is its strength for journalists – but also its weakness.

RSS readers, while performing a similar function, are designed to give you an at-a-glance overview of *what has happened today,* or this week, or this month. The strength of RSS for journalists is its comprehensiveness, and its customisation: it allows you to make sure that you miss nothing; and to make sure that new information is supplied to you in a way that fits your needs. Most importantly for journalists, it allows you to receive 'less public' information that has not already been published on social media. And ultimately, for journalists, that is particularly valuable.

Social networks: setting up lists and dashboards

When you begin reporting on a particular field, area or subject, you should make sure that you are following relevant and useful social media accounts in that area. For journalists Twitter is the dominant tool to use in this respect: it is succinct and fast; but don't overlook Facebook and, depending on your field, social networks like LinkedIn, Tumblr, Vine, Instagram and YouTube to name just a few.

One of the most useful functions in Twitter is the Twitter list: this allows you to add any user to a list which you can then look at separately to your main Twitter timeline. (Facebook also has an option to create lists of friends or interests. You can find guidance on their Help pages at facebook.com/help/135312293276793.)

Lists can be made on any basis. Here are some examples:

- A list of people within a particular industry
- A list of people within a particular geographical area (your 'patch')
- A list of people with a particular role (e.g. fellow journalists, or footballers)
- A list of accounts which are not human (e.g. automated accounts for press releases)
- A list of people you have met in person
- A list of colleagues
- Celebrity accounts
- A list of accounts which are funny and provide light relief.

The @ITVCentral account, for example, maintains or follows 12 lists. These include a list of travel companies across the Midlands (23 members); another of local councils (46); one of 'Reporters/Correspondents/News-desk/Technical/Sales' (58 members); one of 'Anyone and (nearly) everyone working for ITV News' (153); one of local papers (60); a list of BBC accounts (17); a list of MPs' Twitter accounts (88); one of Midlands football clubs (17); and a list of West Midlands Police accounts (273).

Some of these were created by other organisations, such as West Midlands Police, and then 'subscribed to' by @ITVCentral. You can follow lists made by other people by looking at any account and clicking on the 'Lists' button. The default view shows you lists that the account is *subscribed to* (on the left). But there is also the option to see lists that they are a *Member of*. Try browsing both. Once you are on a list page you can click 'Subscribe' to add that list to your lists.

Your own lists can be found in the same way, but you can also view them using a Twitter dashboard like TweetDeck (see below).

To create a list yourself first find someone that you want to start that list with, and click on the cog icon next to the 'Follow' or 'Following' button. Select 'Add or remove from lists . . .' and on the window that appears click 'Create a list' and give it a name. You can also choose whether the list is public or private.

To add more people to the same list follow the same process as above but tick a list you've already created instead of 'Create a list'.

Some people worry about following too many people on Twitter because they might then receive too many updates to cope with, but the Twitter list stops this becoming a problem: instead of checking your main timeline, you can switch between lists just as you would switch between different TV channels.

Using dashboards to switch between lists and searches

Twitter's own website isn't very useful for following updates on the service. Instead you should use a social media 'dashboard' service such as TweetDeck (now owned by Twitter) or Hootsuite. These services also allow you to follow different lists and searches on the same screen, and manage multiple social media accounts too: for example your own professional account and a general account for your section or publication. Make sure you are posting from the right account.

When you log into TweetDeck it presents updates across different columns on the screen. The basic columns might be your general timeline, any @ messages and a column for direct messages. On the left, however, you can add extra columns by clicking on the plus icon. These include tweets that you have favourited, new followers, search results (including hashtags) and, of course, lists.

By putting each list in its own column you can quickly scan across updates in different fields. You can also order them from left to right based on their priority.

Using search

While email alerts, social media and RSS readers work well, there will always be situations when you need to use search engines to find background information, experts or case studies. But search engines are problematic for journalists for a fundamental reason: they

CLOSER LOOK
FIVE TIPS FOR FINDING USEFUL TWITTER ACCOUNTS

Here are five techniques you can use to find the right people to follow on Twitter.

1   Search Twitter biographies only
    There are a number of tools for searching biographies on Twitter, such as FollowerWonk (make sure you select 'Search Twitter bios only' from the drop-down menu).

    Try a range of terms: not just likely job titles but interests, organisation names, locations and other keywords.

2   Browse Twitter directories
    There are a number of directories for Twitter users. WeFollow works well with a general search but adding location seems to exclude a lot of relevant results.

    Twellow allows you to narrow down to the UK, and particular cities, which helps exclude US results, but there doesn't appear to be a way to use keywords and location together. There are categories too.

    A different approach is to search for networks of users around hashtags: Bluenod is one site which will do just that – and even allows you to create a Twitter list based on the results.

3   Find related lists
    It's likely that someone else has already created a Twitter list covering the same or a related area. One way to find these is to look at the users you've already found and see what lists they've been added to.

    You can find these by going to the Twitter user's profile page and clicking on 'Lists' to the left and then selecting 'Member of' in the middle. The resulting URL should look like this:

    https://twitter.com/USERNAME/memberships

but with the username instead of USERNAME. *Guardian* reporter Shiv Malik's list of memberships, for example, can be found at:

    https://twitter.com/shivmalik1/memberships

You can also try to search for Twitter lists themselves. One way to do this is to put your search query at the end of the following URL:

    https://twitter.com/search?mode=timelines&q=

For example, a search for lists with 'welfare reform' in the title would look like this:

    https://twitter.com/search?mode=timelines&q=welfare+reform

Alternatively, you can try some clever use of Google like this:

    site:twitter.com/*/lists/ inurl:YOURKEYWORD

(Replacing KEYWORD with your own keyword.) Or try broadening the search to something like this (replacing the phrase with your own):

site:twitter.com/*/lists/ "mental health"

This will bring back any list pages where one of the tweets mentions that term. Obviously this depends on what people are tweeting about at that moment in time.

4 Search discussions and hashtags

As you start to follow people in your field, you'll come across some terms and hashtags repeatedly. In health, for example, people will be talking about the NHS, cuts, nursing, midwifery, GP opening hours and other issues.

You can search for these on Twitter itself, or use Google with the phrase site:twitter.com (note no space after the colon) which limits results to Twitter.

Make sure you use quotes to get exact phrases only – e.g. 'zero hour contracts' will ensure you don't get results that mention those words in separate places, but be aware it will also exclude misspellings and variations such as 'zero hours contracts' plural.

Hashtags of the same phrases are worth trying too: #bedroomtax and #welfarereform, for example, have both been widely used instead of the full phrase.

You can also try prefixing general terms with 'uk' – #ukhousing, for example, is often used by those within the UK housing industry to distinguish their discussions from those elsewhere.

Watch out for scheduled live chats too – #CABlive, for example, is used for discussions between citizens advice bureaux – and campaigns, like #PaydayWatch.

You can also use a tool like Hashtagify.me to find hashtags related to ones you already know. A similar service, SonarSolo, identifies related terms but goes beyond hashtags and also includes 'mentioned people'. And BuzzSumo identifies key people around keywords or phrases too, while Topsy will allow you to identify 'influencers'.

5 Following followers

Finally, look at the people you've already found and who they're following and listing.

When you're logged in to the Twitter website it normally shows a box on each profile page showing 'similar accounts', but clicking on 'Following and Followers' will give you more suggestions – or you can just add those words to the Twitter account URL: a list of accounts that the *Guardian*'s Patrick Butler is following can be found at https://twitter.com/patrickjbutler/following, for example.

rank content based primarily on how many other pages link to it. This is why search engine results are often dominated by news stories and Wikipedia entries. By definition, you are unlikely to find 'exclusive' or surprising information without using some more advanced techniques.

On these occasions it is very important that you can use the search engine quickly and effectively, and knowing advanced search operators can be key to this.

Search operators

Search operators allow you to specify something about the search results you want to get, beyond the words that you are using. For example, putting quotation marks around a series of words means that the search engine will only look for that *exact pattern* of words: specifying "Michael Brown" with quotation marks means you will not get results where those words are separated, for example *Michael has brown hair* or *Michael William Brown*.

More advanced search operators can specify other qualities, such as the type of site that results come from; the type of document; the time period that it was or was not published during; and whether words appear in the title or URL rather than anywhere in the page.

Most people use search engines by searching for *what they want to know*. However, to use them most effectively you should *describe what you expect to find*. The difference is subtle, but important: here are some things to consider:

- *Who* do you expect might have published this information? (For example, a government body, or a charity? A police force, or a health authority? A school, or a university?)
- *When* do you think this information was published?
- *What type* of document do you expect to contain this information? (A report? A presentation? A spreadsheet?)
- *Where* in the document do you expect certain words to appear? (The body, or the title? The URL?)
- What *specialist jargon* might be used in the document, which you might not find in other reports?
- What qualities do you expect the information *not to have*? For example, it might not have certain words, or not be published within a particular timeframe, or not be published by a particular body.

All these qualities can be described using search operators.

Who published it?: the site operator

Most of the time journalists are looking for information that has some sort of *authority*. It might be 'official' reports, statements or statistics made by government, health or police bodies; or it might be authoritative research done by an academic, or claims made by a charity or union that represents thousands of people.

The *site:* operator allows you to specify the type of source of information by identifying the domain that the information sits on. Here are some examples:

- site:uk
- site:gov.uk
- site:bristol.gov.uk
- site:police.uk
- site:ac.uk
- site:org.uk.

The first example will only bring back results on sites that are hosted on a .uk domain. That includes sites like *amazon.co.uk*, *met.police.uk* and *argos.uk* but it *excludes* sites like *amazon.com*, *sunkist.co.jp* and *spiegel.net*.

The second example is more specific: it will only bring back results on a gov.uk domain. That includes all local authorities in the UK, as well as central government departments and bodies such as NationalArchives.gov.uk and royalmint.gov.uk.

The third example is more specific still: it only brings back results on Bristol Council's domain bristol.gov.uk.

Many official bodies have particular types of URLs: all UK police forces, for example, use the police.uk domain, which is very useful when you want to specify that your information should be published on a police force website (the fourth example above). Universities use the ac.uk domain – useful when looking for academic research or academics themselves (you can also try specifying the domains of academic publishers, for example: site:tandfonline.com). Health bodies use nhs.uk, the military uses mod.uk and schools use sch.uk.

Charities use the .org domain, but this is a little more complicated: while some will use .org.uk some will simply use .org, and some might even use .co.uk or .com, so you may need to try a few different searches if you don't find what you're after. Also remember that you may find experts in other countries as well: US universities use the .edu domain, so site:edu may be worth trying for some searches too.

Sometimes the site operator can help you find details about a particular individual you are reporting on. Online investigator Michael Bazzell says he often uses the operator: 'A Google search of site:craigslist.com and [one phone] number revealed archived expired posts by the [person] promoting himself as a male prostitute'. Another search using site:amazon.com found that the person in question had reviewed books to help with addiction to controlled substances (Bazzell 2013).

What type of document: the filetype operator

Authoritative information often comes in particular types of documents: reports are often published in PDFs, or Word documents. Spreadsheets are published in Excel files or CSVs. Presentations are published in PowerPoint.

To specify this use the *filetype:* operator like so:

- filetype:pdf
- filetype:xls
- filetype:xlsx
- filetype:doc
- filetype:docx
- filetype:ppt
- filetype:pptx

Note that there is no space between the colon and the code used to indicate the document type: xls for an Excel spreadsheet (or xlsx for more modern versions); doc for a Word document (or docx) and ppt or pptx for a PowerPoint presentation.

Bear in mind that documents are sometimes created in one format and saved in another: spreadsheets and presentations, for example, may be exported to PDF format before publishing. See Chapter 10 for more on converting PDFs.

Specifying where words appear: inurl, intitle

Two operators allow you to specify where terms appear: *intitle:* specifies that a word appears in the title of the document or webpage; *inurl:* specifies that it appears in the URL. You can also specify more than one term by using the related operators *allintitle:* and *allinurl:*

The *intitle:* operator can be particularly useful when you have a lot of results and only want to see those where the document is specifically about your keyword (rather than it being mentioned briefly or incidentally). Such a search might look like this:

intitle:"top secret" filetype:pdf

The *inurl:* operator can be useful where your keyword is used in the actual structure of a website, or tends to appear in the name of the website. For example, clinical commissioning groups in the UK all tend to have 'ccg' in their URL, so a search can be narrowed to those by specifying: *inurl:ccg*. Because they are health bodies you can also combine it with another operator like so:

site:nhs.uk inurl:ccg

When was it published?: search tools

Google also allows you to specify a time range for the results it gives you, although this is not done with an operator but instead in the 'Search tools' menu underneath the search box. To use it do the following:

1   Conduct a search as normal.
2   Underneath the search box click 'Search tools' then select 'Any time' from the menu that appears.
3   You can specify periods such as the past hour, 24 hours, week, month or year if you want to exclude older results.
4   However, this functionality is most useful to exclude more recent results (if you want to ignore recent news reports). To do this click on 'Custom range . . .' and select a start and end date.

Note that this only refers to the time when Google *indexed* a webpage (stored it in its database), not necessarily the date when it was actually published.

Specifying specialist jargon, codes and specific names

This technique is not about operators but simply about knowing your field and the sorts of language that tends to be used in official documents. If you want to know about poverty in schools, for example, you will find the word 'poverty' is not often used. Instead you would need to look for other terms which indicate poverty, such as "free school meals" or "pupil premium". And if you want to know about drivers who fail a driving test but still drive away the official term is "Drive off unaccompanied from DTC" (Driving Test Centre).

Likewise if you are searching for a detailed breakdown of crime in Manchester, you might search for specific areas of Manchester such as 'Chorlton' rather than 'Manchester'. Why? Because whereas a national breakdown might mention Manchester, only a detailed breakdown will mention specific areas of that city.

Another technique is to search for unique reference codes if you have them. Schools, universities, police forces and local authorities will often have unique reference codes which are used in official statistics. Documents using these will tend to include statistics.

Excluding results containing certain words or other qualities

Language is a flexible thing, and often the same thing can have many different meanings. 'Golf', for example, can refer to the sport, or to a car made by Volkswagen. 'Table' can be a piece of furniture, or something on a page which shows data.

If your search results are confused by these ambiguities, you can exclude certain results by using the minus operator (without any space after it) like so:

* golf –volkswagen
* table –furniture.

You can also combine this with other operators. For example, the following search not only excludes any mentions of Volkswagen, but also excludes any results on the BBC domain, and any results that have 'championship' in the title:

* golf –volkswagen –intitle:championship –site:bbc.co.uk.

Wildcards: specifying a phrase with some room for ambiguity

If you want to search for an exact phrase you use the quotation mark like so:

"between 2010 and 2014"

But what if you have a broad idea of the phrase but don't want to be so specific? In those cases you can use a *wildcard*: the asterisk symbol. This stands for 'any word or phrase'. Here's an example:

"between * and 2014"

Try this search yourself and look at the results: the phrases in bold are the ones that Google has matched to your search. When I perform this search these include:

* "between 2004 and 2014"
* "between 2010 and 2014"

- "between 2009 and 2014"
- "between 1914 and 2014"
- "between 2013 and 2014"
- "between 1970 and 2014".

In this case the results are all numbers, but that's just because most matches refer to date ranges. Try "between * and then" and most results will match either "between now and then" or "between then and then".

Caches: finding older versions of webpages and pages that have disappeared

Sometimes you may click on a link and discover that the webpage no longer exists, or you suspect that a webpage has been changed and you want to see what it used to look like. In these situations archives and caches can be useful to compare the latest version of a webpage with older versions or to find pages which have disappeared.

For more recent changes, try conducting a relevant Google search and clicking on 'cache' next to the relevant result. This will show you Google's own 'cached' (saved) version of the page. You can also use other services which do this for you, such as CachedView.com.

For older changes the Internet Archive's Wayback Machine (archive.org/web) can give you snapshots going further back. Search for the URL and you will be presented with a calendar showing what dates it has saved that page: click on any date to see the saved copy.

Sometimes pages haven't disappeared but have merely moved. In these cases try copying the last part of the URL (normally containing the page title) and searching for that.

Vertical search engines

Google, of course, is not the only search engine around. And while other search engines such as DuckDuckGo, Bing and Yahoo are always worth a try too, more interesting are the smaller 'vertical' search engines which focus on more specific fields. If you work in a particular field it is worth identifying specialist search engines which cover that field. Here are some examples:

- Skyscanner (flights and airlines)
- IceRocket (blogs and social media)
- BoardReader (forums)
- Blinkx (video)
- SlideFinder or Slideshare (presentations)
- Healthline (health)
- Google Scholar (academic research)
- Bing Scholar (academic research)

- Academia.edu (academic research)
- Eventbrite or Meetup (events)
- Google Tables Search (webpages with tables)
- Zanran (webpages with tables, charts or reports).

Custom search engines

If you regularly search a particular collection of sites you can create your own custom search engine at cse.google.com/cse (or just search for *Google custom search engine*). You just need to type in the URLs of any sites you want to search and then it will give you a link to the new search engine you've just created.

If you want to change your custom search engine at any time just return to Google custom search engine and it should be listed there for you to edit.

Finding sources in search and social media

As well as using search to find background or facts, you are likely to need to find experts and case studies. The techniques listed above can be useful in finding these too – even on social media.

Finding experts

Experts are a particularly useful example. Typical types of expert include the following:

- Insider 'experts' who are employed within the industry full time, part time or on secondment.
- Academic experts who research and/or teach in the field. These may also work within the industry on a part-time, consultancy or secondment basis, and have probably done so in the past.
- 'Observers' – individuals who have an interest in monitoring how a particular industry operates, either because they are concerned about its impact on themselves or their loved ones, or because they see commercial or professional opportunities. This also includes . . .
- Issue campaigners – people who are interested in an issue that relates to their field. They may be nationally focused, or tackling how an issue plays out locally.
- Retirees – people who have retired from any of the above positions. One journalistic trick is to follow who leaves the industry, because they will have insider insights without, necessarily, the contingent concern over keeping their job.
- Students – at the other end of the spectrum are those who wish to enter a field or industry and are studying it. Occasionally individuals in this category will have unique insights through their research, internships or contacts.
- Bystanders – this category is slightly different to those listed above, as their role as 'observer' is generally accidental, and not informed by expertise. However, they also have less reason to skew their description of a particular event.

Experts on any particular field tend to work for a narrow range of organisations: for example, universities, government, charities and think tanks. Many organisations also promote their own experts on specific experts' directories.

To find an expert then, use searches like these:

- professor air safety site:ac.uk
- researcher child poverty site:org.uk
- experts directory law.

Another approach is to look for *research first*, as a way of finding the researcher. Try using Google Scholar or Academia.edu.

If you're looking for industry experts try looking for people who have presented at industry conferences in that field in recent years, or who are active in organising events (sites like Eventbrite, Lanyrd and Meetup come in useful here, but you can also use advanced search techniques to find official websites for conferences, or their schedules). And, of course, you can look at news reports on the subject to identify experts who have already been interviewed on the topic. You can also look for online CVs mentioning the field or organisation you are interested in:

Tesco intitle:"curriculum vitae"
retail expert allintitle:conference schedule

People search and LinkedIn

There are a number of search engines that focus on finding people rather than documents. These include Pipl, 192.com, 123people and Yasni. Often these will connect to social media profiles and other publicly available information.

LinkedIn is a particularly useful tool for finding people in particular roles and industries. The advanced search facility allows you to search by job role, employer and even the strength of their connection to you (i.e. they are a 'friend' on the site, or you have a mutual connection, etc.) Results can be combined with email finding websites such as Hunter.io, VoilaNorbert.com and Email-Format.com.

You can search Twitter biographies using the same techniques and directories listed above for finding useful people to follow. Also useful are tools like Twiangulate, Tweepz and Mentionmapp.

If you are trying to establish relationships between people (such as potential conflicts of interest), Ancestry.com can be useful, although name spellings can be inconsistent (some subscriptions also include access to newspaper archives). If you don't want to pay you may be able to get access through your local library.

Finding case studies

If you're looking for people at the heart of a story – those directly affected by it – then advanced search techniques become particularly useful.

One key technique is to identify who might be affected and what sorts of phrases they might use. For example, if you want to find someone who is a twin you wouldn't search for the phrase "twins": you would search for "my twin sister" or simply "my twin" (with quotation marks). You might also specify that you only want results on message boards or blogs by adding *inurl:forum* or limit results to Facebook pages with *site:facebook.com/pages*.

Jargon and specific language again become important: someone with diabetes might be identified by the phrase "my insulin injection"; someone who is unemployed might be found with the phrase "my JSA" (Jobseekers Allowance).

You can also look for forums and blogs which are dedicated to the particular community you're trying to reach: to reach parents try Mumsnet; to reach teachers try the *Times Education Supplement* forums. Of course these techniques should be attempted alongside analogous approaches in the physical world, such as contacting organisations representing people with diabetes, or physically going to relevant locations, such as jobcentres, and speaking to people there.

Finding people on the scene

There are a growing number of services – such as Geofeedia, Banjo Discovery and Facebook Signal – which are either only available to journalists, or which news organisations subscribe to in order to find local sources and media fast in breaking news situations. It is worth trying to register for a free account with these if you can.

Aside from those, however, knowing some advanced search techniques can help enormously.

Google Street View, for example, can allow you to look at the location and identify local businesses and shops. Find their phone number using an online directory such as Yell.com and call them!

Twitter's *geocode:* operator (see p.69) allows you to search for tweets near a particular location, but remember that only around 1 per cent of users turn on the geolocation feature in Twitter that includes location information with their tweets.

Instagram has a much higher proportion of geotagged content, and you can search Instagram for images in a particular area by using a tool like Worldcam (http://worldc.am) or Facebook Signal's Instagram search feature. Flickr also allows you to search by location at flickr.com/map.

If you're looking for live video Facebook Live can be searched by map at facebook.com/livemap, and if you have the Periscope app you can use its map feature to search too. YouTube – which also allows livestreaming – can be searched by location using geosearchtool.com.

CLOSER LOOK
THE INVISIBLE WEB AND THE DARK WEB

It is important to remember that Google only indexes a small part of the web: most of it is invisible to search engines, and there are two key terms to refer to other parts which it does not see.

The *invisible web* (sometimes called 'deep web') refers to millions of pages which cannot be found by search engines (for example, because they are only generated when a human searches a database, or are password protected, or exist on private networks and intranets).

The *dark web* or *dark net*, on the other hand, refers to pages which are not only invisible to search engines but have also been intentionally hidden. Pages on the dark web can only be accessed using the web browser TOR (it stands for The Onion Router). The dark web is best known for black market and illegal sites such as The Silk Road, which was shut down by the FBI in 2013 and again in 2014. But it also hosts political discussions and human rights activity which users cannot conduct safely in countries where internet usage is censored, monitored or both.

If you cannot find something using Google, it may be worth using specific 'invisible web' search directories such as the WWW Virtual Library and DeepPeep, or searching for databases themselves. Of course, often the fastest approach in this case is simply picking up the phone. As former BBC researcher Murray Dick explains:

> Some research tasks are far better resolved by going straight to source, by finding interactive mediums or sources of expertise far beyond the crowd. This is especially true where search tasks are complex, hard to express in simple terms or unlikely to exist in a convenient place online.
>
> (Dick 2013)

CLOSER LOOK
HUMAN INTEREST STORIES: IDENTIFYING NEWSWORTHY FACEBOOK PAGES AND FORUMS

Many pages and forums can be valuable sources of news stories themselves, if you know what to look for. Here are some examples:

- People often post on the pages of major brands when they have a bad experience (such as finding a spider in their food!).
- Likewise they often seek out online support groups in similar situations.
- Major personal achievements tend to be shared on fundraising sites such as JustGiving, or on the pages and forums for weight loss programmes, campaign pages and other initiatives.
- Journalists often scour tribute pages to find out extra details about people who have tragically died.
- Auction sites like eBay can feature some bizarre items – and related stories.

Some of these situations will raise significant ethical and legal issues. Where someone has a reasonable expectation of privacy, for example, you can be breaking the law if you are sharing their disclosure with a wider audience (even if it is public within that group). Always contact the individuals, and ask if you can get more details for a published story.

Remember that many accusations levelled in these forums may be libellous. Ensure that you seek a right of reply and consider your legal position carefully.

CLOSER LOOK
TWITTER ADVANCED SEARCH

You can search Twitter from a box at the top of Twitter.com. However, there is also an advanced search option at twitter.com/search-advanced. This allows you to specify exact phrases and Twitter accounts that tweets come from or to, or that they mention; that exclude results containing particular words; and that filter results by language, location or date. You can also tick a box if you want to include retweets.

You can use certain advanced search operators to specify these yourself in a normal Twitter search box – and there are some operators which are not even available in Twitter's own advanced search options. You can specify usernames, for example, by using these operators:

- to:
- from:

Add the username you want to specify *without any space*, e.g. from:paulbradshaw to only see results from @paulbradshaw.

To narrow results down to tweets from people on a specific Twitter list, use this operator:

list:

Add the URL of the Twitter list after the operator *without any space*, like so:

list:ITVCentral/itvcentral

To specify that you only want results with a particular type of Twitter card use the *card-name:* operator like so:

- card-name:photo
- card-name:player
- card-name:gallery
- card-name:animated-gif.

To restrict results to a specified type of media or account use *filter:* like so:

- filter:images
- filter:videos
- filter:links
- filter:vine
- filter:replies
- filter:follows
- filter:retweets
- filter:nativeretweets
- filter:verified.

Specifying *retweet* will return results that use RT instead whereas *nativeretweets* will return results retweeted on Twitter itself. Specifying *follow* will only return results from people you follow. You can also use *include:* instead of *filter:*.

To *exclude* results with the specified type of media or account use *exclude:* and the same options above. For example, *exclude:nativeretweets* will exclude results that are native retweets.

To restrict your search to updates using a particular app use the *source:* operator. For example, *source:Twitterfeed* will only show results posted using Twitterfeed.

You can specify a location using the *geocode* operator. This needs three ingredients: the latitude, longitude and range – each one separated by a comma. For example:

geocode:51.527660,-0.102460,15km

You can find the lat/long coordinates of a particular location by using Bing Maps.

You can specify the date or time range of tweets by using these operators:

- since:
- until:

For very specific timings, however, you will need to use a unix timestamp code. This is a series of digits which represents a particular date and time: you can convert any data and time using a tool like epochconverter.com. A search using these timestamp codes will look like this:

- since:1417443899
- until:1417444300.

CLOSER LOOK
DO YOU HAVE PERMISSION TO USE MEDIA?

When you find images or other media on social networks, bear in mind that the user still retains copyright over those (see Chapter 8 for more on this). In some cases news organisations consult their lawyers and take the risk, especially when they assume the images are for public relations purposes. However, that may not be the case. Neil MacDonald, head of web and data at the *Liverpool Echo*, notes that:

> When **celebrities** put images on social media it can be complicated. For example, when there's a news event and someone is sharing an image, we ask for permission to use their image. But with celebrities it's not always clear if the image is for promotion and wider use. Steven Gerrard, for example, has posted images of himself on holiday to his Instagram account. We've had one footballer contact us to say we were using his images and it was his copyright.

Summary

When anyone can seek out information about topical issues online, advanced search skills become a must for professional journalists. Being able to source appropriate, authoritative information quickly, and identify relevant experts and case studies, helps make your journalism better informed, and better illustrated.

The modern journalist needs to be able to manage a number of different sources of information, from multiple lists on social networks to email alerts and RSS feeds. But they also need to be able to seek out information and find appropriate contacts.

There are a range of skills that you can use to make your work quicker and easier, from setting up initial feeds and alerts in your field, to following the right people on social media, and organising those sources into dashboards and lists. And when the amount of information is overwhelming, search operators can help you drill through the noise to find the key information and individuals that will make the difference.

Activities

1   You've been told that you're going to be the new transport correspondent for a regional broadcaster. How would you quickly find and follow key people in that field on social media? What about key feeds or email alerts?

2   The government has announced a new strategy to tackle child poverty. You need to find statistics on child poverty in your area. What search might you use to find those? Think about who might publish them, in what format and where.

3   You're writing a feature about the UK fashion industry and need some expert comment. How can you identify someone who has researched the industry and knows it inside out? How would you find someone who holds a senior position with a major brand?

4   There's a fire in the city centre and everyone is tweeting about it. How do you identify which tweets are from people on the scene? How can you contact someone who may own a small business nearby, but is not on social media?

5   It's a slow news day and you need a heart-warming story about someone raising a lot of money in your local area. Try some search techniques to find it. Think about the sites where a fundraiser might talk about their experience.

Further reading

Bazzell, Michael. (2013) *Open Source Intelligence Techniques*, 2nd edn, CCI Publishing
Dick, Murray. (2013) *Search: Theory and Practice in Journalism Online*, New York: Palgrave Macmillan
Edwards, Vanessa. (2016) *Research Skills for Journalists*, Abingdon: Routledge

Online resources

Cordelia Hebblethwaite's website The Social Media Reporter has a wealth of resources and advice on organising feeds and lists, trends, advanced research tips and verification: https://medium.com/the-social-media-reporter
Craig Silverman's Verification Handbook for Investigative Reporting outlines a number of advanced search techniques and case studies: http://verificationhandbook.com/book2

Bibliography

Bazzell, Michael. (2013) *Open Source Intelligence Techniques,* 2nd edn, CCI Publishing
Dick, Murray (2013) *Search: Theory and Practice in Journalism Online*, New York: Palgrave Macmillan
Sherwood, Merryn, Nicholson, Matthew and Marjoribanks, Timothy. Controlling the message and the medium? The impact of sports organisations' digital and social channels on media access, *Digital Journalism*, 12 October 2016, DOI: http://dx.doi.org/10.1080/21670811.2016.1239546
Wihbey, John. Journalists' use of knowledge in an online world: examining reporting habits, sourcing practices and institutional norms. *Journalism Practice*, 3 November 2016, DOI: http://dx.doi.org/10.1080/17512786.2016.1249004

4 Writing for the web

Chapter objectives

What this chapter will cover:

- Elements to consider in a content strategy

- How online journalism is different to writing for print

- BASIC principles in writing for the web: Brevity, Adaptability, Scannability, Interactivity, Community/Conversation

- Blogging tips and how to choose a topic for a blog

- Longform and immersive journalism

- Search engine optimisation

- Using trends tools

- Social media optimisation.

Introduction

It shouldn't have to be said that the web is different, but I'll say it anyway: *the web is different.* It is not print, it is not television, it is not radio.

So why write content for the web in the same way that you might write for a newspaper or a broadcast? The short answer is: *you don't.*

In the early days of the web many news organisations used to take content written for print and put it online without any changes. This was called *shovelware*, a derogatory reference to the way print content was 'shovelled' onto the web without any thought as to whether it was the best way to tell the story on this new medium.

It was not.

We know, of course, that television news reporting relies on getting *footage* and making a story *visual*. We know that radio reporting relies on recording *sound*. And yet the very first television news bulletins were just radio broadcast on a black screen, while early radio news broadcasts saw presenters simply reading out the most recent copy of the newspaper. It took decades to invent the language of broadcast journalism on radio and TV, and you are part of the generation that is inventing the language of online journalism.

How lucky are you?

Some fundamental principles of good journalism apply whatever medium you work in: answering the '5 Ws and an H' (who, why, what, where, when and how), being factual, clear and getting to the point quickly. This chapter outlines some of the best practice around web writing that has been established since news media began publishing on the web, alongside the changing context surrounding it. That context includes changing consumption behaviours, changing distribution behaviours (search and social) and changing cultures of production including, most notably, blogging.

CLOSER LOOK
WHAT IS ONLINE JOURNALISM?

Online journalism has a number of characteristics which define it compared to print or broadcast journalism:

- The *internet* is used as a platform for stories. This means that people can consume it on any internet-connected device, the types and numbers of which are fast-expanding.
- *Hyperlinks*: the ability to link your story to other information online.
- *Non-linear* storytelling: readers determine how, when and where they consume content.
- *Multimedia*: stories are not limited to any one medium. They might be told using only text, images, audio or video, or any combination of these.
- *Multiplatform*: stories might be accessed on desktop or laptop computers, mobile phones, tablets, e-readers, glasses or watches or any other internet-connected device.
- *Transmedia*: stories can be reported *across* multiple delivery channels. For example, a story might start on Twitter, with more details on a news site, background in a blog post, live video on Facebook and a roundup on email.
- *Real time*: instant connectivity means journalists can go live as soon as a story breaks.
- *Interactivity*: readers can engage with journalists, with content, and with each other
- *Accessibility*: information can be accessed globally and around the clock. It is not typically published at a regular time.
- *Transparency*: links and embedding allow journalists to give access to their sources. Unlimited space allows publishers to upload raw data, documents, full audio, video and transcripts.
- *Measurability*: because content is published online it is possible to measure how people use it in all sorts of ways, from clicks and time spent on a page to the number of shares, likes, comments and other forms of engagement (see Chapter 2 for more on analytics).

- *Autonomy*: in print and broadcast content typically went through an editorial process overseen by more senior members of the team. Online, however, content is sometimes published without editorial supervision – particularly on social media and in live reporting. This places greater onus on the journalist to be accurate, write clearly and understand the legal implications.
- *Accountability*: at the same time, journalists are more accountable to readers who can point out factual errors, spot plagiarism, identify copyright infringement and highlight out-of-date information.

The importance of content strategy

In the 20th century a journalist had relatively few decisions to make about how to treat a story: the medium was already decided, the lengths and formats limited. Online, however, the dizzying array of choices can cause a certain degree of anxiety. Many publishers have developed *content strategies* to prioritise this decision-making process: identifying their objectives and deciding which types of content and formats might best meet them.

For individual journalists a similar process can be a useful approach to ensure you can make decisions quickly and confidently.

Such a strategy begins with the same principles as good journalism on any platform: knowing who you are writing for, and why. If you know who your audience is, you have a good idea what information is most valuable, what knowledge to take for granted, what style is appropriate and where and when is best to reach them.

The 'why' might be a combination of editorial and commercial imperatives: on the editorial side you might consider whether your audience wants primarily to be informed, entertained or educated, for example. On the commercial side objectives might range from reaching a wider audience to targeting more specific ones; and from focusing on "clicks" to a more sophisticated focus on "engagement".

Everything else is based on the who and the why. But your content strategy itself also needs to consider its own how, what, where and when.

'How?' Thinking about format

The nature of the story influences the format you might use to report it. Does the event take place over a geographical area, and will users want to see the movement or focus on a particular location? Then a map might be most appropriate.

Are things changing so fast that a traditional 'story' format is going to be inadequate? Then a liveblog may work better (see Chapter 6).

Is there a wealth of material out there being produced by witnesses? A gallery, portal or aggregator might all be good choices.

Is there some complex science or backstory which needs to be understood? An explainer or backgrounder can work well.

Does the story involve a lot of facts or data? Consider an infographic or some sort of data visualisation (see Chapter 10).

Have you secured an interview with a key character, and a set of locations or items that tell their own story? Is it an ongoing or recurring story? An audio slideshow or video interview may be the most powerful choice of format (see Chapters 9 and 7).

Are you on the scene and is raw video of the event going to have the most impact? Grab your phone and record – or livestream.

'What?' Thinking about medium

Format does not necessarily determine the medium: a liveblog can be text only or image-driven; an interview could be audio, video or mixed media. A podcast can be video ('vodcast') as well as audio-only.

'Where?' Thinking about platform

A liveblog's reporting might be done through Twitter, on your own website or both. Video can be published directly on Twitter or Facebook, on YouTube, Instagram or Snapchat, or on a website, or a combination of these.

The platform has an impact on your choice of style (see Chapter 5 for more on this), on the audiences you might reach and the sort of engagement you might get: remember that platforms like Facebook or Twitter are not just 'channels' for pushing out content, but different places where people engage with you and with each other, exchanging information which can become part of your reporting (whether you want it to or not). See Chapter 12 for more on this.

Watch this: NowThis News's editor-in-chief Ed O'Keefe talks about telling the same story across different platforms in an interview with MediaBriefing, https://www. youtube.com/watch?v=gVemUNXkbVQ.

'When?' Thinking about timing

Just because you can publish your story instantly does not mean that you should. News organisations are increasingly adopting publishing schedules online so that stories which are not time-sensitive can reach the biggest audience. For example, websites tend to experience the largest traffic during the morning rush-hour, lunchtime breaks and late evening before people go to sleep. This led *The Times* to adopt an editions-based schedule around the times 9am, midday and 5pm (Davies 2016), while Toronto tabloid *Twelve Thirty Six* named itself after the optimal time it chose for publishing its email newsletter. There are also particular times of the week where content might perform best: is your article a bit of Friday afternoon fun, something to be used over the weekend or an article to kickstart the week with?

But if it's time-sensitive, get it out now!

In addition, different types of content perform better at different times of day. The *Washington Post*, for example, found that photo galleries (without sound) performed better during the day while people were at work, while video was watched more in the evening when users might not have to worry about colleagues hearing what they were watching (Doctor 2011).

Finally, the type of device can also vary based on the time of day: at the *Wall Street Journal* in 2014, for example, it was noted that almost 40 per cent of traffic came from mobile at 7am, but the proportion was less than half that three hours later (Albeanu 2014). This has led many email newsletters to be published in the morning, while social media publishing tends to also focus around commuting times (see Chapter 5 for more on timing).

BASIC principles

When remembering web writing principles it is useful to think about the mnemonic BASIC. This stands for Brevity, Adaptability, Scannability, Interactivity and Community/ Conversation. Over the following pages we will explore each in turn and how they apply to web production.

B is for Brevity

Brevity has long been a core part of web writing practice. This is due in part to early studies on how people read from screens compared to reading print, which suggested that people read more slowly from the former. More recent research has challenged this, however (Noyes and Garland 2008), suggesting that users have become more skilled at reading from a screen and the differences less pronounced. But the custom of writing with brevity remains.

Why? Partly because the majority of news reading in many countries now takes place on mobile devices, where there are more demands on users' time than might be the case if they were reading a newspaper or magazine.

But also partly because we now know a lot more about how people read more generally. In print we had much less information about the consumption behaviour of readers; online, however, publishers can measure how long the user spends on the page, how far they scroll down and even where their mouse travels and how they interact with the page. Unless you are writing a longform piece of journalism (see p.78), you should be thinking about how to ensure your writing demonstrates brevity.

CLOSER LOOK
THE QUARTZ CURVE

One famous result of the impact of user data on publishing practices is the 'Quartz Curve', named after the business news publisher Quartz, which found that users tended to read very short articles or very long analytical articles much more than they read articles within the traditional 500–800-word length. Editor-in-chief Kevin Delaney told the Digital Editors Network in 2013: 'The place between 500 and 800 words is the place you don't want to be', arguing that this length lacked both the focus and shareability of a short piece and the 'real pay-off' of a longer piece (Jackson 2013).

The Quartz Curve should be treated with some scepticism, as it may not apply in the same way to readers of other publications, but it is still a reminder that assumptions about the 'right length' to write to may have no basis in how people read at all. Measuring what works and what doesn't has become a key part of publishing.

Forms of brevity

Brevity comes at a number of different levels. These include:

- The length of each sentence or paragraph
- The length of the article
- The possibility of 'chunking' a longer piece into a series of shorter parts
- Brevity in multimedia.

At the level of the paragraph, try to stick to one concept per paragraph. Once you've made your point (one or two sentences at most), move on to the next paragraph. Initially this may feel a little bare, but you will be surprised how effective it is. For a good example of an organisation which uses this style very effectively, look at how BBC news reports are written.

At the level of the article if you are writing anything other than in-depth features *shorter pieces* tend to work better online. Because you are not filling column inches or airtime, there is no reason for your article to meet a particular word count such as the standard 500 words. Around 300 words is normally enough to tell a basic news story. Consider using links and embedded media to add the extra background that print articles would normally be filled out with.

If your article is a longer feature, consider 'chunking'. This is the process of splitting a longer piece into smaller chunks, each with a particular focus. Chunking has a number of advantages, including the increased chance of each part of the article being found, more opportunities for search engine optimisation (each part can be optimised separately) and more combined visits across the articles than would be achieved with just one. And of course you can also publish the full, combined longer feature too so people can choose to read it in either form.

Brevity is equally important when producing multimedia material, and similar approaches including chunking are also used in multimedia production. See Chapters 9 and 7 for more.

CLOSER LOOK
LONGFORM AND IMMERSIVE STORYTELLING

In 2012 the *New York Times* published a six-part story about a deadly avalanche. *Snow Fall* was thousands of words long, included galleries, animations, biographies and video interviews with those involved – and was a media sensation.

In less than a week the story received 3.5 million pageviews and was shared over 10,000 times on Twitter. Most importantly each reader spent on average 12 minutes on the page (Dowling and Vogan 2015): a very long time in web publishing.

Snow Fall (Branch 2012) was a seminal piece in the history of online journalism: coinciding with the 'race for the tablet market' (Dowling and Vogan 2015), it made other news organisations look seriously at 'longform' and more interactive or 'immersive' formats for their stories, and turned 'snowfall' into a verb: 'Can we snowfall this?' became a question asked in newsrooms around the world, and the meaning of the term 'longform' changed.

Previously used to refer to content that was too short for a book, but too long for a feature (some publishers had been publishing 'longform' pieces as ebooks called Kindle Singles), 'longform' is now used to refer to any online piece that runs into thousands of words. Longform content often borrows narrative techniques from features and stories, such as the 'hourglass format' (rather than the inverted pyramid) and the 'delayed drop' whereby we are introduced to key characters first before a newsworthy 'twist' about them is revealed (the 'drop'). It also uses documentary film conventions such as raw footage and documents.

Snow Fall also kicked off a technical race to create tools that would make 'snowfalling' an article easier: it had taken the *New York Times* six months and more than ten staff to create the combination of text, video and animation, and they had to do this outside the *Times*'s content management system (Koc 2015). But within two years a number of companies had launched tools to help others create what became known as 'immersive' journalism, including Atavist.com, Shorthand Social, FOLD and a range of WordPress plugins. Accompanying this was a rise in longform editorial platforms including Byliner, Beacon and Longform.com.

In the same year as *Snow Fall* was published, Twitter co-founder Evan Williams launched his own longform publishing platform: *Medium*, with a stripped-back design to make reading as pleasurable as possible and a proactive editorial strategy: Medium limited publishing rights to chosen writers in the early days, commissioned content itself and acquired the longform publisher Matter. Later it would enter into partnerships with magazines to publish on the platform too. This hybrid approach between platform and publisher has led Medium to be called a *platisher* (see Chapter 2 for more on platishers).

Now one of the best-known platforms for longform content online, longer content tends to do well on Medium: in January 2015 the average length of a Top 100 Medium post was 7:25 minutes (Lee 2015). Of course it's not just about length, but the effort invested in writing too: the Medium data team noted that top-performing posts tend to take more time per word to write, and tend to be by people who had invested effort in building up a following (Sall 2014).

What Medium and *Snow Fall* have proved is that, while brevity is important in general when writing for the web, very long articles can also do very well – if you have the material to justify it.

A is for Adaptability

When it comes to creating online content, adaptability is important in two respects:

- First, the journalist needs to be able to adapt the story to the best medium available.
- Second, the journalist needs to think about how the content itself might be adapted by users.

The age of the journalist who *only* writes text, or who *only* produces video, or audio, is behind us. Whatever industry you work in, it is likely you will be expected to take pictures, film video and record audio when needed. You might need to create galleries or maps, publish data and charts, blog about story background, explainers or analysis, host live chats or stream live video.

You must be able to adapt your style not only for different types of reporting and across multiple media, but also across multiple platforms: Facebook, blogs, Instagram, YouTube or anywhere else that audiences gather. Sometimes you will have only a phone to do so.

Henry Jenkins calls his 'transmedia storytelling' a process whereby elements of a story are distributed across 'multiple delivery channels' (Jenkins 2006). His focus was on the deliberate use of channels in the creation of fiction, such as the Matrix franchise, where information was distributed between films, animated shorts, comic books and games. But the same principle applies to news reporting where different information on the same story might be reported on Twitter, Facebook Live, Snapchat and a dedicated news website.

This does not mean that you have to be an expert in all of these media or platforms, but you *should* have *media literacy* in as many as possible: in other words, a good online journalist should be able to see a story and adapt it for the right platform.

The person who eventually films the video, or creates the interactive element, may be someone else within the team. But the *ideas* should come from every member connected with the online newsroom. And, of course, there will be occasions where you are the only person on the ground able to put those ideas into action, so you should at least have the basic ability to record good audio or video from your phone, always grab a decent photo at the scene, write for social media and engage with people online, handle data and understand how interactivity works. In short, all the chapters in this book!

Adaptable content

It is not only the journalist who benefits from being adaptable: *information needs to be adaptable as well.*

If you are creating multimedia content, you can allow users to embed or download it. In 2009, for example, Al Jazeera announced it would be making video footage available for others to reuse and remix under a Creative Commons licence, while in 2011 *Wired* magazine began releasing all of its staff-produced photos under a Creative Commons licence. Both allowed others to build on top of their content.

Sharing the data behind stories is another way to make them adaptable: users can make new charts, infographics and tools from that data, which are in turn useful to your audience and take the story forward. The *Guardian* has been particularly successful at this with its Flickr group for data visualisations of its data (see Chapter 10).

S is for Scannability

Users of news websites are often task-oriented: they may have arrived at your webpage through a search for something specific, or because someone has shared it with them for a particular reason. If they don't find that something fast, they will go elsewhere.

How do they find that something? Research in 1997 suggested that 79 per cent of web users scan pages (Nielsen 1997), looking for headlines, subheadings, links and anything else that helps them navigate the text on screen. By 2006 this scanning behaviour was established enough to be known as the 'F-shaped pattern' (Nielsen 2006): reading first across the top of the page, then across again a little further down, and then vertically down the left edge of the page.

Of course, the tendency to scan across a page is not limited to the web. Over hundreds of years print newspapers and magazines have developed a number of design elements to help people scan the page.

Online news borrows from these traditions, but because it is a medium where users are *active* – scrolling, clicking and zooming as they interact with the page – scannability is key to effective online journalism. There are a number of techniques that enhance the scannability of any webpage:

* Clear, *unambiguous headlines* and subheadings: avoid cryptic or pun-based headings.
* A focus on *the first two or three words* in the headline, intro and subheadings. These should relate to the keywords that your story relates to, such as key people, organisations, places or events.
* A clear *summary* that tells the story quickly. In other words, the 'inverted pyramid' structure recommended in traditional newswriting. Avoid 'setting the scene' unless you are writing a longform piece.
* Using *subheadings* to break up an article. These should be mini-headlines signalling the content to come and giving the reader numerous entry points into the text.
* *Bullet or numbered lists*: see how this bullet list caught your eye as soon as you looked at the page? These work brilliantly online – any chance you get, use them.
* *Indented quotes*, sometimes called 'blockquotes': users often look for direct quotes. Indenting any quote that runs over one line works well to signal at a glance that you have spoken to sources.
* *Numbers*: numerals stand out against text and allow people to quickly find sections of the story which relate to hard figures. In print the guidance is normally to write

numbers above ten as a word. However, some online guidelines ignore this to maximise the opportunities for using numerals. Check your publisher's style guide.

- *Emboldened words*: this is a good way of highlighting key phrases or entities in your piece and again gives the user entry points into the text. Use it sparingly for the first time a name, organisation, place or concept is mentioned. Never underline text for emphasis: underlining should only be used for links.
- *Hyperlinks*: again, this is a quick indication that you have used background material and linked to it.
- *Embedded material*: most content management systems now allow you to embed tweets, Facebook or Instagram updates, YouTube videos, documents and presentations. Sometimes this is more effective than simply linking.
- *Breaking up text* with images, galleries, charts, video, audio, maps and other embedded media.

The last technique – mixing text with other media – is now common practice in online newswriting. Look at articles in a news website like the *Daily Mail*, *Independent* or *Mirror* and you will see they are peppered with non-textual illustration throughout. The ultimate effect is to draw your eye down the page and engage you for longer. Just as a good text article used to mix quotes with facts and background, a good online article does all that *and* mixes in images, tweets or video.

How to write a good link

Links are the lifeblood of the web – and one of the first things people look for when they visit a page: not because they want to leave your site (yet), but because they want to see what value your webpage offers. What they don't want to see as they scan down the page is this:

<u>Click here</u>

It doesn't matter what sits either side of those two words – 'Click here to read' or 'to find out more click here' – because that's not what users will immediately see.

A link should make sense on its own. It should be succinct, and unambiguous. Overheid. nl's guidelines on 'Writing good link text' gives the bad example:

<u>The SP refers to statements which the mayor made in March</u>.

Is this linking to the SP? The referral? Or the statements? They instead suggest:

The SP refers to <u>statements which the mayor made in March</u>.

For the same reason you should always deep link wherever possible. A deep link is a link to a specific page within a site, not its homepage.

Finally, if you are linking to anything other than a webpage – e.g. PDFs, images, Word documents, spreadsheets – it should be made clear, e.g. 'In the report (PDF)'.

CLOSER LOOK
ACCESSIBILITY AND SCANNABILITY

There is a further benefit to making your online journalism scannable: accessibility.

People with limited vision or blindness use screen reading software to read webpages. This will generally read out headings and links first. Adding clear headlines and subheadings means they won't have to listen to 300 words before they hit the part they want.

The biggest blind users of the web are search engines. Search engines, quite logically, place higher importance on headings, subheadings, links and bold text. It helps them index your content, so if you are helping blind users access your content you are helping search engines understand it too.

I is for Interactivity

Interactivity is as core to online journalism as sound is to radio journalism or moving images to television. One of the most basic examples of this is the *link*, which allows users to interact by clicking through to related information. Likewise *embedded media* such as video and audio players and social media updates allow users to interact with multimedia or to follow, retweet or like the social media update directly.

There are many more features of interactivity beyond these basic features – you can read about these in Chapter 11 – but the key question to ask in web writing is *what might a user want to do* while they read your article? And then think about using links, embedded media and other interactive technologies to help them to do that.

C is for Community/Conversation

Community and conversation have always been the lifeblood of journalism. Good journalism has always sought to serve a community, whether it's a local paper campaigning against the closure of a hospital, or a magazine surveying its members to identify their biggest concerns. Commercially, journalism has always needed large or affluent communities to support it. And good journalism – whether informative or sensationalist – has always generated conversation.

Now, in a hyperlinked world, community and conversation are more important than ever. Communities contain contributors who can lead you to a story or a key piece of information; communities contain keen moderators who can help maintain the standard of discussion; they even contain editors who will highlight mistakes, omissions and new details to be incorporated into a story.

Writing for the web, therefore, can often be improved by a consideration of how it connects with that community (see Chapter 12 for more).

Conversation is king

During the mid-2000s the academic Jay Rosen noted that journalism had moved 'from a lecture to a conversation' (Rosen 2004). It is a useful phrase to remember: you should be asking yourself when writing, '*Am I engaged in a conversation – or am I writing a lecture?*'

There is a tendency in online publishing to talk about 'content', and occasionally (although less often now) you will hear media executives say that 'content is king'. But you underestimate your audience and its conversations at your peril. Perhaps one of the most successful media companies so far, Facebook, built its business around conversation, and before its rise the most popular use of the internet was not content services, but email.

People don't want to passively consume content online – they want to use it, produce it and exchange it.

Conversation and community are closely linked: conversation leads to community, but it is difficult to have a conversation without a community to begin with. Writing for the web, then, must involve taking part in – and stimulating – conversations in a number of ways:

- *Comment* on blogs, post on forums, correct and update wikis, converse on social media.
- *Link* to sources (who will in turn know that they are being quoted either through pingback or traffic).
- *Listen.* That means reading blogs, forums and other media in your sector, and then starting from the beginning again: comment, respond, link, open up.

Blogging

Blogging is perhaps the original online-native format: ideal for quick updates, while also well suited to in-depth analysis; used for personal reflection, but also for impersonal lists of useful links; and based on images, audio, video or text, blogs have laid the groundwork for best practice in web writing across the internet.

Blog jargon

One common mistake that people make when writing about blogs is to confuse the term 'blog' with 'blog post'. The blog is the publication; the *post* is the individual article, or what a diarist would call entries. They are the main content of blogs, updated regularly.

The other main content of blogs can be found on *pages*. The About page gives details on the blog's author, history, subject matter, etc. Some blogs will have other pages such as editorial or ethical policies, recommended reading, gallery, etc. Content from pages is not shown on the main homepage, but instead you will typically find pages linked on the main content tabs (About; Contact).

Down the outside column of a blog you might find a *blogroll*: this is a list of other blogs the author likes. It may simply be labelled 'links'. You might also see *widgets*: that perform additional functions from simple static text (such as a biography of the author or a list of popular posts) to donations and online shopping.

CLOSER LOOK
'IS BLOGGING JOURNALISM?'

Is television a form of journalism? Are words on a page a form of journalism? Are sounds a form of journalism? It depends. Blogs are a *platform*. They can *contain* journalism, just as TV, radio and print can. Many bloggers practise journalism, many do not. To ask if blogging is a form of journalism is to confuse form with content. It is like asking 'Is ice cream strawberry?'

G. Stuart Adam's (1993) definition of journalism is an excellent one to use when addressing this: 'Journalism is an invention or a form of expression used to report and comment in the public media on the events and ideas of the here and now.' If a blog fits that description, you could argue it is journalism.

Choosing a focus for a journalistic blog

Starting a blog as a journalist is a good idea: it gives you the discipline to write regularly, and build knowledge on a particular subject. It also makes you think about audiences and helps you to build a relationship with that audience. If you are persistent and dedicated, you can even build up a large enough following, or a strong enough reputation, that publishers might approach you about partnerships or employment opportunities.

However, to make your blog successful you need to make sure it has all the qualities of good journalism. That means it should be well researched, original and published for a wider audience, rather than your immediate social circle.

There are three particular types of blog that can help you ensure you meet those standards: the niche blog, the 'behind the scenes' blog and the 'running story' blog.

The *niche blog* focuses on a specific subject – the more specific the better. Blogging about solar energy, for example, is likely to be more effective than trying to blog about 'environmental news'; it will make you stand out more, and give you more focus. If you cannot choose a niche to begin with, then try to focus more and more as you develop knowledge of a field.

The *'behind the scenes' blog* can provide a useful space for reflection on the stories you are covering, and why you made the decisions you did on the angle you took, the people you interviewed and so on. You can use it to post information that didn't make the 'final cut', and raw material such as full interview transcripts or audio, video, images and even spreadsheets. The BBC's The Editors blog (bbc.co.uk/news/blogs/the_ editors) are one example, providing an insight into the working practices of editors and building trust with users.

The *'running story' blog* sees the journalist report regularly as they take on some form of challenge. Examples might include learning to drive or giving up smoking, making a significant journey or even eating a recipe for each letter of the alphabet. A more feature-based form, this can be very successful but obviously has a limited shelf life.

Of course these three broad types are only examples, and you might combine aspects of each – writing a niche blog which includes reflective postings and a running story. Or you might do something entirely different. The key thing is: just do it. You can tweak and improve as you go.

Avoid blog formats that don't give your journalistic skills enough opportunity to stand out: *reviews* blogs, for example, are extremely common, but the proliferation of reviews online means that journalists are almost never hired based on their ability to write one. *Opinion*-based blogs suffer from the same problem. *Personal* experiences can be interesting to blog about if they are newsworthy or touch a nerve, but it's unlikely you'll have those on a regular enough basis to justify a *professional* blog dedicated to the subject. Giving yourself the challenge of seeking out stories and thinking of creative ways to tell them will be much more worthwhile.

CLOSER LOOK
WHICH BLOG SERVICE SHOULD I USE?

There are a number of blogging services available. *WordPress* is one of the most widely used platforms, and many news organisations' content management systems are WordPress-based, so it's worth gaining experience in using it.

If you want to write analysis or longform reporting, *Medium* is worth considering: the platform also allows you to curate or contribute to 'publications' if you want to collaborate with others. Its social features mean that engaging with other users through comments can help you to build your network.

For photoblogging or video blogging (vlogging), *Tumblr* is worth considering, especially if your audience is young and the content suits the platform's curation-based features.

Avoid general website creation tools like Wix: these are not designed for regularly updated sites based on new content.

Search engine optimisation

Search engine optimisation (SEO) is the practice of optimising your content so that search engines can best understand it and are more likely to suggest it in response to a relevant search query. This does not mean that we are 'writing for search engines': we are writing for people. It is people's behaviour – clicking through to your articles, reading them, sharing them and linking to them – which shapes how highly search engines rank your content. Search engines not only store information about the content of your webpage, but how many people link to it, how many people click on those links and even how long they spend on the page.

It starts with the 'spiders'. Search engines like Google and Bing use 'spiders' (computer scripts) which follow links ('crawling') across the web and store information ('indexing') about the pages that they find (detailed below). That information on millions of pages is then stored in a massive database, which is regularly updated.

When you conduct a search the results are ordered on a search engine results page (SERP). What order those results come in – and which comes top – depend on two key factors: *relevance* and *importance*. The relevance is based on the terms that you typed in, and what the search engine knows about you (for example, where you are in the world, whether you are on a mobile phone or laptop, what you've searched for previously). Importance is based on the webpage itself: a webpage that has been frequently linked to and updated, on an authoritative site, is going to perform well. SEO means, first, making sure that the search engine understands that your page is *relevant* to the search by ensuring the content on the page contains relevant words. Second, SEO means improving the *importance* of the page by making it more likely that people link to it.

When someone searches for something that you've reported on, the search engine uses hundreds of signals to decide how prominently to show your article. These are known as *search algorithms*, and are being constantly tweaked to improve their performance. Every so often a company like Google will announce a major change to an algorithm: for example, in 2011 the 'Panda' update was introduced to tackle 'content farms' (websites which tried to publish a lot of poor quality content in order to sell advertising). In 2012 the 'Penguin' update cracked down on sites that paid or organised for other sites to link to them, and in 2014 the 'Pigeon' update prioritised local results when relevant. It is important to follow industry sources like Search Engine Land to find out when new changes are announced.

The precise details of algorithms are closely guarded, but broadly they measure three things: the content of a webpage; the code underpinning it; and the context surrounding it. I'll explain each in detail below.

SEO level 1: page content

If your page contains *keywords* which are *relevant* to a search query then it is likely to be ranked more highly than another page which has less relevant content. Keywords are just that: key words that people tend to use when searching for something. Understanding what terms people are likely to use for something, then, is an important skill: when the Japanese volcano Mount Ontake erupted in 2014 most people outside Japan searched for "Japan volcano", not "Mount Ontake". As a result, most news reporting used the former phrase over the latter.

The *position* of the keywords is important: an article which mentions Coco Chanel in the headline is likely to be more relevant to a search for "Coco Chanel" than an article where he is only mentioned in the final paragraph. For similar reasons, it is important that relevant keywords are used in the first paragraph.

Also important are subheadings, tables and lists, links, bold or italic text, but avoid repeating the same keyword over and over again: this is called 'keyword stuffing' and is penalised by search engines.

Headlines and the colon

Even the position *within* the headline or subheading is important: having a keyword within the first two words is better than having it at the end of the headline. This has resulted in an increasing use of colons in headlines, such as these:

- Mediterranean migrant deaths: EU has 'moral duty' to act
- General Election 2015: Students being put off voting for Lib Dems over tuition fees U-turn
- Morning sickness report: 1000 abortions a year in Britain due to extreme form of illness during pregnancy.

You can see that this technique is incredibly useful in getting the keywords to the front of the headline.

An online headline will generally be different to the headline that was written for print. For example, the front page print headline 'Yeung guns for Brady' is punchy and punny but doesn't work well online, where the *Birmingham Mail* changed the headline to 'Carson Yeung to block Karren Brady's leaving benefits package'. Note how the use of keywords makes it much easier to find in search engine results – and to understand.

However, this does not necessarily mean the end of the amusing headline. Hashtags in particular have given a new lease of life to puns in headlines. When homes were flooded with sewage in South London social media users coined the hashtag #poonami, leading to headlines like '#Poonami Flows Through Kennington, South London After Sewage Pipe Burst (PICTURES)'. The pun is acceptable because *people were searching for it* after seeing it on social media, so it had become a *relevant* keyword in itself. You'll notice, though, that the headline also manages to fit in plenty of other keywords too.

Headlines also often focus on media: if your article has video, audio, images, a liveblog, map or infographic, then that might be important to highlight in your headline. A headline like 'Video: Calais residents protest for Jungle migrant camp to go' not only helps distinguish your coverage from other reports, but chances are that some people are actively searching for video (it is *relevant*). Likewise 'Infographic: How Apple's iPhone matches up with Samsung's Galaxy' tells us that we're likely to be able to understand this article more quickly than non-visual versions. A similar approach is to use *calls to action* like 'watch', 'meet', 'join', 'hear' – see Chapter 5 for more.

Trending topics

Knowing the right keyword to use is a combination of knowing your audience, and using the right tools. Google Trends (google.com/trends), for example, allows you to compare relative search volumes for different phrases (to add more than one phrase click 'Compare'). The tool defaults to worldwide patterns since 2014, so make sure you change this to your country and a recent timescale to get a more accurate result. Google's Keyword Planner (adwords.google.com/KeywordPlanner) will likewise suggest the most popular searches based on the word or phrase you type in (try a search for your own publication and scroll down to 'Additional keywords to be considered' to find out what other things your readers are searching for).

On social media Trends24 (trends24.in) allows you to identify trending hashtags, while Trendsmap.com shows which terms are trending in different places around the world. For Facebook and Instagram journalists can register to use Facebook's Signal tool (signal. fb.com), which shows trending topics on both platforms. Some newsrooms also have subscriptions to similar tools like Crowdtangle and Storyful which cover multiple platforms.

Sometimes trending topics and user search behaviour can shape content itself: newspapers now routinely publish factual pieces with headlines like 'What is the time of the anti-racism protest march?' for the simple reason that people are searching for that information. It's a reminder that journalism isn't just about surprising stories, but also about answering basic questions that readers have.

SEO level 2: code

The code used on an article page contains all sorts of extra information about its contents that can help search engines. For example, the <h1> tag means 'level 1 heading', and should be used for any top level headings like a headline or website title. There are also tags like <h2>, <h3> and so on for lower level headings and subheadings. If you are making something into a heading by only making it bold, then that's not a very effective way of telling a search engine 'this is a heading': it just thinks it's bold text.

Code is particularly important for images, video and audio. Remember that search engines can't 'see' or 'hear'. Instead, they use a number of clues to try to understand multimedia. This includes:

- The filename: try to avoid using default names like 'IMG5634.jpg' or '241216.mov' and change it to something descriptive like 'LionelMessi.jpg'.
- Captions: make sure these use keywords as outlined above.
- Any text near to the media, such as the paragraph before and after.
- If you are embedding media you've uploaded to services like YouTube, Vimeo, Soundcloud or Audioboom, make sure you've edited the title, description, category and tags to include keywords as outlined above.

Another important element in your webpage code is the <title> tag which indicates the page title: this is normally what is displayed as the page title in search engine results, rather than the headline, and can be written accordingly. For example, the *Wall Street Journal* article 'White House party crashers cause a hangover' would not be very clear in search engine results, and so has a different page title on the web: 'Obama asks for review after Michaele and Tareq Salahi crash White House State Dinner'.

If your article has a *meta description*, that allows you to determine what text is showing *under* the title in search results. This can increase clicks which in turn affects your ranking (see the section on context below).

The *URL* is particularly important. If you are registering a URL yourself try to pick one that contains keywords relevant to your field: something like basketballscores.com is going to have an immediate advantage over something like basketcases.com (although the latter has more personality, which might be more effective in building an audience longer term). Beyond that, most media organisation content management systems – and free ones like Wordpress and Medium – allow you to edit the end of your URLs for SEO. Journalists are encouraged to use this end part of the URL to list keywords that may not be possible to include in the visible headline. The *Guardian* article 'Do your homework if "back to school" means a first phone for your child', for example, has a URL ending first-mobile-phone-child-right-handset-high-school.

The *speed* at which the page loads is now an increasingly important part of SEO: so much so that it has its own acronym: WPO, or web performance optimisation. Similarly, having a mobile-friendly version of pages will increase the likelihood that it is in search results for users on mobile devices.

Using *tags* and *categories* is thought to have little if any impact on SEO, but it does improve navigation (readers being able to click from one article to others with the same tag or category) and create extra 'landing pages' (the category page) which themselves can appear in searches. Categories tend to be broad 'sections' that you cover regularly, such as 'boxing' or 'health'; tags tend to be specific people, locations or organisations mentioned in the article such as 'diabetes' or 'Wayne Rooney'.

SEO level 3: context

The final, and most important, element of search engine optimisation is the context that your page sits in. This includes things like the site that it sits on, how recently and how often the page has been updated and where it is located. But most important of all is how many people link to your webpage, and what keywords they use when linking.

Underpinning all of this is the original Google algorithm, known as PageRank. Named after co-founder Larry Page, PageRank counts how many other pages link to your page, and rates the quality of those links. A link from a long-running and well-established site like the BBC is considered much higher 'quality' than, for example, your friend's webpage which was only set up last week, and that quality is itself measured using PageRank. Put another way, the higher the PageRank of sites linking to you, the higher your PageRank will be in turn.

Don't try to pay for, or swap, links, or take part in 'link exchange' programmes. This is called 'black hat' SEO: many of Google's algorithms are designed to detect if a site has done this and it will issue big ranking penalties if it thinks you have. Likewise posting links back to your site on forums and comments will not work: these typically include a 'nofollow' tag which tells search engines to ignore links.

The best way to have lots of people linking to you is, of course, to write fantastic, compelling, unique content that others want to share and link to. No amount of SEO techniques can avoid the need for great journalism.

Likewise, you can affect some of the other contextual factors by simply being dedicated. Publishing regularly, and persistently, for a long time on a core set of topics is a good strategy for improving your SEO. Search engines look for the same thing we all do: evidence that you care.

ROB HAMMOND, HEAD OF SEO AT TRINITY MIRROR GROUP PLC

Rob Hammond has been head of SEO at regional newspaper group Trinity Mirror since 2014, following a similar role at the Telegraph Media Group.

What key SEO techniques are journalists expected to use?

Broadly, the key technique we advocate is to think from the perspective of a searcher. A core part of effective SEO is psychology; what are people likely to be looking for, when, why and how would they search for it?

We use Google Trends to help answer these questions, more so following the update in June 2015 to include real-time search data, which has become especially useful for breaking news.

We also expect writers to link well and often – to background pieces, tag pages and external sites where relevant. Again this should be informed from the perspective of the reader – what would be useful for a reader, how can you guide them to other content they may find interesting? When done well, this has the side benefit of helping search engines to determine an article's relative importance within a particular topic.

How is SEO factored into story choice and treatment?

Search is a core source of traffic to our websites, and as such we consider it at all stages of a story's development. We suggest stories and treatments in conferences, as well as liaising with editorial teams in event planning and during breaking news events to ensure we get the best visibility in search.

In terms of breaking news and ongoing stories, we use real-time analytics tools such as Chartbeat and Google Trends to identify potential opportunities in search. We also distribute an automated email with the latest search trends and top performing content several times each day so anyone can keep track of what stories are likely to do well in search.

SEO is a key factor in our event planning process, and we look at search trends as well as the performance of past content to suggest different story angles, what might work well and when people are most likely to be interested in a particular story.

How have SEO algorithms impacted on Trinity Mirror?

One of the most significant algorithm changes for us was the change to the 'In the news' box in late 2014. As well as opening up the news results box to non-news sites, we have seen a big boost in visibility for our local news sites since the change.

Sometimes a change in the display of search results can be more significant than an algorithm update though, for example the increase in the number of paid ads seen above natural search results, or further expansion of Google's 'Knowledge Graph' results (answering searches directly on search results pages). One example would be the medals table for the Olympics, which took up the majority of the search results page and sent negligible onwards traffic to publishers.

What common SEO myths do you come across?

Perhaps the most common myth is that SEO is mainly concerned with cramming a long list of keywords into a headline. Effective SEO in news is about getting the focus right on a story; using the right language is essential, but that has importance outside of SEO too. Sticking five loosely related keywords in a headline is never going to be as effective as figuring out what the core one or two concepts are in the story, and working that in naturally within the headline.

Writing persuasive and interesting headlines is just as important in search as any other medium. We can see from data in Google's Search Console that an interesting headline will generally receive more clicks than a boring one in the same position.

Another myth I often come across is the perception that you can 'SEO' an article, as if it's a magic dust you can sprinkle on top of a pre-written article. Whilst there are a number of small things you can do, if search isn't thought of from the start of an article, in terms of what you're writing, why, for who and when it should be published, then search is set up to fail.

Social media optimisation

As social media began to become as important a source of traffic as search engines, a similar skillset of social media optimisation (SMO) began to emerge aimed at identifying ways to improve the discoverability of your content on social media.

SMO can refer to two different things: either optimising material posted *to* social media, or optimising website content itself so that it is *more likely to be shared by others on* social media – and in an ideal world, 'go viral'. In this chapter we will be focusing on the latter (optimising social media updates is covered in Chapter 5).

If SEO attracted criticism for 'writing for machines', SMO has been blamed for the rise of 'clickbait': headlines which promise something they can't quite deliver, characterised as 'You'll never believe . . .'-type headlines.

This has led social media companies like Facebook to alter their algorithms in response: in 2016 Facebook announced it was 'further reducing clickbait' in its newsfeed. Its algorithm would now look for any headline which 'withholds information' and 'exaggerates the article to create misleading expectations' (Peysakhovich and Hendrix 2016).

The technique of writing a headline which makes a reader curious enough to click is known as the *curiosity gap*. Like many online techniques it is not new: in broadcast the 'teaser' is well established, while the 'real-life story' magazine genre, for example, is based on generating a similar form of curiosity. Examples on the website reallyreallife.tumblr. com include 'I swapped a bowl of pasta for a BABY'.

However, it is not the technique that is the problem: it is when the story cannot deliver on what is promised: Facebook's previous attempt to identify clickbait looked for occasions when a user had 'liked' and then quickly 'unliked' a story in their feed, or spent very little time reading it. That is a frustrating experience you do not want to be giving your readers. Instead, you want to be making sure that you have got a story that people will want to share because it is just a great or important story.

If you do have that great story then 'teaser' headlines can work well on social media. In his research on curiosity George Loewenstein not only argues why curiosity is so effective (first a lack of knowledge is identified, and then we seek to 'cure' it), he also outlines five curiosity triggers (Loewenstein 1994). These are:

- Questions or riddles ('Can You Die From a Nightmare?')
- Unknown resolutions ('You'll never guess . . .')
- Violated expectations ('. . . will surprise you')
- Access to information known by others ('Dustin Hoffman Breaks Down Crying Explaining Something That Every Woman Sadly Already Experienced')
- Reminders of something forgotten ('40 Things That Will Make You Feel Old').

If your story has any of these triggers, it may be worth leading on that in your headline.

While teaser headlines have been getting all the attention, however, web publishers have also been moving to longer headlines which give you the whole story all in one go. The *Daily Mail* is one of the best-known practitioners of this technique, with headlines such as: '*Myleene Klass under fire for claiming she released giant crab on Hampstead Heath after it stowed away in her luggage when she flew back from Pacific island of Mogmog*'.

The reason for such a long headline is partly based on the opportunity to include more keywords – in this case 'Myleene Klass', 'giant crab', 'Hampstead Heath', 'Pacific island' and 'Mogmog'. But user testing has suggested these longer headlines also work well in getting people to click through.

Jonah Peretti and the Google penalty

Jonah Peretti is perhaps the best-known name in the field of 'going viral'. Soon after he launched BuzzFeed the site was wrongly penalised by Google and dropped out of search results. Without any traffic from search Peretti was forced to focus entirely on social media traffic. He has continued to do so since, with enormous success.

A famous presentation from Peretti (Saint 2010) outlines some of the techniques that BuzzFeed uses. These include targeting the "bored at work network" (note how a strong sense of audience forms the first part of any strategy), and creating something that is 'easy to understand, easy to share, and includes a social imperative'.

Similar lessons have been drawn by other people. Annalee Newitz, for example, highlights the 'Valley of Ambiguity' (Newitz 2013) where harder-to-understand journalism formats risk not being shared: longform opinion essays, science news on discoveries that are hard to interpret and political news with a complex backstory all fell into this valley. But the same stories might be told in more engaging ways by using more socially successful formats such as debunking, explainers or investigations that reveal a hidden truth (or indeed LOLcats).

The 'social imperative' identified by Peretti – something which motivates the person to share – has also been explored by others. One study concluded that 'Content that evokes high-arousal positive (awe) or negative (anger or anxiety) emotions is more viral. Content that evokes low-arousal, or deactivating, emotions (e.g. sadness) is less viral' (Berger and Milkman 2012). Similarly Alfred Hermida writes about other research which suggests people are more likely to share news that disgusts them: 'Sharing disgust provides an emotional release. It also is a way of confirming with others the boundaries of what is socially acceptable' (Hermida 2016).

Highlighting something wrong with the world, or celebrating something which is right, will be familiar themes for anyone who has ever written human interest stories. At the heart of the best real-life stories is something universal. But there are other types of story which do well too: content which is informational, or which asserts the user's identity, for example. Lists of things that you only know if you come from Bristol, for example, or '40 Things That Will Make You Feel Old'.

These list-based articles have become so common that they have their own name: the *listicle*. These can range from the frivolous and humorous ('11 Random, Amazing Food Videos We Can't Stop Playing On Repeat') to the serious ('12 Charts That Explain Why You'll Never, Ever Be Able To Afford A Home'; '16 Absolutely Outrageous Abuses Detailed in the CIA Torture Report'). They can also work well as a form of *curation*, rounding up the best or most important information about an issue or event (see Chapter 12 for more on curation)

Lists have always been a staple feature of magazines and newspapers (*The Sunday Times* Rich List, or the '25 Richest People in Britain' is one long-running example), but websites have discovered that they perform especially well online, partly because the headline alone immediately promises two of the five qualities of web writing detailed above: brevity (p.76) and scannability (p.80). List formats like slideshows and galleries create more page impressions, according to executive editor of *Huffington Post* UK Stephen Hull, who points out: 'Most of our listicles explain an issue and act as an add-on to a meatier story that uses a traditional journalism format' (Lawlor 2013). The result might well be more readers using the listicle as an entry point to something weightier they otherwise would not have known about.

CLOSER LOOK
NINE COMMON MISTAKES WHEN WRITING FOR THE WEB

The following is a checklist covering common mistakes made repeatedly by first-time web writers. Check this against your own content: if you're not doing any of them, see if you can make your content better by revisiting some of the techniques outlined in this chapter.

- Are you getting straight to the most newsworthy, interesting piece of information in your first paragraph? (Unless it's a longform piece)
- Are you linking to your source whenever you refer to a piece of information/fact?
- Are you linking phrases (e.g. 'a report'), *not* putting in full URLs (e.g. http://university.ac.uk/report)?
- Are you indenting quotes by using the blockquote option?
- Are you using brief paragraphs – starting a new one for each new point?
- Are you using a literal headline that makes sense in search results and includes keywords that people might be looking for, *not* general or punny headlines?
- Are you splitting up your article with subheadings?
- Are you ending your post with a call to action and/or indication of what information is missing or what will happen next?
- Are you embedding linked media such as tweets, Facebook updates, YouTube videos, audio or images?

WRITING FOR EMAIL

Email newsletters and magazines are an often-overlooked part of the publishing landscape, and it is important to remember that writing for email has some specific considerations to take into account compared to writing for the web or writing for social media.

As with all forms of writing, it is important to consider your audience and the contexts in which they are receiving your reporting. With email, it is most likely that someone is viewing your work on their mobile phone, for example. And your email is going to be alongside dozens of other emails demanding their attention, with the user having to make their first decision to open based on the subject line.

The subject line of the email is particularly important. At the *New York Times* – which publishes over 30 different email newsletters and has a team of 12 people working on them – they found that email subject lines 'should be no more than 30 characters to drive the most engagement on mobile' (Teicher 2015).

Being clear about the *purpose* of the email publication – and making that clear on the subscription page and the email itself – is also an important step to ensuring that people open it and use it. Typical formats for email newsletters include: highlighting only the 'most important' recent news, or the 'best of' a particular type of thing; providing useful resources and tips for people in a particular sector; or giving behind-the-scenes insight and analysis. Trying to do more than one of those things all at once may dilute the usefulness of your mailing.

Within the email itself *less* is often *more*: focusing on the three or four key stories (or recipes, fashion disasters, etc.) has been found to be more successful than overloading the email with too much information. The style of writing is also important: having a distinctive voice which stands apart from junk email and connects directly with the reader is crucial to building relationships. Always imagine that you are writing for one person.

Strong images are an important feature of email newsletters, and if the subject is particularly visual you may want to make them the main focus (but make sure they have alt text for those who have images turned off). Animated gifs and emojis can work well too. Don't overlook video, either: vertical video in particular has been found to perform much better within emails (Tinflow 2016).

You can use a range of tools to create templates for your emails, and to distribute them. Some, such as Nuzzel Newsletters, focus on curation, while others, like MailChimp, focus on design and management. Measurement of email 'open rates' (what percentage of users open your email) and other metrics such as CTR (click through rates: the proportion of people clicking on a link in your email) are a crucial element in testing your writing techniques.

And finally, remember that once sent, you cannot edit or correct an email newsletter – so make sure the email is proofread closely (ideally by someone who hasn't written it) and pay strong attention to detail.

Summary

Writing for the web requires a complex skillset: for a start, it is not just 'writing' you are doing, but rather choosing what combination of text and other media might be the best way to tell your story for your audience, at the best time and on the most appropriate platforms.

You need to be able to spot the story angle that will engage people on social media, and inspire them to share it with others – or to identify the keywords that will help the right people find it on search engines. Clarity in writing is not just about the story itself, but making sure the code underpinning it is accessible too.

The sophistication of these options has led to enormous creativity and diversity in journalistic storytelling over the past two decades: the use of links, embedded media, animated gifs and galleries have brought stories to life, while interactive forms like live chats, quizzes, database-driven storytelling and immersive longform features provide ways to bring stories to new audiences. Alongside all of this, blogging has undergone its own transformation, influencing the informal tone of much writing online and a new culture of engagement and transparency.

But that proliferation of options can also be confusing, so publishers and journalists now have to be much more strategic in making these decisions. An effective content strategy is a key element in enabling you to make the right decisions quickly.

With that content strategy helping you, it is important to experiment with all the storytelling techniques you have at your disposal: from distilling a story in a gif or employing effective SEO to designing multimedia interactive experiences. Be brave, take risks and accept that sometimes things will not quite work out – that's OK: you will learn from each experiment and be a better storyteller in the long run.

Activities

1   Write a strategy to help you decide how best to report your stories. It should include who your audience is and what platforms they use when. Then based on that think about the types of stories they might need you to report, and the sorts of formats and media that might best suit those stories. Don't assume you know all the answers: test different approaches (times, platforms, formats, media) and see which ones do best!

2   Take an article you've already written and use the techniques detailed in this chapter to improve it. Are you succinct or too wordy? Have you thought about different media? How might readers want to use your content? Does the story use subheadings and other techniques for scannability? Are you linking and inviting interaction? Use Google Trends to identify what phrases people are using to search for your topic, and make sure that the headline and intro use the same language. Make sure that images have alternative descriptions.

3   Use Buzzsumo, or one of the other tools listed in this chapter, to search for the most-shared content by a keyword relevant to your field. What qualities does that content have? Does it engage the reader emotionally? Is it useful, or informational? Does it use techniques like the curiosity gap or listicle format? See whether some types of content are more shared on certain types of social media.

4   Brainstorm ideas for the following:

   - A blog in a specialist area – does anything else cover this? Could you pick a more specific niche?
   - Five posts for a 'behind the scenes' blog that reflects on your work as a journalist
   - A 'running story' blog – what challenge could you accept?

   Search for similar blogs on Medium, WordPress and using IceRocket. What platforms do they use? How does your blog fit into that field? What makes it different? How can you engage with that community through linking and comments?

5   Use Atavist, FOLD, Shorthand Social, Medium or another immersive or longform storytelling tool to write a longer feature. Think about how images, maps, video and audio can add to your story. Use subheadings and sections to break it up into chapters. Read about different storytelling forms like the 'hourglass' and the 'delayed drop' and experiment with those.

Further reading

Battelle, John (2005) *The Search: How Google and Its Rivals Rewrote the Rules of Business and Transformed Our Culture*, London: Portfolio

Hicks, Wynford (2016) *Writing for Journalists* (3rd edn), Abingdon: Routledge

Kissane, Erin (2011) *The Elements of Content Strategy*, New York: A Book Apart

Rosenberg, Scott (2010) *Say Everything: How Blogging Began, What It's Becoming, and Why It Matters*, New York: Broadway Books

Tancer, Bill (2008) *Click: What Millions of People Are Doing Online and Why It Matters*, New York: Hyperion

Zion, Lawrie and Craig, David (2015) *Ethics for Digital Journalists*, Abingdon: Routledge

Online resources

Buzzsumo Trending Now: app.buzzsumo.com/research/trending

Facebook Signal (registration required): Signal.fb.com

Google Trends UK: Google.co.uk/trends

How to Write the Perfect Headline: The Top Words Used in Viral Headlines, Buffer Social: https://blog.bufferapp.com/the-most-popular-words-in-most-viral-headlines

Search Engine Journal: searchenginejournal.com

Search Engine Land: searchengineland.com

Bibliography

Albeanu, Catalina. 'Desktop isn't dead': tips for multiplatform publishers, Journalism.co.uk, 10 October 2014, https://www.journalism.co.uk/news/-desktop-isn-t-dead-advice-for-multiplatform-publishers/s2/a562754

Branch, John. Snow fall, *New York Times*, 20 December 2012, www.nytimes.com/projects/2012/snow-fallHicks

Davies, Jessica. The Times of London is swearing off breaking news, Digiday, 30 March 2016, http://digiday.com/publishers/breaking-news-commodity-times-adjusts-digital-news-metabolism

Doctor, Ken. The newsonomics of the Washington Post's Reader Dashboard 1.0, Newsonomics, 7 April 2011, http://newsonomics.com/the-newsonomics-of-the-washington-posts-reader-dashboard-1-0

Dowling, David and Vogan, Travis. Can we 'snowfall' this? *Digital Journalism* 3(2), 2015, 209–224, http://dx.doi.org/10.1080/21670811.2014.930250

Hall, Jim (2001) *Online Journalism*, London: Pluto Press

Hermida, Alfred (2016) *Tell Everyone: Why We Share and Why It Matters*, New York: Anchor Books

Holovaty, Adrian. A fundamental way newspaper sites need to change, Adrian Holovaty, 6 September 2006, www.holovaty.com/writing/fundamental-change

Jackson, Jasper. Is this article too long or too short? Why newspapers are writing the wrong articles for the web, MediaBriefing, 17 October 2013, https://www.themediabriefing.com/article/is-this-article-too-long-why-newspapers-are-getting-their-article-length-just-wrong-for-the-web

Jenkins, Henry (2006) *Convergence Culture: Where Old and New Media Collide*, New York: NYU Press

Koc, Elif. Review of interactive storytelling at the New York Times, Future NYT, 10 May 2015, http://futurenytimes.org/reviews/interactive-storytelling

Lawlor, Anna. 5 ways the listicle is changing journalism, The Guardian Media network blog, 12 August 2013, https://www.theguardian.com/media-network/media-network-blog/2013/aug/12/5-ways-listicle-changing-journalism

Lee, Kevan. How to use medium: the complete guide to medium for marketers, Buffer Social, 4 February 2015, https://blog.bufferapp.com/how-to-use-medium

Loewenstein, George. The psychology of curiosity: a review and interpretation. *Psychological Bulletin* 116(1), 1994: 75–98

Marshall, Sarah. Why Quartz does not publish 500 to 800 word articles, Journalism.co.uk, 15 October 2013, https://www.journalism.co.uk/news/-smartden-why-quartz-does-not-publish-500-to-800-word-articles/s2/a554444

Newitz, Annalee. Viral journalism and the valley of ambiguity, Gizmodo, 13 November 2013, https://io9.gizmodo.com/viral-journalism-and-the-valley-of-ambiguity-1463178368

Nielsen, Jakob. Why web users scan instead of reading, Nielsen Norman Group, 1 October 1997, https://www.nngroup.com/articles/why-web-users-scan-instead-reading

Nielsen, Jakob. F-shaped pattern for reading web content, Nielsen Norman Group, 17 April 2006, https://www.nngroup.com/articles/f-shaped-pattern-reading-web-content

Noyes, Jan M. and Garland, Kate J. Computer- vs paper-based tasks: are they equivalent? *Ergonomics* 51(9), September 2008: 1352–1375, DOI: 10.1080/00140130802170387, https://www.ncbi.nlm.nih.gov/pubmed/18802819

Peysakhovich, Alex and Hendrix, Kristin. News feed FYI: further reducing clickbait in feed, Facebook Newsroom, 4 August 2016, https://newsroom.fb.com/news/2016/08/news-feed-fyi-further-reducing-clickbait-in-feed

Rosen, Jay. Top ten ideas of '04: news turns from a lecture to a conversation, PressThink, 29 December 2004, http://archive.pressthink.org/2004/12/29/tp04_lctr.html

Saint, Nick. Jonah Peretti's awesome viral media presentation explained, Business Insider, 13 August 2010, www.businessinsider.com/jonah-perettis-awesome-viral-media-presentation-explained-2010-8

Sall, Mike. When is the best time to publish? Wrong question. Medium Data Lab, 9 December 2014, https://medium.com/data-lab/when-is-the-best-time-to-publish-wrong-question-8f0b15be89c2#.jt7e9g8bq

Teicher, Jonathan. How the New York Times gets 70% email open rates, Contently, 8 September 2015, https://contently.com/strategist/2015/09/08/how-the-new-york-times-gets-70-email-open-rates

Tinflow, Randy. The monster opportunity for vertical video, LinkedIn: Randy Tinflow, 13 June 2016, https://www.linkedin.com/pulse/monster-opportunity-vertical-video-randy-tinfow

5 Writing for social media and chat apps

Chapter objectives

This chapter will cover:

- What social media and chat is, and why it is important for journalists
- How to be professional on social media
- What to write about on social media
- What works well on social media
- The importance of measurement and experimentation
- Specific considerations on Twitter, Facebook, Instagram, Pinterest and Tumblr.

Introduction

Watching the recent history of social media platforms has been like watching a rerun of the history of blogging. Initially dismissed by journalists as a fad, and then attacked as a threat to traditional journalism, now social media is an integral part of what almost every journalist does. Sound familiar?

Ann Friedman, writing about the reluctance of some journalists at the *New York Times* to adopt Twitter, said it was fine to ignore Twitter but only '[if] you have a completely secure job at one of the world's largest print publications and don't see a need to network with other journalists. And don't care if they see your work' (Friedman 2014).

For the rest of us, the choice is clear: social media matters. Not least because it is a required part of the workflow. In 2009 the BBC's World Service head Peter Horrocks made Twitter accounts mandatory for all BBC journalists. 'You are not doing your job if you cannot do these things', he said (Bunz 2010). A year later competitor Sky News installed the Twitter application TweetDeck on the computers of all its newsroom staff in an attempt to make social media 'a part of the fabric of the day-to-day work', as executive producer Julian March put it (l3ahb3tan 2010).

By 2014 it was becoming integrated into the writing of stories themselves: the *LA Times*'s redesign required journalists to 'write three pretweets with each article' (Benton 2014), while the *New York Times*'s leaked innovation report noted that reporters at ProPublica must submit five tweets alongside each story, partly in order to get reporters thinking about how their content might work on social media. The *Huffington Post* and BuzzFeed are among many web native publications that have pioneered these systems.

The reason is obvious: social media platforms like Facebook and Twitter are where our audiences are. Not only that, it's also where our sources, colleagues and bosses are. In 2013, for example, it was revealed that Downing Street was handing out 'Twitter exclusives' to favoured journalists before they were officially announced. And research in 2016 suggested that interacting with readers on Twitter leads to lower levels of perceived bias in the news media (De Zúñiga et al. 2016).

Any journalist who wants to be accessible to possible leads, who wants their stories to connect, and – let's be honest – who wants to impress potential employers and colleagues, takes social media seriously.

This is not just about Twitter. The number of social media platforms – and now messaging and chat applications – has mushroomed over the past decade. From LinkedIn, MySpace and Facebook in 2002, 2003 and 2004, to Twitter and Tumblr in 2006 and 2007, WhatsApp in 2009, Instagram and Pinterest in 2010, Snapchat in 2011, Vine in 2012, Yik Yak in 2013 and video streaming tools Meerkat and Periscope in 2015, the social-savvy journalist has had to keep up with perpetual change – and can anticipate continuing to have to do so for the foreseeable future.

Their use has also exploded. In 2007, when Ofcom first asked people in the UK about their social media habits, just 22 per cent of respondents had a social media profile, and only 30 per cent of those logged in at least once a day. In 2015 almost three-quarters of people had one, and 81 per cent of those checked in daily (Ofcom 2015).

Social networks' role in news consumption has also grown significantly. By 2016 a survey of news consumption in 26 countries was showing over 51 per cent of people saying they used social media as a source of news and 12 per cent saying it was their *main* source of news. Facebook dominated, followed by YouTube, Twitter, WhatsApp and Google Plus, although in Asian countries Kakao Talk, Kakao Story and Line were used more (Reuters Institute 2016).

As a result, not only are reporters expected to manage their own social media accounts, but an increasing number of new jobs are being created to manage the 'branded' social media accounts of media organisations and the raft of new publishers such as football clubs, fashion brands, music labels and charities. *Cosmopolitan* magazine, for example, was reportedly getting 3 million readers a day on Snapchat in 2015 (Sloane 2015), while Refinery29 employed a team of ten people to produce daily content for the app.

One of the main reasons for this has been changes in the way that people now consume information. If the rise of the web was about the spread of desktop computers into a significant proportion of homes and businesses, the rise of social media has been about the spread of the web onto people's phones and tablets. One striking statistic suggests that Americans spend one out of every five minutes on smartphones on Facebook and its subsidiary Instagram (Griffith 2015). In other words, social = mobile.

Amidst this change it's easy to overlook a key consideration when it comes to reporting on social media: social is not the web. And writing for social media is different to writing for websites. In this chapter we'll explain just how.

DEFINING SOCIAL MEDIA

danah boyd (her name is spelt entirely in lower case), one of the leading researchers into the use of social media by young people, defines social networking sites as services that allow people to:

> (1) construct a public or semi-public profile within a bounded system, (2) articulate a list of other users with whom they share a connection, and (3) view and traverse their list of connections and those made by others within the system.
>
> (boyd 2007)

In other words, social networks are about connecting with others and establishing our identity along the way.

Most social media platforms include some sort of blogging functionality – whether those are Facebook 'updates', Twitter's 'tweets' (sometimes called microblogging) or multimedia updates (Vine was essentially video blogging; Instagram is photo-blogging). Social networking does not *have* to involve news or journalism at all – it is pointless to ask 'Is social media journalism?' – but in connecting with others and asserting our identities we often use or report news, and this is why it is so important to journalists.

It is also an important way for us as journalists to connect with others and establish our credibility and personality – not just through using social media to report the news, but also sharing our own experiences, knowledge and insights.

Starting out: creating a professional social media account

Chances are that you will already have a number of social media accounts for personal use. The first thing you need to consider as a journalist is whether to set up separate accounts for professional use – or whether to convert existing personal accounts.

The key thing to bear in mind here is that there is no such thing as a truly personal (even private) account if you are a journalist. If you approach a source and they try to find out more about you there is a good chance that they will stumble across your 'personal' account and make judgements based on that.

These judgements are made not only on your current social media updates, but earlier ones as well. Twitter's Joanna Geary, who worked for the *Birmingham Post*, *The Times* and the *Guardian* before joining the microblogging platform, talks about her early years as a journalist when the top result on a search for her name was an embarrassing post she had made on a message board. This made it more difficult to be taken seriously as a professional when approaching contacts.

Sometimes people will look through your social media history in order to attack your credibility: for example, suggesting that you are not objective because of previously expressed views. Be aware of this when you make updates – and be aware that in the future your job may change, or indeed your opinions.

Even updates on apparently ephemeral platforms like Twitter and Snapchat can be stored, browsed through and searched for relevant comments – especially if your account is hacked (see the section on web security in Chapter 2 (p.38) for more on this).

The UK's first youth police and crime commissioner, Paris Brown, had to resign from her post based partly on comments on Twitter made when she was 14 years old. She told the BBC: 'I'm sure many people today would not have the jobs they are in if their thoughts in their teenage years were scrutinised.' (If you want to delete your previous tweets without deleting your account, there are tools such as TweetDelete which will do this.)

Even if you have a 'private' account you cannot guarantee that people following you on that account will not make copies of what you have said and share those publicly. One extreme example of this is how often the private practice of 'sexting' is sometimes later shared with a public audience. But this also applies to private messages: after being fired by Reuters, Matthew Keys decided to publicly tweet a private conversation he had had two months earlier with Bloomberg social media director Jared Keller, in which Keller had been complaining about his job. Keller left Bloomberg that day (LoGiurato 2013).

You should therefore assume that any updates on all of your accounts – personal or professional – can be seen at some point by everyone. If you want to communicate privately, use a phone or, better still, meet in person.

The simplest option, if you are serious about a career in journalism, is to have one account and use it professionally. That doesn't mean you can't use it in a personal capacity – to communicate with friends, for example – but rather that you should always be conscious that those communications take place in front of a large audience and behave accordingly: being aware of your audience is an essential skill for a journalist.

Edit your profile

Once you have set up a professional social media account, it is worth spending some time on your profile to make sure that it presents the same appearance of professionalism as your updates.

First, it is worth considering the username you are choosing, or editing the one you already have, to reflect the byline you have on any stories you write. Nicknames like '@catfan' or '@bigben' are going to be harder for people to find, while numbers and punctuation like underscores make usernames harder to remember.

If someone already has your preferred username then consider adding a suffix like 'journo' or 'news' to your name to create the new username, or a prefix: Twitter's Joanna Geary was @bhamjoanna when she worked for the *Birmingham Post*, and then @timesjoanna and @guardianjoanna before she joined Twitter and became simply @joannauk. The BBC's Eileen Murphy, meanwhile, chose to use @theeileenmurphy on Twitter when she discovered @eileenmurphy was already taken. When new social media platforms launch it's always worth registering early to make sure you get your username, even if you don't plan to use it quite yet.

The profile picture and any header or banner image across the top should be the sort of image you would send to an employer (if you had to) – and if you don't have that, a more abstract image (i.e. an object rather than you) is preferable to one that gives a bad impression.

Your biography entry should be clear and simple. Try to avoid describing yourself as a 'student journalist'. 'Journalism student' is fair enough (if uninspiring), but 'student journalist' implies that your work stays in the classroom. Clearly, that's unlikely to be the case: more likely than not it goes online.

In that case, then, why not name the websites and publications that you contribute to in your biography. You might say 'freelance journalist writing for X, Y and Z' or 'Sports editor for X' or even 'writer' or 'blogger', and the name of your own site. This also shows that you take your own publication seriously.

Add some keywords to describe the areas you report on (locations or subjects) – this also helps people find you more easily when searching for reporters in your field. And it is absolutely vital that you check closely for typographical or grammatical errors (the same applies to all your updates).

The most important part of your biography is the link. A biography without a link either suggests absent-mindedness (how could you forget?!) or a lack of interest in your profession (how can you not have your own site?!).

That link should be to the best place for people to find and read your work: if you write for one site, then link to your author page. If you write for a range of publications then you should be linking to your own personal site which you (hopefully) regularly update with links to that work. If for any reason you don't have any work online to show (what are you waiting for?) then link to the most detailed social media profile you have: a LinkedIn profile is often the most professional option.

Remember that many social media platforms allow you to include more than one link in your profile. Twitter, for example, will turn any @ names (such as brands you work for) into links to their profiles; and any hashtags will also be linked. You can also use a URL shortener like Tiny URL or Bitly to make links shorter if you need to.

Finally, make sure that you are following people and have posted some updates. A lack of either suggests a lack of interest in the platform.

Social first or social last?

Even before writing for social media it is important to consider whether you are approaching your journalism in a 'social first' mindset, or treating social media as something that comes 'after' the story.

Again, this is a familiar scenario: when journalists first started publishing on the web it was typically done as an afterthought: reporters would file copy for the print or broadcast editions first, and only put news on the web after it had been broadcast or printed.

Now of course most news operations have a 'web first' strategy: stories go live online when they're ready, rather than waiting for the next day or the evening bulletin. This is partly because the audiences are bigger, and partly in recognition of the fact that others will be covering the same story first if they don't.

At many news organisations the same process is happening all over again with social. For example, the *New York Times*'s Michael Roston notes that letting reporters deliver some news first on social 'helps them connect directly with an interested audience' (Roston 2014).

But BuzzFeed's Tom Phillips argues that too many news organisations are still too slow to publish on social media: 'People are on social, so do it on social. Don't wait until you've got the article and a URL. Use social as social. Be first to the joke' (Belam 2015a).

The first consideration in writing for social media, then, is to think about how you might report on stories using social media *before* you have written full articles.

If you are writing a liveblog you might be doing both (see Chapter 6 for more on this). But in many cases it's useful to think of your social media account as an *ongoing* liveblog of 'My life as a journalist': sharing updates about what you're doing, updating interesting news from your field and colleagues and interacting with others. The key thing is not to treat it as merely advertising.

Social media is not (just) about promotion

Imagine if you only ever used your telephone to call people up and demand that they read your latest article: it would be repetitive and annoying, and after a while people would stop taking your calls.

Social media is no different: it is, after all, *social*. And this means interacting with other people, rather than merely shouting at them.

Of course, *one* of the reasons that journalists use social media is in order to get people to read their articles. But you will vastly increase the chances of people reading your work if you adhere to two pillars of basic good practice.

1. Be interested in other people if you want them to be interested in you

This is the most basic rule of social relations: we all know the bore who only ever talks about himself and never asks what's going on in your life. And as a journalist it's simply unforgivable not to be interested in other people: after all, that's your job!

In social media you can show your interest in a number of ways:

- Retweet, share, like or re-blog updates from other people you think your followers will find interesting or useful.
- Reply to people when you want to know more about something they've posted about.
- Reply to people who ask you questions.
- Send messages (public or private) to individuals who you find interesting. It might be that you want to know more about their job, or an experience they've had.
- Follow some people when they follow or message you. Obviously you don't have to follow everyone, but following those who look interesting or who you think might need to privately message you is a simple way to send out a signal that you are interested in what they are saying. If you follow a lot of people you can always use Twitter lists to split them into smaller more manageable groups.

2. Serve your audience first, not your ego

If you use them correctly, social media platforms can be a place for you to build a sizeable audience. But in order to do that, you must make your social media account useful and valuable to that audience.

A simple way to do this is to share the best journalism in your field today. It doesn't matter if that journalism happens to be by you, or a colleague, or someone on another website. Research suggests that people are more likely to click on your links if you tweet a mix of your own and content by other people.

You can also serve your audience by sharing links to background material: that might be official reports, statistics, key quotes or images, audio or video.

And, of course, you can serve an audience by responding to their questions and inviting suggestions for questions you might ask or angles you might cover in pursuing a story. Remember that these invitations can be open (i.e. not directed to anyone in particular) or you can include the names of individuals (for example their @name on Twitter, or simply their name on Facebook) to direct that invitation to them.

What shall I write about?

Andy Carvin, one of the best-known journalists on Twitter, says of his feed: 'I get uncomfortable when people prefer my Twitter feed as a newswire. It's not a newswire. It's a newsroom. It's where I'm trying to separate fact from fiction, interacting with people. That's a newsroom' (Ingram 2012).

If you are struggling to think about what to write about on social media, come back to that quote, where Carvin mentions two key elements of any good social media feed:

- Separating fact from fiction
- Interacting with people.

In addition, I would add the following things that happen in newsrooms:

- Keeping up to date with developments
- Making observations
- Asking questions.

The last two are really just forms of 'interacting with people', but they are worth identifying because they are particular types of interaction that work well on social.

'Curating' the news

'Keeping up to date with developments' is the simplest way to start writing for social media: as a journalist you should be a voracious reader (and listener and watcher) of news in all its forms – and social media is the perfect platform to share that. Indeed, in most cases you need only click the 'Share this' or 'Like' buttons on a story to add it to your feed.

But keeping up to date with developments as a journalist doesn't just mean news reports: it also includes press releases and announcements, livestreams and live broadcasts, official reports and documents, new statistics and new analysis. All of these also can be useful to your audience – and establish your authority in your field. One study of Twitter users found that the greatest motivator for sharing links was 'not the sharing itself but actually seeking information' (Lewis et al. 2014, p.6).

This sharing of 'things you are finding out' has a particular name in journalism: *curation*. It isn't new: on a newspaper you might create 'roundups' of the key stories from the day; in a broadcast bulletin you might round up the week's key stories; and on a magazine you might do the same every month. On social media, you're doing it every hour or more.

One social media platform – Tumblr – is designed precisely as a curation tool. Installing the Tumblr bookmarklet (a button that you add to your browser toolbar) allows you to 'curate' anything from a webpage with a click: it may be a particular image (or series of images), a video or audio clip or a key quote. The site can also be set up to automatically share your latest update to other social media platforms.

Interacting with people

The creative content manager for Twitter, Mark Luckie, notes that: 'Journalists who tweet 20% fewer links—either links to their own stories or to other online content—and 100% percent more mentions, including handles and @replies, actually grow their following by more than 17% over the long term' (Glaser 2013). Interacting with people means first listening to them: make sure you are following key people in your field (see Chapter 3 for more on how to find them), and you should have an idea of what they are doing or what is important to them. This gives you a perfect opportunity to help them where you can (answering a question, for example, or clarifying a fact).

Asking questions is another obvious way to interact with people. If they are at an event, are there many people there? What's been most interesting? If they express anger at something, ask why. If they are excited, ask for more details. All of these are signs of potential stories.

Don't overlook the importance of simple interactions like favouriting tweets, Tumblr posts or Instagram updates, or liking and sharing Facebook updates.

Making observations

Observations are often ignored when it comes to writing about social media. This is something of an oversight when you consider how many social media platforms are visual: after all, what is Instagram but 'my photographic observations'?

Observations help add a more human and personal element to your social media updates (while obviously still remaining professional!). They might be odd things you've seen on your way to work, or a comment on a great film you've just watched. It might be an observation about the train you're travelling on, or the city you've just arrived in (try not to offend the locals!). You might be making observations about the live match you're watching with millions of others right now, or a piece of 'appointment television'.

These observations are not about your traditional reporting role (finding new information) but rather about sharing little bits of your personality so that people can relate to you better, in the same way that you might meet a contact for a drink and talk about a TV series you both like before you get down to business.

In addition, observations train you as a writer to be always on the lookout for the interesting detail, or the worrying contradiction, while training your ability to communicate sharply and, where appropriate, wittily. These skills are particularly important to develop if you write interview pieces, reviews, columns or event coverage, where colour can bring a piece to life.

Some of the best observations are visual, or audiovisual. And again here social media can help you develop a 'visual eye': look out for scenes in everyday life that strike you as interesting. It might be a sign that says 'Apologies for the incontinence' (instead of inconvenience), or the site of a new building that is starting to take shape. It might be video of a visible police presence at a protest, or long queues at the bus stop.

Finally, think about audio too, and develop your journalistic 'ear'. Which sounds 'paint a picture'? It might be announcements at the train station, the sound of people arguing or simply the scratch of your pencil as you vote in an election (the great thing about sound is that it doesn't show who you voted for!).

Having your personality

Observations are just one part of expressing your personality on social media. But personality on social media is a hard thing to get right. Some people confuse having a personality with having an *opinion*. In fact, it's more about *style*. Many aspiring journalists hope to be opinion columnists at some point – but having a strong opinion is not the same as having one which people want to *read*.

Typically opinion columnists are paid to do their job because they have two qualities that set them apart from the mere wannabes: first, they speak with authority (because they do their research); and second, they speak with flair (because they hone their writing until there's no one better). They also don't waffle: every word is made to work for its place.

The same principles apply on social media: what can be duller on social media than having an opinion? *Everyone* on social media has an opinion! So what else do you have? Can you share some interesting evidence? Or can you express something in a way so colourful and memorable that people will pass it on? Try to write drafts of each update and improve upon them before publishing. A writer should not treat 140 characters any differently than they would 800 words, and your first draft should never be the last.

One journalist who was commissioned to write a column (and a book) as a direct result of her Twitter account is *Mirror* reporter Susie Boniface. Boniface tweeted anonymously as @fleetstreetfox, and over time built a significant following based on three key ingredients: first, she shared original information on the industry gained as an insider; second, she wrote from a specific angle: that of a self-declared 'foxy feminist'; and third, she had a distinctive way of writing: bold, sarcastic and sharp-tongued.

Aim for all three – angle, information and style – and you can do well – but a strong voice without anything new to reveal or a perspective to tell it from is only a third of the recipe.

Separating fact from fiction

Using your social media account to separate fact from fiction is one of the most valuable services you can perform as a journalist. After all, it's what is expected of you every day.

There are a number of ways that you can do this. The simplest is to share your everyday processes: for example, you might be working on a piece about immigration and trying to establish some statistics as part of that. When you find those statistics, share them – making sure to link to the source.

Equally you might find a claim by a politician or celebrity about the issue which is not supported by the facts – and make that part of your update.

You can also invite others into your process. For example, if a politician is claiming that a protest was 'violent' you can ask people who were there whether that was their experience. Or you might appeal to legal experts to clarify a point of law.

When doing this you need to make sure you are not merely asking other people to do your job for you.

Think before you retweet: the role of verification on social media

The two roles that contribute most to social media – curating content from elsewhere and separating fact from fiction – can come into conflict if you are not careful about what it is that you retweet. It can be embarrassing when others point out that an update you have shared is not actually true.

Before you retweet, like or share any update from another user, take a moment to check if you are confident it is true. For example:

- If there is a link in the update have you clicked on it and checked that it is what the update says it is?
- Does the story sound 'too good to be true'? If so, be particularly cautious.
- Is the account reliable? Sometimes journalists fall for hoax accounts or satirical accounts which pretend to be those of famous people.
- Is the link on a reliable site? Again, sometimes satirical websites are mistaken for real news, or hoax websites are set up to fool journalists.
- If an image is included use Google's reverse image search feature to find out where that image has been used before.
- Engage with the source and ask further questions first, e.g. 'Where did you hear about this?' or 'Have you got a link to more details?' If they do not respond, assume that they cannot provide more details.
- Consider adding a caveat to your own update, e.g. 'This sounds too good to be true. Does anyone have any more details?' or 'Not sure if this is true, chasing more. If you have details please let me know.'
- Be aware that libel and contempt laws apply to social media too: if you repeat a defamatory statement made by someone else you can be liable too (see Chapter 8 for more on this).

Look out for out-of-date material too. In the wake of terrorist attacks in Paris in November 2015, for example, a seven-month-old story about attacks in Kenya which had happened many months earlier became the top story on the BBC website with 7.5 million views coming from social media. Many – although not all – of these were people mistakenly believing the attack had just happened, or using it to illustrate that the media was ignoring terrorist attacks outside Europe (despite the story coming from the BBC!). But the story also illustrated how powerful social media is, as Martin Belam summed it up: 'Social sharing of one story can make it more read than anything that has been editorially selected to go on the homepage of one of the biggest news site in the world, months after it is published' (Belam 2015b).

Read the section on verification in Chapter 6 (p.150) for more on useful techniques and tools to use.

CASE STUDY: NEIL MACDONALD, HEAD OF WEB AND DATA, *LIVERPOOL ECHO*

When we started the *Echo* Twitter feed we had no evidence on which to base it – so it was just a case of keeping an eye on the metrics to see what worked. That grew to influence what we do, when and everything else.

Finding what people wanted to engage with, and get involved with, led us to become more sophisticated, using relevant hashtags and including the @ names of relevant sites. For example, we will @ fan sites, respected independent journalists who might be interested, as well as any groups mentioned in the article. And research has shown including pictures generates better engagement and responses: even though it takes extra time to find the right image and size, it's worth it.

I used to be a sub editor, which comes in useful when writing for social media. Sub editing is all about writing the right headline in the minimum space to tell the story, in the best possible way, and that helps. But you have to remember that social media is not just a one-way medium. There's nothing worse than a stream of 'Hey! Look at this story!' 'Hey! Look at this story!' 'Hey! Look at this story!'

We've always encouraged reporters to have a bit of personality on social media. You've got to remember who you are, and who you represent. Remember that people want to see the real person and not just you sending out links. And we've done very well, building up a huge following. That audience is used to us asking for their help.

But that engagement can be a balancing act: you need to remember you are a representative of the organisation. If someone has a go at you, you can't just have a go back. Some reporters have gone too far on social media and we've had to rein them in. It's basic journalism common sense: if someone phoned in, how would you speak to them? It's exactly the same.

Validation is important: with the riots in 2011 we had to check reports that things were kicking off in a particular area before repeating them. With the Hillsborough

---

inquiry in 2014 we held back from repeating early leaks because we couldn't be sure they were genuine.

We treat each platform differently but what is universal is that you don't just broadcast: you *engage*. It's a two-way medium. On Facebook we are much more structured in terms of when we put information on – on Twitter we can put three things in quick succession but on Facebook we tend to be posting every half hour. We don't repeat the same URL because you can get penalised for that. Google Plus we are using for livestreams: Google Hangouts of a council planning meeting, or press conferences. We're planning them with reporters and local figures like the mayor.

When we were covering the giant puppets in Liverpool we filmed short video *Vines*, then at the office they downloaded the original video files and edited them together into a longer piece. Likewise when there was a bomb scare a reporter went out and recorded Audioboo interviews with those affected – it was much more interesting to hear from people directly than by way of a text report. We also update YouTube with any new videos, and Flickr has been part of things for a while.

It's fun! It can be serious but it can be a laugh, you can let off steam and engage with people.

CLOSER LOOK
SOCIAL MEDIA'S SECRET RECIPES: ALGORITHMS

Just as Google and other search engines use a special calculation to decide what results to show on the first page when someone searches, social media services use similar calculations to decide what updates to show you, and where.

These are called *algorithms*. Algorithms are closely guarded by social media services for two reasons: first, because they prevent publishers and spammers trying to cheat and 'game' the system to get their content to the top; and second, because they give publishers and spammers a competitive advantage over other social networks.

Despite this many companies conduct regular experiments to try to work out the ingredients that the algorithms use to rank content, comparing, for example, the performance of updates with or without video.

Algorithms are constantly tweaked by social media services (once a week at Facebook, for example) based on their own experiments to see what content users find most relevant and what works best for their adverts, and also the signals that indicate someone is trying to 'cheat' the system. Changes in algorithms can have a big impact. Many 'viral content' sites, including Upworthy and Distractify, saw their traffic plummet when Facebook made changes to its algorithm in December 2013 to emphasize particular qualities that it judged to be indicative of 'higher-quality' content.

What works well on social media

Social media platforms are an enormously competitive environment for journalists, but there are particular strategies that can help make your content stand out from the rest.

Visuals are key

Research published by Twitter found that adding a visual to a news tweet increased the likelihood of it being retweeted by 27 per cent (Rogers 2014), while analysis of 8000 posts on businesses' Facebook pages showed that photos received 53 per cent more Likes and 104 per cent more comments than the average post (Corliss 2012). Statistics vary from study to study but the broad consensus is that visuals are one of the most important aspects to consider when posting an update to social media. In addition, many of the newest social media platforms, such as Instagram and Pinterest (see p.125), are almost entirely visual.

Visuals don't have to be photographs: you can also use charts and graphs, maps, infographics, timelines, typography or a combination of image-and-text.

As a result, a number of tools have been launched to help communications professionals create images that are optimised for social media. Chisel (usechisel.com) allows you to combine text and an image and share it on social media in seconds, while Canva.com allows you to generate graphics at the specific dimensions used by different social media platforms.

Being aware of these dimensions is important: Twitter, for example, will crop images to a landscape format when viewed in a timeline. If you have uploaded an image that is in portrait format most people will not be able to see the top and bottom parts unless they click on the tweet.

You can find a list of various social media platforms' image sizes by searching for Sprout Social's 'Always up-to-date guide to social media image sizes' (King 2014) – but check regularly for changes and keep up to date with announcements from social media platforms when they decide to make a change.

Video sets your content apart

Having video in your social media update helps distinguish it from other updates. On Facebook it has become particularly effective, as Fortune reported in 2015: 'For creators with more than a million Facebook fans, photo posts reach 14% of their audience on average, and text-only updates reach just 4%, according to one manager of content creators. But video posts? They reach 35%' (Griffith 2015).

Twitter has also followed suit: in 2016 the company's advertising arm announced statistics suggesting that video was shared three times more than gifs and six times more than photos (Twitter Ads UK 2016).

Video on social media does not have to be complicated: a brief piece of raw footage is enough to give a flavour of the scene, or you can choose to upload a short video interview directly to social media as a way of promoting the larger article it is embedded in or taken from. You can even film yourself, although there should be a good reason for doing so: this is not television.

In some cases you can illustrate your social media update with third party video: an article about a pop star might be shared on Facebook with a video of his latest single; an interview with a prominent sportsperson might be tweeted with an animated gif of their celebration following a vital win.

If you are using your own footage you have a choice between uploading your video directly to the social media platform – what is referred to as *native video* – or first uploading to a video service such as YouTube, Vimeo or Instagram, and then posting a link to that.

In either case the video will be playable by the user – but the social network may treat them differently.

This is because video has become a significant battleground between social media platforms who are giving preferential treatment to native video in an attempt to eat into YouTube's significant audience and TV channels' advertising income. In late 2013 Facebook started the ball rolling when they began testing auto-playing native video. By 2015 Twitter was joining the competition with support for native video up to 30 seconds.

Facebook's experiment seemed to have worked. According to one report, while in February 2014 three-quarters of videos on Facebook were hosted on YouTube, a year later the tables had turned completely: 70 per cent of videos on the social network had been uploaded directly (Griffith 2015).

Thomas Baekdal conducted an experiment to see how much Facebook was giving preferential treatment to video in his newsfeed. His conclusion was that 'Facebook has twisted the newsfeed so that 30% of your organic newsfeed is being replaced by Facebook video posts' (Baekdal 2015).

Of course, algorithms change all the time, so it may be that at some point Facebook decides to change the weighting given to video. As always, it's important to monitor industry developments to gauge the current thinking.

Meanwhile, you should consider the differences between platforms and how different types of video perform on each. Om Malik argues that Facebook has the advantage of its higher quality 'comments and community':

> The crucial difference is that on Facebook, you see people actually talking (and tagging) their friends . . . which in turn drives up the video viewership and final counts. On Facebook, comments drive distribution. On YouTube, you want to duck for cover.
>
> (Malik 2015)

On the other hand, YouTube content is more easily embeddable by anyone, and good content tends to have a longer shelf life, according to Allison Stern from the video marketing company Tubular Labs: 'On the YouTube side, you get repeat winners. You see longevity in the videos' (Blattberg 2015).

You should also consider creating different video for different platforms. In one BBC investigation by Colin Campbell the team created a 15-second video clip for Instagram, a 29-second version for Twitter and a 40-second version for Facebook pages (bit.ly/ojhbbcfbvideo).

Sell the medium or format of the linked content

Increasingly, when journalists write headlines for the web or for social media, they specify the medium or format involved. They shout VIDEO and AUDIO in caps at the start of the tweet or post; MAPPED or INFOGRAPHIC; INTERVIEW or LIVEBLOG.

Sometimes the medium or format is implied more subtly, with a call to action: we urge users to 'Watch', 'See' and 'Listen'. But we also invite them to 'Join' (a live chat or liveblog), 'Meet' (an interview) and 'Find out' (an explainer or backgrounder).

Part of it is that we recognise that the medium is something special; that users often make a choice based on the medium itself. But it's also about abundance and scarcity.

This is the scarcity principle: on the web, original information is scarce; audio or visual content is scarce; live-ness is scarce. Above all, attention is scarce.

The reason why we brand our content with 'VIDEO' or 'LIVEBLOG' or 'INTERVIEW' or 'LISTEN' is the same reason we used to brand it with 'EXCLUSIVE' or 'PHOTOS'.

Use quotes and digits where you can

Perhaps surprisingly, when it comes to news *tweets* quotes and digits are more effective than videos in leading to retweets. It may be that quotes indicate original information (rather than the reporter's second-hand understanding) and digits indicate facts (rather than opinion).

When reporting on stories, then, it is important to look for key quotes and facts that you come across – whether that is in reports that you are reading, in conversation with sources or in your own articles.

And of course quotes and numbers work particularly well when presented visually. The #BBCGoFigure project, for example, provides a basic visual template to allow journalists to present key numbers from one of the day's news stories. It began as a social media-only project but has been so successful that the BBC now publish weekly roundups of the visuals on their website's Magazine Monitor too, and the format reportedly works well on chat apps.

When it comes to combining images with quotes, BuzzFeed are a good example to look at across all social media platforms – and often articles themselves feature quotes-as-images that the user can easily share. For example, when tweeting about an article covering an appearance by musician Ed Sheeran, @BuzzFeedCeleb used one short quote in the tweet itself and a second quote in one of the images that were added to illustrate the tweet.

Don't just repeat the print headline: tell the story

Print headlines are designed for a different medium, and even web headlines aren't always designed for mobile or social. When you're telling a story on social media, rewrite the headline accordingly: headlines that sum up the story clearly work well here.

For example, when the *New York Times* tweeted the print headline 'The rock 'n' roll casualty who became a war hero', it received 74 retweets. But when rewritten as the more straightforward 'He got kicked out of both Nirvana and Soundgarden. Then he became a war hero', the tweet received 567 retweets.

Keep it short and update regularly

Just because you can write more than 140 characters on Facebook or Tumblr doesn't mean you should. Short posts – below 250 words on Facebook and 80 characters on Twitter – have been shown to work best when it comes to user interaction, so keep it simple and brief. And you can be more ruthless still: posts on Facebook with 40 characters receive 86 per cent more engagement than longer posts according to some studies (Lee 2014).

Action helps too – more verbs, fewer nouns – and 'positive sentiment', i.e. surprise or pleasure, tends to work well too (rather than the traditional downbeat approach of print journalism).

One analysis of the most followed journalists on Twitter concluded that tweeting every day and a 'flurry of tweets about events' were two of the major factors in their followings:

> Think of Twitter like . . . those electronic toys back in the day that needed to be fed and watered . . . Each of the journalists' owned media profiles on Twitter exhibited significant daily activity, as well as distinct spikes in sent Tweets and engagement, including mentions and Retweets, around events.
>
> (Breese 2014)

Updating regularly shows users that you care about the account, and also helps build up a history of engagement (people liking or sharing your posts) which makes it more likely that they'll see your updates next time (that's one of the factors in deciding whether an update gets shown on Facebook).

Emojis, emoticons and chat acronyms

The need to keep communications short online and in text messages has led to a range of creative solutions, often derided as 'text-speak'. The first wave consisted of emoticons (characters which, when used together, look like facial expressions) and acronyms (such as ROFL for 'Rolling on the floor laughing!') but more recently these have been increasingly superseded by 'emojis': small graphics that more directly represent a range of icons, symbols and expressions, rather than relying on combinations of alphanumeric characters such as :-). Emojis have proved so popular that in 2015 Instagram allowed them to be used as hashtags.

Emoticons and emojis can help reduce ambiguity in text-only communication and can also make messages more intimate or personal. However, it is worth establishing whether your audience is familiar with the language being used. Some key questions to ask include:

- Does the intended audience use emojis themselves?
- Does the intended audience use emoticons or acronyms?
- Would they expect you to use emojis or emoticons? Or would they expect you to be more professional?
- Is the use appropriate to the subject matter? (For example, is it a serious story – which may not suit emojis – or a playful one?)
- Is the use justified by the demands of the medium? (For example, do you have a limited number of characters on Twitter?)

As always, it comes down to professional judgement – but when done in the right context it can be fun. In 2015, for example, The Telegraph Football Twitter account took to using emojis in their football coverage: Leicester Football Club were represented by a fox because of their nickname of 'The Foxes', while Chelsea Football Club were represented by a Russian flag and a bag of money because of their wealthy Russian owner.

Users responded with either outright anger and confusion ('Just stop it, please'), or suggested emojis of their own. In short, the approach played into the fierce banter surrounding the sport, and provided something of a social game as supporters tried to work out what the icons meant ('I'm being thick here but I don't get Villa vs Liverpool? Chelsea is very funny though.').

The BBC found their most successful experiment on WhatsApp was when they asked users to show how they felt about the Indian elections by using emojis, while both the *Guardian* and *Huffington Post* live tweeted Barack Obama's 2015 State of the Union Address in emojis using special Twitter accounts @emojibama and @HuffPostEmoji.

A last thing to be wary of with emojis, however, is that the same icons do not always look the same on Android and Apple phones: make sure you check on both before you publish.

Should I post more than once? It depends

When it comes to Twitter the advice is not to be afraid to tweet the same story more than once: in fact at BuzzFeed UK journalists are expected to tweet their own stories three times, changing the wording in order to test what works best (see the section on measurement, p.117). Michael Roston, a staff editor for social media at the *New York Times*, tested the approach in 2013 by tweeting the same story during weekend hours and overnight. The tweets on Saturday and Sunday performed particularly well:

> What that meant to us was that a story that was of great interest to readers on a Tuesday afternoon is likely to be of interest to readers grazing Twitter on a Saturday night who didn't see it the first time around.
>
> (Roston 2014)

But Twitter is a relatively straightforward platform to judge. Other social media platforms have more complex algorithms where posting multiple times may actually reduce the chances of each one ever being seen.

Some guidance exists: one report from LinkedIn suggested 20 posts per month as the optimal frequency – that is, one per day. And there is some evidence that the same sort of frequency works best on Facebook.

The social media management tool Buffer was set up to address just this problem: users can 'buffer' social media updates that they want to share (normally links), and the service would automatically post those at what they have judged to be optimal times and frequencies (14 times per day for Twitter, twice a day on Facebook and Google Plus and once per weekday on LinkedIn). You can change the default settings, and it is worth doing so once you have a better idea of how your particular audience behaves.

However, if you are able to update manually then you should be seeking to post once your previous piece of content has already 'peaked' in terms of engagement rather than timing posts arbitrarily.

Think about timing

Timing has a significant impact on how likely it is that people see your update: after all, if you're publishing at 3am how many people are going to be awake to see it? (Actually, more than you might think: remember that 3am your time may be when users in another time zone are just checking in, and when competition for attention is at its lowest).

This is particularly important on platforms like Twitter which order content almost entirely by time of publication (although in 2016 the service changed this to a 'show me the best tweets first' algorithm), but it is also important on other platforms that factor in other qualities as well: ultimately, the more recent the update, the 'fresher' it is going to be judged, and the more likely it will be put in front of users at that time.

What time is the best time? Well that depends on all sorts of things. First, it depends on the platform you are publishing on – and what research you are reading.

Search Engine Journal looked at a number of industry reports on optimal times for publishing on Facebook, and found advice ranging from 1pm to 3pm to 'the broader suggestion of anytime between 9am and 7pm. It seems that this generally points to early afternoon being a solid time to post, and anytime after dinner and before work being a long shot' (Cooper 2014). Needless to say Facebook has also changed its algorithm since those studies were done. Tweets, on the other hand, are generally considered to be most effective at lunchtime and during the afternoon commute, and the advice for LinkedIn is to post during business hours.

Time of the week is also important: a number of studies seem to suggest that the end of the week is better than the beginning, while there is conflicting advice about weekends: some studies say that weekends are a bad time to post, while others point out that because fewer people post at weekends, there is less competition. A 2011 Facebook report suggested that Saturday links received 85 per cent more clicks, for example (Lavrusik 2011).

The problem with most of the advice on timing is that it generally relates to an audience that isn't yours: most commonly, it tends to be based on US users, and a general audience (or a marketing one) rather than a specific (or media) one.

The other thing about timing is that it depends what you want to happen to your updates. One piece of research, for example, found that 5pm was the best time on Twitter for retweets, but 6pm was the best time for clickthrough rates (CTR): in other words, the rate of people clicking on links to read an actual article. Why? The suggestion was that at 5pm people are travelling and more likely to be checking Twitter and retweeting. At 6pm people are getting home and actually clicking on links to read them. So which is it that you want?

So although timing is important, the best way to find out which times are best for *your* audience is to *test* social media updates *with your audience*. Readers of health industry magazines may be night owls; business audiences may be most active on social media during the 7am commute.

You can get some useful guidance by looking at the behaviour of your existing followers: tools like Followerwonk will tell you when your followers are most active online, allowing you to target updates accordingly. But what they don't tell you is about the people who aren't already following you. Ultimately you will only find out by testing . . .

Ultimately, writing great content is the most important rule of all

Although all the factors mentioned above – timing, media, interaction, brevity – can help increase the chances that people see your content, the best way you can optimise your work is by creating really compelling stories. Many social media platforms will measure what people do with your content: not only whether they click on a link but even how much time they spend reading your content.

And if they spend a lot of time on your content, then research shows they're more likely to come back, which means they will keep seeing your updates.

The importance of experimenting and measuring

Experimentation and measurement are central to understanding what is effective in writing for *your* audience on social media.

The measurement part is relatively easy. But experimentation is more important. Because while you can use measurement to find out which updates perform the best and worst, it requires experimentation to tell you *why*.

Measurement can be done by anyone; but experimentation requires creativity, and strategy. What you test through experimentation is up to you: you can experiment with new ways of telling stories on social media. You can choose to test the timing of updates; the use of media such as images, video or audio. You can test different images, or different text.

Commonly you experiment by trying to rule out various factors that could influence the results: if you are testing timing then you might leave the text itself unchanged between each update. If you are testing different text you may try to keep timing as close together as possible, and so on.

Measuring your audience

A number of tools will tell you when your followers are most likely to be online, or what sorts of words tend to appear in their biographies. Followerwonk, for example, will analyse the followers of any Twitter account and tell you when they are most active, where in the world they are and what words appear most often in their biographies, among other things.

To analyse traffic on Instagram you can use Iconosquare or PicStats.com. LinkedIn Insights will show you demographics for followers of any company pages you run. Facebook Insights will give you a demographic breakdown of fans of any pages that you run, and its most popular time periods, while Wolfram Alpha's Facebook Report is just one of a number of tools that will do the same for your personal page.

One thing to beware of is analysing those that already follow you rather than those who you want to follow you (and, for example, might be online at a different time). It is important to analyse both your own account and those of direct competitors (if you can) to see whether you could be doing anything differently.

Measuring performance

Facebook Insights provides a range of metrics on your page's performance, from *likes* and visits to things like *reach* (how many people an update actually reached – including those who haven't necessarily liked your page) and *engagement* (a combination of likes, clicks, comments and shares). You can look at overall trends and individual posts or videos.

LinkedIn's Insights provide metrics on individual posts and overall engagement on any company pages that you run. Under your *profile* menu you can also access a section called 'Who's viewed your profile' which tells you that but also who's viewed your posts and how you rank for profile views.

Twitter Analytics shows you the most successful tweets for the last few months, but more importantly it gives you raw tweet-by-tweet data that can be downloaded and analysed for any specified period (you can also do this in Facebook Insights). This requires some spreadsheet skills (see Chapter 10) but does give you a lot of control.

Twitter is perhaps the best served social network of all when it comes to third party tools: Twtrland shows how often you are retweeted, and what sort of tweets you post (replies, retweets, links and so on). Along with Twitonomy it will also show how active you are, and who you engage with the most. Mentionmapp shows similar information in a network graph, and Vizify allows you to see what terms you are tweeting about most.

Twittercounter shows how your follower numbers have changed over a particular period, allowing you to overlay that with tweet volume or the numbers you are following.

Tweetlevel shows how engaged your account is and what sort of role it plays (e.g. 'amplifier' or 'curator'). Most have some sort of free level of service, but it's a competitive market, so some tools disappear and others spring up. Look around for the one that fits you best.

All of these tools are to be taken with a pinch of salt, particularly when it comes to the exact measurements, but in relative terms they can be useful for comparisons.

General analytics tools

As well as social networks' own analytics services there are also general analytics tools that can be used to measure the success or failure of different experiments.

Bitly, for example, is best known as a way of shortening URLs, but it will also provide you with analytics on the performance of that URL once you share it: was it clicked, when and where (both geographically and whether it was clicked on in Facebook, Twitter or elsewhere)? Buffer will do much the same.

Google Analytics can be installed on services like Tumblr, but if installed on your website it will also tell you where traffic is coming from.

Summary

Social media has become such an important part of journalism that being able to write for the medium can be considered as important as being able to write for the web. This is partly because in many ways writing for social media is about writing for mobile, given how much social media consumption is done through our mobile phones and tablets.

It is vital to be professional in the way that you use social media, because sources will inevitably judge you based on what they find on your various social media accounts. That means retaining your scepticism as a journalist and seeking to question and verify what you hear through social media. But you should also try to be human, and inject your own personality into what you do.

Remember that you are using social media to serve a community, just as you might serve a community through your reporting online, in print or on air. But you have the ability to interact with that community too, so be interested in them and you will often find that interest repaid.

Some key principles to bear in mind when writing for social media include the following:

- Update regularly – always be looking for things to share
- Experiment with different approaches – and measure the results to see what works best
- Time updates carefully for when your audience is most likely to see or use them
- Look for visuals to illustrate your update – including animated gifs and YouTube video
- Share raw video or audio where you can – consider 'native video'
- Use direct quotes and numbers when you can
- Tell the story simply and clearly – don't merely repeat headlines.

And finally, it is worth emphasising that there are many different social media platforms with different qualities and user bases, and that those qualities and audiences sometimes change. Keep up to date with those changes, but most of all: experiment, and be creative. You won't know if something works until you try it.

CLOSER LOOK
TWITTER

Although we have outlined a number of broad areas of good practice when it comes to writing for social media, each platform has its own qualities which need to be considered as well. Some things that work well on one social media platform don't work well on others.

Twitter, for example, receives a larger amount of attention than it should when it comes to journalism on social media, because it tends to be journalists' own favourite social network. But it is far from the biggest source of either traffic or audiences. When it comes to reaching audiences, other social networks are often much more effective:

particularly Facebook but also Tumblr and, in some markets, visual platforms like Instagram and Pinterest (see p.125).

A useful illustration of the difference between Twitter and Facebook comes from a comparison of the top stories on Twitter and Facebook in 2013: the most-shared stories on Twitter that year were a mix of major breaking news events (photos and a liveblog of the Boston bombings) and celebrity news; but breaking news is absent from Facebook's most-shared pieces, which instead is dominated by listicles like '30 signs you're almost 30' and real-life stories such as 'Two years after she passed away, a woman gives her family an unforgettable Christmas'. BuzzFeed dominates the list with 15 out of the top 20 entries.

In 2014 other publishers were learning BuzzFeed's tricks on Facebook, but the pattern was the same: the most shared story was 'He saved 669 children during the Holocaust . . . and he doesn't know they're sitting next to him', while quizzes like 'Can we guess your real age?' were a major feature. Twitter's top ten list, meanwhile, contained a number of exclusive news stories from 'The secret U.S. casualties of Iraq's abandoned chemical weapons' to 'LeBron James explains his return to Cleveland Cavaliers'.

A comparison of the most popular publishers on each platform shows a similar pattern: the top five publishers on Twitter in January 2015 were the BBC, *New York Times*, Mashable, the *Guardian* and the *Huffington Post*. The top five on Facebook were PlayBuzz, the *Huffington Post*, BuzzFeed, Fox News and NBC News.

Broadly speaking, then, Twitter does very well in *breaking and exclusive news*, whereas Facebook performs better on more timeless stories and pretty much everything else. And then there are the platforms growing more quickly than Facebook. Below we outline some of the considerations to bear in mind for each platform as well as the general techniques outlined above.

140 characters or less

Many people worry about the limitations of social media platforms – especially the maximum of 140 characters on Twitter or only being able to film a few seconds on Snapchat. For users, this brevity is part of the appeal – but for those who like to write or film it can feel like a terrible limitation.

As with any medium, however, limitations can often lead to great creativity. And the best way to learn how to work with those limitations is to look at how others do it.

One of the best examples of what you can do with 140 characters comes from ABC News' digital correspondent in Moscow, Kirit Radia. In one tweet he managed to report:

Recap today: #Ukraine MPs impeach Yanukovich, free Tymoshenko, sked early elex. Govmt flees #Kiev. Police retreat. Pres. defiant. Russia mad.

The tweet demonstrates that it is fine to use abbreviations where audiences will understand the need to do so, as well as the importance of hashtags.

But it is also worth pointing out that you do not always have to fit everything into one tweet: you can tell a story in a series of tweets, by focusing on different elements in each – or indeed you can quote or reply to your own tweets and add further details.

Equally important are elements in your tweet that provide more information than their characters alone. One example of this is an image (which can also contain words), video or audio clip. And in 2015 Twitter introduced article preview cards which allow for a similar effect without impacting on the character limit.

But perhaps the most valuable use of characters is the link. Adding a link in your update allows readers to click through to fuller details whenever you need.

Writing for Twitter is as much of an art as writing headlines – in fact the skills needed are very similar. Headlines are designed to grab a casual reader's attention, and the writer has a limited number of characters in which to do that – but the writer on social media has more competition than ever before to grab that audience.

Twitter @ names

The @ sign on Twitter has a number of uses. Not only can you use the @ symbol to address a public message to someone else, you can also use it to copy them in on a message or to refer to them in the same way as you might link in a web article.

It is important to understand the distinctions between the three uses. Here are some examples:

1   @paulbradshaw where are you?
2   Train delayed. May be late @paulbradshaw @snarkmouth
3   Just met @paulbradshaw + @snarkmouth, what lovely people!

The first update is directed *only at* that person. For a number of years this would not be seen by your followers unless they followed both you *and* the person mentioned. However, in 2016 Twitter changed this and your followers will see that message regardless.

The second update is *directed at everyone* but *also specifically* directed at the users named. This means while all your followers will see the update in their timeline @paulbradshaw and @snarkmouth will *also* see your update in their 'notifications' channel.

The third update is *about/linking to* the users named. It means that anyone reading that update can click on those @ names and find out more about them, even following them if they wish.

If you want to talk about someone it is wise not to start a tweet with their @ name for the reasons outlined above (it looks like it is directed at them).

Sometimes you may wish to ask questions in public in this way so that the recipient is aware that you are expecting them to explain themselves not only to you but to your followers as well, e.g. 'Can you explain why the homeless are being criminalised, @ChiefConPSNI?'

Choosing and using hashtags

A hashtag is any word immediately preceded (without a space) with the hash symbol on Twitter: the hashtag #nursechat, for example (but not # nursechat with a space). The convention was not invented by Twitter itself but instead suggested by user Chris Messina in 2007. Twitter initially rejected the idea as being 'for nerds' (Edwards 2013) but when users began using the tags to refer to news events the platform began to integrate it into their technology, making hashtags clickable.

Now the company even publishes guidelines on using hashtags. These include:

- If you Tweet with a hashtag on a public account, anyone who does a search for that hashtag may find your Tweet.
- Don't #spam #with #hashtags. Don't over-tag a single Tweet. (Best practices recommend using no more than 2 hashtags per Tweet.)
- Use hashtags only on Tweets relevant to the topic. (Twitter 2014)

Any space or special character in a hashtag is treated as the end of the hashtag, so don't use spaces in hashtags. For example, #nurse chat means 'hashtag nurse' followed by the word 'chat'. Likewise a comma, full stop, asterisk, currency sign, question mark or exclamation mark will not be included in the hashtag.

It is also worth remembering that hashtags have to include at least one text character – they cannot be composed entirely of numbers. When the Danish war drama *1864* was being discussed on Twitter, for example, users had to use the hashtag #1864dr because #1864 would not be made into a link.

People are going to have to use the same hashtag for it to be effective, so the shorter the hashtag the better. During the 2015 UK General Election, for example, the most popular hashtags were, simply, #GE15 and #GE.

Hashtags are extremely flexible devices. They can be used in all sorts of ways, here are just some:

- To connect your tweet to a news event (e.g. #sandiegofire, one of the very first hashtags)
- To identify a 'channel' or discussion; examples include #nursechat, or #FF (follow Friday: a regular recommendation of people to follow)
- To identify a place: this can be a big city like #Birmingham but more often it is used for more specific areas such as #SellyOak, or a postcode such as #B42
- For branding purposes, for example, to identify a campaign or coverage as yours: during the annual budget announcement the BBC use #BBCbudget to distinguish their coverage (and for users to distinguish their conversations) from others
- To express an emotion (e.g. #confused)
- To indicate consent for your content to be used in some way (for example, being aggregated into TV, print or online coverage).

Here, for example, is how the *Wolverhampton Express and Star* newspaper tweet a story about football team West Bromwich Albion:

> #wba still want QPR's @phillips_matty despite the imminent arrival of @JamesMcClean_23 #bhambc

Even in this short update a number of editorial decisions are being made: first, to use a hashtag to draw this to the attention of fans of the particular team; second, to use an acronym to save characters. But also a second team – QPR (Queen's Park Rangers) – is *not* hashtagged because those fans are not the target audience (although they would be interested in the story and it would probably do no harm to add a hash to them).

The hashtag #bhambc is a pre-agreed hashtag used to draw the tweet to the attention of the BBC Birmingham and Black Country liveblog team, who will then know they have permission to include that update (if they think it appropriate to their audience).

Both players in the story are on Twitter so their Twitter handles are used. This performs a number of functions: first, it is *additional useful information* for users: it means that they can click through to those profiles, read them and follow if they wish. But secondly, it draws the story *to the attention of* those players. If they retweet or favourite the story then they may bring it to a wider audience – but also if they respond to it (for example, to deny the rumour) then that means a new story (and potentially more accurate reporting – although they could always be lying!).

Various tools can be used to identify relevant hashtags to a particular audience or topic: Hashtagify.me and Hashtags.org are two of the oldest: type in an existing hashtag and the services will suggest related ones.

However, hashtags don't just exist online: they are often used to indicate that viewers of television programmes can take part in discussions online, or to do the same for readers of newspapers and magazines. In 2014 the *Sun* newspaper decided to print daily hashtags alongside its stories after recruiting a dedicated social media team. These included #cordencameron alongside an interview with David Cameron by comedian James Corden, and a piece on a rugby "love cheat" being hashtagged #scrumbag.

During major events hashtags can also serve a graphical purpose: ahead of the 2010 FIFA World Cup Twitter announced the introduction of 'hashflags': when users used special country code hashtags (such as #ESP for Spain or #FRA for France) a flag for that country would be displayed alongside it. They were reintroduced for the 2014 World Cup and have been extended for other events including Ramadan and Eid, Eurovision, the NBA finals, the cricket world cup and elections.

CLOSER LOOK
FACEBOOK

Facebook is known for being a massive player in online news, but the extent of its reach is still easy to underestimate. In 2014 the *New York Times* reported that Facebook had a fifth of the world logging on to the site at least every month, while the site drove 'up to 20 percent of traffic to news sites' (Somaiya 2014). By 2015 it was being reported that Facebook was driving more traffic to news sites than Google (Ingram 2015).

One element to consider is the difference between creating a Facebook profile, and an official Facebook page. Facebook profiles have long had a limit of 5000 'friends', so some prominent journalists have decided to create an official Facebook page instead, allowing many more 'likes'. Pages also allow you to gain insights into your followers and use apps (for example, to run contests).

However, profiles also have a number of advantages: there is a suspicion that they perform better than pages when it comes to being seen by users (this makes sense given that people tend to engage more with people than brands), and an update to Facebook's algorithm in 2016 gave greater weight to friends and family updates than updates from pages. Also only profiles can comment on other profiles, join groups or comment on group posts.

You can also overcome the 5000 friend limit by enabling the 'follow' or 'subscribe' option (Facebook.com/about/subscribe) so people can follow your updates without having to add you as a friend. This is something worth doing anyway.

Actively seeking engagement helps when it comes to Facebook optimisation: if someone has interacted with an update before, it is more likely that they will be shown your future updates. One piece of research found that including questions or seeking input was found to increase engagement by 64 per cent (polls are particularly useful here, when appropriate), but the type of content also helps:

- Posts with journalist analysis received 20% more referral clicks
- Longer posts do better: 5-line posts get a 60% increase in engagement while 4-line posts receive 30% more engagement.

(Lavrusik 2011)

If you're reporting about people or organisations it's worth tagging them in your updates so that they are notified (increasing the chances that they either share the update or engage in another way). Tagging a person is relatively simple: start typing their name (making sure to capitalise the first letter) and a dropdown menu should appear from which you can select them (it helps if you are connected). To tag an organisation – i.e. their Facebook page – type the '@' symbol and then start typing the name of the page.

Facebook's use of hashtags has been declared a flop with no impact on the success of updates.

CLOSER LOOK
INSTAGRAM

Instagram is perhaps one of the best examples of how professional use of social media differs from personal use, and is a particularly difficult social network for many journalists to get their head around. There are two key reasons for this: first, because it is primarily visual rather than textual; and second, because it is not really designed for promoting stories and driving traffic (although the site started to allow links for advertisers in 2015, and many news organisations work around the linking limitation by directing users to the link in its profile, which it changes depending on the story it is promoting).

Instead, as Alexandra MacCallum, Assistant Managing Editor for Audience Development at the *New York Times*, says: 'It's much more about building awareness and, hopefully, loyalty for The New York Times broadly, but particularly for the Times' incredible visual storytelling' (Blattberg 2015), while Cory Haik, Executive Producer for Digital News at the *Washington Post*, says the platform is about building community and having conversations.

The *New York Times*'s first Instagram accounts were set up for food, travel and fashion, followed later by sport, its video team, its marketing department and its events team. The subjects lend themselves well to visuals: the travel desk, for example, 'cuts 15-second videos specifically for Instagram, which serve as vignettes from its "36 Hour" weekend travel guide series' (Blattberg 2015).

Likewise, Wired's 2015 attempt to tell a longform story on Instagram was essentially a photo-feature: 'Left behind in a high-speed world' (https://www.instagram.com/p/9eEdzalWhz) told the story of a teacher in Mississippi across 11 Instagram posts accompanied by long passages of text. Technology website Contently reported that photographer Tabitha Soren was asked 'to capture mostly atmospheric shots'. 'We wanted to set the scene for the story to take place in', photo editor Sarah Silberg told the website (Riley-Adams 2015). When she saw the resulting images, a decision was made to publish them on Instagram rather than the print publication in order to make the most of them and give readers different entry points.

In the UK the BBC's experiments on Instagram have also focused on video: 'Instafax' provides compressed news items or roundups in just 15 seconds, mixing video with text captions, a 'slideshow' approach pioneered by social news startup NowThis News. Other experiments include CNN asking German election candidates to answer questions in 15-second videos; cooking videos from National Public Radio (NPR) as part of #NPRDumplingWeek; and CBS *This Morning* using time lapses as a way of rounding up events.

The *Guardian*, meanwhile, has used its Instagram account to provide 'behind the scenes' shots from journalists on assignment at key events (where there are strong visuals). Katie Rogers, social news editor at the *Guardian* US told Journalism. co.uk:

> I don't see it as this arbitrary 'let's put everything we do every day on Instagram', I want readers to be aware [that] we're using the hashtag when there's movement, when people are travelling, when there's a specific story to follow.
>
> (Bartlett 2014)

Hashtags are more important on Instagram than on other platforms – the *Guardian* uses #GuardianCam, while NPR use #onassignment – as they provide the primary means of connecting images with other media, and allow other reporters to contribute coverage from their own Instagram accounts. Many users add multiple hashtags, with one study (although it did not focus on news) finding that interactions were highest on posts with over 11 hashtags (Seiter 2015). *Wired*'s longform story is a good example of where hashtags can help: once you find the first image in the series, there is no easy way of navigating to the others, a difficulty that a hashtag could have helped solve. Alternatively, Instagram's Carousel feature, introduced in 2017, allows you to upload multiple images as a single scrollable update.

If you already work in a newsroom a good way to get started on Instagram is to share strong imagery or images from the archives: some accounts focus entirely on historical photos. You can also make weekly callouts for photos with particular themes, as NBC News did. Another approach is to seek out live events, share photos and engage with others doing the same (for example, liking or commenting on good photos).

Profiles and interviews can work well on Instagram: a striking photo of the subject draws you in to read the accompanying text. Practical content, such as picture-led how-tos, can also work well – but make sure that users can follow from one step to another by using hashtags, for example. Strong or important quotes from news stories can also be made into standalone visuals.

Photos and video on Instagram have traditionally used a 1:1 ratio (square) format which is important to remember when taking photos or filming for the platform, although this changed in 2015 when the platform decided to begin allowing landscape and portrait ratio media, and in 2016 when Instagram introduced its Snapchat-like (and vertical) Stories feature (see Chapter 9 for more on vertical formats). And while it may be easier to use the Instagram app to take photos, you will get higher quality results by using your phone's own camera app first.

It is worth searching online for tips on creating photos and video for Instagram and recommended apps designed to help you create visuals, such as Boomerang (for gif-like loops), Cinemagram (for turning photos into animated gifs), Hyperlapse (for timelapses), Instaquote and Legend (for combining text with images). See Chapter 9 for more on creating video for social media.

CLOSER LOOK
PINTEREST

Pinterest can be a significant traffic driver if you are publishing in a particularly visual market. For magazines like *Martha Stewart, Cooking Light, Elle Décor, House Beautiful* and *Country Living* it has been a bigger source of users than Facebook. But for hard news organisations it is likely to rank much lower.

Some of this comes down to how Pinterest is often used: as a scrapbook to 'pin' visuals of interest to the user and their friends to shared 'boards'. The site itself describes itself as a place to discover and save creative ideas: recipes, home decor, design, gardening, art and fashion naturally fall into that category.

But that doesn't mean people aren't ready to stumble across news on the site. NPR Pins has over 12,000 followers on the platform; the *Guardian* almost 700,000; while tech news site Mashable has over 1.4 million. And the site can be used to share articles, audio and video.

One simple way to get started is to use Pinterest as another platform to share your stories: NPR Pins (pinterest.com/nprpins) uses boards in much the same way as their website might use sections: education, technology, music and so on. The *Guardian*, in contrast, tends to use boards for individual stories – especially visual ones – such as "A tribute to Andy Warhol" or "UK General Election 2015". Mashable focus on utility, with boards like "The best apps" and "Tips & tricks: social media and tech".

You can also use Pinterest to curate interesting content you come across, in the same way that you might share links on Twitter or Facebook.

Finally, you might use Pinterest as a place to share user content: Al Jazeera's Pinterest account for *The Stream* (pinterest.com/ajstream) collects together videos from users on one page so they can be watched and shared in one place.

CLOSER LOOK
TUMBLR

Tumblr has seen massive growth in recent years – particularly among younger and female audiences. In 2014 the service overtook Instagram as the fastest-growing social platform, with a 120 per cent increase in active users. In comparison, Facebook's active users only grew by 2 per cent.

One of Tumblr's strengths is the way that it combines the qualities of a blogging platform and a social network like Twitter: on the one hand the site is based on sharing media – images, video, audio, quotes, conversations ('chat') and interesting links – but you can also use the service to post text entries, add tags and customise the appearance of your site in the same way that you can a blog (and add Google Analytics so you can track where traffic comes from).

Likewise, while people can stumble across your site as they would any other blog, they can also 'follow' you to see your updates in their Tumblr dashboard, in the same way that you would see updates in your Twitter dashboard. And you can 'reblog' updates from other people if you like them (a good idea if you want people to engage with you), while adding comments.

For that reason many media organisations use Tumblr as they do Twitter: posting images alongside a short description of and link to the story that it illustrates. NBC News, *The Atlantic*, *USA Today*, *Vice* and *Entertainment Weekly* use the platform to publish photo sets based on their most visual stories; *GOOD* magazine's Tumblr is a gif-heavy interpretation of the day's news, while *Vanity Fair* combines gifs illustrating entertainment stories with behind-the-scenes video and links to stories on the official website. *Vogue* and *GQ* and simply go for the photo-and-link-to-the-full-story approach.

If you have a particularly visual section on your publication it may be worth considering setting up a Tumblr dedicated to that: the *New York Times Style* magazine, for example, has its own Tumblr, as does the *Washington Post*'s information graphics and the *Guardian*'s data journalism, and NPR's social media desk has its own Tumblr at socialmediadesk.tumblr.com.

And Tumblr can be used for standalone stories or series, particularly the human stories behind a topical story or issue. The *Guardian* used Tumblr for its 'Benefits Diaries' series, setting up five benefits claimants on Tumblr to write about how welfare changes were affecting their daily life; while 'We are the 99 percent' was a platform for a range of people to write about how their lives were affected by financial inequality. It doesn't have to be serious: 'Young journalist problems' focuses on a series of amusing memes and examples of just that.

Generally, the simplest way to get started with Tumblr is to use it as a scrapbook of interesting images, links, videos and quotes. You can also set up an 'Ask me anything' section on your Tumblr by turning it on in your Tumblr blog's settings. Look at lots of examples and then, when an opportunity presents itself to use it for something more specific, you'll know what to do.

CLOSER LOOK
CHAT AND MESSAGING APPS

In 2014 a number of news organisations began tentatively experimenting with a new wave of 'chat apps'. Tools like WhatsApp, Snapchat, WeChat, Mxit, Kik, Telegram, Yik Yak, Line and Viber differ from traditional social media platforms like Twitter and Facebook because they are not public, and it could be argued that they do not meet danah boyd's definition of a social network.

But news organisations' own chat app accounts are often managed by the same people who manage their social media presences, and typically take advantage of mass messaging functionality which blurs the boundary between private chats and public social media updates.

Although most chat apps are used by media organisations to 'broadcast' key stories, they can also be used to interact with audiences. CBN radio in Brazil, for example, uses WhatsApp as a way for listeners to report news directly to them, while the *Washington Post* used it to set up a group chat for expats to discuss the UK election and the BBC used it in West Africa, where it was hard to get reporters on the ground, for coverage of the Ebola crisis, and users could share first-hand accounts of developments in the area.

The apps have particular potential in parts of the world where most people connect to the web through phones, and a large proportion of those use chat apps. The BBC's Trushar Barot, for example, says:

> We try to triangulate three things. One, a market that we're big in, or generate a lot of interest in. Secondly, where we think a particular app has got quite a lot of strength in terms of its user base. And thirdly, finding a big story that's happening [there].
>
> (O'Donovan 2014)

These three elements led the BBC to use WhatsApp and WeChat in India and Mxit in South Africa during elections, BBM in Nigeria and Viber in Nepal. They even decided to introduce emojis – visual characters – into their reporting in India, with positive results.

The major advantage of chat apps – for the moment at least – is that unlike social media, most users will see your message, and the rate of people clicking through to stories is higher than on other platforms. However, in order to avoid users unsubscribing you must be careful to limit the number of messages you send (even more so in low bandwidth areas). For that reason chat apps work best for time-limited events such as elections (where users are willing to receive a number of updates if it is only over a short period of time) or for once-per-day updates of the most important breaking story on a specific issue.

It should also be pointed out that some chat apps are becoming publishers in their own right: in 2015 Snapchat began covering breaking news when it covered shootings in San Bernardino, California, that left 14 dead, and it already hosts a 'Discover' section where a selection of approved publishers can reach the Snapchat userbase directly.

Activities

1   Have a go at the *New York Times* quiz: Can you tell what makes a good tweet? www. nytimes.com/interactive/2014/07/01/upshot/twitter-quiz.html (or search for the title). How well did you do? Why do you think some did better than others – and why did you get some wrong?

2   Download your Twitter analytics for the last month at analytics.twitter.com (you'll need to be logged in first). See if you can identify the tweet that had the most engagement. Try to identify which tweet had the most clicked-on link, and which

tweet had the most replies or favourites. You will find the skills outlined in Chapter 10 useful here.

3   Tweet the same story four times on Twitter using four different techniques outlined in this chapter (for example, one with an image, one with @ names, one at a different time and so on). See which one gets the most engagement and try to work out why that might be. Remember that there could be more than one reason: what other experiments could you conduct to narrow down which reason it is?

4   Use a tool like Canva.com or Usechisel.com to create a visual for a key quote in one of your stories. See if it performs well on social media.

5   Set up an account on all the major social media platforms and dedicate a day to using each one to share stories, video or images while you work. How do they differ?

Further reading

boyd, danah (2014) *It's Complicated: The Social Lives of Networked Teens*, New Haven, CT: Yale University Press – also available as a free download from danah.org/itscomplicated

Bradshaw, Paul (2016) *Snapchat for Journalists*, Leanpub (leanpub.com/snapchatforjournalists)

Brake, David (2014) *Sharing Our Lives Online: Risks and Exposure in Social Media*, Basingstoke: Palgrave Macmillan

Hermida, Alfred (2014) *Tell Everyone: Why We Share and Why It Matters*, Toronto: Doubleday Canada

Kelly, Nichole (2012) *How to Measure Social Media: A Step-By-Step Guide to Developing and Assessing Social Media ROI*, Indianapolis, IN: Que Biz-Tech

Knight, Megan and Cook, Clare (2013) *Social Media for Journalists: Principles and Practice*, London: Sage

Online resources

Social networks are constantly tweaking their technology – both for commercial reasons (for example, trying to compete with new entrants, or getting people to spend more time on the service) and for editorial reasons (preventing people from 'gaming' the system with poor quality content).

These changes can have a big impact on how you approach writing for social media, so it's important to keep up to date with the company's own blogs, and industry coverage. Here are some links to check regularly:

AdWeek Social Times: adweek.com/socialtimes
Facebook documents: scribd.com/facebook
Facebook for Business: facebook.com/marketing
Facebook media: facebook.com/fbmedia
Facebook newsroom: newsroom.fb.com
Google official blog: googleblog.blogspot.co.uk
Instagram blog: blog.instagram.com
Journalists on Facebook: facebook.com/journalists
LinkedIn blog: blog.linkedin.com

LinkedIn newsroom: press.linkedin.com
Medium blog: medium.com/the-story
Pinterest blog: blog.pinterest.com/en
Reddit blog: redditblog.com
Slack blog: medium.com/@slackhq and slackhq.com
Snapchat blog: blog.snapchat.com
Tumblr Staff: staff.tumblr.com
Twitter media: media.twitter.com
WhatsApp blog: blog.whatsapp.com
YouTube official blog: youtube-global.blogspot.co.uk.

Also worth reading is the Tow Center's Guide to Chat Apps at towcenter.org/research/guide-to-chat-apps

Bibliography

Albeanu, Catalina. Vox: stop worrying about the Facebook algorithm, Journalism.co.uk, 9 June 2015, https://www.journalism.co.uk/news/vox-stop-worrying-about-the-facebook-algorithm/s2/a565399

Baekdal, Thomas. The made up success of Facebook video, *Baekdal Plus*, 2 January 2015, https://www.baekdal.com/insights/the-made-up-success-of-facebook-video accessed 9 June 2015

Bartlett, Rachel. How the BBC and Guardian are innovating on Instagram, Journalism.co.uk, 4 February 2014, https://www.journalism.co.uk/news/-how-bbc-guardian-innovating-instagram/s2/a555771

Belam, Martin. 'People are on social media, so do it on social media' – BuzzFeed's Tom Phillips on #GE2015 at News Impact Summit London, Martinbelam.com, 8 June 2015, http://martinbelam.com/2015/news-impact-summit-tom-phillips-buzzfeed-ge2015 accessed 9 June 2015

Belam, Martin. A sobering stat about just how much Facebook controls distribution to news stories, Martinbelam.com, 17 November 2015, https://medium.com/@martinbelam/a-sobering-stat-about-just-how-much-facebook-controls-distribution-to-news-stories-aa89db9ca828#.uv8xvm8r8 accessed 9 December 2015

Benton, Joshua. The new L.A. Times redesign would like to write that tweet for you, thank you very much, NiemanLab, 5 May 2014, www.niemanlab.org/2014/05/the-new-l-a-times-redesign-would-like-to-write-that-tweet-for-you-thank-you-very-much accessed 9 June 2015

Blattberg, Eric. Inside the New York Times Instagram strategy, Digiday, 13 February 2015, http://digiday.com/publishers/nytimes-instagram-strategy

Boyd, Danah and Nicole Ellison (2007, October). Social network sites: definition, history, and scholarship, *Journal of Computer-Mediated Communication* 13(1), article 11.

Breese, Elizabeth. How to win followers and influence journalism: lessons from journalists with the most followers on Twitter, Muck Rack, 10 July 2014, http://muckrack.com/daily/2014/07/10/how-to-win-followers-and-influence-journalism-lessons-from-journalists-with-the-most-followers-on-t accessed 17 June 2015

Bunz, Mercedes. BBC tells news staff to embrace social media, *Guardian* PDA, 10 February 2010, https://www.theguardian.com/media/pda/2010/feb/10/bbc-news-social-media

Cooper, Belle Beth. A scientific guide to best posting times for tweets, Facebook posts, emails and blog posts, *Search Engine Journal*, 7 January 2014, https://www.searchenginejournal.com/scientific-guide-posting-tweets-facebook-posts-emails-blog-posts-best-time/82749

Corliss, Rebecca. Photos on Facebook generate 53% more likes than the average post [NEW DATA], Hubspot, 15 November 2012, https://blog.hubspot.com/blog/tabid/6307/bid/33800/Photos-on-Facebook-Generate-53-More-Likes-Than-the-Average-Post-NEW-DATA.aspx accessed 9 June 2015

De Zúñiga, Homero Gil, Diehl, Trevor and Ardèvol-Abreu, Alberto. When citizens and journalists interact on Twitter, *Journalism Studies*, 24 May 2016: 1–20, http://www.tandfonline.com/doi/abs/10.1080/1461670X.2016.1178593

Edwards, Jim. The inventor of the Twitter hashtag explains why he didn't patent it, Business Insider, 2013, www.businessinsider.com/chris-messina-talks-about-inventing-the-hashtag-on-twitter-2013-11?IR=T

Friedman, Ann. Should all journalists be on Twitter? *Columbia Journalism Review*, 9 October 2014, www.cjr.org/realtalk/journalists_using_twitter.php

Glaser, Mark. Mark Luckie: Twitter not getting into news business, Mediashift, May 2013, http://mediashift.org/2013/05/mark-luckie-twitter-not-getting-into-news-business

Griffith, Erin. How Facebook's video-traffic explosion is shaking up the advertising world, Fortune, 3 June 2015, https://fortune.com/2015/06/03/facebook-video-traffic accessed 9 June 2015

Ingram, Matthew. Andy Carvin on Twitter as a newsroom and being human, Gigaom, 25 May 2012, https://gigaom.com/2012/05/25/andy-carvin-on-twitter-as-a-newsroom-and-being-human

Ingram, Matthew. Facebook has taken over from Google as a traffic source for news, Fortune, 18 August 2015, http://fortune.com/2015/08/18/facebook-google

King, Kevin. Always up-to-date guide to social media image sizes, Sprout Social, 30 June 2014, http://sproutsocial.com/insights/social-media-image-sizes-guide accessed 9 June 2015

l3ahb3tan, TweetDeck Newsroom rollout continues at Sky News, Poynter, 19 March 2010, www.poynter.org/2010/tweetdeck-newsroom-rollout-continues-at-sky-news/101514

Lavrusik, Vadim. Journalists and Facebook, Facebook, 3 June 2011, www.scribd.com/doc/57043299/Journalists-and-Facebook

Lee, Kevan. Infographic: the ideal length for every social media update, Buffer Social, 21 October 2014, https://blog.bufferapp.com/optimal-length-social-media

Lewis, Seth C., Holton, Avery E. and Coddington, Mark. Reciprocal journalism, *Journalism Practice* 8(2), 2014: 229–241

LoGiurato, Brett. Fired Reuters employee goes scorched-earth on his friend on Twitter, Business Insider, 3 May 2013, www.businessinsider.com/reuters-matthew-keys-dm-bloomberg-jared-keller-2013-5?IR=T accessed 11 June 2015

Malik, Om. How & why Facebook video can overtake YouTube, OM, 8 June 2015, https://om.co/2015/06/08/facebook-vs-youtube-battle-for-online-video

O'Donovan, Caroline. Around the world, media outlets and journalists are using chat apps to spread the news, NiemanLab, 10 June 2014 www.niemanlab.org/2014/06/around-the-world-media-outlets-and-journalists-are-using-chat-apps-to-spread-the-news

Ofcom. Adults' media use and attitudes report 2015, 11 May 2015, http://stakeholders.ofcom.org.uk/market-data-research/other/research-publications/adults/media-lit-10years accessed 17 June 2015

Reuters Institute. Digital news report 2015, Reuters Institute for the Study of Journalism, http://digitalnewsreport.org/survey/2015/social-networks-and-their-role-in-news-2015

Reuters Institute. Digital news report 2016, Reuters Institute for the Study of Journalism, http://reutersinstitute.politics.ox.ac.uk/sites/default/files/Digital-News-Report-2016.pdf

Riley-Adams, Ella. Can Wired make Instagram journalism mainstream? Contently, 17 November 2015, https://contently.com/strategist/2015/11/17/can-wired-make-instagram-journalism-mainstream

Rogers, Simon. What fuels a Tweet's engagement? Twitter, 20 March 2014, https://blog.twitter.com/2014/what-fuels-a-tweets-engagement accessed 9 June 2015

Roston, Michael. If a tweet worked once, send it again—and other lessons from the New York Times' social media desk, NiemanLab, 6 January 2014, www.niemanlab.org/2014/01/if-a-tweet-worked-once-send-it-again-and-other-lessons-from-the-new-york-times-social-media-desk accessed 9 June 2015

Seiter, Courtney. How to gain a massive following on Instagram: 10 proven tactics to grow followers and engagement, Buffer, 10 June 2015, https://blog.bufferapp.com/instagram-growth

Sloane, Garett. Cosmo is getting 3 million readers a day on Snapchat Discover, Digiday, 14 October 2015, http://digiday.com/platforms/cosmo-says-getting-3-million-readers-snapchat-discover accessed 10 December 2015

Somaiya, Ravi. How Facebook is changing the way its users consume journalism, *New York Times*, 26 October 2014, www.nytimes.com/2014/10/27/business/media/how-facebook-is-changing-the-way-its-users-consume-journalism.html?_r=0 accessed 9 June 2015

Twitter. Using hashtags on Twitter, 2014, https://support.twitter.com/articles/49309-using-hashtags-on-twitter accessed 17 June 2015

Twitter Ads UK. Twitter X Video at #smlondon, Twitter Moments, 9 November 2016, https://twitter.com/i/moments/796352806374567937

6 Liveblogging and mobile journalism

Chapter objectives

This chapter will cover:

- What liveblogging is
- Why liveblogging is widely used in the media
- Different types of liveblog
- The ingredients of a liveblog
- Ideas for liveblogging
- How to prepare for a successful liveblog
- Mobile journalism skills
- Mobile journalism kit
- How to verify content at speed.

Introduction

> If journalism is the first draft of history, live blogging is the first draft of journalism. It's not perfect, but it's deeply rewarding.
>
> (Sparrow 2010)

In the modern news environment when news breaks readers don't want to wait for journalists to write a 300-word story: they want to follow developments as they happen. Users also increasingly want communal experiences; to interact with journalists and others affected in real time.

The liveblog allows us to do both of these things, and it has proved enormously successful in attracting and retaining audiences. When 2 million public sector workers went on strike in 2011, for example, it was liveblogged by broadcasters at the BBC, Sky and Channel 4 News, national and regional newspapers, radio reporters, online-only publications and blogs, student publications and even campaigning organisations and the unions themselves.

Research in 2013 found that the *Guardian* website was publishing almost 150 liveblogs every month (Thurman and Walters 2013) and for good reason: the amount of time that people spend on liveblogs, and the amount that they engage, tends to be much higher than on traditional news stories.

While some elements of online journalism borrow from broadcast and print journalism, the liveblog is a format which is very much online-native. As its name suggests, it was largely born in blogging: the first liveblogs were created by regularly updating a single blog post to add new information on a developing story or event. But liveblogging really took off with the rise of microblogging services such as Twitter, which allowed reporters, witnesses and experts to provide real-time updates on news developments without having to write formal news stories or blog posts.

The rise of the liveblog, then, represents not only a way to bring that content into the news site ('curation'), but also the community that is helping to create it.

What is liveblogging?

A liveblog is a continuous series of real-time updates on a newsworthy event. As a format the liveblog is as flexible as the blog itself: what you choose to do with it is up to you; there are liveblogs which last an hour, and liveblogs which last weeks. There are regular liveblogs, and unscheduled ones. There are liveblogs about serious news events like protests and riots, and there are liveblogs rounding up a range of news updates from across a sector or region, but there are also liveblogs done during broadcasts of popular TV shows, or feature-style challenges. Here are just some examples of the breadth of uses to which the form has been put:

- Many of the earliest liveblogs by newspapers were of sports events: football and cricket matches. More recently many news organisations have run liveblogs over several days for events like the Olympics.
- As Greece inched towards a deal over its debt, the 'euro crisis' was liveblogged by the *Telegraph* and other newspapers.
- *I, Scientist* liveblogged the panel discussion 'Are robots really after our jobs?' from University College London.
- The BBC's Local Live project is a daily liveblog rounding up all the stories that are being reported in the region, linking out to local newspaper sites and hyperlocal blogs.
- Many local newspapers run liveblogs summarising everything that is going on in the region and linking to relevant stories as they are published on the site.
- When Nick Hewer took over as host on the long-running TV gameshow *Countdown*, the *Guardian* liveblogged the episode. More broadly, popular shows such as *The Apprentice*, *X Factor* and *The Great British Bake Off* are regularly liveblogged by newspaper websites.
- BuzzFeed's Daniel Dalton liveblogged 'This Is what it's like to watch "Harry Potter and the Prisoner of Azkaban" for the first time'.
- When the owner of Aston Villa football club confirmed that the club was up for sale, the *Birmingham Mail* liveblogged reactions and developments.

- *SchoolsWeek* liveblogged the Public Accounts Committee (PAC) as the head of an academy school answered questions.
- The *Guardian* liveblogged every day of the Leveson Inquiry into the conduct of the British press.

Some liveblogs are done by a single individual; others are done in teams with people on the ground reporting, and 'producers' back at base coordinating. Others are done with the collaboration of hundreds of eyewitnesses, stakeholders, experts, campaigners, reporters from other news outlets and other participants. It all depends on what the story is, and what information is most useful.

It is essential that you differentiate your coverage in some way from any other liveblogs, based on your audience. For example, a local liveblog will focus on how the event affects local people, but a liveblog for a national publisher will take a broader view, and a liveblog for a magazine might focus on the industry or sector that it caters for. Differentiation is done partly through style and emphasis, but largely in where you focus your preparation: what is your expertise, and how do you develop and deploy that live?

When done badly the results can be incoherent, disconnected and fragmented. When done well, however, a good liveblog can draw clarity out of confusion, chase rumours down to facts and draw multiple threads into something resembling a canvas.

Most importantly, it takes place within a network. The audience are not sat on their couches watching a single piece of coverage; they may be clicking between a dozen different sources; they may be present at the event too; they may have friends or family sending them updates from their phone. If they are hearing about something important that you're not addressing, you have a problem.

More static than broadcast, liveblogging does not require the same cycle of repetition that you will see on 24-hour news channels; more dynamic than print, it does, however, demand regular summarising.

Why liveblog?

Liveblogs do incredibly well when it comes to the amount of visitors that they get, and how long they spend on there. At the *Guardian* liveblogs get 300 per cent more views than traditional news reports, and 233 per cent more visitors (some visitors view more than once) (Thurman and Walters 2013), while the *Manchester Evening News*'s Paul Gallagher tells a similar story, saying that liveblogs increase dwell time (the amount of time spent on a page) twentyfold (Bateman 2011).

Research by Neil Thurman throws up a raft of similar statistics: readers spend on average between 6 and 24 minutes on liveblogs: a very long time in news consumption (Thurman and Walters 2013). They are perceived as being more balanced or factual than traditional articles 'because of the range of opinions they present, the links they provide to sources and supporting documents, and their "neutral" tone' (Thurman 2014) and audiences are 'more than twice as likely to participate in live blogs compared with other article types' (Thurman and Walters 2013).

Some news organisations have decided to make their homepage a liveblog – or indeed the whole site. The ITV News site, for example, was relaunched as a form of liveblog in 2012: every update to a story (for example, a new video or reaction) was given its own page, and users could choose to watch all the updates on a homepage, or click through to a particular 'story page' and see all the updates on that story alone. The site increased its traffic sixfold.

But the format also has benefits besides those which are about increasing traffic. It allows print outlets to compete in the 24-hour environment of rolling news. It also allows publishers to cover major sporting events even when they may not have the budgets to obtain live coverage rights (although restrictions may still apply).

And it allows journalists to do more with their time: after all, if your TV writer has to watch the latest episode of *Countdown*, why not get them to liveblog it at the same time? And if a local reporter has to sit through council meetings, why not liveblog those?

CLOSER LOOK
INGREDIENTS OF THE LIVEBLOG

Although a liveblog does not have the formal 'inverted pyramid' structure of most news articles, it does still need certain ingredients and to follow particular conventions.

The headline, for example, will often lead on the fact that it is a liveblog, or at least 'live', followed by the story that is being reported. For example: *Live: Sparkbrook shooting latest – Man dies after gun attack.* Other elements include: a roundup of the key points, an introduction setting the scene, mixed media, and a roundup at the end.

The 'key points'

The top of the liveblog will often include a bullet-point list of key events or points that have emerged during the process of the liveblog. This stays at the top of the liveblog throughout and allows users to 'find their feet' in being able to understand the latest updates.

At the start of the liveblog this bullet list might only have one or two background points, but as things develop those bullets can be added to and changed. Often they will link to stories elsewhere on your site which provide more details.

Having a gallery sit at the top of the liveblog can also have a big impact on pageviews and you should aim to get one into a live breaking story as soon as you can.

The intro: set the scene

The intro typically sets out the background to the liveblog – for example, what is happening, where. A *Health Service Journal* liveblog of a vote in Parliament, for example, has the following introduction:

MPs are to vote today on Clause 119 of the Care Bill, which could give the health secretary powers to close down hospitals within 40 days, plus the rest of today's news and comment.

(*HSJ Live* 2014)

Digital Spy's liveblog for a TV programme final sets a lighter and less objective tone:

It's here! We can't believe it's come around so quickly, but it's time for the Britain's Got Talent final – and tonight, someone (or some people) will walk away a wee bit richer (and a wee bit nervous about performing for the royal family).

(Wightman 2015)

These are often written in advance: preparation is vital to liveblogging (see p.144). For example, when preparing for the UK election debate liveblog reporters at *The Spectator* had written about 'Five things to watch for during tonight's debate'. The *Radio Times* explained 'everything you need to know' about how the debate worked while the *Independent* wrote a backgrounder on all seven leaders. The *Guardian* had even liveblogged the party leaders preparing for the debate. Typically you start anywhere from 10 to 30 minutes before the event itself.

Part of the reason for this is SEO: making liveblogs live an hour or two before the event gives search engines time to find your story and make it available when people search.

The middle: regular updates

Once you've set the scene you can get straight into those live updates. These should be very regular – if you are leaving large amounts of time without an update you've either chosen the wrong thing to liveblog, or you haven't prepared well enough. The *Guardian*'s liveblogs, for example, update about every 10 minutes on average (Thurman and Walters 2013). But for big and fast-developing news events you may be updating more than once per minute.

Some updates will have been pre-prepared: for example, background details, maps, graphics and links. Others will come from outside: for example, user contributions, user-generated content (UGC) and contributions from colleagues.

You should aim for a mix of types of update in order to keep people interested: for example, if you've used too many updates from other people, add one of your own, and if we're hearing too much from you, try to look outside for what other people are saying or doing. After a couple of background details, bring us back to the here and now. Inject images and video to break up constant text updates, and so on.

Some ideas for different types of content you can switch between:

- Summarising and clarifying: what did all those words actually boil down to?
- Contextualising (politically): why are they making that statement?

- Contextualising (facts): what's the background to that statement?
- Factchecking: are they representing the facts accurately?
- Linking: is there a report that the statement is based on? Or an article which explains more about a particular anecdote?
- Colour: is there something about a setting, expression or individual which you might remark on to bring it to life? Wit and personality are important here.
- Social: what are other people saying on social media and via email and comments? How can you bring that into the debate?

Remember that in sporting events the liveblog will still need to be updated during breaks in play, and these can go on for some time. The *Guardian*'s Dan Lucas once had to liveblog a cricket rain break for five hours. 'Then it was nice to have audience interaction' (McEnnis 2015).

The roundup: ending it

Ending a liveblog is just as important as starting it – and can be one of the most difficult parts. Typically you will want to summarise the key points of the event and point the user to links where they can read more. If there is more liveblogging to come you should indicate that too.

Remember that you don't have to end the liveblog when the event itself ends: in some cases the aftermath will be just as interesting, or you can find ways to reflect on what has just happened. After the UK election leaders' debate finished, for example, the liveblogs at the *Guardian*, and BBC didn't stop for another two hours, while on the *Scotsman* liveblog of the debate, host Tom Peterkin used Google Hangouts to discuss the debate with three guests on live video.

After the liveblog is finished

Once the event and liveblog have finished, the headline is often altered to read 'As it happened'. After all, the event is no longer live but now acts as a recording of the live coverage. Some liveblogging tools (see p.146) will also automatically reverse the chronology so that, instead of showing the most recent update first, the liveblog now shows all the updates in chronological order, or users can choose to view it in either order.

You may want to write up a more traditional article on the event if someone else hasn't already done so. Thankfully you have lots of material to use from the liveblog itself, and of course make sure you link to the liveblog in any related articles. As *Birmingham Mail* reporter Jonny Greatrex explains: 'You link out to the content, then back to the liveblog from that content, and get people to loop round your site driving up engagement time and pages per user.'

Ideas for liveblogging

Some people assume that you need to wait for a big news event to start a liveblog, but the format has proved particularly flexible in serving a whole range of editorial demands.

Protests and demonstrations are perhaps the most obvious candidate for liveblogging. They are normally planned and announced in advance, so use a tool like Google Alerts (see Chapter 3) to receive emails when the terms are mentioned, as well as following local campaigning groups and local branches of national campaigns.

Industry conferences provide another useful opportunity to liveblog: whether you're reporting on a particular geographical area or subject there will be industries that play a key role in it. Use a search engine to find industry calendars or a listing of some of the specialist events and organisation services like Exhibitions.co.uk to find them.

Council or board meetings, hearings, committees and other public and semi-public meetings often have significant implications for local communities, sections of society or particular industries. They are also often poorly covered. This provides a real opportunity for enterprising individuals to add value to their readership. In addition, there are more informal meetings of small groups which you can find on sites such as Meetup, Upcoming and Eventbrite.

Court liveblogging can generate enormous engagement from audiences, says *Birmingham Mail* reporter Jonny Greatrex:

> It creates so much interest as it is allowing the audience to see or follow something normally totally obscured: live court proceedings, where the most that people would normally get is a chalk drawing and a TV reporter explaining events in 60 seconds.
> (Personal interview 2015)

If you are planning to liveblog or tweet from court make sure you are confident on your law – particularly contempt of court. The Crown Prosecution Service have issued guidance which says live tweeting or blogging should be allowed (see Chapter 8 for more), but it is still up to the discretion of the judge and some will still not allow it.

Press conferences are an obvious candidate for liveblog treatment. You can also add to this political events such as the Budget, debates or Prime Minister's Questions. The main consideration is that you will be covering the conference alongside other journalists, so your coverage needs to be distinctive. The situation is also likely to be tightly controlled, and as a result dull, so have the facts and evidence ready to challenge what is being said, and bring users into the coverage too.

Product launches and store openings can be very dull affairs, but occasionally generate significant interest – particularly among technology and fashion fans – to justify liveblogging. Your liveblog is likely to use that interest as the basis for some broader editorial angles. For example, launches and openings are social gatherings, so try focusing on the people there: interview them, paint a picture of how diverse or similar they are. Tap into their expertise or enthusiasm; work with them. And think about what people might want to know after the launch/opening: tips and tricks on using new technology? The items that are flying off the shelves? You may need to be ready to contact experts and insider sources too.

What about sporting and cultural events? Look to less well-covered sports, concerts, performances, fashion shows, exhibitions and other events. Be aware of rights deals and other restrictions, however: live coverage rights for certain popular sports, such as Premiership football, may be limited. There may be restrictions on taking photographs of cultural events, or recording audio or video at a music event (see Chapter 8 for more).

Anticipation of an event can be an event in itself. The *Liverpool Echo*'s Friday afternoon liveblogs previewing the weekend's football fixtures are a particularly successful example of this. Really, they are a live chat, with the liveblog format providing the editorial urgency to give it a news twist.

And liveblogs can still be successful even if the event has already happened. When the *Birmingham Mail* received a tip-off about an armed robbery one night, they had no staff available to run a liveblog, but still launched one the morning after covering what reporters were doing as they chased details.

Remember that you don't need to wait for something newsworthy to happen to start a liveblog: you can do something yourself, and liveblog your progress. Ideally it should be something with a beginning, a middle and an end over a limited period of time: running a marathon, for example (if you can hold the phone!), or collecting 1000 signatures for a campaign. It should also involve others: the liveblog format lends itself to outside contributions.

One example of this is liveblogging anniversaries. On 18 June 2015 the *Telegraph* liveblogged the Battle of Waterloo, as it happened two centuries earlier, while the *Birmingham Mail* liveblogged the anniversary of the Birmingham pub bombings. Clearly this takes a lot of research, but can be very creative.

Laurence Dodds, who ran *Telegraph* liveblogs on anniversaries from the fall of the Berlin Wall and the funeral of Winston Churchill to Waterloo and the Battle of Britain, says that he prepared for the liveblogs with a large range of sources: books, interviews with historians, old *Telegraph* newspapers and interviews with living witnesses. He says:

> The mistake I made was to underestimate the time my preparation would take. For Berlin especially I did a lot of original research and interviews, including phoning up the historian of a German football club. Lots of work also went into the multimedia stuff, like graphics and pictures, which I commissioned from the relevant Telegraph teams. I also had a lot of conversations with museums who own the rights to images and old documents.
>
> (Bradshaw 2015)

The key to a good liveblog, says Dodds, is to pick out a few different threads which represent all the sides of the story that you want to tell, and follow them from start to end.

> In part this is determined by which eyewitnesses wrote most copiously. You have to be very selective and ruthless, because there is so much stuff. My strategy wherever possible was to pick one person who best represented each participating group, and stick with them. For example I used Fred Ponsonby in the Waterloo blog and Winston Churchill in Battle of Britain as recurring characters to anchor the action.
>
> (Dodds 2015)

As for breaking news, while you cannot plan for the exact timing of breaking news, you can *prepare* for some news events which may happen at some point. At the most basic level, you should know how to quickly launch a liveblog. But you might also have files prepared for when certain stories break. For instance, most news organisations have obituaries ready to go when certain public figures die. And if there is a major earthquake or other natural disaster, major transport problems, or a terrorist incident, you should have contacts ready to call.

Your role as a liveblogger

One of the key qualities of liveblogging is its networked nature: at the same time as you are covering an event, dozens or hundreds of others may be liveblogging and live-tweeting about it too (or even watching it on television). So you need to quickly evaluate that coverage and decide where your efforts will be best invested and appreciated.

The bottom of the 'value chain' in liveblogging is simply *documenting* what is happening. In an event where you are the only witness, this makes sense. But if there are lots of other people doing the same thing, you may want to spend at least some of your time *filtering and aggregating* (curating) the most informative and insightful updates.

Moving up the value chain, you should also consider adding some *analysis* of what is happening: why is one particular piece of information or statement important, or why is this one not important? What does this mean for the industry or area that you are covering?

You might also decide to *enrich* coverage by adding audio, or video, or other multimedia that adds a new dimension. When the *Telegraph* planned their liveblog of the wedding of Prince William and Kate Middleton, for example, they placed different reporters at key positions on the route and tasked them with producing different media: one might be doing audio interviews with those waiting on the route; later they might add video.

Finally, if the event involves disputed facts or versions of events, you might seek to *verify* that information. This is what often happens during election debates, for example,

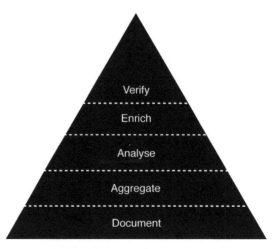

Figure 6.1
Liveblogging: adding value to the network
Source: Courtesy of OnlineJournalismBlog.com

where everyone can watch the coverage and have an opinion, so the main need is for a reporter who can actually check whether the claims being made are true or not. Likewise, during riots and demonstrations there are often lots of claims from those on the ground about what is really happening and why; a journalist's role in that situation is to verify what the truth is, as far as they can see.

Preparing for liveblogging

A good liveblog is well prepared – just as a good TV or radio programme is the result of days spent lining up guests, researching key talking points and preparing key visuals or sounds.

The worst liveblogging is done when the reporter has not prepared anything and knows nothing about the subject. You can spot these liveblogs a mile away: updates are dull, and there are large gaps between them.

How you prepare for the liveblog clearly depends a great deal on the subject of the liveblog itself. You should certainly aim to pre-write some material that can be easily fed into your coverage when things go quiet: for example, the introduction and background details on people, places and facts (why will this affect people; what are the key facts and figures; what has been anticipated, expected, predicted or feared). You might also write separate articles which are published on the same day, such as profiles and explainers, that you can link to in your introduction and coverage.

Visuals are particularly vital to live coverage, and can often be pre-prepared. Typical examples include a map of any route, charts illustrating key facts and infographics combining these.

Information you should be seeking out for different types of events includes:

- *Agendas, schedules and routes*: council meetings tend to publish an agenda online in advance. Likewise industry conferences will have schedules. Even protests will sometimes publish the route that they will be taking in advance. When are the key moments likely to be?
- *Documents*: presentations, transcripts and reports are often published online by organisations in advance of meetings and conferences, or you can ask for these in advance.
- *Jargon*: many events may feature the use of jargon which you will need to be able to understand immediately. Documents can help you identify these in advance, but be prepared to ask for them.
- *Systems*: how do particular aspects work? (for example, voting systems, technologies, inventions)
- *People and places*: make sure you research the key people involved in an event, whether those are speakers, campaigners or delegates. If the event is in a particular building or along a particular route, have some detail on key places so you can add a bit of colour.

Bookmarking is a very useful technique on this front: tools like Pinboard (pinboard.in), Delicious (delicious.com) and Evernote (evernote.com) allow you to add multiple tags to each page or document, and later retrieve material based on one or more tags. Tags might describe the subject, type of document or other qualities. For example, you might tag one webpage with 'report', 'childpoverty' and 'Bristol'.

Prepare the ground

In addition to background information, you should also be preparing other elements to make sure your reporting is the best it can be on the day.

Contacts, for example, are key: knowing *about* people is one thing; *knowing people* is another. Make sure you have some good contacts in the organisations involved: ideally speak to them before the event so you have some quotes ready to go and they know who you are if you phone them during the event itself (for example, to get a reaction to an accusation, or check a fact).

In a similar vein, you should make sure you have good *feeds* set up on social media: for example, hashtags and lists of key people in TweetDeck or other social media dashboards (see Chapter 3 for more on this).

Locations might also be important. If you're going to be on the ground then it helps to know where the local wifi spots are, and which areas are likely to be good for interviews (quiet; good visuals) or where trouble might flare up. Try to recce places before you arrive there – or speak to others who can give you a heads-up.

Finally, make sure that you let people know that you are going to be liveblogging in advance (if it is appropriate to do so): write a preview article highlighting why this event is going to be important or exciting, and at the end mention that you or your organisation will be reporting it, live.

Liveblogging skills

When done well, liveblogging can take in curation, writing for social media, recording video and audio for the web, image editing and verification. Initially you may feel overwhelmed by the various demands, but remember that doing all of these at the same time takes practice, so the more practice you get, the easier it will become.

One of the things that most people struggle with when first liveblogging is simply updating regularly: it can be hard to find things to report when nothing is happening, which is why that preparation is so important: it gives you material to publish or points to mention when things are quiet.

Personality and style are important too. Dan Ripley of the *Daily Mail* recommends: 'Be as human as possible, project your character, inject humour, make it as lively as possible – but you've got to get the details' (McEnnis 2015).

Try to make sure that you have identified any appropriate *hashtags*, or create one if you don't find any being used (you can always change). Remember that even if you don't have time to capture an image or record a sound you can still describe it: try to tell us how things sound, look, smell and even taste.

Direct quotes are particularly useful in liveblogging: try to use those where you can. And focus on updating when something *changes*.

A further skill to focus on is the ability to move quickly in response to developments. If the action switches to another location, you need to go there. Don't be afraid to talk to people: if you see someone important or unknown, you need to be able to approach them and ask specific questions. Knowing *what* questions comes down to research: what would your users want, or need, to know?

You also need to be able to switch focus and check what other people are saying online: there may be other people in the same place posting updates on social media; or there may be experts tweeting from afar, or individuals with key questions based on the coverage. You should also look for examples of individuals or organisations affected by the things being discussed: for example, are there charities or businesses which would be affected? People who have suffered, or succeeded, because of policies or proposed ideas?

A final skillset relates to multimedia. Remember that multimedia in liveblogs is very different to broadcast video or audio, or even photojournalism:

- Video can be (and typically is) raw footage, more like a photograph that moves than a story.
- You don't have to tell us the story as a broadcast journalist would do – sometimes you have to narrate, but really strong online video and audio often lets the subject or pictures tell the story.
- Even if you are not allowed to take images of people because of privacy concerns, you can take images of other things that tell the story: a broken chair; a discarded leaflet.
- Keep it short. It's better to record five one-minute audio clips, each answering a single question, than to publish a five-minute audio. The same goes for video.
- Keep it even shorter. Video on Twitter, Instagram, Snapchat and other platforms is limited by length. That brevity is their strength: play to it.
- But also remember that you can stream video or audio using tools like Periscope or Spreaker. Of course, there should be a good reason to do so.
- Make visuals out of text: tools like Canva and Chisel allow you to create social media-friendly images that bring quotes to life. Wordle allows you to make word clouds out of speeches or documents.
- Make visuals out of background: think timelines and maps.
- Make visuals out of facts: it may be a chart, but equally you can pick a single number and make a visual out of that.

You don't need to record *everything* visually and aurally, but having that in your toolkit will give you some extra options. In particular, look for situations where hearing someone's tone of voice (their pain, confidence or evasiveness) tells us much more than their words alone.

Finally, there is *verification.* Try to go to the source of any facts or claims where possible. You might even speak to researchers who were involved.

At the end of the liveblog you should have performed that vital watchdog role that journalists often claim: holding power to account and giving a voice to the voiceless.

CLOSER LOOK
LIVEBLOGGING TOOLS VS TWITTER

There are many liveblogging tools that seek to make the process easier: Coveritlive, Liveblog Pro and Scribble Live are perhaps the best known. These will give you a dashboard where you can automatically pull in updates from social media (for example, specific users' accounts, searches or hashtags), insert media, conduct votes and moderate comments. But most importantly they all enable you to embed the liveblog on your website. They also make it much easier for users to replay afterwards. This is why news organisations use these tools rather than Twitter alone.

Many of these tools will also 'push out' any updates to social media, so that when you update a liveblog on Coveritlive, for example, your Twitter account will also publish that update, so you don't lose out on engaging through social media.

But also don't overlook other tools that may feed into your reporting: you may want to livestream video or audio. You may need to create maps, or charts. And, of course, there are the tools for following what is going on – and verifying it.

'Mojo': mobile journalism

When AJ+, Al Jazeera's social media unit, reported from Baltimore, US on protests against police brutality, they broke their record for engagement and increased their audience by tens of thousands of people. One of the co-producers, Shadi Rahimi, put the success down to the relevance of their reporting, the speed of delivery on social platforms, conforming to social norms and raw emotive video: 'We know that positive emotions often carry content farther than negative (awe vs sadness), and anger-inducing content is more likely to be shared than sadness-inducing; it produces greater emotional activation' (Rahimi 2015).

Mobile journalism – often abbreviated to 'mojo' – is regularly used to report live – or very quickly – from the scene of an event. In liveblogging, being on the scene makes a huge difference: it allows you to provide colour and quotes that other people cannot get, while it also puts you in a perfect position to respond to developments and verify claims.

Often reporters sent live to the scene of a news event will be expected to do specific things in their work to make sure that the right content is online quickly. *Birmingham Mail* liveblogger Jonny Greatrex outlines six key steps that their reporters need to follow:

1 We need a scene picture immediately
2 We need six to eight paragraphs of colour or scene-setting, which can be self-referencing: 'I am at the shooting in Sparkbrook, crowds have gathered at the police cordon, I am off to speak with people', for example
3 A 10–15 second video clip of the scene, this can then go in every story about the incident
4 Five more pictures so we have enough for a gallery

5   Then a constant stream of copy
6   If someone has died, find out who the dead person is and where their family lives, and get a full, sit-down chat and family album.

Because you can only be in one place at one time it is important to monitor social media as well so you can follow what is happening where, and where you might need to be. You can also use social media to arrange to speak to participants, or invite users to tell you where they think you should go.

* When reporting on a mobile phone or tablet put it in airplane mode to stop the recording being interrupted by a phone call or alert.
* Remember that your main strength is the images, audio and video that you can capture – but also that you don't need to do that all the time. Try to vary the content you are producing, and be prepared to listen just as often as you publish.
* If you are recording audio or video make sure you are close to the subject. This means you can get clearer audio and a steadier shot (see Chapters 7 and 9 for more on audio and video).
* Likewise, try to record in a quiet place with little background noise.
* Mobile journalism trainer Stephen Quinn advises holding the camera with both hands with your arms at your side to keep things steady, and using your body as a tripod, moving at the hip rather than moving your arms.
* Think about ratio. Traditional video uses landscape ratio, so be careful about which way you are holding your camera. But equally your footage may need to work in square or vertical ratio if it is going to be used on social platforms. Know which ratios you are going to use before you begin.
* If you are filming video which is to be used on television then check whether you are using the right frame rate. Some apps (such as Filmic Pro) allow you to select a frame rate which is suitable. And if you can listen to the audio while you record, all the better.
* Avoid using the front-facing camera: it is always poorer quality than the rear-facing one. And avoid using zoom (it results in poorer quality images – although this is changing): move closer if you possibly can instead.

CLOSER LOOK
USEFUL MOJO KIT AND SOFTWARE

The most basic kit for any mobile journalist is, of course, the mobile phone. You will find various articles arguing about the merits of iPhones vs Android phones but both have their advantages and it will depend on the sort of assignment you are on. You can also use a tablet. Apple devices' main advantage is the iMovie app, while Android devices have the advantage of removable batteries and memory cards.

It is always worth making sure that you have a generous data plan which is going to allow you to stream video or send large files, and you may even consider buying multiple SIM cards with different operators in case you are in an area that doesn't have a good signal.

Sound is important when it comes to recording multimedia, so find out how to connect a microphone to your phone (you can get adaptors for most iPhones and Android devices). Remember that you can also use your hands-free headphones as a microphone: try attaching them to an interviewee's lapel.

Depending on how much space you have, and how important it is, you may want some way to fix your device to a tripod (or a monopod/'selfie stick') if you need a steady shot. You might also take small but powerful LED lighting too. Tools like the Padcaster, which has fittings for a zoom lens, lighting, microphone, and tripod, provide a frame for an iPad or iPhone.

Multimedia uses up a lot of power and memory, so consider buying a portable charger unit which you can use to recharge your device if necessary, and have extra memory cards if your phone uses them (iPhones don't, so try to buy a device with lots of memory). You might also want to buy separate devices instead of relying on your phone to do all the work: portable digital camcorders, DSLRs (digital single-lens reflex cameras) and audio recorders can be used to record and then connect to a laptop to upload media.

If you're doing a lot of typing consider getting a small (ideally foldable) portable bluetooth keyboard which you can connect to your phone.

In terms of software clearly you will need the basic social media apps, but see if you can get an app for the liveblogging service too. You can also often get an app for your content management system on your phone (WordPress, for example, has its own app, and the BBC have their own internal app for journalists called PNG). You will need an audio recording app that allows you to upload to relevant platforms, and video editing. Note that while services like Instagram allow you to record inside the app, it is generally better to record video normally and then upload it to those services.

Make sure you also have streaming apps such as Spreaker for audio and at least one video streaming app such as Periscope, Meerkat, Ustream, Bambuser or Qik (some are portrait and allow users to comment live, while others are landscape). Note that you can also stream from a laptop and record using YouTube Live and other services.

Don't forget about apps which can help with other issues as well: a torch, for example, and a battery meter app which will help you reduce power consumption.

MOJO MANIFESTO

TIPS TO BE A SUCCESSFUL DIGITAL JOURNALIST

TIP 1: PHOTOGRAPHY SKILLS

A tweet with an image is twice as likely to be shared, A picture speaks a thousand words - I could go on, but the first tip to being a successful Mojo is to perfect your skills in photography. Having a mirror-less camera or DSLR in your kit still counts as Mojo, in fact its Mojo+.
Your photographic skills will have a profound effect on your visual storytelling. Practice & Master the Art

TIP 4: WORK IN PUBLISHING

The language and editorial discipline you will learn from working in a newspaper or magazine will help greatly with the quality of the content you create. That may be for online or more likely it will be immersive multimedia for mobile. Either way, time spent learning the skill of the print journalist is time very well invested.

TIP 2: RADIO EXPERIENCE

A fundamental part of being a great Mojo is understanding great sound. This includes how to capture it using the correct mics, what Apps or hardware to use and how to edit and mix great sound. Spend some time working in radio. Create your own radio packages and podcasts. They will inform your digital multimedia content for the rest of your career.

TIP 5: SOCIAL MEDIA

The role of the journalist is no longer linear, you must learn to master Social Media platforms. Understand what works best on each platform and how to write and create content for the ones where your audience reside. This will allow you to grow your personal "digital brand".

TIP 3: GRAMMAR OF TELEVISION

When creating great visual stories it is important to understand the grammar of television. Why are shot sizes important, what about angel of view. All these things inform the psychological impact of your story. Sequences are the building blocks of great visual stories and they also form a core part of the editing process. If you are going to learn to shoot - you MUST learn to edit.

TIP 6: HYPERLOCAL & GLOBAL

At times it may feel that you are struggling to develop an audience for your content. Just remember your audience is both hyperlocal AND global at the same time. Pursue stories that have local impact but global appeal.

TIP 7: DON'T FEAR THE TECH

With the pace of new technology moving so fast it is easy to be intimidated by all the latest gadgets. It's important to stay up to date with the latest developments and to be able to spot the opportunities as they develop. Join groups and communities on Facebook, follow influencers on Twitter and subscribe to emails/newsletters/podcasts to keep your self informed.

TIP 8: LEARN TO CODE.

Its not for everyone but if you are good with tech (see tip 7) then you should seriously consider learning to code. Even the learning process will open up the opportunity to join hackathons and meet like minded people with whom you can collaborate on projects and develop ideas.

Blog: http://tvvj.wordpress.com   Twitter: @glenbmulcahy

Figure 6.2

Glen Mulcahy's 'mojo manifesto'
Source: http://mobilevideodiy.com/lesson/mojo-manifesto-by-glen-mulcahy

Ethics of accuracy in liveblogging

In his book *Tell Everyone*, Alfred Hermida notes that when Lisbon was almost destroyed by an earthquake in 1755 it may have taken weeks for the news to reach London, but the way that news spread three centuries ago would still be recognisable in our hyper connected society: 'The initial reports were often embellished and contradictory, much as happens now on social media. In the absence of timely and reliable information, Europeans exchanged stories, opinions, rumours and theories for months following the disaster' (Hermida 2014, p.120). Today, he notes, the same process takes place but 'days become minutes and weeks are hours'.

There will always be concerns about technology and accuracy: when US Senator Gabrielle Giffords was shot in 2011 many news organisations reported on Twitter – incorrectly – that she had been killed. Some blamed Twitter for the error, but the same mistake was made 30 years previously when President Ronald Reagan was shot as he left a Washington hotel. 'People shouldn't see this as a Twitter mistake', said National Public Radio's (NPR's) Andy Carvin, 'rather it was a reporting mistake that could have occurred on any platform' (Taylor 2011).

This, of course, is the point: your standards of accuracy should be the same whatever medium you report on. Liveblogs and mobile journalism place increased pressure on you as a journalist to 'hit the deadline', but you also have increased opportunities and resources to verify the information that you come across.

In some cases the liveblog itself is one of those resources: if you come across information which has not been verified, you might sometimes judge that your audience may be able to help with this. Acknowledging that a piece of information is circulating and putting that into context is important – especially when everyone else can see the same information too. You might simply ask if anyone has any more information, or say that it does not match up with other reports, but most importantly you should continue to update on the status of that piece of information, and seek to check it yourself – through phone calls, getting yourself or a colleague to the scene or checking technical details (see p.152).

Verifying information live

When the telephone first entered the newsroom journalists were sceptical. 'How can we be sure that the person at the other end is who they say they are?' The question seems odd now, because we have become so used to phone technology that we barely think of it as technology at all – and there are a range of techniques we use, almost unconsciously, to verify what the person on the other end of the phone is saying, from their tone of voice, to the number they are ringing from and the information they are providing.

Dealing with online sources is no different. How do you know the source is telling the truth? Well, you're a journalist: it's your job to find out.

The internet gives us extra tools to verify information – certainly more than the phone ever did. The apparent 'facelessness' of the medium is misleading: every piece of information, and every person, leaves a trail of data that you can use to build a picture of its reliability.

Broadly speaking there are three levels of verification of any information online:

1   The *content*
2   The *context*
3   And the *code* underpinning that.

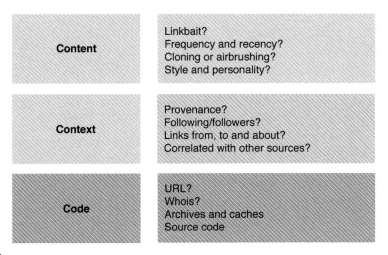

Figure 6.3
Content, context and code: verifying information online
Source: Courtesy of OnlineJournalismBlog.com

Questions to ask of content: too good to be true?

At its most basic level, alarm bells should ring if the information you're looking at seems too good a story. Journalists have found themselves hoaxed in the past by transfer rumours posted on message boards by a football 'agent' (really a bored teenager), by photos showing the Harrods Christmas lights spelling out an offensive message (a simple piece of cloning in Photoshop) and by a social media account pretending to be a newspaper columnist apologising for her latest article blaming a pop star's homosexual lifestyle for his death. Embarrassing emails that go viral can turn out to be PR tricks. Video diaries can be revealed as new forms of fiction.

The more hoaxes you are familiar with, the more likely alarm bells are going to ring at the right time: the website Snopes.com keeps track of the most widely shared ones, and they often share similar qualities.

The frequency and recency of information will give you a clue as to its veracity: the more recent the information, the more up to date it is likely to be (although it may be based on out-of-date information – trace it back to its source). And the more frequently a source is updated (over a long period of time), the less likely it is to come from an opportunistic hoaxer.

Finally do the style and personality of the information match the supposed source? Do they write in the same tone? Do they make spelling mistakes?

Questions to ask of context: verifying social media accounts

The Associated Press's Fergus Bell recommends separating the source and the content when verifying information (see Figure 6.4) (Bell 2015). Thankfully, social and other digital media lend themselves particularly well to verification because, in our activity in

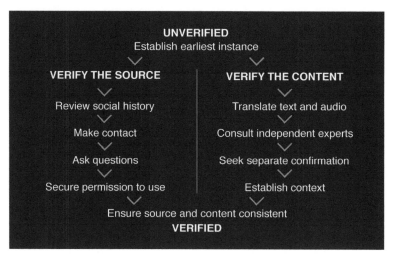

Figure 6.4
Fergus Bell's system for verifying information at the Associated Press

social networks, we effectively verify each other. If your information comes from a social network account, ask yourself some of these questions:

- How long has the account existed? If it's only existed since a relevant story broke then it's likely to be opportunistic.
- Who did the person first 'follow' or 'friend'? These should be personal contacts, or fit the type of person you're dealing with.
- Who first followed them? Likewise, it should be their friends and colleagues.
- Who has spoken to them online? Ditto.
- Who has spoken about them? Here you may find friends and colleagues, but also people who have rumbled them. But don't take anyone else's word for their existence unless you can verify them too.
- Can you correlate this account with others? The Firefox extension Identify is a useful tool here: it suggests related social network accounts that you can then try to cross-reference. The Chrome extension Polaris Insights does something similar for companies.

Finally, of course, you should try to speak to the person. Phone their office or their employer and confirm whether they do indeed have the account in question.

For websites the checks are broadly similar. On Google you can use the advanced search facility to look for other pages that link to the one you're checking. These might include other websites that have rumbled the hoax before you – or are bragging about it. Similarly look at what links the webpage contains to other sites: does this fit with what you would expect?

Questions to ask of code

If your source is a webpage, look at the website address. If it is purporting to be a governmental website it should end in .gov, gov.uk, etc. Health websites may end in .nhs, police in .police, defence in .mod and so on. Academic websites should end in .ac.uk or .edu but this is no guarantee: less reputable 'establishments' have managed to obtain web addresses with these extensions. And of course .com addresses offer no guarantees.

Use a Whois service to find out who the web address is registered to. This isn't immune to fakery but the hoaxer may not have thought about it, and if the details are hidden you may wonder why. Try variations of the domain. For example, when the viral 'Labservative' campaign first began it was not clear who was behind it: the company had kept their details private for the .com address, but they had forgotten to do so for the .co.uk variation. This was followed up by a phone call to the company asking who was managing the campaign.

If you are asking for emails verifying a story, make sure you are forwarded the original email, and not a screengrab, and check the IP address of the email against who it's supposed to be from (you can search online for instructions on how to do this).

On Wikipedia and other wiki-based sources, look for 'history' and 'discussion' links where you can see what changes have been made and the discussions about them.

Finally, right-click on the page and view the source code. Occasionally hoaxers intentionally leave clues here, but you can also find other clues such as the author, date, location and technologies used.

Sometimes looking at the metadata of documents can lead to a great story itself: when the UK's Conservative Party sent a letter from 'more than 5,000 small business owners' to the *Telegraph* praising the party's economic plans, one observer noted that the letter's metadata showed that it had originated from Conservative Central HQ: this was no grassroots movement. Once people realised this, they dug into the names on the letter and found dozens of problems including businesses that did not exist, duplicate names, people who were not business owners at all and people who had never signed the letter and asked to be taken off. It was a major embarrassment for the party.

Verifying media: images and video

The quickest thing to check with any image is: has it been published somewhere else before? Google Images offers a 'reverse image search' which will search the web for images which are the same as, or similar to, an image which you upload.

Also look for cloning and airbrushing. Cloning is the replication and repetition of small areas of a photograph to, for instance, make a crowd look bigger by duplicating faces; or to make an air attack look more dramatic by adding extra plumes of smoke. Airbrushing is the removal of details. Also worth watching for are composite or staged images (there is a whole genre of Google Street View hoaxes that fall into this category).

Inconsistent lighting, eye shapes and light reflections within eyes are all good clues to look for as well. But also look for details which don't match up with the place or date that the video or photo was supposed to be of: you can search for weather reports in that place and time, or other images of that spot (using Google Street View, for example). You can check that accents match that location, or licence plates, or insignia on uniforms.

You can also find out more about an image or video by checking the EXIF data: this is information about when the image was taken, on which camera and with what settings. Jeffrey's Exif Viewer (regex.info/exif.cgi), for example, allows you to quickly see the EXIF data on any web-based image. That information can also be used when speaking to the photographer to check that it was they who took the image (although remember that EXIF data can be faked too).

Some news organisations – such as the BBC, in its UGC hub – have systems that look for Photoshop modification (not necessarily a sign of hoax – a user could simply have cropped or lightened an image). You can also see this yourself by looking under 'details' > 'origin' > 'program name'. JpegSnoop will provide more details on images, and other tools to help you check images include Forensically (29a.ch/photo-forensics) and Ghiro (getghiro.org). Error Level Analysis is another useful tool to detect possible alteration, although it's not perfect. New tools are being created all the time, so search for image verification tools to find others.

CLOSER LOOK
WHAT TO DO WHEN YOU GET IT WRONG: CORRECTING ERRORS

If you do post a liveblog update that later proves to be wrong, what do you do? Should you delete it and risk looking like you're trying to pretend it never happened? Or should you try somehow to correct it while risking the original update still being shared?

Some platforms – such as Facebook – allow you to edit posts, but with Twitter there's no clear consensus on best practice. There are, however, some broad guidelines identified by Nathan Gibbs (2011):

- Capture the error: take a screenshot or archive it using a service like Freze.it
- Publicly acknowledge the error
- Reference the error in the correction
- Notify those who shared the error
- Repeat the correction.

When it comes to liveblogs and articles a report from the New America Foundation recommends corrections are made as early as possible: 'In particular, media outlets should correct online versions of their stories directly (with appropriate disclosures of how they were changed) rather than posting corrections at the end (which are likely to be ineffective)' (Gahran 2012).

CASE STUDY: LISA MACLEOD, *FAST*FT

In May 2013 the Financial Times *launched its own dedicated liveblog: fastFT (ft.com/ fastft). The newspaper's head of operations and associate editor, Lisa MacLeod, explains how the site works:*

*fast*FT is the first place where *Financial Times* stories are published. The day starts at around 5:30am. We are filing content for a specific niche, a specific following: traders, the trading room, so it is important to match the timing of the traders who use the site, matching the rhythm of the market. The site focuses on market-moving information: breaking news, with one to two sentences on 'What does it do for me?'

Some interpretation is needed by specialist reporters. They are quick workers – using the news wires and Twitter for alerts. But if there's a scoop, that is owned by the FT: that's the right platform for those.

Journalists are part of the live news desk, but we use a straight-to-publish content management system, like TweetDeck, which allows reporters to publish quickly. And although the whole thing is online-only, we often reverse-publish reports into print as short pieces.

It's an interactive approach: we use a lot of stats, and it's very visual. We use the Chartbuilder tool which means we can bypass commissioning of graphics. Sometimes an explainer or slideshow is commissioned early along with the news reports. And we have developers coding in the newsroom for anything more complicated.

The idea is to make the updates 'short and sharp', and then they can be picked up by other reporters for FT.com who might add quotes or other details. But sometimes they don't need to; sometimes *fast*FT is all it needs. That means it can create space for reporters to work on other things where something doesn't need a 'traditional' story.

Summary

Liveblogging and mobile reporting have become central to the online output of the majority of news organisations: reporters are expected to be able to report from the scene of major news events using social media and multimedia. Even broadcast reporters used to travelling with camera operators and other technical support are expected to file images and updates from the scene while they wait for their colleagues to arrive (and often after the film crew leaves, too).

These updates from reporters – and from others at the scene, whether witnesses, participants or the authorities – are regularly incorporated into liveblogs: a format that has proved to be one of the most engaging in modern journalism. But liveblogs can also be flexible enough to be used to cover 'softer' stories such as a reporter's personal journey, or a shared TV experience.

The liveblog demands a wide range of skills from the journalist: in hard news you need to be able to report quickly and accurately – to chase the truth behind claims and verify rumours, images and video. You will need to be able to adapt to the best medium for the story, whether that is a simple text report or multimedia, and prepare thoroughly so you know what to expect and how to fill the dryer periods.

In softer liveblogs you'll need to be just as well prepared. You'll need to be able to entertain with a quick wit and a sharp eye for detail, but you'll also need to be an impeccable host, bringing users into the experience and highlighting their most interesting or amusing contributions.

As sports reporter Dan Lucas says: 'To write about it in a format that allows the journalist such unprecedented scope to apply their own personality to the reportage is hard work but fun too' (McEnnis 2015).

At their best, liveblogs represent a rare fulfilment of one of the central promises of online journalism: the ability to connect individuals, to provide a shared experience that helps debunk myths and enlighten individuals, while also offering a platform for a variety of voices to reach the truth about news events.

Activities

1   Find a forthcoming event such as a protest, meetup or conference (use the resources outlined in this chapter). Make a plan for how you would cover that event: this should include what research you can do ahead of the event; what kit you might need; what your role should focus on; and what might be the beginning, middle and end of your live coverage.

2   Come up with ten ideas for a liveblog. Try to apply them to different subjects – not just live events but other feature ideas outlined in this chapter like 'a day in the life' or an anniversary.

3   Pick a major public event and look for three different examples of live coverage in different publications using the liveblog format. How do they differ and why? How are the liveblogs structured in terms of beginning, middle and end? How do they incorporate user-generated content (UGC)?

4   Produce a liveblog yourself using one of the tools outlined in this chapter – or one that you have found yourself. Try to create a mix of text, images and multimedia. Look for opportunities to highlight (curate) relevant content by others if possible. Review the results and identify areas where you can improve. For example, did you update frequently enough? Did you describe what was happening in detail, or quote people?

5   Monitor social media during a TV debate such as *Question Time* (hashtags like #BBCQT are useful), or during a breaking news event or protest, and look for opportunities to factcheck claims that are being made by viewers. Use the techniques outlined in this chapter.

Further reading

Burum, Ivo (2013) *How to Mojo* (iBook): https://itunes.apple.com/gb/book/how-to-mojo/id633249999?mt=11

Burum, Ivo and Quinn, Stephen (2015) *MOJO: The Mobile Journalism Handbook*, Abingdon: Focal Press

Gillmor, Dan (2009) *Mediactive* – free download at https://mediactive.com/book

Montgomery, Robb (2014) *A Field Guide for Mobile Journalism* (iBook): https://itunes.apple.com/us/book/field-guide-for-mobile-journalism/id877677780?mt=13

Online resources

First Draft News focuses specifically on live reporting and has a number of resources around verification: https://firstdraftnews.com/resources

Forensically (image verification tool): https://29a.ch/photo-forensics

Glen Mulcahy's Mobile and Video Technology Blog: https://tvvj.wordpress.com

Google Image Search—click on the camera icon to upload an image and search for it elsewhere on the web: https://images.google.com

Silverman, Craig (ed.) (2014) *Verification Handbook*: verificationhandbook.com

Bibliography

Bateman, Robyn. Digital editors network 2011 #DEN2011, *Journonest*, 23 October 2011, http://journonest.co.uk/2011/10/23/digital-editors-network-2011-den2011

Bell, Fergus. Verification: source vs content, *Medium*, 16 June 2015, https://medium.com/1st-draft/verification-source-vs-content-b67d6eed3ad0

Bradshaw, Paul. How the Telegraph liveblog historical anniversaries, Online Journalism Blog, 1 October 2015, https://onlinejournalismblog.com/2015/10/01/how-the-telegraph-liveblog-historical-anniversaries

Dodds, Laurence. Author interview, September 2015

Gahran, Amy. Prompt, obvious in-line corrections work best online, research indicates, Knight Digital Media Center, 29 February 2012, http://archive.knightdigitalmediacenter.org/?/news_blog/3526

Gibbs, Nathan. How to correct social media errors, *Mediashift*, 12 July 2011, http://mediashift.org/2011/07/how-to-correct-social-media-errors193

Greatrex, Jonny. Author interview, September 2015

Hermida, Alfred (2014) *Tell Everyone: Why We Share and Why It Matters*, Toronto: Doubleday Canada

HSJ Live, HSJ Live 11.03.2014: MPs to vote on Care Bill 'hospital closure' clause today, *Health Service Journal*, 11 March 2014, www.hsj.co.uk/news/hsj-live/hsj-live-11032014-mps-to-vote-on-care-bill-hospital-closure-clause-today/5068769.article#.VciL2PlVhBc

McEnnis, Simon. Following the action: how live bloggers are reimagining the professional ideology of sports journalism, *Journalism Practice*, 6 August 2015, DOI: 10.1080/17512786.2015.1068130 /www.tandfonline.com/doi/full/10.1080/17512786.2015.1068130#abstract

Rahimi, Shadi. How AJ+ reported from Baltimore using only mobile phones, Poynter.org, 1 May 2015, www.poynter.org/news/mediawire/341117/how-aj-reported-from-baltimore-using-only-mobile-phones

Sparrow, Andrew. Live blogging the general election, *Guardian*, 10 May 2010, www.theguardian.com/media/2010/may/10/live-blogging-general-election

Taylor, John. Admitting mistakes and explaining how they happened builds your integrity, @jbtaylor, 10 January 2011, www.johntaylor.co/crisis-communications/admitting-mistakes-explaining-happened-builds-integrity

Thurman, Neil, and Anna Walters. 2013. Live blogging – digital journalism's pivotal platform? A case study of the production, consumption, and form of live blogs at Guardian.co.uk. *Digital Journalism* 1(1): 82–101.

Thurman, Neil. Real-time online reporting: best practices for live blogging, in Lawrie Zion and David Craig (eds) (2014) *Ethics for Digital Journalists*, New York: Routledge

Wightman, Catriona. Britain's Got Talent: it's grand final time – as it happened, *Digital Spy*, 31 May 2015, www.digitalspy.co.uk/tv/s107/britains-got-talent/news/a650162/britains-got-talent-its-grand-final-time-as-it-happened.html

7 Online audio

Chapter objectives

This chapter will cover:

- How online audio is different to radio journalism formats
- Different audio formats used online
- The basics of audio production
- Useful kit to record audio for the web
- Generating ideas for audio stories
- Considerations in live audio streaming
- Podcast ideas and considerations
- Audio slideshows: tips and techniques
- Publishing and optimising audio for the web.

Introduction

Audio is perhaps the medium with the most unrealised potential when it comes to online journalism. Although there was a peak of interest in 2005 as publishers raced to create their own audio programming and 'podcast' was even declared word of the year by the *New Oxford American Dictionary*, by 2010 the focus had moved on to video and social media. In that year *USA Today,* the *Los Angeles Times* and the *Boston Globe* all cancelled their podcasts, followed by the *New York Times* the following year.

But while publishers had stopped investing in podcasts and formal programming, individual reporters had not: audio was being used more and more widely in general reporting. Helped by new mobile-based tools such as Audioboo (later to be renamed Audioboom), Soundcloud and Spreaker, and the increasing use of mobile phones in newsgathering, journalists were embedding audio in articles, sharing sound clips on social media and streaming it live online.

Then, in late 2014, *Serial* changed everything.

Serial was a podcast series about the murder in 1999 of an 18-year-old student. Made by the creators of the well-known radio programme *This American Life*, it became the fastest podcast to reach 5 million downloads and streams on iTunes, topping the charts in four different countries.

Suddenly, podcasting was fashionable again. The podcast networks SoundWorks, Radiotopia, Gimlet Media and Infinite Guest were all launched in 2014; Slate's Panoply (in partnership with the *New York Times*, WBUR and the *Huffington Post*) followed in 2015. One analysis noted that 30 per cent of all podcasts listed on iTunes US had been launched in the 12 months from June 2014 to 2015 (Morgan 2015), most of them in the news and politics category, while the number of Americans who had listened to a podcast within the previous month shot up by 25 per cent (Webster 2014). Between 2012 and 2015 the number of podcasts being hosted on one of the largest podcast hosts, Libsyn, went from 12,000 to 28,000, and the number of downloads more than doubled (Vogt 2016). So much was going on in the field that Nieman Lab launched a regular newsletter to report on developments in the field, *Hot Pod*.

There was a lot to report: BuzzFeed launched its first two podcasts in March 2015 and the *Wall Street Journal* introduced WSJ Podcasts the same year. Broadcaster WNYC announced plans to raise $15 million for a new podcast division, while Al Jazeera and NPR both launched new audio apps. By 2016 NPR's chief operating officer was talking about podcasts as 'a way for us to bring new talents and new voices into public radio' (Doctor 2016) and the *New York Times* was announcing the creation of a new audio team. 'Podcasts as we know them are just one style of audio', it said. 'We plan to experiment with other forms of on-demand audio, including short-form, newsier offerings, and with new platforms like [Amazon's] Alexa and Google Home' (Henig and Tobin 2016).

And audio was hot in the startup scene too: venture capitalists started throwing their money at innovative apps and new ways of creating and sharing audio, hoping that they were backing the 'Facebook of audio'. 2016 saw the launch of audio conversation apps Anchor and Pundit, Clammr – a tool for highlighting the best bits of a podcast – and the mobile editing-and-podcasting app Bumpers FM, among others. By the end of 2016 Facebook itself entered the arena, introducing live audio and partnering with broadcasters including the BBC and LBC. Now there was a whole range of ways for people to create, share and consume content.

What had changed since 2005? Partly the ease with which people could consume podcasts. Although iTunes added podcasts in that year, users still had to download podcasts to their computers and transfer it to their iPods. The iPhone hadn't yet been released and widespread mobile connectivity and use of smartphones were not part of the landscape.

A decade later, the devices and the bandwidth were there for people to use – and *Serial* was the killer content needed to give them that push. Audiences for podcasts have been significantly younger than radio audiences, mirroring a similar generational shift among young TV viewers towards video on demand. And over the next decades, the roll-out of internet-connected cars and speakers promises a massive potential market to come.

How is online audio different to radio?

There are two key differences to bear in mind when comparing radio to audio online. The first lies in the devices we use to *consume* audio online: while radio is typically a 'background' experience, playing as we cook a meal, or work, online audio is a much more 'lean-forward' experience: audio clips in news articles and audio slideshows must be clicked on and listened to: research by Radio Joint Audience Research (RAJAR) in 2015 noted that most podcast listeners preferred to listen while commuting or travelling, or while relaxing or doing nothing, whereas radio listeners tended to listen while studying or doing chores (RAJAR 2015). Podcasts in particular are also typically listened to through headphones on a mobile phone (Vogt 2016).

This is changing – particularly with the rise of internet-connected cars and speakers – but the culture of online audio has been shaped by those early experiences: good audio must take into account the contexts in which it is consumed.

A second difference lies in the way that we *produce* audio. Unlike radio, there is no need for your audio to fill a particular amount of time: content is as long as it merits. If you are producing audio on a regular basis you might consider a podcast, but even then the length does not have to be the same each week. And outside podcasting, audio is very likely to be *irregular*, following the demands of the stories that you cover and which ones benefit from an aural element or treatment.

Different audio formats online

There are a number of types of audio you might consider using as an online journalist:

- Raw audio, to illustrate a story, such as the noise of a protest
- Audio clips, such as the answer to one question or a classic guitar lick
- 'Social' audio, where users can respond with their own audio recordings, using apps like Anchor and Pundit
- Full audio, such as an interview
- Audio for social media: typically clips taken from longer packages and edited to give a taster
- Audio programming, i.e. podcasts, which might have a particular format and multiple elements
- Audio slideshows, combining a gallery of images with audio such as an interview
- Livestreaming audio.

Of course these distinctions are not very strict: podcasts can be illustrated visually like an audio slideshow; a story might embed an audio clip which is so long that it is difficult to distinguish from a podcast. But broadly speaking these categories are useful in thinking about the type of audio you want to produce.

Audio basics

Whatever type of audio you are recording, some key principles apply: you need to make sure that the speaker can be heard above any background noise, that sound levels are good and consistent and, if possible, use a microphone.

Recording equipment

Audio can be recorded directly onto a computer or laptop, in a studio, on a mobile phone or tablet, using a digital dictaphone, or audio recorders such as a Marantz, Edirol or Zoom. All of these have strengths and weaknesses: mobile devices allow for quick publishing when your audio is time-sensitive; studios make for a controlled and 'clean sounding' environment, but often require booking in advance and require more technical tuition. Dictaphones are convenient but audio recorders provide more control over things like levels and audio inputs.

Checking sound levels

Good audio needs to be 'just right': loud and clear enough to understand what is being said, or what is happening. The two extremes to avoid are:

- Audio that is too *quiet*, meaning the listener struggles to hear
- Audio that is too *loud*, so that it becomes distorted and uncomfortable to listen to.

Normally these extremes are avoided by checking the *levels* of the sound coming into your audio recording device or software. On an audio recording device like a Tascam, Marantz or Edirol, there is normally a screen that displays those levels as a series of bars which move as the sound comes in. You will see similar level indicators on audio apps like Audioboom and Ferrite.

It is a good idea to *test your levels* before recording: getting your interviewee to speak into the recording device and checking where those bars go. If the bars 'peak', hitting the line at the top of the levels or triggering a red light on the levels indicator, then it is too loud and you need to move the device further away. But if they remain very low throughout, then you need to move closer.

You can take levels before you start recording, with recording paused, or during an initial few seconds of recording that you edit out later. Sometimes you can amplify audio a little during editing, if it is a little quieter than you would like, but distorted loud audio is harder to fix.

What microphone do I need?

There are three main types of external microphone that you might use in recording audio: handheld mics, lavalier (or lapel) mics and shotgun (or boom) microphones. Lavalier mics are often used for video because they don't get in the way of the shot, but this isn't an issue when you are just recording audio. A handheld mic gives you more flexibility, allowing you to record more quickly, and to record your own questions alongside the responses. A shotgun microphone is normally used for recording 'wild track' (the sound of the surrounding environment).

Different microphones also record in different directions – what is called *directionality*:

- A *unidirectional* or *cardioid* microphone records in one direction (and a little to the sides). This is useful for recording a speaker without capturing other sounds in the room.

- An *omnidirectional* microphone records in all directions, which makes it useful for capturing atmosphere.
- A *bidirectional* microphone records in two directions: forwards and backwards. That might allow you to record a conversation, for example.

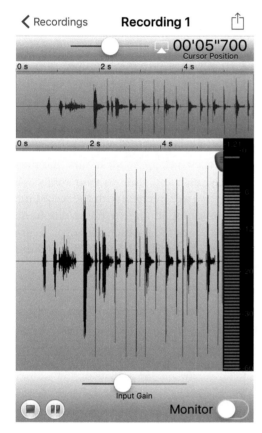

Figure 7.1
The Twisted Wave Recorder app shows levels on the right hand side

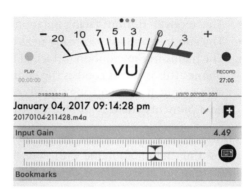

Figure 7.2
Voice Recorder Pro has a very prominent levels gauge

Figure 7.3
Spreaker's audio recording app has a levels indicator in the bottom right corner

Figure 7.4
The Audioboom app takes up most of the screen with the audio levels for your recording

Recording devices like Tascam, Zoom or Edirol have built-in microphones, and often provide the ability to change the directionality of those microphones based on the situation. You can also usually plug in multiple external microphones.

It is likely that at some point you will need to use your phone to capture audio; there are at least three microphones to consider in this respect:

- The 'receiver' or front-facing microphone, which you speak into during phone calls
- The rear microphone, normally next to the rear-facing camera
- The hands-free microphone attached to the headphones that normally come with the phone. This is not as good as the built-in mic, but it does have the flexibility of being able to put it on someone's lapel, or to move it between speakers. In very noisy environments you can also place it right next to the mouth.

It is important to know where the microphones are placed so you don't make the mistake of covering the microphone with your finger when recording. Phone microphones are directional, but also designed to adjust to sound that they pick up, so make sure that they are pointing in the right direction and, importantly, nice and close to your subject. If you are further than a few inches away background noise will interfere with the recording.

In addition to built-in microphones it is worth investing in an external microphone for your phone. You can get adapters, such as the iRig Pre or PRO, which allow you to use microphones with a 3-pin XLR connector, or you can buy microphones with a 3.5mm lead that can plug directly into a phone or the 3.5mm adapter that comes with it.

Watch this: BBC's Nicholas Garnett on using mobile audio to report riots safely
https://www.youtube.com/watch?v=YzTqBo7PyWc

Recording in mono or stereo

Some devices provide an option for recording in mono or stereo. Remember that stereo recordings will take up more space and take longer to upload or download. Audio dramas often make good use of stereo, and podcasts like Radiolab have also used it inventively. However, most situations in journalism don't require stereo recording: voice-based reporting, for example, will be just as good in mono.

Coming up with ideas for online audio

If you are on the scene of a newsworthy event you should certainly be on the lookout for striking sounds, just as you should be looking for opportunities to grab images and video for your report. You might also look to grab a few 'soundbite' single-question clips from people involved.

Beyond reacting to events, you can also plan ahead for stories that will work well on audio. These include:

- Speech-based events, such as debates, speeches, presentations, lectures and conferences
- Interviews where the subject is a good speaker, or whose voice is particularly expressive (the voices of younger or older people, for example, tell us much more about the speaker than their words alone)

- Interviews where the non-verbal reaction is likely to be key (for example, a person's hesitation in answering, or the way that they stumble over their words, or avoid the question)
- Situations involving a range of participants who can contribute a variety of voices to a report
- Stories *about* audio, such as reporting on music and musicians
- Heated discussions, which might involve contributors with a range of valuable perspectives and experiences
- Stories where users can participate in the creation of audio, such as community-driven conversations through social audio platforms.

An experiment in 'viral audio' by NPR found four types of format that work particularly well (Athas 2015): *audio explainers* (like 'How to sound like an Austinite' or 'The scientific reason tomato juice tastes better on planes'); 'Whoa sounds' that are inherently interesting (like 'listen closely: there's a song hidden in this hummingbird's chirp'); *strong narratives* (like 'Listen: this doctor tried to save a boy with the ebola virus') and *snappy reviews* (in one example two reporters go head to head in 'Hot chicken face-off: Prince's vs Hattie B's').

On a more regular basis, you might also think about audio programming *formats*, i.e. podcasting. See the section on podcasting (p.169) for more.

Practicalities will always come into play when deciding which ideas to pursue. If audio is not core to the story, then prioritise the elements which are (such as establishing the facts or getting some quotes). You might, for example, interview someone for your story, and then at the end ask if you can record a brief (30–90 second) clip of them explaining some element of the story.

Some ideas will require more time and preparation than others, and it may be that the story does not justify this (or will be old news by the time it is finished). For that reason you might focus your efforts on audio treatments for stories that are less time-sensitive, or require a deeper exploration.

CLOSER LOOK
AUDIO CLIPS

Audio clips are perhaps the easiest way to get started with online audio. Easy to record with a mobile phone, and ideal for embedding in news articles or sharing instantly on social media, the emphasis is on brevity, rawness and instantaneity rather than studio-quality sound or snappy editing. However, it still needs to be clear, audible and make sense, and you still need to consider the basics of audio outlined above.

There are many apps, depending on what kind of mobile phone you have, which you can install on your phone for recording, editing and publishing clips. Most mobile phones have a built-in audio recorder, such as iPhone's Voice Memos. However, getting that online isn't always easy, and there are a range of useful apps which can be used not only to record but also edit and upload.

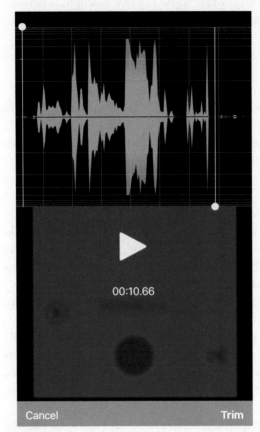

Figure 7.5
Screenshot of Clyp

All-in-one tools like Audioboom and Clyp allow you to record, publish and auto-tweet audio clips within the app, ideal for raw audio from an event, single-question interview answers (you can always record more than one), highlights of speeches or your own analysis. As well as recording on the app, you can upload your own audio, and it is possible to do some editing around the start and end points of your clip.

Other tools focus more on audio production: apps like Ferrite, TW Recorder, BossJack Jr and AudioCopy allow you to record and edit audio, and provide more control over quality, effects and sometimes multiple tracks.

Most apps offer some functionality with the free version, and extra features if you're willing to pay, such as the ability to record or stream for longer, upload larger files or add filters and effects.

Alternatively you might record sound clips using a dedicated audio recording device such as a Tascam or Marantz, or a digital dictaphone. If you use a device like this, the audio will need to be transferred onto a computer, edited, exported and uploaded to an audio hosting platform.

One clever way to add audio to your content is to make a passage of text into a clickable audio clip. The free online tool *SoundCite* (soundcite.knightlab.com) allows you to do this: after following three steps you are given some code which creates a passage of text shaded grey with a play button immediately before it. When the user clicks on the text or play button the audio clip is played. The effect is similar to a hyperlink: when you use a phrase like 'the noisy crowd' or 'her unique drumming style' or 'his phone call to the police', it can be clicked to play audio of that crowd, drumming or phone call.

Tips for perfect audio

Sian Grzeszczyk is a correspondent for BBC Radio Coventry and Warwickshire. Here are her tips for creating strong audio:

- Set out with a clear set of objectives – a shopping list – this will make it easier to edit. If you head out without a clear idea of what you want you'll come back with far too much audio and risk missing the point of the piece.
- Strong audio clips featuring good quotes stand out a mile but make a note while conducting interviews to save time before the edit.
- Always ask for feedback, whether it's a package or a report.
- Take time to listen to how other journalists produce podcasts.
- Aim to be original, stay out of your comfort zone.
- Don't be afraid of mistakes – just make sure you learn from them.

Examples of audio clips in journalism

Audio clips can be used in a range of ways, from being the focus of the story to something additional. Here are some examples:

- BBC World Service host full interviews on their SoundCloud account (soundcloud.com/bbc-world-service)
- BuzzFeed use eight different clips of people with different accents for the quiz *Can You Guess The Accent?* (buzzfeed.com/juliafurlan/so-uh-where-are-you-from)
- BuzzFeed include a clip of a phone call to the police in *911 Audio: Hotel Manager Reports Guest For Being Transgender* (buzzfeed.com/dominicholden/911-audio-hotel-manager-reports-guest-for-being-transgender)
- *Huffington Post* include a 4-minute audio interview with a case study in the piece *Courting Disaster: After Liver Transplant, Anxiety About Health Care Costs Without Obamacare* (huffingtonpost.com/2015/03/03/courting-disaster-lose-everything_n_6784756.html).

> *Watch this:* Smartphone journalism: Audio https://www.youtube.com/watch?v=QmTHmjYNLf4

CLOSER LOOK
LIVE AUDIO STREAMING

Livestreaming audio works well for events where you are expecting a lot of speech, but very few interesting visuals (otherwise you might choose live video). You will need to make sure that you have the bandwidth to support a livestream: ideally you should have access to wifi and be confident that the wifi signal is not going to get swamped by other users.

There are a range of livestreaming audio apps including Spreaker, Mixlr and Boxcast. Most have a time limit on free accounts, but users can pay more to get extra or unlimited time and other features. You should also consider what happens to the audio after the livestream has finished: can you download it and edit parts to use elsewhere?

When planning a livestream, contact the organisers and speakers in advance if possible to let them know that you will be livestreaming it. If you cannot do that, arrive early and ask them before it begins. If it's a public meeting such as a council meeting or scrutiny committee you shouldn't have to ask permission, but it is polite to inform people what you are doing, and a good excuse to make contacts. For private events you may have to check that participants are happy to be recorded. Court cases generally cannot be recorded.

If you are livestreaming something that involves speech, you need to make sure that you are as close as possible to the person or people speaking. Arrive early and get in the best position for this. You might need more than one microphone and some way to position them properly if the people you are recording are in different positions.

The two key parts in any live audio stream are the introduction and the ending. Make sure that you introduce the livestream right at the start, establishing where you are and what's going to happen. You also need to think in advance about how you might end the stream – particularly if your livestreaming account has a time limit.

While the event is taking place you may need to monitor comments on the live feed or on social media in case listeners experience problems or ask questions. You should also make notes about the times when key moments occur, so that you can grab those clips later and either insert them into a text article, or edit them together into an audio package (see, for example, the Guardian Live Podcast, which presents the best bits from events the newspaper has organised).

When the livestream has finished, make sure you point listeners towards other coverage and any later reports that you intend to publish.

CLOSER LOOK
PODCASTS

In its early days podcasting was, like blogging, a way for anyone to connect with an audience online. As a result many early podcasts consisted either of one person speaking directly to the listener, or two people discussing an issue of the day.

As it has grown and developed, however, podcasting has become a much more polished medium, with more variety in the formats that are used, and increasing sophistication in editing. Many newspaper podcasts combine analysis with interviews, discussions and short 'packages', while well-known podcasts like Radiolab and 99% Invisible weave together multiple audio elements into compelling stories. Although there is no one way to make a podcast, there are plenty of examples of good practice, and sources of inspiration for the aspiring podcaster.

What is a podcast?

A podcast is a digital audio file that can be distributed over the internet. The term is a hybrid of of 'iPod' and 'broadcast' but the format is now consumed on mobile phones, tablets and in cars.

Radio shows are often available in this format but podcasts can cover any topic, are not restricted in terms of style and length and can be created by journalists and non-journalists alike. They can be posted directly to a website but some people argue that audio must have an RSS feed to be a 'true' podcast. Audio platforms like Audioboom and Soundcloud automatically provide an RSS feed and subscription facility, as do publishing platforms like WordPress and TypePad, and dedicated podcasting platforms like iTunes, LibSyn and PodBean.

Podcast ideas and planning

A podcast can be about anything at all. It can be an interview, discussion, guide, expert advice or just a way to blog out loud. It can be pegged to a news piece or something timeless.

The best way to get ideas is to think about what your target audience would like and the stories and issues that interest them. Try out ideas on friends and family – and ask users to send you comments and feedback. And make sure you listen to lots of podcasts from a range of sources with a critical ear before setting out to create one (see the list below).

Play to your strengths and to the interests of your potential listeners, and yourself. For example:

- Do you have access to events that might provide lots of useful audio?
- Do you have practical expertise you could share?
- Can you research a subject in depth and access interesting interviews?
- Do you and another presenter have the sort of chemistry that could engage listeners and bring subjects to life? (This takes work and persistence.)
- Do you have an idea for a distinctive format that could work across multiple episodes?
- Are you looking at a deep and rich story that could be spread across many episodes?

One of the most common mistakes made by new podcasters is to assume two friends chatting is enough to make a good podcast. But what might be an interesting conversation for you isn't necessarily the most interesting – or useful – content for someone else. To make your podcast stand apart, it needs to have unique content, i.e. hard work on research. One of the easiest ways to make your podcast stand out is to have guests who have already done that research: experts and academics, people with interesting experiences or skills and those in senior positions at organisations who make decisions that affect others. Having these guests also increases the reach of your podcast to people who want to hear from that particular person.

Twelve podcasts to listen to for inspiration

The list below includes a range of podcasts that should help you come up with ideas and identify good practice. Some are part of a media organisation's wider news output, while others are standalone. Some have been included because they are significant in the industry and regularly discussed. Think about the different formats that are used, and the different ingredients that are combined to make a compelling show. Here are some that are worth listening to:

1 *Serial* (serialpodcast.org): the seminal series that gave podcasting a new lease of life. Make sure you explore the material on the website, too: it's not just about the audio.
2 *This American Life* (thisamericanlife.org): a long-running radio series which has become one of the best-loved and most influential podcasts around.
3 *Radiolab* (radiolab.org): *This American Life* host Ira Glass once said Radiolab had created 'the rarest thing you can create in any medium: a new aesthetic' (Glass 2011).
4 *Freakonomics Radio* (freakonomics.com/archive): created by the authors of the book by the same name, *Freakonomics Radio* discusses economics and science, and how they relate to modern life.
5 *99% Invisible* (99percentinvisible.org): award-winning show on design and architecture created by Roman Mars, it often works with radio stations.
6 *Answer Me This* (answermethispodcast.com): Sony award-winning podcast by Helen Zaltzman and Olly Mann based on engaging with its audience. Its style combines a well-honed chemistry and wit with strong research. Look at how they add supporting material on the website too.
7 *Reply All* (gimletmedia.com/show/reply-all): a show all about the internet that shows how you can do a two-presenter format well.
8 *Death, Sex and Money* (wnyc.org/shows/deathsexmoney): a good demonstration of how picking important themes and strong interviewees makes all the difference when it comes to compelling content.
9 *Partially Derivative* (partiallyderivative.com): a podcast all about data. If you're interested in data journalism, this is a good example of how data can be brought to life in audio.
10 *Song Exploder* (songexploder.net): anyone can talk about music that they like, but getting interviews with those involved makes you stand apart.
11 *Final Games* (soundcloud.com/finalgamespodcast): likewise, there are plenty of podcasts by fans of games, but Final Games speaks to those in the industry, and uses a clever *Desert Island Discs*-type format to hang the interviews around.
12 *Football Weekly* (theguardian.com/football/series/footballweekly): another highly competitive field for podcasts is sport. The *Guardian*'s podcast combines a range of formats (discussion, interview, roundup) with expertise and research.

13 *IRE Radio Podcast* (ire.org/podcast): Investigative Reporters and Editors is an organisation dedicated to improving investigating reporting. This simple podcast tells the story behind individual investigations, and is a useful listen for anyone interested in the field. It also shows how you can make podcasts out of 'behind the scenes' insights.

As well as the podcasts listed above new podcasts come out all the time, so try to listen as widely as possible and look out for new voices and approaches.

How long does a podcast have to be?

There is no set length for a podcast: they can vary in length from a few minutes to over an hour. The regular recording of shorter audio clips, for example, has been called 'micro-podcasting'. Examples include Chris Marquardt, who used Audioboom to provide short regular photography tips, while Mary Hamilton used her walk home from the newsroom to record a podcast about her day. One collaborative micropodcast idea was 'First Pages' (audioboom.com/tag/firstpages), where users were invited to read out the first page of a book they particularly like and tag it with #firstpages to add it to the collection.

One study of podcasts listed on iTunes suggested that the average length had increased from 25 minutes in 2007 to 40 minutes in 2015 (Morgan 2015), but that average included non-journalism formats like 'philosophy' and 'spirituality'. Business news podcasts were among the shortest, with a median time of 15 minutes (Morgan 2015).

Longer is not necessarily better: research a year earlier based on data from podcast app Stitcher suggested the average podcast listener only stayed connected for 22 minutes (Beard 2014). The key question is not how long a podcast should be, but how long *your* podcast *needs* to be: if you have a variety of elements it may need more time; a compelling and complex story might justify a longer treatment (or, better, multiple episodes). Simple subjects may not need long at all.

Once you have come up with an idea ask yourself:

- What does the listener get out of this?
- Who would subscribe to this?
- What is 'aural' about the subject?
- How much variety of 'voices' is there to keep people interested?
- Could you produce content regularly?
- How much editing time might be needed?
- What preparation and research is needed?

Once you are satisfied with the answers to these questions you need to think about practicalities such as equipment and the environment you will be recording in. Clearly having a reliable environment like a studio is useful, but not everyone has access to one and it's not always practical to record in that way. Recording 'in the field' often results in more interesting and livelier sound, so don't be afraid to get out there – but you will have to allow time for editing afterwards.

Always test your equipment before going out in the field and just before you start to record. Make sure you have pressed the 'on' button to record – it might sound obvious but when under pressure this is the most common mistake.

Those without the luxury of a studio need to make sure recording is done in a designated quiet area. Out and about, environmental noise such as the sound of traffic or wind can hamper the quality of audio so be selective about the type of microphones you use and the location. Remember to always carry a notepad and pen – note names, places, spellings and 'killer quotes' that you might want to use as a taster audio clip.

Interviews

Podcasts can have a relaxed, accessible style but when it comes to interviews the journalistic rules of good research and accurate, fair questioning apply. It is not necessary or advisable to give an interviewee a list of questions (the result will be stilted and sound rehearsed) but you can give them a general idea of topics to be covered. If they are particularly nervous of being recorded you might give them a quick trial run for the first question. Be clear about the narrative of your story and the order of your questions while following up on answers that beg further investigation.

When recording an interview:

- Keep control of the microphone
- Don't rustle papers
- Keep eye contact with your interview subject
- Keep questions short – try not to ask 'closed' questions that will elicit 'yes' or 'no' answers
- If they get tongue-tied or make a mistake, record that segment again
- If you want to keep out of the interview don't interrupt, mumble, sigh, laugh out loud or say 'OK' or 'mmmmm, I see'. These can be edited out but it makes the process more time consuming.

Discussions

Discussions are regularly used in podcasts: they provide an opportunity to hear from a range of voices, gain some useful insights and information and, with the right mix of contributors, can be insightful, heated or entertaining.

Be clear about the rules of engagement when you organise a discussion. You don't want people to agree so much that there is nothing to discuss, but equally you want to avoid a 'zoo radio' effect where participants talk over each other and raise their voices.

Be clear about who is hosting the talk and introducing guests, what subjects will be covered and the general length of answer you expect from guests to prevent them monopolising the discussion. It is advisable for the host to agree a signal such as a raised hand to indicate to someone that they need to come to the end of their sentence.

While it is not necessary or advisable to follow a script it is a good idea to make notes and craft an introduction, cues to different subjects and lines that would help to round up the podcast. Guests might also have their own notes if they think there are key facts or points they need to remember. Always remember the listener and talk to them directly. Ask them to share their reactions and ideas across relevant online platforms: your site, forums, blog, Facebook page, Twitter account or anywhere else. This should be a two-way process: online feedback could give you ideas for the next podcast. Name those who have contributed responses and seek out and engage with listeners – this will guard against podcasts that sound self-indulgent and smug.

Editing your podcast

Before editing your podcast it is worth reviewing all your audio and checking any notes you made along the way. It is essential you do this first, particularly if you have several audio projects on the go or if you have left a gap between the recording and editing process.

Several software programs are available to journalists. The most popular include Audacity, GarageBand and Adobe Audition. Audacity is a free software program which is easy to install and good for beginners. It allows you to record directly from your computer – which is a good place to start for those with little experience who want to practise basic skills such as recording, deleting, cutting and moving around audio clips. Audacity is a drag and drop program that can import WAV, AIFF, AU, IRCAM and MP3 files and works with Windows and Mac computers. It also comes with a series of step by step tutorials for the novice. GarageBand (for Macs) is for the more experienced podcaster and offers more features such as the ability to add music and special effects. Adobe Audition is aimed at professional audio producers and has additional functionality. You can also get audio editing apps for mobile phones and tablets such as Twisted Wave Recorder and Ferrite, useful if you are on the move but limited compared to the computer-based options.

Once you have imported any audio to your computer keep copies of your audio files in one folder. When you import your files into a program such as Audacity you will get what is called a 'timeline', which indicates the sequence of your audio and tracks that contain audio clips. There are many tools to allow you to add, overlap and fade between clips. When you are starting out it is a good idea to follow a linear narrative: editing, cutting and pasting your clips in order. You can always leave gaps at the beginning and at the end if you want to add anything such as an introduction, music or another type of clip: many podcasts, for example, have a 'sting' at the start (a brief theme unique to the program) to establish that the podcast has begun. If you make a complete hash of it start over again – that's why you need to keep a copy in your folder.

If your audio is too quiet you should be able to amplify it using the audio editing software's effects options. You can also reduce background noise by selecting a sample of the type of noise you want to remove, and using the 'noise removal' option in the effects menu. But if you have to do this at all, you should of course remember to prevent these problems at the recording stage the next time you go out and record.

If you are on the move a lot, or your subject requires you to be, it might be worth trying out some of the mobile-specific podcasting apps. Some of these, such as Bumpers, focus on recording and hosting your own podcasts. Others, such as Anchor, Opinion, Pundit and ZCast, make it easier for others to join in a discussion that becomes a sort of social audio-based podcast.

When editing remember to:

- Cut with care – be fair and balanced
- Don't cut the context of a quote
- Don't cut the character of the piece – a pause or a stumble may be telling
- Cut out blips such as coughs, hisses and interjections from the interviewer, but don't feel you have to cut out every one
- Select the introductory audio to give meaning to the piece, don't puzzle the listener
- If music is used make sure it does not intrude on audio and is not likely to annoy the listener
- Most music is copyrighted in some way – make sure you know what sort of copyright covers the music
- 'Sell' your audio online with good headlines and explanatory text.

HOW THE ANFIELD WRAP PODCAST MAKES A LIVING

The Anfield Wrap is an independent podcast for Liverpool supporters. Starting in 2011 as a weekly show, usually on a Monday (post weekend match) – it was then picked up by local radio station Radio City Talk, who commissioned a second show for Fridays.

Neil Atkinson, content manager at The Anfield Wrap (TAW) and the main presenter, says they were very quicky seeing 20,000 downloads a week – and it became clear there was demand for more:

'We did history shows – and people wanted more of those, we did comedy shows and people wanted more of those. They wanted more analysis, more tactics, more pre-match, more post match.'

As producing TAW started to take up more of their time they became convinced there must be a way of earning 'at least a couple of quid' from it.

They eventually decided on a subscription model and after four years launched the TAW Player.

'The idea was if you liked the free show– you'd then decide whether to subscribe, and between 8 and 13% do subscribe to TAW.'

Subscription costs £5 a month – with an additional 30 to 40 shows a month available to members, making TAW among the most prolific independent podcasters in the UK.

'You've got Gimlet in the US, but I don't think anyone else in the UK, or anyone linked to football has done the subscription model. What we're trying to do, there's no blueprint or path to follow.'

They've now had over 10 million downloads, clocking up around 100,000 per week, but as Neil explains – that does vary.

'It fluctuates massively. If Liverpool win more people listen and more people subscribe. There's a direct correlation between results and downloads. If Liverpool score a late winner against Crystal Palace – more people listen, more people subscribe.'

Four people now work full-time on TAW with funds coming directly from subscriptions. The subscribed shows are hosted on Amazon, while the free content is on Libsyn.

So far no money is generated through advertising: Neil says that's a conscious decision.

'You can end up managing advertisers' expectations, and that's not our job. Our time should be spent on producing content – and producing good content.'

He also believes it would be wrong to have adverts or sponsorship on the subscribed shows, 'if people are paying money, they certainly wouldn't want that'.

As well being extremely popular – downloaded in 200 different countries – The Anfield Wrap has also been a critical success.

It's been named Best Team-specific Podcast in the World by New York-based lifestyle magazine *Complex* and Best Podcast by the Football Supporters Federation in 2012 and 2015.

Neil puts part of its success down to the way it is produced – which creates authenticity.

'Something I think other podcasters miss is (contributors) being in the same place, the same room, making that the core of the podcast. That's absolutely huge.'

He's not a fan of using Skype for recording phone calls.

'You can't get that rapport, you have people talking all over each other.'

'Football's supposed to be a laugh. It's a collective experience and the podcast should reflect that.'

Another important factor is using broadcast-quality audio.

TAW started out recording in Parr Street Studios, Liverpool – where Coldplay produced two of their albums.

Since then they've worked hard to ensure the quality of their podcasts is on a par with their Radio City Talk show.

'Audio quality's often overlooked by podcasters, but it's massive. People are listening on their commute, on the train – they want to be able to hear what's being said.'

Finally Neil believes their experience from working in radio has improved their podcasting:

'There's more discipline and structure in radio.

'Too many podcasts are, at best, a brilliant conversation. At worst they just sprawl. Having done radio you're more focused on someone listening, someone's opted in. Let's come back to them and where they are.'

Looking ahead Neil says they're focusing all of their energies on making the TAW player and subscription work.

He insists this will be done not through business plans or marketing strategies – but by doing what they've always done: concentrating on content.

'We trust our audience and that they'll come and find us and not the other way around. They want the audio quality to be good – but they don't want us to sound like anyone else but ourselves.'

(Interview by Joe Norman)

Publishing

Choosing a place to put your podcast is a challenge in itself: there are dozens of places to choose from, from general audio platforms like Soundcloud and Audioboom to dedicated podcast hosts like Libsyn, PodOmatic and PodBean. Don't be afraid to upload to more than one and focus on the one you feel most comfortable with. Community can be important: if you feel that the audience you are aiming at is more likely to use one platform than another, use that to guide your decision. And as you gain experience you may look for additional features that are only available by switching platform.

To publish audio on the web you need to save it in an audio file format which is supported by the host, most commonly MP3 or WAV. The site's help pages should explain what formats it supports.

The next question is how potential listeners can find and subscribe to your audio online. Podcast subscriptions are based on RSS technology: most podcasts are made available via an RSS feed so listeners can subscribe to it and are alerted to fresh content. Audio hosting services Audioboom and Soundcloud will provide RSS feeds and services such as PodBean will give you a feed for your podcast too: check the service's help pages for tips on submitting the feeds to podcast indexes. You can also use the built-in RSS feeds on most blog hosts including WordPress, or use Feedburner.

Think creatively about the title and description of your podcast – make it short and snappy if it is a regular podcast and remember to use descriptive keywords to help people find your podcast via search engines. You'll need an image to represent it too. You are then ready to submit your feed to podcast directories.

iTunes might be the best-known place to find podcasts, but it's not the only game in town: Google Play Music is important for Android users, and many podcast fans use dedicated apps to listen to podcasts (called 'podcatchers') like Overcast, TuneIn and Stitcher. Try to submit to more than one. In fact, there are so many podcast directories that there's even a directory of those directories: the website Podcast Places (podcastplaces.com).

Note that many of these directories have certain criteria before they will list your podcast, such as a certain loudness and use of meta tags. Check these when submitting and make sure your podcast satisfies them.

HOW CBC RADIO'S PODCAST PLAYLIST CHOOSES GREAT PODCASTS

Lindsay Michael and Kate Evans are from the CBC (Canadian Broadcasting Corporation) Radio's *Podcast Playlist* (cbc.ca/radio/podcastplaylist), a programme that aims to feature the best in Canadian and international podcasts. Every episode, the presenters select podcasts that are related to a chosen theme, and interview podcasters.

Podcasts are found through searching online, following podcasters on Twitter and looking at reviews from podcasting site The Timbre (thetimbre.com). Selected podcasters are paid a standard rate. Here's what they look for in a podcast:

- It sounds like a lot of care goes into the sound and editing – a polished voice is what people are used to on the radio, however Michael and Evans will mix it up by also including podcasts that are not 'radio-professional'
- Smart and interesting conversation
- The ease with which a podcast can be found and listened to
- The podcast doesn't have to be the highest quality on the best website: great content means more
- Podcasts do have to follow certain radio regulator rules so they do have to edit out swear words for the radio
- Short can be good: podcasts can be 5 minutes in length as long as the content is interesting!

Here's what they avoid:

- Podcasts with bad sound quality, hissing or static
- Lack of editing (i.e. too much rambling) – although 'rambling podcasts' aren't suitable for their work, it is a perfectly acceptable form of podcasting that some enjoy
- Exciting concept with no follow-through
- People imitating other podcasters: 'You will not be a better Ira Glass than Ira Glass, but you will be a better you', Lindsay Michael says
- No story arc or shape to the interview
- Poor use of music (too much)
- Bad jokes.

(Interview by Gurpreet Mann)

CLOSER LOOK
AUDIO SLIDESHOWS

Audio slideshows can be a particularly powerful way to turn an audio interview into something engagingly audiovisual. Likewise, they can also be used to turn a standard picture gallery into something deeper and richer. And with many social networks and advertisers prioritising video, they can also be an easy way to create 'video' content.

Audio slideshows often base themselves around interviews: one person talking about their experiences over a slideshow of photographs provides an extra dimension to what we are hearing. The *New York Times's One in 8 Million*, for example, used the form to tell a series of stories about individual New Yorkers from rookie cops to mambo dancers, while the *Telegraph* used a slideshow to illustrate an interview with the former athlete Denise Lewis about the Olympic gold of Jessica Ennis (see the section below on slideshows (p.180) to find links to all the examples mentioned here).

Another common use of audio slideshows is to accompany a series of photographs with narration from the photographer, or a photographic expert. Examples include photographer Steve Bloom narrating a collection of his images, *South Africa under Apartheid in the 1970s,* and judges narrating award-winning wildlife photography in *Global Views – Lives and Landscapes.*

Art and culture work well for the same reason: David Dawson worked as assistant to the painter Lucian Freud for 20 years, and narrates imagery of his art and working environment in one slideshow for the BBC, while in a *Guardian* piece an interview with the head of an immersive theatre company is run over striking imagery from their latest production.

Audio slideshows are particularly good for bringing historical imagery to life: the *Telegraph* interviewed ten D-Day veterans to narrate an audio slideshow marking the anniversary of the event, while BBC Wales's *The Welsh in Patagonia, 150 Years On* sees two descendants of those who migrated to the area narrate a mix of old and new images of the area and its Welsh settlers.

Choosing a subject for an audio slideshow

The best slideshows combine great imagery with the intimacy of audio reportage and allow the viewer to mull the images and voices without being distracted.

A strong subject is crucial. Typically this will be someone with a powerful or fascinating personal story or, less often, a group of people whose collective experiences bring a subject alive. Vox pops, however, do not make very good audio slideshows.

Sometimes audio slideshows are chosen because the audio or images alone don't have quite enough impact, and the addition of an extra dimension can bring it to life.

Not all slideshows need audio. A striking set of pictures without a narrative attached to them has value as a picture gallery and is popular with readers, often getting high traffic figures. For example, a flower show will have stunning images but little in the way of a story. A story with history and context will need explaining, and therefore commentary from a journalist or from the subjects in the story.

Once you have an idea consider the following:

- Are the pictures likely to have visual appeal (the slideshow will suffer if images are weak or samey)?
- Is there a variety of images? Close-ups, long shots, medium shots
- Remember pictures of people sell a story: portraits, close-ups
- Capture ambient sound for atmosphere (use this to introduce and punctuate your package)
- Is there a strong narrative with a beginning, middle and end?
- Ask the subject to include your question in their answer – for instance, if you ask 'When was the first time you . . .?' their reply might begin 'The first time that I . . .' This allows you to let the subject tell their own story without including your questions
- Think about what might be the first and last image
- Are captions needed to give further information?

- Avoid over-use of literal imagery, e.g. showing a picture of money when the subject mentions 'money', etc.
- Think about length. Is it too short and feels underdeveloped? Or are you making it too long and overindulgent?
- Think about how you deal with images in different ratio (landscape, portrait, square)
- Consider how much to use the Ken Burns effect (a slow zoom towards the image – see below), if at all – don't use it on every image.

Collecting audio and images

An audio slideshow might be made in a range of ways: the journalists might take photographs and gather audio; or they might work on audio in conjunction with a photographer. A third option is where a subject provides the images – for example, if you are interviewing someone about their past, or an archive that they maintain. Or pictures might come from users' submissions, or the photo library of a publisher or news agency.

However you collect the images, it is important to make notes about who is in each image, who took the image, when and where. This information might be needed for captions or for narration.

Paul Kerley, who works with audio and images at the BBC, recommends using between eight and ten images per minute, and around 20 minutes of audio to edit down to a publishable length of 3 minutes or less (Welsby 2010). He also suggests that the story should be built around the images rather than the audio, although other writers differ on this point (Luckie 2010).

Before the editing process, gather all your material and select the strongest images. Listen to the audio – you may need to go back to your first batch of pictures to select another image to illustrate a point.

Software for slideshows

Audio slideshows are essentially video files, so you can use any video software to create them: iMovie, Final Cut, Windows Movie Maker and Adobe Premiere are all fine, and the YouTube Editor can also be used to create them.

Video editing software will often use the 'Ken Burns effect' on still images by default: this is the effect of slowly panning or zooming in on an image, and is named after the documentary maker who used it in his work. It adds motion to still images, which can work if it is a normal video with a still image in the middle. But for audio slideshows it can quickly become repetitive and intrusive. For that reason it is worth finding out how to turn the Ken Burns effect off in your particular software at the start of any project.

The best-known specialist audio slideshow software is Soundslides but a wave of social media- and mobile-focused audio tools are now available including TapeWrite, Explory, Voddio, JamSnap and Korsakow. Some have limited functionality but are quick to pick up; others are more advanced but take more time.

Narrative considerations

When you listen to a number of audio slideshows you will notice certain recurring structural characteristics. Often the package will begin with a few seconds of background noise ('wild track') to 'set the scene' before the subject introduces either themselves or the key narrative event that the audio slideshow concerns. Imagery may mirror this – an establishing shot of the subject's environment followed by an image of the subject or event.

You will want to place your strongest audio clip at the start, and your most attention-grabbing imagery. One of my favourite audio slideshows, by Franzi Baehrle (an MA student of mine at Birmingham City University), begins with the words 'If we could have heard children screaming as they died, burning to death, we couldn't have done it'. The interviewee was talking about taking part in bombing raids over Germany during the Second World War, and that quote was perfect to start the audio slideshow with: when you hear him say that, you drop everything and want to hear the rest!

Likewise, you will also want to end on a strong image and some sort of resolution so that users have a strong memory of the story.

The difficult bit is filling in the middle. Pacing is important: more upbeat stories might move through images more rapidly, while serious or sombre subjects warrant a slower treatment (Luckie 2010). Long shot images with some wild track can be used to shift from one scene to another; close-ups are best for the most intimate moments of the narrative. Details can work particularly well in audio slideshows; objects take on new meaning when juxtaposed with a personal experience.

These are, of course, not rules – and with confidence they are there to be broken – but they can serve as useful guides when starting out.

Audio slideshows: 13 to watch

If you want to watch the audio slideshows mentioned in the section above, the links are given below, as well as a few more. Watch these slideshows and think about why the format was chosen, how the images are used and how the audio might have been edited to work best.

1   The *New York Times: One in 8 Million* (nytimes.com/packages/html/nyregion/1-in-8-million)
2   The *Telegraph: Denise Lewis on Jessica Ennis Gold* (telegraph.co.uk/news/interactive-graphics/9469644/Denise-Lewis-on-Jessica-Ennis-gold-audio-slideshow.html)
3   BBC: *South Africa under Apartheid in the 1970s* (bbc.co.uk/news/in-pictures-18242214)
4   BBC: *Global Views – Lives and Landscapes* (bbc.co.uk/news/magazine-18522990)
5   BBC: *Working with Lucian Freud* (bbc.co.uk/news/entertainment-arts-16849079)
6   The *Guardian: Inside The Drowned Man with Punchdrunk's Felix Barrett* (theguardian.com/stage/audioslideshow/2014/apr/15/the-drowned-man-punchdrunk-felix-barrett-temple-studios-audio-slideshow)

7 The *Telegraph: D-Day Anniversary Audio Slideshow* (telegraph.co.uk/history/world-war-two/10878511/D-Day-anniversary-audio-slideshow-meet-ten-veterans-of-the-1944-Normandy-invasion.html)

8 BBC Wales: *The Welsh in Patagonia, 150 Years On* (bbc.co.uk/news/uk-wales-33620890)

9 ITV: *Mother from Nottingham Talks about the Day Her Daughter Died on Holiday* (itv.com/news/central/update/2016-08-19/audio-slideshow-mother-talks-about-her-daughters-last-day-and-calls-for-tough-new-laws-on-helmets-abroad-after-quad-bike-accident/)

10 *The Atlantic*/Council for Foreign Relations: *The Arab Spring's Aftermath, in 7 Minutes* (theatlantic.com/international/archive/2016/01/arab-spring-anniversary/416301/)

11 BBC: *Classic Cars in Gaza* (news.bbc.co.uk/1/hi/world/middle_east/8622121.stm)

12 Franzi Baehrle (student): *A Better Understanding* (https://vimeo.com/39144821)

13 Hedy Korbee (student): *The Whitford Files* (https://www.youtube.com/watch?v=Eaq5ZP3veHM).

Look for audio slideshows on YouTube for ideas and inspiration. Many of these have been submitted by people who are not journalists but are of high quality.

Publishing and optimising your audio

Getting your audio online is not the end of your editorial process. One of the key differences between radio and online audio is that online audio almost always has a *visual* element: your clip, stream or podcast will be associated with a still – or sometimes moving – image to illustrate it. You also need to think about the *text* surrounding it.

Most audio hosting services allow you to upload a thumbnail image to accompany your audio, and a well-chosen image can make a big difference to whether users click on your audio or not. Having the face of your interviewee or yourself, for example, can draw listeners in more than a rather abstract image, while a well-designed logo can be important in conveying the professionalism and dedication behind your work.

Titles and descriptions are equally important in helping users make a decision on whether or not to listen to your audio (Athas 2015) – and also help search engines understand it (see Chapter 4 for more on this). Descriptions should link to the article that your audio is part of, so users stumbling across your audio on can click through to the full piece, and also any other relevant webpages.

Broadly speaking there are at least three places you need to think about when it comes to publishing and optimising your audio:

- The audio hosting platform (e.g. Soundcloud, Audioboom, Clyp, Facebook, PodBean, iTunes, etc.)
- The webpage on which your audio might be embedded (e.g. your news article or feature, or your podcast's dedicated website)
- Social media (where you might share short audio in full, or a clip from a longer piece).

It is worth selecting a 'must-listen' clip from your audio (in other words, something that has to be heard rather than watched or read) and publishing that separately in order to promote it on social media. The audio tool Clammr (clammr.com) was created specifically to address that problem (it also lets you embed audio clips on websites), while the radio station WNYC created 'audiograms' in 2016 – videos that look like audio players – in order to share short clips online. 'We think shorter, more snackable content is the way to go', Delaney Simmons, WNYC's social media director, told NiemanLab (Owen 2016). The station decided to focus on clips under a minute after looking at their analytics for their audio on social media, using the format as a way to bring listeners in and, hopefully, get them to download the whole podcast.

Sometimes the clips don't need to be from the podcast itself: audio that wasn't included for whatever reason can still be used on social media or in related articles. If you are embedding your audio in an article consider using 'audio' in the headline or subheading to 'sell' the unique content that you have, or calls to action like 'Listen' or 'Hear' (which also work well on social media).

Summary

From podcasts to audio slideshows, audio has been responsible for some of the best-known web-native formats in journalism, but it has also been one of the toughest nuts for publishers to truly 'crack'. Difficulties in finding and sharing audio, measuring audiences and monetising them, plagued the sector for years. But the success of podcasts like *Serial*, and improvements in audio optimisation techniques, have opened up the potential of the form.

In many ways audio occupies a sweet spot: boasting the engagement of video without the associated costs. The challenge for you as a journalist is spotting the opportunities for telling stories through sound, and telling those stories well.

It is important to have a range of options available so that you are ready to respond to those opportunities when they arise. Your mobile phone and tablet should have a range of apps for recording, editing and sharing audio. You should know where the microphones are and have external ones when needed, or audio recorders. Free audio editing software will inevitably come in useful even if you don't intend to use it often.

Sometimes the sound that travels furthest is audio that was made for another purpose. In an article about the difficulty of making audio 'go viral', Stan Alcorn notes that calls to the police and hotlines, voicemails and speeches are often widely shared, describing them as 'bits of audio that serve as evidence in a news story' (Alcorn 2014).

Audio does not have to be complicated: making a note to record and share interesting sounds as you go about your reporting can get you started on developing your audio instincts. Recording just one question on audio after every interview can build your confidence – then record a full interview on audio.

For most journalists the above are the key audio skills that you need to develop: the ability to illustrate or add to a story where audio does it best. If you aspire to a role as a podcaster or multimedia producer, experiment as you develop a style of your own.

Ultimately, whatever your audio aspirations are, try to listen to a range of audio just as you read widely: they'll teach you about not just audio production, but great story-telling too.

Activities

1   Visit a big event such as a music festival or demonstration.

- Try to use a dedicated audio app like Audioboom
- Make sure you test out the app beforehand and that you know how to publish to social media
- Interview participants
- Ask for tips on how to survive a festival
- Think about capturing the atmosphere through different clips of sound
- Get permission to record live music
- Prepare for the event beforehand by checking out the area and identifying good places to capture sound and images
- Capture images that will work well in a slideshow – close-up, colour, variety
- Share some of the results while you're there
- Embed key clips in an article to illustrate the event.

2   Record and interview and source images for an audio slideshow.

- Interview a photographer willing to talk about their work, or someone with an interesting history and photos that illustrate it
- Record some wild track of relevant sounds to add an extra dimension
- Edit the audio into a narrative that grabs the listener from the start, keeps them engaged throughout and ends strongly
- Move the audio into some video or slideshow editing software and add images which amplify or complement the audio.

3   Create a series of short podcast guides to your area.

- Research your local area
- Record weekly reports on local attractions, restaurants, bars and nightlife
- Think about who you might record – do you even need to be in the podcast?

4   Create your own podcast format.

- Brainstorm ideas for what might make for good, regular audio programming. Don't settle for generic or formulaic ideas – what makes it unique, and aural?
- Research your subject and know it well enough to talk confidently and naturally with others – as well as to pick good guests
- Make sure you've got a decent setup: a quiet place to record and a good microphone.
- Check your levels and get recording!
- Edit the results for a sharp final product
- Keep practising – it takes time to develop real sharpness and a good chemistry.

5   Optimise audio for the web.

- Listen to a long audio piece such as an interview or a podcast – this should be by someone you know so you can get permission to work with it
- Identify a clip from the piece that is 'must-listen', then use editing software to pull it out as a standalone piece
- Upload the audio to a hosting platform and choose a strong image to illustrate the clip
- Create an article to embed the clip in, which also links to the full audio
- Repeat the process for social media: write a social media update and include the audio clip (see Chapter 5 for extra tips).

Further reading

BBC Editorial Guidelines: www.bbc.co.uk/editorialguidelines
Hudson, G. and Rowlands, S. *The Broadcast Journalism Handbook*, 2007, Harlow: Pearson
Lubetkin, Steve and Papacosta, Donna. *The Business of Podcasting*, 2015, http://thebusiness ofpodcasting.com
Mills, J. (2004) *The Broadcast Voice*, Abingdon: Focal Press

Online resources

Hot Pod: https://www.hotpodnews.com
Midroll Media Blog: www.midroll.com/blog
On SoundCloud Creator Guide: https://on.soundcloud.com/creator-guide
This American Life: Make Radio: www.thisamericanlife.org/about/make-radio
Transom – Podcast Basics: Transom.org/tag/podcast-basics/

Bibliography

Alcorn, Stan. Is this thing on? Digg, 15 January 2014, http://digg.com/originals/why-audio-never-goes-viral
Athas, Eric. From explainers to sounds that make you go 'Whoa!': The 4 types of audio that people share, NiemanLab, 20 January 2015, www.niemanlab.org/2015/01/from-explainers-to-sounds-that-make-you-go-whoa-the-4-types-of-audio-that-people-share
Beard, Nicolette. Podcasting: storytelling for the 21st century – pros, cons, examples and best practices, TopRank Marketing Blog, January 2014, www.toprankblog.com/2014/01/podcasting-content-marketing
Doctor, Ken. So what kind of a show does podcasting have in store for us? NiemanLab, 16 September 2016, www.niemanlab.org/2016/09/so-what-kind-of-a-show-does-podcasting-have-in-store-for-us
Glass, Ira. Radiolab: an appreciation by ira Glass, Transom, 11 August 2011, http://transom.org/2011/ira-glass-radiolab-appreciation
Henig, Samantha and Tobin, Lisa. An update from the audio team, New York Times Press Run, 6 September 2016, www.nytco.com/an-update-from-the-audio-team

Luckie, Mark S. (2010) *The Digital Journalist's Handbook*, Seattle: AA Books

Morgan, Josh. How podcasts have changed in ten years: by the numbers, Medium, 2 September 2015, https://medium.com/@slowerdawn/how-podcasts-have-changed-in-ten-years-by-the-numbers-720a6e984e4e

Owen, Laura Hazard. Hoping to make audio more shareable, WNYC introduces 'audiograms' for social media, NiemanLab, 8 March 2016, www.niemanlab.org/2016/03/hoping-to-make-audio-more-shareable-wnyc-introduces-audiograms-for-social-media

RAJAR. MIDAS measurement of internet delivered audio services, Autumn 2015, www.rajar.co.uk/docs/news/MIDASAutumn2015LFFinal.pdf

Vogt, Nancy. Podcasting: fact sheet, Pew Research Center, 15 June 2016, www.journalism.org/2016/06/15/podcasting-fact-sheet

Webster, Tom. A major shift in podcast consumption, Edison Research, 14 April 2014, www.edisonresearch.com/a-major-shift-in-podcast-consumption

Welsby, Claire. Top hints and tips for making great audio slide shows for the web, Digital Adventures, 1 November 2010, https://digitaladventures.wordpress.com/2010/11/01/top-hints-and-tips-for-making-great-audio-slide-shows-for-the-web

8 Introduction to online media law

Tim Crook

Chapter objectives

This chapter will cover:

- Key elements of media law to consider when reporting online
- The importance of ethics and useful ethical guidelines
- Contempt of court and guidance for using social media to report from court
- How to avoid breaking copyright law – including the use of Creative Commons-licensed materials
- Database rights and data copyright
- Libel risks specific to online publishing
- Defences to use against accusations of libel
- Privacy issues for online journalists and their sources.

Introduction

It is important to understand that any online journalist publishing in the UK is operating in a country that dropped 18 places between 2015 and 2017 (from 20th to 38th) in the World Press Freedom Index of 180 countries published by the non-governmental organisation Reporters Without Borders. That is below Lithuania, Belize and Tongo. There is no constitutional guarantee of media freedom in UK legislation. Article 10, Freedom of Expression, from the European Convention on Human Rights is highly qualified with conditions, restrictions and penalties, and equally balanced with other rights, and the interests of 'national security or public safety'.

The UK also has three different legal jurisdictions: Scotland, Northern Ireland and England and Wales. There are significant differences in the media law among these three systems. Scotland's legal system has different terminology, processes and concepts. It is also worth noting that the British Crown dependencies of the Isle of Man and the Channel Islands, although part of the British Isles, also have their own separate legal jurisdictions and independent media law systems.

In this chapter we will briefly summarise a range of legal and ethical considerations using the 'SPECTACULAR' mnemonic, before digging deeper into some of those, including contempt, libel, copyright and privacy.

Regulators and guidelines

Conduct and publication are controlled by primary media law in the form of acts of Parliament and case law made by the courts, and secondary media law from a range of regulators:

Ofcom (ofcom.org.uk) is a statutory regulator for licensed broadcasters and can fine, suspend and remove the licence of broadcasting publishers.

IPSO (ipso.co.uk) is a regulator that is not prepared to apply for recognition before the statutory Press Regulation Panel (PRP). It describes itself as 'the independent regulator for the newspaper and magazine industry in the UK'. Most of the country's print and online media groups contract into its content regulation, including the publishers of the *Sun*, *Times*, *Sunday Times*, *Daily/Sunday Telegraph*, *Daily Mail/Mail on Sunday*, *Daily/Sunday Mirror*, *Sunday People*, *Daily/Sunday Express*, the *I* newspaper and regional/local newspaper groups. It has the power to fine for breaches of the Editor's Code and can order corrections. It has started an arbitration scheme for media law disputes where claimants have capped costs of £3000.

IMPRESS (impress.press) is a regulator recognised by the PRP and substantially funded by the family foundation of Max Mosley – a media standards campaigner. It describes itself as 'the first truly independent press regulator in the UK'. It is developing by consultation its own code of standards and ethics, runs a low-cost arbitration scheme and has the advantage that those media publishers agreeing to be regulated by IMPRESS are not subject to exemplary (punitive) damages in media law cases, or to the risk of having to pay the legal cost of all sides even if successful. Micro publishing businesses that have fewer than ten employees and an annual turnover not exceeding £2 million per year will not be subject to these penalties under the 2013 Crime and Courts Act.

The Guardian, the Observer, the Independent (now published online), *the London Evening Standard and the Financial Times* are significant publishers that have not yet agreed to be regulated by any external body. Should any of them join IMPRESS, the mainstream UK newspaper and magazine industry is likely to have the confusing situation of two active and rival regulators with separate codes of ethics and standards

The BBC employs the largest number of journalists of any publishing organisation in the UK, and although from 2017 it became subject to full future Ofcom content regulation, it still obliges its employees to comply with BBC Editorial Guidelines (bbc.co.uk/editorial guidelines).

The Information Commissioner's Office (ICO) (ico.org.uk) regulates the Data Protection Act and Freedom of Information Act. In particular, if you process digital information about other individuals for journalistic purposes your employing publisher or you yourself as a freelance will be obliged to register with the ICO: 'The Data Protection Act 1998 requires every data controller (e.g. organisation, sole trader) who is processing personal information to register with the ICO, unless they are exempt'. For most individuals and organisations, the annual registration fee as at 2017 is £35.

The Information Commissioner fined the *Daily Telegraph* £30,000 for misusing the data it had collected from its subscribers so that it could send hundreds of thousands of emails on the day of the 2015 General Election urging readers to vote Conservative (ICO 2015).

These short summaries and guidance on media law must not be regarded as constituting professional and qualified legal advice. Media law is in many parts an extremely complicated specialism of the law and should you have the misfortune to find yourself in difficulties it is important you seek professional and qualified advice.

SPECTACULAR advice

I recommend that all journalists should adopt an online media law survival strategy represented by the acronym, *SPECTACULAR*, with the letters standing for the following principles:

- *S*erious implications
- *P*rivacy
- *E*thics
- *C*ontempt of court
- *T*esting your copy rigorously
- *A*nonymity
- *C*opyright
- *U*nreasonable language
- *L*ibel
- *A*ttitude
- *R*ights.

Below we go through the key details for each principle. The remainder of the chapter expands further.

Serious implications

S is for *Serious implications* if you transgress media law. Not only can you be financially ruined if sued – you could be criminally prosecuted, fined or even jailed.

The basic detail – key information and points you need to understand

Civil litigation is pursued by a privatised, profit-led legal profession in the UK that operates with very high costs, rewards fees for success and collects high after-the-event insurance premiums from the losing side. Changes to the legal costs regime for defamation and privacy actions in England and Wales have still not been implemented. Legal fees charged by English media lawyers have been researched and surveyed as sometimes being in the region of well over 100 times those charged in other European countries. Damages awarded and agreed are generally seen in the rest of Europe as disproportionate, but in this country lawyers think they are fair and justly remedying.

The arbitration schemes run by IMPRESS and IPSO also engage costs for the defendant publisher. While at the time of publication these are early days in the history of these alternatives of media legal litigation, it is conceivable that arbitration outcomes will still involve several thousands of pounds in legal costs even before any binding award in terms of damages.

Most media law crimes are strict liability, which usually means that the prosecution does not have to prove intention, with construction of meaning by subjective interpretation of the alleged victim, or objective interpretation by judges. The UK judiciary has been observed by sociologists as being mostly male, white, privately and Oxbridge educated and operating as a self-perpetuating elite. The size of audience (i.e. how many Twitter followers you have and your Facebook privacy setting) and number of Internet site visitors will be mitigation in damages and criminal penalties, but not a defence. If defamatory comments under your web postings (damaging to reputation – generally known as libel) have not been moderated (i.e. not checked editorially or legally prior to going live), this does not guarantee you are immune from legal problems. European case law is beginning to be ambiguous about whether moderation has made any difference, particularly if the trolling verges on hate crime abuse (see *Delfi AS vs Estonia* bailii.org/eu/cases/ECHR/2015/586.html). And a recent English case has confirmed that the criminal courts can order the banning of social media reporting of sensitive criminal trials because Twitter and Facebook postings cannot be detached from comments and replies.

In theory there may be defences for what you do, but the power of the state/private claimant and their lawyers' costs are so great, 'the chilling effect' (in the US it is called SLAPP: strategic lawsuits against public participation) means it is easier, less risky and cheaper to surrender, settle and apologise for trying to tell the truth (or at least what you think is the truth). The alternative is to remain silent – generally seen as self-censorship and compliance in a climate of fear.

In England and Wales the legal profession is well over 90 per cent privatised and there is less eligibility for legal aid than at any time since the Second World War. If you were courageous enough to defend and represent yourself, Citizens Advice Bureaux are overstretched and if you are lucky you might have volunteer pro bono lawyers to advise you, but most of these are likely to be law students or the newly qualified.

It is also very important to understand that anything you do and publish in the cyber-digital sphere is subject to another dimension of control and liability. This is the private contract you have with the private corporation that hosts your communications. The terms and conditions of global internet businesses such as Twitter, Google, Facebook and WordPress offer additional legal duties and liabilities. Your service could be withdrawn with devastating consequences when your work and archives have not been backed up. In July 2016, the *Guardian* reported that writer and artist Dennis Cooper learned that his Gmail account had been deactivated – along with the blog that he had maintained for 14 years. He complained that the decision meant two of his transgressive novels had been taken off the internet along with what was described as censorious 'erasing of an unfinished book' (Sidahmed 2016).

Privacy

P is for *Privacy* – have you invaded somebody's reasonable expectation of privacy without public interest justification? If you expose private intimacies to do with sexuality, education and family matters, then you could be breaking the law.

The basic detail – key information and points you need to understand

Privacy is about intrusive conduct related to private information and situations. The UK courts measure the principle of freedom of expression in terms of public interest against privacy rights. This is an equal balancing exercise with an intense focus on the circumstances of each case. Questions that will be asked will include whether there was a duty and entitlement to confidentiality. Article 8 of the ECHR convention talks about the right to home, family and correspondence. The concept of media privacy is so wide-ranging it can include filming digital video on a smartphone at a private location without permission.

Ethics

E is for *Ethics* – the Editors' Code set for IPSO is regarded as a benchmark for ethical and legal communication. IMPRESS has been using this code while it consults and develops its own separate code of ethics and standards.

The basic detail – key information and points you need to understand

There is no harm studying and respecting the IPSO code at ipso.co.uk/editors-code-of-practice. For broadcasters it is very important to respect and understand Ofcom's Broadcasting Code at ofcom.org.uk/tv-radio-and-on-demand/broadcast-codes/broadcast-code.

The BBC's Editorial Guidelines (bbc.co.uk/editorialguidelines) are also very influential. They are the first base for standards and duties for anyone working for the BBC. You need to bear in mind that all of the BBC's content regulation is covered by Ofcom.

Outside any legal obligations in law and regulation, you should also consider moral and ethical values. Professional reputation and audience loyalty will be jeopardised by a publication policy and behaviour that is unpleasant and unfair and only just stops short of breaching law and regulation. It is known by the Latin expression *damnum sine injuria* (injury with no damages). This is about being nasty, discourteous, unpleasant, using people instrumentally instead of intrinsically and not treating other people as you would like to be treated yourself. Professional associations such as the National Union of Journalists and the Chartered Institute of Journalists have a separate code of ethics that sets standards that are in addition to law and regulation (see links at the end of this chapter).

You might like to consider alternative codes of ethics from the English-speaking world that are influential beyond the narrow prism of British journalism. The US Society of Professional Journalists approves and publishes a code (spj.org/ethicscode.asp) that is grounded much more on moral and ethical principles than the mere pragmatism of staying on the right side of existing law. An example of an ethical maxim not normally emphasised in UK journalism codes is: 'Boldly tell the story of the diversity and magnitude of the human experience. Seek sources whose voices we seldom hear' (Society of Professional Journalists 2014).

The US Radio Television Digital News Association updated its code of ethics in 2015 to take into account the 21st century ecology of digital online journalism, and a specific standard unique to online communications is: '"Trending", "going viral" or "exploding on social media" may increase urgency, but these phenomena only heighten the need for strict standards of accuracy' (Radio Television Digital News Association 2015).

Contempt of court

C is for *Contempt of court* – protecting the right to a fair trial without prejudice from media coverage or, as a former Attorney General once said, 'Trial by Google'.

The basic detail – key information and points you need to understand

The key question to ask is, have you created a substantial risk of serious prejudice, or impeded a fair trial, or breached court orders postponing or prohibiting publication?

Contempt of court is a specific criminal offence in the UK with a maximum jail sentence of two years and an unlimited fine. It involves publishing in any way to a third party, including by social media, seriously prejudicial information when criminal cases are active after an arrest, a warrant for arrest or the opening of an inquest hearing. It can also be impeding the process of justice by monstering an arrested suspect and any form of threatening or intimidation of witnesses.

It is, therefore, very important to avoid using online media to comment on any ongoing legal case; whether civil or criminal after arrest, when a warrant for arrest has been issued, or when litigation is being heard in court. As an individual you are unlikely to be aware of any special and additional reporting restrictions that are only known at editor or media lawyer level. Although there are defences to some media law crimes of 'unintentional publication', case law has indicated that the legal system shows little sign of compassion or interest in your 'ignorance of the law' or indeed that you were not directly informed about or had no knowledge of a reporting restriction. It will be assumed that you should have shown 'good faith' in finding out, and your professional status should be such that you had been properly trained about the risks. The good faith essentially means acting responsibly. The pervasive nature and easy accessibility to media archives online means some care should be taken in crime and court reporting to avoid linking to postings previous to arrest and charge that have content that could cause a substantial risk of serious prejudice.

'C' is also for criminal behaviour by committing crimes through conduct and research leading up to your online publication. This could be harassing anyone by causing distress on at least two occasions, computer and phone interception and bribing people for information through treating or promising favours. This is covered by two criminal offences in the UK: agreeing to incite a civil servant, including police officers or members of the armed forces, to commit misconduct in public office, and since 2010, the Bribery Act means that in some circumstances paying sources for information could be a crime with no public interest defence. The Computer Misuse Act 1990 is another piece of legislation making it a crime, for example, to use somebody's computer without their permission to obtain information, or to 'hack' into another person's computer, smartphone or digital tablet having guessed or obtained their password without their knowledge.

Testing your copy rigorously

T is for *Testing your copy rigorously* for any possible breach of media law and ethics before publication. Read, re-read and re-read again. If in doubt, leave it out, seek advice and never, ever take anything for granted. Professional decision-making in online journalism requires legal checking. You need to be defensive. You need to be professional. Lawyers will be risk averse but a *good* media lawyer will help you find a way to publish with the least legal risk. The risks in media law come from all directions and are often unexpected. If you have an instinct that something is wrong – trust it and act on it.

Anonymity

A is for *Anonymity* – in the UK there are many classes of persons who have anonymity for life because of their involvement in criminal processes or legal proceedings. They are often victims or witnesses.

The basic detail – key information and points you need to understand

All sexual offence complainants have anonymity for life, so do victims of people trafficking, female genital mutilation (known as FGM), blackmail victims where the menaces are embarrassing, children (aged 17 and under) in court cases and teachers accused of offences against their students prior to being charged. The list is not exhaustive. It includes the identity of jurors in criminal trials and anything concerning their verdict deliberations. Victims of people trafficking criminal offences were given statutory anonymity in 2016 and there is a growing lobby to ensure that victims of 'revenge porn' have the same legal protection.

All media publishers have to carefully consider the risk of people who know the victims doing their own detective work to put two and two together. This means pixilation, silhouetting and electronic voice distortion is not enough. Actors have to be used. Individual journalists, not just editors, can be held liable for criminal offences. It is very important to avoid including any kind of specific detail that could enable anyone to make the identification. The former editor of the *Sun* newspaper, David Dinsmore, was ordered to pay compensation of £1000 and legal costs of £1500 for approving the publication of the pixelated image of the 15-year-old victim of Sunderland soccer player Adam Johnson. The image had been sourced from her Facebook page (Perraudin 2016). The judge acknowledged that although the paper had altered the photo to disguise her identity, it could have left her identifiable by people familiar with her Facebook profile.

Subsequently, Parliament removed the cap on fines and financial penalties for publishers convicted under the 1992 Sexual Offences Act at the Magistrates Court. The *Daily Telegraph,* which had also published a modified representation of the victim's image from Facebook page, was fined £80,000. The *Telegraph* sold only four copies of the 3 March 2016 edition in the area where the girl lived, and there was no evidence that anyone had actually seen the picture and been able to identify her. But it was accepted that publication of the photograph was likely to lead to her identification (PA Media Lawyer 2016).

What was in the public domain and not subject to a reporting restriction last week or yesterday may not be the case today or tomorrow, and you may not know about it. The English legal system sometimes somersaults between identification and anonymity; for example, in the search for missing youths who could be the victims of sexual offences. The investigating authorities may release names and images in the public interest to secure their safety. As soon as this is done, and the arrest of the suspect has been made, all forms of media must then delete and remove anything identifying the victims previously made public. What is public knowledge yesterday, may be contempt of court and a serious criminal offence today.

Copyright

C is for *Copyright* or Intellectual Property. This is a legal protection for the creation of work and includes a large range of media content.

The basic detail – key information and points you need to understand

You should not steal other people's intellectual property; particularly in words, images and music. The best defence is to always get permission for using other people's creative work. Breach of copyright is publishing a substantial part of an image, script, publication, table or database belonging to another person or organisation without permission unless there is a defence of fair dealing by criticism or review, parody, 'quotation or otherwise' or use in reporting a current event.

However, you must always remember that digital images and photographs are excluded from the 'reporting current events' defence.

You might have a very rare public interest defence where an image discloses something so awful, outrageous and wrong there is no other way of reporting it. You may also have the defence that the material is now in the public domain because the publication is 70 years after the death of the author, 50 years after the date of a broadcast, 70 years after the public release of a sound recording (from 1 January 1963) and 70 years after the death of the director, screenplay author and composer of an original film production. Media publications such as films and online websites often have multi-layered copyright interests where the duration varies. Only photographs and images put into the public domain prior to July 1912 are absolutely safe from copyright liability. Computer programs, coding and software are also copyright protected.

The Creative Commons licence is a vital defence and enabling facility for the use of images and multimedia in online publications where the copyright is owned by other people. For more detail on the different categories of licence available see creativecommons. org/licenses. You need to be cautious about siphoning information from online databases for the purposes of using infographic-style software to produce data journalistic designs and layouts. In the UK database owners are entitled to 'database rights' under a European Union (EU) 1996 Database directive that was implemented in English law a year later.

Unreasonable language

U is for *Unreasonable language* – if your language is unreasonable, then there is a risk you are ringing media law alarm bells.

The basic detail – key information and points you need to understand

Communications on electronic networks such as on the internet or social media like Twitter make you liable under section 127 of the 2003 Communications Act to criminal prosecution for messages that are 'grossly offensive or of an indecent, obscene or menacing character'. That could mean up to six months of imprisonment and a fine of up to £5000. In 2011, over 1200 people were prosecuted under this law. By 2014 the figure had risen to over 1500 with 55 individuals jailed. Examples have included tweeting jokes at airports that have been misunderstood. What you think is a strong opinion could be seen as 'grossly offensive' by the police, Crown Prosecution Service (CPS) and Director of Public Prosecutions (DPP).

Section 127 can also be used for 'message stalking', which you might regard as protesting or a campaign – if it can be proved that your electronic utterances are 'for the purpose of causing annoyance, inconvenience or needless anxiety to another'.

Section 1 of the Malicious Communications Act 1988, which applies to old mail as well as electronic communication, makes it a criminal offence with the same penalties as above to 'threaten', message indecently, grossly offensively or with false, or believed to be false information on the part of sender.

In 2013 the DPP finalised guidelines on when it is not in the public interest to prosecute menacing messaging. Prosecutions are likely if social media communication contains 'a credible threat of violence, a targeted campaign of harassment against an individual or which breaches court orders'. The 'grossly offensive' category is expected to be reserved for racial/gendered orientation or hate crime abuse. See the CPS's *Guidelines on Prosecuting Cases Involving Communications Sent Via Social Media* (cps.gov.uk/legal/a_to_c/ communications_sent_via_social_media).

Libel

L is for *Libel* – attacking anyone's reputation in a serious and inaccurate way can lead to litigation.

The basic detail – key information and points you need to understand

Libel is anything said by image or words that causes serious harm to the reputation of anyone or indeed a business or company by any form of media publication – even an email. Public bodies cannot sue for libel, but individuals in those bodies who are specifically subject to libellous comment can be. The law is unclear on whether trade unions and non-public associations can sue on their own account.

Tweets, re-tweets, blog posts, Facebook updates, Instagram images, video or text, WhatsApp messages, YouTube videos, text messages and 'status' notices and emails 'copied' and 'distributed' to more than a second party, i.e. beyond the traditional single mail correspondent, can all be libellous and represent publications in terms of English law. The old rule was the letter seen by one person was not a libel publication unless opened by a butler or secretary. You should bear in mind that libel in Scotland, which has a separate legal system, includes a damage-to-reputation communication to one person only. In England and Wales libel actions need to be brought within a year of publication, and in Scotland litigation needs to be taken within three years of the published defamation.

The libel can be committed by implication, innuendo and jigsaw juxtaposition identification, e.g. any reader connects a fragment of information online to something said on the radio, television or in a newspaper. You do not even have to name people to get into trouble or even explicitly state or repeat an allegation. The House of Commons Speaker's wife, Sally Bercow, was successfully sued for libel for one tweet when she asked why a former Tory politician was 'trending' and added 'innocent face'. This was deemed to be libel by jigsaw identification/implication because allegations of child abuse had been broadcast by the BBC, and on the internet, and somebody the BBC did not name was being identified in blogs and social media. The libellous meaning is constructed by the victim and your authorial intention is no defence.

In multimedia you have to watch out for something general and libellous being said in commentary being connected to illustrative 'wallpaper' – still or moving images with specifically identifiable people in the *mise en scène* of the imagery.

But there are defences. For example, there are privileged shields where your information and reporting is derived from court or government proceedings. This gives you absolute or higher qualified privilege. Public meetings, press conferences and press releases have a privilege at a lower qualified level. Fairness and accuracy are paramount and you must publish the gist of a person subject to defamatory allegations if they demand it. Other defences include innocent dissemination, truth in substance and fact, honest opinion based on true facts or publication in the public interest. You could have the defence of neutral reportage provided the language of the reporting is balanced and you are not shown to adopt and agree with the libellous allegations being reported.

Editorial decision-making conditions are considered in the evaluation of the public interest defence. There is also a specific web operator's defence for user-generated comments whether they are moderated or not. Complaints need to be addressed within 48 hours. The Defamation Act 2013 introduced a qualified privilege for academic conferences and papers that are peer-reviewed. It is very important to appreciate that malice on your part will probably defeat many of these defences. Malice means deliberately setting out to harm somebody, usually to an unlawful extent. Most of the reforms in the 2013 Defamation Act do not apply in Scotland, and none apply in Northern Ireland.

Attitude

A is for *Attitude* – keep it professional and cautious. It does not mean you have to 'self-censor' and sacrifice your freedom of expression. You can write in an angry way, but your anger needs to be channelled through truthful and lawful writing that is in the public interest. The interest needs to be more than just what interests the public. And being abusive, menacing and threatening is likely to be unlawful.

Rights

R is for *Rights* – other people's, which under the Human Rights Act 1998 are protected in so many ways. Article 10, Freedom of Expression, as a right is equally balanced with Article 8, Right to Privacy, and Article 6, Right to a Fair Trial. At its extreme, digital, online communications could threaten somebody's right to life under Article 2 and the right not to be subject to inhuman and degrading treatment under Article 3. Read them and understand them at legislation.gov.uk/ukpga/1998/42/schedule/1.

CLOSER LOOK
ONLINE COPYRIGHT AND INTELLECTUAL PROPERTY

Copyright resides in two main categories of expression:

1   Authorial/primary works. LDMA standing for: Literary, Dramatic, Musical and Artistic.
2   Entrepreneurial/derivative/secondary works. SFBCT standing for: Sound recordings, Films, Broadcasts, Cable programmes, Typographical works.
    Copyright law in the UK is derived from the 1988 Copyright, Patents and Designs Act, its amendments since then and EU Directives on copyright and intellectual property.

Copyright does not protect slogans, facts, news, ideas or information, but it does offer protection in the way they are expressed. Tables and listings of information are a copyrighted expression of selected facts. So is computer coding, software and online digital databases.

Copyright takes effect as soon as copyright protected material is created. It is the information you select and the way you arrange that information that makes it unique. In order for material to have copyright protection it has to result from independent intellectual, or creative effort. In other words, you must have put some work into it.

Copyright lasts for the duration of the author's life plus 70 years for literary, dramatic or musical works. The situation is the same for directors, screenplay authors and musical directors of films, 70 years for sound recordings and 25 years for published typographical editions. Copyright in databases lasts for 70 years in the case of identifiable authors who have made them with intellectual effort and creativity, and

15 years for databases of information produced as the result of investment. It is important to understand that unpublished manuscripts with no known authorship remain in copyright until 2039. These are known as 'orphan works'. An unpublished work with the identity of the author known always remains in copyright until such time as it is published and then the clock starts ticking for 70 years after the death of the author before the material achieves public domain status.

There is copyright in iconic designs that are the logos of public and private corporations. For example, the design of the London Underground map is copyrighted. Photographing and publishing images of banknotes is a criminal offence unless you have obtained the permission of the relevant authority, for example, the Bank of England.

Journalists have a 'fair dealing' defence if they use quotations and material in the course of reporting current events, criticism or review, and where only a less than substantial part of a literary, dramatic, musical or artistic work is used. What 'less than substantial' means varies from case to case but the general principle is that it is not excessive beyond the purpose of reporting, or reviewing, and does not undermine a copyright owner's commercial interests. It is a matter of quantity and quality.

It is necessary that the quotations are attributed. It should be fairly obvious that publishing a substantial part or key, identifying element of a copyrighted work without permission undermines the defence.

In *Fraser-Woodward vs BBC* in 2005, the High Court decided that 14 photographs of David Beckham and his family taken by a celebrity photographic agency had been used for the purposes of criticism and review in a documentary about tabloid journalism. The judge observed:

> Apart from one which was on screen for about 4 seconds, they were shown for no more than 2 or 3 seconds each, and some of them less than that. On occasion, they were shown as part of a brief still image; on others the camera panned quickly across them or zoomed in relation to them.
>
> *(Fraser-Woodward Ltd vs British Broadcasting Corporation*
> *Brighter Pictures Ltd* [2005])

In another case in that year (*IPC Media Ltd vs News Group Newspapers Ltd*) the court decided that the *Sun* newspaper had not satisfied the criticism and review concept. In a half-page advertisement of its new TV listings magazine it had also reproduced without permission the cover of a rival TV listings title.

Facts rewritten do not amount to a breach of copyright. Blatant lifting of the original work (i.e. another story) with the same words, skill, labour and judgement of the original journalist is a breach of copyright, but rewriting a news story broken by a rival publisher is unlikely to be so.

In 2001 the *Sunday Telegraph* was not allowed to depend on Article 10 Freedom of Expression rights when defending a breach of copyright action involving the former leader of the Liberal Democrats, Paddy Ashdown. The newspaper's political editor had included substantial sections of Mr Ashdown's confidential note of a meeting with the prime minister. The quotations went much further than those normally incorporated in a news report (see www.bailii.org/ew/cases/EWCA/Civ/2001/1142.html).

In theory, there is 'a public interest' defence for copyright under common law and the 1998 Human Rights Act, but it is rarely recognised. The threshold for refusing to enforce copyright on public interest grounds would be 'if the work (the images) were immoral, scandalous, contrary to family life, injurious to public life, public health and safety or the administration of justice'. A small claims court judge ruled in favour of a regional newspaper that had copied images from a website showing the activities of urban explorers in derelict buildings because they illustrated police concern that crimes were being committed.

Image issues

You cannot usually publish a picture without permission from the copyright holder. You should ensure you use images online that you and your colleagues have originated yourself. If you are relying on a Creative Commons (CC) licence for an image derived from Wikipedia, Wikimedia, Flickr, Pinterest or Google Images, make sure that you comply with all the specific terms (see creativecommons.org). The licences usually require a specific attribution such as: '"Creative Commons 10th Birthday Celebration San Francisco" by tvol is licensed under CC BY 2.0'. When publishing on an online platform you can do a number of things that show respect and courtesy to the CC licensing. For example, in WordPress editing you can embed the URL of the source image hosting so that it clicks through. You should use captioning to fulfil attribution, and hyperlinking can also act as source acknowledgement.

The fair-dealing defence for news and current affairs does not apply to images. Image fair dealing only relates to criticism and review. This should mean that you can use images to illustrate your genuine criticism or review of a photographic exhibition or book of photographs. But your selection and publication should not be so excessive that you would defeat the purpose of anyone visiting the exhibition or buying the book of photographs.

All images (photographs, designs, artwork, sculptures, etc.) have rights implications in Europe (including the UK) where made and published/exhibited after 1 July 1912. In the US the position is more complicated because of copyright renewal provisions.

Case law in England and Wales is trying to catch up with the internet and online social media communications. But copyright law still applies to photographic images distributed by Twitter, Instagram or other social media platforms such as Facebook.

If you find user-generated image content on Twitter, for example, you can direct-message the account holder to find out if they originated the image and would be prepared to allow you to use the image with a credit. It is important to establish that the person giving permission has the right to do so and ideally owns the photograph.

Social media images and photographs taken for domestic purposes are protected by a privacy provision in section 85 of the 1988 Copyright, Patents and Designs Act, so it is important to seek permission and check the origin and provenance of such imagery. Family images on a Facebook page connected to somebody involved in a news event could have a copyright belonging to the person who commissioned them as well as the person who was paid to take them. An example would be a wedding or official school photographer.

Although it is becoming a common practice for mainstream news publishers to 'screen-grab' images from television coverage of news events to use in their online publications, a strict interpretation of copyright law is that this could be infringement without the permission of the source provider. Mohammed Al Fayed successfully sued the *Sun* for publishing two stills from the security video-tape of his property Villa Windsor in Paris. The newspaper argued they were running a public interest news story disputing how much time his late son Dodi and the late Diana, Princess of Wales had spent there. The court ruled the information from the images could have been published without infringing photographic copyright (see www.bailii.org/ew/cases/EWCA/Civ/2000/37.html).

The situation appears to be different though when using short clips of digital video or sound from publishers covering a news event. This is derived from a test case in 1991 involving the BBC and the satellite news provider BSB. The case established that within a 24-hour period rival media organisations can use extracts of video for news reporting taken from exclusive rights coverage of public interest sport and news events. In this case, it was the World Cup. Again, the extracts had to include an acknowledgement of the source/origin, and should not be substantial in use; they were to be used after the rights holder had first published, and the rival media organisation had to ensure that such occasional limited news usage did not undermine or compete with the original publisher's commercial interests in buying the rights exclusively. The BSB use was deemed reasonable in terms of using clips ranging between 14 and 37 seconds and only up to four times in any 24-hour period.

The 2016 case taken by the England and Wales Cricket Board and Sky against the Fanatix sports app indicated that an excessive use of short though qualitative clips became a tipping point of 'purely commercial rather than genuinely informatory' usage (*England and Wales Cricket Board Ltd & Anor vs Tixdaq Ltd & Anor* [2016]).

In 2014 the fair dealing defence was reformed to include quotation of works (whether for criticism or review or otherwise) and copying works for the purposes of caricature, parody or pastiche. This has opened up a debate about whether this expands the fair-dealing defence for online photographs and images. It could be argued that in order to quote a statement or event presented on a website, using a screengrab of the relevant webpage for current reporting purposes might qualify under this extension of fair dealing.

However, it is unlikely to change the exclusion of photographic images in current event fair dealing. The government's Intellectual Property Office has said:

> Whilst the exception applies to all types of copyright work, it would only be in exceptional circumstances that copying a photograph would be allowed under this exception. It would not be considered fair dealing if the proposed use of a copyright work would conflict with the copyright owner's normal exploitation of their work. For example, the ability to sell or license copies of photographs for inclusion in newspapers would be a normal exploitation.
>
> (Intellectual Property Office 2014)

Quite detailed research needs to be undertaken to ascertain rights holders in photographic images and legal disclaimers will need to be published to avoid future actions from the owners of what appeared to be orphan works (material previously published with no assigned and traceable ownership/originality). The provenance and original rights in an image can be determined through 'reverse image searching'. Google offers this online service by clicking on the camera icon at the end of the search box at images.google.com. The searching usually locates extant sites where the image was first published online (see Chapter 3 for more image sourcing techniques).

Original images of other images, or two- or three-dimensional works of art, are subject to rights implications where they are taken in private exhibition spaces or from in-copyright publications. However, public architecture and sculptures are deemed to be in the public domain, however recently built and created.

You need to be aware that the use of digital still and video images taken in people's homes, on private and corporate property, are not copyright free. You will need to obtain permission. Sometimes you might be in an environment that you think is public, but is, in fact, privately owned. This could even be a park, shopping mall, railway station, airport or transport hub.

Online journalists should be alert to the growing tendency of significant sports rights-holders to ban the use of gifs and short videos in social media coverage. The International Olympic Committee's (IOC's) decision to engage such a ban for the Brazil Olympics generated considerable controversy The IOC media rules stipulated: 'The use of Olympic Material transformed into graphic animated formats such as animated GIFs (ie GIFV), GFY, WebM, or short video formats such as Vines and others, is expressly prohibited' (Price 2016). The English Premier League tried to control similar social media exploitation in 2014, along with other big and lucrative sporting events.

Twitter is obliged by law to respond to copyright notifications submitted under the US Digital Millennium Copyright Act (DMCA). Section 512 of the DMCA sets out a statutory procedure for formally reporting copyright infringement, as well as providing instructions on how an affected party can appeal a removal by submitting a compliant counter-notice. You can read more about Twitter's copyright policy at support.twitter.com/articles/15795.

Incidental use

There is an incidental use defence in UK copyright when images, designs, words and indeed music, video and broadcasting might be included in a separate publication, whether photographic or filmic or online video sequence. The key expression from section 31 of the 1988 copyright legislation in this defence turns on the idea that the defence fails 'if it is deliberately included'. An example of incidental use would be the filming of a documentary about shoplifting and in a sequence showing somebody being arrested the store's background music is playing, or if the sequence was in an electrical goods shop with large plasma screen televisions, there might be a film or broadcast television service showing on the screens. Obviously if you digitally edited the ironic selection of a scene from a film showing shop-lifting onto the screens, then you would need to obtain the rights for the use of that sequence. It would be different if this was incidental and a rather miraculous showing at the time of the arrest. The mere serendipity of such a coincidence could be argued to be an incidental use.

Moral rights

Most employed journalists producing online publications are not entitled to the Copyright, Design and Patents Act 1988's (CDP's) establishment of the right to be identified as the author or director of a published work and the right to object to derogatory treatment of the work. These are known as 'moral rights', but journalists are still entitled to the protection against false attribution of their work. This means that it would be unlawful for somebody else to claim credit for your work or for a publisher to put your name to a publication that you had no involvement in.

Small claims actions

It is important to appreciate that copyright infringement actions are becoming more frequent and easier to launch. The Small Claims track of the Intellectual Property Enterprise Court (IPEC), a division of the High Court in London, is now operating for actions involving damages of less than £10,000. It means that individual photographers can litigate on their own behalf in a less formal legal process. More than 60 actions are being heard each year. HM Courts & Tribunals Service publishes guidance on taking a case to the Intellectual Property Enterprise Court on Gov.uk (www.gov.uk/guidance/take-a-case-to-the-intellectual-property-enterprise-court).

Music issues

Music publishers, composers, musicians and record companies have two very powerful music licensing organisations – PRS and PPL – actively enforcing copyright compliance in all dimensions of media. If you are involved with a publisher that regularly uses copyrighted music for entertainment, there will be an obligation to pay for an annual licence and probably make detailed returns on the music that has been used. PPL will be anxious that as a music publisher you have control over your own streaming. This could require hosting your music on your own server. There may be difficulties obtaining a music use licence if your music usage is encoded from a host platform such as SoundCloud, YouTube or Vimeo. This is because access to the music is provided to all users of the host platforms rather than your own online publication.

YouTube, owned by Google, operates a system known as 'Content ID' (see support.google.com/youtube/answer/2797370). Copyright owners can use it to easily identify and manage their content. Videos uploaded are scanned against a database of files that have been submitted by content owners. The copyright owners can decide what happens when content in a video on YouTube matches a work they own. After completing a Content ID claim, the copyright owner can: mute audio that matches their music; block a whole video from being viewed; monetise the video by running ads against it, in some cases sharing revenue with the uploader, and track the video's viewership statistics. Content ID processing also operates across Vimeo and Facebook. Copyright owners are also increasingly using services such as Audible Magic to engage with Automatic Content Recognition (ACR) in a range of applications from content identification to media synchronisation.

This issue emphasises that journalistic use of private corporate online platforms is always subject to contractual obligations. For example, Vimeo publishes what it describes as 'community guidelines' with the warning that violations of any guidelines could lead to the removal of videos or accounts.

It is possible to use music journalistically with the current event reporting and criticism and review, as well as quotation fair-dealing defences. However, the music used would have to be relevant, illustrative and short – certainly not a substantial part in length of any track. An EU Directive extended copyright duration for music recordings from 50 to 70 years in October 2013. This means that recorded music released for public consumption prior to 31 December 1962 is likely to be out of copyright, though music compositional and arrangement copyright continues for 70 years after the death of the author. Any musical recording published after 1 January 1963 will remain in copyright until the end of 2043.

Database issues

It is very important to appreciate that data journalism and internet data-scraping software programs generate two risks of copyright infringement in UK media law. Database copyright exists where the database itself is a literary work of an author's own intellectual creation, and a Database Right resides in a collection of independent works, data or other materials which are arranged in a systematic or methodical way and individually accessible by electronic or other means.

The Database Right does not require any intellectual or creative effort. It exists if there has been a substantial investment in obtaining, verifying or presenting the contents of the database, and investment for these purposes means any investment whether in financial, human or technical resources. The information does not have to be confidential. The Database copyright duration lasts 70 years from the death of the author, and the Database *sui generis* Right lasts 15 years from the end of the calendar year when the production of the database was finished.

This means that the extraction or re-utilisation of all or a substantial part of the contents of online sites that qualify under the definition of databases is likely to be a UK copyright infringement. Copying the contents to another digital electronic storage device amounts to extraction. Making the contents available to the public by any means amounts to re-utilisation. This would, of course, include the engagement of computer graphics data journalism software to organise the data extracted in an illustrative form.

There is a fair-dealing defence for Database copyright in terms of current event reporting, for criticism or review, or quotation for journalistic purposes. This could operate where a journalist had extracted database information from different sources and is setting out an analysis or comparison for public interest purposes. The fair-dealing defence for Database Right infringement is explained as extraction by a lawful user, for the purpose of illustration or teaching, or for a non-commercial purpose, where the source is indicated. This would appear to provide a defence for data journalistic illustration provided that the source is indicated. However, it would be wise to check the terms and conditions applying to visitors of online database resources. When the terms and conditions exclude visiting the website for the purposes of data scraping, there is an argument that the journalist researcher is not 'a lawful user' of the site. The ultimate and most effective defence is, of course, the consent and the agreement of online database owners.

Such database arrangement protection does not apply in the US where compilation copyright does not apply to all the data extracted from a copyright database. And in the case of databases not protected by copyright law it could be lawful to 'scrape' all of a database unless the website's terms and conditions make it a breach of contract in relation to registered site members or visitors. The European database right is only available to companies based in EU countries.

CLOSER LOOK
CONTEMPT

As previously explained, media contempt law in the UK is designed to prevent lay jurors being exposed to serious prejudice after criminal or inquest cases become active. The substantial risk period is live after any suspect has been arrested, or in the case of a coroner's inquiry, an inquest has been formally opened. Examples of incidents where publications have been found by the courts to be in contempt include: publishing previous convictions; suggesting the defendant has confessed; suggesting accusations of more serious crimes or crimes they are not facing; suggesting arrested suspects are guilty; saying something so bad about them that you could seriously prejudice the mind of any potential juror against them; joining in a media crowd mentality of libelling and demonising somebody arrested in a police inquiry or wanted by warrant for arrest.

The size of an online audience can be quite small to trigger a media contempt conviction. This was the case in 2011 when the *Daily Mail* and *Sun* newspapers were fined for publishing online photographs of a man on trial for murder and pictured him holding a handgun. The prosecution determined that there had been 190 unique visitors to the images in Sheffield where the trial was being held before the papers removed them.

The Divisional Court observed:

> The criminal courts have been troubled by the dangers to the integrity of a criminal trial, where juries can obtain such easy access to the internet and to other forms of instant communication. Once information is published on the internet, it is difficult if not impossible completely to remove it.
>
> *(Attorney General vs Associated Newspapers Ltd & Anor* [2011])

There are many other case law examples of media contempt convictions. A more recent one is that of the Attorney General's successful prosecution of the Condé Nast *GQ* magazine, which published an article by Michael Wolff during the phone hacking trial of former *News of the World* editors Andy Coulson and Rebecca Brooks.

The Lord Chief Justice ruled that the article:

> implied that Mr Rupert Murdoch was a participant in the phone hacking, that the
> defendants must have been aware of the phone hacking, that the defence was being
> funded by him and conducted on the defendants' instructions so as to protect his
> interests, but in a way that might also secure their acquittal.
>
> (*HM Attorney General vs The Condé Nast Publications Ltd* [2015])

He imposed a fine of £10,000 with £50,000 to pay in legal costs.

Most of the newsworthy cases you are likely to cover will be at the Crown Court, or
High Court of Justiciary in Scotland where lay juries (12 in England and Wales and
15 in Scotland) will decide the facts in terms of the verdict (guilty or not guilty in
England and Wales/guilty, not guilty, or not proven in Scotland).

Where the accused has admitted the offence(s) and there is not going to be a trial,
you will be attending a sentencing hearing for which there are unlikely to be many
restrictions.

But where a not guilty verdict has been declared, the presence of a jury will mean
you have to take great care in observing media contempt law until all the verdicts have
been returned.

Most sensational criminal cases begin with a first and only appearance at the
magistrates' court. This is likely to be a journalistic assignment when you are a general
reporter and unless reporting restrictions are lifted (all defendants have to agree) you
must comply with these very specific rules.

You can report what goes on outside the court, but what you report from beyond the
proceedings is subject to the Contempt of Court Act. This means that again you should
take great care to avoid publishing anything that creates a substantial risk of serious
prejudice or impedance to the administration of justice.

Reporting court cases: some simple ground rules

1 Never report anything said in the absence of the jury until after all the verdicts have
   been returned.
2 Stick to reporting accurately what is said in court and do not paraphrase using
   exaggerated, dramatic and sensationalist language, avoid comment and never present
   allegations as fact.
3 Make sure your reports are fair and accurate. Being fair involves putting the other side
   of the story. Make sure you state that the defendant(s) has pleaded not guilty, and the
   trial is continuing at the end of the day.
4 Always comply with reporting restrictions, reporting prohibitions and postponements.
   For a detailed briefing on the comprehensive details of these restrictions, download
   and read the Courts and Tribunals Judiciary's guide on 'Reporting restrictions in the
   criminal courts' (for England and Wales); the online guide provided by the Judicial
   Studies Board (for Northern Ireland) or the statutory reporting restrictions and

privileges published by the Scottish government, all listed at the end of this chapter. Check and update the guides every year so you are briefed on the latest extension of restrictions, which at the time of publication have included anonymity for alleged victims of people trafficking.

You need to be accredited when visiting court complexes to cover cases. It is advisable to join a professional journalists' association such as the National Union of Journalists, Chartered Institute of Journalists or British Association of Journalists, and be in possession of a press or media card. At the very least have a letter of accreditation from your editor, or tutor if you are a student (although student accreditation is available from the bodies mentioned above).

You should be able to use smartphone devices, tablets and laptop computers to make notes, email or text reports and tweet live reports, but always remember that it would be a criminal offence if you were to use your device to record sound or digital video. Broadcast facilities are being slowly introduced in some courtrooms, but they are organised by complex installation and processes of approval and control. Download, study and keep the Lord Chief Justice of England's guidelines on courtroom tweeting at: https://www.judiciary.gov.uk/wp-content/uploads/JCO/Documents/Guidance/ltbc-guidance-dec-2011.pdf.

The right to take notes in a courtroom is essential for any reporter and you should have a polite reference point confirming this, should a judge or court service staff try to stop you. The 2016 case of *Ewing vs Cardiff Crown Court* (www.bailii.org/ew/cases/EWHC/Admin/2016/183.html) determined that courts should have a very good reason to make orders preventing note-taking in the public gallery. The case involved a non-journalist, but asserted note-taking as part of the open justice principle.

Social media controls

Unlike in the US, which has a constitutional First Amendment, the British courts have more extensive powers to prohibit and ban the reporting of legal proceedings in all kinds of digital and analogue media. In 2016 the Court of Appeal became so concerned about the overwhelming abuse and prejudice being communicated in comments on social media sites during a murder trial, it decided to halt reporting on those platforms. This was because the mainstream media were unable to disable the comment streams of their reports communicated on social media platforms such as Facebook and Twitter.

The first trial of two 14-year-old girls accused of torturing and murdering a 39-year-old woman called Angela Wrightson was stopped, and a retrial ordered in another city. The court approved a court order made by the trial judge to media publishers not to place any report of the trial of the girls on their respective Facebook profile page or pages, to refrain from issuing or forwarding tweets relating to the trial and to disable the ability for users to post comments on their respective news websites (see www.bailii.org/ew/cases/EWCA/Crim/2016/12.html).

It is now far easier for jurors to access media reports and coverage of a criminal case prior to the arrest point and before the strict liability rule applies, making it a potential media contempt to publish content that creates a substantial risk of serious prejudice. Judges countermand this risk by instructing jurors not to do any research of their own. Some jurors have been prosecuted for defying the judge's direction. News media publishers should avoid linking to or reproducing material that has been 'archived' online. The English and Scottish courts have powers under the Contempt of Court Act 1981 to postpone reporting of proceedings (section 4(2)) and prohibit publication of the identities of witnesses whose identification has been withheld from the public before court (section 11).

In 2013, the then Attorney General, Dominic Grieve QC, made a significant speech titled 'Trial by Google? Juries, social media and the internet'. He said:

> Trial by Google . . . is different . . . the internet is a haystack of material, scattered with the odd prejudicial needle, as it were. Trial by Google allows a juror to locate the haystack, find the needle, pull it out and ascribe significance to it that it simply would never have had otherwise.
>
> (Attorney General Dominic Grieve QC MP 2013)

Judges have considerable powers to ensure the right to a fair trial under Article 6 of the Human Rights Act and European Convention and their orders can reach out to all forms of media including Twitter. In March 2016, Mr Justice Coulson ordered the deletion of a tweet by the Health Secretary Jeremy Hunt during the manslaughter trial of an anaesthetist and health trust.

The Law Commission carried out a consultation on a proposal that judges should be given clear powers to temporarily order the removal from the internet of crime reports regarded as seriously prejudicial to any forthcoming trial. This followed an order made by Mr Justice Fulford in the 2012 trial of a police officer accused of the manslaughter of Ian Tomlinson during the G20 protests in the City of London in 2009. The judge had directed the media to remove any archive online reports of previous allegations of violent conduct against the defendant. During the trial, he further ordered that the *Mail Online* remove two archive reports that had been discovered to be still accessible on the internet.

CLOSER LOOK
DEFAMATION (ALSO USUALLY KNOWN AS LIBEL)

There are four basic definitions of libel in common law:

1   What you write exposes someone to hatred, ridicule and contempt
2   What you write lowers someone in the estimation of right-thinking people generally
3   What you write damages someone in their trade, profession or office
4   What you write causes people to shun and avoid your subject.

The Defamation Act 2013 says 'a statement is not defamatory unless its publication has caused or is likely to cause serious harm to the reputation of the claimant', and 'harm to the reputation of a body that trades for profit is not "serious harm" unless it has caused or is likely to cause the body serious financial loss'. Bodies that trade for profit are usually companies and corporations. There have been some test cases indicating 'serious harm' is a higher threshold than mere injury to feelings. The serious harm can be obvious in relation to the words when, for example, calling somebody a paedophile, or terrorist. Claimants are now expected to demonstrate damage to reputation as perceived by others.

Libel actions in England and Wales have to be taken within one year of their publication. Unlike in the US, the burden of defence in libel cases is always on the media defendant. This is also true in privacy and misuse of private information actions. Government bodies and local authorities cannot sue for libel. This was established in the 1993 case of *Derbyshire CC vs Times Newspapers* (www.bailii.org/uk/cases/UKHL/1993/18.html). But this does not mean councillors and executives subject to specific and individually linked libels are also blocked from taking action. This precedent does not apply to associations and 'public interest' bodies such as trade unions.

Even if you do not name someone explicitly, or state the actual nature of a libel, if it is possible to work out who and what you are talking about you are likely to be in trouble. In other words, the construction of understanding a libel can be achieved by jigsaw identification between different media platforms and publications making one liable with the other.

The most famous 'Twibel' in recent years involved the wife of the House of Commons speaker, Sally Bercow, who in 2012 had tweeted 'Why is Lord McAlpine trending? *Innocent Face*'. The late Lord McAlpine had been wrongly accused of historic sexual abuse. The court decided Ms Bercow had libelled by innuendo in the context of multimedia coverage elsewhere (www.bailii.org/ew/cases/EHWC/QB/2013/1342.html).

Online libels are now taking up much more of the business of the courts. *Easeman vs Ford* is an example of a case where a filmmaker had successfully sued an activist and blogger for 'a long-running and extensive campaign of online vilification and harassment' (*Easeman vs Ford* [2016]).

A golden rule when testing your copy is to imagine you are the most sensitive person being criticised and think the very worst interpretation of what could be misunderstood by the language you have used.

When evaluating your copy consider the worst possible 'reading' of your material (known as the bane), make your assessment on one quick and immediate reading (the natural and ordinary meaning expected of your audience), then look for any antidote in terms of putting the other side, indicating that the bane is ridiculous, meaningless satire that nobody would believe, and contextualisation which would ensure that any reasonable reader would not derive any defamatory meaning.

Always be alert to separating fact from comment. Facts have to be proved and if defamatory are the most dangerous parts of your copy. Comment should be opinion, honestly held and based on true facts or allegations made in legally privileged contexts.

Avoid alleging, or imputing, defamatory motive. Not even the prosecution has to prove motive in a criminal trial. It is almost impossible to prove unless admitted. There is a famous legal quotation about how it is as difficult to guess the state of a man's mind as it would be to guess the state of his digestion.

Saying somebody has lied about something means you are saying they have deliberately been untruthful and that is a clear example of a libel. The verb 'lie' implies an intention that it is very difficult to prove in law, and in libel the burden of proof is on you. The claimant does not have to prove they did not lie. So you might be able to prove that they were mistaken in what they said, but how could you prove that they intended to say something they knew to be wrong?

Reporting somebody saying that somebody else lied about something is the same as you saying the other person lied. Repeating or reporting a libel by attribution still makes you liable to libel.

This means that the old sayings 'think before you open your mouth', or in the 21st century 'think before you tweet or text' and 'talk with your brain and not your heart', are very apt. A former editor of the *Guardian* (when it was based in Manchester) was C. P. Scott and his famous maxim, 'Comment is free, facts are sacred', is widely quoted. In media law you should remember that in libel 'facts when substantially true are free, comment when not honest opinion is expensive'.

Specific online libel risks

There are a number of libel risks peculiar to online production and communication. When tweeting be careful about any juxtapositions with hashtags. If you are reporting about an identifiable individual you should avoid any association of that person with #murder, #crooks, etc. When you are producing online postings be very cautious about labelling files with language that is potentially defamatory. Such information is readable in some browsers when activated by the cursor, and file properties are usually discoverable by right clicking.

The same is true when embedding information in HTML that you might think is hidden. In reality, the inclusion of such information in 'alternative text' or click-through URLs could generate defamatory meaning. If you have an apparently innocent image of somebody that clicks through to a visual image communicating something despicable or scandalous then it could be argued that you are constructing an online defamation.

Hyperlinks to libellous webpages on their own should not constitute a repetition of a libellous posting unless the libel is summarised and stated in the phrase encapsulated in the link, or it is quite clear there is a context of encouraging people online to visit the libellous page with the intention of damaging somebody's reputation.

Libel defences

You may be able to avoid getting sued if any of the following defences apply to what you have said or written:

1   The statement you are reporting has *come from a senior police officer or government department* – you may have qualified privilege (subject to explanation or contradiction).

Conditions include fairness and accuracy without malice. The qualified privilege under the 2013 Defamation Act now applies to governments anywhere in the world; authorities anywhere in the world performing governmental functions; and international organisations or international conferences.

2 It was *said in open court, or in the Houses of Parliament.* You should have absolute privilege for court reports and higher qualified privilege for parliamentary reports. Higher qualified privilege means it can only be defeated by malice. Key conditions include fairness and accuracy. Absolute privilege enables you to report malicious statements made in evidence and requires that the reports are 'contemporaneous' – i.e. published to the nearest deadline in respect of court reports. The absolute privilege in court reporting also applies to foreign courts and international courts and tribunals. Qualified privilege also applies to legislatures anywhere in the world.

3 It was *said at a public meeting* (held for a lawful purpose). You should have qualified privilege (fair, accurate and in the public interest) but you need to get or at least be receptive to the side of the person being attacked and report the gist of that if provided. This is what being subject to contradiction or explanation means. Again the conditions of fairness and accuracy are required. This defence has been extended to public meetings abroad.

4 It was *said at a press/media conference* provided this satisfied the recognised conditions of a public meeting above. This means that any member of the media had access to the conference. This could be in the street or on private premises. This excludes one to one interviews. Press/media releases accompanying the conference attract the privilege provided the content is not substantially different from what was said at the conference. Your report has to be fair and accurate. The defence has been extended to press conferences abroad.

5 The statement you are reporting is *substantially true*. The defence will succeed if your report contains substantially untrue imputations that 'do not seriously harm the claimant's reputation'. Remember you have to prove this defence.

6 You are reporting an *'honest opinion'* such as in a review or editorial. The defence needs the following conditions:

   i It is opinion
   ii Report/publication includes 'in general or specific terms, the basis of the opinion'
   iii 'An honest person could have held the opinion' based on a 'fact which existed at the time the statement complained of was published', or 'anything asserted to be a fact in a privileged statement published before the statement complained of'.

This means the opinion could be based on allegations made in a court case, in Parliament, in a peer-reviewed statement in a scientific or academic journal or in a publication satisfying the new public interest defence under section 4 of the Defamation Act 2013. What does the 'honest' part of the defence mean? It means the defence fails if the author of the statement did not hold the opinion, or if the reporter/publisher 'knew or ought to have known that the author did not hold the opinion'.

Get all this right, then you might be let off the hook.

7   You might have a *public interest defence* under section 4 of the Defamation Act 2013. Public interest is not defined in the Act, but the courts have set out ideas in case histories and they include:

- 'What it is in the public interest that the public should know and what the publisher could properly consider that he was under a public duty to tell the public'
- 'In a simpler and more direct way, whether the public was entitled to know the particular information'
- 'The interest is that of the public in a modern democracy in free expression and, more particularly, in the promotion of a free and vigorous press to keep the public informed'
- 'The general obligation of the press, media and other publishers to communicate important information upon matters of general public interest and the general right of the public to receive such information . . . there must be some real public interest in having this information in the public domain.'

This last quotation was from Baroness Hale in *Jameel vs Wall Street Journal* in 2006, and she added:

> This is, as we all know, very different from saying that it is information which interests the public – the most vapid tittle-tattle about the activities of footballers' wives and girlfriends interests large sections of the public but no-one could claim any real public interest in our being told all about it.

This defence is available to the publication of facts and opinions.

For the defence to succeed you need to prove that you 'reasonably believed that publishing the statement complained of was in the public interest'. In doing that you will be entitled to argue 'allowance for editorial judgement'. This is likely to be informed by previous court definitions of 'responsible journalism', which was known as the 'Reynolds' defence. The criteria for responsible journalism included: giving fair opportunity for people criticised to give their side of the story, reporting a gist of this, evaluating the reliability of your source who might have an axe to grind and avoiding sensationalist language and bias.

The critical thing in the field of defamation is, if in doubt, to get professional legal advice before publication.

8   *Qualified privilege* in being a statement published in a scientific or academic journal. The conditions are: (i) statement must relate to scientific or academic matter; (ii) statement was peer-reviewed by editor and one or more persons with academic expertise relating to the scientific/academic matter/issue; (iii) malice will defeat the defence.

9   *Innocent defamation*. This is available under section 1 of the 1996 Defamation Act and applies when as the journalist/publisher you had no warning or reasonable antici-pation that the libel would be communicated on your media platform – this could be a live broadcast or website. The conditions will be developed by case law, but at the time of writing there is little of it available. The defence hinges on the concept of responsibility for publication and will be satisfied if in defence you can show that you

took reasonable care in relation to the publication, and you did not know, and had no reason to believe, that what you did caused or contributed to the publication of a defamatory statement.

The defence has to square with the statute stating that it is necessary that you are 'not the author, editor or publisher of the statement complained of'. In practice if you are responsible for an internet publication you should have a 'notice and take down policy'. You need to remove potentially defamatory material from public access as soon as you have been given notice of the complaint. This is both European and UK law. The Internet Service Provider is usually not regarded as liable as long as the 'take down' is engaged promptly to remove libellous material when notified. Furthermore, the defence is likely to be unavailable if comments and user-generated material is editorially moderated prior to publication.

10 *Operator of website defence* (enacted by section 5 of 2013 Defamation Act in January 2014). This is a new defence for the operators of websites where a defamation action is brought against them in respect of anything posted on their websites, for which they were not responsible. Website operators no longer have to pre-moderate reader comments. This is a 'report and remove' system that people can use if they believe they have been defamed on a website message board.

The system enables website operators to deal with all initial correspondence in-house. See the guidelines that website operators need to comply with in order to engage this defence in The Defamation (Operators of Websites) Regulations 2013 (www.legislation. gov.uk/ukdsi/2013/9780111104620).

The rules for this defence state it will not be necessarily lost when internet postings are moderated.

11 *Neutral reportage.* This has been codified in the Defamation Act 2013 within the public interest defence. Essentially this is neutral reporting of a row/dispute where the sides are libelling each other. Your reporting has to remain neutral by avoiding any explicit or implicit language indicating that you agree or support the defamatory statements. For example, an investigative journalist writing a book about allegations of corruption against police detectives cannot have the defence if he entitles his book 'Bent Coppers'. Section 4(3) of the Defamation Act 2013 gives the defence further statutory underwriting:

> (3) If the statement complained of was, or formed part of, an accurate and impartial account of a dispute to which the claimant was a party, the court must in determining whether it was reasonable for the defendant to believe that publishing the statement was in the public interest disregard any omission of the defendant to take steps to verify the truth of the imputation conveyed by it.

This means when impartially and accurately reporting a spat where libels are being spun, you are not obliged to investigate and confirm the truth of what is being said.

CLOSER LOOK
PRIVACY

The Human Rights Act 1998 means freedom of expression is balanced with the right to respect for privacy. The English and European courts recognise that private information cannot be reported unless it is in the public interest. No-go areas include the nature of health treatment and state of health, work records, education, sexuality and conduct, personal finances, matters relating to home and family, written and digital correspondence and personal relationships.

It now means that people who do not give permission to be photographed in public, and are not the subject of a public interest story, are entitled to privacy protection. The principle is that media privacy law applies when any individual has 'a reasonable expectation of privacy'. Privacy has a wider legal meaning in the European context and covers dignity, honour, reputation (overlapping with libel), identity, family life, home space and private communications (correspondence, email, mobile, Skype, palm computer devices, etc.).

Public interest

The most extensive definition of public interest that can be used to defend against media law actions can be found in the IPSO *Editors' Code of Practice*:

> The public interest includes, but is not confined to:
> Detecting or exposing crime, or the threat of crime, or serious impropriety.
> Protecting public health or safety.
> Protecting the public from being misled by an action or statement of an individual or organisation.
> Disclosing a person or organisation's failure or likely failure to comply with any obligation to which they are subject.
> Disclosing a miscarriage of justice.
> Raising or contributing to a matter of public debate, including serious cases of impropriety, unethical conduct or incompetence concerning the public.
> Disclosing concealment, or likely concealment, of any of the above.
> There is a public interest in freedom of expression itself.
> The regulator will consider the extent to which material is already in the public domain, or will become so.
> Editors invoking the public interest will need to demonstrate that they reasonably believed publication – or journalistic activity taken with a view to publication – would both serve, and be proportionate to, the public interest and explain how they reached that decision at the time.
> An exceptional public interest would need to be demonstrated to over-ride the normally paramount interests of children under 16.

This definition is very significant for UK journalists because their statutory defence of 'for the purposes of journalism' under section 32 of the 1998 Data Protection Act is dependent on any processing of private data being in the public interest.

There is a possibility there could be an increase in litigation against online journalists and publishers for processing data for the purposes of journalism that could be argued to be private information. Actions could be successful where it can be shown that the data process controllers could not reasonably believe the information being processed is in the public interest.

Academics and media lawyers are beginning to call this 'the new libel', meaning that where libel litigation is less likely to succeed (when harm to reputation has to be serious) actions based on data processing of private information that harms personal dignity are more likely to succeed.

Two conflicting privacy standards

In an information age that is understood to be globalised, it has to be accepted that there is no single globalised standard for what is permissible in communicating private information.

UK and European law ordinarily allows legal prohibition of communicating truthful information if it is 'private'. This is not the situation in the US, where such legal censorship would be unconstitutional under the First Amendment. This resulted in the 2016 UK Supreme Court ruling sustaining a court injunction against the English and Welsh media publishing anything that could identify a celebrity connected to a US publication revealing gossip about his private relationships (www.bailii.org/uk/cases/UKSC/2016/26.html).

The difficulty of this division in the exercise of information rights is that it is not even possible to identify in this book the name of the US publication regularly revealing scandals concerning public figures that it would be unlawful to publish in England and Wales. It also means that in the English and European context digital online publishers will be subject to stricter controls in what they can publish compared to their visitors and readers who would be able to access banned information elsewhere in global cyberspace.

Another division has emerged in relation to what is known as the 'right to be forgotten' through the data processing of internet search engines. The European Court of Justice ruled in 2014 that EU citizens are entitled under a 'right to be forgotten' to ask internet search engines to remove links to pages that contain old, inaccurate or even just irrelevant data about them. Any legal obligation to remove such information does not apply to online journalistic publishers and their archives. It applied specifically to Google in terms of it being seen as a 'data processor' rather than a publisher (www.bailii.org/eu/cases/EUECJ/2014/C13112.html). Google has been forced to set up a system of receiving and deciding requests (support.google.com/legal/answer/3110420).

The right to be forgotten does not extend to search engine operations beyond the EU, but efforts are being made to prevent EU internet users bypassing right-to-be-forgotten removals, and in England, the Information Commissioner has directed Google to sever links to professional media sites that report successful right-to-be-forgotten decisions.

Recent case history turns on the interests of children

It needs to be remembered that in the UK Privacy and Freedom of Expression are balanced equally. This led to the May 2015 Supreme Court case of pianist James Rhodes, whose autobiography was blocked from publication because of concern about the impact of his revelations about being abused as a child on his own children. Although he won the case, the fact that his book had been subject to prior restraint through such a long and complex process of litigation indicates how freedom of expression can be held in abeyance until the courts decide the issue (www.bailii.org/uk/cases/UKSC/2015/32.html).

In January 2013, the third husband of the Oscar-winning British actress Kate Winslet won a privacy action against the *Sun* over the publication of images taken of him at a private party that had previously been posted on Facebook. Mr Justice Briggs said:

> The question is whether the publication of the Photographs, or of a more detailed description of their contents than the fact that the claimant is depicted partially naked, would add anything beyond mere titillation. In my judgment it would not.

He said the threat to publish them 'comes very shortly after the belated discovery by the media of the claimant and Miss Winslet's recent marriage, at a time when the claimant finds himself in a temporary blaze of largely reflected publicity'. The judge also engaged the issue of there being no possible reason for exposing Kate Winslet's 'children to a real risk to additional embarrassment or upset from the nationwide publication of photographs (or their contents) depicting their other carer behaving in a foolish and immature manner when half naked' (*Rocknroll vs News Group Newspapers Ltd* [2013]).

This case highlights the sensitivity of the English courts to any matters that concern the interests of children. Hence the 2014 ruling in favour of singer Paul Weller, who objected to the *Mail Online* publishing a photograph of him with his three children taken in a public place in Los Angeles (www.bailii.org/ew/cases/EWHC/QB/2014/1163.html).

The 2016 UK Supreme Court case of *PSJ vs The Sun on Sunday* also concerned itself with the potential harm to the claimant's children of any media exposure of the celebrity's personal sexual relationships being made public (www.supremecourt.uk/cases/uksc-2016-0080.html).

Privacy for online journalists and their sources

The subject of privacy also concerns the confidentiality of the online journalist's investigations, research and communications, particularly with regard to the professional duty to protect sources. The whistle-blower Edward Snowden revealed the extent of surreptitious interception of online data by state intelligence agencies. In the UK, the online magazine *Press Gazette* highlighted police force use of the Regulation of Investigatory Powers Act 2000 to obtain journalists' phone data without any court hearing and scrutiny by an independent judge. While campaigns are being run to improve journalist source protection, you would be advised to follow techniques and advice provided by the Centre for Investigative Journalism. See their pdf guide on Information Security for Journalists that is downloadable at: www.tcij.org/node/1016.

There are practical steps that can be taken to keep confidential journalistic research and communications with sources secure. This includes encrypting emails to keep correspondences with sources secure, using anonymous internet browsers such as Tor to keep web use private and using secure, encrypted operating systems such as Tails (tails.boum.org). Another measure that is inconvenient, though even more secure, is to commit sensitive information to hand-written analogue media and to avoid any form of digital storage, or communication. See Chapter 2 for more on information security issues and techniques.

The Investigatory Powers Act 2016 compels internet service providers to keep meta-communications data for one year and up to 48 state investigatory agencies are able to apply to gain access without judicial approval. The Act stipulates that the application for confidential journalistic or journalist source data has to be approved by a Judicial Commissioner. The communications data stored will include records of all calls, texts, location data and web activity. Judicial scrutiny of the interception will only apply if the stated intention is to identify confidential journalist material or the source of that information. If those are not the stated aims, it can be argued that the police and security services are still free to go ahead and examine journalistic data unchecked. Journalists have no rights to be informed about the applications or access to their information. If the Judicial Commissioner is unable to collect evidence from the journalist affected it can be argued that they can never be in a position to consider all the facts of the case. The process of scrutiny is not the same as when an application for a production order is made to a Crown Court judge under the Police and Criminal Evidence Act 1984 for excluded confidential journalistic material. The new act recognises that UK state intelligence and investigatory agencies can lawfully engage in the interception of the content of digital communications and Electronic Network Exploitation (ENE). This form of electronic interference can involve turning any computer, smartphone and digital device connected to an intelligence target into surveillance and recording machines. But this intervention requires warrant approval at ministerial level and the double lock of Judicial Commissioner approval. Any journalist subject to such investigation would have no right to challenge this level of intrusion. The oversight here is wholly dependent on the effectiveness of the new Investigatory Powers Commissioner and team of Judicial Commissioners. The legislation does require a code of practice that the public interest in protecting journalistic source confidentiality is recognised. State investigators have a legal obligation to seek Judicial Commissioner approval should they stumble across anything they recognise as confidential journalistic or source material when examining bulk data or carrying out electronic interceptions.

The key problem for online journalists is that the Investigatory Powers Act 2016 presumes that information held on mobile phones and electronic devices belongs to the service provider and not the individual or organisation that pays the bill. The legislation enables state authorities to bypass the 1984 PACE journalist procedures, when they want to access electronic data and information.

There are signs that unlawful interception and collection of journalists' data by police forces investigating 'leaks' can be successfully challenged at the Investigatory Powers Tribunal. In 2016, a Scottish tribunal in Edinburgh awarded an investigative journalist £10,000 in damages after concluding his Article 8 and 10 rights had been breached by Police Service Scotland.

Another critical vulnerability for any online journalist is the risk that employers and publishers will not honour the confidentiality and privacy of their professional communications and dealings with confidential sources. This became apparent during the Metropolitan Police inquiry codenamed 'Operation Elveden'. The police revealed that they were able to investigate 434 'leaks of information' because British news publishers had from 2011 surrendered over 20,000 emails and 12,000 documents critical to journalist source confidentiality.

The material was provided by News International (now News UK, publishers of the *Sun*, *The Times* and the former *News of the World*) and Trinity Mirror (*Daily Mirror*, the *People*) without the permission of their journalists or the sources they had been in contact with. This resulted in criminal prosecutions of the journalists and their public official sources; particularly when the sources had been paid for information. All the journalists who pleaded not guilty were acquitted, had their charges dropped or convictions cleared by the Court of Appeal. This was not the case with the sources. One of the sources, a former prison officer Robert Norman, is challenging his conviction in the courts and arguing that his rights under Article 10 of the Human Rights Act entitled him to confidential journalist source protection (www.bailii.org/ew/cases/EWCA/Crim/2016/1564.html).

Privacy – the new criminal libel?

The developments in British media privacy law are extending well beyond initial case law blocking publicity about the private lives of well-known celebrities. Essentially most privacy actions seek to suppress media publicity for truthful information, and this process can only be achieved by a prior restraint civil injunction. Where the private information concerns the reputation of an individual, the law is developing into a telescoping and overlapping of privacy and libel. The 2008 privacy action between Max Mosley and the now defunct Sunday newspaper, the *News of the World*, turned on whether the paper could have been justified in saying his sadism and masochism (S&M) party was Nazi themed. This was undoubtedly a dispute reputation issue. When the judge ruled that it was not, he then went on to conclude that without this public interest dimension of truth, the revelations of Mr Mosley's private sexual activities became a breach of his privacy. This means that it can be argued that the case was both an issue of libel and privacy, though the compensation awarded was for breach of privacy only (www.bailii.org/ew/cases/EWHC/QB/2008/687.html).

The 2016 case of *ERY vs Associated Newspapers Ltd* suggests that privacy law can now prevent news media from reporting that an individual has been interviewed by the police under caution. Mr Justice Nicol observed in his ruling: 'in many cases there has been an overlap between privacy and defamation. A threatened publication may jeopardise both the claimant's reputation and his privacy.' In this case the individual's financial company was under police investigation with involvement from the National Crime Agency. But the judge decided he should not be named as having been questioned by detectives. The very fact he had been suspected of criminal conduct to the extent that the police needed to caution and interview him undoubtedly affected his reputation. But the court decided that a prior restraint injunction preventing publication was justified to protect his privacy. This was judged therefore to be something true and private that was not in the public interest to be published (www.bailii.org/ew/cases/EWHC/QB/2016/2760.html). The judge's ruling has been criticised by a media lawyer as an over-extension of privacy laws (Kean 2016).

The argument that privacy law is becoming the new criminal libel is based on the fact that, in the old law of English criminal libel, even if a media publication successfully defended an action on the basis that it was true it had to go on to prove that it was also in the public interest. Criminal libel was abolished by the Coroners and Justice Act 2009, but it might be argued that the jeopardy is being revived in the current developments of privacy law.

The level of judicial control over the reporting of clear public interest matters is very well demonstrated in the case of the 14-year-old cancer victim who wished to be frozen in a cryogenic state after her death. Her parents had initially disagreed on whether this should happen (www.bailii.org/cgi-bin/format.cgi?doc=/ew/cases/EWHC/Fam/2016/2859.html).

Mr Justice Peter Jackson postponed reporting of the case until one month after her death. He also issued reporting restrictions making it a contempt of court for any media publication to identify the girl, her family or the hospital trust and its staff on an indefinite basis. The control was designed to carry out the wishes of the teenage girl, allow her family time to grieve and shield them from media scrutiny. But the restrictions mean that it will be impossible any time in the future to report the identity of the young person who chose in these unusual circumstances to be cryogenically preserved in a facility in the US until such time that medical science may have progressed and she could be brought back to life.

Summary

Online media law is asymmetrical. This means that it intersects myriad dimensions of private, public, analogue, digital, UK and international forms of law and regulation. It also means it is dynamic, complex and changing.

For the past 30 to 40 years UK media law has been substantially influenced by European law and the rulings of the European Court of Human Rights (ECHR) in Strasbourg and the European Court of Justice at Luxembourg. UK courts have to 'take into account' rulings of the ECHR derived from the European Convention on Human Rights and Fundamental Freedoms that became statutory UK law with the passing of the 1998 Human Rights Act, which came into force from October 2000. Since the UK joined what was then the European Common Market in 1972, all rulings of the ECJ (the European Union Court) have been binding on UK courts. However, the referendum vote to leave the EU in June 2016 clearly means that the situation may well change in the future.

Another unstable and ambiguous aspect of media law is that there are often no clear right and wrong decisions on publication. They are merely arguable in law and not certain. Lawyers will be happy to be paid to argue the issues in courtrooms, but you personally, and your employing publisher, may not care to pay for the huge costs involved. In the digital online information age, we are also experiencing an intense transition and combination of production between analogue printed media and online digital media. The law does not necessarily have an answer and clear policy for both dimensions of publication.

Further reading

Information security for journalists, Centre for Investigative Journalists: www.tcij.org/node/1016

The latest editions of the following are all recommended:

Crook, Tim (2013) *UK Media Law Pocketbook,* 1st edn, Abingdon: Routledge

Hanna, Mark and Dodd, Mike (eds) (2016) *McNae's Essential Law for Journalists,* 23rd edn, Oxford: Oxford University Press

Quinn, Frances (2015) *Law for Journalists,* 5th edn, Harlow: Pearson

Smartt, Ursula (2014) *Media & Entertainment Law,* 2nd edn, Abingdon: Routledge

Thom, Cleland (2016) *Online Law for Journalists,* clelandthom.co.uk

Online resources

BBC Editorial Guidelines: www.bbc.co.uk/editorialguidelines

Courts and Tribunals Judiciary's guide on 'Reporting restrictions in the criminal courts' (England and Wales) April 2015 (revised May 2016), https://www.judiciary.gov.uk/publications/reporting-restrictions-in-the-criminal-courts-2

CPS guidelines on prosecuting cases involving communications sent via social media: http://cps.gov.uk/legal/a_to_c/communications_sent_via_social_media

The Defamation (Operators of Websites) Regulations 2013: www.legislation.gov.uk/ukdsi/2013/9780111104620

IMPRESS: www.impress.press

Information Commissioner's Office: ico.org.uk

IPSO: https://www.ipso.co.uk

Judicial Studies Board for Northern Ireland: Reporting restrictions for courts: www.jsbni.com/Publications/reporting-restrictions/Pages/default.aspx

Ofcom: www.ofcom.org.uk

Ofcom Broadcaster's Code: http://ofcom.org.uk/tv-radio-and-on-demand/broadcast-codes/broadcast-code

Society of Professional Journalists: Code of Ethics: https://www.spj.org/pdf/spj-code-of-ethics-bookmark.pdf

Statutory reporting restrictions and privileges in Scottish courts: www.gov.scot/Resource/0041/00416260.pdf and www.gov.scot/resource/0041/00416261.pdf

National Union of Journalists and Chartered Institute of Journalists have separate codes of ethics.

Bibliography

Attorney General Dominic Grieve QC MP. Trial by Google? Juries, social media and the internet, Attorney General's Office and The Rt Hon Dominic Grieve QC, 6 February 2013, https://www.gov.uk/government/speeches/trial-by-google-juries-social-media-and-the-internet

Attorney General vs Associated Newspapers Ltd & Anor [2011] EWHC 418 (Admin) (3 March 2011), www.bailii.org/ew/cases/EWHC/Admin/2011/418.html

Derbyshire CC vs Times Newspapers Ltd [1993] UKHL 18 (18 February 1993), www.bailii.org/uk/cases/UKHL/1993/18.html

Easeman vs Ford [2016] EWHC 1576 (QB) (29 June 2016), www.bailii.org/ew/cases/EWHC/QB/2016/1576.html

England and Wales Cricket Board Ltd & Anor vs Tixdaq Ltd & Anor [2016] EWHC 575 (Ch) (18 March 2016), www.bailii.org/ew/cases/EWHC/Ch/2016/575.html

ERY vs Associated Newspapers Ltd [2016] EWHC 2760 (QB) (4 November 2016), www.bailii.org/ew/cases/EWHC/QB/2016/2760.html

Ewing vs Crown Court Sitting at Cardiff & Newport & Ors [2016] EWHC 183 (Admin) (8 February 2016), www.bailii.org/ew/cases/EWHC/Admin/2016/183.html

EWHC 472 (Ch), [2005] FSR 36, [2005] EMLR 487, [2005] 28(6) IPD 11, www.bailii.org/ew/cases/EWHC/Ch/2005/472.html

Fraser-Woodward Ltd vs British Broadcasting Corporation Brighter Pictures Ltd [2005] *HM Attorney General vs The Condé Nast Publications Ltd* [2015] EWHC 3322 (Admin) (18 November 2015), www.bailii.org/ew/cases/EWHC/Admin/2015/3322.html

Information Commissioner's Office (ICO). ICO fines Telegraph Media Group for election day email campaign, 21 December 2015, Information Commissioner's Office, https://ico.org.uk/about-the-ico/news-and-events/news-and-blogs/2015/12/ico-fines-telegraph-media-group-for-election-day-email-campaign

Intellectual Property Office (IPO). Exceptions to copyright: education and teaching, Intellectual Property Office, October 2014, https://www.gov.uk/government/uploads/system/uploads/attachment_data/file/375951/Education_and_Teaching.pdf

Kean, Caroline. COMMENT: privacy injunction to stop media reporting police investigation into businessman 'is dangerous and needs to stop', *Press Gazette*, 2 December 2016, www.pressgazette.co.uk/comment-privacy-injunction-to-stop-media-reporting-police-investigation-into-businessman-is-dangerous-and-needs-to-stop

PA Media Lawyer. Telegraph fined £80,000 for publishing 'modified' photo of Adam Johnson sex crime victim, *Press Gazette*, 11 October 2016, www.pressgazette.co.uk/telegraph-fined-80000-for-publishing-modified-photo-of-paedophile-footballers-victim

Perraudin, Frances. Former Sun editor convicted over Adam Johnson victim picture, *Guardian*, 7 March 2016, https://www.theguardian.com/uk-news/2016/mar/07/adam-johnson-former-sun-editor-david-dinsmore-convicted-victim-picture

Price, Rob. The Olympics is trying to ban animated GIFs, *Business Insider*, 5 August 2016, http://uk.businessinsider.com/ioc-announces-ban-animated-gifs-livestreaming-rio-olympics-2016-8

Radio Television Digital News Association. Code of Ethics, Radio Television Digital News Association, 11 June 2015, www.rtdna.org/content/rtdna_code_of_ethics

Rocknroll vs News Group Newspapers Ltd [2013] EWHC 24 (Ch) (17 January 2013), www.bailii.org/ew/cases/EWHC/Ch/2013/24.html

Sidahmed, Mazin. Dennis Cooper fears censorship as Google erases blog without warning, *Guardian*, 14 July 2016, https://www.theguardian.com/books/2016/jul/14/dennis-cooper-google-censorship-dc-blog

Society of Professional Journalists. SPJ Code of Ethics, Society of Professional Journalists, 6 September 2014, https://www.spj.org/pdf/spj-code-of-ethics-bookmark.pdf

9 Online video

Chapter objectives

This chapter will cover:

- How video online is different to broadcast journalism
- Useful equipment and software for online video
- Different online video formats
- Vertical and square video
- Drone journalism, virtual reality and 360-degree video
- Ideas for video online
- How to shoot video
- How to edit video
- Live video tips
- Publishing and optimising video for the web.

Introduction

In an online world awash with text, video has become an important medium for publishers in three respects: to distinguish themselves from bloggers and other new entrants; to perform well on social media; and to enable them to charge more for advertising. As a result, journalists are being asked to capture video on a story wherever possible, while a raft of new specialist positions are being created dedicated to producing more video content.

This is not just happening in print and online-only publishers: TV news organisations have also discovered an appetite for video online that is very different to broadcast television. With broadcast formats not attracting viewers online, many broadcasters are now adopting 'web-first' production methods where video is produced for mobile and online consumption *before* broadcast, rather than vice versa. In the BBC's 2014 Stringer Report, for example, it was said that reporters needed to know that their 'first priority is to provide video for online . . . the video should have immediacy, relevance and character' (Stringer 2014).

Even radio news has become an *audiovisual* medium, with studio interviews regularly livestreamed online, and reporters capturing video for social media. We are all video journalists now.

In many ways the last people to catch up with this rush to video are the audience. A 2016 Reuters Institute report noted that 'growth around online video news seems to be largely driven by technology, platforms, and publishers rather than by strong consumer demand' (Kalogeropoulos et al. 2016, p.5). In looking at 30 news websites the study found that only 2.5 per cent of time was spent on video pages, and their survey of news consumers across 26 countries found that three-quarters of respondents said they only occasionally or never used video news online. What is not clear is how much of this is down to video just not being compelling enough, and how many people only consume video on social media (the statistics only referred to video on news sites).

Certainly social media-focused publishers such as BuzzFeed have decided that video is the future: CEO Jonah Peretti announced in 2016 that from that point on every major initiative would have a video element. 'Having a single "video department" makes about as much sense as having a "mobile department"', he said (Wang 2016).

In many ways having video alongside, or instead of, text is becoming as natural as using photographs to illustrate stories. And just as printing technology made it possible to include photographs in newspapers from the mid-19th century, increases in connectivity and bandwidth have made video increasingly part of the news package online.

But just because we *can* use video, doesn't mean we *should*. There are four ways in which we might do so:

- Some video *illustrates* a story, much as a photograph does (for example, by adding raw footage)
- Some video *adds to* the story, much as a link does (for example, full interviews or answers, explainers)
- Some video *distils* the story, much as a headline does (for example, video for social media)
- Some video *tells* the story, instead of using text (for example, a video report or feature).

Knowing when to use video, why you're using it and how to do it well is what this chapter is all about.

Online video is not TV

December 2010 was an important moment for news video online. At the end of that year the video platform Brightcove reported that for the first time *newspapers* were now streaming more minutes of content online using the service than broadcasters (Brightcove and Tubemogul 2010). Video, it seemed, did not just mean 'TV online'.

It would take some years, however, for journalists to start to challenge techniques absorbed over decades of watching broadcast news reporting. Early video saw some reporters sitting behind desks and reading out headlines as if the audience was tuning into a 6 o'clock bulletin. But it quickly became clear that online audiences were turned off by broadcast techniques – even when those techniques were being used by broadcasters with years of production experience. On the BBC's iPlayer, short news *clips* were getting more traffic than news *programmes* on iPlayer: 'Online, there is often no need for the reporter as an intermediary', noted Alfred Hermida, 'as a user will have already read the story' (Hermida 2010).

Understanding why some broadcast techniques don't work online requires thinking about why those techniques were invented in the first place. Television has no choice in using video, so it has had to invent a number of ways to 'make the news visual', from the 'presenter behind the desk' to having reporters standing 'on the scene' to tell you what they know. These tricks are not needed online: if your story isn't visual, don't use video.

It is also important to understand how people consume news on television, and how they consume online news differently. 'Online video should not ape TV', argues John Domokos of the *Guardian*.

> For a start, you have to imagine how a person in front of a computer is searching for it and looking at it – it might be in a small frame. It's a much more intimate environment. You have to grab their attention very quickly, in a few seconds.
>
> (Domokos 2016)

Mobile phone and tablet consumption complicate the picture further.

For David Dunkley Gyimah, one of the first video journalists in the UK, video journalism signals a revolution, an advance on television news production. His post 'Secret history of a media revolution' describes the mid-1990s innovations at Associated Newspapers' Channel One and the influence of video journalism trainer Michael Rosenblum on what was to follow: reporters who would film themselves; shooting and reporting in digital; 'a digital workflow from filming to editing that would ultimately eliminate analogue tape, the first livestream on the web' (Dunkley Gyimah 2015): all these were pioneered before the web.

The video journalists of the 1980s and 1990s were the first to use lightweight cameras. Unencumbered by heavy equipment, their template for storytelling was to get as close to the stories as possible, and the people in them. This translates well online: a decade after Channel One, freelance reporter Kevin Sites used the same techniques as a 'backpack journalist', filming and transmitting his own reports from war zones across 2005 and 2006.

Then, in 2007, the first iPhone was launched. With the launch of the Nokia N95 in the same year (which was issued to journalists by newspaper groups such as Trinity Mirror), this would extend video production opportunities to journalists and citizens around the world. And when digital single-lens reflex (DSLR) cameras began to include video recording capabilities in 2008, it made it easier for photographers to start producing video too.

As a result, the influence of photography and photojournalism is perhaps as significant as that of TV: David Hedley's research, for example, notes that in solo video journalism 'storytelling strategy reflects the photojournalistic conventions of realism and empathy' (Hedley 2012). Many websites have adopted a documentary and feature-style approach for their video output: the *New York Times* 'photojournalism blog' Lens is a typical example, including video and multimedia under its umbrella.

A third thread is what Dunkley Gyimah calls 'cinema journalism': video which borrows techniques from cinema, and cinéma vérité in particular, rather than broadcasting (Dunkley Gyimah 2016): in a video explaining the concept, online video pioneer Travis Fox is quoted as being influenced by the French director Tony Gatlif (see *Watch this* below).

> *Watch this:* David Dunkley Gyimah talks about 'cinema journalism'. https://www.youtube.com/watch?v=DqVpdyR_7Z4.

Different publications make different decisions on which approach to adopt. Local newspaper sites often prefer newsier angles focused on events, people and sport, using solo video journalism techniques. Look at the YouTube channels and Facebook pages of the *Liverpool Echo* and the *Yorkshire Evening Post* and you will find coverage of local charity runs, farm shows, interviews with footballers, store openings and CCTV camera footage. National newspapers lean more towards a mix of video journalism, photojournalism and cinema journalism.

The journalist themselves can sometimes be the focal point in video blogs – as long as they have something interesting to say and a visual kicker. For example, cinema critic Mark Kermode does a twice weekly video blog for the BBC while the journalists at *Stuff* magazine blog about gadgets they are testing. The magazine industry in particular has taken strongly to video, with many publishers having their own TV studios and many magazines posting video to branded video 'channels' on their own site, YouTube and various social channels.

More recently innovations in HTML5 and JavaScript have created an opportunity to create more interactive forms of video. In *The Fallen of World War II*, for example, users can pause the video at key points and roll their cursor over elements on-screen to more deeply explore the data being presented. YouTube annotations now allow video creators to add clickable on-screen 'hotspots', while interactive video tools like Touchcast and Interlude are providing opportunities for producers to add similar functionality to their video (see p.240).

But perhaps the biggest shift in the move from broadcast to online video has been the rise of vertical and square video.

Vertical, square and circular video

There is nothing about video which means it has to be horizontal: after all, painters have used portrait and square formats for centuries, and photographers don't limit themselves to one ratio. In the 1930s film pioneer Sergei Eisenstein even wrote about 'rethinking the rectangle' (Bordwell 2009). Still, vertical video online has had to face down a range of insults, summed up best in the 2012 parody 'public service announcement' video *Vertical Video Syndrome*.

One of the biggest factors in changing this has been Snapchat. Snapchat has been vertical-only from the start, and in 2015 it announced the numbers to back that up, when it told advertisers that vertical ads on the platform were viewed to the end nine times more frequently than horizontal ones. That same year live (and mostly vertical) video apps Meerkat and Periscope also launched (see the section on live video, p.243) while YouTube updated its mobile apps to play vertical video too. Facebook followed the next year, when it found that people watched for longer and with sound turned on when presented vertically in feeds (Peterson 2016).

Publishers were running the numbers too: Jon Steinberg, the chief executive of the *Daily Mail* in North America told the *New York Times* that they found higher engagement, satisfaction and completion rates when using the format. 'We're working to get to 100 percent of our videos vertical', he said (Manjoo 2015). Video production company founder Randy Tinflow found similar statistics in email publishing: fewer users dropped off when they didn't have to rotate their phones to watch video (Tinflow 2016). In trying to satisfy both a mobile and a desktop audience the *New York Times* even went as far as to create three versions of one video piece on Justin Bieber: horizontal, vertical and square (Wang 2015a), while NewsWhip found that 18 of the top 20 videos on Facebook in September used a halfway-house *square* ratio (Corcoran 2015).

By 2016 vertical video was accounting for 29 per cent of video viewing time (Newman 2016). The BBC was piloting vertical video in Snapchat and in the BBC News mobile app, rounding up the latest stories under the title 'Ten to watch'. Watching the videos featured on the app (at pinboard.in/u:paulbradshaw/t:tentowatch) is illustrative: some videos are filmed for vertical, and others are filmed for horizontal and cropped for a vertical ratio. They are a useful lesson in how composition and the rule of thirds remain important in shooting vertical video, along with captions for the large number of users who keep the sound turned off.

In the same year Snapchat launched Spectacles, glasses that filmed in *circular video*. Circular video works by presenting *part* of that circle of footage in the rectangular frame you are viewing 'through', which means it works in both horizontal and vertical. A video of the format in action was included on the homepage of spectacles.com, and can also be seen at youtube.com/watch?v=AynCKhsYtXA.

Choosing to film in vertical, square or even circular will ultimately come down to the platform you intend to publish on, and the subject you are covering. Outside Snapchat and organisations' own mobile apps, most video journalism is still filmed in horizontal ratio, with a significant proportion of video 'snippets' being re-edited in square ratio for social media platforms like Instagram and Facebook. When you have the option to choose vertical or horizontal, that doesn't mean you should always take it: you might find that a wider shot is more effective to capture the subject you are filming.

The best way to make an informed decision is to consume as wide a variety of videos as possible. Vertical and square video promise to be the scene of enormous creativity in the next decade as video makers experiment with the best ways to tell stories in unconventional ratios. Snapchat, along with Instagram, is likely to be the scene of much of that development, so make sure you are following journalists and media organisations on both platforms to see what conventions are being followed – and invented.

What equipment do I need to make video?

What kit you need depends on what sort of video journalism you're planning to do. You can get started with a laptop and a built-in webcam, or a tablet. But most video journalism is now done using a good mobile phone: it's light, portable and image quality is good enough for most situations. For this reason it is also the best way to get started with video journalism and learn the basic techniques. Make sure you have a phone with enough memory and battery power (see Chapter 6 for more).

If you're interested in specialist video journalism roles, once you are confident with a mobile phone you might want to look at more powerful kit. A *DSLR* camera with video capability is used by some video journalists as a middle-range option: DSLR cameras give you more control than you get with a mobile phone, and give you a greater 'depth of field' (although there are ways to achieve similar effects on a mobile phone). Some cameras are also networked, meaning you can upload to the web via wifi or transfer wirelessly to your phone, tablet or laptop. You can also buy special memory cards (such as the Eyefi) that will add this functionality to a camera.

At the high end are dedicated – and expensive – video cameras. These provide more control than a DSLR – or do so without having to buy extra attachments – and are closer to broadcast journalism equipment. For that reason they are best for projects that might need to be broadcast as well as placed online.

For active first-person video you might want to look at devices like the *GoPro*, which is designed for capturing activities like skydiving, skiing, cycling, scuba diving and watersports. You might even want to get a *drone*, or a special *360-degree* video camera (see p.226). And, of course, for an animated video you don't need a camera at all.

A *microphone* makes a big difference. Audio is very important when recording video: mobile phones aren't great at recording sound more than a few inches away, so having a microphone helps you deal with situations where background sound is a problem, and makes your video sound more professional generally. A *lavalier* – or lapel – mic can be fixed on a person's collar and is ideal for pre-arranged interview situations, but make sure it is not rustling against the material. A *handheld* microphone is what you see reporters using on television, and allows you to record either yourself or anyone you interview. A *shotgun* microphone is useful for picking up atmospheric sounds. If you are filming with a mobile phone in a noisy environment you can also use the hands-free microphone in the headphones that come with the phone: however this should be a last resort. See Chapter 7 for more on sound and microphones.

Find out if the microphone will work with your mobile phone, or if you need an adapter. The iRig adapter, for example, allows you to use broadcast microphones with iPhones or Android devices.

If you want a steady shot consider buying some sort of *tripod*: these range from small flexible portable tripods like the 'GorillaPod' series, which can be wrapped around a post, to extendible 'selfie sticks' or traditional camera tripods. You may need a grip, adapter or case to connect your phone to the tripod through a 'mounting hole'.

Lighting will be important if you are filming in a poorly lit environment, or are filming inside: you might notice that one of the qualities of many successful YouTube vloggers is good lighting (you can even get light meters for mobile phones). *Headphones* can make a difference: use them to listen to the audio feed while you film. And then there are *lenses*: remember that zooming on a mobile phone generally reduces the quality of the image. Instead, for mobile phones you can buy lens kits which can be placed over the mobile phone camera, such as the Olloclip.

Figure 9.1
Photo of 'GorillaPod'-type tripod used to attach phone to a wire fence
Source: Courtesy of Joe Tidy

Some video journalists use a separate audio recorder to capture audio, which can then be edited into the footage later on. This is a useful backup plan in case your camera microphone does not record as well as you expect.

Don't forget the little extras like lens covers, extra batteries and memory cards – and your charging leads!

CLOSER LOOK
DRONE JOURNALISM

Drones – remote control unmanned aircraft – have been eagerly taken up as a way of getting striking aerial footage without the cost of hiring a helicopter. As well as breaking news, the devices have been used to 'provide glimpses of natural disasters that would otherwise be too hazardous for journalists to obtain, and to offer unique perspectives that enrich news storytelling' (Holton, Lawson and Love 2014). The *Manchester Evening News*, for example, used drones in coverage of a fire at the city's dogs' home, while the

BBC has flown them along the tunnels of transport project Crossrail, and inside and around both Canterbury and Lincoln Cathedrals.

BBC drone operator Neil Paton says the best stories for using drones include industrial and transport pieces; housing stories; agricultural, environmental and rural affairs; and stories that involve big subjects (Pedret 2016). But there are costs involved: aside from the drone itself you will need to explore insurance: the BBC insures its drones against causing damage up to a cost of £20 million, and recommends insuring against at least £5 million. Risks include invasion of privacy, reckless piloting, being hacked and issues around airspace controls and regulation (Collins 2015).

After an initial period of experimentation, a range of guidelines and rules have been established that limit how you can use a drone. In the UK you need the permission of the Civil Aviation Authority (CAA) to fly a drone, and this has to be renewed annually. They cannot be flown over congested areas without authorisation, and cannot fly within 50 metres of any person, vessel or structure not controlled by the pilot. In 2015, for example, a man was fined £1800 for illegally flying drones over professional football matches and London landmarks (Gayle 2015). Check the latest guidance on the CAA's drones section for more information on the rules. You can also find BBC guidance on the use of Unmanned Aerial Systems on their Safety Guidelines pages, and the Professional Society of Drone Journalists has a range of resources on their website (dronejournalism.org) including a code of ethics.

Privacy is a particular factor to take into account. Paul Egglestone from the University of Central Lancashire says they often discuss the ethical differences between using a drone to obtain footage compared to standing on a step ladder and using a long lens. 'We've all seen those shots looking down at festivals for example – they are mostly illegal as things stand' (Hartley 2015).

Other factors to take into consideration when using drones include wind speed (avoid speeds over 20 mph), strong rain, extreme temperatures – and the battery life. It is recommended that two operators should control the drone: one to direct the flight and the other to control the camera.

CLOSER LOOK
360-DEGREE VIDEO AND VIRTUAL REALITY

While drones provide opportunities for videographers to *film* in places they've never been before, 360-degree cameras create opportunities for *viewers* to *explore* video and images in ways they've never been able to before. And virtual reality is allowing them to experience places even drones can't go.

Most use of 360-degree video and photography involves spectacular or exclusive scenes that a user is going to *want* to explore (nature and historical documentary reporting, environmental and travel journalism all suit the medium well), as well as large public events: Vice News used it to cover a rally by 60,000 protestors, while the *New York Times* used it to cover vigils in Paris in the wake of the terrorist attacks in November 2015. It can also be used to immerse viewers in more personal stories: Gabo Arora and Chris Milk, for example, used 360-degree video in *Waves of Grace*, which follows an Ebola survivor in Liberia as she narrates her story. And *Clouds Over Sidra* shows a refugee camp through the eyes of a 12-year-old girl. This intimacy – without the presence of a reporter – can be part of 360-degree video's appeal.

Behind-the-scenes 360-degree video can also tap into users' natural curiosity: talking about the potential for using the technology on the election campaign, for example, *Washington Post* video directory Micah Gelman says: 'Viewers can experience what it's really like to be on the campaign trail by seeing not just the candidates but what the candidates themselves are seeing' (Wang 2015b). This means thinking carefully about the environment you're shooting in, and what is visible – including any crew, and yourself. If you need to remotely control the camera from a distance to keep yourself out of shot, you'll also need to make sure it's protected. There are ethical considerations around making sure that people have given consent to be filmed. Broadcasting guidelines on consent are useful here.

Virtual reality (VR) is often used synonymously with 360-degree video – partly because the VR apps and devices (such as Google Cardboard or Oculus Rift headsets) are also used for 360-degree video. But there is a difference: some will insist that virtual reality video is *simulated*: in other words, the footage is virtual, not real.

VR is useful for allowing users to explore environments that cannot be filmed, whether that is reporting on space or other planets, science reporting on what goes on inside our bodies, places from the past that no longer exist or predictions about the future that might never exist. Associated Press used VR to explore what happens in the brain of someone with Alzheimer's disease, for example (Kreinberg 2016), while the *Wall Street Journal* created a VR roller coaster ride through 21 years of the NASDAQ stock exchange: 'We could have done a flat chart of the NASDAQ. We have done that numerous times. But virtual reality lets you feel the change in your gut', said developer Roger Kenny (Bhatia 2015). VR is a more expensive and intensive process, involving research and planning as well as the creation and editing of the visuals themselves alongside any narration, and with a much smaller audience able to experience it, that makes it the less likely option for most projects.

YouTube started supporting 360-degree video and VR in 2015, and Facebook the year after, saying that 360-degree and immersive video would be a key focus for the news feed. WordPress and Twitter joined a few months after that. But you can also find content on specialist apps such as Within, Jaunt VR, NYT VR and Discovery VR. You do not have to buy expensive headsets to experience VR: Google Cardboard headsets (and others based on the same idea) can cost as little as a film rental. Likewise, you don't need expensive tools to get started: the Google Street View app is a good way to get creating 360 images on your phone, or you can record 360 video using apps like Splash. For longer and higher quality 360-degree footage, however, you will need a 360-degree camera.

Software

Software plays as big a role in video journalism as hardware, particularly when it comes to mobile apps. The key factors to consider are what kind of computer or phone you use, budget, expertise – and the kind of video journalism you will be producing. Video uses up a lot of memory so it is likely that you will need additional storage (portable hard drive) plus a high processor speed.

There are, broadly speaking, four things which video journalists use software for:

1 Recording (including social media apps like Instagram or Snapchat)
2 Editing
3 Altering (adding filters and effects, slowing or speeding video, changing frame rate, adding interactivity)
4 Publishing (including YouTube, Vimeo, etc.).

Some software covers more than one step in the process: the Vine Camera app, for example, allows users to record, edit and publish video; Snapchat to record, alter and publish. YouTube's video editing tool can record, edit, alter and publish all in one.

Generally speaking it is better to record video outside any app or website first: this generally results in higher quality but also more control to do other things. On a phone the built-in camera app is fine for most cases. However, if you need extra control over things like frame rate, resolution or audio you can use an app like Filmic Pro.

Editing software at the entry level includes iMovie on the iPhone, iPad or Mac and Windows Movie Maker on PC. For more advanced editing options you might explore Adobe Premiere and the Final Cut and Avid suite of products. You can also do basic editing online using the YouTube Editor. Many television journalists use Avid while Final Cut Pro is popular with documentary and independent filmmakers.

If you are using an iPhone the iMovie app is extremely good for editing and publishing/ emailing without having to move your footage onto a laptop (Final Cut Pro is also available as an app, but is vastly more expensive). On Android, editing apps include KineMaster, Quik and PowerDirector, but as new apps are added and updated all the time it's worth trying a few to find the one which has the features that you require.

In addition to basic editing it is worth exploring more specific video apps that provide particular features. Legend and Gravie, for example, allow you to animate text against a still image or video. This is particularly useful for creating titles. If you are shooting vertical video you might need a specific editor for that (InShot, for example), or an app that will allow you to run multiple vertical videos next to each other to create a horizontal one (PicPlayPost, for example). Other apps allow you to turn multiple images into video slideshows, turn video into animated gifs, record your screen, create time lapses or slow motion, record stop motion animation or even animate virtual characters. And, of course there are lots of apps which will apply all sorts of filters and effects to your video.

Publishing software is important to ensure you can get your video online quickly on the move. If you're uploading to YouTube then you will need the YouTube Capture app on your phone and, crucially, to be logged in; likewise any social media accounts. Many news organisations now have their own apps for uploading video too, used only by employees.

All of these apps give you huge creative options when it comes to your video: the key thing is to be clear what the purpose of your video is and never to use a feature *just because you can*. Like the best writing, the best video is simple, clear and doesn't get in the way of the story.

Step 1: Coming up with online video ideas – and planning them

One way to come up with ideas for online video is to simply come up with lots of story ideas – then look at those ideas with the eye of a video journalist. That means looking for stories that have a strong visual element. It might be a striking setting, a compelling character or lots of action. Here are some examples:

- *An interview*: if the person is good on camera, or visually interesting, or their expressions are key to the story, video can work well
- *Events*: protests, marches, sporting events and openings can provide decent visuals – but remember that a few seconds might be enough
- *Demonstration*: if you or an interviewee need to explain how something is done, or how something works, why not film it?
- *Reaction*: if you think someone's reaction is going to be strong – whether that is their reaction to a question, or their reaction to some good or bad news – then capturing it on video can tell us much more than any amount of words
- *Colour*: anything which is colourful – literally, or figuratively (such as a colourful character) can work well on video.

Remember that video does not have to be complicated, or long: start by filming short 3–6-second clips that might go on social media while you're out reporting to 'set the scene'. Try combining multiple 1–2-second clips to create a short montage (see how some of the most successful creators on the video service Vine (now closed) used this approach). Moreover the clips can be used on other social media as well.

Video formats used online

Video can take a range of forms and formats online. Here are just a few to look at and think about:

- *News clips*: often provided by agencies, mainstream broadcasters and sites such as YouTube
- *Embedded video*: a video player embedded in a text article that enhances the story, for example, a charity parachute drop
- *Part of a multimedia or interactive package*: a video that could have narration, interviews, pictures and graphics to illustrate the story
- *Guides*: 'how to' videos are popular on magazine websites and YouTube

- *Screencaptures*: PewDiePie built an enormous following by capturing what was happening on his screen while playing computer games – but that alone isn't enough: you have to be informative, useful and entertaining all at the same time
- *Vlogs*: video blogs
- *Livestreams*: live video from an event or studio
- *Video shows*: internet channels such as Current TV
- *Documentary features*: see Vimeo's Documentary Film subsite for examples (vimeo.com/documentaryfilm)
- *Motion graphics and animation*: often used to explain something in a way that might be clearer than using real-life settings and presenters
- *Explainers and backgrounders*: video can be a good way to explain how something works, or how we got to this situation in the first place
- *Time lapse*: condensing minutes, hours, days or months into a video which is sped-up
- *Round-ups and previews*: if you're looking ahead to an event, or rounding up the highlights of the week, this can be done on video – but still try to find a way to make it visual.

Once you have an idea for a video ask yourself: who would want to watch this and why? The story might be good but it might be better served through text, still images, audio or a combination of all three. Think about practicalities such as resources and time. Think about images and footage that can be used and how they will propel the story. Some news organisations have their own studio to record interviews, reviews or live video. But are you adding any visual value to a story, or would it be more interesting to film somewhere else?

Interviews can be a compelling feature if the subject or person is interesting or if there is an element of exclusivity about the video: Q&A-style questioning of officials is unlikely to elicit good video although specific responses used as clips in a package might add balance. Remember that intimacy works particularly well online and if the issue is appropriate and the subject is willing it may be better to let them tell their story themselves straight to the camera, rather than putting yourself between the story and the viewer.

A simple way to get started with interviews is where you ask just one of the questions on camera: the response might only come to 30 or 90 seconds, but that's a good length for embedding in a broader text piece.

Features and news packages need research and planning. It is not necessary to storyboard your feature in the prescriptive way of a film director so that each and every shot is prefigured (unless you are planning to invest time in a documentary-style piece). Stories have a habit of changing and developing. However, think about the people, the places, the action and still shots you might want to use. Before setting out make a checklist and consider the following:

- What's the story?
- What pictures will you need? (think about locations)
- Can you shoot the story on your own? (think about transport)
- Have you packed the right kit and tested it?
- What kind of environment are you going into? (think about terrain, weather, lighting, safety)

- Have you researched interviews in advance and made appointments?
- Plan ahead: video stories take more setting up than print. For instance, you can't film a story about forestry in a series of lumberjacks' and activists' offices. You have to arrange to meet them in a forest.
- Have you permission to shoot video? Think about government buildings, public spaces such as schools or copyright material such as music that may be playing in the background
- Permission slips – you will need contributors to sign a form giving permission to publish or broadcast their interview
- Parental consent – needed for interviews with children
- Identification – court reporting rules apply to video
- Think about balance, right of reply and visual libel. This is an easy trap to fall into when you juxtapose images with voiceover without thinking how the two fit together (see Chapter 8 section on libel, p.206)
- Think about third party footage. The preponderance of cameras now means that you may find useful footage from other people – or even a CCTV camera. Google 'Man stuck in lift 40 hours' for an example of how one story was brought to life by using CCTV footage.

CASE STUDY: THE *HUFFINGTON POST*'S MARIAH STEWART ON USING 6-SECOND VIDEO TO COVER THE FERGUSON PROTESTS

In 2014 the streets of Ferguson, Missouri became the site of regular protests against police racism following the killing of an unarmed black teenager by a white police officer and the subsequent court case. As riots broke out the 6-second video platform Vine became an important place to follow what was happening. Mariah Stewart *became one of the best-known journalists using the platform.*

'When all of the events started to take place here in Ferguson, I immediately took to social media to get the word out. Twitter and Instagram were my go-to platforms for live-posting actions: at first I preferred Instagram over Vine because Instagram offered me a longer amount of time to shoot. However, Instagram doesn't translate on Twitter well. My colleague, Ryan Reilly, suggested that I use Vine so that people who didn't have the app could easily view it on my Twitter feed.

'It was a good idea. I quickly realised the time length didn't matter and that Vine was better at reaching a bigger audience.'

One of the advantages of Vine is that the short videos upload much more quickly, particularly when internet connections are slow or under heavy demand. Channel 4 journalist Alex Thomson, for example, used the platform to post short updates from the Ebola crisis in Sierra Leone and 'fill in the wider framework' that had to be left out of broadcast reporting (Perraudin 2014).

'I'm so thankful for online journalism', says Stewart. 'We're able to do so much with it that television simply can't. When people read my articles and see the embedded video they can instantly replay the clip over and over again. It's nice to have a videographer on the ground, but sometimes all you need is a short video to get the job done.'

Watch Mariah's Ferguson coverage, including embedded Vine clips, at https://pinboard.in/u:paulbradshaw/t:mariahstewart

CLOSER LOOK
YOUTUBERS AND JOURNALISM

While the news industry was getting to grips with online video, a whole new generation was busy inventing a web-native approach to video production outside of traditional media: 'YouTubers'.

Typically presenter-led and published regularly to a demanding schedule, YouTubing is in many ways more like traditional television than the more content-led and irregular approach to video taken by print and online journalists. As with traditional broadcasting, the platform and medium has already been chosen, so YouTubers must regularly fill a certain amount of screen time regardless of whether the content itself best suits the medium. They must also ensure that the production quality is high enough to meet audience expectations. While the tone may be informal, the approach to lighting and sound is often thoroughly professional, with tight editing and jump cuts used to keep the pace fast.

Content that is *useful* tends to do well on YouTube. As a result many successful channels closely resemble traditional magazine sectors and article formats, from makeup tutorials by people like Lauren Luke (signed up by the *Guardian*) and Claudia Sulewski (signed up by *Teen Vogue*) to cooking shows like SORTEDfood and tips-based channels like HouseholdHacker. Stampy and Dan Middleton manage to combine useful gaming tips with clear, entertaining delivery and, equally important, prolific and persistent publishing. Channels like Veritasium and Numberphile build on a rich history of popular science.

The regularity of publishing means you need to think creatively about the show's 'format' (examples include Jung & Naiv's 'naive' interview format, and the YouTube channel 'Cooking with dog'), make sure that content is compelling and original, find an engaging style that is your own, and regularly come up with strong ideas. But one of the key qualities of YouTubers is the way that they engage with their community.

Hannah Witton, whose videos on sex, body image, gender and sexuality receive tens of thousands of views says: 'You need to get involved with the community. I see some of my viewers as friends.' But dealing with comments can be difficult. 'You have to focus on the lovely comments. Not everyone can love you.'

YouTube may be the focus, but other platforms are important too. Anna Gardner, who runs the ViviannaDoesMakeup channel on YouTube, feels that the focus on 'YouTubers' is misleading. 'I'm actually a blogger', she said at the Rethink Media conference in 2015. 'I have a blog [winner of the Best Beauty Blog at the 2014 Bloglovin' awards], and Instagram account, and YouTube as well.'

There are also many video producers inventing a new visual language on other platforms: Vimeo is well established as a platform for longer form video production drawing on documentary styles. Vine helped video creators explore shortform and looping video. Twitch created a platform for video game playthroughs, talk shows and live e-sports tournaments before expanding into radio, music and creative walkthroughs. And more recently Snapchat has taken YouTube on directly, teaming up with the Tribeca film festival to showcase the best video, and supporting top creators directly.

Commercially, many successful channels make money from a combination of YouTube ads and collaborations with brands (sponsorship). But you need to be aware of advertising regulations: the Committee of Advertising Practice has a specific section on its website devoted to video blogs which is worth consulting (Committee of Advertising Practice 2015). Any coverage that is paid for must be disclosed. Outside of advertising some YouTube channels are used to build a customer base for events and merchandise. But it takes time. 'There is no magic formula, just be consistent', says YouTuber Lily Pebbles. 'Don't take your foot off the pedal.'

Step 2: Shooting video

It is not enough to just switch the camera on and start shooting. You might capture hours of material but find in the edit that you have badly framed shots, no close-ups, jerky footage and invasive ambient sound. Think about the different elements of the story you need.

In other words, shoot to edit. For example, you might be covering a protest by parents at the closure of a local school. A shot of people chanting with placards or of people marching only tells one part of the story. Think about the composition of visuals that will tell the story and give it context: footage of the school and its location, close-ups of individuals and their placard messages, interviews, a shot that shows how big the demonstration is and the reaction of bystanders. Is the protest holding up traffic? Are there police?

Framing video: composition

A variety of shots always helps in video, and there are three shots in particular that you should practise and become familiar with. Keep the camera still and always get these three shots before doing moving shots:

- Wide shot – stand back and establish the scene
- Medium – move closer in to the point where people can be easily identified
- Close-up – used for interviews, usually just head and shoulders.

If you are using a mobile phone make sure it is focusing on the right part of the image by pressing on that area of the screen. You should see a circle or square appear briefly to indicate that the phone is focusing there. If you press and *hold* on an area of the screen you should see *AE/AF LOCK* appear: AF means Auto Focus: the focus will be locked on that point of the screen. AE means Auto Exposure: you can move your finger up or down on the screen to lock the exposure (how much light you want).

Think about composition: when people first start filming video they tend to put the subject in the centre of the screen, but look at professional video journalism: you'll notice that often the subject is slightly off to one side.

This is the *rule of thirds*, also used in photography. The rule of thirds imagines the shot is divided vertically and horizontally into thirds by lines. Where the lines cross, you put the focus of your shot. For example, if someone is being interviewed they should be off-centre and their head below the top line so they don't look like they are being squeezed into the shot.

Most cameras will show you a grid on the viewfinder to help you use the rule of thirds, and you can turn it on on a mobile phone too by going to your camera settings and looking for the Grid option.

Traditionally TV reporters have avoided letting subjects look straight into the camera, which gives the impression that they are staring at the viewer directly. Instead they will ask them to speak to the off-camera interviewer, and give room between the person being interviewed and the direction that they are looking. If there are shots of the interviewee, they will often be positioned on the opposite side of the shot (if the interviewee was on the right, the interviewer will be on the left), looking 'back' at the interviewer.

However, because of the intimacy of online video many videographers ask the interviewee to speak directly into the camera: after all, vlogging and YouTube have now made us much more used to seeing people speak this way, and many more people are comfortable with speaking to camera. You can use either approach but make sure you do it consistently and give clear instructions to the interviewee.

Shooting to edit: thinking about sequences

Sequences are a key technique in telling stories through video. For example, to tell the story of a successful athlete, a sequence might start with a clip of the athlete walking out onto the track, followed by a clip of her taking up a starting position, followed by a clip of her feet flying off the blocks. By combining the three shots you are able to condense time and make the story more visually varied and interesting. By contrast, imagine how much longer and less interesting a single shot of the athlete walking out, taking up position and running would be.

To create sequences you first need the footage to edit together, so shoot a variety of different shots for your story, with an idea of how they might fit together into sequences (a storyboard is useful, but bear in mind that news events might throw up surprises that you need to be prepared to go with). David Burns recommends shooting at least four times

CLOSER LOOK
'SHOOTING' VIDEO WITH YOUR COMPUTER

Some video is created entirely on computer. A number of online tools, for example, allow you to create animations and presentations that can be used for backgrounders and explainers. These include PowToon (powtoon.com), Moovly, GoAnimate and Animaker.

If you want to record what is taking place on your computer you might also look at screencapture and screencasting software like CamStudio, Jing and Screencast-O-Matic. There are also tools for streaming on platforms like Twitch, such as Open Broadcaster Software (OBM).

Another way to create video without a camera is to record an interview via video chat. Again there are plenty of tools for doing this including software that will record a Skype chat. YouTube Live's Google Hangouts On Air option will not only livestream a video chat on your YouTube channel and Google Plus pages, but the video will be saved there too, allowing you to edit it, and download if you wish. It also has a screencasting option and allows you to install extensions for extra functionality such as being able to draw on screen.

as many close-ups as wide or medium shots: these satisfy the viewer's desire for detail but are also easier to edit together (Miquel 2012).

For those starting out the following advice is helpful:

- Use the autofocus and auto lighting function
- If filming with a mobile phone, turn airplane mode on: you don't want filming to be interrupted by a phone or message alert
- Make sure you know where the microphone is on the phone – and then make sure you're not covering it
- Use a tripod, or at least steady a mobile phone shot by holding your elbows by your side. This is key to professional-looking video (but not necessary if, for example, you stumble upon a news story and setting up a tripod would mean missing key footage)
- Avoid sweeping shots left and right (or panning) – too much movement is distracting
- Avoid too much zooming in and out for the same reason
- Capture movement *in* the frame; don't be tempted to create movement by moving the frame around
- Along the same lines, try to ensure that subjects enter and leave the frame rather than you following them
- Don't follow a wide shot with another wide shot: use a variety of angles
- Remember close-ups work well online
- Leave yourself at least 10 seconds of video at the beginning and end where the shot does not move. One of the first rules of editing is not to cut on a shot that is still moving
- Remember to choose a shot, press record and film it then *stop* recording and set up for the next shot. Inexperienced camera operators tend to leave the camera rolling and end up with hours of useless footage.

Once the basics have been learned, consider experimenting with the following: a piece to camera (for example, a video piece for a blog) and shooting cutaways (often used in interviews, when there is a shot of the interviewee's hands or room, for example). You should also get in the habit of shooting enough supplemental footage that illustrates the story or point a person is making.

It is easy to make mistakes in a stressful situation particularly when you are on your own with no one else to rely on. Common pitfalls for even the most experienced video producers are:

- Forgetting to turn the camera on
- Choosing the wrong environment (e.g. a dimly lit office or in front of a bright light)
- Umming and aahing while interviewing: remember to keep quiet
- Allowing interviews to go on too long – keep interviews short and to the point with open questions that prompt your interviewees to give decent responses
- Letting the interviewee make time-specific references which may not make sense later – don't be afraid to brief the interviewee to avoid that type of reference
- Videoing someone in front of distractions, e.g. traffic or a poster with easily read text
- Letting the interviewee grab the microphone.

CLOSER LOOK
TIPS FOR ONLINE VIDEO JOURNALISM

1 Always have a camera with you.
2 Be clear about what the story is, and what your film is doing.
3 Show, don't tell, and don't try to ape TV formats.
4 The internet is an intimate medium, get close to your subject, allow them to tell their story, instead of using soundbites
5 Be fair to your characters and subjects.
6 Speak to real people, real voices, rather than talking heads.
7 Try to get actuality – real life happening in front of your camera, instead of set up shots and GVs (general views).
8 Be ruthless with your edit, keep it short and tight and take advice from people who weren't on the shoot.
9 Watch quality documentaries and keep up with what others are doing.
10 If you're starting out, upload to YouTube, video blog, and share on social networks.

(From John Domokos, video producer at the *Guardian*)

Step 3: Editing video for the web

If you are capturing short video clips for use alongside a text article or on social media, then it is likely that the 'editing' is done at the planning stage. A common technique, for example, is to ask an interviewee to introduce themselves at the start of the clip, and to include the question in their answer (for example, 'My advice to people wanting to get into the sport is . . .'). The resulting video should only need to be 'topped and tailed' (removing unnecessary footage at the start and end of your clip) to be usable straight away. Doing this for each question separately can give you a series of brief videos that can be inserted into an article for extra colour.

For longer video packages you are likely to have to edit together more than one clip, in a different order to which they were filmed. This is called 'non-linear' editing.

Non-linear editing software such as iMovie or Final Cut allows the journalist to cut, split, move and delete video and audio to construct the story. First, however, it is a good idea to look at all the raw footage and decide what elements are needed to construct a story with a clear beginning, middle and end. This can be a time-consuming process: don't be tempted to start editing straight away. You may have forgotten a particular sequence or the significance of a quote might not have been clear at the time of recording. Beginnings are particularly important: Mukul Devichand of BBC Trending says 'You only have 7 seconds to engage people: if you don't, they will go elsewhere' (Hayward 2015).

Logging and the rough-edit

Start by looking at the footage. You may have more than an hour's worth that you need to edit down to three minutes or less. You may have several hours of footage from which you want to construct a long feature. In these situations, save yourself time by going through the footage and logging the clips you want to use. This process is called a rough-edit.

Log the clips by giving them catchlines (labels) and create your log by hand or electronically (most software programs allow you to do this). Note the 'in' and 'out' points (the precise time) of each clip by looking at the digital time display on your video camera or phone. Be selective about your clips and choose establishing shots, a range of close-ups and mid-shots and have a mix of short, killer quotes and longer, more descriptive elements from interviews. Try to be disciplined. You may need to drop footage of an interview if two people make the same point.

Import and edit

When you first create a project in your editing software you will need to import the clips you are using. If you are on a mobile phone clips can be imported from your camera roll. Most editing tools have a drag and drop, cut and paste system which allows audio, music and titles to be added. They also have a timeline where clips are added to create a narrative and where you can layer video and audio clips so that, for example, you can add ambient sound.

Decide what order you want your clips to go in and place them on the timeline. You can look at your clips frame by frame, cut them and split them in two. With most tools you can also separate the audio track from the video, allowing you to show 'illustrative' video over relevant audio from a different clip: for example, you might have interviewed someone talking about a protest, and you want to show your footage of the same protest over that audio.

Think about pacing – you need to draw the viewer while getting to the point. Online audiences tend to have a shorter time threshold when they view a story online because they have the facility to click to something else. Keep the pace lively and keep in mind the length of your video.

For example, a shot lasting 30 seconds in a 3-minute video is generally far too long as you may find that the story gets squeezed or becomes incoherent. This is a tough area to make rules about: the content should dictate the style and length, but journalists also often overestimate the value of their own content, so be ruthless: just because you've invested effort doesn't mean it has to be used. Consider transitions if you feel clips are at the right length but put together seem jerky. The software program you use will give you a number of options for transitions such as dissolving and fading in and out. Don't be tempted to use more elaborate transitions: remember the focus is the story, not your knowledge of editing software.

How long should it be?

One advantage of producing for the web when compared to television is that there is no rule about length – you don't have a schedule to worry about. But should we keep it short?

Research by video hosting company Wistia suggests that increasing the length of a video *does* have a negative impact on engagement: anything longer than 2 minutes leads people to engage less with a video (Fishman 2016). If you're making a short video, then, it is best to keep it under that threshold.

A good example of this is *Fortune* magazine's YouTube video series 'My Breakthrough Moment in Leadership'. In each video a different business leader describes their 'breakthrough moment'. Because it's simple the videos generally sit around the 1-minute mark, and the completion rates (how many people watch to the end) are very high.

For longer more feature-based videos, however, try a length between 6–12 minutes: 'Every second counts between 2 minutes and 6 minutes, but there's hardly any drop-off between 6 minutes and 12 minutes', the Wistia analysis notes (Fishman 2016). It may not seem long to you at first but think about how much footage you will have to shoot and edit on your own.

Beyond that length there has been an increasing focus on 20–30-minute video by news organisations: the *Guardian*, for example, has a documentary department that commissions independent film-makers and production companies, while the *New York Times*, *The Economist* and *Der Spiegel* are among other organisations investing in similar content.

Adding audio

Many online video journalists like to dispense with voiceovers where the journalist introduces a piece or adds running commentary. They prefer to let the visuals of the story, the narrative of the video and the people in the piece tell the story. The argument is that voiceovers hold up the story (because people want to see action, not talking heads) and that their use is too much like broadcast television (this is a stylistic preference).

However, there is nothing to prevent a journalist recording a separate piece of audio to run with the video if it helps to give context and add meaning to the story. This can be recorded on to the phone or camera itself or separately using a microphone attached to your computer.

Adding audio on mobile can be problematic: iPhones will only give access to audio that is stored as music on the phone, so it is easier to record audio as a video clip and then dispose of the visuals in the editing. Android phones are more flexible.

Don't be tempted to add loud music to add to the dynamic of the piece or music with lyrics that will detract from the message: the listener might feel like they are being emotionally manipulated, or simply not like your taste. It is also likely to raise copyright issues. Remember to get permission if you use music and other copyrighted material. If you do need to add music there are many websites where you can download copyright free music for free (search.creativecommons.org allows you to search some of these, such as ccMixter) – and upcoming musicians are good sources of free music if you feel it adds to the story, but make sure you give them a credit.

Clever use of audio or natural sound can make your story much more evocative. Don't show a picture of a baby crying without letting your viewer hear the sound. This is known as letting your package *breathe*. And try not to show pictures of people talking if your voiceover prevents the viewer hearing what they are saying. This is known as *goldfishing*.

Adding interactivity

There are a range of tools and techniques for adding interactivity to a video. The iPad app Touchcast, for example, allows presenters to draw on the screen, overlay clickable video clips and live social and news feeds on top of the video, and use 'green screen' techniques to change the backdrop. Eko Studio allows video editors to add choices into their videos so users can choose their own path, and there are dozens of other tools and apps that offer other interactive features: search around and experiment when new video apps are released.

YouTube offers a number of interactive features through 'cards' and 'end screens'. Cards can add polls to your video, and link to other videos, playlists or channels, or to certain websites. End screens also offer some of these plus subscriptions.

If you are willing to learn a bit of code then you can add custom interactivity, for example, using HTML5 and JavaScript libraries. See Chapter 11 for more.

Creating titles and credits

Your program will allow you to create titles and credits that you can type and place on the video. Interviewees should have their name and title clearly displayed, set left or right, at the bottom of the screen. Be sure to use credits for byline purposes and for commissioned material such as archive footage and music. Check the size of the text – it can appear very small online. As with transitions, resist the temptation to choose more elaborate caption designs. Keep the typography and colour simple – and the focus on the story, not your telling of it.

Step 4: Publishing video online

Video files need to be compressed into a file format that works online. MOV is popular among journalists but there are other formats such as MPEG and MP4 and AVI. Most multimedia organisations host video themselves and will have guidelines on formats and other considerations depending on the content management system they use. Others will allow you to upload video directly to a video sharing site such as Vimeo or YouTube, which accepts all of the above file formats and many more besides.

The compression process can leave your crisp video footage looking blurred, so experiment to see how compressed it needs to be. High definition (HD) is nice, but it too will need to be compressed and it also uses up far more memory (HD comes in more than one size) and takes longer to upload. If your story is time-sensitive, the HD version can wait: get it up as fast as you can.

Once you've uploaded to a site like YouTube, take time over settings like the title, description, tags and categories (see below) and licence. Videos will default to a YouTube licence, but if you choose a Creative Commons licence this means that other people can find your video in the YouTube Video Editor or in Creative Commons searches, and make new content. This can help you to reach new audiences and make it easier for people to collaborate with you. For the same reason it is a good idea to leave embedding on: World Press Photo research found that videos that are embeddable receive five times as many hits as those that are not (Campbell 2013).

Video optimisation

Uploading a video to the web should never be the end of your video production process: it is vital that you add extra information that helps search engines to understand what your video is about, and makes it easier for users to find.

First in the list should be your *video title and description*. Use the same SEO principles outlined in Chapter 4 to make sure that these help search engines to understand your video content, but remember that videos are also normally displayed in search engine results and in searches within YouTube and Vimeo: so a strong title and description can increase the chances that someone clicks through to watch your video.

The same applies to any article containing your video: don't just publish the video on its own without any text; ensure you write something that introduces the video and makes it easier for search engines to understand.

It's important to remember that YouTube itself is the second biggest search engine after Google, so chances are that many people will come across your video there rather than in the article it relates to. For that reason remember to use your description to link from your video to any article it appears in, and also to link to other relevant pages such as your author page.

Choose a good thumbnail for your video: this can be changed in the video settings. More broadly, take some time to optimise your channel as a whole: add a welcome video, a channel description, links to social media and other YouTube channels, and create sections if relevant. Playlists can be used to gather related videos together.

When it comes to social media make sure you make video that people want to watch all the way through: Facebook, for example, takes into account not only how many people have watched a video but also for how long, so it's better to have a short video that people watch in full, than a long video that people are going to give up on. If a user turns on the sound or makes the video full screen that also helps. The AJ+ video *Drowned Syrian Boy Symbolizes Refugee Crisis Sweeping Europe* is a good example: only 2 minutes long, with captions throughout, it was viewed over 20 million times on Facebook (see 'What works well on social media' in Chapter 4 (p.111) for more on the types of content that people tend to watch and share most).

Captions have become a key feature of video created for social media: in 2016 Digiday reported that as much as 85 per cent of video views on Facebook were happening with the sound turned off. Gretchen Tibbits, chief operating officer for LittleThings, told the website that while the first 3 seconds were critical, because Facebook counted 3 seconds as a 'view', '[t]he video also has to be designed to capture attention without needing sound' (Patel 2016).

Live videos are given particular weighting while they are still live, but are less likely to be seen afterwards: Facebook has found that users watch videos three times longer while they are live compared to when they are no longer live (Kant 2016).

CLOSER LOOK
CHECKLIST TO CONSIDER WHEN POSTING VIDEO

- Write titles like headlines, with keywords that make them searchable
- Write descriptions like the first paragraph of a story, and add useful links
- Make sure categories and tags are correct
- Choose a good thumbnail
- Consider using a Creative Commons licence
- Remember to cross-promote online video in print or broadcast
- Use captions for social media: most video is watched with the sound turned off
- Create shorter versions for social platforms where relevant, linking to the full video online
- Consider using shorter clips within a text article, as well as publishing the 'full video interview' as a separate piece, allowing users to choose how they consume the content and providing more opportunities for discovery
- Consider 'chunking' longer video into parts that can be found and viewed separately, but link to each other
- Consider uploading to multiple platforms: social networks like Facebook and Twitter tend to prioritise 'native video' uploaded directly to the platform, rather than links to videos elsewhere.

Live video

Live video has been available to journalists online for over a decade: livestreaming services Bambuser, Qik, Ustream and Justin.tv all launched in 2007, while YouTube announced its own livestreaming service YouTube Live in 2011 and the video game livestreaming platform Twitch launched the same year. But it was the launch of Meerkat in 2015 that really kicked off the rise of live video for mainstream publishers.

Meerkat's innovation was to connect live video to a person's Twitter network and allow other users to comment on the stream. Although services such as Twitcasting had offered much the same years earlier, the market in 2015 was bigger and hungrier for live video.

Within a month Twitter had launched its own live video app, Periscope. And just five months later Facebook had launched Facebook Live. The race was on, with the trend spreading to other platforms too: in October Twitch launched Twitch Creative, an attempt to expand outside video game playthroughs, and in 2016 Tumblr and Instagram added live video capability too. In just 12 months live video postings on YouTube had increased by 130 per cent (Shead 2016).

Publishers have been quick to take the opportunity to go live: in April 2016 BuzzFeed famously spent 45 minutes livestreaming two employees trying to make a watermelon explode with rubber bands: with over 800,000 viewers watching at one point, that made it the most-watched Facebook Live video ever (within a month the record was smashed by a woman laughing in a Chewbacca mask).

Facebook Live was put to more serious use in June the same year, when *BBC Newsnight* decided to stream a 'day of Facebook Lives' in the wake of the UK's EU referendum result. Normally limited to 45 minutes of airtime, the team essentially used Facebook Live to create its own 24-hour channel for one day. Similar 'parallel' broadcasting could be found during that year's Euro championships and Olympics as TV presenters invited viewers to continue watching on their Facebook page, while on radio a phone-in with the Newcastle manager on BBC Newcastle was streamed on Facebook Live and attracted 100,000 views.

A more in-depth use of live video was demonstrated by *New York Times* journalist Deborah Acosta, who used Facebook Live to stream her quest to find the person who had taken photographs she found on a pavement. 'Reporters are always solving mysteries', wrote *New York Times* public editor Liz Spayd. 'But what made this unique is that Acosta did so both with her audience watching and with some offering up real-time clues' (Spayd 2016).

Facebook's push on live video prompted the company to share best practices in the medium (Facebook 2016). These include:

1 Tell people ahead of time when you're going to broadcast
2 Go live when you have a strong connection
3 Write a compelling description before going live
4 Ask your viewers to follow you and receive notifications when you go live
5 Say hello to commenters by name and respond to their comments
6 Broadcast for longer periods of time to reach more people
7 Be creative and go live often!

Also worth remembering – again – is that audio is just as important in live video as in recorded video. It is often the first thing to be forgotten, so make sure you give it as much consideration as the visuals.

Summary

Online video is not one form of journalism: it is several. It is the solo journalism of Kevin Sites and the longform video popularised by Vice News; gamers on Twitch and lifestyle vloggers on YouTube engaging with their communities; BuzzFeed's social-savvy video and broadcasters livestreaming long after their programme went off air; and reporters including raw footage in their text reports, or animating backgrounders to explain the context of their story. It can be vertical, horizontal, or square; raw, edited or live; 6 seconds or feature-length.

Some of the techniques of broadcast journalism simply aren't appropriate online, and often the story is best told by taking the reporter out of the way. But other techniques remain: the need for a strong story, engaging characters and ruthless editing to tell a story succinctly. Beyond broadcast, it is important to take lessons in storytelling from cinema and documentary too: the importance of sequences, for example, and narrative in longer pieces. And remember, good video means clear audio.

As video journalists we are publishers too: it is important to make sure that we think about how our video is understood by search engines and why people might share it on social media; how people might interact with it, and the contexts that they might experience it in, from an article to a YouTube page to a social media update.

But all good video starts from one thing: an idea. You don't need to be piloting drones and filming 360-degree video to create compelling content; you just need to keep an eye out for stories that can be made better with some moving imagery. Keep it simple to begin with, and build from there.

ALASTAIR GOOD: HOW I SHOT THE CALAIS CAMP STORY

'The refugee/migrant camp in Calais had been growing steadily for some time. Estimates varied between five and ten thousand people who had travelled from the southern part of the globe to escape war, persecution and poverty. They were all hoping for just one thing: the chance to make a dangerous journey across the Channel to Britain.

'One of my contacts in an aid agency working in the camp called me to say that bulldozers were due to move in to clear the camp the next day. I pitched the story to my editor and was on the Eurostar by the afternoon.

'Just as I arrived into Calais my contact called to say that there had been a last minute reprieve as a judge had ordered the clearance could not continue until the number of unaccompanied children in the camp could be accurately assessed.

'These days it is hard to get commissioned to cover foreign stories with the restriction on budgets and the need to spend money on stories that are likely to be the most popular. With that in mind I decided to stay.

'When travelling and working alone with a lot of expensive camera equipment, security is an ever present issue. I called my editor and told him where I was going and when I expected to return, that way if I didn't get in touch that evening then he would know something had happened and begin making enquiries.

'I also took down the address of my hotel on my phone so I could show that to taxi drivers and get a ride back as well as marking the hotel location on a paper map. Smartphones are great until they run out of batteries or signal so I always try to make sure I have a paper map of where I am.

'I unpacked my camera from its case and carried it in a plain looking rucksack.

'Most of the people I approached spoke some English and were willing to talk but at the mention of the video camera they immediately refused. I could attempt to film them anonymously, from the back or just their feet while recording the sound of their voices but I always try to steer away from that if I can. One of the values of video journalism over print or radio is seeing the emotion on the faces of people and anonymous interviewees can also call into question the authenticity of the story.

'I called my contact and she said she would be able to help me with a young Afghan girl who had walked with her mother for months to reach the camps, but that wouldn't be until the next day.

'One big part of the story at the camp was that people outside didn't really understand the scale of it: since I'd been there three years previously it had grown from a collection of tents and an old farmer's shed to a sprawling shanty town complete with restaurants, shops and even a barber shop.

'With this in mind I decided to film a walking tour of the camp with my voice as a guide to what we could see. I could have filmed myself speaking to camera cut with shots of the camps but for web video you don't want to waste the audience's time with unnecessary scenes so I thought that I could show more of the camps if my commentary was audio only. This style of video is also more immersive and gives the viewer the impression that they are walking around the camp themselves.

'I wanted to record the audio live as I walked around. I could have shot the pictures and then written a script to record later but I always feel those voiceovers lack an immediacy that reporting from the ground in the moment captures. Doing it this way meant a good few false starts as I ran out of things to say or people walked into the shot.

'The next day I went back and interviewed the young girl, initially I had thought I would combine her interview with the footage I'd shot the previous day but the tone was very different and so I decided to make two separate pieces.

'The Calais assignment taught me the value of being able to react to changing situations on the ground: I'd had to go from reporting a breaking news situation to making a more long-tail piece that the Telegraph could use in all stories about immigration as we waited for the next announcement over the camp clearances.

'On my way out of the camp on the second day I called a taxi and waited where I had been picked up the day before. I saw a young man with a stills camera looking anxiously up the road and so I introduced myself. It turned out he was a freelance photographer trying to get back to the centre of Calais but he'd been mugged in the camp and had his money stolen.

'I offered him a ride in my taxi, it seems obvious but in the cut throat competitive world of modern reporting it is important to stick together and help each other when you can.'

(Source: Alastair Good, video journalist, telegraph.co.uk/journalists/alastair-good)

Activities

1   Analyse how video journalists covered the EU referendum. The EU referendum generated hours of coverage not just from broadcast media, but print and online outlets as well. Here's an illustration of the different ways that the media created video specifically for the web:

- BuzzFeed partnered with Facebook to host a series of EU 'Townhall Live' debates using Facebook Live. The streams are embedded in this follow-up post: https://www.buzzfeed.com/matthewchampion/buzzfeed-eu-live – notice shorter clips have also been published on BuzzFeed UK Politics' Facebook page and embedded too.
- The *Telegraph* and *Huffington Post* partnered with YouTube to host their EU debate. You can see how highlights and clips are embedded in this article above the debate liveblog: www.telegraph.co.uk/news/2016/06/14/the-telegraph-eu-debate-with-boris-johnson-and-alex-salmond-all
- The BBC created a number of explainers including: 'How much does the UK spend on the EU?': www.bbc.co.uk/news/uk-politics-eu-referendum-36419806
- The *Guardian*'s animations team created this explainer: 'Brexit for non-Brits': https://www.youtube.com/watch?v=7H9Z4sn8csA
- The FT held a series of interviews with key figures, including this one with John Major: https://www.youtube.com/watch?v=yVlVGEuXw94
- ITV took a 'Fact Check' section from its broadcast bulletin and published it as a standalone piece online: https://www.youtube.com/watch?v=lADts6eD9Tc
- The *Huffington Post* used 360-degree video to show a protest after the referendum vote: https://www.youtube.com/watch?v=BntZF4CeQyg
- They also used user-generated video and video calls to create a piece on 'These young people voted for Brexit': https://www.youtube.com/watch?v=mzdhMoaCpQ4
- Finally, this video of Professor Michael Dougan wasn't produced by any media organisation, but was watched over half a million times on YouTube, and 7 million times on Facebook: https://www.youtube.com/watch?v=USTypBKEd8Y.

All these video journalists have taken different approaches. Analyse these videos and ask:

1 Who tells the story?
2 What is the point of the story?
3 Why do you think they took this approach?
4 Was it successful?
5 Why do you think it was/wasn't successful?

2 Video an event. Get permission to shoot video at an event such as a toy, gadgets or wedding trade show.

- Start with establishing shots of the venue and people as they pour in
- Take mid-shots of exhibits, displays
- Interview exhibitors and customers using close-ups
- Find the most popular stand and video someone testing a product (it could be you)
- Find out what the themes and trends are and close the video with a good quote.

3 Broadcast your blog.

- Decide how long your video will be – keep it short.
- Pick a subject you were going to write about.
- Make some notes of key elements you want to include.
- Try not to read from a script, keep it natural. If you fluff your lines start again – or carry on and just cut out the mistake in editing (people are used to jump-cuts in online video) or leave it in to keep it raw and informal.
- Post it to your blog and YouTube – read comments and respond – appropriately!

Further reading

Burgess, Jean (2017) *YouTube: Online Video and Participatory Culture*, Cambridge: Polity Press
Burum, Ivo and Quinn, Stephen (2015) *MOJO: The Mobile Journalism Handbook: How to Make Broadcast Videos with an iPhone or iPad*, Abingdon: Focal Press
Lancaster, Kurt (2013) *Video Journalism for the Web*, Abingdon: Routledge
Tu, Duy Linh (2015) *Feature and Narrative Storytelling for Multimedia Journalists*, Abingdon: Focal Press
Weight, Jenny (2012) *The Participatory Documentary Cookbook*, http://i-docs.org/2012/04/14/the-participatory-documentary-cookbook-community-documentary-using-social-media

Online resources

BBC Editorial Guidelines: www.bbc.co.uk/editorialguidelines
BBC Safety Guidelines: Unmanned aerial systems [drones]: bbc.co.uk/safety/resources/aztopics/unmanned-aerial-systems
Docubase (an interactive documentary directory): http://docubase.mit.edu
Glen Mulcahy's Mobile and Video Journalism Technology Blog: tvvj.wordpress.com
Mobile Video DIY: http://mobilevideodiy.com/learn
Vimeo Video School: vimeo.com/blog/category/video-school
YouTube Creator Academy: creatoracademy.youtube.com

Bibliography

Bhatia, Gurman. Virtual reality news is becoming a reality in many newsrooms, Poynter, 30 September 2015, www.poynter.org/2015/virtual-reality-news-becoming-a-reality-in-many-newsrooms/372330

Bordwell, David. Paolo Gioli's vertical cinema, David Bordwell's website on cinema, August 2009, www.davidbordwell.net/essays/gioli.php

Brightcove and Tubemogul. Online video & the media industry, Brightcove, 22 December 2010, https://files.brightcove.com/brightcove-whitepaper-online-video-and-media-industry-q3-2010.pdf

Campbell, David. Visual storytelling in the age of post-industrialist journalism, World Press Photo Academy, April 2013, www.worldpressphoto.org/sites/default/files/upload/World%20Press%20Photo%20Multimedia%20Research%20Project%20by%20David%20Campbell.pdf

Collins, Mary M. News drones: risks and rewards, NetNewsCheck, 10 December 2015, www.netnewscheck.com/article/46302/news-drones-risks-and-rewards

Committee of Advertising Practice. Video blogs: scenarios, Committee of Advertising Practice, 19 August 2015, https://www.cap.org.uk/Advice-Training-on-the-rules/Advice-Online-Database/Video-blogs-Scenarios.aspx#.Vdxx6flVhBc

Corcoran, Liam. Five quick things to know about successful Facebook videos, NewsWhip, October 2015, https://www.newswhip.com/2015/10/five-quick-things-to-know-about-successful-facebook-videos

Domokos, John. Author Interview, September 2016

Dunkley Gyimah, David. The secret history of a media revolution being exposed at~ Dublin MojoCon? and presentation at Apple Store, Lnd., David Dunkley Gyimah, 15 February 2015, https://medium.com/@viewmagazine/secret-history-of-a-media-revolution-dublin-mojo-conference-and-global-talk-at-apple-store-ldn-4ee266cec3af#.llklydtv7

Dunkley Gyimah, David. Where might we go with a 21st century visual journalism model? David Dunkley Gyimah, 9 May 2016, https://medium.com/@viewmagazine/what-we-learn-from-tarkovsky-in-a-new-form-of-journalism-dc836b32d7ee#.ypj2fhf4a

Facebook. Tips for using Facebook Live, Facebook, April 2016, https://www.facebook.com/facebookmedia/best-practices/live

Fishman, Ezra. How long should your next video be? Wistia Blog, 5 July 2016, https://wistia.com/blog/optimal-video-length

Gayle, Damien. Man fined for flying drone at football matches and Buckingham Palace, *Guardian*, 15 September 2015, https://www.theguardian.com/technology/2015/sep/15/man-fined-in-first-uk-drone-conviction

Hartley, Sarah. The journalists taking flight with drones, Beacon, 12 May 2015, https://www.beaconreader.com/sarah-hartley/the-journalists-taking-flight-with-drones

Hayward, David. Making great online video: don't imitate TV, David Hayward, 8 October 2015, https://medium.com/@david_hbm/making-great-online-video-don-t-imitate-tv-748e3dabfdfc#.td4yi7mqn

Hedley, David. Social moments in solo videojournalism, *Digital Journalism*, 13 September 2012, http://dx.doi.org/10.1080/21670811.2012.716630

Hermida, Alfred. Lessons from the BBC on online video that works, Reportr.net, 20 September 2010, www.reportr.net/2010/09/20/lessons-bbc-online-video-works

Holton, Avery E., Lawson, Sean and Love, Cynthia. Unmanned aerial vehicles: opportunities, barriers, and the future of 'drone journalism', *Journalism Practice* 9, 2015: 634–650, http://dx.doi.org/10.1080/17512786.2014.980596

Kalogeropoulos, Antonis, Cherubini, Federica and Newman, Nic. The future of online news video, Reuters Institute for the Study of Journalism, 28 June 2016, http://digitalnewsreport.org/publications/2016/future-online-news-video

Kant, Vibhi. News feed FYI: Taking into account live video when ranking feed, Facebook Newsroom, 1 March 2016, http://newsroom.fb.com/news/2016/03/news-feed-fyi-taking-into-account-live-video-when-ranking-feed

Kreinberg, Jake. Behind the scenes on our first animated VR experience, *AP Insights*, 1 August 2016, https://insights.ap.org/whats-new/behind-the-scenes-on-our-first-animated-vr-experience

Manjoo, Farhad. Vertical video on the small screen? Not a crime, *New York Times*, 12 August 2015, www.nytimes.com/2015/08/13/technology/personaltech/vertical-video-on-the-small-screen-not-a-crime.html

Miquel, Cesar. Fundamentals of shooting visual sequences, IJnet, 10 October 2012, https://ijnet.org/en/video/fundamentals-shooting-visual-sequences

Newman, Nic. Journalism, media and technology predictions 2016, Reuters Institute for the Study of Journalism, 11 January 2016, http://media.digitalnewsreport.org/wp-content/uploads/2016/01/Newman-Predictions-2016-FINAL.pdf

Patel, Sahil. 85 percent of Facebook video is watched without sound, *Digiday*, 17 May 2016, http://digiday.com/platforms/silent-world-facebook-video

Pedret, Carla. What journalists need to know to fly a drone, Online Journalism Blog, 11 February 2016, https://onlinejournalismblog.com/2016/02/11/what-journalists-need-to-know-to-fly-a-drone

Perraudin, Frances. Vine shifts from comedy clips to a valid journalistic tool, *Guardian*, 23 November 2014, https://www.theguardian.com/media/2014/nov/23/vine-comedy-clips-journalistic-tool-alex-thomson

Peterson, Tim. Facebook now officially showcases vertical videos in mobile news feeds, *Marketing Land*, 26 August 2016, http://marketingland.com/facebook-now-officially-showcases-vertical-videos-in-mobile-news-feeds-189401

Shead, Sam. YouTube live video views are on the rise as Google takes on Facebook and Snapchat, *Business Insider*, 30 August 2016, http://uk.businessinsider.com/viewings-of-youtube-live-videos-are-up-80-2016-8

Spayd, Liz. Facebook live: too much, too soon, *New York Times*, 20 August 2016, http://mobile.nytimes.com/2016/08/21/public-editor/facebook-live-too-much-too-soon.html

Stringer, Sir Howard. 2022: Towards 500 million, BBC, 20 May 2014, http://downloads.bbc.co.uk/mediacentre/howard-stringer-report.pdf

Tinflow, Randy. The monster opportunity for vertical video, LinkedIn Pulse, 13 June 2016, https://www.linkedin.com/pulse/monster-opportunity-vertical-video-randy-tinfow

Wang, Shan. The New York Times wrestled with many dimensions of video to visualize the making of a hit, NiemanLab, 8 September 2015a, www.niemanlab.org/2015/09/the-new-york-times-wrestled-with-many-dimensions-of-video-to-visualize-the-making-of-a-hit

Wang, Shan. In revamping its video strategy, the Washington Post steers clear of imitating TV, NiemanLab, 11 September 2015b, www.niemanlab.org/2015/09/in-revamping-its-video-strategy-the-washington-post-steers-clear-of-imitating-tv

Wang, Shan. BuzzFeed is separating its entertainment and news divisions, pushing both further into video, NiemanLab, 24 August 2016, www.niemanlab.org/2016/08/buzzfeed-is-separating-its-entertainment-and-news-divisions-pushing-both-further-into-video

10 Data journalism

Chapter objectives

This chapter will cover:

- Why data journalism is in demand in the news industry
- What data journalism is
- How to come up with data journalism ideas
- Where and how to find data
- How to tell stories with data
- How to clean 'dirty data'
- Data visualisation techniques, types and tools
- The importance of statistical literacy
- Mistakes to avoid in data visualisation.

Introduction

It is extremely difficult to make a mark in the current journalism jobs market. With the biggest employers cutting staff and thousands of graduates competing for new roles, it's fair to say you need every advantage you can get.

So the story of Josh Katz is all the more striking.

While most students spend years trying to get through the doors of the most famous newspapers, the *New York Times asked* Josh Katz to do an internship there. And when he did, he ended up creating the newspaper's most popular piece of content that year – even though it wasn't published until 21 December. When his internship ended, they gave him a job – as a staff editor on a new project.

Why was Josh in such demand? He had data journalism skills. And equally importantly, he had an idea for a project that would end up being shared by millions of users across the US.

'How Y'all, Youse and You Guys Talk' – a data-driven interactive feature based on data about dialects around the US – was launched on the *New York Times* site on 21 December 2013, when most readers were winding down for Christmas. Within ten days millions of users had accessed it – more than any other piece of content in the 355 days before it went live.

Data journalism has the ability to create rockstars. In fact, former *Guardian* data editor Simon Rogers calls it 'the new punk'. In 2012 data journalist Nate Silver, who began writing about baseball data before founding the political data blog FiveThirtyEight, became perhaps its most famous 'star' within the media industry when he started to drive an enormous proportion of traffic to the *New York Times*, who had bought his site. At one point 71 per cent of politics story views were on FiveThirtyEight posts. But the site was also driving traffic across the whole site:

> Earlier this year, approximately 1 percent of visits to the New York Times included FiveThirtyEight. Last week, that number was 13 percent. Yesterday, it was 20 percent. That is, one in five visitors to the sixth-most-trafficked U.S. news site took a look at Silver's blog.
>
> (Tracy 2012)

A year later, after a best-selling book and approaches from the film industry, Silver was poached by ESPN, allowing him to return to his love of sport. 'Nate disrupted the traditional model of how to cover politics', said the *New York Times* public editor Margaret Sullivan (Sullivan 2013). And along the way, like any good punk, he managed to stir up the status quo. 'Punditry is fundamentally useless', he once said (Allen 2012).

What is data journalism?

There are a lot of preconceptions about data journalism. Some people think it is technical, or mathematical, or investigative. In reality, it doesn't have to be any of those things.

The most famous stories of this generation – from the MPs' expenses story in 2009, to WikiLeaks's 2010 Afghanistan and Iraq warlogs and Cablegate, to revelations about extraordinary rendition and torture of terrorism suspects, widespread surveillance and tax evasion – have all been data journalism stories.

But data journalism is also behind everyday reporting, from school league tables to the most popular pet names, from clown crime waves to places to avoid eating. It is used on TV and radio, newspapers and magazines – and, of course, online.

Yes, data journalism can be about statistics and spreadsheets. But data journalism is also used by music journalists, entertainment reporters and new fashion publications. Sometimes the resulting story might not mention any numbers at all. Susanna Kempe of Emap's fashion website WGSN says:

> The fundamental difference is that an old-fashioned publisher is about publishing the past, what has happened, and what we do is all about saying what will happen. And because of that we enable our customers to be successful in the future. It's a dramatic shift.
>
> (Smith 2011)

Data journalism is, basically, any journalism that involves structured information. And when everything is online – from government spending and last month's weather to music sales, fashion gossip, social network connections and sports performances – that basically means the world is your oyster. Here are just a few examples to illustrate how diverse data journalism can be:

- Which singer has the best vocal range in the UK – No, it's not who you think (*Mirror*)
- London fashion week – which colours are always in style? (*Guardian*)
- Why Chelsea FA Youth Cup winners could struggle to make the grade (*Telegraph*)
- Live counter: watch how much NHS money is going into private hands (*Mirror*)
- Revealed: Manchester United have suffered more injuries than any other Premier League side (*Telegraph*)
- What the world eats (*National Geographic*)
- How much energy does the 'greenest government' get through? (*I, Scientist*)
- Universities where students sign up to 'sugar daddy' dating site to pay fees (*Telegraph*)
- Britain's top-selling singles, ranked by beats per minute (*The Times*)
- Has austerity caused more food banks to open? (*Hunger In London*)
- From Poppy to Sherlock: the UK's most popular pet names (*Guardian*)
- Presidents' speeches getting dumb & dumber (Vocativ)
- Prostitution and the internet: more bang for your buck (*The Economist*)
- Nobel Prizes by country since 1901 (Business Insider)
- Holy shrinkage Batman! Your ears are shrinking (Ampp3d)
- The fallen of World War II – data-driven documentary about war and peace (independent)
- 12 charts that explain why you'll never, ever be able to afford a home (BuzzFeed)
- Sex by numbers: how do you measure up? (*Telegraph*)
- Dog map: find the top pooch in your postcode (BBC)
- What the numbers say about who will win at the Oscars (BuzzFeed).

In short, if there's information about it online, you can do data journalism with it. That means not just numbers and statistics, but words and speeches, colours and images, sounds and video and even people's connections with each other.

A brief history of data journalism

Data journalism is not a new thing either. In 1821 data journalism dominated the front page of the very first edition of the *Guardian*: the paper led on a table of school spending in Manchester. And in the US in the late 1840s *New York Tribune* editor Horace Greeley commissioned a piece of data journalism on politicians' travel expenses. Computing power made its initial splash in journalism in 1952 when a UNIVAC computer the size of a garage was used to predict the presidential election for CBS News (quite accurately, as it happened). Then, more significantly, in the 1960s Philip Meyer used social science methods to investigate the causes of riots in Detroit.

Meyer became a pioneer in the field, the author of a seminal work – *Precision Journalism* – and the father of what became known as computer-assisted reporting (CAR). CAR was a precursor to data journalism: its techniques centred largely on working with spreadsheets and databases on your own computer. What changed in the 21st century was that computers became networked, and publishing moved from one-way media like newspapers and TV to the interactivity of the internet. The phrase 'data journalism' – sometimes 'data-driven journalism' – was coined to describe this new and broader method (given that computers were now 'assisting' almost all journalism).

Adrian Holovaty was central to this change, and if there is a year for the birth of modern data journalism it is probably 2005, when Holovaty launched ChicagoCrime.org (although the term was not coined until years later). ChicagoCrime.org combined a number of the qualities of the new method: first, its data gathering was networked, and automated: every weekday, his computer program would go to the Chicago Police Department website and gather all crimes reported in Chicago. Second, the data could be viewed in any way the user wanted: users could browse by crime type, ZIP code and city ward. Third, it was strongly visual: it had a map that people could interact with.

Holovaty himself was influenced by the BBC's Backstage project, which opened up its content for developers to remix. And predating both was the work of MySociety in the UK, which opened up data on the activity of politicians and made it easier to hold power to account – the classic watchdog role of journalism – with projects like TheyWorkForYou, Democracy Club and WhatDoTheyKnow. The site was even threatened with legal action by politicians who didn't like citizens being able to see how they voted.

Getting started with data journalism skills

Data journalism can involve all sorts of skills and people, from those who are good at getting information in the first place, to those who can pull stories out of it (analysis), those who can write the stories, make information visual, or make data interactive.

A diagram showing the various stages that *might* be involved in any data journalism project is shown in Figure 10.1.

DON'T PANIC!

Data journalism can involve a range of skills, from data gathering skills to programming, visualisation and design. But you don't need to use all of those skills all of the time, and most data journalism stories either involve a small number of skills, or a team of people who cover a number of skills between them. There are very few data journalists who have them all. In fact, those people who *do* have all these skills are so rare that they are known in the industry as 'unicorns' (because they don't really exist).

The key with data journalism is to start with simple projects that build different types of skills. For example, creating a 'top ten' table might help you build basic spreadsheet skills, then you might try creating some charts using a free online tool. In another project you might move onto mapping, or you might work with a bigger dataset, or acquire data in a different way.

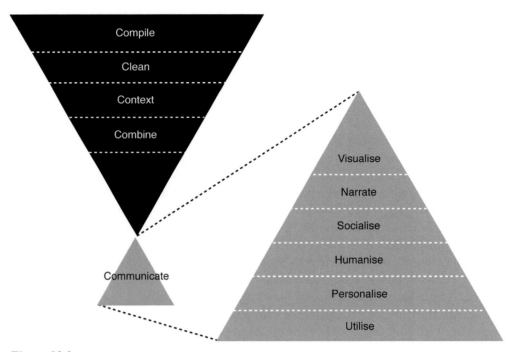

Figure 10.1
The inverted pyramid of data journalism

The main principle is to learn by doing projects that excite you: don't learn tools for the sake of learning tools, or you'll quickly get bored or frustrated. Be driven by your passion.

Coming up with ideas for data-driven journalism

Data journalism ideas start in exactly the same way as every other journalism idea:

- You are either reacting to new information (data)
- Or you have an idea or lead and decide to seek out the information that allows you to write a story about it.

The MPs' expenses stories, for example, were primarily *reactive* data journalism: the *Telegraph* had a disk full of information on expense claims, and needed to find the story in them. The same is true of the WikiLeaks warlogs and diplomatic cables, but also softer, press release-driven stories like 'From Poppy to Sherlock: the UK's most popular pet names' (*Guardian* story based on data supplied by John Lewis pet insurance).

Reactive stories can also come from new data releases: 'Parts of Rhyl and Wrexham remain in top 10 of "most deprived in Wales"', for example, is based on new government data.

More *proactive* data journalism stories tend to start with a question. 'London fashion week – which colours are always in style?' is exactly that: a question. Likewise 'Which singer has the best vocal range in the UK – No, it's not who you think'. Having a hypothesis helps: 'Presidents' speeches getting dumb & dumber' (Fox et al. 2014) is a story that comes from testing a hypothesis – but be prepared to change your hypothesis as you start to look at the evidence (perhaps they started with the hypothesis that speeches were getting more complicated, for example).

Sometimes proactive data journalism begins with someone complaining about something, or an observation of unfairness. The Atlantic story 'In Champaign-Urbana, Illinois, 89% of those arrested for jaywalking are black' is one of those: it is based on a hypothesis that there were disparities between two communities in the number of arrests. Likewise FiveThirtyEight's 'The long migration of English football' looks at whether there has been a move from teams in the north to teams from the south of England dominating the Premier League.

And proactive data journalism often follows up on current news stories: a national announcement about child poverty may be followed up by an analysis of regional data to give readers a local picture of the situation. A sports team struggling in a world cup tournament may be illustrated by a historical overview of their decline over time. A politician's claim about immigration may be factchecked against the reality. In these cases it helps to be able to react quickly.

To come up with a data journalism story idea it is worth trying both approaches:

- To be *reactive* you need to be regularly checking new sources of data, whether that's government data releases, company reports or press releases.
- To be *proactive* you need to be curious about the world around you, and issues that are already in the news.

Stage 1: Finding data

If you want to be alerted when new sources of data are published, there are a range of places that will provide alerts. Typical sources include:

- National and local government
- Bodies that monitor organisations (such as regulators or consumer bodies)
- Scientific and academic institutions
- Health organisations
- Charities and pressure groups
- Business
- The media itself.

In the UK, for example, government statistical releases, research, transparency data and Freedom of Information releases are all published centrally on the gov.uk site's Publications page (gov.uk/government/publications), where you can subscribe to email or RSS alerts based on keywords, categories, information types or a combination of those. For example, if you are interested in sport, media or the arts then it is worth getting updates from the Department for Culture, Media and Sport.

The Office for National Statistics (ONS) provides alerts in its media centre, as well as a release calendar so you can plan ahead, and NHS Digital has a publications calendar too. For other bodies data may be announced in press releases, so it is worth seeing if they provide an alert facility or asking to be added to their mailing list.

Many countries have open data portals such as Data.gov (in the US) and Data.gov.uk, and regions and cities sometimes do too: London's is at data.london.gov.uk and Birmingham's is at data.birmingham.gov.uk.

As well as formal open data portals, watch out for projects that seek to open up data from the outside: OpenCorporates, for example, provides open data on millions of companies around the world. OpenCharities does the same for the charities sector, and OpenOil for the oil industry. OpenDataCommunities.org provides open data on hundreds of local authorities. Try searching for 'open data' and your topic to see if there's a portal providing data.

Try searching for 'disclosure logs' of particular organisations, where they publish Freedom of Information requests and, sometimes, the data provided in response. These not only provide useful data, but also ideas for stories (such as repeating a request a year later) – see p.257.

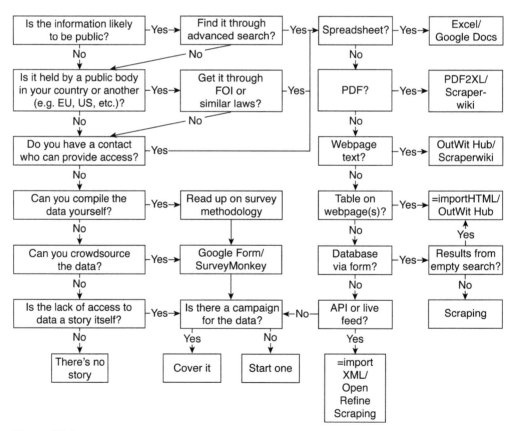

Figure 10.2
Datagathering flowchart

CLOSER LOOK
FREEDOM OF INFORMATION

A great way to get data for exclusive stories is to use the Freedom of Information (FOI) Act 2000 to request information from public bodies including data and documents. The Act covers police and justice, hospitals, GP surgeries and health bodies, schools, colleges and universities, public transport bodies, the military, arts councils, local councils and central government, the BBC and pretty much any organisation run with public money. Bodies have to respond to your request within four weeks, but there are also exemptions, such as if the request would cost too much to fulfil, or it would breach someone's right to privacy.

The online tool WhatDoTheyKnow is particularly useful for FOI: you can submit FOI requests easily through the site, as well as find similar FOI requests and the responses to them. However, your request will be public, so if you don't want other people to see it you can also use the site to find out the relevant email address to send your FOI request to.

Another useful site is FOI Directory (foi.directory), run by Matt Burgess, the author of *Freedom of Information: A Practical Guide for Journalists*. This also lists the email addresses of various public bodies to send FOI requests to, and provides guides and updates on using the law.

When requesting data through an FOI request, it is always useful to specify the format that you wish the information to be supplied in – typically a spreadsheet in electronic format if you want to avoid having to convert PDFs or Word documents. You should also request as much detail as possible: try asking for breakdowns by incident, day, week, or month rather than aggregate totals.

Heather Brooke's book *Your Right to Know* (2007) is also a key reference work in this area, providing guidance on using FOI in different sectors and phrasing your request so it is not refused under one of the exemptions.

Finally, remember that FOI is not the only law you can use to request data. The Data Protection Act 1998 allows you to request data held about yourself (for example, a source could use it to find out what information the police or hospital holds about them), and the Environmental Information Regulations (EIR) allow you to request information from public bodies if it relates to environmental issues.

APIs and unusual data formats

Some organisations will provide data via an 'API' in formats like XML and JSON. API stands for 'Application Programming Interface' and is basically a standardised way for apps to interact with that data. It makes it easier for web developers to write scripts that 'fetch' data from the API and display it in maps, charts or tables whenever someone uses their app or website (many news organisations now have their own APIs to make it easy for people to make apps out of their content).

For journalists, however, it can be hard work. If you are using an API see if there is some option to get all the data in a bulk download. Look for a 'documentation' page, which explains how you can query the API for different bits of data and specify the format you get it in. If the data is in XML or JSON look for online converters that will turn it into a spreadsheet format you can work with (Open Refine is very good for this – see the section on cleaning, p.260).

Ultimately, some APIs are more helpful than others, but if you have a friend or colleague who understands programming, or are willing to learn some yourself, it can make a big difference (see Chapter 11 for more on APIs).

Using search engines to find data

If you are using a search engine to find the data you are looking for, it helps to specify certain things such as the type of file you want (for example, spreadsheet) and the type of domain it is on (for example, government sites). This will ensure your results aren't dominated by news stories that don't contain raw data.

You can do this through using the *advanced search* facility: on Google this is at google.com/advanced_search (or just search for 'Google advanced search') or you can use 'search operators' such as *filetype:* or *site:*. Note that there is no space between the operator and whatever filetype or domain you want to specify.

Here are some examples of how you might use these:

- *Yorkshire schools filetype:xls*
- *"disclosure log" site:ac.uk*
- *alcohol licensing applications site:bolton.gov.uk*
- *"hate crime" site:police.uk filetype:pdf*
- *twins site:nhs.uk filetype:xls*

There's a lot more you can do with search operators, such as specifying words in the URL or title, excluding words and specifying number ranges. See Chapter 3 for more operators. For an extensive guide to Google search see googleguide.com/advanced_operators.html.

Remember that Google only searches a small part of the internet and there may be other search engines that give better results for different searches, or that might search more narrowly. Specialist 'vertical' search engines include Microsoft Academic Search (academic.research.microsoft.com) and Google Scholar (scholar.google.co.uk), which might help you find field experts.

Gathering data yourself

There are two basic approaches you can take in gathering data: compiling it from other sources such as newspaper or other reports (secondary research, as used by the award-winning Migrants Files and the Bureau of Investigative Journalism's Naming the Dead project) or collecting it yourself through methods such as observation or surveys (primary research).

Whichever method you use, you should understand the potential weaknesses in the methodology and seek to address them. The selection, size and generalisability of the sample; the selection and phrasing of questions; the environment; the use of a control group; your own presence; and myriad other factors must be taken into account to ensure that your methods stand up to scrutiny.

Needless to say there are countless books covering research methodology and you should read these if you are to do any research of your own. Even if you don't, they will give you an understanding that will prove very useful in looking at the methods used to gather other data that you might use.

Live data

Sometimes news organisations use live data in their data journalism, particularly in sports and elections, but also sometimes to analyse live feeds from social media to determine what public opinion is like on those platforms, a process called 'sentiment analysis'.

Preparation is key to live data projects: where will you get the data from, and how will you filter it? (Sometimes live data is 'scraped' – see below.) How can you visualise it most clearly? And how do you prevent it being 'gamed' (users intentionally skewing the results for fun or commercial or political reasons)?

Also, if you are using sentiment analysis be aware that it has a number of weaknesses. In particular, it is not an exact science and is not always good at detecting irony or sarcasm ('Oh what a brilliant shot that was'). You should also be careful not to suggest that public sentiment on one social media platform is the same as public opinion (not only are social media users not representative of the wider population, but people may not say things in public that they might express in a private survey). Any coverage should make these weaknesses clear and be careful that results are not presented as representative of the general public.

CLOSER LOOK
SCRAPING

'Scraping' is the process of automatically gathering information from webpages or online documents. It can be especially useful in data journalism because it allows you to combine data from potentially thousands of webpages into one easy-to-analyse spreadsheet. Data that would otherwise take weeks to compile can be compiled for you – and updated regularly.

The technique was used for the *Mirror*'s article 'Which singer has the best vocal range in the UK?': a scraper was used to gather information from over 260,000 sheet music arrangements on the site musicnotes.com, and then identify the highest and lowest note for each artist. It was also used by the Bureau of Investigative Journalism to gather figures on rape convictions from over 80 police reports.

To scrape information it must be in a consistent format. So, for example, results from searching a database can be scraped because each page of results has the same structure, but profile pages on different council websites cannot, because each site will use its own way of presenting that information.

For more challenging scrapers you will need to learn some basic programming, but there are also a number of tools which will scrape websites for you without any programming knowledge. These include OutWit Hub and Import.io.

Stage 2: Cleaning data

Data can suffer from all sorts of problems that make it 'dirty data': it might be misspellings or variations in spelling, odd punctuation, mixtures of numbers and letters, unnecessary columns or rows, duplication or anything else. Because you are trusting a computer to perform calculations for you, you need to check that it understands things the same way you do: a computer, for example, will see 'New Town', 'Newtown' and 'newtown' as three separate towns when they may be one.

Even simple changes to your data can make a big difference. Spreadsheet software, for example, assumes that your headings are in your first row: deleting unnecessary rows before those headings and making sure the headings only fill one row can help with analysis. Likewise, Excel will assume any empty row is the end of one table, and will only sort, filter or calculate up to that point. Removing empty rows solves that problem.

The more detailed your data, the more likely that it will need some form of cleaning. If each town only appears once, for example, then there's no opportunity for confusion. But if each town is named multiple times there is scope for it being mistyped (if the data has been manually entered by someone).

Some tips for cleaning your data include:

- Use a spellchecker to check for misspellings. You will probably have to add some words to the computer's dictionary.
- Use 'find and replace' (normally in the Edit menu) to remove double spaces and other common punctuation errors.
- Remove duplicate entries – if you are using Excel there are a few ways to do this under the Data tab – search for duplicates in Help. Sorting can also help identify these.
- Watch out for extra spaces at the beginning and end of text; they are often easy to miss and may prevent matching in some programs.
- Sort your data by any numerical columns from largest to smallest: look out for unusually small or large numbers that may be errors (for example, a decimal place is in the wrong position).

Some aspects of cleaning are more about formatting. For example, if you have a full address or name in one column and want to split it into separate columns, try using the 'Text to columns' option under the Data menu.

Cleaning tools

For cleaning challenges that take up a lot of time it is worth exploring a dedicated cleaning tool like Open Refine (openrefine.org). Open Refine (formerly Google Refine) is particularly useful when you create a new project and select your dataset: in the preview stage you can choose to merge heading rows, ignore initial rows, remove empty rows and even merge sheets or files (select more than one when creating the project).

Once the data is imported you can perform 'common transforms' such as removing double spaces and inconsistent formatting across an entire dataset, but Open Refine also has a 'cluster and edit' option which will identify entries that are similar (such as the New Town/Newtown/newtown example above), and mass-edit them. If you're willing to learn more advanced techniques you can perform customised transformations on cells, such as splitting on certain characters or creating new columns based on existing data.

Learning Open Refine and associated cleaning techniques is one of the most underrated aspects of data journalism: a little time dedicated to learning these techniques can save you an enormous amount of time and manual work later on. You can find various tutorials on Open Refine at onlinejournalismblog.com/tag/google-refine.

Also useful in this respect is the tool DataWrangler (vis.stanford.edu/wrangler), although it is no longer supported.

Converting PDFs and other files

Part of cleaning may involve converting PDFs or other documents into spreadsheet format. Again you can find various tools that will perform this for you. Tabula (tabula. technology), for example, was designed by journalists to help extract tables from inside PDFs, and PDFtoExcelOnline.com offers free PDF conversion up to a certain limit. If you have Adobe Acrobat you may be able to use that to do larger conversions; otherwise you can buy PDF conversion software from companies such as Wondershare, Nitro and iSkysoft.

Stage 3: Questioning and contextualising data

> More than 12,000 flight plans were now stored in my computer. I was trying to narrow things down – find the pattern that lurked beneath all this data and the identity of the CIA's planes that might be involved in rendition. When I started my investigation, I had almost no information but now I was almost swamped. I turned to a software programme called Analyst's Notebook, a tool used normally by the police or intelligence organisations to solve complex financial crimes or even murders. Its job was to find connections within exactly such a mass of data.
>
> (Grey 2006, p.107)

Once you have the data in front of you it can be easy to be overwhelmed by the possibilities: typically any dataset will have many different stories in it, and it may be tempting to start looking at one, only to be distracted by another, and then another, and before you know it a whole afternoon has passed you by.

For example, say you obtain a dataset showing every callout by police to educational establishments in the country. The data shows when the callout was made, what sort of crime was involved (e.g. assault, drugs, theft), the type of institution (school, college or university), its name and the police force involved. Here are just some of the stories you could tell:

- 'Police called out 300 times in a year to school X'
- 'University X worst in country for police callouts'
- 'Police callouts to colleges for drug crimes double in a year'
- 'Violent assault tops the table of police callouts to schools'.

So before you begin questioning your data, decide what the most important *newsworthy* aspect of the data is *for your audience*. A number of factors will influence this: if a particular issue is topical, or something has happened recently, that may decide it. If one story is likely to be less surprising than another, drop it in favour of the more surprising. You might also choose to explore more easily answered questions first, before tackling more challenging ones.

In the stories listed above, for example, it is perhaps more surprising to hear about police callouts to schools than to universities or colleges, so we might decide to focus on that. And looking for the worst schools is more concrete than identifying broader trends. Make sure you stay focused on finishing that particular story before you move on to others.

Of course once you have the main story you can always look for other details to provide background to that: we might lead on the fact that one particular school has a lot of police callouts, but later on in the piece mention that callouts generally have halved, or doubled, or that theft is on the increase but drug crimes are dropping.

Asking the questions

You can ask questions of data in a number of ways:

- By sorting and filtering it
- By using 'wizards' such as a pivot table
- By using functions and formulae.

Sorting and filtering your data will tell you simple stories such as who's top and bottom, in which categories. It is relatively easy to do: to filter, go to the Data menu and select the filter button. Drop-down menus should appear at the top of each column which you can now use to filter on any of those.

Sorting is also done within the Data menu. If you are sorting make sure that you haven't selected a whole column first or it might try to sort *just that column* which will mix all the data up (you don't want this: you want to sort all the data, but based on the values in one column). All you need to do is make sure you select one of the cells in your data, and the program will detect the rest.

If you need to aggregate data into a number of entries or total amounts by a particular category or name (which can then be sorted), then pivot tables are the best way to do this (assuming you have adequately detailed data). Make sure you are somewhere in your data and then select pivot table in the Insert menu (or the Data menu). A new sheet will be created with an empty table. You then fill this table with the things you are interested in (put those in the Rows area) and what aspect you want to calculate about those (put these in the Values area and then customise whether it calculates a total sum, count of entries, average or something else). For more about pivot tables see the ebook *Data Journalism Heist* (leanpub.com/DataJournalismHeist).

All other questions can usually be asked using formulae. These always begin with an equals sign and normally refer to cells in your spreadsheet like so:

$$=SUM(A2:A300)$$

The word SUM in that formula is called a 'function'. Spreadsheet software has hundreds of functions that perform all sorts of tasks, from adding up numbers (which is what SUM does), to calculating averages (AVERAGE and MEDIAN), counting how many entries there are (COUNT and COUNTA), testing whether a cell is blank (ISBLANK) or a particular type of value, or whether it meets a particular criteria (IF). Functions can also be used to extract data from cells (such as particular characters) and clean them up, and they can also be used to combine data (VLOOKUP). For a full guide to using spreadsheet functions to find stories, see the ebook *Finding Stories in Spreadsheets* (leanpub.com/spread sheetstories).

CLOSER LOOK
QUICKLY GENERATING AVERAGES AND PERCENTAGES USING SPREADSHEETS

Spreadsheet packages can save you a lot of time as a journalist. Excel and the free spreadsheet software Google Sheets can quickly generate an average or percentage from sheets of numbers using formulae.

To calculate a percentage divide the whole by the part. For example, if you want to find out what proportion 10 is out of 100, the formula would be =10/100.

The result is normally shown as a decimal: 0.1. You can format this to display as a percentage (10%) by clicking the % button – or you can right click on the cell and select Format cells . . . then choose *percentage* from the options given.

Most formulae in Excel use cell references rather than actual numbers. The formula looks to see what values are in those cells, and uses them to perform a calculation. For example, if you wanted to divide the number in cell B2 by the total in C2 to get a percentage, the formula would be:

$$=B2/C2$$

To calcuate a percentage change, you need to first work out the *change* (new figure minus older figure) and then divide that change by the older figure. For example, if sales of a particular outfit increased from 100 to 110 then the change is 10 (110–100). Divide that change by the older figure (100) to get the percentage change: in this case, 0.1 again, or 10 per cent.

Another useful tool to play with is spreadsheet *functions*. To see how a function works create a new spreadsheet with two columns: column A called 'Name' and column B called 'Age'. Fill those columns with the names and ages of ten people that you know (try to use a wide range of people with different ages).

In a separate cell type the following formula:

=AVERAGE(B2:B11)

This will generate a mean average from all the numbers between cells B2 and B11. B is the first column; the number 2 refers to the row: you can adapt these cell references to different cells when your data covers a different range. Now in another cell try this:

=MEDIAN(B2:B11)

This will give you the median (middle) value of all the numbers in those cells.

Try sorting the data by the age column to order the names by age. Try sorting by name, too.

To find formulae for other calculations use a search engine to search for the phrase 'spreadsheet function' followed by the sort of action you want to perform. For example, 'spreadsheet function calculate average' or 'spreadsheet function rank values'.

Putting the data into context

One of the most important things to look for in your data is *what isn't in it*. For example, if we are looking at police callouts to schools the one piece of data that's missing is the number of pupils at each school. Without that information we might simply be highlighting the fact that schools with more pupils call the police out more often: not because it is a troublesome school, but simply because there are more people who might become involved in something that requires the police.

Similarly, whenever you are dealing with absolute figures you can expect that the biggest areas will generally have the most of anything. In the UK, for example, Birmingham is by far the biggest local authority in the country, so when it topped a table for the most CCTV cameras it was no surprise at all. What was surprising was that nearby Sandwell Council had the most CCTV cameras *per person*. And when it comes to policing, the Metropolitan Police will generally be spending the most and dealing with the most crimes.

Having basic data to hand – the populations for every local authority or police force, or the number of students at each university or school – will help you put that information into context quickly.

If you need to convert total figures into numbers per person then the calculation is easy: total events (crimes, callouts, etc.) divided by the relevant population (pupils, residents, etc.). You can do this manually but there are ways to combine the data more easily (see p.266).

Correlation is not causation

When first starting out on data journalism many people try to establish the *causes* of things. You should avoid doing this unless you are very confident with statistics, because it is very difficult to do, and easy to get wrong.

The main problem is that just because two things happen together, you cannot prove that they are related. If there are a lot of crashes near speed cameras does that mean that the cameras have failed? Or was that the reason why they were put up in the first place? If there's a lot of crime near schools with high levels of poverty, does that mean that the poverty is causing the crime, or vice versa (only wealthy people can afford to move out)? Or are both caused by a third, unmeasured variable?

Normally to establish causation you need to be able to control various factors (called variables), and typically journalists cannot do that.

So by all means report the facts – that there is a lot of crime near schools with high levels of poverty, or crashes near speed cameras – but don't speculate on cause and effect unless you can back that up to a statistician. And always seek to quote an expert who can provide some factual context.

CLOSER LOOK
BIG DATA

Work in data journalism and you'll probably come across the phrase 'big data'. There's very little agreement on just how 'big' a dataset needs to be to be classified as big data, but it is often used to refer to data that represents all users of a particular service rather than a sample.

One of the major issues of big data is that it will be too big to analyse in standard spreadsheet software like Excel. Instead you will need to use a query language like SQL to 'ask questions' of the data file (rather than opening it), or create a filtered subset of the data (for example, a specific time period or location), which is then small enough to analyse in a spreadsheet.

Another major issue with big data is the potential to identify correlations that are misleading. Put another way, if you have lots of different pieces of information, it's much more likely that you'll find connections between them. But it's also much more likely that you'll find 'false positives': connections that are merely coincidental (called the multiple comparisons problem).

CLOSER LOOK
STATISTICS

If you're dealing with numbers it is important to have some basic statistical literacy. Averages are a good starting point: what is an average? Well there are three types of average: the *mean* is what you get when you add up all values and divide by the number of people, organisations or events involved. But mean averages can be misleading: an average wage might be skewed by a few very big earners at the top. The *median* is a much better average when dealing with man-made figures: this is the mid-point at which half of values are higher, and half are lower. Finally, there is the *mode*: the most commonly occurring value, useful to identify best-sellers.

If you are not clear what type of average someone is talking about, ask the person who has supplied the data.

Another useful term to understand is *margin of error*. This indicates how accurate the data is: for example, if someone says that the number of people unemployed in your town is 14,000 but the margin of error is plus/minus 2000, then that means the real figure could be anywhere from 12,000 to 16,000.

The reason for this is that some statistics are based on *samples*: the larger and more representative the sample, the more accurate the results are going to be when generalised to the wider population. But it is still generalising, and that introduces room for error. In fact, even the margin of error is typically only the range within which the survey is expected to be right 19 times out of 20.

For an accessible read on the subject see Darrell Huff's *How to Lie With Statistics* (1991) or Ben Goldacre's *Bad Science* (2008) and blog (badscience.net).

If you are in any doubt about your figures you should double-check your findings wherever possible with statisticians in the field you're covering. The Royal Statistical Society has local groups you can speak to, and regular events and projects to help improve statistical literacy in reporting.

Stage 4: Combining data

There may be a number of reasons for combining data: you may need to put figures into context, for example, by adding populations to your data. You may have been given codes in one dataset, and need to combine it with another dataset that explains what those codes mean. Or you may want to combine spreadsheet data with a map to create a visualisation or mashup (see the section on visualisation below, p.270).

If you need to combine data in a project, and there's lots of it to combine, one common way to do so is spreadsheets' VLOOKUP function. This 'looks up' a particular value (for example, a school name) and brings back data associated with it (for example, its pupil numbers). Another method is to use Google Fusion Tables' 'Merge tables' option. You will find tutorials on both approaches online.

To merge data the two datasets you wish to combine will need a common 'field' (column). Normally this might be the name of the organisation, institution or area that both have in common (for example, the column of school names or police forces).

But because names are often slightly different in different datasets (a police force might be called Avon and Somerset in one but Avon & Somerset in the other) you may get some gaps, and need to fix those manually after the initial automatic combining. For that reason, if you have ID codes in both sets, these are often better fields to match on.

CLOSER LOOK
MASHUPS

Sometimes when data is combined online it is called a 'mashup'. Wikipedia defines a mashup as 'a web page or application that uses or combines data or functionality from two or many more external sources to create a new service'. Those sources may be online spreadsheets or tables, maps, RSS feeds (which could be anything from blog posts or news articles to images, video, audio or search results) or anything else that is structured enough to 'match' against another source.

This 'match' is typically what makes a mashup. It might be matching a city mentioned in a news article against the same city in a map (to show those news stories on a map); or it may be matching the name of an author with that same name in the tags of a photo; or matching the search results for 'earthquake' from a number of different sources. The results can be useful to you as a journalist, to the user or both.

One quick way to get playing with mashups is to mix two maps together using the website *MapTube* (maptube.org) which also contains a number of maps for you to play with. But if you want to create your own it's likely you'll need to learn about programming and APIs (see Chapter 11).

PAMELA DUNCAN, THE *GUARDIAN*

Ask a room full of journalists why they chose their job and you will get multiple answers. One response you're very unlikely to hear, however, is 'because I just love working with numbers'.

I, like many others, am an accidental data journalist. My first data story was a 2011 piece about the pension lump sums and termination payments due to members of the outgoing Irish government. To write the story we had to work out, using a rather complicated set of guidelines, how much each would receive. The resulting story showed that outgoing TDs (the Irish equivalent of MPs) would receive €13m in goodbye money and €4.2m in recurring annual pensions thereafter, and listed each politician's individual payout. I may not have realised at the time that it was a data story. But I had been bitten by the data bug and I have been using data to tell stories ever since.

Having started working as a data journalist with the *Irish Times* I moved to the *Guardian* in November 2015. Since then I have covered a diverse range of topics from Brexit to the dispersion of asylum seekers around the UK, from perception gaps to the gender gap, from electroconvulsive therapy to a major NHS data loss.

All these stories have something in common. They were all written using one or a combination of the following building blocks:

1   **Straight data:** Pulling existing data from reliable sources which are then analysed.
2   **Requesting and/or building datasets:** For example, using multiple Freedom of Information requests (a word of warning on this one: it's vital to balance the time it is likely to take against the importance of the story you'll get back).
3   **Scraping:** Coding can be a great asset to a data journalist. Scraping – using code to pull down data programatically – is one of its most common uses in data journalism.
4   **Cleaning:** Like it or not part of being a data journalist involves cleaning up the errors that find their way into datasets.
5   **Visualisation:** Being able to create your own visualisations helps you identify the news angles in your dataset, helps the news desk because you can quickly identify suitable graphics, and helps your story because you can rid your text of excessive numbers.
6   **Attention to detail:** Remember that all the tools you use are only as good as the person entering/analysing the data so it is key that you check, check and check again.

But even just learning the basics in Excel will get you far. I ❤ Excel. In my opinion every journalist should learn to love it too. Why? Because it can help us all conquer our dislike of numbers and make us better journalists.

Stage 5: Communicating the story

When it comes to telling data journalism stories most people immediately think of data visualisation – but there are other ways to tell the story too. These include:

- Write the story
- Bring it to life on screen or in audio
- Create something that is personalised to the user
- Create a social experience (such as a crowdsourcing exercise, or the ability for others to make things with your data)
- Create a tool that people can actually use.

It's important to think about which method suits the story best, which one will work for your audience and which one is practically achievable.

Narrating: writing a story that uses data

The simplest way to tell a data story is to just *write* it. Data stories fill newspapers and magazines every day, from short updates (such as the BBC's #BBCgofigure social media data stories) to longform features. Visual illustration helps, but it may not be the focus.

When writing up a data story, try to make the numbers relevant. Avoid shouting about big numbers which have no context. One news story, for example, reported on the Metropolitan Police spending £35,000 on the speaking clock in two years. But is that a lot? Not much? (Actually it only works out as each officer calling the clock once or twice each year). The 'big number' story is often a last resort for the reporter who has not much of a story at all.

Instead, try to write about numbers in concrete terms that people can imagine. When the *Mirror* wrote about the NHS 'wasting £25 million a year by paying over the odds for basic supplies like toilet rolls and syringes' they led on the fact that 'Saving on loo rolls would pay for 700 nurses' (Hayward 2014b). Another story about parking charges generating £3.9 million for hospitals ran under the headline 'Nurses charged almost £200 a month just to park their cars at work' (Hayward 2014a): now that's something we can imagine and relate to. And when the *Evening Standard* wrote about attacks by prisoners on wardens they led on the five attacks every day rather than the 4000 attacks in the previous two years. Why? Because we can *feel* those five attacks much more than we can 4000.

A good data story should also have more than just numbers. You should seek out quotes too: if it's a critical story you should certainly seek a response to the figures (they might point out a mistake that you've made, but don't take their word for it!); if it affects real people let's hear from them; and if it needs contextualising by an expert, ask them too.

Humanising: finding case studies

If your story has victims, and their stories are compelling, then be prepared to put the data into the background and focus on the victims. Strong case studies can bring a data story to life in a way that the numbers will not, and sometimes the data is just a way of identifying who is particularly affected, and establishing that they are not an isolated case.

If you can get them on camera or on audio, consider telling your story using multimedia. This is how broadcast media tell data stories: by starting with the person, and then filling in the facts.

In short, the case study tells us why we should *care*, then the data tells us why this *matters*.

Making data journalism social

As a raw material, data can be extremely social. Users may want to create and share new things with it, whether that's a chart drilling down to a particular aspect of the data, or an impressive infographic or map. The *Guardian* datablog, for example, maintains a Flickr photo pool where users can share visualisations they have made with *Guardian* (or any other) data.

Users may also be affected by the issues represented in the data, and want to contribute their story to your reporting. When the Center for Investigative Reporting, for example, pulled together data on the backlog of disability benefit claims for armed forces veterans, they also appealed to veterans willing to 'share your experience applying for disability benefits' to take a few minutes to fill out a form to tell reporters more.

Because social distribution is such a major part both of publishing and newsgathering, it is important to think about the social dimension of your story, and whether to share the data that underpins it. Ultimately you stand to benefit not only from more readers, but also users volunteering their analysis, technical skills and personal experiences. What have you got to lose?

CLOSER LOOK
HOW TO PUBLISH A SPREADSHEET ONLINE

Google Drive (drive.google.com) is a free website which allows you to create and share documents. You can share them via email, by publishing them as a webpage or by embedding your document in another webpage, such as a blog post. This is how you share a spreadsheet:

1   Open your spreadsheet in Google Drive (sheets.google.com).
2   Click on File > Publish to the web . . .
3   A new window should appear giving you some options. You can publish the entire document, or just one sheet, for example; and you can publish as a link to the live document, or get code to embed it. Click 'Publish' (you should also make sure '*Automatically republish when changes are made*' is ticked if you want the public version of the spreadsheet to update with any data you add or delete).
4   Now a link should appear in the middle of that window. If you want to share that, copy the address and test that it works in a web browser. You can now link to it from any webpage.
5   Alternatively, you can switch to the Embed tab to get the code to embed your spreadsheet in a webpage. Copy this and paste it into the HTML of a webpage or blog post to embed it (embedding may not work on some third party blog hosting services, such as Wordpress.com).

Another alternative is to create a HTML table using a service like Tableizer (tableizer. journalistopia.com). All you have to do is copy the data you want to put in that table (including headings), then paste it into the box on Tableizer. Click 'Tableize it!' and you will be given HTML that can be copied and pasted into a blog post or article.

Data visualisation

At their best, graphics are instruments for reasoning about quantitative information. Often the most effective way to describe, explore, and summarize a set of numbers – even a very large set – is to look at pictures of those numbers.

(Tufte 2001, p.9)

Data visualisation is so widely associated with data journalism that often the two are assumed to be the same thing. But while you can do data journalism without the visualisation, it is much harder to do visualisation without data journalism.

Broadly speaking there are two typical reasons for visualising data: to find a story, or to tell one. Quite often, it is both.

In one example, designer Adrian Short obtained information (via an FOI request) on parking tickets from Transport for London that showed the number of tickets issued against a particular offence plummeted from around 8000 to 8 in the space of one month. But the drop only became obvious when Short turned the raw data into a stacked area chart.

Data visualisation can take a variety of forms, from traditional bar charts, pie charts, line graphs and maps to more striking formats such as coxcomb diagrams, network graphs and treemaps and new formats such as word clouds.

In larger organisations the data journalist may work with a graphic artist to produce the visuals that illustrate their story – but in smaller teams, in the initial stages of a story, or when speed is of the essence they are likely to need to use visualisation tools to give form to their data.

The key to successful data visualisation is to be clear what sort of story you are trying to tell: opting for fancy impressive chart types is pointless if the charts don't actually *work*. In journalistic terms, it's the equivalent of using long fancy words just to impress people, while everyone is confused about what you're actually saying.

Broadly speaking there are four types of stories you may want to tell with charts:

1   Stories about composition: for example, '95% of spending goes on party conference'
2   Stories about comparison: for example, 'Manchester attracting more tourists than Birmingham'
3   Stories about relationships: for example, 'Larger schools see more police callouts'
4   Stories about distribution: for example, 'Police callouts peak at 9pm'.

As you can see, the last two categories make for stories that are less concrete and harder to tell (and when it comes to relationships you are touching on issues about correlation vs causation, so be careful). For that reason, most stories are either about composition or comparison.

Different types of visualisation fit different story types, for example:

•   Stories about composition can be told with pie charts or tree maps. Or if it is composition over time, stacked area charts. Composition of words can be communicated with a word cloud.
•   Stories about comparison can be told with bar charts or column charts. If the story makes a comparison over time, a line chart works well. If the comparison is geographical, a map may work.
•   Stories about relationships can be told through scatter charts or bubble charts. Network diagrams can also be used to show relationships between actors in a network.
•   Stories about distribution can also be told through scatter charts, or histograms. If the distribution is geographical, maps can work well.

In some cases your visualisation may *not* be trying to tell a story, but instead helping the user to find it (in other words, the visualisation is exploratory). In this case, again make sure that it is the best chart for that purpose. For example, maps work particularly well for finding 'outliers' in data where distance is not obvious: Tony Hirst, for example, used a map to visualise MPs' travel expenses, allowing him to spot MPs who were claiming more than their near neighbours, but not necessarily showing up as big claimers overall. The general principle when designing such visualisations is 'Overview first, filter, then zoom', meaning that it should provide an overview of the whole, but then the facility for a user to filter and zoom in to more details on something of interest.

Once created, a useful framework for checking your visualisation is Kaiser Fung's 'Trifecta Checkup' to help clarify visualisations.

1   What is the practical question?
2   What does the data say?
3   What does the chart say?

He writes: 'All outstanding charts have all three elements in harmony. Typically, a problematic chart gets only two of the three pieces right' (Fung 2010).

CLOSER LOOK
TIPS FROM A PRO: DAVID MCCANDLESS

David McCandless is a writer and designer and author of the books *Information is Beautiful* (2010) and *Knowledge is Beautiful* (2014). His work has appeared in the *Guardian*, the *Independent* and *Wired* magazine. These are his five tips for visualising data:

1   Double source data wherever possible – even the UN and World Bank can make mistakes.
2   Take information out – there's a long tradition among statistical journalists of showing *everything*. All data points. The whole range. Every column and row. But stories are about clear threads with extraneous information fuzzed out. And journalism is about telling stories. You can only truly do that when you mask out the irrelevant or the minor data. The same applies to design, which is about reducing something to its functional essence.
3   Avoid standard abstract units – tons of carbon, billions of dollars – these kinds of units are overused and impossible to imagine or relate to. Try to rework or process units down to 'everyday' measures. Try to give meaningful context for huge figures whenever possible.
4   Self-sufficency – all graphs, charts and infographics should be self-sufficient. That is, you shouldn't require any other information to understand them. They're like interfaces. So each should have a clear title, legend, source, labels, etc. And credit yourself. I've seen too many great visuals with no credit or name at the bottom.
5   Show your workings – transparency seems like a new front for journalists. Google Drive makes it incredibly easy to share your data and thought processes with readers, who can then participate.

Utilisation: making tools from data

Increasingly, data-driven journalism is not just about telling stories but is making products that people can use, from searchable databases to apps. This is such a large area that we'll need a whole new chapter to explore it – you'll find this covered in Chapter 11.

Charts

One of the basic principles of data visualisation is to avoid using 3D effects: these not only add unnecessary visual information but it can actively distort the chart. Tilting a pie chart, for example, makes the slice furthest away smaller than it should be (because of perspective).

Although pie charts are perhaps the most commonly used chart, they are also the most commonly *misused*, and one of the least effective. This is because comparing the slices of a pie chart is sometimes harder than, say, comparing different columns in a column chart, or slices in a treemap (a treemap is a rectangular pie chart).

For this reason you should avoid having too many slices (stick to five or less by focusing on the top five, or grouping together 'the rest' into a separate category), and avoid bar charts where the slices are too similar in size. If you can create a treemap instead, then that is often preferable.

Generally, avoid trying to pass on too much information in a single chart. Remember that you can always use more than one chart, or combine them into an infographic. Staci Baird, for example, compares graphics' role to that of headlines and photos in attracting readers, while warning that 'overly complex graphics will quickly convince readers to ignore your article' (Baird 2010).

Colour is another area where simplicity is best: avoid the 'rainbow effect' of using a different colour for every part of the chart. Use a strong eye-catching colour for your 'story' data point (for example, the column, line or slice that your story focuses on) and a less striking colour for all the other points. In a column or bar chart you can give the same colour to all the other columns as long as they are labelled; in a line or pie chart try different shades of the same colour, or semi-opaque colours.

And finally, be careful about scale: always have a baseline of zero on pie charts, and think carefully about baselines on line charts. Starting from other points can be misleading (for example, making differences look more pronounced than they actually are).

The Wall Street Journal Guide to Information Graphics (Wong 2010) offers a wealth of tips on elements to consider and mistakes to avoid in both visualisation and data research. Here are just a selection:

- 'Choose the best data series to illustrate your point.'
- 'Filter and simplify the data to deliver the essence of the data to your intended audience.'
- 'Make numerical adjustments to the raw data to enhance your point, e.g. absolute values vs percentage change.'
- 'Choose the appropriate chart settings, e.g. scale, y-axis increments and baseline.'

- 'If the raw data is insufficient to tell the story, do not add decorative elements. Instead, research additional sources and adjust data to stay on point.'
- 'Data is only as good as its source. Getting data from reputable and impartial sources is critical. For example, data should be benchmarked against a third party to avoid bias and add credibility.'
- 'In the research stage, a bigger data set allows more in-depth analysis. In the edit phase, it is important to assess whether all your extra information buries the main point of the story or enhances [it].'

There are many, many tools for creating online charts. Google Sheets allows you to create charts that can then be embedded on webpages. Datawrapper.de was created by a German journalist as a very quick way for reporters to create basic charts. Tableau Public is more powerful – which means it takes longer to learn – but does give you many more options and more control. You can also use infographic tools like Infogr.am to create charts and add extra detail.

If you want particularly impressive or interactive charts, it is worth exploring JavaScript. D3 is one of the best-known JavaScript 'libraries' (basically a collection of commands) for making interactive charts, and certainly covers many chart types. Factmint.com does all the basic charts and is a particularly easy way to get started with JavaScript. If you find a chart you particularly want to create then look for a JavaScript library dedicated to that type of chart.

Remember also that you can use photography creatively to represent numbers. For the data visualisation project '100 Years of World Cuisine' (visual.ly/100-years-of-world-cuisine), for example, a collection of containers were each filled with a volume of tomato juice to represent the casualties in each war, and the resulting scene was photographed by Marion Kotlarski.

Maps

As soon as people get hold of geographical data, they want to map it. But just because you have some geographical data doesn't mean you *should* map it.

Here's why: maps, like all methods of visualisation, are designed for a purpose. They tell *particular types of stories* well – but not all of them.

There is also more than one type of map:

- Mapping with points is where each row in your dataset is given a location on your map. For example, if you were mapping businesses' food hygiene inspections then a pointer would be placed at the location of each business.
- You can create heat maps to indicate the density of points.
- You can create route maps to indicate connections between points.
- Mapping with shapes is where each row in your data relates to a particular *region*: this might be where your data relates to police forces, health bodies, local authorities or countries. Often shapes are coloured to indicate a value: these are called choropleth maps.

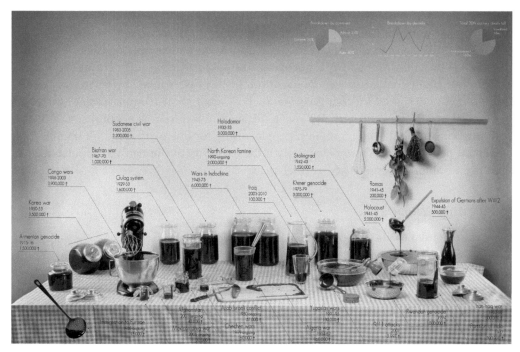

Figure 10.3
'100 Years of World Cuisine'
Source: Marion Kotlarski. Project: Clara KayserBril, Nicolas KayserBril and Marion Kotlarski

The key rule is this: make sure you are clear what story you are trying to tell, or the story that users will try to find. The test is if a map does that job best.

As with charts there are a range of online tools which you can use to create maps: Carto and Google Fusion Tables are perhaps the most widely used in the industry, and both can map with points or shapes, or create heat maps. Tableau Public will also create maps. BatchGeo is particularly quick and easy to use if you want to map fewer than a couple of hundred points, and of course you can use Google Maps itself to create a custom map.

At a more advanced level there are tools like ArcGIS and Mapbox, or JavaScript mapping libraries like Raphael, Kartograph and Leaflet.js.

Mapping points and heatmaps

To map points you will need as precise a description of locations as possible. Ideally this should be a latitude and longitude; if you have postcodes you can find tools online that will convert those into latitude and longitude references: bear in mind that these will not be exact and you may need to clarify that they are only indicative of general location. Beware of placenames which also exist elsewhere: for example, there is a Cambridge, Massachusetts as well as a Cambridge, England.

As with charts, you want to avoid using too many different colours or shapes for markers: try to keep colour coding as simple as possible, and avoid using markers or size for information that's already communicated through colour.

Heatmaps are useful where you do not want to indicate specific points (for example, for privacy reasons) or want to indicate general concentration rather than specifics.

In some cases, a map will not be the right approach: for example, if users cannot find themselves on a map or the story is not about the visible distribution or clustering of those points, but about comparison or composition. In this case you are better using a visualisation device designed for that purpose, such as a bar chart (comparison) or pie chart (composition). A map can actually give a misleading impression of comparison due to varying population density: 5 million people voting for one party can look smaller than 1 million people voting for another party if the 5 million live in densely populated cities and the 1 million are spread across rural areas.

Mapping shapes

Shapes are harder to 'draw' than points on a map. This is because shapes are actually data too: a description of the coordinates and paths needed to draw each shape. As a result, drawing a map with shapes invariably involves merging data: your data about those places, and the data containing the descriptions of those shapes.

This second set of data is often called 'shape files'. The mapping tool OpenHeatMap, for example, has a number of shape files stored in its database, including shapes for countries, US states and UK constituencies and authorities. This means that you can upload your own data and mix it with those shapes to generate maps that combine the two: shapes coloured according to a specified field in your data.

You can also merge your data with shape files using Google Fusion Tables or Carto. Both use a language called KML (Keyhole Markup Language) to describe shapes. Once you upload your own data to Google Fusion Tables you can go to *File > Find a table to merge with* . . . and search all other public tables that share some information (for example, the name of the regions).

The final option is to draw the shapes yourself. In Google Maps Engine Lite once you have drawn your maps (shapes, points or routes) you can export as KML – then import when creating a new Fusion Table.

There's also another option that doesn't involve shape files at all: you can find an image showing all the regions you need, then edit it in image editing software or create an image map (see Chapter 11 for more).

Colouring map shapes

When choosing to colour-code shapes in a map it is a good idea to use a tool like Colorbrewer (colorbrewer2.org) to help you choose the colour palette. This will suggest colour combinations that work for users who are colour-blind, and also suit the type of data you are showing (ordinal, for example). Consider making shapes semi-transparent so the detail underneath can still be seen.

Word clouds

If you are working with text rather than numbers there are ways to visualise that as well. Word clouds, for instance, show which words are used most often in a particular document (such as a speech, bill or manifesto). This can be particularly useful in drawing out the themes of a politician's speech, for example, or the reaction from people online to a particular event.

Word clouds work best when more than one is used to draw comparisons: they have been used in the past to compare the inaugural speeches of different presidents, or the election manifestos of different parties.

Word cloud tools include Wordle, Tagxedo and Tagul. But remember you can also use bar charts to compare frequencies – often with more clarity. Word frequency tools like Wordcounter.com will tell you how many times each word is used, which you can then use in a chart.

Network diagrams

Network diagrams show relationships between different entities: these might be people, companies, bands or anything else. Based on *network analysis* they can be very useful in showing power relationships. Channel 4's Who Knows Who project, for example, used network diagrams to show 'the connections between politicians, celebrities and business leaders, and where power really lies in the UK'. Similar ideas have been developed by They Rule in the US (theyrule.net), Who Runs HK in Hong Kong and Reuters's project Connected China.

Tools for creating network diagrams are harder to learn than basic chart tools. Google Fusion Tables and Kumu are perhaps the easiest, while Gephi is one of the most widely used (and the one you can find most tutorials for).

Infographics

Infographics combine various elements of visualisation into a coherent whole. In addition, an infographic typically adds typographical elements to highlight key figures, or illustrate the facts with quotes from case studies or experts.

The key challenge when creating an infographic is to combine those elements in a way that is not overwhelming or confusing. For that reason it helps to have basic design or layout skills and understand principles of contrast, repetition, alignment and proximity (sometimes called the CRAP rule):

- *Contrast*: pick your most important element (whether that's a chart, a map or a figure) and make it much bigger than all the other elements: perhaps four or six times as big. The clear contrast will tell the user where to look first.
- *Repetition*: try to make other elements on the same screen the same size. This will make it easier for the reader to move between elements. You should also repeat colours: use one colour for emphasis and a second or third colour for other elements. Shapes and line thicknesses should also be kept the same throughout to ensure consistency.
- *Alignment*: align different elements with each other. It helps to have a basic column structure (for example, your main element might take up three 'columns' while all other elements are aligned within one column each).

- *Proximity*: don't leave large gaps between elements, but do leave enough room for the design to be readable.

If your infographic is longer than one screen, you should treat each screen as a distinct 'page' on that infographic. Think of these as chapters: each one should have its own introduction (an element of contrast). And as a whole, the infographic's chapters should form a beginning, middle and end that take the user through the infographic.

Summary

If you want to get an edge in a highly competitive journalism jobs market, data journalism is a hugely desirable skill to have. Data journalism skills can help you produce exclusive stories that hold power to account, or create attention-grabbing visuals and interactives. If you're very good, you can do both.

There are lots of different ways to get into data journalism. You can focus on finding stories in new datasets released by government organisations or other bodies, or develop your visual skills by creating compelling maps and infographics. You can develop skills in finding new data – for example, by using FOI or scraping. Or you can focus on interactivity and develop coding skills.

The best way to get started is to start simple – and pick a subject or story that you're passionate about, whether that's a hard news subject like crime or health, or a softer subject like fashion or music. Whatever it is, there will be data about it somewhere. Once you've mastered one simple skill, try to master another, but never ever feel under pressure to be a master of everything: even the best data journalists have gaps in their skillsets.

Because of the wide variety of skills involved, data journalism often involves collaboration. Look out for mailing lists and meetups where you can ask questions and share your work with others who might be able to build on it. Designers or developers might be interested in creating things with the data you have found; or you might be able to find data collected by others that you can work with.

Ultimately data journalism gives you the opportunity to make a real difference with your journalism – and you don't need anybody's permission to do so. The power available online and in your laptop is quite incredible, and yet many journalists fail to make the most of it. With data journalism, you can use that power in all sorts of exciting ways – and invent new ways too.

Activities

1 Submit an FOI request to your local authority or police force using the website TheyWorkForYou.com. FOIs are best for requesting documents or statistics – you could, for example, ask how much they have spent on PR in the past three years, or to see any policy documents relating to dealing with complaints. Search WhatDoTheyKnow to see what other FOI requests have been submitted to that body – and the responses. This will help you formulate your own.

2   Use the advanced search techniques outlined in this chapter to find a useful spreadsheet about your local area or a subject of interest. Try to come up with a list of possible story ideas that you could get from it.

3   Look for 'expenditure above £500' on a UK council website, or find a detailed spreadsheet (not aggregate totals) on another subject. Try out some basic spreadsheet techniques to calculate a total, work out a mean average, and a median average. See if you can create a pivot table to find out which company gets the most money, or which department spends the most. Use a search engine to find tutorials that explain ways of solving these and other problems in a spreadsheet.

4   Look at a piece of research that has been released recently by the government or a pressure group. How was the information gathered? How big – and representative – was the sample? How long a period did the research cover? If any of that information is missing, try to get hold of it – and if they won't provide it, ask why.

5   Put a recent speech by a politician into a word cloud creator (such as Wordle) and create a word cloud (you can normally find speeches on GOV.UK's publications section, or on political parties or politicians' own websites). What does it imply about the politician's priorities, or the point they're trying to make? Now try to create a bar chart showing the frequency of the top five or ten words instead (wordcounter.com will tell you the frequency). Which is better?

Further reading

Amin, Lucas and Montague, Brendan (2013) *EIRs without the Lawyer*, London: Centre for Investigative Journalism
Blastland, Michael and Dilnot, Andrew (2007) *The Tiger That Isn't*, London: Profile Books
Bradshaw, Paul (2014) *Scraping for Journalists*, Leanpub (leanpub.com/scrapingforjournalists)
Bradshaw, Paul (2015) *Finding Stories in Spreadsheets*, Leanpub (leanpub.com/spreadsheetstories)
Burgess, Matt (2015) *Freedom of Information*, Abingdon: Routledge
Kirk, Andy (2016) *Data Visualisation: A Handbook for Data Driven Design*, Abingdon: Routledge
Miller, Claire (2014) *Getting Started with Data Journalism*, Leanpub (leanpub.com/datajournalism)
Wong, Dona M. (2010) *The Wall Street Journal Guide to Information Graphics*, New York: WW Norton

Online resources

Flowing Data: flowingdata.com
Guardian Datablog: theguardian.com/data
Investigative Reporters and Editors: NICAR-L mailing list: ire.org/resource-center/listservs/subscribe-nicar-l
Junk Charts: junkcharts.typepad.com
Online Journalism Blog: onlinejournalismblog.com
The Numbers (*Wall Street Journal*): blogs.wsj.com/numbers

Bibliography

Allen, Mike. Hill aides change plane tickets due to cliff – Nate Silver: 'Punditry is fundamentally useless' – Bush 43 to be Grandpa in spring – Purdum, Vilsack, Bernanke b'day, Politico, 13 December 2012, www.politico.com/playbook/1212/playbook9656.html?hp=l6

Baird, Staci. '10 tips for designing infographics', Digital Newsgathering, 24 April 2010, http://digitalnewsgathering.wordpress.com/2010/04/24/10-tips-for-designing-infographics

Fox, E. J., Spies, Mike and Gilat, Matan. Who was America's most well-spoken president? Vocativ, 10 October 2014, http://cms.vocativ.com/interactive/usa/us-politics/presidential-readability

Fung, Kaiser. Junk charts talk, Junk Charts, 3 May 2010, http://junkcharts.typepad.com/junk_charts/2010/05/junk-charts-talk.html

Grey, Stephen (2006) *Ghost Plane: The Inside Story of the CIA's Secret Rendition Programme*, London: Hurst

Hayward, Stephen. Nurses charged almost £200 a month just to park their cars at work, *Mirror*, 12 July 2014a, www.mirror.co.uk/news/uk-news/nurses-charged-200-month-just-3848184

Hayward, Stephen. Saving on loo rolls would pay for 700 nurses, *Mirror*, 9 August 2014b, www.mirror.co.uk/news/uk-news/nhs-flushes-25m-down-toilet-4029928

Smith, Patrick. Interview Susanna Kempe CEO of fashion forecaster wgsn on digital data driven subscriptions, MediaBriefing, 14 July 2011, www.themediabriefing.com/article/interview-susanna-kempe-ceo-of-fashion-forecaster-wgsn-on-digital-data-driven-subscriptions

Soper, Taylor. Nate Silver's advice to young journalists: learn to code now, GeekWire, 25 April 2014, www.geekwire.com/2014/nate-silver

Sullivan, Margaret. Nate Silver went against the grain for some at the Times, *New York Times*, 22 July 2013, http://publiceditor.blogs.nytimes.com/2013/07/22/nate-silver-went-against-the-grain-for-some-at-the-times/?smid=tw-share&_r=0

Tracy, Marc. Nate Silver is a one-man traffic machine for the Times, *New Republic*, 6 November 2012, www.newrepublic.com/article/109714/nate-silvers-fivethirtyeight-blog-drawing-massive-traffic-new-york-times

Tufte, Edward (2001) *The Visual Display of Quantitative Information*, 2nd edn, Cheshire, CT: Graphics Press

Wong, Dona M. (2010) *The Wall Street Journal Guide to Information Graphics*, New York: WW Norton

1 Interactivity and code

Chapter objectives

This chapter will cover:

- What is interactivity?
- Ways to think about interactivity in your journalism
- Tools for adding interactivity to your stories
- The debate over whether journalists should learn how to code
- Basic web design concepts: HTML and CSS
- What different programming languages do
- Basic programming concepts you need to understand
- Understanding APIs
- JavaScript journalism
- Bots, news games and other forms of interactivity.

Introduction

In his book *Online Journalism* (Hall 2001), Jim Hall argues that, in the age of the web, interactivity could be added to impartiality, objectivity and truth as a core value of journalism. It is that important.

Interactivity is central to how journalism has been changed by the arrival of the internet. Whereas the news industries of print and broadcast placed control firmly in the hands of the publishers and journalists, online your users are an integral part of the journalism process – whether you like it or not.

This is partly because the web has grown up on devices (computers, mobile phones) with cultural histories of utility, very different to the cultural histories of television, radio or even print. We do not, typically, switch on our computers or phones and sit back, waiting to be entertained: these are 'lean-forward' devices that we actively *use*.

But that's not all. Interactions with our content are key to the commercial side of publishing too. We rely on users to help our stories rise up the search engine rankings and get found on social media; advertisers increasingly look for evidence of 'engagement' with users beyond mere pageviews. Early research on interactive formats suggested that users spent more time on the page when information was presented in this format (DiSEL 2005) and also recalled more process-related information (in contrast, users appeared to recall slightly more basic factual information when information is presented in normal HTML (Ruel and Outing 2004)).

There has been a long history of writing on the potential of interactivity for journalism. However, advanced interactivity was initially work-intensive and so used only with large stories and investigations. For example, news organisations began creating 'clickable interactives', which presented a range of audio, video, visual and textual resources around a story and allowed users to explore them in the order they preferred.

As technology improved and news organisations experimented more, interactive formats moved beyond merely offering a choice of media. Indeed, the concept of offering a choice of elements (video, audio and so on) is no longer limited to special interactive features: 'longform' and 'immersive' formats (see Chapter 4) now provide users with options to 'dig deeper' into galleries, video or audio, while similar options are often also given in normal web articles.

Interactives, then, began to focus on creating a coherent 'path' through the story and interaction now increasingly revolves around data-driven elements (see Chapter 10 for more). Meanwhile, interactivity has moved beyond the webpage, taking in standalone 'web apps', mobile-based interactivity, personalisation, automation and bots.

In this chapter we will look at the range of ways that online publishers have integrated interactivity into their content, the increasing importance of programming skills for journalists and the tools and techniques that can help you bring readers into your storytelling.

What is interactivity?

If you look at the dedicated 'interactive' sections of publications such as the *Guardian* (theguardian.com/interactive), BBC (bbc.co.uk/news/11628973) and *Telegraph* (telegraph. co.uk/news/interactive-graphics) you will find such a wide range of formats that it is difficult to pin down exactly what is meant by 'interactive'. The *Guardian*, for example, includes cartoons and photo essays within the section, although neither provides any particular opportunity for interaction. Multimedia and visual content is often mixed, and so confused, with genuinely interactive journalism, so it is important to identify how interactivity is distinctive.

Liu and Shrum (2002, p.54) define interactivity as 'The degree to which two or more communication parties can act on each other, on the communication method, and on the messages and the degree to which such influences are synchronized'. Downes and McMillan (2000) address similar ground in their attempt to break interactivity down into six 'dimensions':

1   Direction of communication
2   Time flexibility
3   Sense of place

4 Level of control
5 Responsiveness
6 Perceived purpose of communication.

Put more simply, interactivity is not an either/or quality. Instead most online journalism exists on a *continuum* of interactivity, which mainly revolves around two aspects: communication and control.

On the communication side, interactivity means allowing users to communicate with the news organisation, with individual journalists and – crucially – each other. While much has been written about the arrival of two-way communication between journalist and reader using facilities such as comments, social media and journalists' emails – it is equally important to recognise the emergence of a three-way communication structure: between journalist and reader, and between reader and reader.

Ultimately, the attraction for news websites is the same as that in print and broadcast: the ability to gather people with a passion for the same issue in the same place.

Thinking about control

Control in interactivity can relate to *when* someone consumes their media (time-shifting), or *where* (providing podcasts that people can listen to on their phone, for instance). It can also mean control over *input* into a story – everything from allowing comments on a story to letting readers vote on what should be covered. And it can mean control over the news *output*: the BBC's personalised homepage, for example, allows you to customise the news you get based on your location, fields of interest and particular organisations such as sports teams.

These control options are illustrated in the checklist below. It provides a framework to prompt you to think about how you make your own journalism interactive.

For example, if you are working on a piece of journalism you might ask:

- How can I give the user control over the space in which this is consumed? Make it downloadable, perhaps?
- How might I give the user control over input? Perhaps by blogging or writing on social media about the idea for the article and inviting suggestions for angles, sources, research, etc.?
- How can I give control over output? Allow users to enter their postcode and find out about how the story affects them?

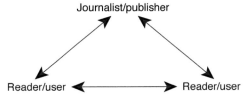

Figure 11.1
Three-way interactivity
Source: Courtesy of OnlineJournalismBlog.com

Ways in which you are giving the user control over ...

Input	For example: reporter contact details, comments form, user-generated content invitation, voting, forum, wiki, chat
Output	For example: linking, 'chunking', choice of medium, playback controls, RSS feed, personalisation, database search, user choice, filtering, zooming
Space	For example: mobile-optimised content, publishing on multiple platforms, RSS feed/subscription
Time	For example: storing and republishing ephemeral content

Figure 11.2
Interactivity: a checklist of user control

Control over time

One of the main features of the internet as an interactive medium is the way it allows users control over the time that they access information: you are not limited by printing press availability or broadcast schedules.

It is important to consider whether your content is optimised for mobile phones: *responsive design* helps ensure that your content works regardless of the device used to access it.

Control over input and output

With linear media such as TV, radio and print, it is the producer, editor or journalist who structures how content is presented (the output). Digital media allows the audience to take some of that control. Examples include:

- At a basic level, *hyperlinks* allow the reader to dictate their experience of 'content' through their choice of clicks (see Chapter 4)
- With online video and audio, the user can *control playback*: pause, skip forward, etc.
- Having *multiple media elements* in a story sometimes allows users to choose the medium they want to focus on
- If it has been split into 'chunks' (see Chapter 4), the user can choose which bit of a longer video or audio piece they experience
- *RSS* allows users to create their own media product, by selecting feeds
- *Database-driven content* allows the user to shape output based on their input – for example, by entering their postcode they can read content specific to their area
- *Interactive data visualisation* allows the user to filter and zoom into areas or subjects of interest to them

- *Interactive editorial formats* allow the user to influence output in a range of ways. This may be as simple as selecting from a range of audio, video, text and still image options. It may be playing a game or quiz, where their interaction (e.g. what answers they get right, how they perform) shapes the output they experience.

In terms of *input* the news media has a rich history of user-generated content (the letter to the editor; the radio phone-in). However, these forms are still *'reactive'* rather than interactive 'unless journalists or other readers (in subsequent letters) respond to the initial communication' (Schultz 1999). Online, input is much more integral: journalists can expect input on anything that they create, and often invite input at the very start of the reporting process (see Chapter 12).

Input can also form part of the publishing strategy itself, as explained in Chapter 12. Indeed, you will notice that interactivity has become so embedded in online journalism practice that you will find its principles outlined in all the other chapters of this book. These include:

- Linking and embedding (writing for the web, Chapter 4)
- Allowing audiences to interact with each other and the journalist or publisher (community management, Chapter 12; liveblogging, Chapter 6)
- Allowing users to explore and interact with data (data journalism, Chapter 10)
- Allowing users to control multimedia (audio (Chapter 7) and video (Chapter 9); writing for social media (Chapter 5).

For the remainder of this chapter, then, we will focus on those technologies of interactivity not covered elsewhere, the role of programming and the 'journalist-coder', and interactive storytelling forms.

Creating interactivity with third party tools

Although some interactivity requires programming skills (see p.293), many of your ideas around interactivity will be achievable using third party tools that you can find online. Often the first step to creating something interactive is to ask the question 'Is there a tool for that?'

There are websites that will help you make video or audio interactive; others will do the same for images. There are tools to create interactive timelines, maps, sliders, quizzes and polls. There are services that will help you create a story with multiple paths, or make a dataset or map searchable.

Some of these tools come and go. But more often than not, you will find a similar service has sprung up elsewhere: good ideas are hard to keep down.

Technologies of interactivity: polls

Polls are one of the simplest forms of interactivity, and are often very easy to add to a page or within social media updates (both Facebook and Twitter include the ability to post a poll or vote).

It is important to distinguish between polls and quizzes (see p.286): in polls, users are invited to vote on a question (asking how they feel, or what they want to happen), and are then presented with the overall results. Typically this has two purposes: first to 'feel the pulse' of the audience (reader-to-journalist interactivity); and secondly to give the audience an opportunity to find out how other readers feel (reader-to-reader interactivity).

Both have issues that you must be careful to acknowledge and address. First, it is important not to confuse self-selecting poll respondents with the wider population or even the readership of your publication. Most survey respondents do not represent that wider population or meet sufficient standards (Wu and Weaver 1997): research on online polls has found that women are less likely to participate (Zhao and Leung 2013), while polls can be hijacked by people who do not normally read your publication, or artificially manipulated.

In 2012, for example, blogger Russell Phillips explained how he had consistently rigged online polls by News.com.au so that they had a 50/50 split. Despite repeatedly alerting NewsCorp, nothing was changed and journalists wrote stories based on the poll results – until finally his article made it onto the front page of Reddit months later (Phillips 2012). Martin Belam recounts similar regular attempts to skew BBC polls in the mid-2000s (Belam 2013), while in 2014 it was revealed that the British spy agency GCHQ had developed tools to manipulate online polls (Greenwald 2014). This problem is sometimes called 'freeping' after the website Free Republic, which directed its users to swamp a number of online polls with their votes.

Second, it is important to ensure that readers understand the limitations of polls: if 90 per cent of respondents said they agreed with something, you must not report that '90 per cent of people' agreed with it: it is 90 per cent of those who responded to that particular poll. The BBC has very useful guidelines on the use of polls that you should read before using any poll results – including those conducted elsewhere – in your coverage (BBC 2016).

For both these reasons it is important to only use online polls within a fun context where the results are not taken too seriously. Robert Niles points out that 'Polls won't tell you anything useful about your readership's *collective* behavior, [but] they can engage your readers to share *individual* stories' (Niles 2007).

They can also be useful entry or exit points for a frivolous story: the *Guardian* began adding a poll to the top of transfer rumour stories in 2015 that invited users to vote on whether the rumour was credible or not, while The *Manchester Evening News* used polls at the end of its transfer rumour posts to invite fans to vote on whether they would welcome the proposed transfer target.

There are countless websites for creating and hosting polls and poll widgets. Perhaps the best established is Polldaddy (polldaddy.com), which is also integrated into WordPress (en.support.wordpress.com/polls). For self-hosted WordPress sites there are also dozens of plugins offering poll functionality, and, of course, you can use programming to design your own, with dozens of polling APIs available (see programmableweb.com/category/polls/api for a list). Another option is to create a poll within a tweet or Facebook update and embed that update within your post.

Technologies of interactivity: quizzes

Quizzes have become a key tool in publishers' storytelling arsenal. The success of the *New York Times*'s interactive quiz 'How Y'all, Youse and You Guys Talk' (see Chapter 10) and the dominance of quizzes in top-performing posts on Facebook have helped establish the format as an effective way to reach large audiences.

Quizzes have always worked well within print magazines, but online the added attraction of instant results (no adding up scores!) and shareability have made them hugely popular on social media, while the data generated by quizzes adds a commercial factor – and privacy dilemma – that should not be underestimated. The rise of data journalism has also provided a new reason to turn to the quiz: they are excellent for finding the parts of any dataset that directly affect the reader.

BuzzFeed in particular has been a major force in pioneering and popularising the quiz as a storytelling device. In 2014 Digiday reported that 96 per cent of users who started BuzzFeed-sponsored quizzes finished them, and in some cases more than a third of users completed quizzes twice (Van Hoven 2014). BuzzFeed managing editorial director Summer Anne Burton told the website that strong visuals, including typography and choice of colour, were important factors in establishing the personality of the quiz.

Playbuzz's chief content officer, Shachar Orren, notes that the personal element is key to the format's success: 'Whether it's a listicle or a quiz or a poll, it's "about you", and that makes you far more likely to be interested and engaged in it, and more importantly, share it with others' (Corcoran 2014).

Adding an extra dimension of interactivity, both BuzzFeed and Playbuzz have created quiz creation tools and guides so that users can add their own quizzes to the site (providing control over input as well as output).

Quizzes can have one of a number of purposes. These can include:

- Giving the user a chance to test themself (how much do they know)
- Providing a more fun way to take in information (what do they *not* know)
- Providing an insight into their character or other qualities (what type of person they are)
- Providing an answer to a question, such as the political party whose policies most closely match your own, or how the latest budget announcements will affect you
- Telling a story in a different way, by communicating story elements through the answers, or using the quiz experience to replicate some other experience.

They also tend to fit into particular genres: BuzzFeed's guide (Calderon 2015) lists four types: trivia quizzes, personality quizzes, polls (see above) and checklists. Another genre – 'guessing game' quizzes, such as 'Can we guess where you're from?' – is specifically identified by research on Playbuzz (Libert 2015).

Empathy can be an important element in a quiz. The *Mirror*'s quiz 'Could you pass David Cameron's English test (and avoid deportation)?' (Mulroy 2016), for example, uses the format to allow users to experience the challenging nature of the questions for themselves, while ABC's 'Metadata quiz: Who has Will been talking to?' (Ockenden 2015) explores the issue of privacy by placing readers in a position of 'spying' on their reporter in order to see how personally revealing metadata is.

Personalisation is another strength of the format. In order to address the 'it will never happen to me' attitude to hacking, for example, the *New York Times* created a quiz feature that asked: 'How many times has your personal information been exposed to hackers?'

(Keller, Lai and Perlroth 2016). As users tick boxes to say whether they have used particular accounts, insurance providers, or credit cards, the page counts up the number of times those companies have been hacked. The quiz has also been regularly updated to reflect new hacking revelations.

Some quizzes can serve to both test knowledge and add to it. The regular 'Quiz of the week's news' published by the BBC, *Telegraph* and *Guardian*, for example, tests how much you know, but also highlights news stories you have missed or forgotten about. Likewise BuzzFeed's 'How privileged are you?' is simply a checklist designed to challenge the reader to reflect on aspects of their own privilege they may be taking for granted.

Increasingly, quizzes are being integrated into reporting rather than published as a standalone piece of content. In the *Seattle Times* investigation into police killings, 'Shielded by the law' (Miletich et al. 2015), a quiz (where users can 'explore the data' by guessing key stats from the investigation) is just one element of a long feature that also includes video, audio and interactive visualisation. The *Guardian* US interactive 'Can you guess the voter turnout in your state?' (Popovich 2016) uses an initial quiz question as a way of introducing a personalised article on local issues affecting election turnout. The BBC interactive 'Which world leaders are you most like?' pretends to be a personality quiz but it's nothing of the sort: instead, it's a clever way to take the user through an overview of world leaders.

There are dozens of free tools online to create interactive quizzes, including those created by BuzzFeed and Playbuzz (playbuzz.com/create). Riddle (riddle.com), Apester (apester.com) and QuizWorks's Online Quiz Creator (onlinequizcreator.com) are just a few. The WordPress content management system includes a quiz 'shortcode' (see en.support. wordpress.com/quiz-shortcode) and you can also create your own quizzes using basic programming techniques (see p.293), or WordPress plugins.

At their most complex, quizzes can become 'choose your own adventure'-style interactive narratives: see the section below on multiple path stories (p.292) for more.

Technologies of interactivity: image maps

Images can be made interactive by turning them into 'image maps'. In an image map specific areas of that image become clickable, with different things happening when a user clicks different areas. Examples include:

- A group photo, where users can click on each face to access more information about that person (text, video, audio or other media)
- A photo of a key scene at an event, with people, buildings and items which all might have a story behind them, and which can be clicked to find out
- A geographical map, where users can click on different places to read about them
- A floorplan showing the layout of a key site in a story: users can click on different parts to find out what happened there
- A diagram illustrating a process or concept: users can click to find out more about a particular stage or element
- An infographic where users can click through to the original data, animations or interviews about key facts or quotes.

In 'Turning the camera around: health care stakeholders' (NPR 2009), for example, NPR turned the camera on lobbyists in the audience for a hearing on a healthcare bill. Users could roll over each highlighted person to see their name and how much their organisation had spent on lobbying the previous year. The *New York Times* used a similar technique for a profile piece on mayoral candidates (Barbara and Giratikanon 2013).

The *Guardian* used an image map of London's skyline to show how it was going to change as new buildings were due to be added to the city (Fenn et al. 2014), while KENS Television used an image map to allow viewers to explore an image from a 'ghost tour' of a hotel (Welsh 2016).

Image maps are, fundamentally, navigational devices: a way of turning an image into a vehicle for navigating information about an issue or story.

In fact, perhaps the best-known image map is one you probably never think about: your computer's 'desktop' interface. Of course there isn't really a blue cloth littered with folders inside your monitor: it's just an image that *resembles* a desktop to help you navigate the information contained within your computer.

You can create an image map in a number of ways. One is to use the HTML tag <map>, for example (you will find plenty of tutorials online). The Image Map Generator (image-map.net) and Image-Maps.com are just two of various online tools that will generate the code for you.

However, there are also various tools that allow you to turn an image into an interactive image map even more easily – and with more multimedia options. JamSnap, for example, allows you to add sounds to images. But perhaps the best-known image map tool is ThingLink (ThingLink.com). The site (which also has a mobile app) allows you to upload an image and then add 'hotspots'. These can be linked to extra textual information, links or they can trigger audio or video clips over the top of the image. In 2016 news organisations began to use the premium version of the tool for 360-degree images too. World Maritime News has a regular 'interactive image' feature using the tool, which has included diagrams ('How well do you know ship parts?'), maps ('Top 5 longest shipping canals in the world') and photos ('How to deter pirates').

The Knight Lab tool StoryMap JS (storymap.knightlab.com) also provides similar functionality. Although it is designed for making maps interactive (see below), it also has a 'StoryMap for Images' option at storymap.knightlab.com/gigapixel.

Technologies of interactivity: interactive maps

Although images *of* maps can be made interactive by using image map tools, it is important to distinguish these from working maps that are *not* static images and can be made interactive in different ways.

The main difference with working maps is that, typically, users can pan across and zoom in and out of a map in order to see more or less detail. Perhaps the major advantage of a map is its potential for *personalisation*: users can zoom in to the areas where they or their friends live, or areas that are of personal interest to them. For that reason maps work well for stories that involve a number of locations, which different users might want to explore in different ways.

As detailed in Chapter 10, you can choose to locate points on a map, illustrate different areas, create heat maps or draw routes.

Locating points on a map makes sense if users will want to look at incidents or organisations near them, such as how local schools perform, or whether someone was arrested for a particular crime. Or if the map shows a *clear distribution of those points*, and this is the story you are trying to tell (for example, fast food vans near the sports stadium are failing food hygiene inspections; or there are more burglaries in one area than another).

Illustrating areas on a map is useful when your story relates to facts or figures relating to bodies that have a geographical 'footprint', such as a local authority, police authority or health body.

Interactive map tools range from simple tools like BatchGeo where you can paste a few rows of addresses and get a quick result, to more advanced tools like Carto, Google Fusion Tables and Tableau Public. There are also tools that allow you to enter each address manually (such as Google Maps) to create a custom map or share routes, or the Knight Lab tool StoryMap JS (storymap.knightlab.com). Mapping is a popular form of interactivity, so it's well worth exploring a few different tools to find the one that does what you need, and that you can use. There are also dozens of libraries in JavaScript (see p.300) and other programming languages that make mapping easier and more interactive, if you want to develop those skills.

Working with the public

Interactive maps need not be generated from in-house knowledge alone – inviting users to contribute (crowdsourcing) can be a key ingredient in fostering interactivity. For example, when a number of motorists started contacting the BBC about problems with their cars following visits to petrol stations, journalists decided to ask viewers, listeners and website visitors if they had experienced similar problems. As responses poured in, the corporation was able to gather data from viewers and website visitors and compile a map of cases richer than that held by any motoring organisation or transport department. That data allowed them to pinpoint the particular petrol stations where the problems had originated, and kicked off an investigation by Trading Standards, which found that contaminated fuel was the cause. Other examples include the *Manchester Evening News* plotting information from users about congestion and roadworks on its travel map, the *Hartlepool Mail* using readers' contributions to map potholes and derelict areas of the town and BBC Radio Berkshire using maps during floods in the area to show which places were the worst affected, along with data about the location of emergency services.

How to involve users in mapping

There are three broad approaches to mapping contributions from users. The first is to process every contribution manually – taking emails, phone calls, comments and texts and entering them into the map yourself. This has clear advantages in being able to verify the information and keep the map working properly, but obvious disadvantages in the amount of time it requires for a journalist and how long it takes for the map to be updated.

A second approach is to publish the map in editable format – that is, allow anyone to edit the map directly, using a tool like Google Map Maker. This obviously has the advantage of not requiring any further work from the journalist other than checking the map regularly and correcting any mistakes. However, it does require a certain level of commitment and technical competence from users, and you may find users accidentally editing each other's entries and the title of the map itself.

The third approach is to part-automate the process in a way that addresses the weaknesses above. You can, for example, create a Google Form for users to fill in. Watch out for duplicate entries from different people entering the same information. Another option is a 'crowd-mapping' tool like Crowdmap.com that makes it possible to create collaborative maps (see Chapter 12 for more on crowdsourcing).

Ultimately, as the BBC's Bella Hurrell explains: 'We have learnt that we should proceed with caution – maps are not always the best interface for exploring content as there can be a lot of clicking involved and not all users find mashup type maps that intuitive.

'So as journalists we need to consider where they will add value, rather than using them because we can.'

Technologies of interactivity: timelines

Where your story involves a series of events, it can also be presented in an interactive timeline. Typically you will need to format the events as structured data, using a spreadsheet with columns for different elements (for example, one column each for the title, description, date or time, image, video, link and so on). This spreadsheet can then be converted into an interactive timeline using one of a number of tools.

These tools include Knight Lab's Timeline JS tool (timeline.knightlab.com). This gives you a spreadsheet template and will display your entries on a single scrollable line, or as a series of cards that can be 'flicked' through. Similar tools include iSpring, HSTRY, Timetoast and Timeglider. You can also find tools such as StoryMap JS (storymap.knightlab.com) and TimeMapper (timemapper.okfnlabs.org), which will place your timeline on a map.

Technologies of interactivity: sliders

Interactive sliders allow you to compare two images (which are overlaid on top of each other) by dragging a slider to change the amount of each image that is visible. They are best known for 'before and after' situations: for example, the story 'Third runway at Heathrow cleared for takeoff by ministers' (Johnston 2016) featured a slider that users could move to see either more of the 'current flight paths' image, or more of the 'proposed flight paths' image.

The slider is positioned in the middle to begin with, so that 50 per cent of each image is visible ('before' to the left of the slider; 'after' to the right). The act of clicking and dragging the slider one way or the other 'reveals' more of one image at the expense of the other, and vice versa.

Sliders can also be quite flexible for other uses as well. The BuzzFeed article 'There are more male MPs right now than the total number of female MPs ever' (Datoo 2014) uses a slider to allow you to compare two charts: one showing the number of male MPs in Parliament, and another showing the number of female MPs.

Creating an interactive transition between two images does not have to be done with a slider. The *Guardian* section 'Photography then and now' (theguardian.com/artanddesign/series/photography-then-and-now) gives users a choice: they can click the image to initiate a slow fade between one image and another, or use a slider just above it.

The tool Juxtapose JS (juxtapose.knightlab.com) from Knight Lab makes it very easy to create sliders. For more control there are some very simple JavaScript libraries (see p.300) and code that you can adapt, such as Twentytwenty, imgSlider, Cocoen and CodyHouse's Image Comparison Slider.

Technologies of interactivity: multiple path stories

Interactive stories have a rich history in literature, from children's 'Choose your own adventure' books to seminal works such as Julio Cortazar's 1963 novel *Hopscotch*. In these books readers are invited to make choices that in turn determine which chapters of the book they read, and in what order.

As soon as technology made it possible, authors were exploring the potential of *hypertext* (links) to create the same experiences on digital platforms. By 1997 Espen J. Aarseth was coining the term 'ergodic literature' to refer to these 'choose your path' narratives (Aarseth 1997).

Of course almost all online journalism offers *some* element of choice to users through hypertext: stories published online routinely link to background material and related stories, or provide a choice of embedded media that users can choose to explore. However, there is a difference between offering these choices as an *extra* element to a *linear* story, and making those choices *integral* to the user's experience of an *interactive* story.

There are now a number of tools that make the process of creating 'ergodic journalism' that much easier. One of the best established interactive story creators is Twine (twinery.org). Journalism student Alex Iacovangelo used the tool to create a story about what it is like to live with Crohn's disease (Iacovangelo 2015). Textadventures.co.uk also offers similar functionality, while Conducttr (conducttr.com) promises more gamification features.

But you don't need bespoke tools to create ergodic stories: if you can create links, you can create interactivity. Another journalism student, Ben Jackson, created an interactive game exploring what would happen if ebola hit London by simply creating a page for each choice the user made (Jackson 2014).

Another option is to 'reveal' different parts of your page based on answers to questions: BuzzFeed used this technique to create a 'choose your own adventure' story around the challenges of leading a political party, in 'Can you survive a week as Jeremy Corbyn?' (Phillips et al. 2015). 'Can you navigate a day with depression?' (Dalton 2015) uses the same techniques to illustrate the challenges of mental health issues.

The same approach can be used on social media: instead of creating a route through different webpages, Terence Eden created a route through multiple Twitter accounts: at each point in the story users could click through to a different Twitter account (he had to create each one) to see the results of their choices (Tamblyn 2015).

There has been a particular focus on interactivity in video, too. Channel 4 News's 'Two billion miles' (twobillionmiles.com) places the viewer in the position of a refugee trying to make it to safety, presenting different video footage based on the choices that the user makes.

Video services like Eko Studio (studio.helloeko.com) and Rapt Media (raptmedia.com) allow creators to insert choices within their video that shape the story that the viewer experiences, while YouTube cards (see Chapter 7) allow you to create a similar experience. One of the earliest uses of the feature, Corey Vidal's 'Blend Your Own Adventure' (Vidal 2009), uses YouTube cards to give users a 'choice' of the ingredients Corey is going to blend on-screen (each card triggers a further video where he selects or blends those ingredients). To achieve the result, Corey needed to create dozens of videos for the various combinations of just seven ingredients that might be selected.

Ergodic stories work especially well for stories where empathy is important. They can be particularly effective in putting the user in the position of an individual at the heart of a story, and engage them in the choices and consequences involved. In a world where complex issues are often oversimplified, interactivity allows us to dig deeper, demonstrating that often there are no easy answers, and many grey areas.

Creating interactivity with programming

Third party tools limit what you can do with interactivity, and often create problems with long-term maintenance. What happens, for example, if the site hosting your content (as often happens) closes down?

Although these tools are useful for exploring ideas of interactivity there will probably come a point at which you want to take more control, do more things and learn more skills. And for that you will need at least some programming skills.

Of course, entire books have been dedicated to individual programming languages, or specific parts of them, and this chapter is not intended to teach you how to write in JavaScript or HTML. However, it should give you the basic principles and context required to start your journey into coding for interactive journalism.

CLOSER LOOK
SHOULD JOURNALISTS LEARN TO CODE?

If you have particularly ambitious ideas for data journalism projects – especially those that involve tools or personalisation – then you'll need to learn programming. But there is also an ongoing debate within journalism about whether *all* journalists should learn programming.

There are a number of arguments in favour of learning coding. First, journalists rely on the internet and computers (including phones) to do their work, so understanding

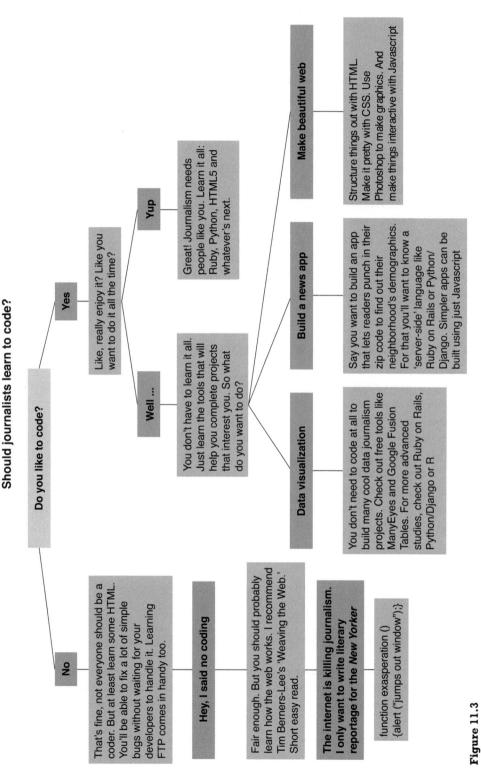

Should journalists learn to code?

Do you like to code?

No

That's fine, not everyone should be a coder. But at least learn some HTML. You'll be able to fix a lot of simple bugs without waiting for your developers to handle it. Learning FTP comes in handy too.

Hey, I said no coding

Fair enough. But you should probably learn how the web works. I recommend Tim Berners-Lee's 'Weaving the Web.' Short easy read.

The internet is killing journalism. I only want to write literary reportage for the New Yorker

function exasperation () {alert ("jumps out window");}

Yes

Like, really enjoy it? Like you want to do it all the time?

Yup

Great! Journalism needs people like you. Learn it all: Ruby, Python, HTML5 and whatever's next.

Well ...

You don't have to learn it all. Just learn the tools that will help you complete projects that interest you. So what do you want to do?

Data visualization

You don't need to code at all to build many cool data journalism projects. Check out free tools like ManyEyes and Google Fusion Tables. For more advanced studies, check out Ruby on Rails, Python/Django or R

Build a news app

Say you want to build an app that lets readers punch in their zip code to find out their neighborhood's demographics. For that you'll want to know a 'server-side' language like Ruby on Rails or Python/Django. Simpler apps can be built using just Javascript

Make beautiful web

Structure things out with HTML. Make it pretty with CSS. Use Photoshop to make graphics. And make things interactive with Javascript

Figure 11.3

'Should journalists learn to code?' flowchart

Source: Courtesy of David Holmes and PandoDaily

how those things work is important to make sure your journalism isn't limited in key ways.

Journalists are regulated and restricted by code in all sorts of ways:

- Code affects what information you can access (just knowing advanced search operators can make a big difference in your newsgathering skills, but there are also APIs, the invisible web and the dark web)
- Code affects how well you can filter the information coming to you – vital when you're facing information overload (for instance with RSS or email)
- Code affects your ability to verify sources and documents
- Code affects your ability to protect sources
- Code affects your ability to empower sources to help you and each other
- Code affects your ability to engage users.

Second, all journalists have to use content management systems which often require a little bit of coding if you want to do anything special. Knowing what's possible also means you can communicate with key colleagues such as web designers and web developers when the content management system doesn't do what you need it to do.

Coding can also be an enormous time saver, allowing you to automate some processes and making some stories possible which otherwise would be impossible. As the *Guardian*'s Charles Arthur says:

> When I was really young, I read a book about computers which made the point – rather effectively – that if you found yourself doing the same process again and again, you should hand it over to a computer. That became a rule for me: never do some task more than once if you can possibly get a computer to do it.

It can also be extremely satisfying, as *Guardian* colleague Mary Hamilton adds:

> I love coding when it works well, I love that moment of unlocking something or creating something new and useful. I find it oddly exciting, which is probably why I carried on doing it after the first couple of times.

Coding gives you something extra in a very competitive jobs market: not just now but in the years to come as well, as technology companies become media companies, and vice versa. As Nate Silver says: 'If you're an aspiring journalist who knows how to code really well, you are in a very hot market' (Soper 2014).

But most importantly, coding allows you to be a better journalist. As journalist Mark Donoghue says:

> Journalism taught me how to ask questions. Computer Science taught me the importance of asking the right question.

Journalism taught me how to communicate. Computer Science taught me how to think.

Journalism taught me how to identify problems. Computer Science taught me how to solve problems.

The arguments against journalists learning to code tend to revolve around the argument that programming is a distraction from the 'core' role of journalism: often perceived to be content creation rather than platform creation. However, journalism and publishing have always been intertwined – particularly in the last decade or so. And in fact one of journalism's core roles is platform creation. As Kovach and Rosenstiel outline in their ten principles of journalism:"It must provide a forum for public criticism and compromise' (Kovach and Rosenstiel 2007). If journalism was merely content creation we would not open up comment threads or host forums; we would not arrange Q&A discussions and editorial events. Coding gives you greater control as a publisher, and as a journalist. In some cases it enables you to publish in the first place.

One of the strongest arguments for coding's role in journalism is that journalists need to understand the systems that govern society and their own work. And code is now one of those major systems. If we expect journalists to understand public administration and the ways that governments are given and exercise power, then they should also understand how code represents power.

And in that sense code is very much about the core role of journalism: which is to hold power to account.

If you want to start learning coding there are many, many resources online, including interactive tutorials on a range of languages and skills on sites like Codecademy, Mozilla Developer Network and Khan Academy. It's also a good idea to join one of the many local meetups for people interested in programming: the Hacks/Hackers network is specifically dedicated to journalists interested in data and coding, and has meetups in cities all around the world, but you can also search sites like Meetup for groups on web design, JavaScript, R, Python, Ruby and coding in general.

CLOSER LOOK
WHAT DIFFERENT PROGRAMMING LANGUAGES DO

There are a range of programming languages, each of which is used in different contexts for different purposes. Those that you will hear mentioned most often include HTML, CSS, JavaScript, PHP, Python, Ruby and R. Very few journalists learn all of these languages but instead focus on one particular part of the web development process.

HTML (HyperText Markup Language) and CSS (Cascading Style Sheets) are the starting point for most people learning how to create interactive experiences. These two languages are used to create and format webpages, so you will need to know these in order to create anything web-based.

JavaScript is used to add interactivity to those webpages: for example, it can be used to add extra content to your page based on what the user does, or change the properties of elements on the page.

PHP, Python and Ruby can be used to deliver content from a database in webpage format, among other things. This can be in response to what a user does – for example, entering details into a form and receiving personalised content – or based on other information, such as information fed in from a live database. Many news apps (see p.313) use these languages.

Python is used in NPR's App Template (github.com/nprapps/app-template), for example, to generate static files which are then published online. The data journalism outlet FiveThirtyEight uses R in a similar way to create charts and underpin interactives (Flowers 2016).

It should also be mentioned that PHP, Python and Ruby are all not just used to deliver information to webpages. Many journalists use these programming languages to gather, clean and analyse information in the first place (see Chapter 10 for more on these processes). The programming language R is also widely used for these purposes, and can also be used to generate webpages by using R Markdown.

Programming is often split into two types: 'frontend' and 'backend'. 'Frontend' refers to what happens in the user's browser when they view pages on your website. This end is normally described using HTML, CSS and JavaScript.

'Backend' refers to what is happening on the computer that hosts the website, typically called the *server* (it 'serves' up the website): for example, the server may hold a database and applications that check information supplied by the user. Interactions with that computer and its applications and databases are typically described using PHP, Python, Ruby and other languages.

CLOSER LOOK
PRIVACY AND CLIENT-SIDE OR SERVER-SIDE
INTERACTIVITY

Interactions on your website can be described as being either 'client-side' or 'server-side':

- The *client* is (usually) the browser that someone is using to view your webpage.
- The *server* is the computer hosting your website, which could be anywhere in the world.

If an interaction takes place entirely within the browser, without any information being requested from your server, then it is described as 'client-side'. *Client-side* interactivity has a number of advantages, including speed but also privacy: it may be important that information supplied as part of an interactive experience (such as someone's birth date, sexuality or opinion) is not stored anywhere. However, note that if the user chooses to share the results on social media this may also have privacy implications.

If information has to be processed by an application or database on your server, this is a *server-side* interaction. The advantage of this approach is that you might want to quantify interactions in more detail: for example, in order to count votes or to provide a breakdown of the choices made by users. Note that users must be informed of any use of personal data, in line with data protection laws (see Chapter 8 for more).

The basics of programming: HTML and CSS for journalists

HTML is the basic language of the web: it is the language that turns plain text into working webpages. Alongside that, CSS adds colour, style and movement (see p.299). The distinction is important: HTML is about content and structure; CSS is about how that looks.

HTML is used to do the following:

- Turn text into linked text (hyperlinks)
- Create tables
- Insert images, video, audio and other media
- Add emphasis such as italics or bold text
- Create headings and subheadings.

You can recognise HTML easily because it is written between triangular brackets called chevrons, like so: *<strong>*. This is called an HTML tag. The tag <strong> makes text strongly emphasised (it will generally look bold). Here are some other common HTML tags:

- <html> creates a HTML page
- <head> creates invisible information about the page, including <title>, which creates the title of the page
- <body> creates the visible part of that page
- <em> makes text emphasised; <strong> makes it strongly emphasised
- <h1> makes text into a level 1 heading, the most important heading
- <h2> makes a level 2 heading, which is slightly less important than a level 1 heading. Similar tags will create headings at levels 3 down to 6
- <ol> begins an ordered (numbered) list
- <ul> begins an unordered (bullet) list
- <li> begins a list item in one of those lists
- <img> inserts an image
- <a> makes text into a link
- <table> creates a table. Within that table you can also create a row with <tr> and table data cells with <td>.

When you use one of these tags, it is like pressing a button to turn bold 'on', or to turn a list 'on'. Most tags, then, also need to be turned off, by repeating the tag but with a slash at the start, like so:

- </strong> to turn strong emphasis off
- </h1> to indicate the end of your heading
- </li> after each list item, and </ol> to indicate the end of the whole list
- </a> at the end of the text you want to link
- </td> at the end of each table data cell, </tr> at the end of each row, and </table> at the end of the whole table
- </html> to end the HTML page.

Most of the fundamentals of HTML can be learned very quickly indeed: it is a very simple language, and there are plenty of free courses, videos and other resources online that you can use to learn it. But the most important thing is to try things out and experiment, learning through trial and error.

Style, not structure: CSS

One thing that HTML should *not* be used for is to change the style of the text. Sometimes, for example, people use tags like <h1> to make text bigger, but that is considered bad practice. Remember that HTML tags are about meaning, not style: the <h1> tag means text is more important than normal paragraphs or <h2> text. The <strong> tag is used to indicate that text should be emphasised strongly; the fact that it *appears* bold is a side-effect of that.

Appearance is controlled using a different language: Cascading Style Sheets (CSS). CSS is used to:

- Specify the colour and typeface of text
- Specify the *size* of elements, such as text, images, shapes and lines
- *Position* elements on the page
- Present your content differently based on the user's device: for example, depending on whether it is being viewed on a mobile device or desktop computer.

Normally CSS does this by *targeting* HTML tags within the page. For example, it might be used to say 'make all links green' or 'make all <h1> text 30 pixels high' or 'give all images a 1 pixel-thick red border'. Here is an example of some basic CSS code:

h1 { font-size : 18px; }

The text at the start specifies the HTML tag that the stylesheet is targeting for the style that follows. This is followed by a pair of curly brackets containing the property *attribute* and *value* that you want to apply to content within that tag. In this example, the CSS is saying that it wants to make any text within <h1> tags 18 pixels large.

Each style has two parts: first the property (font-size in the example above), then a colon, and then the value of that property (18 pixels in the example). Finally, a semi-colon indicates the end of that particular instruction.

You can apply more than one style to a single tag. In the example below, the CSS is specifying three things: a background colour, the colour of the text itself and the font size:

h1 {background: #00FF00; color: #FF0000; font-size: 18px;}

You can also target HTML elements more specifically. You can target elements that are contained within a *combination* of tags (for example, linked text within lists), and you can also target HTML tags based on additional properties. HTML tags often include attributes and values such as *class='headline'* or *id='navigation'* which are added for this purpose.

Like HTML, CSS is a simple language to learn, with plenty of resources online. And like HTML, the best way to learn is by trying things out and learning as you practise.

'JavaScript journalism'

JavaScript is widely used in publishing as the basis for all sorts of interactivity. Most of the examples mentioned in this chapter – including quizzes like 'How Y'all, Youse, and You Guys Talk' and the *Guardian*'s 'Photography then and now' sliders – use JavaScript, and many of the tools, including Juxtapose JS, Timeline JS and StoryMap JS, are JavaScript-based as well (the JS in the name stands for JavaScript).

The *Washington Post*'s Ray Daly even argues that 'JavaScript journalism' deserves to be recognised as a genre in its own right (Benton 2013). By way of illustration, he points out that after an almost entirely text-only 19th century, in the 20th century we came to accept that photography was a major element in news too. In the 21st century many news websites now have more lines of JavaScript than lines of text. His talks on the subject are well worth watching if you want to learn more (see the 'Online resources' section at the end of this chapter).

Typically most JavaScript interactives work by 'listening' for things to happen on a page, such as a user clicking on a particular object, scrolling down the page or entering information. These are called 'events', and when one of these events happens, part of the JavaScript is triggered. Here are some examples of typical interactions that are created with JavaScript:

- When a user clicks on an image, fade it out slowly and fade in a different image in the same place
- When a user scrolls down the page, move a video clip in from the edge
- When a user hovers over a video clip, turn the sound on
- When someone hovers over a particular part of a map, show a box with information about that area
- When someone clicks on a correct answer, add 1 to their score
- When someone reaches the end of a quiz, display their total score.

Some JavaScript interactions work in a similar way to CSS, by targeting different parts of the page. For example, JavaScript can be used to change the transparency property of an image to create the effect of 'fading out' or 'fading in'. They can also be used to add or remove text, images or other elements to or from part of the page.

Other JavaScript interactions work by storing information, which is then used to determine what the page does next. For example, a JavaScript quiz will store your score and then change it based on your actions (choosing a right or wrong answer), before displaying it back to you at the end, or using it to choose a more humorous result (such as 'which animal are you' or 'how old we think you are').

This ability to store information is central to some of JavaScript's most powerful editorial applications. It opens the door to more personalisation, for example: choosing your town from a list might trigger the display of information specific to that area; entering your wage details into a web form can allow an interactive feature to calculate the impact of a new budget announcement on your household.

Another powerful feature of JavaScript – and other languages like Python, R and Ruby – is that you can find lots of 'libraries' of code made by other people to solve similar problems (see p.303). One of the most widely used JavaScript libraries, for example, is jQuery, which has a lot of built-in methods for creating animation and interactivity. Another is D3, which makes it easier to create interactive charts and data visualisation. There are also JavaScript libraries for creating interactive maps, sliders, quizzes, apps and other types of content.

Which programming language should I learn?

Journalists starting out in interactivity and data journalism often ask which programming language they should learn. Really, there is no single answer: it depends what you want to use programming for. Journalists focused on *finding* stories often learn languages like Python, R and Ruby, which can be used to write scripts that gather information, clean it, analyse it and visualise it. Journalists focused on *telling* stories often learn JavaScript because of its widespread use for interactivity. But all these languages can be used for both purposes: PHP, Python or Ruby are often used in 'backend' web development to create more advanced database-driven applications, for example.

The key thing is to find a project that you are passionate about, and use it as a basis for exploring programming techniques. Keep things simple to start with – a quiz or counter, for example – and then look for tutorials on how to create it. It also helps to break down your challenge into smaller tasks: for example, 'How do I store a score using JavaScript?'

Programming concepts it helps to understand

If you're looking to get into coding, chances are you'll stumble across a raft of jargon, which can be off-putting, especially in tutorials that are oblivious of your lack of previous programming experience. Below are some concepts you're likely to come across – and what they mean.

Variables

A variable is a way of 'containing' information so that you can use it in a line of code. To give some examples:

- You might create a variable to store a person's age and call it 'age'.
- You might create a variable to store the user's name and call it 'username'.
- You might create a variable to count how many times something has happened and call it 'counter'.
- You might create a variable to store a user's score
- You might create a variable to store something's position
- You might create a variable to store a list of possible answers
- You might create a variable to store data for a chart.

Variables can be changed, which is their real power. A user's name will likely be different every time one piece of code runs. A score can change when someone selects a correct answer. A counter can increase by one every time something happens. A list of items can have items added to it, or removed.

They can also be combined or used as the basis of calculations: an age (one variable) might be calculated based on a birth date (another variable).

Strings, integers and other types of information

Programming is very strict about classifying different information, which affects what you can do with it. Typical types of variables, for example, include:

- 'Integers' (whole numbers) and 'floats' (numbers with decimal places)
- Text – generally called 'strings' and indicated by quotation marks like so: '17 August'
- Lists or 'arrays' – explained below – normally indicated by square brackets and commas like so: ['Manchester', 'Glasgow', 'Paris']
- Dictionaries or 'dicts' – explained below – normally indicated by curly brackets, colons and commas like so: {'Age' : 23, 'Name': 'Jane'}.

This is important because problems can occur when code encounters information in the wrong format. For example, you cannot perform a calculation with strings or in some cases combine text with numbers.

To prevent these problems in those cases, coding often involves telling the code to treat '7' as a number and not a string, or even to convert the string 'seven' to its numerical equivalent. Computers are great at performing tasks repetitively but need to be given explicit instruction as to what they are to do.

Functions, methods

Functions and methods are generally one-word recipes to do things that would otherwise take many lines of code to explain. Here are just two examples:

- The function *length* or *len* in some languages means 'give me the length of the thing I specify'.
- *Split* in some languages means 'split this thing into one or more things based on a criteria I specify'.

Most functions need extra information called an *argument* or *parameter* in parentheses after it. For example in this code:

length('Paul')

the function is 'length' and the argument is 'Paul'. 'Paul' is used as the specific ingredient which 'length' will give you the length of (four characters, in this case).

Many functions come ready to use in the programming language from the start. JavaScript, for example, has built-in functions including *length*, *split*, *search* (look for characters in a specified string of text) and *replace* (replace characters in a specified string of text). Python's built-in functions include *len*, *split*, *sum* (add up a series of numbers), *max* (give me the biggest number in a list) and dozens of others.

As well as built-in functions, you can create your own functions in your code. If you want to do anything more than once it is a good idea to create a function to save you writing that code over and over again.

A third type of function or method is one created by other people, and shared in a *library* – see below.

The *documentation* for a function or method should tell you more about what exactly it does – and what arguments it takes. These are called parameters in general, but they both mean the same thing – it's just that one term is used for the general ('This function has one parameter: an object to be measured'), and another for the specific ('Taking the argument "Paul"'). If you ever need to know what a function or method does, search for 'documentation' and the name of the function and language being used.

Libraries

A library is a collection of code that has been made available for other people to use. Just as a real-life library (called a 'package' in R) contains lots of books to help people do things (cooking, gardening, DIY), a library in programming makes it easier for people to perform certain tasks. Put another way: libraries are a way of using other people's code, and can save a lot of effort.

Each library is focused on a particular type of problem. If you can think of a problem, it's likely someone has created a library to deal with it: drawing a map; scraping information from a series of webpages; converting a document; charting data or putting it into interactive tables; creating animations or effects.

Within that library will be a collection of functions and methods (see above) that have been created to help solve parts of that particular problem. In a mapping library, for example, there might be functions which draw the background map, and other functions which help place a marker on that map, and another function which controls its shape and colour, and so on.

To be used, most libraries have to be *imported* – typically by using a bit of code that links to the file containing the library.

Why do people share libraries? Well it's part of the culture of programming to contribute back into the community. Sharing your code means others can help you improve it, or build extra features on top of it. It also helps build people's reputations. But most of all, it means everyone can make things more quickly and effectively than would be the case if no one shared their work.

Lists/arrays and dictionaries/dicts

Lists and dictionaries are special types of information that can be enormously useful in programming – but also confusing for those not used to them.

The terminology varies: in some programming languages lists are called *arrays*, and dictionaries are called *dicts* ('objects' in JavaScript).

A list or array is just that: a list of items, which looks like this:

['Asia', 'Africa', 'Europe']

Lists are enormously useful both for:

- Storing information (for example, in scraping, or a user's answers in a quiz)
- Repeating actions (for example, plotting or mapping each number or location in a list). See 'Loops' below.

A *dictionary* is similar: it is also a type of list, but with this key difference: a dictionary is a list of *pairs*.

Each pair has a label (called a *key*) and a value, connected together by a colon, for example:

'Age': 24

The term *dictionary* is useful: think of it as a collection of words with an associated definition. Another way to think of it is as column headings (age, name, location) and values (18, Sarah, Chicago).

Each pair in a dictionary is separated by commas and the whole is placed in a list in curly brackets like so:

{'Age': 23, 'Name': 'Jane'}

This makes it particularly useful for storing data that has more than one label. For example, you might store a list of ages as a simple list. But if you wanted to connect each age to a name or location, you'd need a dictionary to do that.

This is precisely the logic behind the data format JSON, a format used by a number of APIs (see p.305).

Loops

As mentioned above, one of the great things about lists is that they allow you to repeat actions many times – one of the main uses of programming.

To do this you normally use a *loop*. The loop starts at the first item in a list, performs some action with it, then repeats that action with the second item, and so on until it comes to the last item.

Examples include:

- Taking each location in a list and placing it on a map
- Taking each number in a list and sizing a bar in a bar chart to that amount
- Taking each item in a list of names and adding it to a partial URL to form the full URL
- Taking each URL in a list and running some code to grab information from it.

These are called *for loops* because they repeat *for* each item in a list. A second type of loop is a *while loop* which will repeat as long as (*while*) something is true or false. For example:

- Moving an image forward a pixel (animating it) 'while' someone's score is below or above a certain value
- Continuing to advance the timer 'while' it is below a certain value.

Understanding APIs

API stands for Application Programming Interface. APIs are often used to fetch information from another source, or connect your interactive with something else such as a social media account.

Typical APIs with journalistic uses include:

- Social media APIs (What are people saying/sharing in a specified location/with a particular term?)
- News APIs (What content has been published by a specified journalist/with a specified category?)
- Political APIs (How has a specified politician voted? What constituency does a specified person represent?)
- Location APIs (What is the latitude and longitude for this postcode? What is the local authority?)
- Crime APIs (What crimes have occurred near this location on this date? What were the outcomes?)

Here are some examples of how APIs have been used in journalism:

- A ProPublica investigation used the Facebook API to connect their data with the person's Facebook profile. This could then provide personalised data about their school, and tell them which of their friends had used the same app.

- One interactive used the *New York Times* articles' API to find stories about certain neighbourhoods, and place them on a map (using another API: Google Maps).
- A BBC investigation used the political API TheyWorkForYou to see which politicians had asked the most questions in Parliament (the API allowed them to request information on every question asked).
- A series of interactives published in Trinity Mirror's local news websites invited users to enter their postcode to find out about issues affecting their local area in the run-up to an election. The tool used a location API to convert that postcode into the right local authority area, which they could then provide information on (see 'Find my seat', p.316).
- A number of interactive apps and maps will detect the user's location and use a crime API to return information on the crime rates in that area, or use a social media API to show social media updates near that location.

APIs are particularly useful in programming, because they allow you to ask lots of questions and get lots of answers (generally as structured data), often based on live, or the most recent, data and without any middleman.

The coding is often focused on the presentation of the resulting information – for example, on a map, or in a chart, or in a timeline.

A question to an API is normally formed as a URL, and examples are often provided on the API's *documentation* pages. For example, the URL to ask the UK police API about crimes during a specified month at a specified latitude and longitude is:

http://data.police.uk/api/crimes-at-location?
date=2012-02&lat=52.629729&lng=-1.131592

If you split this URL where you see a question mark, everything after that question mark should contain the question that you are asking: the *query*.

How to form a query is normally also explained in the documentation pages. In the example above the query specifies a date (using *date=*), a latitude (*lat=*) and a longitude (*lng=*). Each piece of information is separated by an ampersand (&).

API keys and limits

Some APIs also require you to register for an *API key*. This is a sort of password which is used to ensure that you don't use the API too much. An API key normally comes with some sort of limit on the number of queries you can make (usually in the thousands). You typically use your API key by including it in the URL in the same way as other pieces of information, for example, *&key=AjkasjfajsfaiHIHU872832*.

Tools to write, find and share code online

To write code you only really need a basic free text editor. Built-in applications like Notepad or Textedit are OK, but it is better to download alternatives that have been made with coding in mind. These text editors – such as TextWrangler, Atom and Sublime Text – often include colour coding to help you differentiate between code and text, and highlights to tell you when tags haven't been closed. They also include many useful keyboard shortcuts and menu options to save time with repetitive tasks (Collins 2016).

Once you've written your code you need to remember to save it with the right extension: .html, .css or .js for HTML, CSS or JavaScript files respectively.

There are also web-based 'code playground' services, which speed up the process of coding and testing code. Codepen (codepen.io) and JSFiddle (JSfiddle.net), for example, split the screen into three windows where you can write HTML, CSS and JavaScript at the same time, and a fourth window where you can see the resulting working webpage. The results can be previewed live, and shared with others – or downloaded in a zip file that can be unzipped as separate HTML, CSS and JavaScript files.

Some of these services also allow you to browse experiments by other users, which you can then 'fork'. *Forking* means to 'clone' code in order to explore and adapt it. It is a good way to learn how other people have created a particular effect, by changing small parts and seeing how it affects the page.

One service that is particularly widely used to share code, collaborate, fork and publish is *GitHub* (github.com). You will find GitHub pages for individual journalists such as Condé Nast International's Jacqui Maher and ProPublica's Derek Willis, but also for organisations, teams and dedicated data journalism outlets like FiveThirtyEight. Here are some examples to check out:

- Derek Willis: github.com/dwillis
- Jacqui Maher: github.com/jacqui
- FT Interactive News: github.com/ft-interactive
- *Guardian*: github.com/guardian
- *Wall Street Journal* graphics team: github.com/WSJ
- ProPublica: github.com/propublica
- NY Public Radio: github.com/nypublicradio
- BBC News Labs: github.com/BBC-News-Labs
- FiveThirtyEight: github.com/fivethirtyeight
- The Upshot: github.com/TheUpshot
- BBC England data unit: github.com/BBC-Data-Unit
- WNYC Data News Team: github.com/datanews.

GitHub is something of a social network for code: you can use it to follow individual people, or projects. You can also create groups on the site (by setting up an 'organisation' account), and use it to collaborate with others.

Once you have set up an account, try visiting one of the examples listed above. Each GitHub organisation account page will have sections for 'Repositories' (projects) and for 'People'. The People tab allows you to see each person who is a member of that organisation, click through to their page, see what they're contributing to and 'follow' them. Following someone means you will be alerted when they make a new contribution to the project (this could be adding new code, or new files).

You can also follow individual projects by switching back to the 'Repositories' tab, going to a repository page and looking for the 'Watch' button towards the top of the screen. Clicking this allows you to opt in to notifications when the repository is updated.

There is some jargon to get used to on the site. For example:

- *Repositories* (or 'repos' for short) are collections of code and files. If it was on your computer, you'd simply call it a 'folder'.
- *Cloning* on GitHub means creating a copy of a project on your computer, normally to experiment with it yourself or to try to understand someone's code.
- *Forking* is very similar: this also creates a copy of someone's project. But this copy will be on GitHub too. When you fork a project, it's often because you want to maintain a link with the original. For example, you can *fetch* any updates to the original project in order to keep your version up to date. And it's much easier to submit a *pull request* (see below).
- *Branching* is a way of creating a copy of your own project, in order to try some different ideas. If your ideas don't work, you've still got the original version and can delete the branch. But if it works well, and you want to reintegrate it into the original, you can submit a *pull request* (see below) to do so. Branches also allow different people to work on different parts of a project, for example, adding new pages.
- A *pull request* is a request for your changes to a project to be included in the original version. For example, you might add a line of code, or correct some errors in the text, and want that new line, or that correction, to be reflected in the main project. If your pull request is accepted, then that is what will happen.
- *Version control* is a broad term for a system used to track different versions of files within a project. One of the reasons GitHub is so useful is it makes it easier to compare differences between different versions of the same file, and to revert to previous versions if you make mistakes.

One of the main uses of GitHub is to collaborate on projects, or to adapt work by others. Many news organisations make some of their code 'open source' (available for others to reuse) on GitHub pages, and so it can be very useful knowing how to find, reuse and build on that code. Examples include Quartz's chart creation tool Chartbuilder (github.com/Quartz/Chartbuilder), Vox Media's site generator Autotune (github.com/voxmedia/autotune) and New York Public Radio's Audiogram, a tool for generating shareable videos from audio clips (github.com/nypublicradio/audiogram).

GitHub also includes a way of easily publishing webpages from your files, called GitHub Pages (pages.github.com). This can be particularly useful if you need to test some code out but don't want to buy web hosting yet, and it can also be used to showcase your GitHub account in a more polished way. SRF Data, the data-driven journalism unit of Swiss Radio and TV, has a GitHub Pages site at srfdata.github.io, for example, while Guardian Digital Development can be found at guardian.github.io/developers.

CLOSER LOOK
COUNTERS

A JavaScript counter is a very simple way to add animation to a story and bring a key number to life. Normally placed in the middle of the story in the same way that you might have a graphic explaining a 'key statistic', the counter will start from one number (often zero) and begin increasing that number at a rate determined by the code that has been used to create it. The code may also specify a number at which the counter will stop.

Halfway through a *Telegraph* article about Apple (Titcomb et al. 2016), for example, a counter is included that explains: 'Apple made £37.47bn in profits in the last year. Since you started reading, that's . . .'—and then comes the counter. The user can watch as Apple's profits-while-reading accumulate.

The *Mirror* and its data journalism offshoot Ampp3d pioneered the use of counters in the UK, employing them in stories such as 'Live counter: watch how much NHS money is going into private hands' (Cocco 2014), 'Watch Wayne Rooney's earnings add up in real-time' and 'Watch how many foreigners enter the UK. Every. Single. Second.' (Now no longer online.) The last example used *multiple* counters to illustrate how headline figures about the number of foreign visitors failed to mention that most of those visitors were tourists. While the counter for tourists moved quickly, the counter of migrants did not, because the numbers were much smaller. It was a clever way of putting figures into context.

To create a counter a simple calculation is required: take a total amount (for example, £37.47bn in the Apple case above), and divide by the period of time that amount covers, in seconds (in the example above that would be the number of seconds in that year). That gives you the number *per second*, and you can set the counter to increase at that rate.

CLOSER LOOK
NEWS GAMES

Tell me and I'll forget; show me and I may remember; involve me and I'll understand.

(Proverb)

Games – and more generally *play* – have become an increasingly important element in journalism. In 2010 the seminal book *Newsgames* (Bogost, Ferrari and Shweizer 2010) identified seven types of newsgame: editorial; infographic; documentary; puzzle; literacy newsgames; community; and platforms. Five years later Maxwell Foxman looked beyond games to address the concept of 'play' in news (Foxman 2015): newsgames, he argued, were just one of four categories of game *mechanics*: the other three being badges, points and prizes; quizzes and questions; and situation-specific designs and packages.

Games have been used particularly often to explain or demonstrate complex systems. Early examples include the *Gotham Gazette*'s Budget Game, where users had to try to balance the city's budget, and *The Economist*'s Energyville game, which tasks players with maintaining a city's energy supply in reaction to various financial, environmental and technological changes. Online publication Fusion commissioned a mobile game about rigging elections to complement its documentary on the same topic (Lichterman 2016).

Philip Trippenbach, the co-founder of GameCamp who worked as an interactive producer for news organisations, notes that games are less useful for telling the facts of what happened in a given past event, but have enormous potential to explain how things work (Trippenbach 2009). Still, some – such as Al Jazeera's games on illegal fishing (Ruhfus 2014) and Syria's electronic armies (Ruhfus 2016) – use gamification techniques (Kohn 1999) such as points and missions as an innovative way to deliver a series of pieces of content.

CLOSER LOOK
BOTS

Short for 'robot' – specifically an internet or 'web robot' – a 'bot' is just a computer script, normally created to perform repetitive tasks. This broad description can cover such a wide range of terms that you may find it being used to talk about very different things in different contexts.

One common type of bot is a 'crawler' or 'scraper', which explores multiple webpages or documents and collects information about them: the 'Googlebot', for example, was created by Google to build its search directory (you can find more about scrapers in Chapter 10). Others will monitor information online and respond to it (for example, by changing prices based on demand). Bots are also used for nefarious purposes: for example, to make it look as if more people are viewing webpages or clicking on adverts.

In the context of interactivity and news publishing, however, the term 'bot' is normally used to refer to something that users can interact with. Examples include:

* A bot which automatically publishes updates on a particular social media account when it receives new information from a feed (such as new articles)
* A bot which can supply article suggestions in response to a query from a user
* A bot which attempts to provide answers to questions given by users.

One of the earliest uses of bots in journalism was the 'Twitter bot'. Bots have tended to automate three particular aspects of journalism: *alerting*, *aggregating* and *monitoring*.

The result is a level of coverage that would be unlikely to be provided by human reporters alone.

Alerting is relatively simple: many website Twitter and Facebook accounts are actually updated by 'bots', which automatically publish every time a new story appears on the publication's RSS feed (see Chapter 3 for more on RSS).

Aggregating can take a number of forms. The @North_GA news bot, for example (now suspended), aggregated RSS feeds from a number of news sources in the northern part of the state of Georgia. Others automatically retweet material matching a particular search (for example, updates with a particular hashtag or phrase, or stories matching a particular search term on Google News).

Monitoring often involves a script that tracks what public figures or bodies are doing or saying: @stopandfrisk, for example, fetches and tweets data from the New York Civil Liberties Union on police use of stop and search (Lokot and Diakopoulos 2015); while the Facebook page Sir Keir Starmer in Parliament (facebook.com/keirstarmerparliament/) posts an update every time the politician does something in Parliament (as recorded by TheyWorkForYou). Some include a threshold: WikipediaLiveMonitor (@wikilivemon) monitors edits on Wikipedia and tweets when the frequency of edits on a page is unusually high (indicating something newsworthy), while other Twitter news bots tweet when an edit is made from an IP address associated with the Houses of Parliament or other public body. Your Reps On Guns (@yourrepsonguns) retweets politicians when they mention firearms or related terms.

Lainna Fader, engagement editor at *New York Magazine*, notes that the obsessive repetition of bots makes them useful 'for making value systems apparent, revealing obfuscated information, and amplifying the visibility of marginalized topics or communities' (Fader 2016).

An analysis of 238 Twitter 'news bots' (Lokot and Diakopoulos 2015) identifies further uses of news bots, including *critique and opinion* (@NYTanon, for example, critiques the use of anonymous sources in the *New York Times*, and @cybercyber highlights the overuse of the term 'cyber' in news reporting) and *entertainment* (some bots, such as @DrunkBuzzFeed, 'remix' content with amusing results).

The first wave of Twitter bots was largely based on automated technology: tools like Twitterfeed (now closed) made it simple to connect an RSS feed to a Twitter account. Later, services including IFTTT and Zapier made it easy for people to connect all sorts of services (for example, to update a Facebook page whenever a Google spreadsheet was added to it).

A second wave of *chatbots* came as a number of messaging platforms opened up their platforms to developers. The chat app Telegram was one of the first, launching a bot creation API in June 2015. '[Bots] can do anything', the company announced. '[T]each, play, search, broadcast, remind, connect, integrate with other services, or even pass commands to the Internet of Things' (Telegram 2015). TechCrunch and Forbes Telegram bots would invite users to choose particular topics, authors and sections to subscribe to, but could also ask questions like 'Who is Jack Dorsey?' or

'What is Disrupt?' (Bernard 2016). The BBC realised it was an opportunity to reach audiences in places where the BBC Uzbek language website was blocked (BBC News Lab 2016).

Messaging app Slack added a bot directory six months later. The *New York Times* used it to create a bot for election alerts while Digg's Slack bot provided story recommendations based on keywords (Wang 2016). Bots could also be used for internal purposes: nyt-campfinbot (github.com/newsdev/nyt-campfinbot) was created to notify *New York Times* reporters about filings to the Federal Election Commission's website.

In 2016 the trickle became a flood: Kik, Line, Skype, Facebook Messenger and Viber all introduced bots, while Twitter added bot functionality to direct messages (Power 2016) and Amazon Lex was launched to help people create bots for its Alexa platform. Facebook's launch of bots on its Messenger platform included a demonstration of CNN's app. The *Guardian* used the platform to create a Sous-Chef Messenger bot that provided recipes to users when they suggested an ingredient or keyword. Bots, it was said, were the new apps.

Why the big rush? For publishers a big driver was the realisation that people were no longer adding new apps to their mobile phones (Frommer 2014), and the 'new frontier' on mobile was *within* those apps that people already spent most of their time using. For the chat apps it was the rise of 'messaging as platform': in China people were already able to pay for goods, services and *content* within chat apps like WeChat, and Western chat services saw an opportunity to expand. But a third trend was related to technical capability: artificial intelligence (AI) was now at a stage where it could be used to power bot technology, opening up all sorts of new possibilities. Even some Twitter bots have become more sophisticated and able to respond to queries in different ways.

As with any rush, a number of services also popped up to make it easier for people and companies to create bots, including Chatfuel (chatfuel.com), Botsify (botsify.com), Api.ai and Gupshup (gupshup.io). These tended to offer basic automation, as well as ergodic functionality (users choose from a limited number of options). But the real challenge is designing bots that respond to the wide range of language used by users: the Slack scheduling bot MeeKan reportedly needed over 2000 sentences just to deal with one meeting request.

Simple bots can be relatively easy to create with these tools, and it is also easy to create automated bots using IFTTT or Zapier to connect an RSS feed or Google spreadsheet to Slack, Twitter or other services. The key is to decide what you want to do this for.

Lokot and Diakopoulos (2015) suggest four elements to consider when designing a bot: the input; the output; the algorithms that turn inputs into outputs; and the function or intent. 'These categories and their subcategories can act as a starting point for the decisions a newsroom team might have to make in defining and building a bot.'

CLOSER LOOK
CLICKABLE INTERACTIVES AND MULTIMEDIA INTERACTIVES

Clickable interactives or multimedia interactives provide a special interface to allow users to explore elements of a story. The BBC's 'UK military deaths in Iraq', for example, allows you to filter and click on profiles of servicemen and women who died in the country between 2003 and 2009, while the *Telegraph*'s 'Walls around the world: the barriers being built to divide people' invites you to click on different construction projects to find out more about their political context.

Most clickable interactives are created using programming in languages such as HTML5 and JavaScript. The more complex your interactive, the more advanced your technical skills are likely to need to be.

One of the potential disadvantages of clickable interactives is that they can become out of date if new information is not incorporated. Some ways to address this include incorporating a live feed from a database or dataset that itself is updated (see 'News apps' below). Remember that you may need to plan for the long-term maintenance of the interactive, including manual monitoring and corrections.

CLOSER LOOK
NEWS APPS

ProPublica's Scott Klein describes a news app as 'a big interactive database that tells a news story' (Klein 2012). But the database is just what powers the app: from the user's point of view the 'app' is typically the webpage, which allows users to connect with and explore the information in that database. The webpage therefore provides, as one data journalist describes it, 'windows into the data behind a story' (Davis 2012).

Unlike a mobile phone app, a news app – or 'interactive news application' (Boss and Broussard 2016) – requires no download and can be viewed on the desktop as well. Interaction with the data comes through selecting options from drop-down lists, typing into a form, clicking on a map or chart or even allowing access to background information from your computer such as your location or operating system.

ProPublica has been responsible for some of the best-known news apps. Dollars for Docs (projects.propublica.org/docdollars), allows users to find out if their doctor has received money from drug companies or device manufacturers; Cruise Control (projects.propublica.org/cruises) tells the story of problems on cruise ships while allowing users to search ships' health and safety records; and The Opportunity Gap (projects.propublica.org/schools) allows parents to compare school districts.

NPR launched its seven-person news app team in 2012: its projects include Playgrounds for Everyone (playgroundsforeveryone.com), a guide to accessible playgrounds driven by user contributions. In the UK the *Financial Times*'s news app The UK Economy at a Glance (ig.ft.com/sites/numbers/economies/uk) is a dashboard that pulls economical data from a range of sources into one page, while the *Guardian* explored the housing crisis by allowing users to see just how much of the country was outside their budget in Where Can You Afford to Buy a House?

Because they need to communicate with a database, news apps often require more web development time than other interactive features, sometimes involving multiple members of the editorial team. The *Chicago Tribune*'s Brian Boyer, for example, says their team often writes code in pairs: 'Most projects don't take more than a week to produce, but on longer projects we work in week-long iterations, and show our work to stakeholders – reporters and editors usually – every week' (Boyer 2012). These demands mean that apps often tackle longer-lasting issues or problems outside the news cycle.

The editor of the *New York Times* interactive news team, Chase Davis, recommends addressing three questions before building a news app: Who is my audience and what are their needs?, How much time should I spend on this? and 'How can I take things to the next level?' Examples include:

> Solve a generic problem; create a new way to engage users; open source parts of your work; use analytics to learn more about your users; or even find cases like [property valuation web app] Curbwise where part of your app might generate revenue.
>
> (Davis 2012)

News apps face an issue around archiving and future-proofing: as Meredith Broussard notes, archiving news apps presents a particular challenge of software preservation rather than merely preserving static web content, given that apps typically consist of a combination of code, data and media which may reside on different servers (Broussard 2015). Any news app creation, then, should consider such future-proofing and archiving challenges.

CLOSER LOOK
PERSONALISATION

The interactive quiz 'How Y'all, Youse and You Guys Talk' was the *New York Times*'s most successful story of 2013 – but it wasn't the first time a personalised interactive had become a massive viral hit. Two years earlier a similar interactive by the BBC, 'The world at seven billion', became the most clicked, shared and 'liked' news story on Facebook of 2011, and the fourth most popular on Twitter.

The key to both was personalising the experience to the user. Instead of merely saying 'Here is some interesting research', the *New York Times* interactive *demonstrated* it, on *you*. In classic storytelling, it followed the rule of 'Show, don't tell'.

Similarly, instead of just reporting on the world's population reaching a landmark, the BBC decided to relate it directly to the user. By entering your date of birth you would be given your own position in those 7 billion (for example, the 4 billionth person alive on Earth at that time).

A particular success was to make that personalisation *social* too: upon completing the interactive, users were invited to 'share this page' with a customised message that said 'My number is . . .' with their specific number and the hashtag #whatsyournumber.

Personalisation can work in all sorts of ways: when the *New York Times* created a story on the best and worst places to grow up, they made the text change depending on where the user's computer was located. 'Consider Middlesex County, Mass., our best guess for where you might be reading this article', the text might read (if that was where you were). 'It's one of the better counties in the US in helping poor children.'

Other interactives ask the user to type in a postcode or zip code to find out what health, or education, or crime is like near them. *Time* magazine used research on cycles in baby name popularity to ask 'How popular will your name be in 25 years?' again based on the user typing it in. And the Daily Bread interactive by Where Does My Money Go? (wheredoesmymoneygo.org/dailybread.html) asks you to drag a slider to indicate your salary, and then tells you how much of that goes on tax, and how much of that tax is spent on defence, health, the environment and so on.

CLOSER LOOK
MAKING DATA JOURNALISM USEFUL WITH WEB TOOLS

Some interactives seek to do more than just tell stories or personalise them: they actively seek to empower users. During the 2015 UK election, for example, a number of developers created Voting Advice Applications (VAAs) such as Who Should You Vote For?, PositionDial.com, YourCandidates.org.uk and WhoGetsMyVoteUK. Vote for Policies was typical of these in offering to help you 'Compare policies from each party in their own words, and make an informed decision about who to vote for' while Who Shall I Vote For? was a 'quick, interactive and insightful quiz' to '[d]iscover whose policies match your personality'.

Sometimes tools are not about decision-making, but helping users connect with others, or hold power to account. VoteSwap told the user what kind of constituency they live in and whether it was worth swapping your vote with someone in a constituency where it was likely to have an impact. Three days before the election it was reported that over 13,000 Labour and Green supporters had used the site to swap votes. Ask Your Candidate helped users ask questions of prospective parliamentary candidates and Democracy Club CVs allowed users to ask candidates for their CV and share them on that site.

HOW WE DID IT: FIND MY SEAT, PATRICK SCOTT, TRINITY MIRROR DATA UNIT

During the 2015 UK General Election the Trinity Mirror Data Unit created a special interactive tool that allowed readers to find out more about their own constituency. The tool was used across all their titles including the national Mirror *newspaper as well as the* Liverpool Echo, Birmingham Mail, Manchester Evening News, Newcastle Chronicle *and north Wales's* Daily Post. *Patrick Scott was part of the team that created it.*

The main problem when it came to the data was getting it broken down to the correct geographical areas. Obviously because we were doing the project in conjunction with the election the most relevant breakdown was for parliamentary constituencies, so any data we used had to be available in that format. This was probably the main constraint I was under and meant that we couldn't display some of the data for Scottish and Northern Irish constituencies because it simply wasn't available.

[Statistical site] NOMIS was fantastic in this regard because it provides very flexible options when it comes to picking the areas you want your data to cover. It's also pretty much the definitive source for the measures I was interested in anyway so, in the main, I didn't have to stray too far away from there when it came to getting the data. The main exception to this was the house price figures which I sorted into constituencies myself using [the programming language] R and the Land Registry's price paid data.

The goal with all the measures was to draw them from the official channels (NOMIS, Office for National Statistics, etc.) so as to keep them authoritative and reliable.

In terms of managing the whole thing it was just a case of keeping a master spreadsheet in as tidy a condition as I possibly could. This involved grouping different measures into themes by colour and lots and lots of use of Excel's Rank function. If nothing else it taught me that constituency codes are far, far easier to match up than constituency names.

When it came to the visuals the main challenge was to distil all the information we had into something that was easy to understand and relevant to the conversations surrounding the election debate as well as to each individual who used the search tool. Find My Seat ended up being effectively split into two parts with the top part giving basic information like the name of the constituency the person lived in, who their MP was, who won last time and who was standing this time. The second part was the more detailed 'issues' section where we attempted to build up a picture of what was happening in each constituency in terms of the economy, the cost of living, immigration and pensions.

Because Trinity Mirror sites don't have paywalls we are reliant on pageviews and advertising to bring in cash. In this sense interactives like Find My Seat are good because it is content that can be used across the group and promoted throughout the build-up to the election without needing to be updated. I think it had about 250,000 uses across the group while it was up and running. It probably did well in terms of dwell time too.

(Interview by Antia Geada)

Summary

Interactivity is a central feature of online journalism as a genre. The best online journalism exploits the potential of the medium to create the most effective way to communicate information and engage the user. Typically, that involves allowing the user some degree of control over input or output, or the time or space in which they can experience the story.

As interactivity has become more and more established within journalism, certain formats and generic qualities have emerged. The quiz, for example, is now established as one of the most engaging and basic formats, and interactive maps have become commonplace. Data-driven journalism has led to the rise of 'news apps' that allow users to explore the data in their own way, while calculators add an extra dimension of personalisation. As the form matures further, expect more formats and practices to establish themselves within the storytelling toolkit.

This increasing role of interactivity has also led to increasing demands for journalists who either understand how coding works, or who can code themselves. Most journalism takes place within teams, and being able to communicate with developers or designers in that team, or adapt to situations that require a little coding, is an important advantage in a competitive jobs market.

One of the most difficult ethical demands on journalists is to make complex issues clear to audiences, and engaging, without oversimplifying them. Interactivity allows us to connect with people at a personal level while also providing opportunities to explore the complexities of important stories, and ultimately empowers users as active citizens. Journalism that does not allow users to interact with the issues, facts and stories involved risks being seen as flat and frustrating: a disappointing user experience that reflects on the news brand as a whole.

Interactivity does not have to be difficult. With dozens of third party tools that you can use to make sliders, maps and other formats, it's easy to get started: developing a creative mindset around storytelling ideas is the most important thing to begin with. And there are new developments every month in interactivity that bring new possibilities to make an impression on both your audience and your employers – make sure you explore them.

Activities

1   Map out possibilities for interactivity. Choose an issue you have recently read about – or that you are reporting on – and use the checklist of user control outlined in this chapter to list ideas for giving the user control over time, space, input or output. Then go through this list of interactive formats and write down ideas for exploring that issue using as many formats as possible:

    1 Polls
    2 Quizzes
    3 Maps
    4 Image maps
    5 Timelines

      6 Sliders

      7 Multiple path stories

      8 Bots

      9 Clickable interactives

     10 Counters

     11 Newsgames

     12 Personalisation

     13 Calculators

     14 News apps.

2 Brainstorming newsgames. Draw up a storyboard for an interactive game around a particular issue. Think about the following:

   - What are the key issues?
   - Who are the key characters?
   - What are the challenges that they face?
   - What factors do they have to weigh up in making decisions?
   - What sorts of storylines exist around this topic? (history, present, future).

3 Create an interactive map. Use Google Map Maker, Crowdmap or another mapping tool to create a map of incidences of a particular event, for example, crimes, failing schools, accidents. Consider the type of information you need and how it needs to be formatted, and what story the map is telling.

4 Create a basic bot. Use IFTTT.com or Zapier to create a bot that will automatically update a Twitter account, Facebook page or Slack channel when something happens. The article '22 essential IFTTT recipes for Twitter' (cnet.com/uk/how-to/22-essential-ifttt-recipes-for-twitter) is just one of many that outline the process and the options. Look for other examples of recipes and tutorials online.

5 Create an interactive timeline of online journalism. Use one of the interactive timeline tools mentioned in this chapter, or another that you find online, and create a timeline for the key moments in web history outlined in the opening chapter of this book. Try to find or create images, video, audio or other elements to illustrate each moment. Tweet the results to me @paulbradshaw!

Further reading

Bogost, Ian, Ferrari, Simon and Shweizer, Bobby (2010) *Newsgames*, Cambridge, MA: MIT Press

Foxman, Maxwell. Play the news: fun and games in digital journalism, Tow Center for Digital Journalism, Columbia Journalism School 2015, http://towcenter.org/wp-content/uploads/2015/02/PlayTheNews_Foxman_TowCenter.pdf

Woolley, Samuel, Boyd, Danah and Broussard, Meredith. How To Think About Bots, https://motherboard.vice.com/read/how-to-think-about-bots

Online resources

BBC Editorial Guidelines: Surveys, Opinion Polls, Questionnaires, Votes and Straw Polls, bbc.co.uk/editorialguidelines/guidance/surveys

For Journalism (data journalism resources for all): forjournalism.com

Watch Ray Daly talking about 'JS journalism' at http://js-journalism.org

Dan Nguyen: Build a web portfolio from scratch with Github pages: https://dannguyen.github.io/github-for-portfolios

Playbuzz Academy: publishers.playbuzz.com/academy

Playbuzz interactive tools: playbuzz.com/create

Bibliography

Aarseth, Espen (1997) *Cybertext – Perspectives on Ergodic Literature*, Baltimore, MA: Johns Hopkins University Press

Barbaro, Michael and Giratikanon, Tom. A viewer's guide to the mayoral candidates, *New York Times*, 4 April 2013, www.nytimes.com/interactive/2013/04/14/nyregion/mayoral-candidates.html

BBC Editorial Guidelines, Section 10: Politics, Public Policy and Polls, www.bbc.co.uk/editorialguidelines/guidelines/politics/opinion-polls, accessed December 2016

BBC News Lab. Bots in news labs, BBC News Lab, 12 July 2016, http://bbcnewslabs.co.uk/2016/07/12/bots-in-newslabs

Belam, Martin. What can news organisations like news.com.au learn from the BBC's approach to online voting fraud? Currybetdotnet, 29 January 2013, www.currybet.net/cbet_blog/2013/01/news-voting-fraud.php

Benton, Joshua. Arguing for a new genre: 'JavaScript journalism', NiemanLab, 30 July 2013, www.niemanlab.org/2013/07/arguing-for-a-new-genre-javascript-journalism

Bernard, Travis. Check out the new AI-powered TechCrunch news bot on Telegram messenger, TechCrunch, 15 March 2016, https://techcrunch.com/2016/03/15/check-out-the-new-ai-powered-techcrunch-news-bot-on-telegram-messenger

Bogost, Ian, Ferrari, Simon and Shweizer, Bobby (2010) *Newsgames*, Cambridge, MA: MIT Press

Boss, Katherine and Broussard, Meredith. 'Challenges facing the preservation of born-digital news applications', IFLA International News Media Conference, Hamburg State and University Library, 20–22 April 2016, http://blogs.sub.uni-hamburg.de/ifla-newsmedia/wp-content/uploads/2016/04/Boss-Broussard-Challenges-Facing-the-Preservation-of-Born-digital-News-Applications.pdf

Boyer, Brian. How the news apps team at Chicago Tribune works. In Gray, Jonathan, Bounegru, Liliana and Chambers, Lucy (eds) (2012) *The Data Journalism Handbook*, 1st edn, http://datajournalismhandbook.org/1.0/en/delivering_data_2.html

Broussard, Meredith. Preserving news apps present huge challenges, *Newspaper Research Journal*, 36(3), September 2015: 299–313, http://doi.org/10.1177/0739532915600742

Calderon, Arielle. Everything you need to know about creating BuzzFeed quizzes, BuzzFeed, 3 September 2015, https://www.buzzfeed.com/ariellecalderon/buzzfeed-quiz-guide

Cocco, Federica. Live counter: watch how much NHS money is going into private hands, *Mirror*, 7 October 2014, www.mirror.co.uk/news/ampp3d/live-counter-watch-how-much-4389075

Collins, Keith. How to use coding apps like a pro to work magic with text, Quartz, 20 August 2016, http://qz.com/759600/you-dont-have-to-be-a-programmer-to-harness-the-power-of-text-editors

Corcoran, Liam. How PlayBuzz went viral, NewsWhip, October 2014, https://www.newswhip.com/2014/10/playbuzz-went-viral

Dalton, Dan. Can you navigate a day with depression? BuzzFeed, 7 December 2015, https://www.buzzfeed.com/danieldalton/again-again

Datoo, Siraj. There are more male MPs right now than the total number of female MPs ever, BuzzFeed, 21 October 2014, https://www.buzzfeed.com/sirajdatoo/women-mps-in-parliament

Davis, Chase. How to build a news app. In Gray, Jonathan, Bounegru, Liliana and Chambers, Lucy (eds) (2012) *The Data Journalism Handbook*, 1st edn, http://datajournalismhandbook.org/1.0/en/delivering_data_2.html

Digital Storytelling Effects Lab (DiSEL). HTML versus Flash: what works best – and when, Digital Storytelling Effects Lab, Fall 2005. www.lauraruel.com/disel/DiSEL_report_one.pdf

Donoghue, Mark. Author interview, 2011

Downes, Edward J. and McMillan, Sally J. Defining interactivity: a qualitative identification of key dimensions, *New Media and Society* 2(2), June 2000, DOI: 10.1177/14614440022225751

Fader, Lainna. A brief survey of journalistic Twitter bot projects, Points, 26 February 2016, https://points.datasociety.net/a-brief-survey-of-journalistic-twitter-bot-projects-109204a8d585

Fenn, Chris, Powell, Jim and Mead, Nick. How is London's skyline going to change? An interactive guide, *Guardian*, 29 March 2014, https://www.theguardian.com/artanddesign/ng-interactive/2014/mar/london-skyline-changing-now-future-pictures

Flowers, Andrew. 'FiveThirtyEight's data journalism workflow with R, useR!', 2016 International R User Conference, 15 June 2016, https://channel9.msdn.com/Events/useR-international-R-User-conference/useR2016/FiveThirtyEights-data-journalism-workflow-with-R

Foxman, Maxwell. Play the news: fun and games in digital journalism, Tow Center for Digital Journalism, Columbia Journalism School 2015, http://towcenter.org/wp-content/uploads/2015/02/PlayTheNews_Foxman_TowCenter.pdf

Frommer, Dan. Most smartphone users download zero apps per month, Quartz, 22 August 2014, http://qz.com/253618/most-smartphone-users-download-zero-apps-per-month

Gillmor, Dan (2006) *We the Media*, Sebastapol, CA: O'Reilly Media

Greenwald, Glenn. Hacking online polls and other ways British spies seek to control the internet, *The Intercept*, 14 July 2014, https://theintercept.com/2014/07/14/manipulating-online-polls-ways-british-spies-seek-control-internet

Hall, Jim (2001) *Online Journalism*, London: Pluto Press

Hamilton, Mary. Author interview, 2011

Iacovangelo, Alex. Living with Crohns Disease – Part 1, Philome.la, June 2015, http://philome.la/_Alex_Iaco_/living-with-crohns-disease---part-1

Jackson, Ben. Interactive game: Ebola in London, *The Jackson Review*, 8 November 2014, http://bjacksonuk.com/2014/11/ebola

Johnston, Chris. Third runway at Heathrow cleared for takeoff by ministers, BBC, 26 October 2016, www.bbc.co.uk/news/business-37760187

Keller, Josh, Lai, Rebecca and Perlroth, Nicole. How many times has your personal information been exposed to hackers? *New York Times*, 22 September 2016, www.nytimes.com/interactive/2015/07/29/technology/personaltech/what-parts-of-your-information-have-been-exposed-to-hackers-quiz.html

Klein, Scott. News apps at ProPublica. In Gray, Jonathan, Bounegru, Liliana and Chambers, Lucy (eds) (2012) *The Data Journalism Handbook*, 1st edn, http://datajournalismhandbook. org/1.0/en/delivering_data_2.html

Kohn, Alfie (1999) *Punished by Rewards: The Trouble with Gold Stars, Incentive Plans, A's, Praise, and Other Bribes*, Boston: Houghton Mifflin

Kovach, Bill and Rosenstiel, Tom (2007) *The Elements of Journalism: What Newspeople Should Know and the Public Should Expect*, New York: Three Rivers Press

Libert, Kelsey. What Playbuzz can teach you about creating viral quizzes, Inc., 18 June 2015, www.inc.com/kelsey-libert/what-playbuzz-can-teach-you-about-creating-viral-quizzes.html

Lichterman, Joseph. Can you make learning about gerrymandering fun? Fusion teamed with mobile gaming devs to try, NiemanLab, 20 October 2016, www.niemanlab.org/2016/10/can-you-make-learning-about-gerrymandering-fun-fusion-teamed-with-mobile-gaming-devs-to-try

Liu, Yuping and Shrum, L. J. What is interactivity and is it always such a good thing? *Journal of Advertising* 31(4), 2002, http://dx.doi.org/10.1080/00913367.2002.10673685

Lokot, Tetyana and Diakopoulos, Nicholas. News bots: automating news and information dissemination on Twitter. *Digital Journalism*, 15 September 2015, DOI: 10.1080/21670811. 2015.1081822

Miletich, Steve, Willmsen, Christine, Carter, Mike and Mayo, Justin. Shielded by the law, *Seattle Times*, 26 September 2015, http://projects.seattletimes.com/2015/killed-by-police

Mulroy, Laura. Could you pass David Cameron's English test (and avoid deportation)? *Mirror*, 19 January 2016, www.mirror.co.uk/news/uk-news/quiz-could-you-pass-david-7203301

Niles, Robert. Best practices for online polls, *Online Journalism Review*, 10 December 2007, www.ojr.org/071210niles

NPR. Turning the camera around: health care stakeholders, NPR, 2009, www.npr.org/news/specials/2009/hearing-pano

Ockenden, Will. Metadata quiz: who has Will been talking to? ABC, 19 August 2015, http://mobile.abc.net.au/news/2015-08-19/metadata-will-ockenden-contacts-quiz/6694234

Phillips, Russell. The Ubermotive guide to media influence, Ubermotive, 14 October 2012, https://www.ubermotive.com/?p=68

Phillips, Tom, Jewell, Hannah, White, Alan and Curry, Paul. Can you survive a week as Jeremy Corbyn? BuzzFeed, 3 October 2015, https://www.buzzfeed.com/tomphillips/can-you-survive-a-week-as-jeremy-corbyn

Popovich, Nadja. Can you guess the voter turnout in your state? *Guardian*, 11 October 2016, https://www.theguardian.com/us-news/ng-interactive/2016/oct/11/voter-turnout-presidential-election-states-2012-2016

Power, Rachael. Twitter's direct message chatbots: our verdict, MarketingTech, 4 November 2016, www.marketingtechnews.net/news/2016/nov/04/twitters-direct-message-chatbots-our-verdict

Ruel, Laurs and Outing, Steve. Recall of information presented in text vs multimedia format, Poynter, September 2004, www.poynterextra.org/EYETRACK2004/multimediarecall.htm

Ruhfus, Juliana. Why we decided to gamify investigative journalism at Al Jazeera, Medium, 1 October 2014, https://medium.com/@julianaruhfus/pushing-the-boundaries-of-news-why-we-decided-to-gamify-investigations-and-current-affairs-db6b13d64a46

Ruhfus, Juliana. Gamifying the Syrian cyberwar: 6 important lessons I learned, Medium, 4 October 2016, https://medium.com/@julianaruhfus/hacked-syrias-electronic-armies-can-we-at-al-jazeera-create-immersive-news-experiences-in-a-ceceaf3d98d9

Schultz, Tanjev. Interactive options in online journalism: a content analysis of 100 U.S. newspapers, *Journal of Computer-Mediated Communication* 5(1), September 1999, Page 0, DOI: 10.1111/j.1083-6101.1999.tb00331.x

Soper, Taylor. Nate Silver's advice to young journalists: learn to code now, GeekWire, 25 April 2014, www.geekwire.com/2014/nate-silver

Tamblyn, Thomas. A guy has created an interactive adventure story on Twitter, *Huffington Post*, 13 January 2015, www.huffingtonpost.co.uk/2015/01/13/man-creates-interactive-adventure-story-on-twitter_n_6461166.html

Telegram. Telegram Bot Platform, Telegram Blog, 24 June 2015, https://telegram.org/blog/bot-revolution

Titcomb, James, Hope, Christopher, Swinford, Steven and Mendick, Robert. Apple tax: Downing Street says tech giant 'welcome' to come to UK after EU orders Ireland to claw back £11bn, *Telegraph*, 30 August 2016, www.telegraph.co.uk/technology/2016/08/30/apple-ordered-to-pay-11bn-after-european-union-tax-investigation

Trippenbach, Philip. Video games: a new medium for journalism. In Charles Miller (ed.) (2009), *The Future of Journalism*, London: BBC College of Journalism

Van Hoven, Matt. 96 percent of users who start BuzzFeed sponsor quizzes finish them, Digiday UK, 13 April 2014, https://digiday.com/media/buzzfeed-quizes

Vidal, Corey. INTERACTIVE: Blend Your Own Adventure [START HERE] + Will It Blend? YouTube: Corey Vidal, 5 May 2009, https://www.youtube.com/watch?v=DcJFwy7KPBA

Wang, Shan. A friendly new Slack bot from Digg lets you ask for articles around keywords, domain names, and more, NiemanLab, 17 March 2016, www.niemanlab.org/2016/03/a-friendly-new-slack-bot-from-digg-lets-you-ask-for-articles-around-keywords-domain-names-and-more

Welsh, Stacey. INTERACTIVE: Do you believe in ghosts? Explore South Texas hauntings and decide, KENS5, 2016, www.kens5.com/features/interactive-do-you-believe-in-ghosts-explore-south-texas-hauntings-and-decide/345056471

Wu, Wei, and Weaver, David. On-line democracy or on-line demagoguery: public opinion 'polls' on the Internet. *Harvard International Journal of Press/Politics* 2(4), 71–86

Zhao, Kevin and Leung, Louis. Factors Influencing online poll participation, *International Journal of Cyber Behavior, Psychology and Learning* 3(2), April–June 2013: 1–12

2 Community, social media management and user-generated content

Chapter objectives

This chapter will cover:

- What is community management?
- Why media organisations are creating new roles in community and social media management
- How to plan a community management strategy
- Different stages in a community's development – and what to focus on in each stage
- How to identify key objectives in community and social media management
- Content ideas for engaging with your community
- How to research your community
- Why terms and conditions are useful in community management
- Measuring what works.

Introduction

In 2012 specialist magazine publisher Future Publishing was preparing to launch a new title. *Mollie Makes* was aimed at a new generation of young people who enjoyed crafts. But for this magazine, instead of hiring an editor, working on their first issue and preparing for an expensive print run, they tried something different: they employed a community editor first.

The community editor was to engage with the communities they were aiming the magazine at, find out what they were interested in, build relationships and 'build a buzz' around the magazine. It certainly seemed to work: when the print version of the magazine launched it quickly became Future's fastest growing title in the last decade, and Future began to adopt the practice for other new titles too.

Three years later Cates Holderness, the community growth manager for BuzzFeed, demonstrated the importance of her role with a simple act that resulted in record-breaking visits to her employer's website. It started when a follower of BuzzFeed's Tumblr account pointed Holderness to a Tumblr post about a dress. 'Is this dress white and gold', she asked, 'or blue and black?' When the image – and the debate surrounding it – was posted on BuzzFeed, the piece went viral. Massively viral. It was shared 16 million times in a few hours immediately after it was posted, and a number of subsequent posts tripled that number within the week. At one point 670,000 people were on the site at the same time. So many people were talking about the dress that it spawned its own hashtag – #thedress – and some sites even liveblogged the whole affair.

But this wasn't a piece of content created by a staff member: this was a piece of content that came from the community. It relied on relationships with users and Holderness's ability to take the pulse of the community, spot something interesting and highlight it to a broader audience.

Future and BuzzFeed are just two of a number of publishers and broadcasters who see community management as a key part of the editorial team, whether as part of pre-launch audience research and promotion, stimulating, moderating and responding to discussions across multiple social media accounts and forums, or acting as a channel for users to contribute directly to the website, broadcast or print publication. But what exactly is community management?

What is community management?

Community management refers to a broad range of practices. For some publishers community management is about building relationships with readers and working with them to produce the best possible journalism. For others it is more like a public relations role, focused on maintaining their brand across social media, or a commercial role focused on spotting money making opportunities. And in other cases community management is simply about managing the vast amount of audience interaction taking place across their comment threads, forums and social media accounts.

Staff who work in these roles can have a variety of titles, from 'social media editor' or 'community editor' to 'moderator', 'host', 'head of audience engagement' or any mix of the above. And the skills needed can vary widely. Some people make a distinction between externally facing roles, which they class as 'social media management', and roles that feed back into the organisation: the classic 'community management'.

Writing in 2012, for example, Richard Millington said:

> Whisky magazine, PCGamer magazine, and, to a lesser extent, The Economist, do [community management] very well. These magazines have people responsible for fostering genuine relationships between members, organizing events for the audience, subtly influencing the discussions, moderation, building up stars, documenting the best material, creating content about the community.

These are typically the exceptions.

Many news organizations have highly active commenting areas 'have your say!' – but very little in the way of a community. They attract online audiences, crowds, and, occasionally, mobs. News organizations don't want community managers. They want very good moderators.

(Millington 2013)

But since 2013 things have changed. And for the purposes of this book I will be looking at both community managers and social media managers, partly because roles often evolve from one type into the other, and the skills often overlap. One thing they have in common is this: they are responsible for the way that the media organisation interacts with its audiences.

In addition to these specific roles, however, *all* journalists need to have community management skills – and always have. Malmelin and Villi (2015), for example, identify four different roles that journalists adopt when collaborating with the audience community:

- Observer
- Developer
- Facilitator
- Curator.

The observer monitors the audience community's discussions to identify interests, needs and concerns. The developer helps improve the online platform(s) and service so that users are more likely to contribute. The facilitator helps start and maintain online discussions and feed those back to the editorial team. And the curator might highlight the best work by members of the community, both online and in print.

Community management is simply a recognition that journalists need to make sure that they have strong relationships with readers who are then much more likely to help with stories (either as sources or experts). In 2011, for example, research on financial and business journalists found that 81 per cent of respondents were 'engaging on a regular basis with their digital readers, thus fostering online communities' (Greenslade 2011).

Local reporter Georgia Graham says:

My work online is basically a constantly evolving community strategy aimed at reaching new people and finding new stories without alienating the stalwarts who actually buy the paper. Contacts I meet online through social networks take as much work to develop as those I meet for a coffee every couple of weeks, and rightly so. Now I am as likely to be direct messaged a story as I am to find one on my voicemail but it took 8 months of online activity, attendence at meetups and interaction with local issues and organisations to build up.

(Graham 2011)

Brighton journalist Sarah Booker agrees. She says,

Online communities are a great way to know your patch whether geographical or niche. A prime example of a journalist working with a community to improve a documentary about NHS food is Mark Sparrow. He joined message boards and Facebook groups for the Cystic Fibrosis community. I doubt his documentary would have been as rich without the input from that community and the two men I assume he found there who featured on the programme.

(Booker 2011)

In some cases news organisations have explicitly required journalists to engage with their audiences. The Times Group in India, for example, tied participation on WhatsApp with journalists' pay while the *Guardian* has monitored the impact of journalists' participation in comment threads to ensure a healthy conversation.

Why community management?

Community has always been a key part of journalism, but the internet has had two key roles in heightening its profile: first, interactive technologies now make it easier for communities to participate in journalism. But second, we can now also measure their impact: research as early as 2005, for example, identified that when users felt that a website 'Looks out for people like me' (which included a strong sense of community, interaction and a variety of perspectives and publishers caring about their visitors), this helped drive website usage, while 'Connects me with others' also attracted views (Gordon 2008).

In 2009 the then editor of the *Guardian* Alan Rusbridger used the term 'mutualisation' of journalism to refer to the process of bringing readers into the journalistic process. In a more commercially minded example, in 2012 the head of regional newspaper group Johnston Press was saying that they intended to have half of their content created by 'citizen contributors' by 2020. Audiences are no longer an amorphous mass of passive receivers of content: their behaviour is key to the success of the company.

Researchers Nando Malmelin and Mikki Villi (2015) argue that audience communities represent a 'strategic resource' for publishers – the skills and competencies that gives the organisation a competitive edge – and as a result something that should be carefully cultivated.

More specifically, they identify two main advantages for publishers in working actively with the audience community:

- First, it helps strengthen engagement with, and loyalty to, the media brand.
- Second, it gives journalists a deeper understanding and knowledge of their audience, making them quicker to respond to trends and better at identifying stories they know will interest that audience.

As one interviewee put it: 'If we didn't have a community producing contents and subjects that they themselves are interested in 24/7, we wouldn't be able to keep up to speed on what's important to our target audience' (Malmelin and Villi 2015, p.7).

Lewis, Holton and Coddington (2013) use the term 'journalism of reciprocity' to refer to a range of practices adopted by journalists in engaging with communities of users. They

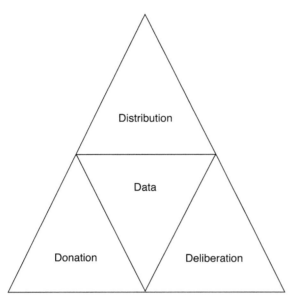

Figure 12.1
The four Ds of user involvement shows different ways that users might contribute, from distributing or donating content, to deliberation (reacting and interacting) or providing data about themselves and their interactions with the content
Source: Based on Krumsvik 2017

argue that these processes lead both to *instrumental* outcomes (goods, such as news stories) and *symbolic* outcomes (such as perceptions, thoughts and behaviour: for example, contributors feeling more important, or subjects of stories changing their behaviour or opinion).

More widely, a focus on communities can also benefit society as a whole. Recent research on user interaction on news sites found increased opportunities for citizens to engage with issues through online forums and social media. In one piece of research into local media's role in civic engagement one TV journalist suggested that the web was in many ways more effective than print had been:

> If you get on to the Yorkshire Post and you click on to a piece about Leeds City Council, you can read the piece and then there may be 200 comments from different people . . . So from that point of view, it's becoming much more important.
>
> (Firmstone and Coleman 2014)

These benefits are so integral to journalism's role that the authors of *The New Ethics of Journalism* (McBride and Rosenstiel 2014) listed 'Engage community as an end, rather than as a means' as one of three guiding principles for journalists.

Thinking about community management: the POST process

A useful framework to draw on when thinking about how you approach communities is the POST process for social media strategy outlined by Forrester Research (Bernoff 2007). This involves identifying:

- *People*: who is the community (or intended community), and where do they congregate online?
- *Objectives*: what do you want to achieve?
- *Strategy*: how are you going to achieve that? How will relationships with users change?
- *Technology*: only when you've explored the first three steps can you decide which technologies to use.

A similar process is outlined by the community management expert Richard Millington in his book *Buzzing Communities*:

1   First, collect and analyse data on your community's progress and health
2   Second, establish goals
3   Third, create an action plan
4   Fourth, track progress.

Identifying your community

In order to be a community manager you must first have a community. That may sound obvious, but different types of publications and programmes have very different audiences, and different levels of community. A specialist magazine, for example, is likely to be able to identify its community very clearly. But publications with much broader audiences – for example, national newspapers – struggle to do so.

In reality, a national publication is likely to appeal to several different communities, and will need to identify, and work with, each one separately. The *Telegraph* is well known for having a particularly strong readership in the military; another section of readers works in the financial sector. Its health coverage attracts doctors, while its fashion and gardening coverage attracts communities with those interests; and it has a strong community of rugby fans. These are all separate communities: there is no community of 'Telegraph readers'.

The smaller the community, the easier it is to identify and work with. You can categorise communities into five broad types:

- Communities of location (these are likely to be smaller than a traditional 'patch', e.g. hyperlocal)
- Professional communities
- Communities of interest (hobbies, interests or lifestyles)

- Communities of cause (what changes are your audience trying to advance – or prevent?)
- Communities of issue (what problems or concerns do your audience share?).

Key to the definition is whether members of that community communicate with each other regularly: 'When audience members have more regular communication amongst themselves, they can be said to form an actual community; otherwise atomized media consumers simply form a crowd' (Malmelin and Villi 2015, p.3).

Once you have identified a community, try to identify where they communicate and gather. There might be a Facebook group dedicated to their interest or cause, or there might be hashtags used regularly within their profession. There might be key blogs, forums or mailing lists that are keenly read.

Look for specialist social networks such as LinkedIn for professionals, SoundCloud for musicians and profession-specific networks such as Doctors.net or *The Times Higher Education*'s forums. Look for the communities in every corner of the net – don't expect them to come pre-labelled. For example, the forums of local football clubs and local newspapers often contain corners devoted to topics other than football and news.

One technique is to start with a few key individuals and trace what they do: Who do they follow on social media and who follows them? What platforms do they use and what groups do they belong to (search for their username: people tend to use the same one)? What hashtags do they use? What lists are they included on, and who else is on those? Who comments and links to their blog?

In Facebook Insights you can add pages to a 'Pages to watch' section. Facebook also offers a separate Audience Insights tool, which allows you to find out what a specific demographic on Facebook does. You can use this, for example, to find out about people on Facebook in the city you cover, or in your country with a particular hobby, or a combination of interest and location. You can even drill down to people matching particular relationship statuses, education levels and sexuality – and then see what pages they like, their occupations and other details.

If the community is on your own site, Facebook page or forum then look at data on their activity: Who is most active and when are people generally active? *How* active are they? What do users do: do they lurk without contributing or do most people do more than that? Do they stay with the site or forum over a long period of time or is there a high level of 'churn' (people leaving and being replaced by other users)?

Don't overlook the offline world too: What meetups and events exist in that field? What are the key organisations or places? Meeting in person is much more effective in building relationships than online communication, so try to meet whenever you can – even if it's just for a coffee to find out more about their world.

As you get to know the community try to identify what motivates it. In his book *The Art of Community* (2009) Jono Bacon identifies four different types of motivations:

- Utility-driven communities (people who want useful content, for example, to improve themselves or to further their career)
- Socially driven communities (people who are a member of a community because of the social support that it gives them, or how it contributes to their sense of identity)

- Change-driven communities (communities who share a desire for change)
- And emotionally driven communities (people who basically want to have fun, or experience other emotions).

What motivates your community clearly links to the content that you might produce for it. Utility-driven communities might be interested in reading tutorials and tips, or interviews that explain how a person achieved success. Socially driven communities might want content that they can share with others, such as the latest gossip. Or they might want content that helps them express a particular identity (such as the latest trends). Change-driven communities might want to be kept up to date with possible opportunities or threats to that change. They might want to be alerted to causes that they should be involved in. And emotionally driven communities may simply want amazing real-life stories, entertaining interviews or articles that help them to experience new emotions (for example, travel pieces, or sex tips).

Objectives in community management

As mentioned above, objectives vary enormously in community management from the superficial, promotional social media role to roles that genuinely seek to give a platform and a voice to your community.

The biggest challenge within community management is what are called 'transaction costs': in other words, the time and sometimes money needed to effectively engage with, and mobilise, people in your community. For this reason, if you are creating a community management role yourself, it is important to be clear what your reasons are for creating that role. If you are being hired to perform the role, find out what your employer's objectives are in doing so. If you don't know then you can end up being distracted by too many tasks.

Ideally you want to identify an objective which your audience shares. Jono Bacon (2009) identifies some typical ways of pitching projects to users which can improve the likelihood that they will work together:

- 'Solve this (common) problem'
- 'Become an expert'
- 'Join/don't be left out'
- 'Change/improve X'
- 'Influence X'.

The benefits of membership and activity need to be clear, and mutually beneficial.

Community management strategy

You will need specific strategies to implement for your own specific community. Once you've identified and are following the community, try to find your best role within it.

Table 12.1 Some common objectives for UGC and associated strategies

Objective	Example community management strategies
Users spend longer on our site	Give users something to do around content, e.g. comments, vote, etc. Find out what users want to do with content and allow them to do that on-site Acknowledge and respond to communities Showcase communities' work on other platforms, e.g. print, broadcast Create a positive atmosphere: prevent aggressive users scaring others away
Attract more users to our site	Help users to promote their own and other UGC Allow users to cross-publish UGC from our site to others and vice versa Allow users to create their own UGC from our own raw or finished materials
Get to the stories before our competitors	Become part of and contribute to online communities
Increase the amount of content on our site	Make it easy for users to contribute material to the site Make it useful Make it fun Provide rewards for contributing – social or financial
Improve the editorial quality of our work	Provide space for users to highlight errors, contribute updates Ensure that we attract the right community in terms of skills, expertise, contacts, etc. Involve users from the earliest stages of production
Users keep returning to the site	Give users a sense of identity and belonging Set up regular email alerts or newsletters Stimulate online discussions

Note: UGC = user-generated content.

Remember that the community is not here to serve you: barging in and asking for case studies will get you the same response as in any physical social space: blank stares and muttered insults.

Lewis et al. (2013) distinguish between two useful concepts in community management: direct reciprocity and indirect reciprocity:

- *Direct* reciprocity is a simple relationship where two members both benefit from an exchange.
- *Indirect* reciprocity, in contrast, refers to acts where an exchange benefits not the *giver*, but another member of the social network.

Examples of direct reciprocity include liking or sharing a social media post, upvoting links or linking to other blog posts in your field. When doing this you might expect that the other party will link back, retweet your Twitter updates or upvote your links.

Examples of indirect reciprocity might include a source passing a story on to a journalist that will not benefit them personally (indeed, it might harm their career or family life), but does benefit others in their community. Or a journalist sharing the information behind a story not because it benefits them directly, but because others in their community can benefit from it. Ultimately, they may still benefit indirectly: the journalist picks up new leads from new sources, for example.

Direct reciprocity is considered a *basic* building block of online community. Examples include retweeting or replying to non-journalists on Twitter, according to Lewis et al., which might provide a useful starting point for establishing 'a pattern of responsiveness and mutual concern' (2013, p.5).

But indirect reciprocity – one person helping another, who helps another – is the more productive, long-term approach: 'By working collectively, members expand their capacities to relay information more quickly and accurately, to connect one another with sources, to match resources with individual and community needs, and to build trust' (Lewis et al. 2013. p.6).

The simplest way to find a place in a community is through solving problems. Listen for questions that people are asking, or complaints that they make. A key skill of a journalist is to find the answers to questions, or get responses to complaints – so that's likely to be one way you can contribute. Those answers and responses, of course, also make for good story ideas and content (which can help you attract other members of the community).

Listen, and link to good content from your community where relevant (whether that is on social media or on your website). This does two things: first, it demonstrates good attribution and demonstrates that you are not looking to take credit for yourself that belongs to others. And second, it makes other people aware of your work: a link to another blog generates a 'pingback', which alerts the author to your piece. Twitter users are notified if their tweet is retweeted by you, Facebook users if you 'like' their update, and so on. Comments are an extension of the same principle of acknowledgement.

You might also see the need for physical meetups or other events – don't be afraid to get stuck in and organise one.

What stage is your community at?

Richard Millington distinguishes between four different stages in online communities. What stage your community is at will influence how you spend your time.

1   The *inception* stage is when a community is just starting. In this stage growth is slow and there is no sense of community on your site. Most or all of the activity is initiated by you and there is little engagement.
2   In the *establishment* stage the community initiates at least half of the activity. There is now a limited sense of community, some engagement, and you are getting growth from referrals (people linking to you).
3   In the *maturity* stage 90–99 per cent of activity comes from the community, and there is a strong sense of community with high levels of engagement.
4   Finally, as the community grows too large it might move into the *mitosis* stage, splitting or growing into more specific groups, which individually are now back at the inception stage.

Millington suggests that the stage of development should determine where you focus your own activity as a community manager: in the inception stage, for example, he recommends spending 40 per cent of your time on growing that community: encouraging members to join, keeping them active and initiating and prompting discussions as you build relationships with members. A quarter of your time, meanwhile, is spent on moderation.

Similar strategies have been adopted by successful hyperlocal publishers. Writing about the first year of the Dutch hyperlocal network Dichtbij, Bart Brouwers notes that community managers were 'expected to spend half of their time reaching out to citizens (mostly through social media) and being out and about in their cities' (Jimenez 2012)

When a community moves into the establishment stage Millington suggests only 25 per cent of your time should be spent on growth, as you encourage members to invite their friends and share discussions and content. Other activities – strategy, content, relationships, activities and technology – now take on a more prominent role as you plan for scale.

And in the maturity stage the focus is on avoiding scaling problems: building processes into the community, organising events and building the profile of the community.

Finally, in the mitosis stage as the community starts to splinter, Millington recommends identifying and creating popular sub-groups, promoting and supporting them and managing leaders of those groups (and helping to train them).

Notably, in all four stages Millington suggests only spending 10 per cent of a community manager's time on content.

Codes of conduct: terms and conditions

Having clear rules for acceptable and unacceptable behaviour is very important if you want to make sure people don't fall out and accuse you of favouritism. Codes of conduct or terms and conditions (T&Cs) don't have to be complex, but they show that decision-making isn't arbitrary and should make it easy for people to identify whether or not something is acceptable.

T&Cs also help you legally: showing that you are a responsible publisher can help as part of a legal defence. Some issues to consider include hate speech, discrimination and incitement, data protection (what do you do with information you have about users?) and copyright (what happens if someone says content has been taken and used without permission?). See Chapter 8 for more details.

CLOSER LOOK
THE SCALING PROBLEM AND THE FOUR TS

'Scaling' a community is notoriously difficult: it is one thing to maintain a relation-ship with 100 people; quite another to do the same with 1000 or 10,000. Jono Bacon recommends 'four Ts' which can play a major role in scaling any community:

1   *Tasks*: give community members specific tasks to help them organise the community as it grows. For example, one person might be in charge of a particular section or topic, or skill.

2 *Teams*: putting members into teams helps them focus on each other, but make sure teams can communicate with each other.
3 *Tools*: creating tools can make certain tasks easier.
4 *T&Cs*: terms and conditions are important in setting ground rules about what is acceptable, and acting as a reference point when disputes break out.

Writing for communities: community management strategies

There are various pieces of content you can write that can help connect you to the wider community. Here are just a few ideas:

- *The best people/sites to follow in your field*. Sites often create a list of key individuals or sites/resources in your field. Not only does this create a shared sense of identity, but it helps others in your community find useful resources, and creates an impetus for people to highlight things you have missed.
- *'How I did it' tutorials and tips*. Tutorials can be very useful for particular communities, creating a role for you within them. They also take readers 'behind the scenes' and strengthen the relationship.
- *Discussion highlights*. If there is a regular online discussion in the community, there may be an opportunity to summarise it. Make sure that members are happy for you to do this, though.
- *Interviews with prominent community members*. Interviews are a great way of making contacts and also bringing yourself to the attention of the interviewee's community.

Live content: chats, Q&As and votes

Live content is a particularly good way of bringing a community together. That might be a live chat, a vote or poll or a Q&A where members of the community can post questions to a prominent or interesting individual.

Polls and votes are easy things to do – but not necessarily do well. The benefits need to be clear. In some cases longer surveys can be more productive than shorter ones: the *Lancashire Evening Post* grew its reader interaction by creating a large survey on the environment, which it promised to present strongly in its paper. Associate editor Mike Hill told Journalism.co.uk that a 40-question survey on local environmental issues gathered 1000 responses, a significant rise from the average hundred answers to the site's daily poll. 'Quite often when you are asked to fill in these surveys you don't want to because it's being used commercially, but because this [research] is for editorial, people want to respond' (Oliver 2008).

Reddit's AMA – Ask Me Anything – is a particularly successful example of the Q&A format being used in an online community, leading to partnerships with other media organisations, while the *Guardian* frequently hosts live Q&As in its careers section.

Hashtags can be used as a way of 'hosting' chats on Twitter: the nursing community hashtag #nursechat is used to organise a weekly discussion on the platform while the BBC's Jeremy Bowen and *Wall Street Journal*'s Sam Dagher have both hosted hashtagged chats #AskBowenBBC and #AskWSJSam on Twitter. These also provide an opportunity to curate the 'best bits' in an article the next day.

A particularly creative use of hashtags comes from *Real Crime* magazine: each Friday from 1pm the magazine used the #RealCrimeFriday hashtag to tell the story of an unsolved real crime case before inviting followers to pitch in with their own theories as to what happened.

Live chats often succeed based on the quality of the participants: if you can organise special guests that will help. But you should also consider inviting participants directly to get things started. The first time you host a discussion like this you may not get much participation but as with so much online publishing persistence is key: by doing it week after week people will come to realise that you are committed to the issue.

Similarly, liveblogs can be a great way of serving and attracting a community. At some point you may be attending meetups, conferences, hackdays or other events in your community (or even organising them). You should aim to preview, liveblog and/or review those events (whichever is most practical). And you can always organise live events online too: the music magazine *NME*, for example, hosted a 'listening party' to mark the 20th anniversary of the release of Nirvana album 'Nevermind', which they liveblogged.

Crowdsourcing

Crowdsourcing is the process of inviting users to help you complete a task: normally finding, interrogating or classifying information. The term comes from a combination of the words 'outsourcing' and 'crowd', and has been successfully used in a range of contexts ranging from science to politics.

In journalism it is often used in one of two ways:

- The 'wisdom of crowds' approach, whereby a news organisation seeks a diverse range of expertise to help solve a problem.
- And the 'Mechanical Turk' approach, where a news organisation needs a lot of users to perform a similar task.

The Florida News-Press, for example, used the 'wisdom of crowds' approach when it wanted to investigate high charges for connecting newly constructed homes to the water supply. Short on in-house resources to investigate the leads, it asked its readers to help. 'Readers spontaneously organized their own investigations: Retired engineers analyzed blueprints, accountants pored over balance sheets, and an inside whistle-blower leaked documents showing evidence of bid-rigging' (Howe 2006).

In a smaller experiment the *Guardian*'s Charles Arthur asked readers to predict the specifications of Apple's rumoured tablet (Arthur 2010). Over 10,000 users voted on 13 questions, correctly predicting its name, screen size, colour, network and other specifications – but getting other specifications, such as its price, wrong.

The Mechanical Turk approach is generally used when a news organisation has a lot of documents and wishes to involve users in poring through them. The *Guardian*'s MPs' expenses app is one of the most famous examples. This provided an interface for users to investigate MP expense claim forms that used many conventions of game design, including a 'progress bar', leaderboards and buttons.

Users can, however, be sceptical of crowdsourcing projects, seeing them as a way of getting users to do lazy journalists' work for them. For that reason it is important to make sure that there is some benefit for the user, and that it is clear that the journalist is working hard too.

In the MPs' expenses example above the organisation invested significant resources into creating a tool, which made it easy for users to participate in the activity. There was also a clear civic benefit to the project – users were helping to hold power to account – and it was clear that journalists would then pick up leads and work on those.

You should always be one of the biggest contributors to any crowdsourcing project, leading by example. And always make it clear what will happen to the work of users, regularly providing updates on progress so that users can see the results of their work (or that of others).

Curation and user-generated content

User-generated content (UGC) is central to a lot of community and social media management and reporters are increasingly expected to monitor content generated by the reader community to 'curate' (select and combine) the best examples. In 2013, for example, Trinity Mirror created 12 new roles for 'community content curators', while at the BBC an entire team is dedicated to sourcing, stimulating and verifying UGC.

News organisations regularly highlight the 'best tweets' of that day or week from readers, or use comment threads on forums and Facebook to draw out users' experiences. It is important to let people know when their comments have been used, or ask permission if they may not be aware that it may be used in that way.

There are various tools for curating content: Storify, for example, allows you to search Twitter, Flickr, Instagram, Facebook and YouTube and combine elements from all of them into a single embeddable thread. It will even automatically notify those featured in the story. If you are just curating tweets then Twitter has the 'Collections' facility to help you do that (dev.twitter.com/rest/collections). And Pinterest allows you to collect images and other media on one board.

Photo pools on Flickr or shared hashtags on Instagram can be a particularly simple way to engage with communities. The *Guardian*, whose experiments with Flickr include inviting users to upload their 'message to Obama' (later published as a book), have comprehensive internal guidance on setting up Flickr groups. Written by Meg Pickard, it includes the following dos and don'ts of setting up and running a Flickr group.

Do this:

- Ask yourself: 'Are people really likely to bother participating?' if not, then it's not worth doing
- Check whether anyone else is already running an identical group – if so, join it, don't duplicate it.

- Make it clear what the group is for – e.g. is there a particular format or type of shot? Remember that while setting constraints can be limiting, they can also be extremely helpful and make it easier for people to join in or know how to participate.
- Invite people to join the group, but don't spam. Invite people who have a known or proven interest in the topic.
- Participate in the group. Respond to questions, comment on photos and keep looking for good things or people to invite to the collection. Add images yourself whenever possible – good community requires participation, not just a platform.
- Recognise and respond to good or interesting submissions or perspectives, even if you don't feature them on the [newspaper] site.
- Act as a good Flickr member: report issues where you find them and encourage good behaviour.
- Be a good ambassador for the [newspaper] on the foreign turf that is Flickr.com. Behave well and be welcoming, funny, polite and intelligent.
- Above all, always treat Flickr users with respect and fairness.

Don't do this:

- Create something you wouldn't want to be involved with yourself, or can't really see the point of.
- Make a group and then walk away.
- Seek to exploit Flickr users or give them any indication that you would want to do so.
- Be afraid to remove items from the group pool if they're not appropriate, or remove members from the group if they cause trouble.

(Meg Pickard, personal correspondence, 2011)

Neil MacDonald, head of web and data at the *Liverpool Echo*, notes that it's important to highlight great content but using readers' content needs to be handled carefully:

We publish a photo from our Flickr groups every day, and will put a shout out for contributions to projects. We published a calendar of pictures from the group, and held an exhibition in our atrium. But Flickr has also been the source of most issues around social media. Posting images to the group means you agree that it can be used by the newspaper, but in the past some newspaper staff have used images which were posted by group members, but not to the group itself. That's not right. In one case we ended up shutting a Flickr group down because staff broke those agreements twice. We had to show that we took those breaches seriously.

(MacDonald 2014)

Moderating forums and comment threads

Comments are a central part of most media organisations' online strategies, with clear benefits for publishers in reader loyalty. However, the quality of comments is notoriously variable, leading some organisations to turn off their comment sections.

Much of this is due to how – or if – the comments are moderated. Research by the Engaging News Project found that nasty comments are reduced when journalists interact with comments (Steiner 2015). They recommended that journalists:

- Respond to questions
- Ask questions
- Provide additional information
- Encourage and highlight good discussion.

The research also found that the layout of comments made a difference, with commenters preferring a structure that allowed them to pick out different types of comments.

It is useful to have policies in place regarding when comments on a story should be turned on, when they should be turned off and what types of stories moderators should focus on. For legal reasons comments are often turned off when a story relates to a crime where someone has not yet been convicted, while particularly controversial subjects such as immigration, abortion and the Israel–Palestine conflict can lead to such heated (and generally unenlightening) comments that they are either turned off or pre-moderated (where comments only appear after they have been checked). The same applies to forums.

In the last few years a lot of commenting on news stories has moved from the news site to social media platforms, and there is some evidence that this has increased their quality and quantity (Hille and Bakker 2014). In these situations, remember that you can embed tweets (and Twitter collections – see above) or Facebook threads into news articles, bringing the discussion back alongside the content.

Journalists are also increasingly encouraged to participate in discussions elsewhere online. At the *New York Times*, for example, an audience development team monitor stories' social media performance not only to see what is being read most, but also to pick up editorial leads. In one case an article about college admissions was being intensely discussed on the Facebook page of conservative media personality Laura Ingraham.

> Recognizing her as an influencer, the social media team deployed [the author of the piece] to her page, where he answered the question Ingraham posed in her Facebook post about the story . . . The Times has set up its [analytics] account so as to be alerted when influential social media accounts post a Times article.
>
> (McDermott 2015)

As always the key question to ask is: what is your objective? If the story stands to benefit from reader comments, corrections or clarifications, comments can be very useful.

The Society of Editors and the World Association of Newspapers and News Publishers (WAN-IFRA) both offer free moderation guides online: see the links in the 'Further reading' recommended at the end of this chapter.

Blog networks sections

Some organisations bring their communities onto their sites by creating specific sections, or partnering with blogs in the field to create content networks.

The *Guardian*, for example, has blog networks for media, fashion and the environment among others, while the *Birmingham Mail* works with a network of hyperlocal blogs in the city. *Vice* has its own network of independent Australasian blogs and the *Huffington Post* has a blogger network too.

The practice is particularly common in the magazine industry: *Glamour* magazine has a 'Young and posh' blogger network that brings together '23 chic bloggers, all in one place' while Condé Nast's *Details* brings together over 60 fashion and lifestyle bloggers in the Details Style Network. Hearst, on the other hand, created a 'blog council' for its parenting magazine *Redbook*, made up of five 'mom bloggers'.

The main benefit for bloggers is exposure, but some will not need that, and it is easy for people to lose interest: you should be careful that the relationship is maintained beyond the initial enthusiasm and you continue to think about ways to work together. You should also always be on the lookout for new members as others stop blogging or move on.

Guest posts and cross posts

A common content strategy in community management is to invite someone to contribute a guest post, or to 'cross post' on your site something that they have already written elsewhere (which you think your readers will find interesting).

With guest posts you are suggesting the topic. It is key to keep the proposal simple: if it is a busy person who doesn't have a lot of time it should not appear too onerous.

One approach is to have a series of guest posts or contributions along a particular theme. This means that new contributors may already be aware of the series, and it is easier for them to look at previous examples to understand what is being asked of them. You should probably write one or two yourself to show how it's done.

One example of this is the *Guardian*'s 'Cine-files' series, which profiles independent cinemas around the country. This is not only simple to do but it has a clear benefit: it means the paper can cover a much broader geography than if they were limited to London-based reporters. Elsewhere in the paper the 'Clip joint' series invites users to suggest their favourite film scenes along an identified theme, such as 'training montages' or 'tense mealtimes'. Not only do readers get the pleasure of the final list, but the discussion around it – and competition to be included – is all part of the fun.

Another example relates to a series about community management itself: the Online Journalism Blog's series 'Lessons in community from community managers' (online journalismblog.com/tag/community-editors) simply asked a particular community manager for their top three tips for others interested in the field. The format was simple and short, and after a few weeks community managers began to volunteer to contribute.

Some news organisations dedicate entire sections to guest contributions: the *Guardian*'s Comment is Free is perhaps the best known example, where dozens of experts are invited to write about topical issues and The Conversation, launched in Australia in 2011, acts as a platform for academics and researchers to write in a similar vein. The site has since expanded to the US and UK.

The guest post format has also found its way onto YouTube, where prominent YouTubers will often appear in each others' videos. The advantage is clear, and applies whether in

CLOSER LOOK
GETTING COMMUNITY MANAGEMENT JOBS

Community management jobs are often filled from within the communities themselves. *Gawker Media*, *The Atlantic* and *Daily Kos* have all hired from their comments, while Samir Mezrahi, Ellie Hall and Dorsey Shaw were all hired by BuzzFeed because of their Community posts.

This makes sense: these people are already demonstrating that they can connect with a community, and don't have to begin from scratch when it comes to building relationships and reputations.

However, this doesn't mean you have to build your reputation in someone else's community: another common practice is hiring people who have built their own communities and reputations through blogging, YouTube and other platforms. When ESPN agreed to acquire FiveThirtyEight, for example, ESPN weren't just buying the brand and Silver himself: they were buying his audience too. And when the *Guardian* hired Lauren Luke to produce makeup videos part of the attraction would have been the thousands of subscribers her YouTube channel boasted – and her ability to interact with them.

video or online: by involving guests you are also attracting their audience with them, while they benefit from exposure to your audience. It is the classic 'duet' tactic borrowed from the music industry.

Measuring what works

> If you don't collect data you're probably reacting solely to the vocal minority in your community.
>
> (Millington 2012)

It is easy to focus your community management activity on what you think resonates with your community, or on the problems that appear most pressing. But it is important to keep returning to your objectives and asking 'Am I achieving what I set out to do?'

Measuring the effectiveness of your work is crucial to community management – and it helps strengthen your case if you are asked what your role is for, or want to ask for extra resources in doing it.

Some objectives can be easily measured: are you getting more users, or are users reading more pages or spending more time on your site? Are people engaging more – whether that's sharing links, commenting or replying? Some measurements are very specific: a 'conversion rate', for example, measures how many people are 'converted' from mere visitors to users who perform some sort of action (such as subscribing, registering or making a purchase). Conversion might also be about retention: for example, is a user still active a month or a year after registering?

Try to be critical about what you measure: lots of users or registrations are not always a sign of health. Regular activity is a much better indication. Likewise, does it matter if lots of people read your material if most of them never finish, and never return?

Measurement is normally done through analytics packages such as Google Analytics and Chartbeat for websites, and Twitter Analytics, Facebook Insights and Bitly for social media (see Chapter 2 for more on analytics). You may also have access to databases indicating registrations and other activity. All of these can help you identify where your attention is needed most: not necessarily where users are most vocal, but where they are quietest.

Measurement can also help you identify what stage your community is at, and whether you still need to be focusing on growth, or can begin to shift towards moderation, or training. And at that point, you can reassess your objectives, tweak your strategy and do your job even better.

Summary

Community management and social media management are vital elements to any media organisation's success: not only does it allow publishers to get to know their audiences better and identify potential opportunities, but it also helps journalists work with audiences to spot developments more quickly, and to report in ways that relate more closely to readers.

But communities have always been a key part of news production, as contacts. It is just that networked media allows journalists to manage a much wider range of contacts than ever before, and also allows potential sources to check out journalists' activity and get in touch.

Roles in the field vary widely. You might be helping establish best practice for other journalists, or working with the advertising department to identify ways to make money on social media. You might be organising events or commissioning content. When the series 'Breaking Bad' ended, for example, social media editors at the *Wall Street Journal* used a Google Form to ask readers how they thought the show should end, and illustrated the best ones in an article. The website also runs a book club: 'The WSJ Book Club is led by guest authors, the first one being Elizabeth Gilbert. Guided by Gilbert, participants read "Wolf Hall" by Hilary Mantel, then engaged in discussion online via the hashtag #WSJbookclub and the Facebook group' (Stone 2014).

At a local level breaking news editor Ben Turner (@BreakyWakey_Ben) will put out a 'shout out' most days – 'Normally around a particular themed day like "Burger Day" – to get daft song titles, film titles, etc.', explains the *Liverpool Echo*'s web editor Neil MacDonald:

> He also puts shout outs around events people are attending. Bake Off is very popular with our followers so he'll ask people to 'send us your baking triumphs and disasters'. Or when we recently had a lot of spiders appearing in people's homes he asked people to send in pictures. When there was a crash on the M53 he asked people if they were involved, and so on.

This variety is what many social media and community managers love about the job, but it can also be distracting: it is important to make sure that you are measuring the impact of what you do, as well as the activity of the community itself to make sure what you do is working.

But when done well, community management can fulfil some of journalism's most important functions: holding power to account and acting as a voice for the voiceless. And you can't ask for more than that.

Activities

1 Pick a news organisation or magazine and identify all the channels they use to communicate with their audience. Do they treat them as an audience, or as a community? Do they have different channels for different communities? What sort of content do they use to engage? What could they do better?

2 Use Facebook's Audience Insights tool to find out what type of people use Facebook where you live: their age, occupations and favourite pages. Then look more specifically at people with a particular occupation, interest or age group and see how their interests change.

3 List some of the objectives that you have for engaging with communities (both online and offline) as a journalist. Now list the objectives that that community might have (for example, is there a local campaign? Or do they have professional objectives? Or family concerns?) Try to identify where the two might overlap.

4 Lurk in an online community for a few days to get a feel for how people interact, who the key individuals are, the key talking points and what sort of role you might be able to play in it that isn't being played already. Write a piece of content that fulfils that role (for example, solving a problem, summarising a discussion, an interview with a key individual).

5 Decide on a measurement that will help you asssess whether your strategy is succeeding. Measure it before you begin, and then regularly afterwards. This may take months, so wait until you've been doing things for a couple of months before deciding if it's working.

Further reading

If you are handling UGC you need to be aware of the risks involved. FirstDraft News's guide *Journalism and Vicarious Trauma: A Guide for Journalists, Editors and News Organisations* is linked from firstdraftnews.com/vicarious-trauma-guide, while the Dart Center for Journalism and Trauma provides guidelines at https://dartcenter.org/resources/developing-your-own-standard-operating-procedure-handling-traumatic-imagery

Millington, Richard (2012) *Buzzing Communities*, Feverbee, https://www.createspace.com/4014863

Bacon, Jono (2009) *The Art of Community*, Sebastapol, CA: O'Reilly

Rosenbaum, Steven (2014) *Curate This: The Hands-On, How-To Guide to Content Curation*, Magnify Media

Society of Editors (2014) *Moderation Guide*, www.societyofeditors.co.uk/userfiles/files/SOE-Moderation-Guide.pdf

WAN-IFRA (2013) Online comment moderation: emerging best practices, wan-ifra.org/reports/2013/10/04/online-comment-moderation-emerging-best-practices

Online resources

Feverbee: feverbee.com

Bibliography

Arthur, Charles. Forecasting is a notoriously imprecise science – ask any meteorologist, *Guardian*, 29 January 2010, www.theguardian.com/technology/2010/jan/29/apple-ipad-crowdsource

Bacon, Jono (2009) *The Art of Community*, Sebastapol, CA: O'Reilly

Bernoff, Josh. The POST Method: a systematic approach to social strategy, Groundswell, 11 December 2007, https://web.archive.org/web/20100322200608/http://forrester.typepad.com/groundswell/2007/12/the-post-method.html

Booker, Sarah. Author interview, 2011

Firmstone, Julie and Coleman, Stephen. The changing role of the local news media in enabling citizens to engage in local democracies, *Journalism Practice* 8(5), 2014: 596–606

Gordon, Richard (2008) *The Online Community Cookbook*, Newspaper Association of America Digital Media Federation

Graham, Georgia. Author interview, 2011.

Greenslade, Roy. Journalists foster online communities, *Guardian*, 21 July 2011, www.theguardian.com/media/greenslade/2011/jul/21/digital-media-marketingandpr

Hille, Sanne and Bakker, Piet. Engaging the social news user: *Journalism Practice* 8(5), 2014, www.tandfonline.com/doi/abs/10.1080/17512786.2014.899758#.VcStXPlVhBd

Krumsvik, Arne H. Redefining user involvement in digital news media, *Journalism Practice*, 19 January 2017, http://www.tandfonline.com/doi/full/10.1080/17512786.2017.1279025

Comments on news sites and Facebook

Howe, Jeff. Gannett to crowdsource news, *Wired*, 3 November 2006, http://archive.wired.com/software/webservices/news/2006/11/72067

Jimenez, Antonio. In the Netherlands, a patch-like hyperlocal network is making money and nearing profit, NiemanLab, 7 June 2012, www.niemanlab.org/2012/06/in-the-netherlands-a-patch-like-hyperlocal-network-is-making-money-and-nearing-profit

Lewis, Seth C., Holton, Avery E. and Coddington, Mark. Reciprocal journalism, *Journalism Practice*, 3 December 2013: 1–13

MacDonald, Neil. Author interview, 2014

Malmelin, Nando and Villi, Mikko (2015) Audience community as a strategy resource in media work, *Journalism Practice*, 9 June 2015: 589–607, www.tandfonline.com/doi/full/10.1080/17512786.2015.1036903

McBride, Kelly and Rosenstiel, Tom (2014) *The New Ethics of Journalism: Principles for the 21st Century*, Los Angeles: Sage

McDermott, John. The NYT dispatches reporters to social conversation hotspots, Digiday, 19 March 2015, http://digiday.com/platforms/nyt-deploys-journos-interact-readers-platforms

Millington, Richard (2012) *Buzzing Communities*, Feverbee, https://www.createspace.com/4014863

Millington, Richard. News organizations and community managers, Feverbee, 29 November 2013, https://www.feverbee.com/news-organizations-and-community-managers/

Oliver, Laura. Lancashire Evening Post grows online reader interaction through surveys, 22 January 2008, https://www.journalism.co.uk/news/lancashire-evening-post-grows-online-reader-interaction-through-surveys/s2/a530949

Steiner, Katie. Before turning off comments, try these research-based strategies, Mediashift, 2 March 2015, http://mediashift.org/2015/03/before-turning-off-comments-try-these-research-based-strategies

Stone, Melanie. Social media editors in the newsroom: what the job is really like, Mediashift, 17 March 2014, http://mediashift.org/2014/03/social-media-editors-in-the-newsroom-what-the-job-is-really-like

Index

Page numbers in *italic* refer to figures and tables.

Editing Digital Video

Robert M. Goodman

Patrick J. McGrath

McGraw-Hill
New York   Chicago   San Francisco   Lisbon
London   Madrid   Mexico City   Milan   New Delhi
San Juan   Seoul   Singapore   Sydney   Toronto

The McGraw·Hill Companies

Cataloging-in-Publication Data is on file with the Library of Congress.

Copyright © 2003 by The McGraw-Hill Companies, Inc. All rights reserved.
Printed in the United States of America. Except as permitted under the United
States Copyright Act of 1976, no part of this publication may be reproduced or
distributed in any form or by any means, or stored in a data base or retrieval
system, without the prior written permission of the publisher.

1 2 3 4 5 6 7 8 9 0   DOC/DOC   0 9 8 7 6 5 4 3 2

P/N 140636-0
PART OF
ISBN 0-07-140635-2

*The sponsoring editor for this book was Steve Chapman and the production supervisor
was Sherri Souffrance. It was set in Century Schoolbook by MacAllister Publishing
Services, LLC.*

Printed and bound by RR Donnelley.

 This book is printed on recycled, acid-free paper containing a minimum of 50
percent recycled de-inked fiber.

McGraw-Hill books are available at special quantity discounts to use as premiums
and sales promotions, or for use in corporate training programs. For more information,
please write to the Director of Special Sales, Professional Publishing, McGraw-Hill,
Two Penn Plaza, New York, NY 10121-2298. Or contact your local bookstore.

To my students, and my mother for enrolling me in typing class.

Patrick J. McGrath

To all the editors I've met and worked with who have influenced my ideas about editing.

Robert M. Goodman

CONTENTS

Contents

Contents   **ix**

Contents

Contents

PREFACE

This book is designed for anyone who wants to learn to edit digital video. It doesn't matter which system or software or operating system you choose to use. Buy whatever meets your needs. If you haven't already purchased an editing solution, we'll help you understand what's important and what's not.

Editing is a language that uses pictures and sounds instead of words. The DV footage on the CD in this book is for the exercises we created to teach you the grammar of editing. Simply copy these files to your hard drive and bring them in to your editing program. It's not absolutely necessary that you have a working system before reading this book. However, you will learn faster if you're able to do the exercises.

Editing digital video is easier than it looks. Everyone starts out confused and fearful. You can learn as you edit. However, once you grasp the underlying concepts of digital editing, the process will cease to be a mystery. You must have faith and courage. Everyone makes a breakthrough sooner or later. Afterwards, all the aspects of editing will become clear to you. Nothing will stand in your way. We've seen this happen hundreds of times with our students. Our methods will help you achieve your breakthrough faster.

Learning to edit is like learning to play a musical instrument. It's a craft and practice is important. The more you edit the easier it becomes to please yourself and an audience. Music and editing share another trait. Both can create deep emotional responses from audiences. There are few things in life more rewarding than sitting in the back of a room and watching other people be profoundly moved by the story you have told.

No matter what the story is, the editor's job is to tell it well. To us, that means editing that's invisible. Anything B acting, camera work, lighting, music, or editing that calls attention to itself rather than serving the needs of the story is detrimental.

Shape the story. Give your audience what they need to see and hear when they need to see and hear it. You must be their guide and representative long before your friends sit down in your living room or audiences buy tickets to see the results of your hard work.

Robert M. Goodman

Patrick J. McGrath

ACKNOWLEDGMENTS

We would like to thank the following people for their generous contributions that have made this book possible: Brian McKernan for encouraging us to write this book; Bob Turner for writing the foreward and being a vocal advocate for editors; Kimberly Hyndman, our intern for her help with the cross-reference section; Bob McGrath for designing the illustrations; Adam Gooder for writing The Dicey Question script; Michael Kelly and Vanessa Montesano for their performances in the exercise; J. Winfield Heckert for lighting the exercise scene; Mark Moskowitz, Jennifer Rew, Jeff Kreines, Frank Black, and Steve Owen for their insights; Beth Leach and Daniel F. McGrath, Sr. for their photographs; Bob Ellis, Seth Levi, and Charles Dyer for their suggestions about films to watch; Daniel Goodman for reading the manuscript and offering his valuable criticism; Johanna Goodman for her patience always; Katey and Amanda McGrath for their encouragement; Mike Kushner and Joyce Acciaioli Rudge for their title graphics; Ned Levi for his assistance; and Rob Crites, Melanie Wright, Mimi Janosi, Vlad Hartman, and Justin Maynard, at The Art Institute of Philadelphia for their support.

FOREWORD

Find Magic in Your Bag of Tricks.

Every editor develops a bag of tricks for special occasions. When an editor is confronted with an unworkable sequence, a scene that is lacking, a rhythm that feels monotonous, the editor will reach into his bag of tricks and find the magical solution to the dilemma in question.

Yes, I do believe in magic, as does every editor and every artist who has ever created magic. You will know when it happens because of the natural high it creates—the euphoria that bubbles up. In many ways, this is what the art is all about. It is true that sometimes you can create magic and your conscious mind is barely aware of it. I know editors that have been given profound natural talents and when you ask, they cannot explain why they chose a cut the way they did or why they chose a sequence of shots, but as an assistant, I have noticed their body language when they perform magic, and they are feeling it when it happens.

Everyone can experience the creation of magic. Most of the time, it comes after you have mastered the craft portion of your art. I believe the difference between craftsmanship and art is that craftsmanship can be taught. Craftsmanship is mastering tools and techniques. It is not easy to become a master craftsman, but with passion, dedication, and hard work, I promise you, it is achievable. Becoming an artist and mastering your art is a different matter. To an artist, art seems to just happen. Part of this is due to a God-given talent that cannot be learned. It is inside you. The other part is more of a path of discovering art and finding what is within you.

When you talk to editors, most will admit that some of their best edits "happen by accident" or "just happen while playing around", or "discovered by breaking the rules". The "rules" are the basic tenets of editing. Craftsmanship involves mastering these tenets, established by the craft's long tradition and understanding of what works and what does not. Sometimes, magic can be found by choosing to ignore one or more of those tenets. Artists know when to try this. Most of us, when confronted with some works of modern art for the first time, have reacted to these pieces with the impression that someone just threw some paint on a canvas. As we mature, we understand this is not the case. Frequently these works are from artists who mastered their craft and then choose to break the rules that they mastered. The power that was discovered generated the magic that inspires people to fill museums to experience this work of art.

Frequently sculptors try to explain that their art is to discover what exists inside a stone. Editors go through the same exploration and discovery when presented with the camera original. Editors remove the extraneous—hopefully until the essential truth is revealed. Interestingly, the style of this revelation is the part of the editor and the part of the sculpture that is left on the work of art, and is part of its beauty. Magic occurs when you stop removing at the perfect time.

This book was created, in part, because digital video editing has given major new powers of experimentation to the editor. The opportunity to try new things quickly is a wonderful technological gift to an editor. I have been an editor in the period prior to this technology and I know the depressing, artistically bereft feeling when "good enough" was said too often, because the cost was too great to try a different cut. The constant feeling that you know you could have made this project better, if only . is a terrible burden for an editor. In the days of linear editing, when your choice would be to destroy what you created to try something different and, when it did not work, have to rebuild the sequence you originally created, was frequently too time-consuming and the tools you created too expensive to try. When editors are at a point in their career that they know what could be, if only they could be given experimentation time, can be a frustrating and painful period. Fortunately, today's technology reduces much of this past frustration. It offers opportunities to try new cuts and greater prospects to discover some magic.

Goodman and McGrath do a good job of teaching the craft of editing. Their book points you to areas where you can find the art as well. It is hard to continually find the magic without mastering the craft. While mastering the craft is difficult and takes a long time, hopefully as you journey you will constantly discover magical sparks that keep you moving forward.

Each time a bit of magic occurs in the lives of editors, or when they experience the magic performed by another, they can slip that knowledge into their bag of tricks, and pull it out at the appropriate time in the future. This magic could be a technique of the editor's craft that created magic under a specific set of circumstances, or it could be a broken rule. An editor will never know when he/she can use this magic trick again, but a great editor collects them and knows when to reach into his or her bag of tricks and pull one out.

Here is hoping that your bag of tricks grows large and rich with magic.

BOB TURNER

CHAPTER 1

The Whole Truth and Nothing But the Truth

The Big Picture

Digital video editing is the process of transferring video and other materials into an editing system; assembling sequences of pictures and sounds (first in a rough fashion and then polishing and refining the show); creating and adding titles, graphics, and effects to enhance the show; adjusting and mixing the sound; and finally outputting the finished show back to videotape or other media so audiences can see the results. This is what you're interested in learning otherwise you wouldn't be reading this book.

Our goal is to teach anyone, amateurs or professionals, how to edit on any digital video editing system and achieve results. It's a difficult task made more difficult because there are over 200 different answers to the question, "what is a digital video system?" There are video-editing appliances (self-contained devices designed to be connected to a monitor and digital video recorder or camera); computer software running on Mac, Windows, Linux, and other operating systems; and integrated systems that combine proprietary hardware with software. For the purpose of this book, all of these are examples of digital video editing systems. We'll call them *editing systems* throughout this book.

Manufacturers use different terms to describe what are universal operations, tools, and features. It would be extremely difficult to write a book explaining the principles of digital video editing using every manufacturer's terminology. Even if we could write that book, it would be impossible to read. To help you sort out these infuriating differences, we've provided a guide in Chapter 11, "What Are They Talking About?"

This book isn't a replacement for your editing system manual, nor is it a guide to a specific system. Instead, we'll present principles that enable you to use any system successfully. This is a results-oriented approach to digital video editing that works no matter which editing system you choose to use.

Words can create confusion so we'll define and use terms based on two criteria: our 40 years of combined experience in editing and what's appropriate under the widest set of circumstances. Our focus on teaching principles is prone to failure because of the variety of editing systems available, unless you have some familiarity with the editing system you plan to use. So start playing with it. Acclimate yourself with the buttons, tools, user interface, and terminology that are part and parcel of every editing system.

No single approach to teaching or learning works for everyone. Anyone contemplating editing digital video should realize that he or she will be working in a computer-based environment. It's crucial that you understand your learning style as it relates to computer software. Understanding yourself and how you best learn is a valuable asset. Software programs change constantly. You must be able to learn new features or a new program rapidly and successfully.

Styles of Learning

This section identifies a few of the learning styles we've spotted over the years. See if you recognize any that match your personality:

The Book Method.   You must read the book first, see it in print, and understand as much as possible in order to proceed on a computer. You like the big picture. You seek a well-written book. If this describes you, you've bought the right book! Read *Editing Digital Video*, the manual for your editing system, and then get started.

The Recipe Method.   You prefer step-by-step instruction. You like to see each task broken down so you can carefully follow a path. Your editing system's tutorial should be your first stop. Follow the instructions in that software or printed tutorial. To help you learn, we've provided footage and exercises in this book.

The Research Method.   You like to jump right in and start working, relying on your experience to work intuitively on a computer. You are the type of person who looks up information only when you run into a roadblock. The index in your editing system manual (and in this book) will prove invaluable.

The Reinforcement Method.   You like to scan the table of contents in the manual to get a general idea of how things work. You glean as much information as you need and then proceed to work in an organized manner. When you are finished exploring, you like to debrief yourself by reading the editing system manual to cement the information into your mind.

The Project Method.   You're the type of person who needs a reason to immerse yourself and learn. This is the sink-or-swim approach. You need a project with a deadline, the pressure of performing under stress, or the motivation of proving yourself in a professional situation. You will use whatever is available and any and all methods to learn. You are independent and resourceful. You rely on experience and ingenuity to take a project from beginning to end, which is its own reward.

The Trial-and-Error Method.   You like to jump right in and start. Your favorite tools are two features: undo and context-sensitive help which are included in most software programs. If this describes you, make sure you purchase an editing system with extensive levels of undo and help. This book serves as an extension of that help system.

The Classroom Method.   You prefer the discipline that an instructor-led course imposes on you and enjoy learning in a group setting. Courses on editing are available at training centers and colleges. Most offer a curriculum that presents material in an organized way over time. You still need to learn the software by yourself, but you're aided by the organization that a class provides. Our methods are being used to teach editing in classrooms everyday.

The Buddy System Method.   You're the type of person who needs a tutor or peer to work with you through the lessons. You find the comfort and encouragement that comes with a partner necessary. Under the theory that two minds are better than one, you prefer to explore things from two perspectives. If this describes you, grab a partner and this book, and start dancing.

The Mentor Method.   This is similar to the buddy system, but you'd prefer to have an expert for a tutor. You need someone who can provide what few of your peers possess—subject knowledge and a disciplined approach to learning. If you can find an expert with the right credentials and experience who is also a capable teacher, this is probably the fastest way to learn editing. However, private lessons given by an expert editor are expensive. We think reading this book is a good substitute for having us sit beside you, but if you still want private lessons and can afford it, feel free to contact us via e-mail at info@camcase.tv.

You can choose from many styles and methods of learning. Most people use more than one method to learn effectively. It's important to recognize the approach or approaches you prefer—the ones that work best with your experience, skill, interest, and pocketbook. Success is important in the beginning because this is when you learn the fundamentals that last a lifetime.

What Is Editing?

Editing is commonly defined as collecting, preparing, and arranging materials for publication. It may also mean to revise or correct and eliminate or omit. Those definitions are just as valid in the world of film and video. To us, digital video editing is the process of collecting, arranging, and bringing materials together to tell a story using pictures and sounds. The word *materials* should be understood as video footage, photographs, illustrations, animations, title graphics, sound, music, or anything else you can incorporate into the finished product. For lack of a better word, we'll use the word *show* to describe the finished product. This is because when you're done, the first thing you'll want to do is *show* the results of your hard work to someone else.

The ultimate goal of editing is to tell stories. Writers use words and sentences to craft stories; editors use pictures and sounds. Joining disparate shots together is fundamental to editing. In one of the oddities that persists in the film and video industry, the simplest way to join two shots together is to *cut* from one shot to another. It's called a cut because film editors once had to cut and splice together strands of film to join two shots. What's important to know is that the act of placing one shot next to another can create an emotional impression that's greater than the sum of the parts.

Why Should You Not Edit?

Before we discuss the reasons to edit, we should mention that not everything needs to be edited. Some things that you've shot may not need to be edited or perhaps never should be edited. If you record something for documentation purposes, it probably doesn't have a beginning, middle, or end beyond the start and end of the tape. It's perfectly okay to realize that a particular piece of footage doesn't need to be edited. For instance, imagine that you recorded your child speaking at his or her graduation. If the only footage you shot is of that speech, you don't need to edit it. Just watch it later. It may be important to save for posterity, but it is not worth editing. If you only have one shot, whether or not it tells a story in and of itself, it doesn't need to be edited.

However, if you shoot your child getting dressed, putting on his or her cap and gown, walking to the podium, and all of the other events leading up to and after the speech, you'd have the material to tell a personal story. Trying to tell a story when there isn't one is a frustrating exercise. The rule is that if it interests you and/or others, and if you have enough interesting shots, you probably have enough material to edit a show.

Figuring out what is or isn't an interesting shot is the subject of Chapter 7, "Setting the Table." We'll discuss how to identify shots and camera angles and how to use these elements to tell stories. The camera is the principal tool we use to record pictures and sounds. This chapter will help make anyone a better cameraperson even though it's written from an editor's perspective. The truth is you can't tell succinct stories that hold the audience's attention with one shot from one angle.

You can tell stories using just the camera and avoid editing altogether. However, it's not very efficient. This approach is called *in-camera editing*, which can be difficult to do. All the scenes must be shot in the exact order the audience will see them and everything you shoot will appear in the finished show. This approach is the opposite of shooting something from one angle or perspective. However, the end result is the same; you do not need to edit the material.

To pull this off, you must have good intuition and an awareness of what will be the *important* or decisive moment before it happens so the camera will be rolling when it does happen. You'll also need to visualize how the material you've just recorded can be joined to the material you're about to shoot. This is easier to do with certain kinds of stories. A wedding is one example. It's a ritual event with important moments that are easily anticipated. Plus, it takes place in a preset order in a few locations. We know a filmmaker named Doug who makes a living shooting weddings that he edits entirely in the camera. After the last dance, he takes the tape from his camera and hands it to the client. The client gets a well-shot story about their wedding that requires no additional editing. What this filmmaker does is akin to performing on a high wire without a net. Doug's in-camera editing ability relies on his careful attention to craft, years of practice, and finely honed skills.

In the past, many amateurs were forced to shoot this way because they had no access to editing equipment. Fifteen years ago, even simple editing equipment was beyond the means of most home users. A basic system used to cost more than $35,000 and required enormous technical expertise. Plus, the technology wasn't very good. Amateurs who were adept at conceptualizing and shooting carefully could manage to tell good stories when the story lent itself to in-camera editing (such as a wedding, graduation, or travelogue). Digital editing has made in-camera editing unnecessary. It's not worth the effort.

Why Should You Edit?

The most efficient approach to telling stories with a camera is to follow the Hollywood model. Shoot what you want, in the order you want to shoot it, and then assemble those elements into a story. This approach came into vogue shortly after the birth of filmmaking around the turn of the twentieth century. Filmmakers quickly discovered that audiences were sophisticated enough to make the mental leap from one shot to another—from one angle to another—without losing grasp of the story. Audiences understood what was going on even when a lot of material was left out. Filmmakers realized that joining disparate shots together gave them more control over how the story was told and on the impact their stories had on the audience, turning editing into an important tool. Another early realization was that editing could alter how an audience perceives time and space.

Although the reason for editing, which most often comes to mind, is to create stories, it's actually only one of the four reasons for editing, which include the following:

1. To build stories from the material you shoot.
2. To fix mistakes or eliminate technical errors.
3. To increase or decrease the duration (running time) of a show.
4. To combine multiple stories or videotapes on one tape. This could mean adding commercials to a television program or compiling several shows on a single videotape.

Examine the list. You'll notice that three of the four reasons are not creative; most editing tasks are technical. Fixing mistakes, cutting for length, or combining things are what most editors do day in and day out. It's an interesting fact that when an editor finally has the opportunity to build a story, he or she often ends up fixing mistakes, adjusting the length, and combining things.

The tongue-in-cheek definition of an editor, hanging in editing rooms around the world, is the person who takes out-of-focus, badly framed, and poorly shot footage of people mumbling, bumping into furniture, and forgetting what to say, and turns that footage into a compelling story with lasting value for which the director will take all the credit. There's a kernel of truth in this definition, although we prefer to say that editing is about taking the best of what you have at hand and telling the most compelling story you can create for the audience.

It's the Audience, Always!

The truth is that the audience is the only entity editors should consider. If you're doing something for yourself, it's easy to watch the footage and imagine the story. However, if you plan to show it to someone else, you'll need to edit. Few people have the patience to watch all the footage.

Nearly every show that people watch (whether it is film, television, or video) is a linear experience. It doesn't matter whether you are making a commercial, documentary, drama, music video, or wedding. The audience cannot change the order of events and must watch the show over a period of time. Editors create organized successions of images so the audience sees and hears one piece of information at a time in the order that the editor decided, which is the order of the show. The audience has to listen and watch these pictures and sounds over time. Therefore, as an editor, you must organize those images in a way that satisfies the needs of the audience. You have to take the audience's point of view.

What do audiences prefer? They usually prefer stories with beginnings, middles, and ends. Stories with conflict and resolution. Only a few books are worth reading about storytelling; Aristotle's *Poetics* is one of these, even though it was written in 325 B.C. Several other more recent books are also listed in our suggested reading bibliography.

This book will help you learn how to edit stories. In the process, you'll also learn the technical side—how to fix mistakes, cut for length, and combine things. The beauty of digital video editing is that it's easier now than ever to do the technical tasks. Fixing mistakes often meant starting over from scratch. Lengthening and shortening shows was a nightmare in the days of linear video editing. Combining things required foresight and planning. Today, it's a breeze to do these things because digital video editing offers random access.

The show the audience sees may be a linear experience, but the process of creating one is not. Digital video editing is nonlinear. All of your materials are available at any time in any order. Random access to your material allows you to build shows the way you want. You can decide to start working on the beginning, middle, or end. You can work within small structures like a three-shot sequence and combine that with other three-shot sequences until you've built a scene or a sequence of scenes. Whenever you're ready, you can put the sections together.

Why Digital?

Digital video editing gives you the ability to change the digital video files stored in your editing system in any way, shape, or fashion. The information in those files is stored as binary data, which means that the file contains a series of numbers that can be either ones or zeros. The power of digital video editing extends beyond simply changing the order of a series of shots. You can change the colors, luminance, contrast, and even the size and shape of the image itself down to the smallest part of the picture information, which is called a *pixel*.

Digital video editing, or *digital editing* for short, encompasses what professionals call *nonlinear editing* (NLE). We prefer digital editing because nonlinear is defined by something else and digital editing is broader. In today's world, you can manipulate so much more than just a sequence of shots. A typical editing system enables the operator to manipulate multiple layers of video, audio, text, and graphics in a completely nondestructive way. Digital editing is the umbrella term for this new way of doing things.

The person who operates these editing systems in a professional environment often becomes a *superuser* because it's no longer enough to be just an editor. You need to be an expert in graphics, audio, effects, editing, compositing, and compression because it all falls under the umbrella of digital

Pixels Everywhere

Pixel is an abbreviation for *picture cell* or *picture element*, which can refer to an individual sample of red, green, or blue in the picture, or to the luminance. To get an idea of what a pixel looks like, look at a computer monitor under a magnifying glass. You'll see a picture comprised of a grid of small rectangles, which are the pixels in a monitor. If you have image-editing software such as Adobe Photoshop™, JASC Paintshop Pro™, or something similar on your computer, you can zoom in or enlarge an image until the pixels become visible. You'll notice this picture is also comprised of rectangles, which are more pixels. If you still don't believe that pixels are everywhere, grab a newspaper or magazine and look at those images under a magnifying glass. They won't be rectangular pixels, but they are pixels nonetheless.

The Ultimate Network

Some television news organizations are already creating programs shot, edited, and broadcast by individuals scattered around the globe. The footage for the story is stored on a huge array of hard drives at a centralized location. The producers, editors, and graphic artists can be anywhere, even in separate places. Everyone accesses a low-resolution version, or *proxy*, of the footage via a computer network if they happen to be at the central location or via the Internet if they're not. The producer creates a rough version of the story, records the narration, and sends the narration and instructions (just the sequence of events) to the central server. The editor then takes the producer's rough edit and narration and polishes the story. An editor or a graphics specialist adds the titles and graphics. The story is then played directly from the central server's hard drives to a transmitter. The transmitter sends the signal to a television set so the story can be seen.

video editing. The digital environment also permits another model, the *networked approach*, which lets groups share access to the same material. Digital files can be stored at a central location that is linked to everyone's computer so multiple experts can have instant access to the same material. Each person can perform a specialized task and make the results accessible to everyone.

The Precepts of Digital Video Editing

Six universal principles—nondestructive, lossless, random, intuitive, layered, and unrestricted—separate digital editing from past approaches.

The first principle is that digital editing is nondestructive. The reason for this starts with the media used to record pictures and sounds. Most professionals call unrecorded media (film or videotape) *raw stock*. After recording, video professionals refer to it as *original source tapes* or *camera source tapes*. Film professionals call exposed and processed motion picture film *camera negative*, *footage*, or *source footage*. For our purposes, we'll refer to any recorded material shot by you or someone else with a camera as an original source tape.

If you remember what we said earlier, the first step in the editing process is transferring material into your editing system. The digital information recorded on your original source tapes is copied to your editing system's storage drives. Those original source tapes can then be placed into storage because the material you'll be editing is the copy on your editing system.

Nondestructiveness goes even deeper. The copies of your original source tapes stored in your editing system are called *media files* because they contain pictures and sounds (media) as digital files. A media file can store all the information on a videotape, from one scene, one shot, or one frame of your material. Typically, a media file holds several shots or a scene. Your editing system makes it easy to mark and name sections of the media file that you feel are useful. These pointers identify a subsection of the media file and are called *clips*. Even though a clip is an object that can be copied and moved in most editing systems, a clip merely tells your editing system where to find the section of the media file you want to play.

The media file is separate from and remains unchanged no matter what happens to the clips. There's another level. If you decide to manipulate the picture by changing the colors or distorting the image, the editing system creates a new media file (see *rendering* in the index if you want to jump ahead). Your original media files remain pristine until you decide to delete them.

No matter how often a digital media file is copied, the copy is always identical to the original. There's no difference between the two because the files are composed of ones and zeroes that can be easily duplicated. Scientists call this a *lossless* process, meaning that nothing gets lost. Digital editing is lossless with regard to copying files. This isn't true if you copy analog materials, such as VHS tapes or traditional photographs. Analog materials degrade slightly whenever you copy them; the image quality gets worse. It's noticeable because the contrast goes up and the sharpness goes down. You

Figure 1-1
Each clip points to a media file that contains the actual pictures and sounds.

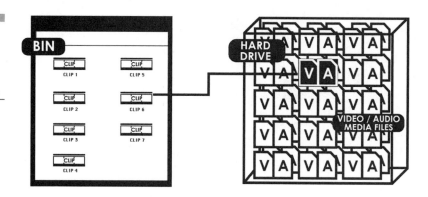

Understanding the Heart of the System

Imagine you go to a diner in New Jersey with friends. You find an open booth and sit down. A jukebox is in front of you on the wall. It's actually just a shiny box with buttons on the front, song titles listed on a series of pages, and a place to put your money in if you want to listen to music. The jukebox in your booth lets you play a CD. The CDs, which are digital and represent the digital media files in your editing system, are stored elsewhere—in a player in a back room of the diner. However, you can control the songs you hear in your booth even though you can't actually see or touch any of the CDs. Instead, you select the songs you want to play by punching in a number code listed next to the song. It costs a dollar for three songs. If you put a dollar into the jukebox, you can select and play three songs. What you're about to do is play back digital media files.

You go through the list and select J12, a Whitney Houston song, P12, a hit from Smokey Robinson and the Miracles, and B2, a Michael Jackson tune. You've chosen three songs to be played in a specific order. All three songs are from different media files. Each album (CD) is a digital media file. The songs are clips. You don't want to play the entire album, just one song. That one song is a subset of the album; it's one section of a digital media file. Each song you've chosen is a subset of the Whitney Houston album, the Smokey Robinson album, and the Michael Jackson album. After you press the buttons, the jukebox tells the playback device to retrieve the master CD, find the subset (the track) that has the song, and play it back for you. The jukebox points to a digital file (the CD) stored in the back of the diner. The process is repeated for every song you choose and the jukebox plays the songs in the order you decide.

If I gave everyone around the table some money, all of my friends could play their own versions of the files stored in the diner's jukebox. Everyone could play the songs on the jukebox in a different order even though no one is actually playing the CDs (digital

Figure 1-2a
Tabletop Jukebox

media files); instead, they are selecting numbers. The numbers that identify the songs relate to the CDs, which are stored in the player in the back of the room. If the owner of the diner took the CDs out of the player and left the slots empty, the jukebox in the booth would still take your money. You could still punch in your choices and make a sequence of your favorite hits. However, you wouldn't hear anything. Without the digital media files in the back room, there's nothing to play. Of course, as soon as the owner puts the CDs back, the songs play.

Figure 1-2b
Selecting a song

It should be clear to you that there's a difference between the song sequence you create by punching in numbers and the digital media files. The sequence determines how the digital media files are played, but the two are completely separate. This is exactly how digital editing systems work.

can prove it to yourself by making a photocopy of a photocopy of a photocopy of a photograph. Professionals call these successive copies *generations* and call the change in image quality *generation loss*. Thankfully, generation loss has been consigned to the past with digital editing. (It's okay to smile.)

Randomness is another principle that functions on several levels. Digital editing systems let you take any approach that works for you. You can start with the pivotal moment in the story and cut that sequence. Or you can start with the end of the story or create the titles first. Whichever approach works for you or however you'd like to edit, digital editing systems make it possible. Sound first, graphics second, pictures third? If it makes sense to you, you can do it. Experienced editors can follow the most efficient path, which might mean switching approaches midway through a project. The technology doesn't force you to follow the same approach for every project. Instead, you can use the one that works best for you.

The next level of randomness is that you can access your material in a random manner. Think of it this way. When audiocassettes were popular, the fast-forward and rewind features were important. CDs made those functions obsolete. The relationship between digital and analog editing is similar. There's no waiting. Every track of your material is instantly accessible.

The concept of intuition is difficult to accept when you're learning your way around an editing system. It seems to be anything but intuitive. The following analogy will help you understand why we believe this is a universal principle. In order to understand digital video editing, it's helpful to look at the methods that were used to edit video and, prior to that, film.

Film editing is done by hand. The process is simple. An editor looks at the film and physically cuts strips of celluloid with a sharp blade. To isolate the piece he or she wants, the editor cuts out that section and puts it aside. The remaining pieces of film are then glued or taped back together, or stored as separate pieces. The image for this phase of editing is of an editor holding film in his or her hand while cutting it with a blade. In the history of editing, this is the Iron Age.

With the arrival of videotape editing, the videotape recorder became the primary device for making edits. To make an edit, the editor had to find the piece he or she wanted on the original source tapes and copy that section to a new tape on a second recorder. The image for this phase of editing is of an editor systematically playing back tapes on one machine and electronically transferring the images to another machine for rerecording. In the history of editing, this is the Machine Age.

With digital video editing, the computer has become the primary device. To make an edit, the editor only needs to rearrange the sequence in which media files are played. The image for this phase of editing is of an editor seated in front of computer display moving objects on the desktop. In the history of editing, this is the Information Age.

Digital video editing is intuitive because all of the tools are laid out in front of you on the computer desktop. Manual dexterity, which was once required for film editing, doesn't impede or improve your ability to edit digital video. There's no need to learn sophisticated mechanical equipment, which was once a requirement of videotape editing, because it all happens in the computer. Digital editing will become more intuitive because computers are becoming more powerful and the user interface is becoming more sophisticated. We are at the beginning of an exponential trend. So, if it doesn't seem very intuitive now, just wait a year.

The principle of layering has a single meaning for beginners though it will acquire multiple meanings later. Film editing is about cutting and pasting, like writing a book by hand. It has the advantages of random access. Film editors who moved to videotape editing lost the ability to work in the manner that felt most comfortable to them. Videotape editing wasn't random. It operated in a strictly linear mode. Editors were forced to start at the beginning and move forward until the show was finished. A good analogy is that some people prefer to write in long hand because it's easy to erase or scratch things out, revise, and make notes. Typewriters are limiting by comparison. Word processing offers some of the freedoms of long hand; you can erase and revise, but it doesn't permit layering. There's no way of making layered notes, which is easy to do in long hand with different colored inks. To overcome this limitation, most people print out their documents and then scribble on the hard copy because they can't scribble on the computer screen. Paper lets you put notes on top of notes. Digital editing also lets you do layering. You can mark up your work, jump back and forth, and leave notes to yourself. It offers the same freedom as paper and pencil even though you're working with pictures and sounds.

Digital editing is unrestrictive and noncommittal. The editor is never forced to make a permanent decision. You can have 2 versions or 200 versions of the same show. You can use the identical material to tell a story three different ways in three different lengths. Best of all, it's easy to accomplish all of this because you can copy, cut, and paste with ease. Make as many versions as you want, if you want to take the time to do it, and see which one plays best with the audience.

The flip side is that you are never really done. You don't have to commit to one version until someone says that time is up, your energy or interest wanes, or the money runs out. Another facet of this principle is that digital editing enables you to see the finished product before you have to commit to it. Digital editing can be a disaster for anyone incapable of making a decision. There are no limitations on how many ways you can slice the pie and few consequences for trying them all out.

Hardware and Software—The Facts

Editing systems have two parts—hardware and software. The hardware is the computer. Even though an editing appliance might not look like a computer, it is one. The computer lets you store and play pictures and sounds in digital files called *media files*. These files are stored on large hard drives. Fast, powerful hardware is required to ensure quick, efficient, and error-free retrieval of the files. If the hardware is up to the task, the editor sees smooth, nonstop playback of the pictures and sounds stored on the hard drives.

Digital editing doesn't happen in a vacuum. The pictures and sounds stored on an editing system must eventually be played elsewhere. It's impractical for people to come to where your editing system resides to watch your show. They'll want to watch it in a more comfortable venue. Hardware (called an *encoder*) that converts the digital media files into standard television signals is at the heart of a digital video editing system. Your editing system has to be capable of displaying video on a computer and television. This may seem simple and obvious, but the technology to make this possible is magical and phenomenal. Without it, digital video editing is nothing but a file management computer game with no lasting purpose. If people can't watch your show on a screen apart from your editing system, what's the point?

Software is what allows editors to manipulate media files to their heart's content without ever having to know anything about computers. It's the go between. Most people think of software as the user interface even though that's only a tiny fraction of what software does for us. There are sophisticated software programs and simple ones. The degree of sophistication determines whether you have a lot of tools or just a few to perform the tasks necessary to create a finished show. Some software programs are intuitive and easy to use. Others are complex with a multitude of features. There are over 200 choices and the decision of which one to use is very personal. Most editors end up using whatever is available to them. Every editing software program includes a basic set of functions and tools that enable you to successfully edit a finished show as long as you become familiar and proficient with the program.

The Big Three—Speed, RAM, and Storage

Computer manufacturers are in the business of selling speed. Every year, the speed of the *central processing unit* (CPU), which is where all the work gets done, increases dramatically. Every year, the manufacturers mount a new advertising campaign to convince consumers to buy a new computer and replace the obsolete one sitting on their desk. If you're using your computer for word processing and e-mail, you can safely ignore their advice.

However, as soon as you decide to enter the world of digital video, you'll discover the truth in those ads. The reality is that computers can never be fast enough, or have enough memory or storage space to satisfy the enormous demands digital video places on computers. Digital editing is taxing, and editing software uses every bit of your computer's processor and memory in a neverending search for more resources.

If you're wondering why, look at it this way. One second of full motion video is made up of sixty still images. There are 30 frames—2 fields per frame, 2 separate images—that must be processed and displayed from a file on a hard drive. Any current computer can display a single still picture. Digital video requires the computer to display 60 pictures every second in perfect time to maintain smooth motion. That requires a lot of processing power. Not only does the motion have to be smooth, but the sound also has to be in perfect sync with the picture. Digital video places a lot of demands on a computer because the picture and sound files must be accessed, retrieved, and displayed at your command. To us, that it happens at all is magic.

We're constantly impressed that when you press Play, the editing system actually retrieves the thousands of images stored in multiple files and plays them back with full motion and sound. We think nothing of it, but it's a marvel. You are asking a lot of your computer when you press Play. We won't accept video that appears to be too slow or fast or that stutters. We expect everything to be smooth and perfect.

To manage all of this data, you need fast CPUs that can move the data stored in large files on your hard drives through the computer and process them quickly. Digital video editing involves reading files and writing new ones. Speed has an impact on how quickly the computer is able to do the calculations needed to create transitions and effects and how fast a new file can be written to store the results. We call this creation of new media files *rendering*. Most shows require a lot of rendering. Newer, faster computers write and create files more quickly than older computers. Another fact of life is that with every new editing software release, you gain more tools and features, although you may also need a faster computer to run the new version efficiently. For example, every successive version of Apple's Final Cut Pro software uses the full capabilities of the company's latest computer models to maximum advantage. As features are added, the need for speed and the minimum hardware requirements go up. You just have to accept the rule—newer, faster computers will always read and write digital video files faster and more efficiently. The corollary to the rule is if your editing system does everything you need it to do today, it will still do it a year from now, although it's bound to be slower than the shiny new systems in those ads.

There's no such thing as being too thin or too rich. When it comes to *random access memory* (RAM), there's no such thing as having too much. The more memory you have in your computer, the better it will run.[1]

---

[1] A technical note: If you don't do any compositing, a gigabyte of RAM is the maximum amount necessary for computers running the Mac or Windows operating system.

Remember that the computer is processing 60 pictures a second and each picture is composed of hundreds of thousands of pixels. The pixels change with each new frame. Memory determines how often your computer can update those pictures. All of the pictures on screen, including the interface's buttons, tools, menus, and viewers, are kept in memory to display them. Even though most of what's on screen remains static, the editing system interface uses up a lot of memory.

The overhead to run the program, along with all those pictures and sounds the editor is trying to manipulate, translates into a neverending need for more memory. If all you had to do was look at a blank blue screen with text, you wouldn't need much. However, every time you open a window, add a layer, or preview an effect, you use up more memory. The amount of memory in your editing system also has an impact on how many video and audio tracks can be played in real time. The more memory you have, the more layers you're likely to be able use. That's why we say you can never have too much and should have as much as you can afford.

Storage is more forgiving. Your needs will depend on the type of projects you plan to do. If you're editing 30-second commercials, you'll need a lot less storage than if you're editing feature-length films. The most common digital video format and the one with the smallest storage requirements is the DV format. One gigabyte of hard-drive space stores about four and a half minutes of DV footage. To hold one hour of DV footage, you'll need about 13 gigabytes of space. If you're using the 1,080/24P *high-definition* (HD) video format, you'll need 334 gigabytes, which is nearly 26 times the space for one hour of storage. The rule is that bigger pictures need faster connections to move them through the system.

It's easy to see, even with DV sources, that projects with a lot of footage will quickly eat up drive space. Any original source material to which you need instant access should be on your editing system. Thankfully, storage seems to get bigger, faster, and cheaper every year. The DV format works well with the typical drives found in computers of recent vintage. You can purchase as much space as you need very cheaply. It's all relative, but even storage suitable for the 1,080/24P HDTV format, which has very high data transfer rate requirements and huge files, is inexpensive. At the moment, you can purchase a terabyte (1,000GB) of 1,080/24P HD storage for under $10,000. Ten years ago, a fast 75MB hard drive cost over $10,000.

The Concept of Workflow

Workflow is the process of creating a show. This process starts with looking at your original source material and ends with looking at the finished show. It's the soup to nuts—from culling footage to editing and layering the elements that go into a show. Workflow is the process, the approach, and the pathway from beginning to end. Workflow is how you get results.

Workflow forces you to ask the following question: How do I gather and view the material, organize the project, and do my job (edit the show)? This order of events is critical to success. Some events in the workflow are universal (part of the underlying structure common to all of digital editing), whereas other events depend on the type of show you're editing. Workflow is flexible. It can accommodate your personality and what you're making. There's latitude to adjust your workflow (change the order of events) to maximize your efficiency.

Every workflow starts with raw materials and ends up with a finished show. You must take the footage and transfer it into your editing system. The material must be categorized so you can find what you need. You must isolate the footage into shots that are clean, clear, and understandable. Those building blocks are then used to create sequences that make sense to the audience. Then you'll need to sit back and look at the show before you start trimming and working on the pacing. It's all part of making the story work for the audience. Transitions, titles, and other layers that can make the story more interesting are added afterwards. The audio is tweaked and mixed. The last step is to output the show for distribution.

Workflow begins with input and ends with output. Your editing system is a tool. You bring source material into the system, manipulate, fine tune, polish, and output it to its final destination. That's the basic process—the general workflow. You can change things around for special projects, but this is the approach editors usually take.

This approach is efficient because you don't want to spend a lot of time making detailed decisions before you have a sense of the overall show. For example, you could spend hours working on a multilayered effect in the first third of the show only to discover when you're nearly done that the sequence in which that effect appears is detrimental to the flow of the show and the entire sequence must be dropped. All the work you did on that complex effect is wasted because it will never appear in the finished show. It makes no sense to layer graphics before you trim and polish. Digital video editing is like building a multitiered wedding cake. You build and stack the layers, and then ice the cake. Transitions, effects, and graphics are the icing. Don't waste your time icing until after the cake is built.

There are also creative workflows that are dynamic, changeable, and essential to success. We'll look at creative workflows in Chapter 5, "Styles and Workflows," through the prism of the different types of video you can make. Each requires an adjustment of the creative workflow to keep your creative juices flowing. However, certain principles are inviolate—you must have input before you can have output.

This book has a workflow, too. We know you need to understand certain things before other things can happen. Yet, as creative people, we believe in random access. If you want to jump ahead to Chapter 5 because you have burning desire to learn the best way to edit a music video, have a passing familiarity with your editing system, and possess a basic sense of editing, go for it. You can always come back to a chapter later or look up what you don't understand in the index. However, if this is your first introduction to editing, you should follow the order of the book. It will give you a solid foundation for understanding the principles and practices of digital video editing.

Do the exercises so you understand how a simple trim can make a difference in how the audience perceives meaning. The exercises will also help you understand what a shot is and how to isolate it. If you don't know a lot about editing, you need to learn these basics. It's best to learn them in the flow that we've created for this book so you can learn to walk before you learn to run.

All About Practice

Learning to use your editing system takes time, but it can be a lot of fun. After you've completed your first project, you'll understand the reward that comes from completion. To become proficient, you must practice. Digital video editing requires knowledge and experience. Experience comes from repetition. Your level of skill will improve as you flex the hand-eye coordination muscles used in editing. So much of what is necessary develops from learning to see the raw materials from an editor's perspective and being able to use the tools. You're only as good as your ability to imagine the story you want to shape. Once you've learned the basics and trained yourself to see, you'll begin to develop the skills necessary to attempt more complex editing projects. The more you do it, the easier it gets.

Don't be alarmed if you feel you're not making progress or getting it as quickly as you'd expect. In our experience, everyone learning to edit for the first time struggles in the beginning. It can be very foreign. However, as time goes by, you will have a breakthrough and the process, technology, concepts, and principles of digital editing will become absolutely clear. It's not unlike the experience of learning to ride a bike. Suddenly, you don't need those training wheels and balancing your bike seems effortless. After your breakthrough, you'll be able to edit naturally with ease. It's a wonderful feeling that erases the memory of what it was like before the possible seemed improbable. Everyone has a breakthrough. Some have it sooner, others have it later. It's part of the guarantee you make to yourself when you identify your method of learning and follow that path.

Summary

Digital editing systems let you take the approach to editing that works for you. All your materials can be accessed randomly. Shuttling tape is a thing of the past. Digital editing offers a layered approach to working with pictures and sounds. It's nondestructive, so it's nearly impossible to make an irreversible error. The joy of digital editing is that you can experiment and create as many versions as you want or have the time to make.

Important Points to Remember

- A digital copy is an exact replica of the original; there is no generation loss.
- Every editing system consists of hardware and software.
- Digital editing uses up all the resources in a computer: speed, memory, and storage.
- Editing success relies on following an efficient workflow. Workflow is the process of creating a show.
- Digital editing is intuitive because all the tools are on the desktop in front of you.
- Undo is only surpassed in importance by the play/stop key.
- Learning to edit takes time. To become proficient, practice.

What the Heck Is That?

A Typical Editing System—If Only There Were Such a Thing . . .

A typical editing system consists of video stuff and a computer. The video stuff includes a video monitor or television set, speakers, and a digital video source, such as a camcorder or recorder. A cable connects the video source to the computer. If the source uses the miniDV, DVCPro, or DVCAM video-tape format, you'll only need one cable (an IEEE-1394 cable, which is also called a Firewire or iLink cable) to connect the video source to the computer section of your editing system. Both the audio and video information recorded on the tape are simultaneously transferred over this cable. Recorders that play other videotape formats may use a *serial digital interface* (SDI) or *high-definition serial digital interface* (HD-SDI) to transfer audio and video to an editing system. These digital links are two-way streets that can send information to your editing system and receive information from your editing system.

The computer components include a keyboard; a mouse or some other pointing device; a computer monitor or monitors; and a minitower or desk unit with the *central processing unit* (CPU), memory, drives, and connectors that typify a computer or, if it's an editing appliance or proprietary editing system, a box of some sort with a manufacturer's name on it. Sometimes a box filled with hard drives called a *storage tower* or *hard-drive array* is also connected to the computer.

If the blade is the tool of film editing and the machine is the tool of video editing, then the computer screen is the tool of digital editing. Your first task when learning to operate an editing system is to familiarize yourself

Figure 2-1
Basic layout for a DV editing system.

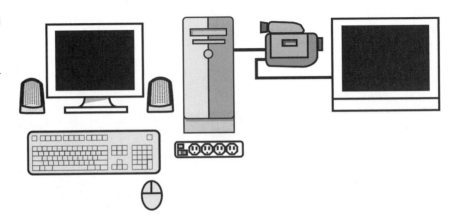

with the desktop. The desktop is the workspace that appears on the computer's monitor(s).

You need to teach yourself to see what is on the screen in front of you. As a student once explained to us, 9 times out of 10, the answer you want is somewhere on the screen. To be successful at editing, you need to learn where the information you want is located and be able to interpret and act on that information using the tools your editing system provides. You need to learn to recognize the buttons, tools, menus, and windows on the desktop. The best way to do this is to explore the four corners of your desktop. Imagine that you're stranded on an island and have to take stock of where you'll be living for who knows how long. You'd want to see everything there is to see. The same thing is true for the desktop of an editing system.

A better analogy for the desktop is the cockpit of an airplane. All of the pertinent information appears on the computer screen. Digital video editing is like flying a plane by instruments alone. Pilots call this *flying blind* because you can't look out the window. In digital editing, there's no window and nowhere else to look. There's just one place for you to focus your attention. The only way to interact with a digital editing system is through the desktop.

The Desktop Interface

Digital editing puts everything you need in one central location—the desktop. Every task is performed here. All the tools and information appear here. The interface—the way you access the tools—varies from manufacturer to manufacturer. Some interfaces are simple and intuitive. Others are complex with a multitude of features, buttons, displays, windows, and menus. Simple interfaces are ideal for beginners.

Figure 2-2
Advanced layout for a DV editing system.

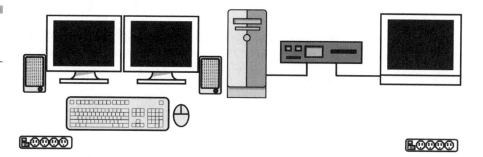

Whether you're using a simple or complex editing system, it's important to understand and learn the interface. This isn't obvious, even to experienced computer users who are just starting to learn digital editing. It's antithetical to anyone with previous film and videotape editing experience. Film editing is tactile and difficult to forget once it is learned. Videotape editing is conceptual. There's so much to think about—from the operation of tape machines to the intricacies of time code lists—that without daily practice, these skills fade from the editor's mind. Digital editing is visual and therefore requires the operator to be knowledgeable only to the point of being able to find what he or she is looking for on the desktop.

However, once you learn digital editing, it is easy. You don't have to use an editing system everyday to remain proficient, which is a big plus for casual users. You don't need to retain information. All you have to know is where to look.

One aspect that can be frustrating is the bewildering variety of jargon. The terms used to describe the identical tools, functions, and features vary from system to system. This is partially due to the convergence of the film, video, and computer industries. Manufacturers snatch terminology from one or more of these industries. Understanding where a term came from can help you translate it into something you understand. If you have a background or expertise in one of these industries, look for an editing sys-

Figure 2-3
Basic elements of the editing system desktop.

tem that uses terms that are familiar. It will make it much easier for you to learn to edit.

Keep your goal in mind—to learn the user interface. Be aware of how the edit screen is laid out, where things are located, and what the menus do. We call this *learning the four corners of your editing system*. There's a lot of information to be found on the desktop. Our goal is to teach you how to become familiar with all those tools, menus, and help functions.

In the beginning, you'll have a much easier time learning the interface if you can simplify the desktop. Remember that even fighter pilots learn to fly simple planes first. After you understand the interface and can locate the major tools, learn the keyboard shortcuts and buttons that will let you soar.

Interface Design

Every editing system has a unique user interface. Some elements are common to all programs, others are not. Among the commonalties, all digital editing systems are graphic in nature and display source materials in windows.

Interfaces can be separated into three categories—abstract, iconic, and virtual. Text-based interfaces are abstract. Interfaces that rely on graphics or pictures are iconic. Virtual interfaces replicate the look and feel of electronic or mechanical devices. Here are three ways we've seen a five-band audio equalizer tool recreated inside an editing system. The abstract approach uses five lines of text, one for each band of audio. Underneath each line is a space where you can type a positive or negative number from 1 to 10. The iconic version uses *sliders* (which are basically little bars that move up or down) underneath the *bands*. The virtual version is a three-dimensional picture of an equalizer with sliders and meters like something you might find in an electronics store. Assuming all three ways produce identical results in terms of audio quality, the choice of which one to use is a matter of personal preference.

It may not seem important, but the design has an impact on your ability to understand information. For example, it's common to check the amount of available storage space before you start a new show. You need to know if you have enough room for new materials without deleting what's already stored in your editing system. In a system with an abstract interface, the amount of free drive space is likely to be presented as a number. It may represent how many gigabytes of empty space are available or how many minutes of video can be stored. An iconic version might use a bar graph to present how much free space is available on each hard drive. The virtual version might have a picture of a hard drive with the available space indicated in one color and the occupied space in another. The information is the same. However, we can understand the message faster if the presentation matches our preferences. Some people need visuals, whereas others are more comfortable with numbers. It helps to know which you prefer because it can influence your decision to use or purchase a particular editing system. There's no single answer. Choose what works for you.

The way tools are accessed is another facet of interface design. Some systems are keyboard driven. Others are mouse driven. Both methods can be well designed. A well-designed interface lets you work longer than a poorly designed one. Unfortunately, most users discover whether an interface is well designed after spending long hours in the cockpit, flying the plane.

What we look for in a keyboard-driven system are mnemonic, easy-to-remember keyboard shortcuts. Pressing the letter P rather than the letter E to play back a clip makes more sense because P for "play" is easy to remember. Manufacturers are faced with the challenge that there are more tools (over 26) than mnemonic letter keys in most editing systems. Ideally, the tools have been assigned to the keyboard in some logical fashion. If you can figure out the logic (using the first letter of the name of the tool or operation is popular), you can be more efficient.

The other important criteria are handedness and complexity. Some of us are left-handed and others are right-handed. Some editing systems place the most often used commands—Play, Play In Reverse, Mark In (where to start), and Mark Out (where to end)—on the left side of the keyboard. If you're left-handed, your stronger hand ends up doing most of the work, which is great. However, if you're right-handed and the most frequently used keys must be accessed with your weaker left hand, you may be very unhappy. The same is true if the situation is reversed.

Any keyboard shortcut that uses more than one finger to execute a command complicates matters. Shortcuts that rely on using the Control or Command keys plus the Shift key plus a letter are more complex than ones that use a single letter. Complex shortcuts are harder to remember. They also require more manual dexterity and are difficult to type quickly. Pressing and holding a combination of keys with one hand may also cause problems such as carpel tunnel syndrome because editing is often repetitive.

Editing systems designed for professionals allow the operator to remap the keyboard to compensate for handedness and complexity. A left-handed editor could decide to change the key to mark an in from the letter I to R

and the key to mark an out from the letter *O* to *E*. This lets a left-handed person to use the identical fingers, on his or her stronger hand rather than the weaker one, to do the most frequent task during an edit. Reassigning keyboard shortcuts enables an editor who uses certain tools more frequently than others to assign those tasks to a single-key shortcut. At the end of the day, the editor in the cockpit who presses 10 percent fewer buttons is 20 percent less tired.

Consider the Interface Before You Buy

If you haven't purchased an editing system yet, get opinions from people who've used the ones you're considering. Most of the popular systems have e-mail lists and user discussion groups on the Internet. There's a lot of chaff (misinformation) surrounding the kernels of wheat so read carefully between the lines of what's written and form your own opinions. The most vocal people tend to be those who are evangelists for or crusaders against the product.

You should keep in mind that the simplicity or complexity of the interface has little or nothing to do with the tool set. Some systems have simple interfaces and powerful tools. Other systems have complex interfaces with many tools that are actually just bells and whistles. These are featurs that let manufacturers make impressive claims, although you'll rarely, if ever, use them.

Edward Tenner, author of *Why Things Bite Back: Technology and the Revenge of Unintended Consequences*, stated, "Things are needlessly complex because featuritis sells products. People buy them for a feeling of control, then complain that they are hard to manage. But show them something simple and rugged and most of them will call it boring."[1]

After years in the cockpit and more than a few long days that lasted well into the night, we believe bigger and bolder is better. Think about it this way. In feature films, the transition from one shot to the next is a cut 90 percent of the time. You don't need a lot of tools, just the right ones. However, just as there are different types of learners, no system can satisfy every editor.

---

[1] Katie Hafner, "Comforts of Home Marred by Tyranny of Digital Controls," *New York Times*, 28 April 2002, National Edition, P.1 and 38.

A major issue for mouse-driven systems is precision. The size of the target, which is the area of the desktop that's active (the area that can detect the mouse and execute an operation or open a tool), determines the degree of precision. If the target area is too small, the editor must be very precise in positioning the mouse. If the mouse buttons are tiny, the editor is forced to be precise. In practical terms, the editor moves the mouse in ever tightening patterns until he or she hits the target. This type of motion can cause repetitive stress injuries. Equally frustrating, although rarely injurious, is when the precision is set too low and anywhere you place the mouse triggers an action. The least tiring setting is somewhere in between.

Another factor to think about is whether the mouse buttons are used effectively. Some editing systems make the tools you're most likely to need in a particular context readily accessible by placing them on a mouse button. For example, after a clip is selected (highlighted), the mouse button could launch a menu that lets you choose to copy, delete, or change the clip's speed or direction. Interfaces that reduce the number of steps required to execute a task are well designed. A well-designed interface lets you work longer than a poorly designed one.

What You're Likely to Find on the Desktop

The following are the basic elements that appear on nearly every editing system desktop. We've used commonly accepted names for these elements. Your editing system may not use the same ones even though these elements are universal. If the editing system you're using has different names and you're not sure how to relate those names to the ones we're using here, see Chapter 11, "What Are They Talking About?" Chapter 11 has a crossreference table that should help you keep everything straight.

The Project

The *project* is the main organizational window that contains information about a specific show. Computers use hierarchical structures. Files are stored in folders or directories on a drive and most editing systems follow this model. The project is usually the highest level in an editing system's hierarchy.

Figure 2-4
Trims bin holding
film clips.

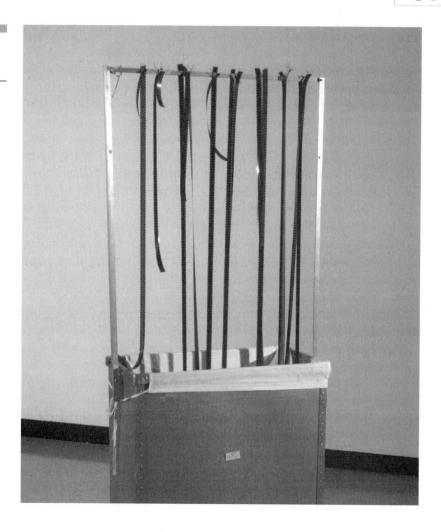

Projects typically store information about the following: all of the sound and picture elements, which are the principal building materials for the show you are editing; the sequences of sounds and pictures (called *timelines*) that you create; and any changes you make to technical settings, such as audio sample rates or video formats, or to user settings, such as the arrangement of the windows on your desktop or the color scheme. The project window is often the first window opened and the last window closed in an editing system application.

The Bin

The *bin* window is a folder that holds clips. The name bin comes from the world of film editing. Many editing systems actually use an icon that looks like a film bin (a square trashcan with a cotton liner) to represent the directories or folders that the editing system creates to store clips. Film editors hung the clips they were working with (long strips of film) from a rack above the bin. As the editor cut shots out of the film reels, the pieces he or she planned to use were hung in the bin. The shots that were unusable were tossed on the floor, which is where the phrase "left on the cutting room floor" originated. The digital equivalent of a bin serves the same purpose, but is much smarter.

The word *clip* is widely used to describe the icons that represent the audio, video, and graphics stored in an editing system. Clips are actually database entries that point to the digital media files stored in your editing system. The clip (refer to our jukebox explanation in Chapter 1, "The Whole Truth and Nothing But the Truth") is not the media file even though it may appear to be the same. Often video clip icons display a single frame of the video file. That frame is a called a *thumbnail* or *picon*. Picon comes from combining the words *picture* and *icon*.

Every system has at least one bin. Some have a set number of bins, for example, one for each category of material, such as audio, effects, graphics, titles, transitions, and video. Other systems let you create as many bins as you like. Bins are just files or folders that help you organize your source materials.

Typically, you can display the contents of a bin in several ways. The text view displays the clips in a database or list view. Most editing systems track a lot of information about each clip. There are categories (or fields) for the

Figure 2-5
Timeline window.

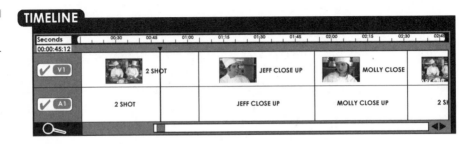

name of the clip, the name of the media file, the name of the original source tape, the duration of the clip, any comments you've made, the creation date of the file, and other technical information. Quite often the list can be sorted by category and/or searched to find the clip or items you need. The picture view displays the clips as a series of picons. These static images represent a full motion video and audio clip. Another potential way to display the bin is a variation on the database view, which includes a picture alongside each text entry.

The Viewer

The *viewer* window is used to play the clips. Controls like those found on a VCR to play, pause, stop, fast-forward, rewind, and shuttle are typically placed under the viewing screen. There are often buttons to mark an in (a start point) and an out (an end point.) Some systems have one viewer window for source materials (the clips) and a second viewer window to play the show or whatever resides on the timeline.

The Timeline

The *timeline* window is where you arrange clips in a sequence that tells a story with a beginning, middle, and end. This comic-strip arrangement represents your finished show. The audio, video, and graphics clips are typically arranged in separate bands (usually horizontal), which are framed by a scalable ruler marked in units of time.

The Top Row

The *top row* is a drop-down menu bar that appears at the top of the desktop. Most computer programs place important functions on the top row or main menu. This is where you are likely to find major operations, such as opening a project, saving a project, importing files, outputting your finished show, and one of the most useful functions, help. This menu functions as your central command center. Professionals know that learning the top row is how you begin to understand the structure of your editing system.

Tool Palettes

There are two types of tool palette windows: a row or rows of mouse buttons or roll-up windows with tabbed folders. Both offer quicker access to specific tools. Most editing systems, though not all, use at least one mouse button bar that floats and can be moved anywhere you need it. Some button bars dock to the top menu. The roll-up window palettes are often used in addition to a button toolbar. Adobe and Apple use this approach.

That's it—there are just six primary elements. Of course, it's more complicated than that because, well, we're not really sure why. Perhaps it's because those six windows seem to multiply like rabbits. We'll discuss this more later.

One Viewer or Two

Every editing system follows either a single- or dual-viewer model. Single-viewer systems follow the flatbed model. A flatbed editing table is the device most editors use to edit film. It has a single screen that displays the pictures and sounds. Dual-viewer systems follow the videotape model called *source record*. The simplest type of video editing system can be made by connecting two recorders together. One videotape recorder plays back the original source tapes and the other one records what's being played on a new tape called an *edit master*. The only way to see and hear what's being played or recorded is to connect monitors to each of the recorders. To help editors keep track of what's what, the monitors were labeled. The one connected to the recorder playing the source tapes was labeled *source* and the other monitor was labeled *record* because that's what that recorder was doing.

In a single-viewer digital editing system, everything you need to see, whenever you need to see it, appears in one window. The viewing screen does double and triple duty. The clips play in the viewer. The timeline (your show) plays in the viewer. The title and effects appear in that window. It all happens in one viewer. If you're working on a system with a single computer monitor, desktop space could be at a premium. This approach uses the least amount of real estate. An extra benefit is that the arrangement of the windows on your desktop rarely changes.

However, single-viewer systems can be confusing for beginners unless close attention is paid to what's being displayed. Every editing system has some kind of indicator to let you know whether you're watching a clip or the timeline. You don't want to mix them up and inadvertently do something on the timeline that you meant to do on a clip.

Editing systems based on the source record model are easier to learn. One of the viewers—the one that represents the record monitor, which we'll call the *results* viewer—is permanently linked to the timeline. Consequently, the results viewer always displays the results of your actions. The other viewer, the source viewer, plays clips. It's usually easy to tell them apart because they have different buttons and information displays. The convention is that the source viewer is always on the left and the record viewer is on the right. Why? That's just the way it is.

Some systems let you make the source and results viewer windows different sizes. If your system permits that, make the results viewer larger. You'll be able to see the difference between the two viewers instantly, and it's nice to have a bigger screen to evaluate the results of your work.

In some systems, whenever you double-click on a clip, a new viewer window opens. It's easy to imagine how quickly your desktop can become overrun with multiple viewer windows. You should open as few windows as possible. Each viewer requires *random access memory* (RAM). If you use up the RAM in your system, you may notice that clips don't play smoothly. Overlapping viewer windows can also cause problems. The best solution is to avoid these problems. Besides, too many open windows can be confusing, especially for beginners. You're trying to learn where all the pertinent information is located on the desktop. Filling up the desktop with unnecessary windows only gets in the way of your learning.

There's another difference between single- and dual-viewer editing systems. Those with multiple viewers are often more customizable. This can be good or bad depending on your needs and skill level. Even if the only thing you can change is the size and placement of the viewers, beginners can get themselves into trouble. You don't want to move the windows around just because you can. It's important to keep the windows in the same place every time you use the system, as you're learning the geography of the desktop.

You'll also learn faster if your desktop is kept clean and uncluttered. A simple workspace lets you focus on editing. If you're using editing software on a computer, it's also a good idea to choose a neutral color for your desktop. Patterns and photographs only make it more difficult to get real work done. Avoid anything with bright colors and fine detail. Those backgrounds make it difficult to see video clearly. Beyond the obvious distractions of having too many lines and colors, there's a physiological problem.

It's impossible to see colors accurately after you've been staring at strong bright colors. The best choices for desktop backgrounds are shades of light blue or gray. One computer graphics expert went to the trouble of painting his workspace pure gray to avoid any interference that light reflecting from his walls might cause while he and his clients were making critical decisions about color. It's not necessary to go that far. Using a neutral desktop background is enough.

The Four Corners

Look at the desktop. The major elements on your desktop should be recognizable. However, it's not enough to just know the center of the desktop. You need to learn the four corners of this cockpit. Do you know what all those icons and buttons do? What's that window in the upper right-hand corner for? What's that little icon on the lower right-hand corner of the timeline do?

Explore the terrain. The name of the icon or tool usually appears when you place the mouse over an object. Press buttons. Open menus. If you want an explanation of what something does, use the help function or check your editing system manual. Eventually, you'll understand what all the functions and tools on screen do. However, you shouldn't feel compelled to learn it all at once. The only thing you need now is a vague sense of where to find things. Where are the tools? How are the menus categorized?

Editing is simple. Finding the tools you need while you're editing is the problem. Learn early to explore the entire desktop. Don't neglect something just because you don't expect to use that feature very often. Remember that you're only as good as your ability to find things on the screen so it's important to teach yourself the four corners.

Train your eye. If the answer is somewhere on the screen, you don't want to have to spend a lot of time searching for it. You want to be able to go to the correct corner immediately. That's another reason to avoid constantly changing the desktop. Editors who maintain a consistent workspace are more efficient because they don't have to interrupt their creative flow to remember where they moved something. For most of us, the location of a tool is easier to remember than its function. Focus your attention on the screen. Use the help feature. Train your eye so you don't interrupt your creative flow. The answers are on the desktop.

In a digital environment, you learn to edit through the interface. The desktop is the interface and the tool. The items on the desktop change radically in many editing systems whenever an operation requires different tools. If you're bringing new source materials (inputting) into your editing system, you need a tool to control the camcorder or recorder and bins to hold the material. If you're working on the audio mix for your finished show, a mixer tool, audio meters, and the timeline are important; there's no reason for any bins or source viewers to be open. Each phase of editing requires different tools. Each tool opens a window, which allows you to perform a task. As your proficiency increases, making the choice of which windows to open and which ones to close becomes easier. To avoid confusion, especially when you're just learning, only open tools that are absolutely necessary.

Even professional editors get confused. If you're working with multiple layers of audio, video, and effects, it's easy to get lost or make a mistake. The solution is to take a step back. Use the undo feature. If you haven't found it, look for it. Undo is one of the most important features in any editing system.

Undo is like the trail of crumbs you leave behind as you wander deeper into the forest so you can find your way out later. Most of the changes you make to the interface or your show can be undone. Editing systems without an undo feature are rare. Very simple editing systems may only permit one or two undo operations. Others can track every keystroke you make from the time you launch the application until the moment you close it. So if you've taken one too many steps into the forest, the best thing to do is to back up. The alternative is to go back to the top menu and restore the project to the way it was before you last saved it.

Taking Control of the Four Corners

Digital editing systems can be bewildering. The desktop is filled with tool palettes, information windows, icons, folders, and viewers. All of them open at once and as you work, windows start multiplying. How can you avoid confusion as you learn the interface?

Reduce the clutter as much as possible. Close unnecessary windows. If you're doing simple editing, close the meter, mixer, and effects windows and anything else that has nothing to do with basic editing. It's best to keep the number of open windows to a minimum since every open window requires RAM. More importantly, real estate on the desktop is limited. There's no sense filling it up with useless windows.

Resize the useful windows to reflect their importance. For instance, if you're organizing clips into bins, the timeline and results viewer should be small. Bins and the source viewer should take up most of the real estate. Scale the viewers down to create more open space. Make the picons in the bin just big enough to see clearly.

The arrangement of windows and tools on your desktop is called a *screen layout*. If the windows aren't locked in place, be careful where you move them. Use the default screen layouts that came with your editing system as much as possible. Different tasks require different tools and the screen layout may change depending on the mode of the editing system. It can be beneficial to modify the screen layout. Once you've figured out what works best for you, leave it alone. You want everything in your screen layout to be in its familiar place every time you edit.

Consistency makes it easier to remember where to look in the cockpit. If you move things around, make sure you return them to their proper places before you shut down your editing system. Many times the screen layout is saved every time you exit the program. The screen layout reverts to that position the next time you open your editing system. Ideally, you want all the windows and tools to be in their familiar places the next time you edit. After you've learned where the useful information is located on the desktop, you can edit with ease. Recurrence equals confidence.

Start with the Top Row

One of the first steps you should take is to familiarize yourself with the menus in your editing system. The most important one is the top row. This is the drop-down menu common to most software running on the Windows and Mac platforms. If your editing system is based on either platform, the top row is usually visible at all times. Some categories are universal, such as File, Edit, and Help. Help is a category you should use *early and often*.

Others are more specific. For example,

- Bin, Clip, Tools, and Window (Avid XpressDV)
- View, Mark, Modify, Sequence, Effects, Tools, and Windows (Apple Final Cut Pro)

- View, Album, Toolbox, and Setup (Pinnacle Studio)
- View, Program, Track, Tools, Media, Windows (Media 100 iFinish)
- View, Collection, Element, Storyboard, and Window (Incite)

There are as many variations as there are systems. We recommend that you make it a point to use the top row menu. This is where you can learn the functions, features, and structure of your editing system. All of the standard computer functions (Open, Close, Save, Save As, and Exit) are available from this menu. The great part is that some of the tools familiar to every computer user perform the identical function in a digital editing system. Digital editing can be seen as word processing with pictures and sounds. The cut, copy, and paste functions (and in most instances, the identical keyboard shortcuts are used) work the way they do with text in a word processor or with video clips on a timeline. We've known some editors to eschew the mouse buttons and edit using only the Control (Command for Mac users) *C*, *X*, or *V* commands.

Chances are when you need to do something beyond making a cut, the tool will be accessible from the top menu. As you step across the top menu and look at what appears under each category, you may not understand what some tools do or what a particular option means. That's to be expected. You just need to get a sense of the logic. For example, in Final Cut Pro, you'll find audio pan and gain under Modify. In XpressDV, it's under Tools.

We recommend that beginners start by using the top menu to perform tasks. It doesn't matter if your editing system runs on the Mac or Windows platform or if it's an editing appliance. The feature or function you're looking for will often be spelled out on the top menu. It's the best place to start.

Even seasoned professionals should use the top menu until becoming an expert on the system. Remember that most of the features and tools are used infrequently. No one should expect to be fluent with all of them. All that's required is ability to find the feature or tool. Using the top menu bar is the most reliable way to access all the tools.

The mouse is an important tool for editors. However, don't let yourself become dependent on it or it will hamper you later. Develop your skills by using the keyboard to learn where the tools are located. After you're familiar with the menus, you can branch out and learn the keyboard shortcuts and then the mouse commands.

The Fast Way? Learn Shortcuts

The easiest way to learn the keyboard shortcuts is to use the top row menu. The shortcuts are listed alongside the menu command. If you see that you're using a command repeatedly, learn the shortcut. Shortcuts bypass the process of selecting a choice on a menu. As the word implies, shortcuts are faster. Whenever you see yourself repeatedly accessing the same menu, scrolling to make a selection, and clicking on the selection, switch to a keyboard shortcut. The most widely used shortcut is the spacebar. In nearly every program, and in nearly every situation, the spacebar is a shortcut for the ALL STOP command. Pressing the spacebar brings everything to a halt.

Other popular shortcuts are slowly becoming universal, such as the *I* key to mark an in point and the *O* key to mark an out point. Common-sense keyboard shortcuts help make editing faster and easier. Chapter 11 includes application-specific shortcuts for many common tasks.

J–K–L

The *J–K–L* group of shortcuts are also growing in popularity. These shortcuts are used to play clips backwards and forward. *J* plays a clip in reverse, *K* is the pause key, and *L* plays a clip forward. In some systems, pressing *J* or *L* repeatedly makes the clip play faster or slower. The *J–K–L* group is so powerful because an editor can play a clip backward and forward at varying speeds with one hand.

If you have any touch typing ability, develop your keyboard shortcut skills. In many systems, the *J–K–L* shortcut is directly below the shortcut keys *I* and *O* used to mark ins and outs, respectively. This means that for those who can touch type, nearly 60 percent of the editing functions can be accessed with one hand. It's easy to see that a touch typist can really soar with a little practice. Shortcut conventions familiar to anyone who uses a word processing program are also used in many digital editing systems. Shortcuts for Cut, Copy, and Paste, Save, Open, Close, and Delete are universal.

Keyboard shortcuts are excellent for quick, precise editing. However, they only work if you use them. Beginners tend to rely on the mouse, which is fine, although the mouse can only take you so far. Frank Black, a professional editor, remarked, "Anyone can edit with a mouse, but you can make a living with the keyboard."

Most of you aren't planning to earn a living editing. However, the most efficient way to work is to edit with your right hand on the mouse and your left hand on the keyboard. Left-handers should reverse that suggestion. To be really proficient at any endeavor, you need to use two hands. Editing with one hand or just the mouse is slow, unproductive, and inefficient. It's amazing to us that students who wouldn't think to play a computer game with one hand routinely use only the mouse to edit.

A Word About Tool Palettes

Tool palettes are common on digital editing systems. The functions on the palette are usually available from the top menu bar or through a keyboard shortcut. It's important to know which tools are only accessible from a tool palette. These tools require the mouse.

If you find important tools that are not duplicated elsewhere, the tool palette needs to be in a convenient place. Screen position is important. If you can, move the strip or window to where it will do the most good. Burying the tool palette means finding it will be a nuisance.

Two Hands Are Better Than One

It's common sense—people who use two hands are more productive. Most digital editing systems have a mouse and keyboard. Some people use the mouse to access tools on the desktop and ignore the keyboard. Others prefer to type keyboard commands and avoid the mouse. Experienced editors know that the most productive approach is to use whatever gives you the faster access to the tool you need. The technique of using both hands is simple to learn: Keep one hand on the mouse and the other on the keyboard. Over time you'll develop your own style—accessing tools with the buttons or keys you find most comfortable.

The best time to start developing your own style is when you begin learning the system. Don't rest one hand in your lap or use it to hold up your head. If you need to think or if you're tired, take a break. Video-game aficionados who play with one hand aren't competitive. Editing works the same way; two-handed editors win every time.

Look for a place where it won't be buried or covered by other windows. It should also be close to other tools involved with the functions on the tool palette. For example, if the majority of the tools are editing tools, this tool palette should be as close as possible to the timeline and results viewer since this is where those editing tasks will be performed.

Personalize the Interface; Make It Work for You

Most editing systems permit some customization. An open system lets you change the screen layout and other aspects of the interface to suit your preferences. The purpose of this is to make the interface more comfortable for you. A degree of openness provides flexibility and power because the system can be altered to suit the task at hand. On the other hand, we depend on interfaces that are consistent. Interfaces that change frequently are constantly confusing.

Organization Is Important

Like most desktops, yours is probably filled with windows for projects, bins, viewers, and timelines. The default screen layout worked best for the team who created your editing system. Screen layout is largely a personal preference so some systems let you choose from several options. Another option called the *custom* option is often available. This lets you position and size the windows and store the arrangement.

Without discipline and consistency on your part, your desktop can end up looking different every time you use the system. This can be confusing when you're learning to edit. Imagine how you'd feel if every time you drove your car, the speedometer moved to a new place. Change for change's sake will give you a headache. Decide on a screen layout that works for you and stick with it. It makes you less efficient, not more, to move the windows around on your desktop every time you edit.

Size the windows to maximize the real estate on your desktop. Position each window where it won't obscure other windows. You need to be able to locate the windows quickly and see what you're doing within the window. Create an arrangement and then live with it.

Some editing systems have default screen layouts that change to reflect the task at hand. In other systems, you'll have to create them. The optimal screen layout for editing a show is different than the optimal layout for mixing a show. What you need to see and where you need to see it often changes dramatically. If you can save multiple custom layouts, name the layout for the task or operation for which its been optimized, for example, mixing or 3-d effects.

Customizing Your Keyboard

Professional editing systems let editors remap the keyboard. You can move shortcuts around the keyboard or even create custom shortcuts. Custom shortcuts are the ultimate keyboard shortcuts because they belong to you alone. These shortcuts are your personal power keys and are usually stored in a user preference file. If you save that file on a diskette or CD, you can reuse your settings at any facility with the same system. Then when you sit down to start editing, you can load your settings and your personal editing cockpit will appear in front of you.

As you work, you'll discover that you use some buttons and commands more often than others. This is a reflection of the type of work you do. Inevitably, you'll also find some shortcuts that don't make sense to you or shortcuts that are useful but cumbersome because they require too many

Out for a Long Drive

Digital editing is like taking a long drive in your car to a place you've never seen. It's a visually stimulating experience. You are excited about what's in front of your windshield, but you must still pay attention to the dashboard. It's also tiring because you have to sit for a long time. Editing is similar. Editors spend a lot of time sitting in front of a monitor watching footage and paying attention to the controls. You need a good chair and monitors should be placed at eye level. Eye strain, aching arm or wrist joints, and numb butt are common complaints. A good mouse pad, a keyboard at the proper height, and proper wrist support can alleviate many problems. Make sure your workspace is comfortable. You'll be glad you did.

Tips

The project window must be open in many systems. It often serves as a table of contents for the project or a place to maintain a list of recently opened files. This element rarely has an editing function beyond opening or closing a project or application. Reduce its size or roll it up to minimize clutter.

- In a single-viewer system, position the viewer in the upper-left center of the desktop to avoid hiding it.
- Place an editing tool palette near the timeline and results viewer where most of the editing takes place.
- Save preference file settings under your own name.
- Save screen layouts under the name of the task you've optimized it for.

keystrokes. We don't think it qualifies as a shortcut if you have to use multiple combinations of the Control (command), Shift, Alt, or Option keys. These shortcuts are candidates for remapping.

Remapped keys work great because they are designed logically and reflect the style and intelligence of the designer, you. For example, Avid master editor Jennifer Rew remaps her keyboard so that Shift-*I* clears in points and Shift-*O* clears out points. We're sure you'll discover shortcuts that make your life as an editor easier.

Summary

Editing is simple, but learning the interface takes time. An editor is only as good as his or her ability to find and use the proper tools. Remember, it's easier to locate something if it's in a predictable place. During an emergency, pilots don't have time to think about where they should look and what the warning lights mean. Similarly, you don't have time when you're in the digital editing cockpit. You just want to go to where you need to go. Remember that learning the interface thoroughly is a lifelong process. However, all you really need to know is where to look.

Important Points to Remember

- The desktop is your center of attention.
- Nine times out of ten, the answer is on the desktop.
- If you prefer a virtual interface, avoid text based abstract interfaces.
- Don't be fooled by simplicity. Bigger and bolder is better!
- Use the top row to understand the editing system's structure.
- Train your eye to find buttons or information on the desktop.
- Avoid confusion. Unclutter your desktop. Close any unnecessary windows.
- Open and close viewers and tools in the same place every time. Consistency makes learning easier.
- Learn the keyboard shortcuts for repetitive tasks.
- Edit with two hands.
- Customize with care.

Beginnings, Middles, and Ends

Now that you're comfortable (or still gaining confidence) with your editing system's interface, it's time to learn how to use this tool. Editing involves telling stories with pictures and sounds. Therefore, you should know something about storytelling and about how editors use pictures and sounds to tell stories. This chapter will help you understand the basics of editing. However, experiencing editing is even more valuable. Editing is an art. As with all the arts, creativity and craft are important. The craft of editing involves learning techniques and practicing those techniques until you achieve competency.

To help you become a competent editor, we've developed a series of exercises to open your eyes to the power of editing. The footage for these exercises is stored on the CD. You can use this material to supercharge your imagination or work with your own footage.

The Tradition of Storytelling

Every story has a beginning, middle, and end. It doesn't matter whether the story is a lengthy drama or a joke. People prefer stories that have resolution because real life rarely does. Storytelling has a long tradition that dates back to the dawn of human history. Since ancient times, those who could tell, perform, depict, and, much later, write down stories have been cherished for their abilities. Digital video fuses oral storytelling, performance, painting and photography, and writing in what is the culmination of a 10,000-year tradition. You have the most powerful storytelling tools ever conceived in your hands. Use them to amuse, illuminate, or memorialize. Above all, tell stories that celebrate our shared existence.

Making Pearl Necklaces

Stories are built by stringing together shots in the right order, as if they were pearls in a necklace. When each pearl in is the right position on the silk cord, we no longer focus on the individual pearls; instead, we admire the necklace. We appreciate its symmetry and treasure the beauty of it as a whole.

Editors arrange pictures and sounds to tell a story. Using the materials at hand, the editor must find the logic or structure that will unfold the story from beginning to end over time. The story can be brief (shorter than a minute) or epic in length. No matter what you're editing (shots of your children playing, a wedding, the coronation of a king, or the next Hollywood blockbuster), the audience sees the finished show as one continuous sequence. The when (the order in which the audience see the images) and the how (how long the audience sees the images) are as important as the what (the content of those images).

Each shot is a pearl that needs to be placed in the correct spot on the timeline. When clear, clean, and understandable shots are selected, all that remains is for the editor to make sure each shot is in its proper place and on the screen for the appropriate amount of time. The audience only sees what the editor arranges.

Although the story appears to unfold for the audience, the structure is perfectly clear to an editor working on a digital editing system. The timeline is a visual representation of a story's structure. Arranging and rearranging shots on a timeline is as easy as shuffling a deck of cards. Select any shot, move it, shorten it, lengthen it, or move it again to shape the story. With practice, the shows that you edit will keep the audience involved until the fade out at "The End."

Are You a Bricklayer or Sculptor?

There are two approaches to the craft of editing. Some editors build shows one shot at a time. They add shot to shot to shot until the last shot is placed on the timeline. Others carve shows out of the entire block of material. These editors chop, chip, and slice to hone and shape the show.

Actually, few editors slavishly adhere to either of these approaches. Sometimes an editor acts as a bricklayer building the show one shot at a time, and then in the next minute acts as a sculptor carving, honing, and polishing. The truth is digital editing makes it so easy to switch back and forth between building and carving that you never have to make a choice. However, you do need to know what each approach entails. It also helps to figure out which one is more appealing to you because that's the approach you should use to start editing a project.

Building

This method is like building a brick wall or stringing pearls on a necklace. The editor adds shots one at a time to the show. To do that, the editor goes

Figure 3-1
Building a show,
shot by shot on
the timeline.

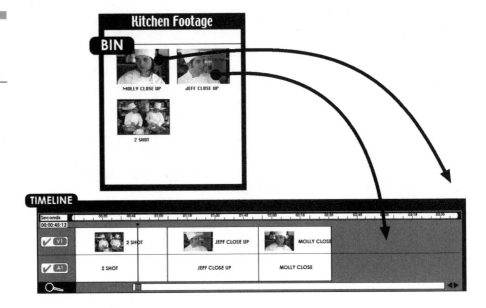

through all the footage and isolates the shots. The details of how to do this appear in Chapter 7, "Setting the Table." In brief, the editor looks at the material, finds the beginning and end of each useable shot, and creates a copy of each shot called a *subclip*. The subclips are named, saved, and stored in bins. Once all the shots have been isolated, the editor can start placing them in the show. Each shot is added in succession from the start. As the editor slowly adds shots, he or she can play and review the results. This method is similar to linear video editing. The editor places a first shot, proceeds to the second, the third, and so on. This method works well with any show that has a detailed script. The exercise you're about to start editing uses the building method.

Carving

This method follows Michelangelo's approach to sculpting marble statues. For Michelangelo, each block of stone contained a human figure. All he needed to do was chisel away the excess marble and reveal the figure trapped in the stone. The editor starts by placing all the material, or at least a manageable portion of it, on the timeline.

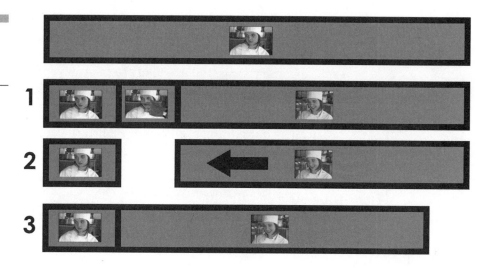

Figure 3-2
Carving video in steps to remove unwanted material.

As the editor watches the material, the sections that are unusable are marked and deleted from the timeline. This is the opposite of what a builder does because the carver is looking for the moment when the material ceases to be interesting. Afterwards, the editor reviews the now much shorter timeline. Editors repeat this process, carving away excess to reveal more of the essence of the material. This method enables the editor to find the structure of the show through the material. Once everything on the timeline is carved to the bone, the editor begins the process of moving those materials around to order the story.

The Editing Exercise

The goal of this exercise is to make as many edits as possible to practice using your editing system while building a simple dialogue scene. You can use the footage on the CD or shoot your own version of the script. This is an easy project designed to let you get your fingers wet.

Editors refer to their first attempts to assemble the show as a *rough cut*. It's called a rough cut because it's rough around the edges. This stage is important because it is where you create a basic structure to give the story a beginning, middle, and end. The flow from shot to shot can be polished later.

You should be comfortable when you edit. Make sure your chair, keyboard, mouse, and monitors are at comfortable heights. Hopefully, you've been wandering around the four corners of your editing system desktop exploring everything, and are ready to take on your first assignment.

The process of transforming original source materials into a finished show is called *workflow*. Here's our workflow for this exercise:

1. Turn on your editing system and launch the application.
2. Create a new project.
3. Copy the clips from the CD into your editing system.
4. Create a new timeline.
5. Edit the shots on the timeline.

Turn on Your System

Like many endeavors in life, starting is the hardest part. Turn on the power to your editing system. If you're using an editing appliance, that could be a single switch labeled on. Or there could be switches located on each piece of equipment in rooms filled with equipment. In our experience, beginners often forget to turn on all of the peripherals connected to the editing system, such as the speakers, monitors, external hard drives, and camcorder.

There's a simple solution to this problem. If you don't have an uninterruptible power supply or surge-protected power strip, purchase one and plug everything into it. This way one simple switch turns everything on.

Editing systems are less expensive than they once were, but the cost to purchase them are still substantial. A high-quality surge protector is cheap insurance for home users. Professional users should have an uninterruptible power supply that gives you enough time to save your work before shutting down the system.

After you turn on your editing system, launch the editing application.

Create a New Project

Every editing system has its own way of creating, organizing, and saving projects. You need to be aware of where your system stores project files so you can find them. If your editing system follows a structured approach, any projects you create will be stored in specific directories. Other editing

Organization Tips for Open-Style Editing Systems

If your editing system doesn't have its own rigid (default) file structure, you need to set one up. Never listen to your evil twin calling you a geek for being organized. You're an editor so you'll have the last laugh later.

- Create a directory (Windows) or folder (Mac) on your editing system for all of your projects. Label it Video Projects or whatever makes sense to you. Then make a subdirectory or subfolder within that directory for each project. This will simplify the process of opening, saving, importing, exporting, and retrieving files. Believe us, this works.
- Create a file structure.

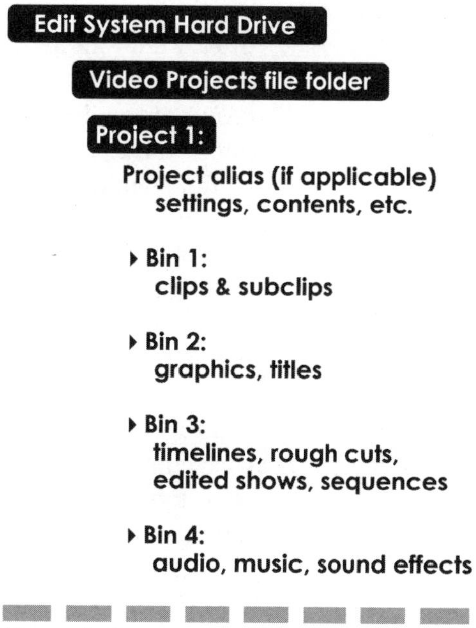

Edit System Hard Drive

Video Projects file folder

Project 1:

Project alias (if applicable) settings, contents, etc.

▸ **Bin 1:** clips & subclips

▸ **Bin 2:** graphics, titles

▸ **Bin 3:** timelines, rough cuts, edited shows, sequences

▸ **Bin 4:** audio, music, sound effects

Figure 3-3
Recommended file structure.

systems take an open approach and don't have a default structure. We've even experienced the embarrassment of not being able to locate a project after saving it on one of these editing systems. As silly as it is to say, make sure you know where your editing system stores its files.

Open systems store project files anywhere and everywhere. As the editor, you must impose order on the editing system by saving your work in the specific directories you create. If you're working on an open-style editing system, read the organization tips in the sidebar.

Create a new project. Name it *The Dicey Question*. Save it.

Get Set to Edit

For this exercise, the only windows and tools that should be open are those used in basic editing. Nothing extraneous should be open, such as titler, audio mixer, or effects windows. Most editing systems default to a basic editing setup. If you have an editing system that lets you modify the layout of the desktop, arrange the windows so they make sense and you're comfortable.

You should have a project labeled *The Dicey Question* open. The project window is the primary organizational window in most editing systems.

Create a bin called *Kitchen Footage*. You'll only need one bin to store clips for this exercise. The footage was shot in a kitchen (hence the name).

Expand the file labeled edv.zip on the CD on your hard drive and copy the material into the bin. There are detailed instructions on the CD.

Your Kitchen Footage bin should now have three clips. Look to see if the clips are in your bin. If the bin can display picons, you will see a picon for each clip. We recommend changing the picon to a picture that's more representative than the first frame of the clip. Look in your editing system manual. If your system doesn't accommodate picons, don't worry about it. Identify each clip by name. They should be called *2-Shot*, *Molly MCU*, and *Jeff MCU*. MCU stands for *medium close-ups*.

Viewer

Watch all of the clips to acquaint yourself with the footage. Normally, there would be multiple takes of each shot in this scene involving two kitchen workers. As the editor, you would have to watch and evaluate all of them trying to find the one take that has the most emotional impact. This is an exercise so you're stuck with our choices.

Pay attention to the motion control buttons on your editing systems viewer or viewers. Play the clips in forward and reverse. Go to the head and tail of the clip. Try out all of the buttons to familiarize yourself with their functions. Most editing systems display the time code somewhere on or near the viewer. Locate the time code display; it will become important later.

Timeline

In most editing systems, the timeline window is near the bottom of the desktop. This window presents a graphic representation of each shot in your show arranged along a line. There's usually a ruler marked in time increments and a timeline cursor (an indicator line or bar) that you can grab with the mouse and move anywhere along the timeline. Track indicators for monitoring audio and video are usually placed on the left side of the window. You'll need them as you edit.

Find the magnifier or scaling tool that expands or contracts the amount of time displayed within the window. A timeline displays the clips on tracks. They can be viewed as a tight group—thin slices of time along a lengthy (in duration) timeline. With the magnifier, the timeline can be scaled to display the same clips as long slices of time. Whether the slices appear to be thin or wide depends upon the amount of time (check the ruler) displayed in the window.

Monitoring

Check your video monitor and speakers to make sure what appears on your desktop appears on these devices. Our thoughts on monitoring appear in Chapter 10, "Getting It In and Out."

Make a New Timeline

Whether your editing system calls it a storyboard, composition, sequence, or program, find the tool or menu that creates a new timeline and make a new blank timeline.

Label the Show

Label the timeline as soon as you make it. Make it a habit to save the timeline before you edit anything onto it. Some systems prompt you to name the timeline, whereas others don't. If yours doesn't ask you to save the timeline, go to the file menu and save it. Use a unique name—one that reflects what you're doing. This exercise could be called *DQ Rough Cut*, *Dicey One*, or *Jeff and Molly Scene*. Call it what it is. Avoid at all costs the ubiquitous name *Untitled*, which is by far the number-one choice of beginners worldwide.

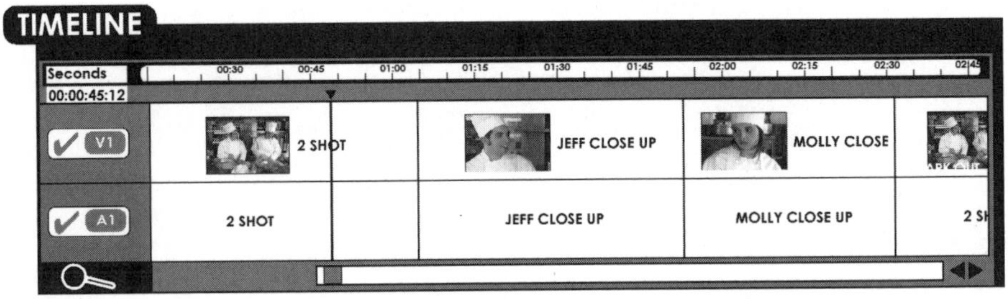

Figure 3-5
A timeline with clips.

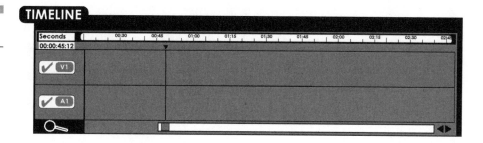

A Once Over in the Cockpit

Let's take a brief look at the timeline before we start editing. The timeline should be placed along the bottom of the screen where it usually resides. Look at the number of tracks displayed on the timeline. This exercise requires one audio track and one video track. In this scene, each character speaks in turn so you only need a single track. A second audio track is optional.

Remove Excess Tracks

If there's a way to turn off or remove unwanted tracks, do it now. There's no sense in having empty tracks that take up space on the desktop if you're not using them. The minimum track arrangement on some editing systems is one video and two audio tracks.

Track Selection Buttons

Clips can only be edited onto the track or tracks that are active. This exercise uses both an audio and video track. Make at least one audio and one video track active. Look for a button or light that tells you the track is in fact on and that the clip you edit onto the timeline will appear there. If you're not sure, try it out.

The track activation light is a significant indicator. An editor always needs to know which tracks are active. When you're doing a complicated edit with a dozen tracks, it's important to be able to quickly identify which tracks will be affected when you make an edit.

The track activation light is the equivalent of the high-beam indicator in your car. Train your eyes to see the track lights. Unfortunately, on some editing systems, this indicator is very small and insignificant. If you haven't trained yourself to see it, you probably won't find it.

Playing and Marking Clips

Watch all the clips to see how the scene unfolds. Normally, you'd make notes about each shot and take in order to help decide which one or ones have the most emotional impact.

For this exercise, start by loading the clip called 2-Shot in your editing system's viewer. In this exercise, the 2-Shot serves as the master shot because it shows the scene in its entirety. Play the 2-Shot. Then play the other shots of Molly and Jeff. These shots are labeled Molly MCU and Jeff MCU.

Mark the Source Shot

If you use the building approach, the first step in the process is to isolate the section of the clip you want to place on the timeline. This is done by marking an IN (beginning) and an OUT (end) point on the clip. Play the clip in the viewer. Set an IN mark where you want the shot to begin. Continue playing the clip. Set an OUT point where the shot ends.

Start the kitchen scene by marking Jeff's opening line on the master—the 2-Shot clip. Load the 2-Shot into the Viewer. Play the 2-Shot and stop it where Jeff's opening line begins. Mark an IN point. Go to the end of the clip and mark and OUT point. Check your IN and OUT points.

Many editing systems have a feature that lets you play only the portion of the clip you marked. It's called *Loop Play* or *Play In to Out*. This tool is useful for checking what you've marked.

Find the buttons or keyboard shortcuts that clear (remove) the marks. When a shot you've marked doesn't start and end the way you want, you'll need to clear the marks you've made. Then you can redo the process of setting the marks. The idea here is to select only the very best part of the shot. If you're not sure what the phrase *best part* of a shot means, be sure to read Chapter 7.

Pay attention to how your editing system indicates an IN and OUT mark. What do these marks look like? Teach yourself to recognize the marks in the viewer windows.

Use the keyboard or mouse buttons to set and clear the marks. We suggest that you start using the keyboard shortcuts for marking an IN and OUT point and use your other hand to scroll through the footage.

Before we continue, try doing what editors call *marking a clip on the fly*. This means to mark IN and OUT points as the clip plays. Some editors prefer to do it this way because they find it helps them determine the natural rhythm of the shot. With the 2-Shot loaded in the Viewer, mark an IN and OUT point for Jeff's opening line as the clip plays. Use *Loop Play* to check your marks. If necessary, redo the process until you're satisfied with the IN and OUT point for Jeff's opening line.

Prepare the Timeline for an Edit

Make sure the track or tracks on which you want to place Jeff's opening line are active. Pay attention to the track indicator lights or buttons on the timeline.

Mark an IN Time on the Timeline

There are two ways to set an IN time on the timeline. You can mark the spot using an IN point or simply place the timeline cursor where you want the edit point to be.

For the kitchen scene, mark an IN time at the beginning of the timeline or move the timeline cursor to the beginning of the timeline.

Every edit has four edit points. The source clip and the timeline (the record side) each have IN and OUT points. However, it only takes three of the four points to make an edit. Your editing system is smart enough to calculate the fourth point. For example, we asked you to set an IN and OUT mark for the source clip, which is 2-Shot in this case. Then we asked you to set an IN time on the timeline (the record side). Your editing system, knowing the duration of the source clip, will calculate the OUT point.

Editing Clips on the Timeline

Most editing systems have two modes: *overwrite* and *insert*. These work in a manner similar to typeover and insert in a word processing program. There are usually keyboard or mouse buttons for each mode. You should be able to identify these buttons on your editing system. We suggest you use the keyboard buttons.

Overwrite Edit

An overwrite edit places a clip on the timeline and covers over anything already in the spot. If there's nothing on the track, it doesn't matter. An overwrite edit never changes the overall length of the show. It's similar to a linear video edit in that the source video covers over existing material. *Overlay* is another commonly used term for this mode.

Insert Edit

An insert edit places a clip on the timeline and pushes everything after the edit point forward. Any existing material will be pushed down the timeline. If there's nothing on the track, it doesn't matter. An insert edit always extends the length of the show. Some editing systems refer to this mode as a *splice* or *ripple* because the act of inserting a shot has a ripple effect from that point onward.

We're Making Straight Cuts in this Exercise!

The edits you'll make in this exercise are called *straight cuts* and both modes will work since this scene is assembled shot by shot. Each clip that you'll apply to the timeline has video and audio tracks. The duration of the tracks will be identical in length. When you look at the timeline, you'll see the video and audio tracks stacked one above the other. The length of the video track should be even with the audio track for every clip you place on the timeline. When you edit a new clip on the timeline, it should be snug up against the previous clip.

Remember, the idea here is to edit a conversation between two kitchen workers, Jeff and Molly. You'll be cutting what Jeff says followed by what Molly says using the script as a guide. It's just "he said, she said" until you reach the end. The shots have to be in the proper order and any action must be matched. Concentrate on the audio. Make sure you don't clip any words when you're marking the IN point and OUT points for each character's line of dialogue. (See Figure 3-6.)

The First Edit

Play the clip with the master shot, which is a two-shot. Use the 2-Shot to establish the location and situation. Mark an IN and OUT that include Jeff's opening line, "Hey, where did you learn to chop so fast?" Edit that portion of the 2-Shot onto the timeline by pressing the proper button to insert or overwrite a clip, now. Congratulations! You've made your first edit and you're on your way.

The Second Edit

Play the clip with the close-up of Molly saying her lines. Mark an IN and OUT that include her lines, "Same place as you, here, remember? Come on, soup's on in half an hour." You'll see a mistake (pay attention to her chef's hat) when she turns away from the camera to look at the soup. To fix this mistake, move the OUT point earlier during her pause.

Figure 3-6

A t imeline with 3 straight cuts of video and audio.

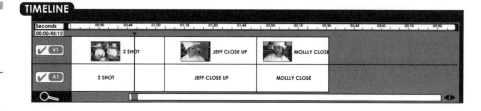

The Drop-and-Drag Approach

Yes, it's true. You can use the mouse to place shots on the timeline. Most editing systems let you click the mouse on the shot you want and drag it to the timeline. It's easy and intuitive.

We have some concerns with this method of working because it's often confusing for beginners. Dragging a shot is just a way to move the clip. In most cases, it doesn't allow you to select overwrite or insert mode. It won't define an IN or OUT point for precision. Any marks on the timeline are irrelevant during a drag-and-drop move. Clips can be dragged to an IN mark if there is one or to the timeline cursor. You can butt up a clip next to an existing clip, or drag a clip to an empty area on the timeline and close up the gaps later.

We recommend using the mouse or keyboard buttons until you learn your editing system. Relying entirely on the mouse is problematic. As your confidence grows, and if the situation warrants it, the drop-and-drag method of editing can be an asset.

The Third Edit

The audience still needs to hear Molly's second line. The only other shot you have is the 2-Shot. Play the 2-Shot and look for Molly's second line, "C'mon, soup's on in a half an hour." Then mark an IN and OUT. You'll want to match the movements Molly makes in both shots in order to match the action. You may have to adjust the in point of the 2-Shot or change the OUT point for Molly's close-up to match the action perfectly.

The Fourth Edit to the End

Play the close-up of Jeff and find his line, "Oh. I mean, you've got really nice hands." Mark an IN and OUT and edit the shot onto the timeline. Continue building the scene, line by line, with "A she said, he said" until you get to the last line in the script.

You have another opportunity to match action. Try cutting between the 2-Shot and Molly's close-up as she reaches for the kitchen towel near the end of the scene.

Review the Exercise

Once you finish building the scene, review your work. Play the timeline and ask yourself these questions:

- Are the audio edits clear and understandable? Are there any abrupt or awkward pauses from one line to another?
- Do the shots flow naturally from one character to another and maintain the rhythm of the conversation?
- Are there any frames of black between shots that shouldn't be there?
- Did you cut on the action?
- Are there any jump cuts that break the continuity between the shots?

The goal here is to create an illusion of reality. This reality is based upon the characters and their actions happening in real time. If a continuity break occurs at any point, the scene will cease to appear real to the audience.

Invariably, you will encounter minor problems. If you do, go back and look at the individual edit points. Make a list of what you want to fix. If you're unsure about whether the scene is working, play the rough cut for another person and get his or her response.

Is the Audio Clean?

The audio portion of the rough cut should sound clean, clear, and natural. You should correct any audio problems at this point. You can do this in several ways. You can play the timeline until you reach the first edit that has an audio problem. Stop here and delete all of the clips on the timeline that follow. Starting from this point, re-edit the clips onto the timeline just as you did before until the scene is complete. The practice will be good for you.

The alternative is to delete just the clip or clips causing the problem. Here's the fastest way to do this. Make sure your editing system is in insert mode. Highlight the clip and delete it. The clip should disappear and the duration of the timeline should get shorter. Position the timeline cursor at the edit point. Find the clip with the line of dialogue you need and mark an IN and OUT. Edit the clip onto the timeline. If you have to replace more clips, repeat the process. If you're not sure what the insert mode is called in your editing system, look it up in Chapter 11 "What Are They Talking About?"

Play the timeline again to make sure you've fixed the problems. Once you're satisfied with the audio, this exercise is complete. In Chapter 4, "Polishing the Necklace," we'll discuss the tools and techniques editors use to adjust and guide the audience through the story.

Save Your Work

You should save your work at this point. When you save a project, you're updating all of the information and storing it for retrieval. Get in the habit of saving your work frequently or use the auto save feature found in most editing systems. We recommend that you set the auto save interval to five minutes or less when you're editing and building shows. Longer intervals are fine for tasks such as viewing footage.

What Am I Saving and Where?

It's important to understand how your editing system saves projects and timelines. Some editing systems may save a timeline as a separate file on your hard drive. Other systems may save the timelines within a bin or project file. You need to know where these files are stored on your editing system so you can find them and back them up. Save anything and everything associated with a project in the directory or folder you created in your Video Projects directory (folder).

Never Leave Without a Backup

You should always make a backup copy of your timelines, bins, and project files and store it somewhere other than on your editing system's hard drive. Computers are notorious for developing problems. Files become corrupted. Hard drives fail. Sometimes the computer will not start. Save your project on a removable media such as a floppy, CD, or tape. It's the only insurance you have. Do it at the end of every editing session. Customarily, the last thing an editor does is save and back up all the assets of the project: bins, timelines, show settings, titles, and effects. There's no need to copy the media files. Those files can be replaced at any time by recapturing the original source tapes.

What's Really Going On?

Hopefully, you've just completed the exercise and watched the kitchen scene. When the audience sees the scene, they'll believe that Jeff and Molly were in the same room at the same time talking to each other. The question is do they have to be? The answer is no.

It wouldn't matter if we decided to shoot the 2-Shot on Tuesday, Jeff's close-up on Wednesday, and Molly's close-up on Thursday. This style of editing was perfected during the Hollywood studio system era for that very reason. On the day Molly's close-ups were being shot, Jeff probably was off working on another picture.

The editor creates the illusion that the scene is happening in real time by joining shots. These shots could have been photographed at different times and in different places, so they appear to flow in a natural sequential order. This is the most important point in this book. *Editors create the appearance of reality through editing. It's an illusion. The end result only has to look real to the audience.*

As the editor, your job is to fool the audience into believing that what they're seeing is real. To be an editor, you must understand the basic principles of editing.

How Does Editing Work?

Editing works because the audience will always find a relationship between adjoining shots. Lev Kuleshov identified this principle, which bears his name. Editing depends on the Kuleshov effect. The shots in the kitchen scene could have been photographed days apart, but the audience sees it as a continuous conversation because they assume the conversation is taking place at the same time in the same room. The audience accepts the illusion that the action is happening in real time in a real space until the editor breaks the rules.

Two Flavors—One Illusion

Editing comes in two flavors: continuity and montage. Continuity editing is the standard approach used in motion pictures and television, including the exercise you just edited. It gives the audience a clear sense of place and action using matching shots to tell a story. The goal of continuity editing is to make the audience believe the story is unfolding in real time.

Our kitchen scene exercise uses three continuity techniques: an establishing shot, shot reverse-shot, and matched action. Jeff and Molly's 2-Shot establishes the space in the kitchen. The audience's ability to recognize and comprehend the image is what editors refer to as *reading a shot*. An establishing shot lets the audience know where the characters are interacting. Shot reverse-shot describes the back and forth dialogue between Jeff and Molly in close-ups. The audience assumes that Jeff is looking at Molly because he looks off screen in the direction we expect her to be. Plus, if you draw a line across Jeff's eyes in the close-up, you will see that his eye line points to Molly and her eye line points to him. It's a trick that lets the audience know they are looking at each other. The other technique we asked you to do was to cut on matched action.

At the beginning of the scene, we asked you make an edit to hide the production mistake in her close-up. She turns her head in the close-up and finishes turning her head in the 2-Shot. Her motion hides the cut. This is another trick that lets an editor hide the seams.

By now, you're probably wondering about the other style, montage. How is montage different from continuity? The definition of montage holds the answer.

What Does Montage Mean?

Montage is a word that confuses people for good reason. In Europe, editing is called montage. The confusion dates back to the 1920s and 1930s. Two Russian filmmakers, Pudovkin and Eisenstein, developed separate theories about editing. Pudovkin's theory of analytic montage (montage is used here in the European sense to mean analytic editing) said shots should be linked together in an unobtrusive manner to guide the audience through the story. In Hollywood, his theory became continuity editing.

Eisenstein's theory of dialectic montage (dialectic editing) was that from the collision of shots, a concept arises, which the audience will figure out. Conflict or counterpoint is the basis for his five types of montage in which meaning is created from shots that don't necessarily have meaning by themselves.

Here are a few examples. See if you can determine the meaning:

- Show a shot of two lovers embracing. Cut to a train entering a tunnel and blowing its whistle.
- Show a close-up of a man looking down and then a close-up of a plate of spaghetti. Cut back to the man looking down.
- Show a shot of a man in bed. He turns off light. Cut to a man opening his eyes.

In *Roger and Me*, the editor cut between wealthy executives talking about how well they were doing and scenes of poverty in Flint, Michigan, to establish a cause-and-effect relationship between the worker's poverty and the executive's wealth. Juxtaposition creates meaning.

Image advertising for products such as perfume, beer, or cars provides some great examples of Eisenstein's approach to montage. Drink Acme Beer and the beautiful girl will be yours.

Perhaps the biggest source of confusion dates back to the 1930s. Hollywood editors developed a way to show the passage of time or place, which they called a *montage sequence*. Examples of these sequences include pages flying off the calendar, seasons dissolving from spring to fall to winter, or generic shots of Paris that let the audience know the characters are in Paris. The images in a montage sequence could be anything that makes a thematic statement. These sequences, which are usually set to music, are also used to represent a character dreaming or recalling past events.

We define montage as any editing style that ignores the strict rules of continuity. Montage editing puts unlike shots together and asks the audience to figure out the relationship between them.

Five Guidelines of Editing

1. Find the shot with the emotional moment—the one that contains the truth or heart of the story. Once you have that shot, edit all the other shots to make that moment shine.
2. Shorter is nearly always more interesting than longer.
3. Give the audience just enough time to read the shot and then make an edit. The time it takes to read a shot depends on the complexity of the image and the audience's familiarity with the subject or object. The

more familiar they are, the shorter the shot can be. For example, a shot of the White House can be much shorter than shots of other buildings.

4. Use motivated cuts. If a person glances off screen, moves his or her head or eyes depending on the closeness of the shot, the editor can cut to what the person is looking at. When someone talks about something, show the audience what he or she is talking about (see the explanation of *cutaways* in the section "Cut Away from the Action").

5. Always give the audience the best view of the action. Use close-ups and other angles to condense the action. Varying the shots lets the editor create rhythm, pacing, and visual variety.

Realistic Action, Real Time, Real Space

If you want people to see the events depicted on screen as real, the audience must believe that the action, time, or space is continuous from shot to shot. Continuity is an illusion that the sequence of images on screen is happening in real time.

To maintain the illusion, the flow of action in one shot must match the flow of action in the next. Editors look for cues to motivate a cut. For example, Molly turns her head. If the editor cuts from the outgoing shot in the middle of Molly's turn and if her head position matches the outgoing shot in the incoming shot, the audience believes they're seeing the action happen in real time. If Molly's head is turned farther away than it should be, the audience perceives a break in time. The speed at which she turns her head gives the audience a sense of time. Emotional action is as viable as physical action. In the exercise, Molly's eyes often convey more information than her words. Seeing her reactions strengthens the emotional continuity of the scene. The audience senses her emotional engagement and are in turn engaged. If the cuts occur at the right moments, the audience will believe that what is taking place on screen is real.

The rules for continuity of space are more flexible. We've all come to accept that a subject can be in one location and in the very next shot suddenly be somewhere else. For example, in a police show, the fact that a detective is in the victim's apartment in one shot and back at headquarters in the next is acceptable. The audience doesn't need to see the detective exit the apartment, exit the building, enter his car, drive to headquarters, exit the car, enter the police station, walk to his desk, and sit down. The audience assumes all of those steps happened because he's a real person. The audience won't realize that continuity has been broken until the editor places the shot of the detective at the headquarters between the two shots of the detective in the victim's apartment.

Here's how you can take theory and put it to practical use.

Techniques for Continuity Editing

Remember that any shot that makes the audience believe the illusion will work, no matter when or where it was photographed. If you want to edit using continuity, it helps to have several angles. When you only have a few shots, it's difficult to condense the action. The lighting and color balance of the shots should match. Pay attention to the screen direction of your subjects. If someone's looking to the right in a wide shot, he or she should be looking to the right in the close-up. This helps the audience understand where the subjects are in relation to each other. Dialogue between characters should be edited so sentences, questions, and answers flow naturally. Dialogue is the simplest motivation for a cut. The other motivators are to cut on physical or emotional action.

Matched Edits and Jump Cuts

To create continuity, cut the shots in the order of the action to make space and time believable. If the audience can follow the action as it progresses, they will perceive the action as continuous. If an action in one shot carries over to the next shot, an editor would say the two shots have *matched action*. For example, a subject walks across the street in one shot and continues to walk in the same direction in the next shot.

This matched edit suggests to the audience that there's no gap in time or space from one shot to another.

A jump cut makes it clear that a gap in time or space exists. Avoid joining shots that will reveal duplicate or broken action. This is a visual tip-off that the action isn't happening in real time. The illusion of continuity can be broken if two shots are edited together that are supposed to be similar but aren't. For example, if the subject is resting his or her chin on his or her hand and in the next shot, the subject's hand is resting on his or her heart, a cut will make the subject's hand appear to jump. If the color balance or lighting or framing is off because the shots were photographed at different times, the audience will notice. They will sense that what they're watching has been manipulated—is not taking place in real time—and therefore the action and characters no longer seem real.

Cut on Action

Cut on the subject's movement to hide the edit. Include part of the action in both shots for a smoother transition. The speed of the action and the position of hands, feet, or objects should match. The audience won't spot small differences because they're focused on the action so you have some leeway. It's best to edit during the action, not during a pause. Professional editors bury mistakes by cutting on action. If the pros have a mantra, it would be cut on action. *Run Lola Run* is filled with examples of cuts made on action.

Cut on Exits and Entrances

A clean entrance or exit is when there's at least one frame in the shot without a subject or object. Make the cut before the subject or object comes into the frame or after it goes out of the frame. Take advantage of clean exits and extrances. That way, you don't have to match action and can still condense time.

Cut on Motion

Motion (subject or camera) makes any edit less noticeable to the audience. This is because the center of attention is the motion. If the subject doesn't move, you can cut from a moving shot to a moving shot as long as the motion of both shots goes in the same direction. Moving camera shots include tracking, dolly, truck, and arc shots, which are all described in Chapter 7.

If the subject is moving, you can cut from a static camera shot to a moving shot as long as the subject and camera move in the same direction or speed.

Cut Away from the Action

An editor has three ways to cut away from the main action: inserts, reactions, and cutaways.

The *insert shot* should not be confused with insert as it's used in linear video editing to describe making an edit on selected tracks. It should also not be confused with the type of clip placement in digital video editing that extends the duration of the timeline. We understand your pain.

The insert shot, also called a cut-in, gives the audience specific plot information, such as the ticking bomb under the hero's chair or a clock on the wall. These shots, which are almost always close-ups, can be written into the script, because an insert shot is one of the rare instances of direct picture instruction a writer is permitted to include.

An insert shot lets the editor break away from the action without breaking the continuity of the scene. After an insert shot, you can pick up the action wherever you want because it's a netural shot that hides jump cuts and errors. No one in the audience will know that the continuity of action has been broken. For example, during a car chase scene, a shot of a traffic light turning red is an insert shot that would allow the editor to change the screen direction of the cars. The *reaction shot* is any shot that reveals someone's reaction to off-screen sound or action. A reaction shot lets the audience know how one character is responding to another character and can enhance the emotional impact of the story. These shots are usually close-ups so the editor can once again break continuity with impunity. Reaction shots are a staple of horror films because an editor can cut to a screaming woman and the shot that follows can be anything anywhere.

Cutaways are any shots that cut away from the action or conversation. The term comes from television where it's used in conjunction with interviews. Cutaways are used to illustrate what a person is saying and to provide more visual variety than the ever-present talking head.

Most of the time, an editor edits interview footage on the basis of what's being said. As a result, the short version of the interview is filled with jump cuts. This sliced-and-diced version can make the interviewee look like his or her head is popping around the screen. Cutaways let you cover all those bad visual edits and speed up the pace of the interview.

What's Missing in Digital Editing?

In the Iron and Machine Ages, film- and video-editing technology forced editors to think. Locating shots meant the editor had to search through reels of film or videotape. Fast forwarding through a reel took about seven minutes. Rewinding was twice as fast. Scanning was slower.

Today, you can jump anywhere in an instant. There is no waiting. Editors need time to think. So the next time you're at a loss for a solution, watch the clips in real time or scan slowly through the material. You may be surprised at what percolates up from your subconscious.

Pace and Rhythm

Pace and rhythm are to a show what symmetry is to a pearl necklace. After the basic sequence (the structure of the story) is laid out, the pace and rhythm must be refined. Pace is dependent on the timing of the individual shots—the rhythm on the interplay between the shots on the timeline. If either element is incorrect, the audience will notice the individual shots. To build a necklace, the clips must be trimmed ever so slightly, so the correct image is on the screen for the correct length of time.

In the next chapter, we'll show you how trimming lets you turn a simple "he said, she said" story into something with more emotional impact.

Summary

Editors tell stories by arranging pictures and sounds. The editor's job is to create a compelling reality using the tools and techniques of editing even though everyone knows it's only an illusion. Whether you build or carve, editing is both art and craft.

Important Points to Remember

- It doesn't have to be real. It only has to look real.

- Shorter is nearly always more interesting than longer.

- Find the shot with the emotional moment—the one that contains the truth or heart of the story—and then edit to make that moment work.

- Cut the shots in the order of the action and condense the action.

- Cut on subject movement to hide the edit. Include part of the action in both shots for a smoother transition.

- Cut on clean exits and entrances.

- Cut on motion. If the subject is static, cut from a moving shot to a moving shot. If the subject is moving, cut from a static shot to a moving camera shot.

- Use close-ups and other angles to give the audience the best view of the action.

- Cut as soon as the audience reads the shot.

- Use motivated cuts. Look for cues in the emotional, physical, or spoken action.

- Use reaction shots to enhance the emotional impact and condense time.

- Use cutaways in interviews to cover edits, illustrate the person's comments, increase the pace, and create visual variety.

Polishing the Necklace

Editors structure, hone, and polish. At every step, the editor watches the show looking for ways to adhere to the rule that *shorter is nearly always more interesting than longer*. After the pearls are strung, hone and polish become the editor's watchwords.

Hone and Polish

Revision is about trimming. When anyone talks about trimming, the words *shorter* and *leaner* are sure to be used. A butcher trims off fat. A tailor trims fabric. If you ask a hairdresser or barber for a trim, there will be hair on the floor. The editor's goal is to make the best show possible. After the structure is in place, the next task is to make it shorter and stronger. Editors achieve this by eliminating extraneous scenes and shortening the duration of the shots.

Every show needs to be honed and every editor has his or her own approach. For some people, tightening up the show is straightforward; for others, it has no end. Typically, an editor will play the rough cut, make some trims, and then work on something else for a while. When the editor is ready to watch with fresh eyes, he or she will repeat the process until the show has been trimmed to satisfaction.

Every frame an editor removes has an impact on how the shot works in the show. The editor watches and asks whether the length of this shot slows the story down. Is this the best part of the shot? Does the audience have enough time to read the shot? Will the audience respond to this shot? Does this shot skew the scene toward one character? These are just a few of the many questions that should come to mind as you consider how each shot works in conjunction with the others. These questions are answered through trimming.

If you want a shot to end sooner or stay on the screen longer, the edit points must be changed. The process of changing the edit points is called *trimming*. The edit points are the IN and OUT points of a clip on the timeline. They appear at the transition line between clips. This transition point is called the *cut point*, or *edit point*. It represents the end of one clip and the beginning of another.

Polishing the show also involves trimming. In this phase, the editor makes subtle adjustments to reveal the emotions of the characters and to hide the edits so the audience never notices the stitching. These tiny trims make the difference of whether a show leaves the audience smiling, crying, or just bored.

Trim to Shorten

Trimming can be done any number of ways in most editing systems. You can use editing tools to accomplish the goal of changing a shot's IN and OUT points. Or, use the trimming tools which can be simple or sophisticated. Don't worry if you find the trimming tools to be confusing or difficult at first. Even the best ones are not particularly intuitive. It takes time to feel comfortable using these features, and some editors do well without ever using a trim tool. Like everything else in the digital environment, a variety of tools and techniques are available that will get the job done. Choose the ones that feel right for you. Here are two simple methods that can be used to shorten a show.

Remove and Replace

Remove and replace works on any editing system whether or not it has trimming tools. The editor removes the entire shot, video, and any associated audio tracks from the timeline. Use the feature on your editing system that removes a clip and closes the gap. Some editing systems call this *extract* or *ripple delete*. Ripple delete refers to the consequences—removing the clip ripples through the rest of the show.

Set new IN and OUT points for the clip. Remember to make the clip shorter. Then re-edit the clip into the timeline in its original location. The editing system should be in insert mode—the one that changes the length of the show and moves all of the shots after the edit. Play the section you've just trimmed to make sure the new edit works.

Some editing systems offer a refined version of this method. Check to see if yours is among them. Load the clip you want to trim into a viewer from the timeline. Set new IN and OUT points. Then press a button or keyboard shortcut, or use the menu to apply the change. As soon as the change is applied, the timeline is updated to reflect the trim. This works well for lengthening or shortening clips.

Carve Away

The simplest way to trim is to mark the unwanted frames from the head or tail of the clip and remove them. This is the carving approach. Split the clip and use ripple delete to remove the extraneous frames. This can be tricky because you are changing the overall length of the show. Make sure all the tracks are selected when you do this or you may inadvertently create lip-sync problems later on in the show.

The remove and replace or carve away methods let you to change the IN and OUT points. These simple methods are the easiest way to reach the goal of making the show shorter and flow more smoothly. If you need or want more flexibility and control, your editing system may have special features just for trimming.

The Trim Window

Trim windows (or the trimming tools) are intended to make it easier to do precision work. Typically, this is a window that displays the outgoing and incoming clips side by side and enable the editor to select to which tracks the trim will apply. There are buttons to trim frame by frame and forward or backwards. Often, pressing the plus (+) or minus (−) key on the number pad will add or subtract the number of frames you enter. Single-frame trim buttons or even an input bar for typing in a frame number may also be available.

Trimming requires trial and error so most editing systems have a loop play function. Loop play repeatedly plays the area around the edit until you decide to stop it. The side (outgoing or incoming) to which the trim will apply is selectable. The editor can choose to trim the outgoing clip side, the incoming clip side, or both sides at once. The outgoing clip is always on the left side and the incoming clip is always on the right side.

Trim windows usually have the following features:

- Two-screen viewer
- Track selectors
- Plus (+) and minus (−) trim buttons
- Play loop (repeat play)
- Left-side/right-side selector

For some editors, including many accomplished professionals, the trim window is confusing and less than intuitive. If you're among those folks, don't use it. That's the beauty of digital editing, figure out what works for you and ignore the rest.

Try Shortening the Exercise

Watch the rough cut of the kitchen scene you edited. Do any of the shots feel long? Try shortening them. Make sure all the tracks (audio and video) are selected. You can probably improve the flow of the scene by removing a few frames here and there. It's amazing to see the difference even a one frame trim can make.

Timeline Trim Tools

Trimming clips always takes place on the timeline. Before you do anything, remember to select the tracks you want to trim. If you don't pay attention, the relationship between the audio and video track(s) may change and create lip-sync problems. Teach yourself to look at the track selector buttons. You need to be aware of which tracks are active or inactive and what impact trimming will have.

The timeline cursor should be positioned over the transition you want to change. Transitions have a left, or outgoing, side and a right, or incoming, side. An editor has a choice to usedo a two-sided trim, which will affect the left and right sides, or a single-sided trim, which will affect one side or the other.

Two-Sided Trim

A two-sided trim is easy and safe because it doesn't affect the length of the show. The editor trims the left and right side of the edit point at once. The clip on one side gets longer and the other one gets shorter by an equal number of frames. It's like the old saying, "What one hand gives, the other takes." The edit point moves forwards or backwards on the timeline, which is why editors call this a *rolling edit*. The edit point rolls back and forth on the timeline. Some editing systems have a shortcut called *extend* that does the same thing. Because the overall length of the show doesn't change, this type of trim maintains lip sync. Trims done in a music video are almost exclusively two sided.

Figure 4-1
Before and after a
two-sided trim of the
video and audio
tracks.

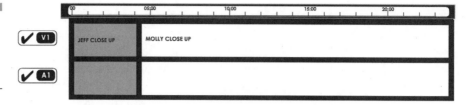

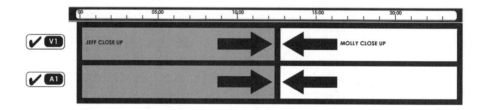

Single-Sided Trim

A single-sided trim changes the overall length of the show, which makes it easy to get into trouble. If you highlight the left side of the edit point, you can shorten or lengthen the outgoing shot. This subtracts or adds frames and affects the timeline from that point forward. All the clips from that position move as a whole to the left or right on the timeline as a result of your trim. The same is true when you shorten or lengthen the incoming shot on the right side. It is dangerous to make a single-sided trim on one track only. You will lose all lip sync from that point forward. There may be special circumstances when such a trim will work. If you're brave, go for it, but realize that you may run into a lip-sync disaster.

Watch Out, Lip Sync Ahead!

Editors use the term *lip sync* when the sound is synchronized to the picture (when the image of a person's moving lips matches the sounds he or she is making). Digital video is transferred into your editing system as data that

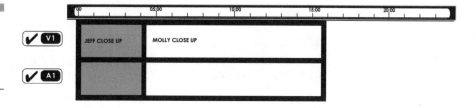

Figure 4-2
Before and after a
single-sided trim of
the video and audio
tracks.

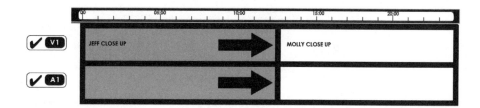

has both audio and video information. The way the data is stored (as one file or as separate audio and video files) depends on the editing system. The same is true for how the editing system treats clips with audio and video tracks. Some editing systems automatically lock the video and audio tracks together. Other editing systems treat the video and audio tracks as separate elements.

The video track is normally stacked on top of the audio tracks in the timeline. When a clip with audio and video is placed on the timeline, all of the tracks line up, one over the other. This clip is in sync. If any of the tracks (video or audio) move forward or backwards in relation to the others, they will no longer line up, which means that lip sync has been lost. If the tracks are normally locked together and you unlock them to work with picture and sound independently, you can create lip-sync problems.

Here are some reasons why editors lose lip sync:

- They edit on one track and forget to include the others (for example, they insert video without the audio or audio without the video).

- They remove a clip and forget to include all the tracks, above and below, especially the empty ones.

- They trim one side of an edit on the video track and do not include the audio tracks.

Figure 4-3
Before and after a
single-sided video
only trim, which
causes lip sync to
be lost.

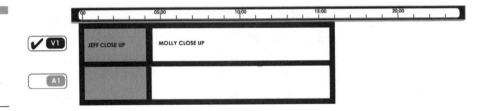

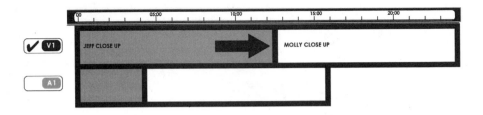

How to Prevent Lip-Sync Problems

Keep locked tracks locked and lock unlocked tracks whenever possible.
Many editing systems maintain lip sync by locking the video and audio
tracks together until the editor decides to unlock them. If you unlock
(unsync) the clips, take extra care whenever you make an edit. If the clips
are normally unlocked, lock the tracks together whenever possible.

If you do anything on the video track that pushes or moves the clips,
remember to include the audio tracks or repeat the operation on the audio
tracks. For example, if you trim five frames from the video, don't forget to
trim five frames from the audio.

Warnings and Alarms

If you lose lip sync, most editing systems issue an alarm. For example, say
a clip you just adjusted throws the audio tracks out of sync. The system
might alert you to the error by turning the audio tracks bright red or displaying a number that tells you that this track is now so many frames out

of lip sync. These alarms and indicators should be treated as idiot lights. You'll need to take steps to fix the problem.

To fix lip sync, you'll need to trim one track back (or forward) to line it up with all of its other tracks. You can always check which way to move by matching the time code from the source clip. This always works because the source time code on the video track and the audio track are always identical when the tracks are in sync. The footage came from the same tape so both the audio and video started out with the same time code address. Here's an example. The timeline cursor is positioned at the beginning of a clip on the video track. The time code indicates that the clip begins at 00:12:15:25, but when you check the audio track below it, the time code is at 00:12:15:20. Oops, they're out of sync! If you trim (shorten or remove) five frames from the video track only, the clip will be back in sync. Some editing systems automate this process to make moving or trimming clips back into sync easier. However, avoiding the problem is still the best solution.

Trimming for Interpretation

Editors make decisions about what should be seen and heard at each moment. If you completed the exercise in Chapter 3, "Beginnings, Middles, and Ends," you have already edited a rough cut of the kitchen scene. The interplay between Molly and Jeff bounces back and forth without any subtly. It's just "he said, she said," and after bouncing back and forth a few times, it gets boring.

The reason for this is simple. The important part in life (or a show) is not what a person says, but rather the manner in which the person says it. What's left unsaid may be even more important. The reaction of others to what a person says also provides emotional clues for the audience. The editor's job is to learn to control these emotional ebbs and flows.

One way that an editor controls those ebbs and flows is with overlap edits. An overlap edit is when the video from one clip extends over the audio of another clip. Overlap edits are also called *split edits*, *L*-cuts, or *J*-cuts. You can see why overlap edits are called *L*- and *J*-cuts by looking at the timeline. If the video precedes the audio, it forms an *L*. If the audio precedes the video, it forms a *J*.

Overlap edits create a tighter, less obvious transition. This is especially true if the cut is jarring or abrupt. This technique enables the editor to shape the audience's point of view and cross-structure the picture and sound to increase the emotional reaction of the audience. Robert Altman is the master of overlapping edits. His film *Gosford Park* is a wonderful example of this technique.

Polishing

Polishing a scene means changing the edit points ever so slightly to create a dynamic rhythmic flow. If this is done correctly, you can steer the audience's attention to the intent of the scene. Is the kitchen scene Jeff or Molly's scene? Whose point of view would you like to show to the audience? By using overlap edits, you can leave one character on the screen longer than the other which creates empathy with the audience.

An Exercise in Interpretation

If you've just finished editing the kitchen scene rough cut, give yourself a break before you do this exercise. Editors need to get away from the world of the desktop every now and then. After you assemble a scene, get up and do something else for a while. Getting away is a healthy thing to do, and it gives you a new perspective when you return.

When you're ready, play the scene. The edits are probably fairly clean even though the scene itself may be a bit dull due to its back-and-forth nature. The actors are only shown talking, which is less interesting than seeing how the characters react to each other. Remember, in a conversation, when one person talks, the other person listens. How does the listener feel? What's Jeff doing when Molly's talking to him? Audiences read reactions by looking at the character's eyes. Unless you, as the editor, show Jeff's face as he listens to Molly talk, the audience can't see his reactions.

This exercise helps you create interesting moments in the show using overlap edits. Your goal is to see if you can swing the scene and the audience toward one of the characters. For example, overlapping Molly while Jeff speaks shows the audience how Molly feels. Try to overlap the edits to strengthen the flow and see if you can swing the scene toward Jeff or Molly.

Making an overlap edit is easy. Overlaps are useful for shaping scenes and tightening edit points. Once you've experienced what an overlap can do, you'll understand how powerful this tool can be. An editor makes an overlap edit by trimming two sides of an edit point. As both sides of the transition are trimmed, the edit point shifts so the picture from one clip extends over the sound from another clip. When only the video track is selected, a two-sided trim will make overlap edits.

How to Make an Overlap Edit

1. Go to the edit point.
2. Access your trim tools, which could be a tool palette, menu, or mode.
3. Both sides of the edit point should be active, or selected, to trim. Check the indicators.
4. Select the video track only. Deselect the audio tracks. If the video is automatically locked to the audio, you'll have to unlock the tracks to proceed. When the video and audio tracks are unlocked, you'll be able to trim the video track with ease, rolling the edit point left or right.
5. Find the spot just after Jeff says, "You have nice hands." Grab the edit point using the mouse. Roll it to the right, covering Molly's words. You're extending Jeff on the video track. If the audio is affected in any way, stop. Use undo, check the track selectors (video only), and try again.

Figure 4-4
Before and after an overlapping edit.

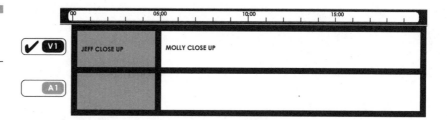

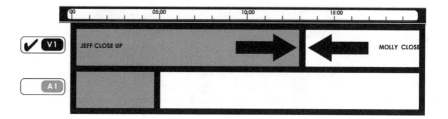

6. Look at the timeline. You'll see that the video clip overlaps the audio. Practice this a few times. If your editing system has a continuous loop play function, use it to repeatedly play this edit point. Watch how Jeff reacts to Molly's line.

7. Try to swing the scene to Jeff. Then try to swing the scene to Molly. Have fun!

Advanced Trimming Tools

Most editors use these advanced trimming tools infrequently: *slip* and *slide*. Both perform two-sided trims. On most editing systems, the trim windows for slip and slide are even less intuitive than the standard trim window.

Slip

Slip is used to move the beginning and end point of a shot without changing the length of the shot on the timeline. This type of trim is great for moving a shot back and forth to find the optimum section within a certain duration. To perform a slip, the IN time at the head and the OUT time at the tail are changed. Anything removed from one side is added to the other side to maintain the duration. The contents change, not the duration.

Figure 4-5
Before and after
a slip.

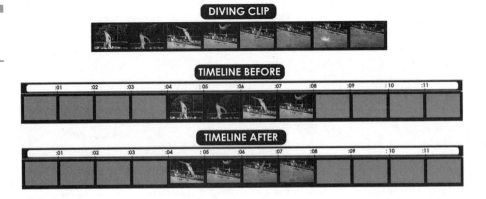

For example, say there's only room for a four-second shot on the timeline. The shot in question depicts a person falling off a platform into the water. In the natural course of editing, the current out point falls midway through the splash. In slip mode, you can move the shot back and forth to find the most interesting four seconds, which is the full splash in this case. The starting point of the shot is set by the length that this clip can occupy on the timeline (four seconds).

Slide

Sliding is similar to slipping in that there are two edit points. In this trim mode, the selected clip doesn't change at all. Its IN and OUT points will remain intact. However, the IN and OUT points of the adjoining clips on either side do change. One side is trimmed shorter and the other side is extended. As a result, the selected clip appears to slide along the timeline. If it moves forward on the timeline (to the right), the clip to the right of the selected clip is shortened, whereas the preceding shot is extended. For example, if an insert shot of a ticking clock should appear later in the show, the editor could slide the clock shot along the timeline.

Figure 4-6
Before and after
a slide.

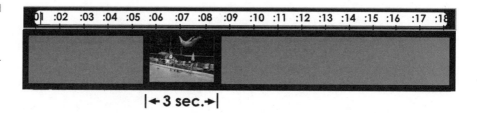

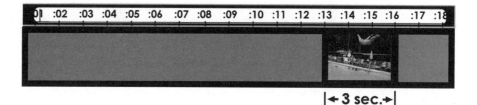

Audio

Audio is often considered the poor stepchild of the images in editing. However, audiences are far more forgiving about image quality than they are about audio quality. If the sound isn't clean and clear, audiences will instantly complain. Spoken words must be intelligible. The relationship between people's voices, music, and other sounds should be properly ranked so the audience hears the most important element first at each moment. Editing audio is not particularly different from editing video. However, the tools to adjust audio are different. As a final reminder of the importance of sound, mixing the show (that is, blending together all of the audio tracks on the timeline) is the editor's last task. Once the mix is complete, the show is complete.

Is It Picture to Sound or Sound to Picture?

It's easier for beginners to cut pictures to a soundtrack than to silence. If you have narration, lay it down first. Then edit the pictures to illustrate the audio track. If you have music, edit the pictures to the beat.

On the other hand, the word *audio* never appears in the phrase *digital video editing*. Digital video is about telling stories with pictures. When you edit the video track first and match sound to those pictures second, your show will rely on imagery to tell the story. The bottom line is that you should never rely on one element to tell the story. Make both the visual and aural stories work.

Sound Sources

Editors work with the following sound elements: sync sound (audio directly linked to the images), ambient sounds (background noises), sound effects (sounds that mimic identifiable noises), music, and voice-overs (narration or commentary).

An Audio Recording Tip

The general rule is that if your pictures aren't good enough, get closer. The corollary rule for audio is that the microphone should be as close as you can possibly get it. The lens on a camcorder has a zoom feature, which can make images appear closer without moving the camera. Audio has no zoom. If you want to record high-quality audio, you must move the microphone closer to the subject.

Organizing Audio Tracks

Most digital editing systems have more audio than video tracks. Most systems can handle eight audio tracks. A conventional arrangement of audio is (from top to bottom) one track for narration, two tracks for sync sound (digital video is usually recorded in stereo so there will be two tracks), sound effect tracks, and music on the last two tracks. Even if your editing system has fewer tracks, the voice tracks should be at the top and the music tracks should be at the bottom.

The audio tracks are edited with the video when an editor is cutting sync sound material, such as shots of people talking. It's a good idea to place each subject's voice on a separate track. This approach gives the editor the most flexibility. To edit the audio from a clip onto a separate track, you'll need to learn how to patch the audio to a specific track or tracks in your editing system. Check your editing system manual for instructions.

Visualizing Audio

A major benefit of the digital environment is that most editing systems enable you to see sound. You can display *waveforms* on the audio tracks. An audio waveform is a graphical representation of the sound energy (see Figure 4-7). The picture looks like a drawing of a mountain range. The peaks are very loud sounds and the valleys are very quiet sounds.

Figure 4-7
Audio waveforms
on the timeline.

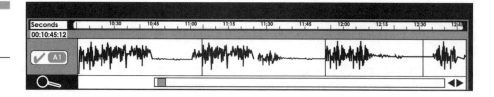

Audio waveforms are extremely useful when you're editing. Deciding where to make an edit using sound as the criteria can be difficult. An editor can't hear any audio when the track is paused. Quiet sections of the audio tracks are often hard to hear. The beauty of audio waveforms is that you can see where the audio becomes quiet, where a sound starts, and where a sound ends. If you prefer to edit by carving, we suggest you turn on the audio waveform feature to do it. Carving away every cough, sigh, or vocal click on the audio track is easier when you can see them.

Audio Adjustment Tools

The first step in the editing process is to place the clips in their proper order —in other words, to string the pearls. After the order has been established, the editor can begin adjusting the audio for volume (loudness), placement (pan position) or quality (equalization).

Adjusting Volume Levels

Some editors adjust the volume levels as they go, whereas others adjust the levels after all the pearls have been strung. This is entirely up to the editor. We suggest that you wait until afterwards to smooth out the levels. The exception would be any clips in which the volume levels are so loud or soft that it becomes distracting to the editor.

Levels for the entire track or just a specific clip on the track can be adjusted. If you need to adjust one portion of a clip (for example, an extremely loud section), split the audio track for that clip before and after the part to be adjusted. This approach is often easier than using the rubberband tool to make the changes. Later, when you have more experience with rubberbanding, you may decide to not bother splitting the track. There are two common approaches to adjusting sound levels in a digital editing

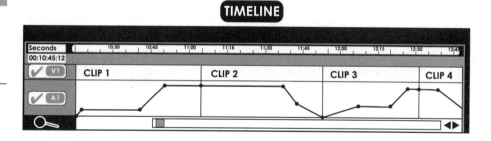

Figure 4-8
Audio levels on
the timeline
resemble stretched
rubberbands.

system: faders and rubberbands. Faders refer to the controls found on a traditional audio mixing board. Some editing systems recreate a mixing board on the desktop as a virtual mixer. The mouse is used to move the faders, or what some people call *sliders*, to make a change. The zero point on the scale, which is the default level, appears in the middle of the range. The plus values are above zero and the minus values are below zero. When the sound is too soft, the level is raised by moving the fader up into the plus values. When the sound is too loud, the fader is moved down into the minus values.

Of course, as with all things digital, the values for the sound level can also be typed in as numbers. For example, if you want to lower the volume level to a particular value, you could type that exact value, pull the virtual fader down with the mouse, or type the amount to subtract from the fader's current value (see Figure 4-8).

Rubberband refers to the way the line representing the audio level behaves when the editor grabs a point on a line with a mouse. The line runs horizontally across the audio track. If the editor grabs the line and moves it up or down, the volume will be affected. The point at which the editor makes this change is called a *node*, or *key frame*.

This approach to controlling volume levels is visual, intuitive, and fun. The process of controlling the sound using this visual method is called *rubberbanding*. This is because the volume level line behaves like a rubberband; it's always a straight line between nodes. If you delete or undo a node, the volume line will spring back to a straight line between the next two nodes. If you have a strong index finger and a comfortable mouse, this method works great.

Adjusting Pan Controls

Pan is short for the panoramic placement of sound either to the left or right speaker in a stereo system. The default position on many editing systems is that all tracks are panned to the center. In this instance, the sound from all the tracks will be heard on both speakers. Other editing systems default to track 1 panned left and track 2 panned right as discrete channels. In this arrangement, the audio on track 1 will be heard on the left speaker and the audio on track 2 will be heard on the right speaker. This odd/even approach carries over to all the tracks in the timeline. All the odd tracks are panned left and all of the even tracks are panned right. The panning controls are usually identical to the volume controls. Nearly every editing system that uses rubberbanding for volume control uses it for pan control as well.

In most cases, voices should be panned to the center. If the music was recorded in stereo, it should be panned to discrete channels. Pan adjustments beyond this should be left to the mix stage. The only other reason to use the pan control while you're editing is to send the sound to one speaker so you can hear it better.

Adjusting Sound Quality

Sometimes the quality of the sound will need to be adjusted. This can happen if there's extraneous background sound or the microphone used to record the audio was placed improperly or was improperly adjusted. The *equalization* (EQ) tools may be able to help correct these problems. EQ lets an editor adjust specific bands of audio frequencies. When it is properly used, an editor can shape the audio so it sounds more pleasing and uniform with the other clips.

Most editing systems have minimal controls that are capable of adjusting low and high frequencies. This can help you clear up rumbling noises at the low end and hiss at the high end. In the midrange, EQ can improve the voice quality. A voice track that sounds flat and dull can be adjusted to sound crisper and clearer. If you discover that one or more of the people who appear in the show need EQ adjustments, save your EQ settings so you can use them again. Label each setting you save using the name of the person. That way it's easy to remember that whenever Steve is heard, Steve's EQ should be applied to the audio clip.

If you have an audio problem that can be solved with EQ, we suggest you try to make the fix as you're editing. The reason for this is simple. If the audio problem can't be solved, the footage may be unusable in the show. You need to know whether you can fix it before you build a show around that material. Once you've figured out that you can adjust the person's audio and get good results, you don't need to apply the EQ adjustment to every one of his or her clips until you're ready to do the mix.

It takes practice and good ears to be able to adjust EQ properly. Try the preset EQ filters that may be included with your editing system. Filters to eliminate wind noise or tape hiss are commom. Experiment with other presets, such as telephone EQ or music bass boost, when you need an audio effect. Most editing systems have just as many audio effects as video effects, although editors tend to ignore them.

What's the End Result?

Your finished show ends up with one soundtrack even though the timeline may consist of two or two dozen tracks. Voices, ambient sounds, sound effects, and music are mixed together into one coherent unit called the soundtrack. Digital video soundtracks are in stereo at a minimum.

Mixing is simply the process of blending together all the audio elements using the volume and pan controls.

Mixing Your Finished Show

The workflow for the soundtrack requires you to edit the sync sound with the picture. Narration and ambience are usually added next. Music and sound effects are typically done last. The exception is when you edit a montage to music or use a beat or click track (just the rhythm of the music) to determine the rhythm of the edits. Once all the materials are placed on the timeline, everything is mixed together.

Place your speakers at a comfortable level. Start at the beginning of your timeline and play the show. Listen to each sound and adjust the level to achieve a good blend of sounds. Always mix to the voice tracks. Sometimes voices will be buried in the music. If this happens, don't increase the volume on the voice tracks. Instead, lower the music tracks. Sound effect tracks should be loud enough to add dimension to the show without being overwhelming.

Take your time. Listen to the show carefully. There should be loud and soft sections. Don't be afraid to lower the volume. Silence can communicate and create an emotional response, too. As we mentioned previously, sometimes what's left unsaid or unheard is important.

Monitoring

Never adjust the volume controls on the speakers when you're editing. The speaker is your audio monitor. It's there so you can make decisions on how things sound. If you change it at every turn, you won't have a reliable reference to determine whether the sound on the timeline is too loud or quiet. The speaker volume should be set at a level that is loud enough to be comfortably heard in the room in which your editing system resides.

Metering Audio

VU (Volume unit) meters are used to measure analog audio levels. An audio meter is a tool that measures the amplitude of the sound in decibels. It's used to make sure the sound level isn't too low, which would result in an audio recording with a reduced dynamic range, or too high, which would result in an audio recording with distortion. For example, a good voice level on an analog VU meter should fall between −3 and 0 dB on the scale. A signal of +3 dB would be too distorted to use. (See Figure 4-9.)

Figure 4-9
Audio levels
displayed in digital
or analog scales.

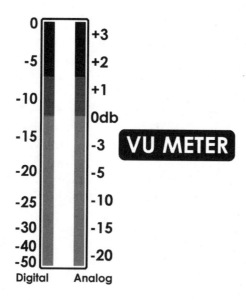

The same scale with different requirements is used for digital audio recording. A digital meter displays a graphic representation of the amplitude of the sound. The scale is different from the VU meter, although you'd never know that. A good voice level for digital audio should fall between −22 dB and −14 dB. Levels set to 0 dB on a digital meter will be too distorted to use.

Measurements are useful if you are familiar with the scale. Use your senses and listen carefully. After all, reading the temperature in Fahrenheit or Celsius degrees doesn't change how cold you feel; it's just a reference number.

Why Mixing Boards Exist

Professionals prefer the feel of tangible faders over mouse clicks, rubberbands, and data entry. This is one reason why mixing boards still exist in professional audio studios.

In a digital editing environment, an external audio mixer can serve as a sophisticated patch panel with volume, pan, and EQ controls. The editor can easily bring in multiple audio sources using a mixing board. When the show is output to videotape, the mixing board enables the editor to monitor both the output of the editing system and the sound being recorded on tape by switching back and forth between using one button.

There are smart digital audio mixing boards that can be connected to editing systems like other peripherals. The idea is to give the editor control over level changes from the audio board or editing system. In our opinion, this is equivalent to using an ergonomic hand controller instead of a mouse to play video games on your computer. It's a nice touch, but completely unnecessary.

Do You Need More Tools?

If the soundtrack needs more sophisticated mixing, for example, on a feature film or for 5.1 surround sound for a DVD, the mix won't be done on a digital video editing system. Instead, the audio tracks will be exported from the editing system to a *digital audio workstation* (DAW). The DAW provides far more control over the soundtrack than the basic audio tools included in editing systems. Read the section on audio in Chapter 10, "Getting It In and Out," if you need to do this.

A Few Audio Tips

- *Know where the show will be played.* Forget how good it sounds on the speakers attached to your editing system. If the show will be output to videotape, the audience will likely see and hear it on an inexpensive television set. If this is the case, don't bother doing a complicated audio mix. Instead, make sure everything is audible when heard through a small inexpensive speaker. Most of the audience won't hear or appreciate your well-crafted stereo mix.

- *For a quick mix, pan all of the audio tracks to one channel.* For stereo, pan all the tracks to the middle. This is a simple but effective method if you don't have time to do a complete mix and you're satisfied with the volume levels.

- *Always check your mix by listening to the show in different settings using different types of speakers.*

- *If you're encoding audio for streaming, remember that the soundtrack will likely be heard on a tiny mono computer speaker.* Your EQ and audio mixing efforts will be lost during compression and/or playback.

- *If you are mastering to a DVD, the mix is of the utmost importance.* Every nuance is likely to be heard.

- *An external audio mixer may be helpful if you have multiple sources, such as audiocassette decks, digital audiotape (DAT) tape recorders, and videotape recorders that need to be connected to the editing system.* Instead of patching each device into your editing system every time you need to input a sound element, an audio mixing board can simplify the task. On the output side, an audio mixing board can distribute the audio signals to multiple VCRs for recording and monitoring.

Summary

Trimming is the tool that gives editors creative control over the show. Hone the show by removing all the unwanted or unnecessary material. Then, polish the show by trimming it to enhance the impact.

Sound is just as important as the picture. Audio conveys information and can enhance the emotional impact of any scene. Audiences are unforgiving of poor quality audio. If audiences can't hear what people are saying, they'll complain immediately.

Important Points to Remember

- The simplest way of trimming to shorten is to mark unwanted frames and remove them.
- The trim window is a precision tool for adding or subtracting frames.
- Pay attention to the lip sync warnings on the timeline.
- Don't sweat lip sync. Learn how to fix and prevent the loss of lip sync.
- Use overlap edits to shape scenes for interpretation.
- Never adjust the volume controls on your speakers after you've set a comfortable level for the room; adjust the volume level of the track to make adjustments.
- Separate sound elements on individual tracks of the timeline.
- Add background sounds to the voice tracks first and then build from there.
- The voices should be the most prominent audio element. Mix the other tracks up to the voice track.
- Digital audio meters use a negative scale. 0dB is maximum overload.
- Listen and watch the level indicator of the audio meter to avoid distorting the sound.

CHAPTER 5

Styles and Workflows

What's Technique?

Different shows require different approaches. The process of editing should reflect the type of show you want to make. This is called *technique*. If you use the same technique in every situation, you are guaranteed to move slowly. The purpose of this chapter is to present techniques for editing commercials, family history programs, music videos, nonfiction, and scripted narratives quickly and efficiently.

Digital editing gives editors the freedom to develop their own techniques. Digital editing does not have any inherent restrictions that force you to take a specific approach because of technical limitations. This is a big change. The machines used for linear video editing were limited and limiting, requiring editors to follow only one path. Digital editing has some technical considerations, although none of these affect creative choices. This means that editors can approach a project any way that suits them. This new independence is allowing creativity to bloom.

The approach to editing you take depends on a number of factors. Your experience as an editor has the biggest impact. You may be influenced by your favorite films or perhaps have studied the work of a particular filmmaker or filmmakers. In this visual era, you are what you watch. Television and cable provide a continuous stream of visual creativity. Commercials, promos, graphics, and effects are showcased everyday in your home. This constant barrage of imagery has made all of us more visually sophisticated and has altered our expectations about pacing and patience.

Two Means to the Same End

Editing can be approached in two ways: building and carving. A good metaphor for the building approach is to think of the editor as a bricklayer. The shots or clips are the bricks. Bricklayers take one shot at a time and slowly build the story. Carving is the opposite approach. Think of the editor as a woodcarver shaping a tree stump into a bench. The material is the stump and the woodcarver gradually slices away, honing and shaping the story into what he or she desires. It doesn't matter which approach you prefer. The decision is entirely up to you.

Good editors often use both approaches at various times. Builders piece together scenes and watch them. Then, they'll often begin carving away unnecessary bits and pieces. Carvers slice away to let the decisive moments shine. They fine tune scenes later by moving and trimming on a shot-by-shot or scene-by-scene basis. Going back and forth between building and carving is how you achieve the seamless quality that distinguishes editing at its finest.

How to Use This Chapter

A roadmap gives a driver a feeling of confidence. The route is clear; you know where you're going and how you have to get there. You want the comfort of a map the first time you drive somewhere. After you make the trip a few times, the route is embedded in your memory and the journey becomes routine.

Editing is never routine. The story, material, and genre change with every new project. You can choose to take the superhighway or stay on the back roads. Every genre has its own editing superhighway (a *workflow*) that can move you from start to finish with the least amount of trouble. We've provided guidelines (our versions of editing superhighways) for music videos, commercials, documentaries, and narratives to help you gain confidence. We feel that the steps we've outlined represent the best way to slice the apple. As you gain experience, you may decide to modify our suggestions to accommodate any quirks in your editing system or the type of projects you do. In any event, reading and following the workflows for the genres we've included will help you learn how to develop your own workflows for other types of shows.

A Practice Workflow Project: A Digital Family History

This simple project illustrates the workflow for a show that documents your family's history. It's a fun project anyone can do and that teaches you the concept of workflow. The project involves recording an elder storyteller as he or she recounts family history and editing his or her interview. The interview provides the structure for the show.

For this example, we'll use your grandmother. However, it could be anyone in your family who knows how to tell a good story. At family gatherings, these are the people who take center stage and tell tales that weave facts, characters, and events together with humor and emotion. The wit and wisdom of these gifted storytellers lend credibility to stories that will become legends to future generations of your family.

Recording family stories with a digital camcorder is an excellent way to preserve the past for future generations. Digital editing gives you the opportunity to turn what you record into an entertaining and informative show. This is your chance to become the family storyteller in a new medium: digital video. After you edit the show, you can send your relatives copies on videotape, DVD, CD, or stream the finished show on the Internet.

Interview Your Grandmother

Record your grandmother speaking to the camera or looking off screen toward the interviewer. The position of her eyes doesn't really matter. The audience for this show will be your family; they'll be glad to see and hear her so no one will notice.

Let her talk as much as she wants and record everything. The order in which she tells her stories is unimportant. She can start or stop whenever she wants. If Grandma goes on a tangent, you can edit that out later and, under these circumstances, anything she says on camera is valuable. You may want to prompt her memory from time to time or ask her to repeat things.

Make her comfortable. For some people, the responsibility of being recorded can be awkward or artificial. If your grandmother becomes self-conscious or nervous, parts of the interview may be unusable. Of course, that's the purpose of editing—to remove any parts that go off track. Most of us go off track now and then and your grandmother is no exception. You may want to try recording her over several days or weeks in short sessions. The most important part is to record as much as possible for as long as possible. If all goes well, she'll recount a lot of past history, weaving family myths and legends with wonderful character descriptions of your relatives. Her stories will become a unique and timeless resource for everyone in your family.

Editing Workflow—The First Half

First, evaluate the material. Then break the interview down into individual segments. You can accomplish these tasks using either the building or carving approach. Choose one. We'll explore both ways to complete the first half of this practice project. Experience tells us that half of you will carve and the other half will build.

Carving the Interview Place the interview clip or clips on a new time-line. The clip length may be limited in your editing system. Try to get as much as possible in one long clip. Use multiple clips if necessary.

Next, mark an IN and OUT point where the interview becomes unusable. Remove the section and close the gap. This may require splitting the clip at the IN and OUT point and then deleting it. (See Figure 5-1.)

Play the timeline. Remove any portion that you or your grandmother would not want anyone to see. Anything that's not part of the story should be cut out (such as coughing, drinking water, or answering the phone). Play the entire interview and remove all of those sections.

At this point, you should only have stories about your relatives—for example, the time your uncle got into trouble as a teenager, how your mother and father met, or what your grandfather did during the war. Each of these stories will be on the timeline.

The final step in this phase is to change the order of her stories so her interview has a dramatic flow. Start with something short or exciting that will peak your family's interest. Try to balance her stories to give her interview a clear beginning, middle, and end. Put her best stories at the end. You might decide to follow a chronological order or perhaps the family tree.

To change the order of the sections on the timeline, highlight the story you want to move and use the cut command. After you've found an appropriate place for the story, use the paste command to move it there. This phase is complete when you're satisfied with the order of her stories.

Figure 5-1
Carving an
interview clip.
1. Isolate unwanted
material;
2. Remove it; and
3. Close the gap.

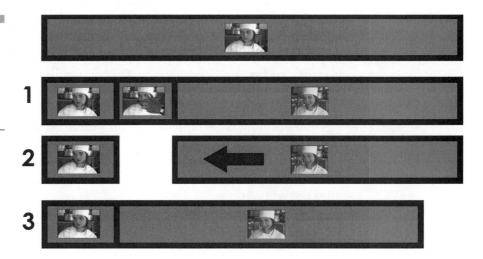

Building the Interview with Subclips   Play your grandmother's interview clip. Mark an IN and OUT point at the beginning and end of her first story. Then make a subclip (a copy) of that story. Name it and store it in a bin. Go to the beginning of her next story and repeat the process.

Go through her entire interview and break it down into separate subclips, one for each story. Each subclip you make should be saved with an appropriate name. If her interview has many stops and starts, you may have some subclips that are parts of stories. Label them so you know that they are only part of a story.

You should make sure that every IN and OUT point is clean. In this context, *clean* means that her first and last words are complete. None of the syllables should be clipped or chopped off.

Then arrange the subclips in the order you want to present your grandmother's stories. Build the timeline by placing the subclips in the order you want. Start with something short or exciting that will peak your family's interest. Try to balance her stories to give her interview a clear beginning, middle, and end. Put her best stories at the end. You may decide to follow a chronological order or perhaps the family tree. The first phase is complete after you've placed all of her stories on the timeline.

The Second Half

The first step in the second half of this workflow is to cover any jump cuts. A jump cut will be self-evident. Your grandmother will appear to jump around. This happens when extraneous sections of the interview are removed and a break in continuity occurs.

If you see a jump cut, you'll want to add family photographs or perhaps footage from an old home movie at that point. See Chapter 10, "Getting It In and Out," and the appropriate sections in your editing system manual to learn how to bring photographs or other materials as clips into your editing system.

Select the photograph clip you want to use to cover a jump cut. For example, your grandparents' wedding picture could be used to cover a jump cut in her story about how she met your grandfather. After you've selected an image, place it on the timeline as a video-only overwrite edit. You don't want to insert the image because that would push everything on the timeline after the edit out of sync.

Continue adding photograph and home-movie clips as video-only over-writes to cover any jump cuts. You can also enhance the stories she tells with these materials. Remember that her interview is the centerpiece of the show so it's not necessary to include any of the sounds associated with home-movie clips. If possible, lock her audio track. This will prevent you from inadvertently editing her narration in these sections.

Next, add transitions between your grandmother and the photographs or home movies. You should use a transition the first time you cut away from your grandmother to a photograph or home movie. It's a good idea to be consistent. If you use a dissolve, dissolve away from and then back to your grandmother. You may decide to add transitions between a series of photographs or simply cut from one to another.

After that, add music. Music helps set the mood. You can select music that matches the time period she's talking about. If your grandmother is telling a story about her life in the 1950s, a popular song from that era would add emotional impact.

This point is the perfect time to create and add the titles and text you feel are necessary. This could include identifying people, dates, or locations. Titles are usually placed on a separate video track. Add transitions to mix the titles in and out. When taken altogether, these small touches will create a lasting family treasure.

The final step is to do an audio mix. Any music you add should be at a low volume and in the background. After all, your grandmother is the star of this show. Each music selection should fade in and out. If your grandmother isn't speaking, for example, during the opening titles or a montage of photographs, you can raise the volume of the music. If you keep the settings consistent for your grandmother's voice, you probably won't need to do anything to her track. With your editing skills, her memories can come alive in a visual story that your family will treasure.

Music Videos

No visual form is more suited to digital editing than the music video. Arranging, cutting, and moving lip-synced shots in time with a music track is technically complicated to do with traditional film or video editing systems. Digital editing systems make editing music video montages exciting.

Background

When Richard Lester, the director of the Beatles' film *A Hard Day's Night*, combined the band's performance with a montage, he created the music video art form. Until that moment, films portrayed performances as actualities that took place in a reality created within a continuous scene. From Fred Astaire to Elvis, when a person sang, he or she sung on camera in one location. Any shots that showed other actions were presented as parts of the scene. The first theatrical film to include sound, *The Jazz Singer*, can be seen as a music video. It shows Al Jolson performing songs and playing the role of a Jewish cantor who breaks into Vaudeville to the disappointment of his father. Most filmed performances followed an approach that developed in the 1930s. The singer or band was shot from the audience's point of view at a stage show or nightclub. The view was from one side of the proscenium. In *Anchors Away*, Gene Kelly experimented with a montage sequence in the "New York, New York" sequence. Three sailors sing and dance all over New York in what was an innovative approach to the performance. Richard Lester added to this tradition. He cut away from the actual performance and showed a variety of action shots, chases, and sequences. The performers became characters in a visual narrative rather than just musicians or singers. Lester used montage editing to cut these shots to music.

The elements of a music video involve a performance to a lip-synced audio track and other nonperformance scenes. The difficulty of editing a music video revolves around the technical problem of lip sync. Performers do not actually sing the song on camera; instead, they mimic the vocals while listening to the song being played back from a CD or *digital audiotape* (DAT). The video or film footage has to be resolved (synced) to the music track by the editor.

Syncing the footage can be done at the beginning, middle, or end of the editing process. No matter when the editor chooses to do it, it must be correct. Viewers implicitly trust that the performer's lips are in sync with the song. If this is lost, the magic and suspension of disbelief are lost.

Music Video Organization

Transfer the music from the CD (or DAT tape) and all the footage. Create separate bins for the following elements: performance, scenes, locations, studio music, sequences, and so on. The bins can also reflect themes and concepts in the song.

Music Video Workflow—The Building Method

This method works with material shot on video. It doesn't work with film unless every take is resolved (synced) with the music. If the film is transferred to tape, this method can be used. All the takes must be resolved, which requires an incredible amount of work. Of course, with a music video shot on film, there's probably a budget for an assistant to do this so it may not matter.

Step 1—Edit the Performance Footage Takes   Performance footage that includes sync sound recorded in the field (music playback in the background) is cut like dialogue—it follows the lyrics. The soundtrack should be the audio from the music playback as recorded by the camera. The best takes, shot angles, and actions are cut using the actual field sound as a guide for continuity. Compare different takes from different scenes and match them by following the lyrics. The editor must evaluate each take. Multiple takes require more time to watch. Once the best take is selected, mark IN and OUT points.

Butt the shots together, line by line, verse by verse, and shot by shot to create a performance video of the talent singing to the music. As long as the performers singing are reasonably close to being in sync, you should have little trouble editing. This technique enables you to start editing right away. Editing using this approach allows you to concentrate on selecting the best shots of the vocals immediately. You don't have to worry about resolving lip sync until the next stage in the process. This technique works well with hip-hop or songs with a number of verses.

Step 2—Resolve the Lip Sync by Adding the Music   The next step is to add the audio tracks from the CD to the timeline. This can be tricky because you have to establish lip sync from the start of the show. Mark the IN and OUT times on the source audio clip (the tracks imported from the music CD). Edit this onto the timeline (audio only), making sure you don't delete the audio and video tracks you've already placed on the timeline. Use other tracks, such as tracks 3 and 4, if tracks 1 and 2 are in use.

Time code or markers can help you line up the sound with the picture. If your system has the capability to add markers, put a mark somewhere near the start of the source audio clip. Pick a word that is distinctive with visible lip movement. A *plosive* word (a word that contains a *P* or *B*) is the easiest to find. Next, place a mark on the identical word in the edited performance piece on the timeline. Then align the two marks. Your IN points should both be at the beginning of the song, and the marks should correspond to each other.

You will have to adjust the show IN time to make sure the sync marks match. Don't change the music clip IN time. A little trial and error will work.

If your editing system doesn't have markers, the easiest way to do this is to use the sync words to set a temporary OUT point at the word on both the music clip and the timeline. You will move the OUT point later.

Go to the beginning of the music source clip and mark an IN point where the song starts. Your editing system should be able to calculate the duration between the IN and OUT points. Let's say it's 25 seconds. In order to match the beginning of the song on the show timeline, go to the OUT point and subtract that duration in seconds. This will be your IN point. Then mark the end of the song clip and move your temporary OUT point. Make an audio-only overlay (overwrite) edit, rolling out the entire music clip until you reach the end.

You can do this another way if your editing system can trim audio tracks. Mark an IN point on the source music clip and the timeline audio track using a matching word in the lyrics. Make an audio-only edit and add the music to the timeline. Your show should have music from the CD in sync from that point on to the end of the song. Then on the timeline, trimming only the music tracks, trim back to the beginning of the song. The idea is to extend the music back toward the start. Don't move the music track; just make it longer at the beginning.

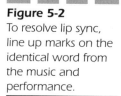

Figure 5-2

To resolve lip sync, line up marks on the identical word from the music and performance.

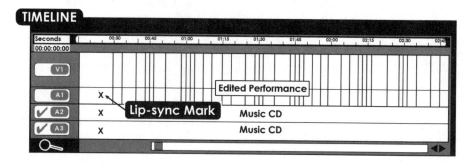

Step 3—Adjust Lip Sync by Slipping Shots That Are Ahead or Behind Play the show and listen only to the CD music track with the reference audio tracks turned off. Look at the show from the beginning to the end. You will notice that some pictures are out of sync with the lyrics. These shots are ahead or behind the music. The next step is to adjust the video track by trimming the start and end of the out-of-sync clips. You can do this by re-editing the clips onto the timeline or by trimming them on the timeline:

■ *Re-edit method* Replace the clip in the timeline by re-editing it. It must have the identical duration, though it will have a different start time. Usually, this will be earlier or later by a couple of frames. Start with five frames. Overlay the edit onto the timeline. Undo it, change the IN time, and repeat this if the lips don't match. Using trial and error, and the undo feature, repeat the process until the lip sync is correct.

■ *Trimming method* This is one of the best reasons to use the slip mode. *Slipping* is a film editor's term that means to adjust the beginning (IN point) and end (OUT point) of a shot without changing the duration of the shot. This is what needs to happen in this case. The out-of-sync shot needs to be adjusted, not lengthened or shortened. Changing the duration would move the other shots (to the left if the new shot was shorter or to the right if it was longer). Consequently, everything from that point on would be out of lip sync. The impact of a change in duration ripples through your show to the end. The solution is to avoid changing the IN point unless you change the OUT point by an equal amount. If you take something away from one end of the shot, you must add it to the other end. The duration must remain consistent to maintain sync.

A Production Tip

Never let the performers sing to an audiocassette. Always use a CD or DAT copy of the song. Audiocassette recorders won't play back at a consistent speed; consequently, you'll have lip-sync problems when you edit.

Go into the slip mode on your editing system. Adjust a shot by a few frames and play it back. Check to see if it's in sync. If it's not, slip the shot a bit more.

Step 4—Isolate Shots from Non-Lip-Sync Footage; Make Subclips
What non-lip-sync shots are called depends on the editor's experience and background. Some people use the term *B-roll shots* and others use the word *cutaways*. In a music video, these shots can be from any scene or performance. These are often shots that relate to the themes portrayed in the song's lyrics. They could be shots of a dance performance or other action. Cut this footage, looking for the dynamic movements. Select shots that have action that occurs within the frame or from outside with camera movement. Look for strong design elements such as color, composition, and focus. After you identify these gems, mark an IN and OUT point, and make a subclip.

Subclips Most editing systems let you subclip (or make a copy of) all or part of another clip. You need to make subclips of individual shots to use the building method. If you're not sure how to recognize a shot or make a subclip, read Chapter 7, "Setting the Table," before continuing.

Music video are usually shot with a lot of coverage. This means that the editor should have a wide variety of choices of shots with different framing and angles. The more shots you have to work with, the more creative you can be. Break down all the non-sync footage into single-shot subclips. Save these subclips in a bin.

Because these subclips are isolated shots, they can be edited on the timeline without any further adjustments to the IN or OUT points. Place them on the timeline as video-only overwrite edits. Use the actions within the

A Tip—Get Organized

The fastest way to find what you need, when you need it, is to get organized. Save any subclips you make into bins. Label the bins so you can easily find the shots you need. For tips on organization, check out Chapter 6, "The China Closet."

shots to create a rhythm or follow the rhythm of the music. Cut the pictures to the words, beat, or hits in the music. Drum hits, cymbal crashes, and guitar notes can all trigger an edit point.

Effects Subclips As you isolate shots for the music video, experiment with adding effects to your subclips. A number of effects, such as motion, are applied to individual clips. If you think a shot would be more dynamic or fit the music better in slow motion or as strobed motion, this is the time to try it out. Clip effects are usually made and stored as copies of the original clip. Reversing the motion of the clip changes a zoom in to a zoom out. You can modify a clip in hundreds of ways. Have fun!

Music videos require many individual shots. You should have more clips and more versions of those clips than you will ever be able to use. You can build faster if you have more choices. The more time you have to play, the better the final result will be.

Step 5—Add Clips and Subclips (Video-Only) to the Timeline The next step is to add (assemble) these selected shots to the timeline. These edits are going to fill in areas where there is no video or cover portions of lip-synced shots. At this stage in the music video process, cut the picture to the synced track. While the audio track remains fixed, make video-only overwrite (overlay) edits. Don't insert video clips into the timeline. An insert edit moves the adjacent clips and causes a loss of track alignment and lip sync. When you push one clip, you also move the adjacent clip, which results in a ripple effect from that point to the end. As you add subclips to the timeline, you'll see your music video come together.

Editing systems usually have a way of grouping shots. For the fun of it, you could drag a group of shots onto the timeline. This saves a lot of time. Plus, the purely random nature of placing a group of subclips on the timeline can sometimes reveal interesting cuts. This is the equivalent of throwing paint at a canvas, except if you don't like the result, you can press Undo.

Step 6—Add Transition Effects Your music video should almost be complete. The final step is to add transitions. Music videos get a lot of their punch from the rhythm generated by cuts made on the beat or counterbeat. Transitions such as dissolves or wipes are rarely used because they break up or slow down the rhythm of the editing. However, sometimes the music dictates the use of transitions. If this is the case, add your transitions now.

Music Video Editing Tips

- Put the music on the timeline. Cut the picture to the music.
- Always do VIDEO ONLY edits. Lock the audio tracks to avoid accidents.
- Use the overwrite (overlay) mode to make sure everything stays in sync.
- Always trim both sides of an edit to maintain sync.

Music Video Workflow—The Carving Method

The carving method works great when time code playback is used during production.

Step 1—Make a New Timeline   Make a new timeline with a starting time code of 00:00:00:00.

Step 2—Edit the Music Clip   Edit the music clip on to the audio tracks of the timeline. The song and the timeline should both start at 00:00:00:00.

Step 3—Find the Start of the Song   Determine where the music starts on the clip of the performance. Set the music start as your IN point. Make a mental note that this is where the song starts. It's much easier to find the start if the song begins at 00:00:00:00 on your camera slate. Watch the performance clip and look at the time code on the camera slate. Because there's usually some preroll, the clip will probably show the slate starting before the music begins at around 23:59:50:00. Go about 10 seconds forward to the 00:00:00:00 spot. If possible, put markers on the timeline to mark this important point on the clip.

Step 4—Make a Video Edit of the Lip-Synced Performance   Match the audio track on the lip-sync performance to the music tracks that are already on the timeline. Use a video-only overwrite to place the lip-synced performance on the timeline. When you play the timeline, the performance should be in sync with the music (see Figure 5-4).

Figure 5-3
Step 3: Find and
mark the start of
the song.

Figure 5-4
Step 4: Edit the
source clip onto
the timeline.

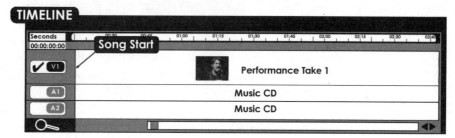

Production Tips: Time Code Playback

- The time code display must be recorded by every camera on every take of the artist lip syncing to the music. It doesn't matter whether you do it as a head or tail slate.
- The time code for audio playback should start at 23:59:45. The song should start at 00:00:00:00.
- Match the timeline's starting time code to the song's starting time code.

Step 5—Add Additional Takes If your edit system handles multiple video tracks, edit each take of the performance on a separate track. Use the time code slate, shown in Figure 5-5, recorded by the camera as the sync point.

You can add any part of a lip-synced performance to the timeline as long as you know the time code for that portion of the song. For example, if you want to edit the third verse, determine the time code when the verse begins from the point of the song start. If the verse begins at 2 minutes and 15 seconds from the song start, overlay that section on the timeline at 2:15:00.

Step 6—Remove the Unwanted Sections After you place all the performance pieces on the timeline, you can begin to carve away the sections you don't want. Set an in and out for what you want to remove and delete it. Make sure you use the mode that leaves a **gap** in the time line. The clips on the video track should not move (see Figure 5-6). If they do, the clips will be out of sync with the audio track.

Your timeline should have a stack of video tracks that are all in sync with the audio. It should be relatively easy to compare one take with another using the track-monitoring controls. Decide which takes or parts of takes are better than others. Cut away all the bad material to reveal the most dynamic performances. This method, which is somewhat of a process of elimination, works well when the singer performs the song several times in a variety of locations. (See Figure 5-7.)

Step 7—The Final Steps To complete your music video, follow the final three steps in the building method workflow.

Figure 5-5
Time code slate
recorded on camera.

Figure 5-6
Step 6: Unwanted
parts of the
performance
removed.

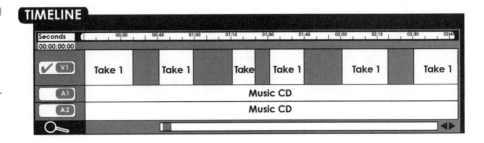

Figure 5-6
Step 6: Unwanted
parts of the
performance
removed.

Figure 5-7
Step 6: Video tracks
stacked to compare
useful takes.

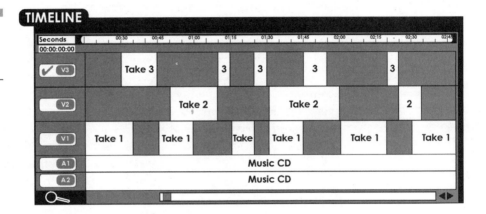

Commercials

If you can't keyframe movement,
you've got no business cutting spots.

Jennifer Rew, Master Editor

Commercials are fun 30-second puzzles for editors. The game is to tell the story within clearly defined limits. There's no such thing as a 32-second commercial, at least not one that will ever be broadcast. You can do whatever works within the time limit, but you cannot go out of bounds.

Commercials rely on finesse—often layers of finesse. The editor's job is to create eye candy that people can watch over and over again. You must understand how to do effects on your editing system. Being able to move logos and other graphics across the screen is an absolute necessity to be considered competent. Top commercial editors are compositing and editing experts. The vast majority (over 70 percent) of the work that commercial postproduction facilities do involves layering and/or compositing. About 80 percent of the time, the audio tracks—voice, music and effects—are added after the picture is cut.

One of the great things about commercials is that they're usually finished at the end of a shift. They require minimal organization beyond religiously labeling every alternate timeline you make. These days deadlines are extremely tight from bid to production to air. There's a lot of pressure to perform, but once it's done and approved, the job is done for good.

Background

The most common length for a commercial is 30 seconds. Advertisers have also experimented with shorter lengths at 10, 15, and 20 seconds. Longer commercials were in vogue on broadcast television when advertising time was relatively inexpensive. Today, one- and two-minute commercials are used primarily for direct-response selling or what are called *short-form infomercials*. What characterizes every commercial is the amount of attention that everyone involved in making commercials pays to each and every frame. There are 900 in a 30-second commercial. Nine hundred images and thirty seconds of sound.

A lot of attention is paid to the details because advertisers expect the target audience (potential customers) will see the commercial dozens of times. The more often a potential customer sees an ad, the more likely it will influence his or her behavior. The cost of making a commercial is a tiny fraction of the money involved to buy air time to broadcast the finished spot. There's no room for flaws because the audience will see that same 30-second spot over, and over, and over again.. You'd think that since everyone knows this, commercials would be better than they are.

Commercial Categories and Styles

Editors who understand advertising craft better commercials. The advertiser's intent determines the category in which a commercial falls, such as image, issue, or sales advertising. Some or all of the following styles are used to create commercials within those categories: animation, comedy, dialogue, effects heavy, music driven, problem/solution, product demonstration, slice of life, and testimonial.

In major markets such as New York, Los Angeles, and Chicago, editors are often selected for their ability to handle a particular style. An editor who understands comic timing might not be the right person to do an effects-heavy commercial, and vice versa. Every commercial relies on timing. Editors need to look for the rhythm within the scenes. Acting, camera work, music, and narration all have inherent rhythms. No matter which category or style is being used, the editor must cut to a visual as well as a musical beat. Professionals count every beat in every shot they place on the timeline. This is crucial because the story must be told in seconds. Everything must be honed, trimmed, and polished until it's perfect.

Image Advertising Image advertising aims to raise the audience's awareness of a company, product, or service. The advertiser wants to create or enhance lasting favorable impressions in the audience's mind often by associating a specific picture or motif with the product. Image advertising offers a lot of room for creativity. Nearly half of all the national advertising campaigns are in this category.

In the opening seconds, or first act, the target audience needs to recognize that this commercial has something in it for them. From an editor's perspective, the goal is to create an environment the customer recognizes or to one that he or she aspires. The middle portion, or second act, of the commercial presents the message. The closing seconds, or third act, links the message to what's being sold. For example, an image ad for a luxury car might begin by establishing wealth. The car might be at the edge of the scene or not shown at all. The images that follow convey understated elegance. Again, the car is not the subject. Not until the final moments does the car achieve screen parity with the lifestyle.

Eye movement and rhythm are key to timing the shots. There are rhythms within the frame and in the juxtaposition of shots. Your goal is to exploit the flow between, among, and within the images. Transitions, superimpositions, and color effects can be used to enhance the flow. A good way to establish the timing and mood is to cut the commercial to music, using a beat track or a sample of something similar in style to what will be composed after you complete the picture edit.

Issue Advertising Commercials that advocate causes, raise matters of public concern, or recommend or attack political candidates fall in the category of issue advertising. The opening of these commercials frame the message. You don't need to waste time getting the audience's attention. People who are interested in the issue automatically pay attention. After the setup, the message must be proved. These commercials wrap up by rephrasing the message in a way that sounds decisive or conclusive. Issue advertising takes the approach: Tell them what you're gonna tell them, tell them, and then tell them what you've told them. Any style works for this category.

Sales Advertising The majority of commercials are timely advertisements about products and services. These commercials fall into the sales category. The style most often used here follows the problem/solution or cause/effect approach. The opening, or first act, grabs your attention and sets up the problem. The middle section, or second act, delivers the message in a dramatic fashion implying that what's being advertised is the solution to the problem. The call to action—the how, when, or where the audience can purchase the solution—is the close, or third act. As an editor, you'll want to edit in a way that keeps the tension going until the end of the commercial.

Workflow for Commercials with Sync Sound

1. Isolate and trim the sync sound shots.
2. Assemble them using script continuity.
3. Evaluate performance and eliminate extraneous material as needed.
4. Trim the sync sound shots for time.
5. Look over B-roll and graphics for the setup and close.
6. Build the open and close.
7. Record a scratch voice-over track, if necessary, and add to the timeline.

■ Advice from an Expert

Mark Moskowitz has created more commercials over the past 20 years than anyone we've met. He's personally produced, directed, and edited over 4,000 commercials for political candidates and hundreds more that sell goods and services. We asked Mark what advice he'd give to editors about commercials. He replied, "Anything, any kind of footage can work. Too many agencies are infatuated with making full- screen movies. Storytelling is fine though it rarely sells. If the footage doesn't work or it's just bad or too long, then you can always do something else with it. Use freezes, layer the footage, kill all the dialogue or on-camera talent, and record a voice-over. Just think about it creatively."

8. Trim the commercial for time, providing space for the composer to help sell with music flourishes.

9. Create alternative versions with more product shots, less onscreen dialogue, and more action.

10. Show the two best versions to the client and have him or her pick one.

Workflow for Commercials Without Sync Sound

1. Record a scratch track or the actual voice-over track. Most of the information will be conveyed by the audio, with the exception of commercials that use emotion or image to sell.

2. Lay the voice track on the timeline. Trim it for time.

3. Insert shots that fit the voice-over track to show what is being said.

4. Make cuts based on where the viewer's eye is being led in the frame.

5. Tighten or open up the voice-over, if necessary. Remember to leave space for music.

6. Build transitions—if needed—as you go.

7. Use type or graphics to reinforce the message. If the words are important, put them in the center or on the right-hand side of the screen.

8. Create alternative versions with more product shots or action.

9. Show the best two versions to the client and have him or her pick one.

Mark's Advice on Agency Commercials

"Cut the best spot using the boards as a guide. Ninety percent of the time, once the agency sees the footage cut at its best, they never look at the boards."

Workflow for Impressionistic Commercials Without Sync Sound

1. Build a European montage based on the motion and rhythm within the shots.

2. Record the narration track.

3. Lay the narration track on the timeline. Trim it for time.

4. Recut where necessary to fit the narration.

5. Tighten or open up the narration, if necessary. Remember to leave space for music.

6. Build transitions—if needed—as you go.

7. Use type or graphics to reinforce the message. If the words are important, put them in the center or on the right-hand side of the screen.

8. Create alternative versions.

9. Show the two best versions to the client and have him or her pick one.

Mark on Choices

"Often you have 30.5 seconds or 31 seconds and have to make an extreme compromise. Recently, we had a fantastic take of someone [speaking] to the lens that was 31 seconds long. We had a less than good take that was 29.5. I opted to use the 31-second take because the end was so great. That meant I had to cut away in the middle and lose a phrase, weakening the power of the to-the-lens performance. I thought the sacrifice was justified because the last eight seconds on camera were just so good. Now, as long as I did that, I made my cutaway ring hard with the message so I was covered in case I really had destroyed the intensity of the spot."

Documentary and Nonfiction

Undertaking a documentary is like taking a journey with no set destination or performing acrobatics on a high wire without a net. A vague outline or treatment describing the characters or situations is often the only guide during production. Hence, the structure of the show must be created during the editing phase. As a result, the editor becomes the most influential person in the success or failure of these shows.

What Is a Documentary?

"A documentary is a film without women. If there is a woman, it's a semi-documentary," according to Harry Cohn, the head of Columbia Pictures, as quoted by Fred Zinneman in his autobiography.

The standard definition of a documentary is a show about political, social, or historical subjects presented in a factual and informative manner using actual footage or interviews accompanied by narration. However, the most successful examples of the genre today feature fascinating characters who face great conflicts under unusual circumstances in a tale that unfolds before our eyes. Great nonfiction stories often have more dramatic arcs than fictional films because truth really is stranger than fiction.

According to the *Oxford English Dictionary*, the word *documentary* was associated with film for the first time in 1930 by Paul Rotha. However, anecdotal evidence suggests that John Grierson, the founder of the British documentary movement, was the first person to use the word in 1926 when he reviewed Robert Flaherty's second film *Moana*. Flaherty achieved fame in 1922 with the release of *Nanook of the North*, which is an ethnographic study of an Eskimo family that was seven years in the making. Grierson defined these types of films as the "creative treatment of actuality." The French also lay claim to earlier usage of the word as a way to describe travelogue films.

What is or isn't a documentary is as murky as the origins of the word. If you ask filmmakers to define what qualifies as a documentary, there will be as many answers as there are filmmakers. Documentary is a loosely defined word with no definite meaning. For many people, documentary conjures up boring shows they were forced to watch in high school. Many filmmakers shy away from the documentary label because of the bad connotations associated with the word. We prefer the label *nonfiction*.

Nonfiction is a clearer description and an appropriately broad term. The subjects of these shows are real people, real events, and real life. Any show based on factual rather than fictional characters or events can be classified as a nonfiction film. No matter which word you use, this genre provides a peerless opportunity to showcase an editor's storytelling skills. The editor is given more responsibility for the storytelling than in any other genre. Consequently, nonfiction offers greater personal rewards and risks. The show's success or failure often depends on the editor's ability.

Nonfiction Storytelling

Most nonfiction is either character or subject driven. Surprise gives these stories their power. The audience can rarely predict the outcome. The most satisfying nonfiction stories (the ones with the widest appeal) are inherently dramatic and are told in three acts.

Conflict is the basis of drama. Change, whether the change occurs in the characters or the situation, holds the audience's attention. Classic themes, such as man against man or man against nature, drive the drama in many nonfiction shows. For example, every show about a social issue pits one or more sides against the other (man against man) whether the topic is abortion or hearing implants for deaf children.

The first act introduces the characters and conflict. The second act explores how the characters confront the central conflict. In the third act, the characters' actions should resolve the conflict. If you think this sounds like a description of the rules for fiction, you are correct. There's not much difference between nonfiction and fiction storytelling other than the characters and circumstances are real rather than invented in nonfiction.

Nonfiction Styles

Nonfiction covers a wide range of styles. That's to be expected considering that fiction can be subdivided into categories, such as action, biography, comedy, drama, fantasy, horror, mystery, romance, and suspense. Nonfiction is no different. Some of the many possible categories of nonfiction include advocacy, biography, culture, education, ethnography, history, how-tos, investigations, nature and wildlife, news, observational, performance, personal quests, reality television, social issues, sports, satire, and travelogues.

There is a subtle difference between shows that employ the conventions of fiction and those that adhere to the true spirit of nonfiction filmmaking. Nonfiction, at its most compelling, is a voyage of discovery for the filmmaker and the audience. It is a voyage in which neither party is sure of the destination until they arrive.

What most people think of when they hear the word *documentary* is actually called *direct cinema*, *cinéma verité*, or *observational nonfiction*. These shows are created from footage that was shot using a fly-on-the-wall approach. The filmmaker often shoots the subject or subjects of the story over long periods of time. The finished show tells the story without narration or commentary from the filmmaker. To edit this type of story, use the unscripted (visual continuity) workflow that is explained later in this chapter. Building or carving works equally well.

In contrast, most of the nonfiction shows on cable and broadcast television are scripted and bear only a passing resemblance to classic nonfiction. Biography and history programs rarely embark on a voyage of discovery; the outcome is predetermined. The same is true of programs that explore a brief period of time or singular event, such as a wedding, the penguin mating season, wander around a city with police officers for a night. Dramatic effect is added by intercutting two or more stories or points of view. Production schedules, limited budgets, and formulaic approaches often preclude anything more than a shallow treatment of the subject. To edit shows of this type, follow the "Workflow for Scripted Nonfiction" in this section.

Criteria for Nonfiction Success

We've watched hundreds of nonfiction films at festivals and markets around the world, which is unfortunately where most of them will remain, playing to limited audiences. The few shows that move beyond the festival circuit and reach a wider audience in theaters or television all share certain characteristics. Editors who remember these criteria craft better shows.

Strong characters are extremely important. What's a strong character? Anyone who's compelling on camera or says things in an interesting manner. It helps if the person is photogenic or was shot in unusual or intriguing surroundings. The strongest characters are those who have the most at stake in the outcome of the story. People facing life and death issues are more compelling than people making decisions about whether to get a Happy Meal or a Blue Plate Special.

The story must have a distinct beginning, middle, and end. Conflict, crisis, or controversy should drive the plot. Timely stories or stories with new information about topics of continuing concern can hold the audience's attention without much of a plot. However, the stories that employ a dramatic three-act structure with twists that trigger each act are more powerful.

Passion and emotion are necessities. The story or the characters should move the audience, touch their hearts, and spur them to think, feel, or explore the subject more. The filmmaker's passion for the subject must be clear to the audience. There should be a strong sense of authorship, which can be expressed in the style or manner of the presentation and/or in the approach to the subject. Authorship answers the following questions. Why did the filmmaker want to make this show? Why is the subject critically important? What does the filmmaker have at stake? Sometimes the only evidence of authorship is incredible access into people's lives and worlds that few have seen before.

The last criterion is an indefinable something. Just as some people have charisma that draws others to them, some nonfiction shows are oddly compelling. These shows excite audiences and ignite discussion well beyond normal proportions. No editor can add the secret ingredient, although it's easy to kill if it happens to be present.

Editing Nonfiction

From an editor's perspective, there's observational nonfiction and everything else. Observational nonfiction, or cinéma verité, grew out of early ethnographic studies like *Nanook of the North*. The philosophy that the camera should be a fly-on-the wall and record what happens without influencing the events developed with the appearance of smaller, more ergonomic film cameras and portable audio recorders in the 1950s. The edited show is supposed to be an unvarnished truthful record. However, the presence of a camera always changes people's behavior. The decision to include some scenes and leave others out is prejudicial. The audience's perception of truth relies on the filmmaker's perceptions. The process of valuing some material as more important than other footage ensures that truth is relative. The category of everything else includes shows crafted from archival materials, interviews, recreations, and other footage that illuminates or provides context for the story.

Stories that grow and develop out of the material rather than being imposed upon the material produce more powerful shows. Mimi Edmunds, a former producer for CBS's *60 Minutes* who currently teaches at the University of Southern California, says, "You'll find that there are at least three or four stories—sometimes more—in producing a documentary. One, the story you think you want to research. Two, the story you actually research. Three, the story you shoot in the field. Four, the story you edit and write in the editing room. The story you start out with is rarely the exact one you end up with in the final product."

Workflow Is Critical

The best nonfiction stories unfold in the edit suite; this is a task that is easier said than done. Editing nonfiction projects can be overwhelming because shooting ratios (the amount of material shot versus the length of the finished show) are often quite high. Shooting 20 hours of footage for a 90-minute show is not uncommon.

Workflow is critical for nonfiction. An editor can easily be buried by the complexity of a job and the avalanche of material. The editor must view all the footage. You cannot take a shortcut for this first step. Logs that were made while the material was being shot can help prioritize the order in which you view the material. However, you'll need to make your own logs.

The method you use to do this depends on how much storage space is available in your editing system. If all the footage can be transferred, we suggest that you use your editing system's logging tools. The search and sort functions of an editing system can be an enormous help when you're looking for specific material; it's usually easier than flipping through page after page of handwritten logs. If not enough space is available, it's often possible to log the material without transferring it to your editing system's storage drives. The alternative is to use logging software, which can control the recorder, capture the time code information, and create a batch transfer list for your editing system.

It's All About Structure

As you watch the material, evaluate it with a critical eye. Pay attention to the shots, angles, and quality of image and sound. Is the material visually interesting? Can you tell the story using only this footage? Is there enough action to hold the audience's interest? Interviews should be evaluated for

Transcripts—Yes or No?

A *transcript* is a written or typed copy of all the spoken words in the material. Transcription services are readily available. These services employ fast typists who listen to an audiocassette copy of your material and create a record of the words in your choice of word processing programs. Some services can mark the beginning of each paragraph with a time code address that corresponds to the location where those words were spoken.

Some producers and editors swear by transcripts. It's easy to print out the document and circle all the best quotes. If the document has time code addresses, it's simple to find those sections. If you string together the best quotes from each of the interviewees, then the show is half-built, right?

Many editors would blanche at this suggestion. To them, transcripts are something to swear at rather than swear by. That approach is terrific if you're creating a magazine article or a story for print. However, reading a transcript is not the same as watching someone say the words. Most of the time what's of interest is the way people say what they say rather than the words they've spoken.

Think about any conversation you've ever had with someone you care about. What's left unsaid often illustrates the emotional feelings that fill the gaps between the words. Those gaps filled with silence or hems and haws are often more important than the mundane things most of us say to each other. No transcript can ever reveal those nuances.

The danger of using transcripts is that it's easy to rely on them and ignore the real goal. We're making shows for audiences to *watch*. Inflection, energy, and nonverbal cues make the interviewe compelling. It's not the words, but the individual's expression that counts.

Having said that, a transcript can be a lifesaver when you have too much material to look at in the time allotted for editing the show. If you find yourself in this situation, think of the transcript as a log someone else has made. Find the places in the transcript that seem promising and watch those sections of the material. As you do, make notes about the person's inflection, energy, and any important nonverbal cues. The challenge is that this approach makes it harder to sense the emotional arc of the entire interview. This shortcut helps you get the job done, though excellence is rarely achieved using this method.

the person's inflection, energy, and nonverbal cues above and beyond what's being said. It's important to note the camera angle and any image or sound quality issues. Sound quality is more important than image quality for interview footage. In the back of your mind, you should also start thinking about ways to organize the material. Is it chronological? Are there multiple points of view or themes?

The next step is to decide whether to base editing continuity on the sound, picture, or narration. You must be realistic about the material you have to work with; otherwise, there's no point in doing this step. If you have many strong interviews, perhaps the best way to begin is to start by building the audio track. On the other hand, if you have great action footage, you should probably try using visual continuity. The best examples of shows cut using visual continuity are observational nonfiction because all of the footage is action based—in other words, it depicts people doing things. If the interviews and footage are mediocre, narration may be the best approach. This decision determines how you'll begin putting the show together. However, before you do anything, you must get organized.

Advice from a Nonfiction Filmmaker

Jeff Kreines has been making cinéma verité films for 30 years with his girlfriend/partner Joel DeMott. Their film *Seventeen*, which made many critics' top-ten lists and was called "one of the best and most scarifying reports on American life to be seen on a theater screen" by the *New York Times*, won grand prizes at many festivals, including Ann Arbor and Sundance (more information can be found at www.perforatedtruth.com).

Jeff's advice about nonfiction filmmaking is that: "Transcriptions and scripts are anathema to good nonfiction filmmaking. Get to know your material by watching it and taking notes on what affects you, and start editing. Don't edit on paper; make your film by editing the film itself. And though it's easy to do, never use cutaways—any shot that starts off looking like a cutaway must include some actual sync in it, or it's cheating. Whenever possible, always lap your cuts (as we film people call it—video people call it an *L*-cut or a split edit)—it helps make things flow. *Bulworth* (a Hollywood film, heavily influenced by cinéma verité) is a great example of this—beautifully edited."

Get Organized

The more material you have, the more organized you'll have to be. If you've never edited a large project, we suggest you read Chapter 6, which goes into more detail about organization and bin management. Organization makes it easier to find what you want when you want it.

The structure you have in mind for the show should influence how you organize your materials. For example, for a show that relies on audio continuity, every interview subject should have a separate bin. Lengthy interviews may need to be split up into several bins to reflect the topics or themes raised in that person's interview. If some topics are raised by more than one person, you may want to create a set of bins that are organized by these topics. Copy, rather than move, clips from the interviewee bins into the topic bins. Some editing systems allow you to organize your bins in a hierarchy, which helps with complex projects. The rationale for all of this is explained in Chapter 6.

The process of organizing your material will help you become more familiar with it. As you watch the footage and make clips, you will begin to discover the themes and story threads that are present in the material. Don't be afraid to modify your original ideas about the organization or structure of the show. Let the material be your guide.

Workflow for Scripted Nonfiction

The editor's job for this type of show is to conform the material to the guidelines laid out in the script and improve on it, if possible. The decisions of where to start and how you choose to proceed are based on personal preference. The structure is predetermined by the script or, in the case of a series, by the bible that outlines standards for that series. The workflow is the same for any other scripted show. Start anywhere you like. If you prefer to build, pick a pivotal scene or a section of the script that appeals to you. Subclip the material and start building the scene shot by shot. If you prefer to carve, string all the material together in script order and watch it. Eliminate anything extraneous. When you've finished the rough cut, sit back and watch the show again. A quick glance at the timeline will tell you if you must contract or expand the show to meet length requirements. Trim the shots to adjust the pacing and rhythm. Add transitions where necessary. Create and add titles, graphics, and credits.

Mix the audio and output the show. The workflow for scripted nonfiction is as follows:

1. View and log the material.

2. Read the script. Make notes about the materials you have—where they do or do not fit with the script.

3. Break down the material into subclips and organize them into bins that reflect the needs of the script.

4. Isolate and trim all the sync sound footage.

5. Evaluate the interviews. Create a bin and make subclips of the best parts of the interview. In a news environment, editors look for succinct statements (under seven seconds) that capture the essence of the interview. These snappy statements are called *sound bites*. Copy any subclips you make (short or long statements) into separate bins.

6. If narration is called for, record a scratch track. Break it down into subclips based on the placement of the narration in the script.

   For shorter shows, try the following technique. Record the narration track with pauses in place for the interviews. The script should indicate the duration of each interview. Edit the narration track onto the timeline. Fill the gaps in the narration with the interviews. Add your cutaway or B-roll shots and you're done.

7. Start assembling the show using the script as a guide. It doesn't matter where you start. Whether you begin with picture, sound, or narration depends on the strength of the material. Scripted shows usually depend on narration. If this is the case, place the scratch narration track on the timeline in script order. Leave space between each section of narration; these gaps can be tightened or expanded after you begin filling in the pictures.

8. Insert the shots indicated in the script and line them up with the voice-over. Build a rough assembly of the show.

9. If the script includes interview material, go through the bin with the best of the interview sound bites and select the ones that enhance the story line the most. Place them on the timeline in the appropriate places.

10. Tighten or open up the narration sections as necessary. Remember to leave breathing room. Listening to uninterrupted talking is very tiring for the audience. There should space for music, natural sounds, and/or sound effects that can add depth and emotion to the soundtrack.

11. Play the show. If you have to fulfill a length requirement, expand or contract the show as necessary.

12. Trim for pacing and rhythm.

13. Add transitions as needed.

14. Create and add titles, graphics, and credits.

15. Mix the audio and output the show.

Workflow for Unscripted Nonfiction

Digital video has triggered an explosion of independent nonfiction film-making. Professionals now compete with anyone who has an abiding interest in a subject or cause and a digital camcorder. The benefit of this is that more voices and views are being heard than ever before.

However, more people are competing for the shrinking funds available to nonfiction filmmakers. It takes an average of five years to fund and complete a feature-length nonfiction show. Many shows take much longer. There's often no separation between production and post. Instead, the process is fluid. The filmmaker raises money, shoots, edits, and raises more money to shoot and edit more until the project is completed or his or her interest wanes. Professional editors are being asked to take on additional responsibilities that were once reserved for producers because budgets demand it. In many cases, filmmakers are choosing to edit their own work for all the reasons you're reading this book. Our workflow for unscripted nonfiction takes these real-world factors into account.

Prep Prep Prep

1. View the material. Make notes about the materials you have. Ask yourself, whose story is it and what is the story? Determine whether visual or audio continuity can be used or if narration will be required.

2. Categorize the material into bins that reflect the structure and continuity approach you'll use to begin editing the show.

Begin Roughing Out the Show   You can rough out the show in four ways. You can build or carve using visual continuity or build or carve using audio continuity. The steps for carving visual continuity are denoted by the letter *C* next to the number. The steps for building visual continuity are marked by the letter *B* next to the number.

Workflow for Visual Continuity

3C. Think about a logical structure for the material. The possibilities are endless. However, the most common structures are based on chronology, location (everything that happens in a particular place), action (cause and effect), or point/counterpoint.

3B. Find and select a pivotal or emotional scene in the material to begin editing. Build that scene by isolating shots and making subclips. Cut the picture. Ignore the audio.

4C. Put all the material on the timeline using the structure you arrived at in Step 3C.

4B. Select a second pivotal scene to build using the same process you used for the first scene.

5C. Watch the show. Look for repetitious or extraneous material and carve away those parts. Carve until only the essence of the material is left.

5B. Figure out how to get from scene one to scene two using the footage you have in hand. This will be the structure of the show (the path from scene one to scene two) if you've chosen the most telling scenes. It's common to discover in the editing process that you need another pivotal moment or a different one to begin or end the story.

Workflow for Audio Continuity

3C. Evaluate the interviews. Develop a logical structure for the show. The most common ones are based on chronology, themes, or point/counterpoint (one person raises an issue and another person answers it).

3B. Evaluate the interviews. Decide whether to use transcripts. Create a bin for each interviewee and make subclips of the best parts of each interview. Copy those subclips into a separate bin labeled Selects and the name of the person.

4C. Place all the interviews on the timeline in a logical order.

4B. Place all the selects on the timeline. Watch the show. Eliminate repetitious or extraneous statements.

5C. Watch the show. Carve away any repetitious or extraneous material.

5B. Rearrange the clips until you find a structure that tells the story. Watch the show. Look for repetitious or extraneous interviews and eliminate them.

6BC. Play the timeline. Make decisions about whether the person should appear on camera or whether other visuals would illustrate his or her words better.

6BC. Play the timeline. Does the audio track tell the story? If it doesn't, you may need to add narration (either an on-camera personality or voice-over) or action sequences to make the story come alive for the audience.

Ask the Tough Questions   These steps are of the utmost importance. The first step within this category is 6v (v for visual) if you're editing the show using visual continuity or 7a (a for audio) if you're editing the show using audio continuity. It's the editor's job to ask the tough questions that the audience will surely ask.

6v/7a. Ask yourself what other material might add impact to this story. Make notes and suggestions for the filmmaker. What footage would you'd like them to shoot the next time they have a production day? Offer ideas about stock footage that could strengthen the show.

7v/8a. Play the timeline. Ask yourself whether the material you have tells the story? If it does, move to the polishing stage. If not, you may need interviews or narration (either an on-camera personality or voice-over) to make the show come alive for the audience.

Polish the Show   No matter how you get here, follow these steps to complete the show:

8v/9a. Trim the show for pacing and rhythm. Leave room for music, natural sounds, and/or sound effects that can add depth and emotion. If you edited on the basis of audio continuity, remember that the audience needs breathing space. Listening to uninterrupted talking is extremely tiring.

9v/10a. Add transitions, if necessary.

10v/11a. Create and add titles, graphics, and credits.

11v/12a. Mix the audio and output the show.

Fiction

When editing fiction, you have a script and footage that follows the script to guide your efforts. Fiction films have been shot the same way since sound was first introduced in 1927. Scenes are shot out of sequence to accommodate the schedule of the highest-paid actors. Production schedules are arranged to minimize the number of days that the most expensive actors must work. The schedule also needs to minimize the number of times the cast and crew must physically move to a new set or location. Moving hundreds of people and equipment costs a lot of time and money.

The Continuity Challenge

The challenge on set and for the editor is to maintain continuity. Whenever scenes are shot out of sequence, continuity is difficult to maintain. A *script supervisor* is on set at all times to prevent continuity errors from being made. This person, who should be called the *continuity supervisor*, serves as the liaison between the director and editor. Script supervisors provide detailed information about how the script was shot. They keep logs and mark the production script to let the editor know which shots and takes cover specific portions of the script. The editor's job would be far more difficult without this information.

Despite all the best efforts of the crew, small and large continuity errors frequently occur. It seems inevitable that small errors will occur over a long production schedule, such as a glass on a table being half full in the master shot and empty in the close-up. Sometimes it's just too expensive to correct a minor mistake. On occasion, major errors will also sneak by.

Here are a few examples we've seen. An actor exits through a door, which was established in an earlier scene as the closet door. Wonder where he's going? An actor's blue jacket in the master shot becomes his red jacket in the close-up. That would be easy to fix on a digital editing system. A scar on a character's left cheek migrates to his right cheek at different times in the same scene. Hmm? A quick search on the Internet will turn up several web sites devoted to the continuity errors spotted by audiences.

Continuity errors are good for a laugh—unless, of course, you're an editor. Another challenge is logistic—organization. Feature-length productions can generate a lot of footage. A typical production might have 40 or 50 scenes and thousands of shots, each with multiple takes. All of the material must be viewed, logged, and organized. The script supervisor's logs are the editor's bible for these productions.

Managing the Edit for a Feature

It's difficult to manage a show that could be two or three hours long. No desktop has enough space to work easily on a timeline of that length. Imagine trimming a few frames off a shot while trying to control a timeline filled with thousands of lip-synced clips. It would be unimaginably difficult. Therefore, it's imperative to break up a project of this size into manageable sections. These sections should be organized along the lines of the structure of the show.

The basic building block is a shot. Feature films are photographed and edited one shot at a time. A series of shots creates a scene. A series of scenes creates a sequence. A series of sequences creates an act. The acts constitute the finished show. Each of these units, from the shot to the show, has a beginning, middle, and end.

A workable method of editing a feature film is to organize your work around sequences. The average sequence is approximately 10 minutes, which is about as long as a timeline can be easily managed on the desktop. The process begins with scenes. Create a timeline for each scene. Organize the clips associated with each scene in their own bins. Once the scene is edited, save the timeline.

After all of the scenes are completed, create a new timeline. Then assemble the sequence by placing each scene on the timeline from beginning to end. Follow the same procedure to build each act. Create a timeline for each act and assemble the completed sequences in the proper order. Add shots or scenes that can serve as transitions between the sequences, if necessary. The advantage of this method is that you can gauge the flow of the story at every step.

A Note About Film   If the show is being shot in film, the sound elements will arrive on separate tapes. More information about double-system sound appears in Chapter 10. It should suffice to say that as the editor, you'll have to sync the audio up to the film before you can cut one frame of dialogue. Most of the technical editing issues involved in feature filmmaking are beyond the scope of this book. However, the workflow is straightforward.

This Might Sound Familiar . . .

The workflow for editing fiction follows the same workflow we presented in Chapter 3, "Beginnings, Middles, and Ends." In that chapter and the one that follows, we show you how to edit the sample footage we included in this book. The production of that simple scene follows the time-honored tradition of a shooting a master and other angles for coverage. On the CD, you'll find a master shot (the two-shot) and a close-up of each character.

Editing this scene should give you a taste of how to edit fiction. The workflow is the same despite the briefness of this scene. The editing approach to one scene is repeated dozens of times when you're editing a feature film. However, before we go over the workflow, let's look at the big picture.

An Editor's Viewpoint of Structure

The shots build the scenes. The scenes build the sequences. The sequences build the finished show. Well-made films have no extraneous shots, scenes, or sequences. Everything has a purpose and advances the story.

About Sequences   A group of scenes with a shared theme or idea forms a sequence. The sequence breaks the larger story into smaller pieces easier for the audience to grasp. In literature, novels have chapters. Chapters separate ideas, events, or experiences from others in a book. The chapters in a film have their own special integrity and structure. A sequence performs the identical function in film and video stories, separating the story into digestible chunks.

Editing Prep

- Organize the footage.
- Watch the footage and make notes about your first impressions. Consider performance, camera work, usefulness, and continuity.
- Above all, look for shots that capture emotional moments.
- Remember that you are the audience's advocate.

A typical sequence lasts about 10 minutes in a Hollywood feature film. We've all seen films with a bank robbery sequence or a miss-the-plane-at-the-airport-sequence. Each contains several scenes that separately and together have a beginning, middle, and end. Each scene within the sequence enhances the story line in the sequence and overall story.

About Scenes The material you have in hand will help you decide the order in which you build a scene. Of course, experience plays a big role here. Action scenes can be built or carved depending on the situation. Dialogue scenes tend to go together like stringing pearls, one at a time. Scenes that contain both action and dialogue require a different approach. You can build each portion separately and combine the pieces later or in stages. It's also possible to assemble the material as one scene, working on both sections concurrently. The power of digital editing is that you can develop an approach that works for you. It's also easy to change your approach to suit the material or meet new requirements.

Fiction Workflow

Start by assembling any action shots that open the scene. Refer to your notes and use the best takes. Pay attention to continuity. The aphorism "cut on action" works here. Add to the flow by placing cuts in the action. These cut points will be hidden in movement. This approach works well if you need to match action using different takes.

Assemble the actors' best takes using the script for continuity. Edit with straight cuts. You might want to keep each character's voice on a separate audio track as you build the scene. It's also fine to place all the voices on the same track. You can easily move them later.

Edit in any insert or cut-in shots that are important for story purposes. These include close-ups or details (such as a close-up of a pistol) that are required for the audience to make sense of the scene.

Continue by adding action shots to the scene if they are available. Assemble them in the order called for in the script.

Listen to the audio and adjust the rhythm to accommodate the actor's natural flow. Add frames at cut points to create pauses to enable the audience to think.

If you want the audience to have time to study someone's face for emotional clues, don't cut away immediately after the character speaks. If you want to tighten up the scene, shortening the shots can change the rhythm or shift the focus away from, or to, a character.

Once the scene plays with a coherent audio track, create overlapping video edits with *L*- and *J*-cuts. Overlapping edits, which only change the video track, are simple to do and let you steer the scene from one character's point of view to another's.

For example, in a conversation, you can change the audience's interpretation by allowing them to see how one character reacts to the other. This is an easy way to show the audience that a character is lying or is nervous when questioned.

Begin trimming the action shots for rhythm, emotional adjustment, and continuity. Fine tune the flow after each character's dialogue is complete.

Linger on action if it helps depict a character's motives. Staying with a character can also help cement the point of view. Shorten shots if you want to increase the pace of the scene or deemphasize a character's prominence.

Add video-only cutaways and reaction shots. Cutaways are any shots that cut away from the action or conversation. They are used to fix continuity problems, compress time, or build rhythm. Reaction shots reveal a character's response to other characters or objects in a scene.

What Makes a Good Cut?

Walter Murch, an Academy Award winning editor, wrote, "In film, a shot presents us with an idea, or a sequence of ideas, and the cut is a 'blink' that separates and punctuates those ideas. At the moment you decide to cut, what you are saying is, in effect, 'I am going to bring this idea to an end and start something new.' If the cut is well-placed . . . the more thorough the effect of punctuation will be."[1] Murch feels there are six criteria that determine a good cut. The first three, in order of importance (by percentage), are emotion (51 percent), story (23 percent), and rhythm (10 percent). This adds up to 84 percent.[2] The three technical criteria hardly matter.

[1] Walter Murch, *In the Blink of an Eye: A Perspective on Film Editing*, 2nd edition (Los Angeles: Silman-James Press, 2001), 18.

[2] Ibid., 18.

Complete the scene by adding ambience to fill in any ambient holes. Ambience is what you'd hear if you were sitting in the room or location where the scene is taking place when everyone stops talking. It's the noise of the place. An ambient hole is a gap on the audio track. In a digital environment, if nothing is on the track, there's dead silence. Except for in outer space, dead silence doesn't exist. The audience will notice the absence of sound. Use what sound recordists call *room tone* and add it to the audio track wherever there's a hole. Add sound effects and music to help tell the story.

The Next Steps—Sequences, Acts, . . .

Complete all the scenes that should be included in a sequence. Place each one, in turn, on the timeline. You can place them one after another to build the story. If there's parallel action, you can intercut scenes. It's usually easier to cut between completed scenes than to build an intercut sequence from scratch. After you've built the sequences, you can assemble them on a timeline. Once you have all the acts, you can assemble the show. If you edit in sections, even the longest and most complex story can be easily managed.

The China Closet

Editing revolves around finding and retrieving the moving images, photographs, drawings, sounds, and music stored in files as digital information scattered on your editing system's storage drive or drives. Think of storage as a china closet. Editing a short program is like making dinner for yourself. You don't need a lot of dishes. You probably don't care if you use a soup bowl for salad if that's what you grab first. However, when you start editing longer programs, it's like hosting a dinner party for a dozen guests. To set the table properly, you must be able to find all the dishes. An organized china closet makes setting the table easier when you're expecting company.

Organizing Projects

Ideally, everything you need for a show should be instantly available and easy to find. Your editing system is designed to keep track of the media files (still images, motion pictures, or audio) stored on your hard drive and let you work with icons called *clips*, which represent the pictures and sounds, rather than filenames. Whenever you access a clip, whether it is a still image, video, or music, your editing system's database will locate the appropriate media file and play it.

Editing systems can help you organize the clips so you can easily find the shots, sounds, or images. However, you need to provide the intelligence. Everyone has a different sense of organization. Give two editors identical material and they'll categorize it differently. However, all professional editors will organize the material in some fashion. Shorter projects require less organization than longer projects. This is equally true whether you measure the length by the duration of the finished show or by the amount of time the editor has to complete it. Good organization (that is, an approach that works for you) lets you find what you need quickly and enables you to edit much faster.

Computers use hierarchical structures that consist of files stored in folders or directories on a drive. Nearly every editing system uses this model. Typically, everything associated with making all the versions of a single show is stored in a *project* file.

Projects

The *project* is usually the highest level in an editing system's hierarchy. Projects usually contain information about the sound and picture elements, which are the principal building materials for the show you are editing; any

Technical Settings Versus User Preferences

Two distinct settings are prevalent in most editing systems: technical parameters and user preferences. Technical parameters are associated with a specific project. For example, the footage for the Mimosa Project was recorded with a miniDV camcorder (NTSC)* in the 16:9 aspect ratio with an audio sample rate of 48 kHz (16 bits) on two stereo tracks. The technical settings for this project must reflect the settings used to record the footage. These technical parameters are usually set when you create a new project and before you start bringing material into the project. If they don't match, most editing systems will either resample the material to match the parameters you set or prevent you from inputting the material. The approach to changing and storing these settings varies from manufacturer to manufacturer.

For our Mimosa Project example, the timeline must use the 29.97 frame rate of NTSC to maintain its time database. The viewers must be set to the 16:9 mode so the footage is displayed properly on the desktop. The frame size must be set to 720×480 pixels, which is standard for miniDV. Finally, the audio sample rate must be 48 kHz to avoid resampling the audio tracks. The important point to remember is that technical settings always refer to a single project.

In contrast, user preference settings control the appearance of the desktop, the mapping of the keyboard, and the layout of the windows on the desktop. These settings store any modifications you make to your editing system's user interface. When you open the application, the user interface reflects your preferences. To sum it up, the difference is that technical parameters apply to one project, whereas user settings apply to all projects.

---

* The television standard used in North America created by the National Television Standards Committee. See page 251.

sequences of sounds and pictures (timelines) that you create; and any changes you make to technical settings, such as audio sample rates or video formats, or to user settings that depart from the default settings in your program, such as the placement of a window on the desktop or color schemes.

Although not every editing system works this way, most do. Even if yours doesn't, the project model is still an excellent way to think about organization. The idea is to put everything you need to build a finished show in one box.

The first step after launching your editing system is to open or create a project. The first time you create a project, your system may create a file, folder, or directory to store information. The second step is to name the project. This may seem obvious, but beginners often overlook this step. Editing programs usually label a new project using a default name, such as Untitled, New, or Project_1 if you don't provide a descriptive name.

Every project should have a name that helps you identify what the project or show is about. Call it what it is—for example, the Smith's wedding, a commercial for Acme Widgets, or perhaps the title of the program. It really doesn't matter what you call it as long as you take the extra step of calling it something. If you're just practicing, call the project *Practice* or *My First Lesson*. Get in the habit of naming things. It's the single most important action you can take to feel in control of your editing system.

In many editing programs, only one project can be open at a time. Think of a project as a large empty table in the reference section of the library. This is where you gather all of the elements in the course of doing research. After a while, the table is covered with books, magazines, notebooks, lists, photocopies, reference books, photographs, microfilm, and audio CDs. Most of the things you need to write your report are on the table in front of you. However, some things are scattered throughout the library. Those materials are readily accessible because you have a list at your fingertips that tells you where they are located in the library.

This table is your central work area. This is where the materials you need are gathered and laid out. Is the material stacked and organized or cluttered and disorganized? The speed and efficiency with which you get the job done depends on how quickly you can access your materials. This is why an orderly project table is important.

The more organized you are, the fewer challenges you'll encounter as you edit. You don't have to follow any specific organization or go overboard, but you do need to figure out how to organize the materials you plan to use in a way that makes sense to you.

This begins with the creation of the project (how you name it) and continues until you finish editing. The best way to avoid frustration is to organize your materials in a consistent fashion. Professionals label things appropriately, which means they name an item using its most distinctive characteristic.

Names

Names and labels are at the heart of organization. Nothing is more important. You should get in the habit of assigning names that enable you to remember what an item is. Throughout the editing process, you will have to find pictures, shots, sounds, graphics, and other materials stored in your system. You'll be glad later when you can retrieve something quickly because you took the time in the beginning to give it a recognizable name.

Here are some basic rules about naming that will help you avoid problems:

- *Use all uppercase letters, all lowercase letters, or capitalize the first letter of each word.* Be consistent no matter which approach you decide to take. This is very important because some computer operating systems will treat Wind Surfing, Wind surfing, WIND SURFING, wind surfing, and WINd surFING as five different names, whereas others will see them as five identical names. This issue also arises whenever you sort a list of names or search for a name. Therefore, you must use upper- and lowercase letters consistently when labeling things.

- *Use unique names.* If you decide to use the title of your show as the name of the project, don't use it for anything else. No matter how tempting it might be to label the completed timeline that you will output to tape *My Hawaiian Adventure* because that's the title of the program, don't do it. It will only cause confusion. It's easy to end up with hundreds of things that need to be labeled and it can be challenging to come up with distinctive names for all of them. However, it's worth the effort it takes if you can avoid looking through a dozen items with the same name, time after time, trying to figure out which one of them is the one you really want. In our experience, taking a few moments to come up with unique labels can save you hours.

- *Use descriptive names.* It may be standard practice in Hollywood to label every shot using a scene number, shot number, and take number, but it's not very effective for most digital video editing projects. Hollywood does it because it makes it easier to match up a piece of film with the sound recording. Sound is recorded separately in film production. In video, sound is recorded on the videotape. You rarely need to match up pictures with sounds or do what's called *synchronizing picture to sound* or *syncing the dailies*. Hollywood's second reason for labeling footage with numbers is that it matches the scene numbers marked on the script. However, unless you can recall from memory what Scene 2, Shot 1, Take 3 looks like, you're better off using a name that indicates the subject or describes the action. Amherst Church, Long Shot (abbreviated LS), or Linda Answers the Phone is more helpful than Scene 2, Shot 1, Take 3.

- *Always label your materials.* Every videotape, audiotape, CD, or DVD should be identified with a reel number and descriptive name. Editing systems identify a particular shot using a reel number, which indicates on which tape the material was originally recorded, and the location of the shot on the tape. A clock, called a *time code number*, is automatically recorded on every frame of video to enable editing systems to find the exact location on the tape.

Time Code

Digital video cameras record picture and sound along with a clock to identify each frame of video. The clock starts at zero, runs in a continuous sequence until the end of the tape, and is designated in military time (0 to 24 hours). Two types of clock are commonly used in video. One is called *nondrop frame time code*. The miniDV video format uses *drop frame time code*. Drop frame is the version designed so the time clock number on the tape corresponds to the time of day on a wall clock. The drop frame clock is adjusted by two frames every minute on the minute, except on 10-minute intervals, which in effect slows it down. It's like leap year where every four years the calendar is adjusted by one day. In video, this occurs every minute except for the tenth minute. The hours, minutes, seconds and frames are separated with semicolons or periods in drop frame time code to differentiate it from non-drop frame time code which uses colons.

Reel numbers are used whenever you transfer material into your editing system. The time code identifies every frame of video and indicates the passage of time. The reel number is the top level of a hierarchy that you must create because the time code number on your original source tapes aren't necessarily unique.

Professional cameras let the operator set the starting point of the time code. Most professionals set the hour number to match the tape's reel number and to give the tape a unique time code. This procedure works because most cameras record on tapes that are shorter than an hour. The tape in the camera and the tape box are marked with a reel number. So, reel

non drop frame

05:10:00:18

drop frame

05;10;00;00

Figure 6-1
Three ways of presenting the same time.

three would have a starting time code of 3 hours, zero minutes, zero seconds, zero frames. If the tape is an hour long, the time code at the end of the tape would be 3 hours, 59 minutes, 59 seconds, 29 frames. Professional recorders all read and display time code. Therefore, in a professional environment, it's easy to see that reel three (the one with the hour three time code) is in the recorder. However, camcorders for home use automatically set the time code to zero every time a new tape is placed in the camera. There is no provision for the operator to change the time code.

Shooting Tip

It's important to avoid time code breaks on your original source tapes because it creates havoc for editing systems. There are two methods to prevent this from happening. The first one—the safe and sure method—is to record black on every new tape before you use it. Turn on your camera or recorder and put in a new tape. If you're using a camera, leave the lens cap on. Disconnect the microphone or turn the audio recording level down. If you can't do either one of those, put the camera in a quiet place while you're blacking the tape. Press the record trigger on the camera, or press record and play on the recorder.

The alternative is the overlap method. Any new recording must overlap the old one by a few seconds. Camcorders automatically use this method whenever you stop and start recording. However, if you rewind and play the footage to review it or take the tape out of your camcorder, you can inadvertently miscue the tape. To check this, use the video cassette recorder (VCR) controls on your camcorder and rewind the tape about 10 seconds. Play the tape, paying close attention to the time code at which the old recording ends. Then rewind the tape and press play again. This time, press stop about three seconds before the old recording ends. Switch the camcorder back to camera mode and start shooting again.

Time code breaks on miniDV tapes occur because home camcorders automatically reset their clocks to zero hours, zero minutes, zero seconds, zero frames whenever the camera senses blank unrecorded tape. If the camcorder senses video, it automatically sets the clock to match the number already recorded on the tape. When you begin recording again, the camera reads the time code on the tape and continues with the sequence.

(continued)

(continued)

An unintended consequence of this approach is that if you don't record over the last few frames of the previous recording, you can end up with a tape that has more than one zero starting time code. This creates problems when you attempt to transfer the material into your editing system. The system has no way of differentiating between the first occurrence and second occurrence of a minute one time code number if the reel numbers are identical. The solution is to label the tape with two reel numbers. For example, the first zero start on the tape could be reel 01A and the second one could be reel 01B.

You may not have tapes with multiple starts, but you will have tapes with identical time code if you use miniDV or other consumer video formats. Whenever you shoot more than one hour of footage for a show, you'll have two tapes with the identical time code. They both start at zero and end at 00:59:59:29. This is why reel numbers are so important.

It should be obvious why each tape needs a descriptive name. Remembering what Scene 1, Take 3 looks like is not any easier than remembering what's on reel 006. However, if reel 006 is also labeled *Outdoor Scenes, Amherst*, you'll have an easier time finding that long shot of a church in Amherst that you want to copy to your editing system's storage drives.

Bin Organization

Editors organize pictures and sounds by categorizing them. This process is like creating an outline, organizing a stamp collection, or filing things so you can find them later. The containers are called *bins*. Bin is the name film editors gave to the piece of furniture they used to store sections of film. It had a bar and clips to hold the strips of film, which hung down into what looked like a trashcan. Most editing programs let you create bins, which work just like folders or directories in a computer.

Bins store video, audio, or graphics clips. You can create as many as you like within a project in most editing systems. Some editing systems let you nest bins within another bin or within a folder. No matter how your editing system works, it is essential to make bins and categorize them if you want to edit with ease.

The point of organizing your source materials in bins is to make the materials easy to find. You can organize footage into themes, locations, the time of day, characters, people, or by the type of media—graphics, effects, audio, video, and stills. The types of categories you can create are only limited by your imagination. Every time you make a bin, label it. Be sure you use unique names.

Organize your material for easy retrieval. If you're editing a documentary, it may be appropriate to create interview, photograph, stock footage, B-roll footage, title, and artwork bins. For a commercial, it might be more appropriate to create bins for testimonials, product shots, and graphics. Again, the important thing is to find a method of organizing the material that works for you. It's easy to copy or move clips from one bin to another and just as easy to delete them. Remember that in most editing systems deleting the clip doesn't delete the media file; it only deletes the pointer to the media file.

Bins merely contain the pointers to the media files that are stored elsewhere. Copying and moving a digital media file takes a considerable amount of time. Copying and moving an icon that tells your editing system where to find and play a media file takes no time at all.

Bin Categories

Table 6-1 shows some examples of bin categories to help you start thinking about organization.

Organizing your materials becomes easier with every project you do. After all, the possibilities are limitless.

Bin Views

Think about how you'd like to work with your material. Most bin windows can alternatively display the clips in the bin as a text-only list, as a text list with tiny pictures that represent the contents, or as resizeable pictures of the material.

Figure 6-2

Bin category
suggestions.

Interiors	Exteriors	Music	Sound Effects
Bride's dressing room	Groom's alcove	Waiting room	Chapel
Titles	Credits	Photographs	Drawings
Stunts	Visual effects	Graphics	Transitions
Testimonials	Interviews	Standups	B-roll
Bridal dinner	Wedding ceremony	Reception	Honeymoon
Wine tasting	Opening ceremony	Closing ceremony	Speeches
Monday	Tuesday	Wednesday	Thursday
Friday	Saturday	Sunday	Selects
Reel 001	Reel 002	Reel 003	Reel 004
Camera one	Camera two	Camera three	Program feed

The List View   The list view can display all or part of the information that an editing system maintains in its database. The information is presented as a database with categories, such as the name of the clip, the IN and OUT time codes, the clip duration, the audio sample rate, the date the media file was created on the hard drive, and the comments. There can be as many as 30 different categories in some editing systems. You can choose to show them all or display only selected categories. You can also move the categories around in most editing systems so you can rearrange the way things are displayed to suit your needs. Most list views can also be sorted by any category in ascending or descending order. The list view is a powerful tool despite its lack of visual information because it gives you access to the database.

The following section includes the categories or fields that appear in the list view of six editing systems. You should note that some categories are standard. This confirms that most editing systems follow the model we described earlier.

Adobe Premiere List View   This list view contains the following database categories: Name, Date, File Path, Log Comment, Media Type (still/movie), Video Info, Audio Info, Video Usage (in the timeline), Audio Usage (in the timeline), Duration, Time Code (first frame of source), Reel Name, Notes, and Labels (fields you can rename).

Apple Final Cut Pro Browser List View   This list view contains the following database categories: Name, Alpha, Anamorphic, Audio Format, Audio Rate, Audio, Aux TC 1–2, Capture, Comment Field (4), Composite, Compressor, Data Rate, Description, Duration, Frame Size, Good, In, Out, Label, Label 2, Last Modified, Length, Log Note, Media Start, Media End, Offline, Pixel Aspect, Reel, Reverse Alpha, Scene, Shot/Take, Size (File), Source (file location), TC, Thumbnail, Tracks, Type (clip, subclip, merge clip, sequence, bin, effect), and Video Rate.

Avid XpressDV Bin List View   This list view contains the following database categories: Name, Tracks, File Start, File End, Audio, Audio Format, Color, Creation Date, Target Disk ID, Duration, IN-OUT (duration), Lock, Mark In, Mark Out, Offline, Project, Tape, Video Resolution, Comments, and Your Headings.

Incite Details View   This detail view contains the following database categories: Name, Comment, File Name, Tape/Reel, Available Tracks, Type (Audio, Video, Graphic), Status (Playable/Offline), Data Rate, Master Clip In, Master Clip Out, Master Clip Duration, In, Out, Duration, and Speed.

Media 100 iFinish List View   This list view contains the following database categories: Name, Reel Name, In Time, Out Time, Tracks, Comments, Keywords, Color, Length, Source In Time, Source Out Time, Source Length, Date, Source Media File Name, Input Setup, Quality, Standard (NTSC/PAL), ColorFX, MotionFX, Audio Frequency, Audio EQ, Rendered Media File Name, Source Media File Size, Rendered Media File Size, and Audio In Channel (#).

Pinnacle Studio Album Details View   This album details view contains the following database categories: Thumbnail, Time Code Start, Scene Name, and Keyword.

The Picture View   The picture-only view hides the database. The only text visible is usually the name of the clip underneath the picture icons, or *picons*. One of the advantages of digital editing is that you can display clips as pictures and edit without ever looking at the statistics in the list view. This is the primary method many editors choose because it's a visual approach.

There are two important considerations when using the bin this way. The first is that the picon (the still image) should display a frame that actually represents the content of the clip. Unless you change it, this image is usually the first frame of the clip. Look in your editing system's manual to see how to change this image so that it reflects what the clip is all about. Pick a frame that shows the subject or principal action in that clip. For example, if you have a bin that has clips of a diver making a series of dives, the default frame (the first frame of the clip) probably shows the diver standing at the back of the diving board with her hands down preparing to dive. All the picons for the clips would look identical in the bin. However, by adjusting what's called the *representative frame,* or *poster frame*, you can select a frame that shows the diver in midair. This way when you edit the footage, you'll be able to instantly identify the dive she is doing and select the clip you need.

The second consideration has to do with the number of clips in the bin. Professionals usually decide to display no more than 25 to 30 clips on a full-screen bin window. If any more clips are displayed, the picons become too small to see. If you find yourself squinting at tiny picons or scrolling through a bin with a vast number of clips, it's time to divide it up by moving some of the clips to another bin.

On a single monitor editing system, the bins can't occupy all the real estate on the desktop. If you're working with a single monitor system, you should reduce the number of picons in a bin to less than a dozen. If you have a very large monitor, you may be able to increase this number.

The Combination View   A compromise approach is to view the bin as a list with picons beside each entry. The challenge is that the picons are often very small and hard to see. If the picons are made large enough to see, the list can become less useful. You'll see fewer items in the bin window and the picons tend to slow down scrolling. Some people find this approach to be a happy middle point. We prefer to switch between the list view and the

Expand Your Desktop

Adding a second computer monitor to your editing system is often the best solution to the desktop real-estate problem. Professional editing systems often have two computer monitors. One is used for the bins and the other is used to display the timeline, tool palettes, and viewer windows. Check the manual for your editing system to see if it supports two monitors. You may need to add a second graphics card to your computer in order to do this. If you plan to do a lot of editing, it's usually worth the extra expense to have the desktop space that two monitors can provide.

picon view as often as necessary. Most systems make it easy to switch from one view to another. It's all a matter of preference. Some people are more comfortable using pictures, whereas others are more comfortable using numbers and statistics to find the material they want.

Digitizing and Transfer

The first and most fundamental of all editing tasks is transferring your source materials from tape, disk, or camera into your editing system. This is usually the very next task after you create a project and make a bin. It takes time—real time. There's simply no way of getting around it. The footage you recorded with your camera has to be played at normal speed to be transferred, or captured, on your editing system's storage drives.

The only editing systems capable of transferring materials at speeds faster than normal are expensive professional systems that are primarily used for television news operations. In these environments, the need for speed is paramount and manufacturers have developed a method of transferring video at four times normal speed. In every other application, a one-hour tape takes one hour to transfer to an editing system.

Unfortunately, most people are confronted by the task of connecting their editing system to a video recorder before they start using their new editing

Making Connections

Connecting analog or professional equipment is more complicated. Many editing system manuals take several chapters to deal with this aspect of digital video editing. Detailed installation instructions are necessary to set up the interactions between your computer, the special boards that digitize video, the external hard drives, speakers, video monitors, and more. A long list of things might need to be set and adjusted before everything works together as it should. Cabling everything together can become complicated and messy. If setting up a stereo system is beyond your capabilities, consider using a turnkey editing appliance. These editing appliances are intended to iron out most, if not all, of the complications. However, if you can follow directions, you should have no trouble setting up an editing system.

system. It's ironic that the first phase of editing is technical, not creative. New users can be turned off and miss out on the joy of editing. Thankfully, digital video camcorders with Firewire connections make it simple. You only need one cable to connect your camera to your editing system. In the past, transferring the material you shot with your camera into your editing system was complicated. This is no longer true.

The Basic Steps

Whether you're using an editing appliance or a computer-based system, the process of transferring materials into your editing system remains the same. The procedures are universal. The following section describes the basic steps to input (copy or digitize) video into your editing system.

Video recorded in a digital format is transferred (copied) to your editing system's storage drives using Firewire or another transport standard, such as *serial digital interface* (SDI) or *serial digitl transport interface* (SDTI). If the material is in an analog format, such as the VHS, BetaSP, or audiocassette format, it must be converted from an analog to digital format in order for the system to use it. This process is called *digitizing* because the video and audio signals are transformed into digital data. Special hardware is required to convert the signals.

Nearly every editing system opens what we'll call an input tool when you want to copy video into your editing system. The input tool is a window that has remote controls for your camcorder or recorder and that asks you to enter information about the material you want to transfer into your editing system. Most systems let you decide where (on which drive) the digital media files you're about to input will be stored. Some systems let you adjust audio and video levels (analog video only) during this process. Some systems may also have meters or instruments that let you evaluate technical quality while you input the footage.

However, every system asks you to enter some basic information about the footage before you input it. Even the most basic system lets you type in a reel name and description. Sophisticated editing systems store as much information about the footage as you'd care to enter.

Enter a Reel Name   However, the most important category, the one that should always be filled in, is the reel name. The reel name is the name you assigned to the tape. This is the name that's marked on the tape and tape box. Professionals generally use three characters that consist of numbers (001) or a combination of letters and numbers (AC1) to name reels. This is because every editing system can handle three characters for a reel name, but not all are capable of using or storing longer descriptive names.

Check the Inputs   Next check to make sure that the video or audio inputs shown on the input tool (or under the system settings) match the type of connection you're using to connect video or audio sources to your system. These input settings may or may not be accessible from the input tool in your editing system. You're likely to see DV, Firewire (IEEE-1394), Composite Video, Component Video, or something else listed on an input setting preference. It doesn't matter what it's called; it just matters that the settings in the editing system match the physical reality of how the video source is connected. The cabling should match. If you're not sure how things are connected, check the installation manual or installation section of your editing system manual to refresh your memory.

Set or Create a Bin   You need a destination for the materials you input. The destination for a clip is a bin and in most systems you have the luxury of choosing which bin you want to use. The bin you select is often called the *target* or *destination bin*. Some systems will automatically pick the last bin you opened or highlighted. In other systems, you have to change a preference setting. Others let you select any available bin in your project using the input tool. We're not aware of any systems that let you input material unless you have at least one bin open. There may be a few exceptions, but we haven't seen them. Therefore, if you don't have a bin in your project, create one and name it. We suggest that you use the name of the tape for the name of your target bin and that you make a new bin for each tape you input into your editing system. The reason we suggest doing this is explained in the section "Batch Input Organization." If you're working on a system that only has one bin, you don't need to set a target bin and can ignore this step.

Select a Target Drive   If your editing system has multiple storage drives, select the one you want to use. The best choice is the one that has the most free space. Every editing system has a way to check how much is available on your storage drive or drives. You should make sure that you'll have enough space for the material you want to input. If not enough space is available, you can free some up by deleting material you don't need anymore or inputting less footage.

It's never a good idea to work with storage drives that are completely full. There won't be any room to store the titles, effects, and transitions you'll want to create later. Most systems seem to get finicky when their storage drives are too full. We know it's a computer and that it can't really get finicky. However, this is the easiest way to describe the odd things that always seem to happen when we fill the drives to the max.

Determine the Quality If you're using miniDV and a Firewire input, most editing systems won't let you adjust the quality or don't offer this feature. Therefore, you can skip this step. However, a few systems give you the option of inputting a low-resolution version, which increases the amount of footage that will fit on your editing system. The idea is that after you've edited your show, you can replace the low-resolution version with the normal version. Since the only footage you replace is what is in your finished show, you don't need much space.

If you're digitizing analog or *high-definition* (HD) formats, you may have the opportunity to select a quality level or level of compression. More information about compression can be found in Chapter 10, "Getting It In and Out." The rule is the higher the quality, the less compression has been applied. The highest possible quality is uncompressed. Of course, uncompressed material also takes up the largest amount of storage space. Highly compressed material takes up the least amount of space, although it has the worst image quality.

The rule of thumb is to use the lowest acceptable quality if storage space is an issue. You can always reinput the footage later at a higher quality after you've gone through all the material and decided what's important.

Select the Tracks When you're using miniDV and Firewire, most systems don't let you select input tracks, so you may be able to skip this step. If yours does, it's probably to accommodate the extra two audio channels available on some miniDV camcorders. Some systems must transfer the video track otherwise they lose the time code track. This becomes an issue if you need to make two passes to transfer all four of the audio channels into your system. A second copy of the video track wastes a lot of space.

Editing systems that let you select individual tracks can save space. Audio requires very little. Therefore, if you need sound but not the picture, input only the sound, or vice versa. The one track you must never turn off is time code, if your editing system will let you turn it off. If there's no time code, you have no way of tracing the media file back to the original source tape.

For Professionals Only: Set the Remote/Local Switch Most professional videotape recorders have a remote/local switch. When this switch is in the local position, the front-panel controls operate the recorder and the remote control is disabled. Check the switch and make sure the switch is set to the remote position. The input tool can only control the recorder when this switch is set to remote.

Input Checklist

- Enter a reel name.
- Check the input settings.
- Set or create a bin.
- Set a target drive.
- Check the available space.
- Choose a compression rate, if applicable.
- Select the appropriate tracks, if applicable.
- Set the remote/local switch on professional recorders to remote.

The Five Input Methods

After you've gone through the input checklist and confirmed that all the settings are correct, it's time to run a test. Use the single-scene input method. There's no point to doing more than one until you're sure everything works.

Single-Scene Input   These are the steps for copying a single scene into your editing system:

1. Put a source tape in the recorder. Open the input tool. Type in the reel name written on the tape label. Using the input tool to control the recorder, find the beginning of a scene. You should be able to play, rewind, fast forward, and shuttle. When you find the beginning of the scene (the first one on the tape will do), press the Mark In button. You should see the time code number for the location of the beginning of the scene in the In field. Next, find the end of the scene. Press the Mark Out button. Once again, the correct time code number should appear in the Out field.

2. The next step varies depending on the editing system you're using. Type in a name or description of the material you're about to input. On some systems, you may need to save the log entry before you can press the input tool record button to start the process. On others, you can

press record without saving the log entry. In either case, as soon as you press record, the video recorder should automatically go to the in point using rewind or shuttle, and cue the tape a few seconds before the in point. The recorder should then go into play. When the tape reaches the in point, your editing system should begin copying. The system should stop copying as soon as it reaches the out point and you should see a clip appear in the bin.

3. Before you input anything else, you should check that clip by playing it. You may have to close the input tool before you can play the clip. Watch to make sure there aren't any problems with levels or the quality of the picture and sound. You should prove to yourself that everything works.

Batch Input   The batch input method is designed to save labor—yours. The idea is to log all the scenes on a tape and input them afterwards. If you follow our shooting tip about keeping a log of where major scenes begin and end on each tape, you can shuttle the tape and find the in and out points for the scenes you want very quickly.

Name and save each entry before you find the next scene. Scenes can be as long as 5 to 10 minutes in length. Some systems limit the file sizes you can copy so check your manual. Every log entry you save should appear in the bin. Go through the entire tape and log all the scenes you want.

At this point, you're ready to input all the clips you logged. Usually, there's a separate command for batch input. You may need to select the clips in the bin you want before you can do a batch input or there could be a menu option to input any clip without a media file. Regardless of how it works, before you do a batch input, it's a good idea to input one clip as a test. If everything is working correctly, you can hit batch input and walk away. The process will take the same amount of time as the duration of the material you're inputting. If you have 50 minutes of footage, you could go to lunch and come back. Always do one clip first so you can walk away.

Input On the Fly   If you're in a hurry, you can input on the fly. This approach is fast but not foolproof. Put the video recorder into play and press the record button on the input tool. The editing system will start transferring the material to the storage drives. However, you must make sure you stop inputting before you reach the end of the recorded material on the tape. A time code break or a loss of time code will cause most editing systems to reject the material you've just attempted to input and you'll have to do it all over again. If you've previewed what's on the tape, write down the last time code number on the tape, so you can stop before you get to the end.

Log and Import   You can watch your tapes and create a log before you start to edit. Using a spreadsheet or word processing program, you can type up a list of scenes with a starting and ending time code for each one. All the editing systems that can import log files have instructions on how you can do this in their manuals. You can also buy specialized logging programs to do this.

After you've logged your footage, you simply import the list into your editing system. Your list appears in a bin without any media attached. It should look identical to the way the bin looked in the batch input method before you did the batch input. The final step is to do a batch input. This approach doesn't save time, but it does avoid tying up an editing system with a task, such as logging, that could be done elsewhere on less expensive equipment.

Scene Detection   Scene detection is a popular feature on some miniDV editing systems. You put in a tape and press the record button. Your editing system splits up the footage into scenes for you. Typically, this feature only works when miniDV is the video source. MiniDV camcorders record the time code and a time of day for each frame. Most of the systems use the breaks in the time of day clock to decide where the scenes begin and end. A few systems use camera movement or abrupt differences in the subject matter to trigger a scene change. Your satisfaction with this automatic process will depend on how your editing system detects scene changes and on your camera operator's shooting style.

Shooting Tip

Take a small notebook with you when you're shooting. Write down what's on each tape. You don't need a lot of information. The beginning and ending time code for major scenes or location changes are more than enough. This comes in handy when you want to transfer material into your editing system. You can create a log file or use the input tool to build a list based on the notes you took. Later, you can use the editing system to do what it does best—break down scenes into shots. If you're using the miniDV format, a notebook is essential because the tape boxes are so small. Most people can barely write a reel number on a miniDV tape let alone a list of scenes.

If you're in a hurry, this can be a timesaver. However, you might lose your familiarity with the material. One of an editor's most important jobs is to look at the footage. At some point, you have to see all of it, evaluate it, and make decisions. The best time to start this process is during the input phase. Scene detection can be useful as long as you watch your footage.

Batch Input Organization

The best approach for a long-form project or any project with more than one source tape is to create a separate input bin for each tape. Label the bin using the reel number or tape name. This is done for several reasons. Most editing systems are incapable of batch input across multiple open bin windows, so it's a disadvantage to log scenes from one tape into separate bins. Batch input typically works within a single bin. Plus, only one tape can be in the recorder at a time. The most efficient approach is to input all the scenes you need from a particular tape once rather than continually putting the tape into the recorder and taking it back out again.

Another reason for this is that we've almost always had to reinput footage at some point. A media file becomes corrupted or is accidentally deleted, or the shot we need drops frames because the media file is fragmented across a hard drive. The handles (extra frames at the head or tail of a shot) aren't long enough to do the dissolve we want. Reel number bins can simplify the process of locating what is missing. Every editing system has a way of indicating when a clip is offline, and when one file becomes corrupted, there's bound to be more.

Yet another reason this is done is that no one is perfect. We all make mistakes such as leaving out scenes we meant to input. In fact, that happens regularly on big projects. If you have bins organized by reel number, you can quickly check the log in the bin against your paper or electronic logs and spot your mistakes.

After you've input all the original source material, you'll want to organize the material into categories so you can begin editing. We suggest you copy the clips rather than move them from your reel number input bins into the bins you'll use to organize and edit your materials. The point is to keep your reel number database intact. So don't move the clips, copy them. Take advantage of your editing system's strengths. It's much easier to create bins and organize clips on the desktop than it is to do on paper or when you're logging footage.

Logging

Most editing systems let you log your footage before you copy or digitize it. This is done for two reasons. On longer shows, it's easy to run out of storage room and you may need to be selective. The more important reason is that the editor must know the footage. You can't edit a show unless you know the footage intimately. The only way to do this is to watch the material repeatedly. Viewing, taking notes, and thinking about the material doesn't have to happen in front of an editing system. The only things you really need to do this job are a monitor, video recorder, and notepad.

In professional situations, this approach is often the most cost-effective solution because it doesn't tie up an editing system. A well-prepared editor or producer can cut the time it takes to edit a show in half simply by knowing what's useable and what's not to tell the story. However, there are times when this isn't true. Under extreme deadline pressure, it may be quicker to input all the footage and make it work as you go. If you have a limited amount of footage, it can be faster and easier to input everything and then use your editing system to organize the material.

The process of logging can occur while you're shooting (in the field) or afterwards during the editing phase. A detailed log kept throughout production is extremely useful, although not every situation lends itself to that approach. This log can record when shots start and end in time code, a description of the shot, whether it's excellent, good, bad, or unusable, or anything else that will enable you to make a decision later about whether to input the material into your editing system. The more you shoot, the better your logs have to be. Large projects, such as feature films, television series, or long-form documentaries, generate vast quantities of footage. Logs provide the first level of organization and can substantially reduce the time it takes to edit these shows.

In the not too distant past, we suggested that everyone keep detailed logs. We don't feel that this is necessary any more. It made sense when editing systems were expensive, hourly facility rates were high, and storage space was precious. Producers who kept detailed logs saved themselves a lot of money. Today, editing software is less expensive than professional logging software and runs on ordinary personal computers. Storage is cheap. Scene-sized files are more efficient than shot-sized files in a digital environment. All you really need are organizational logs that enable you to find major scenes, locations, or interviews. It takes less time to break down long scenes in an editing system than it does to keep detailed shot logs.

Input Advice

■ *Scene-sized files are more efficient than shot-sized files in a digital environment.* Hard drives work best with medium-sized files. There's less wear and tear on your camcorder and on your original source tapes, if you input scenes instead of shots. You don't want to capture an entire tape as one clip because the file size makes it inefficient. Five-second clips are even less efficient. They are time consuming to input and the file size is inefficient.

■ *The best approach is to input scene-size files.* You can break down the scenes later into individual shots using the power of your editing system.

Summary

Organize your editing projects to fit your needs. Long complex shows require more organization than short simple ones. The purpose of being organized is to be able to find materials when you need them.

Important Points to Remember

■ Use unique, descriptive names to label projects, timelines, bins and clips.

■ Organize materials into separate bins.

■ Always label source footage tapes. This becomes the control number (reel number) for your editing system.

■ Transferring material into your editing system happens in real time.

■ Use batch input for efficiency.

■ Logging your materials is important whether you do it before or after its transferred into the editing system.

Setting the Table

Stories are made from clear, clean, and understandable shots. Every piece of footage has one section that reveals the essence—what that shot is about. Your job as an editor is to identify and select the tip of the iceberg (the portion of the footage that lets the audience believe they are looking at an iceberg) instead of showing them all the ice. To do that, you must be able to recognize the types of icebergs floating in the ocean. Learning how to spot these tips comes with experience.

Editors tell stories by stringing shots together. Shots build scenes, which depict all the action in one location at one time. A series of scenes creates a sequence. A succession of sequences builds an act. Acts form the show. Whether you number the acts, or call them the beginning, middle, and end, or the setup, conflict, and resolution, one thing is clear: Acts, scenes, and sequences rely on a basic building block—the shot. Everything starts with the shot.

Shots communicate action or describe the subject. The audience must be able to recognize and comprehend that image. Editors refer to this as *reading a shot*. Some shots can be read quickly, whereas others require more time. The editor's job is to give the audience enough time to read a shot before replacing it with a new one.

What's a Shot?

A shot is the shortest section of recorded footage, as measured in time, that is capable of communicating a single action, feeling, or thought to the audience. This chapter will help you learn to identify the shots in your sea of footage.

Describing Shots

Everyone involved in the production of a show, from the writer to the camera operator to the editor, uses standard definitions to describe shots. The primary way of distinguishing one shot from another is by the size of a human being within the frame. Well-run productions use these shot designations throughout the production process. The production version of the script includes abbreviations for the shots the director plans to shoot. The shot abbreviations carry over to the producer, script continuity clerk, or assistant cameraman's logs of what was actually shot. The editor who must log and evaluate the footage uses the same system. This is a shared language used to describe and categorize basic framing. As an editor, you need to learn this language.

What Are the Standard Shots?

The following is a list of common shots. Descriptions and abbreviations are provided for each shot. The first groups are the ones defined by how much of the human body fits into the frame or what's more accurately called the *field of vi*ew. The field of view is the area that the camera records.

Long Shot (LS)

A LS is any shot taken at a considerable distance from the subject. People appear smaller than the height of the frame. A long shot is often used for *establishing* (EST) or master shots. This shot is also called a *wide shot* (WS) because the field of view is very wide; it does not refer to the focal length of the lens. The amount of space below the feet differentiates a *medium long shot* (MLS) from a long shot (LS) or *extreme long shot* (XLS). Most of the time the LS is the only designation used.

Full Shot (FS)

An FS is framed to include the human figure from head to toe.

Medium Full Shot (MFS)

An MFS is framed to start at the knees.

Medium Shot (MS)

An MS is framed to start at the hips.

Medium Close Shot (MCS)

An MCS is framed to start at the waist.

Close Shot (CS)

A CS is framed to start at the chest.

Close-Up (CU)

A CU is framed to start at the shoulders. This is also called a *head-and-shoulders* (H&S) shot.

Medium Close-Up (MCU)

An MCU is framed to start at the neck.

Extreme Close-Up (ECU or XCU)

An ECU is framed above the chin.

Figure 7-1
Framing of four
common camera
shots.

A Shooting Tip

Frame any shot defined by the human body with room below the demarcation. You don't want to line up the bottom of the frame with the knees, hips, waist, chest, shoulders, neck, or chin. The idea is to include them in a pleasing composition.

Conceptual Shots

This group doesn't rely on field of view. Instead, the shots that follow are conceptual. Any of the field-of-view shots we just defined could work under the right circumstances.

Establishing (EST)

An EST is any shot at or near the beginning of a show or scene that establishes the environment in which the action takes place. This shot can also establish the relationship between the details seen in closer shots. Most EST shots are long shots.

Master

A master shot is a single shot that covers all the action in a scene. This designation is for the director and editor. It doesn't have an abbreviation like the others. The master is the editor's first opportunity to see the scene in its entirety. Many editors use the master as the starting point of the editing process. Because the master is usually a wide shot, the editor will build impact by overwriting (overlaying) closer shots that maintain continuity. Other editors watch the master shot and build the scene entirely from the closer shots. They'll use the master shot as a last resort if they don't have enough coverage (closer shots).

Reaction Shot

A reaction shot reveals someone's reaction to an off-screen sound or action.

Reverse

Any shot from the opposite perspective.

Bridging or Cutaway Shot

A bridging or cutaway shot is used to cover a break in continuity, such as time or place.

Two-Shot

A two-shot shows two people.

Three-Shot

A three-shot shows a group of three people.

Tracking Shot

A tracking shot is any shot in which the camera moves with the subject to maintain distance and framing. The word *tracking* came into use because the camera was usually moved over tracks.

Camera Movement

Camera movement should improve the audience's understanding of what's being shown on screen, not make them nauseous. The editor has to understand where the show will be seen and compensate for it. Motion that wouldn't bother anyone if viewed on a 30-inch television monitor can be horrendous when it's seen on a 60-foot screen in a theater.

A Shooting Tip

Handheld camera work is always the last resort. Professionals keep the camera on a tripod unless they have a specific reason for taking it off. The only reason to dispense with the tripod is when you have no other way of getting the shot. Camera moves should start on a static shot and end on a static shot.

Professional camera operators begin each camera move with a hold (a well-composed stationary shot) and end each move with another hold. This gives the editor four possible shots. The editor can use the static shot at the beginning, the camera move (as is or in the reverse direction), or the static shot at the end. This also makes it easier for the editor to find a place to cut on matched action.

Pan Right or Pan Left

This describes a shot in which the camera rotates horizontally. A pan is like turning your head to the right or left to see beyond your normal field of vision.

Tilt Up or Tilt Down

This describes a shot in which the camera rotates on its horizontal axis. A tilt is equivalent to looking down to see your feet or up to see the ceiling. This is also called a *pan up* or *pan down*.

Pedestal Up or Pedestal Down

This describes a shot in which the position of the camera is raised or lowered with respect to the floor. A pedestal is equivalent to holding a camcorder on your shoulder and bending or straightening your knees to change the height of the camera.

Dolly In (D/I:) or Dolly Back (D/B:)

This describes a shot in which the camera moves closer or farther away from the subject. A dolly move alters the audience's perspective—the relationship of the subject to the background.

Zoom In (Z/I:) or Zoom Out (Z/O:)

This describes a shot in which the focal length of the lens is lengthened or widened. This really isn't a camera move. A zoom often substitutes for a dolly move even though a zoom flattens or expands the depth rather than altering the perspective.

Track Left or Track Right

This describes a shot in which the camera moves left or right relative to the subject. This is a dolly move except instead of getting closer to the subject (moving forward or backwards), the camera slides right or left. In television studios, this shot is called is a truck left or truck right.

Arc Left or Arc Right

This describes a shot in which the camera circles left or right in relation to the subject. This move combines the dolly and the truck to form an arc.

A Shooting Tip

Beginners misuse the zoom by recording their efforts to find a pleasing composition while zooming in and out or using it to follow the action. You'll get more interesting results if you use the zoom to find an appropriate focal length to frame the action before you begin recording. To follow the action, move your body and the camera.

Swish Pan

This describes a shot in which the camera is panned rapidly to blur the picture. Swish pans are used mostly for transitions or occasionally as a point-of-view shot. This is also called a *whip pan*.

Camera Angles

Describing a shot fully requires more information than its field of view or conceptual designation. The angle of the camera to the subject is important when you start editing. If a shot's angle or field of view is too close to the preceding shot, the transition between the two shots will be jarring.

Eye level is a relative height. Camera operators aren't uniform in height and have minimal contact with editors. Besides, it wouldn't help you to remember how tall they are anyway. Any shot at the approximate eye level of an ordinary person is considered to be at eye level.

The other possibilities are predictable. *Low angles* (L/A:), *high angles* (H/A:), and *overhead* angles are the most common ones. In a low angle shot, the subject looks down at the camera. The opposite is true for high angle shots. From this perspective, the subject looks up at the camera. An overhead angle provides a bird's eye view of the scene. An *aerial* is an overhead shot taken from an airplane, dirigible, or helicopter.

Points of View

The other angles you're likely to see fall into the point of view category. The most common one is an *over-the-shoulder* (O/S) shot. This medium shot frames one person's face with another person's head and shoulder. Nearly every interview on television at one point or another uses this shot to confirm that the interviewer is in the same room with the person being interviewed.

Another common technique is to briefly substitute the camera for a character in the scene. This is called a *point of view* shot. The selective use of a *handheld* camera or a device like the *SteadyCam*, which smoothes out handheld camera moves, can make the audience believe that they're seeing through the eyes of a character in the story.

In a *canted* or *dutched* shot, the horizon is diagonal rather than horizontal. A canted shot is another way to pull the audience into the story. In real life, we expect the horizon to be level. This is why people thought the world was flat. When the horizon isn't horizontal, the audience feels like their bodies have been tilted. If your story takes place on a boat, a canted shot could make the scene more believable.

Eye Level Versus Eye Line

A distinction must be made between *eye level*, which is a camera angle, and a *subject's eye line*. It's important to know the subject's eye line when you're evaluating footage. This is an imaginary line that is drawn across the subject's eyes. This is crucial for editing because the eye line (not the eye level) tells the audience where the person is looking. As an editor, you need to be able to match up eye lines if you want the subjects in two close-ups, for example, to appear as if they are looking at each other.

Camera Transitions

The shots listed below are useful for making smoother transitions or establishing a relationship between the subjects of those shots.

Rack Focus

Rack focus refers to any shot in which the focus shifts from one subject or object to another in the frame.

Pan to Reframe

Pan to reframe refers to any shot in which the camera makes a small pan adjustment to improve the composition.

Pan to Cover Action

Pan to cover action refers to any shot in which the camera pans to keep the subject or action in the frame.

Pan to Connect Two Subjects, Thoughts, or Objects

This refers to any shot in which the camera pans from a subject or object to another subject or object. This transition links the subjects together in the audience's eyes.

About Aspect Ratio

Two common aspect ratios (or frame shapes) are used in digital video. The 4:3 aspect ratio is used by the vast majority of television sets in the United States. This has the shape of an almost square rectangle. The width is four units to every three units of height. The aspect ratio can be written as 4:3, 1.33:1, or 1.33. The latter number is the result of dividing 4 by 3 in order to express the ratio as a factor of one. All of the shapes described by those numbers are identical.

The 1.33 ratio is also called the *Academy Format*. This is the shape of the frame in 35 mm motion picture film. However, theaters don't project the full frame. Instead, they use a metal mask in the projector to crop or hide part of the image. In the United States, theaters use a 1.85 mask, whereas in Europe, a 1.66 mask is common. The mask lets the projectionist position the film in the projector with leeway and hide the frame line. These masks change the aspect ratio of the original film to a shape that's more rectangular.

The rectangular shape is closer to the way human beings see the world—hence, the reason for the other aspect ratios typically used in film production. Panavision cameras record images on 35 mm film in a 2.35 aspect ratio and Cinemascope cameras record images on 35 mm film in the 2.5 aspect ratio. Both have very narrow rectangular shapes that create wide-screen images like the ones we see with our eyes.

Figure 7-2
Three common
aspect ratios.

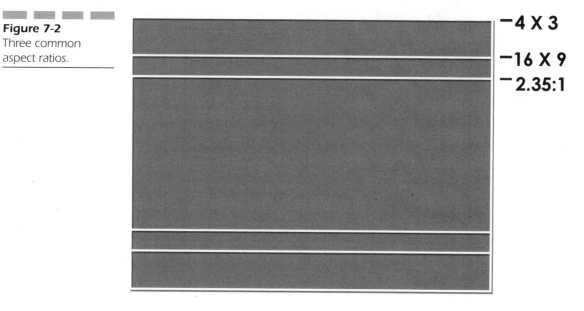

−4 X 3

−16 X 9
−2.35:1

Figure 7-3
The picture area
cropped in different
aspect ratios.

−4 X 3

−16 X 9
−2.35:1

The newest aspect ratio for digital video is the 16:9, 1.78:1, or 1.78 aspect ratio. Again, all those numbers describe the same rectangle. The shape is a narrower rectangle than the one used in the past for video. This aspect ratio, a compromise between 1.66 and 1.85, was designed for high-definition television (HDTV). The purpose was to match the aspect ratios used for feature films so when the film was shown on television, the audience would see everything the audience saw in the theater. The 1.78 aspect ratio, which is midway between the European 1.66 and the U.S. 1.85 ratio, is the compromise solution.

The Rules of Composition

Editors evaluate shots for quality. One criterion is how well the shot is composed. Determining whether something is well composed often depends on the arbitrator and his or her "I'll know it when I see it" answer. However, there are rules to help you understand what to look for as you begin evaluating footage.

The Rule of Thirds

This is the most widely used rule of composition. The rule of thirds is based on the principle of the *Golden Mean*, which was first articulated by the ancient Greeks. The frame is divided into thirds horizontally and vertically. Objects that are placed along the lines create pleasing compositions. The points where the lines intersect are the most interesting places in the frame. This is where you should place any objects that you want to emphasize.

The 180-Degree Axis of Action Rule

By following the *180-degree Axis of Action Rule*, you ensure that the screen direction of the subjects remains consistent. For example, in a two-shot of a man and a woman, the man looks right and the woman looks left. If the camera operator follows the 180-degree rule, the man will look right and the woman will look left in the close-ups. This enables the editor to cut from the two-shot to a close-up. If the camera operator breaks the 180-degree rule, the editor can't cut from the two-shot to the close-up without calling

attention to the cut because the screen direction of one or both subjects will be reversed in the close-ups. As a result, the man may look left instead of right and the woman look right instead of left or the man and woman may have the identical screen direction (both looking right or left) in the close-ups.

This is an example of the consequences. In the two-shot, the man looks right. We cut to his close-up. He looks left. Where is the woman? Cut back to the two-shot. Now he's looking right again and she's on his right. If you continue to do this, the poor fellow will keep flip-flopping around.

The rule works because the camera operator draws a line through the subjects. The line represents the diameter of an imaginary circle around the subjects. The camera is placed on one side of the circle, which is why it's called the 180-degree axis of action rule. The camera can move anywhere on that 180-degree side of the circle as long as the camera doesn't cross the diameter line. If it does cross the line, the screen direction of the subjects will be reversed.

Framing Subjects

Framing is another criterion editors use to evaluate the quality of a shot. The subject should be framed so that there is breathing room or a modicum of space around them. The following sections describe the four space considerations for good framing.

The Essential Area

The essential area is the portion of the frame that will always be seen. Some editing systems can display a grid in the viewer indicating the portion of the image that is within the essential area or title safe. For video production, the essential area is considered 80 percent of the picture's center. This area will be displayed on every television no matter how badly the television set is aligned or misadjusted. In film production, the entire negative is rarely projected. Instead, as we mentioned in our discussion of aspect ratios, the projectionist masks part of the image. In video or film, the boundaries of the essential area are determined by what the audience sees.

If important objects or subjects fall outside the essential area, the editor should mark the shot as unusable. If the audience can't see it, the shot is worthless.

Look Space

Audiences become uncomfortable when subjects are framed too close to the vertical edge of the frame. Proper framing provides extra space in the direction that the subject looks. For reasons that should be obvious, look space is also called *noseroom* when the subject is a person.

Walk Space

The same rule that applies to look space applies to walk space. Proper framing provides extra space in the direction the subject is moving.

Headroom

Headroom refers to the space between the top of the subject's head and the edge of the frame. In general, if the subject's eyes are placed on a line that is one third from the top edge, the proper amount of headroom will be present. (See the rule of thirds.)

Isolating Shots

Editors evaluate material by looking for shots that communicate clearly are well-framed and have pleasing compositions. As you watch your footage, ask yourself the following questions. Does the shot communicate anything? Will the audience be able to read it? If the footage contains action, where does it start? Where does it end? What's the subject of the shot? What are the best parts? An editor's guiding principle is to look for shots that are clean, clear, and understandable.

Now that you understand what you're looking for, isolating shots (locating the tips of icebergs) should be a lot easier. When you spot an iceberg tip, mark an IN point. Then look for the OUT point. Play the IN to the OUT point. Use loop play (play in/out) when you're first learning to isolate shots, if it's available on your editing system. Consider whether the shot you've marked can start later or end sooner. If it can, adjust the IN and OUT points. Each shot should start at the last possible moment and end at the first possible moment. After you've trimmed the shot all the way down, you have the tip of an iceberg. The final step is to save the tip and name it.

Here are a few tips to help you get started as you begin isolating shots in your footage. Mark an IN point where the action starts. Mark an OUT point where it ends. Mark INs and OUTs at the beginning and end of moving shots, such as pans, tilts, or dollies. With interviews or testimonials, make each succinct statement a shot.

Creating Subclips

Subclips are fragments of a longer clip. If you've followed our suggestions about how to transfer footage into your editing system, each clip in your editing system contains a scene. You'll need to break the scene down into smaller shot-sized portions, which are called *subclips*. You can subclip (make copies) of a larger clip on most editing systems. The idea is to create multiple clips, which contain individual shots, from the larger clip, which contains the entire scene.

For example, the birdhouse scene from your trip to the zoo might include close-ups of different birds. The scene clip is called BIRD HOUSE. Find the moment where the first close-up begins, which is of a blue parrot, and mark an IN. Locate the end of the close-up and mark an OUT. Play from the IN point to the OUT point using loop play to determine if the shot you've marked is clean, clear, and understandable. Your IN and OUT points should only include the essence of the shot. Change your IN or OUT points if it will make the shot clearer, cleaner, or more understandable. Then, name and save this subclip to a bin.

Naming Subclips—Short and Unique

Subclips should have short unique names. Some editing systems automatically fill in the name of the original clip and add the word *copy* or a number to differentiate the new subclip from the original one.

In our example, the editing system is likely to name the subclip of the close-up of the blue parrot as BIRD HOUSE1. As you can tell, that's not very descriptive. A better name would be BLUE PARROT because it describes the clip. Later, when you're searching for shots, BLUE PARROT will jog your memory and help you recall what the shot looks like. The best choice for naming a subclip is to use a simple description.

It's common to have multiple shots of the identical subject with different fields of view or different angles. In this case, you'll need to find another aspect, beyond a description, to name these subclips and differentiate between the four BLUE PARROT shots.

A good strategy is to use the shot descriptions. For example, you might have BLUE PARROT—ECU, BLUE PARROT—MCU, BLUE PARROT LOW, and BLUE PARROT TILT. This information will make it easier to identify the shots whether you're using a list view or picon view of the bin. If possible, label the picons with the name you've given the subclip. Picons are often small. It can be difficult to differentiate between two shots that have a nearly identical picon, such as BLUE PARROT TILT and BLUE PARROT—ECU.

Figure 7-5
Subclips are portions of a larger cl ip.

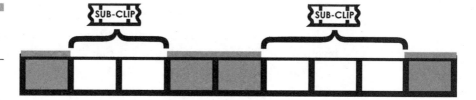

Tips for Subclips

- Don't get carried away with naming subclips. Call them what they are.

- Any name you use is more descriptive than the name your editing system will assign by default. Too much typing impedes creativity.

- Subclips are short, nondestructive copies of your original clips.

- Always leave your original clip as is.

- Always make new subclips from the original clip. In some systems, modifying the IN and OUT points on the original clips can make it confusing and difficult to reset them to their original lengths.

- Deleting the original clip deletes all the copies and subclips you make in most editing systems.

- Remember that subclips are pointers to the media files, not the media files.

Moving shots present another challenge. Imagine what the picons will look like for these four shots: PAN TO CITY BUS, ZOOM TO CITY BUS, FOLLOW PAN OF CITY BUS, and CITY BUS—MS. In this example, the picons, which are still images, will end up being identical. The descriptive name is the only way to tell these subclips apart unless you play them.

Another tip is to use the conceptual shot descriptions where appropriate. For example, say you plan to use a shot of a city street for the EST shot in your show. Make a subclip and name that shot CITY STREET—EST, which is your description for editing purposes.

Another Reason to Name Subclips

On most editing system timelines, the clips are arranged one after the other with their names displayed. Some editing systems can display a still or picon of the first frame in the clip or display picons for every frame in the clip, which uses up a lot of memory. If your editing system cannot display a picon and the clips aren't named, you'll have a lot of trouble editing on the timeline. Editing is easy when you have descriptive names and extremely frustrating when you don't.

Picking Picons

A very fast way to edit is to arrange the subclips (shots) in the bin in the order you want them to play. Then edit all of them as a group onto the timeline, maintaining that order. If you've created clean, clear, and understandable subclips, your work is nearly done. Play the timeline. Then improve the rhythm and pacing by trimming or making overlaps.

This method relies on selecting picons (the picture icons) that accurately represent the shots. You need to find the frame that represents the tip of the top of the iceberg.

Editing systems automatically select the first frame of the clip or subclip. If this is a slate, the visual reference that a picon provides becomes useless. Check your editing system manual to learn how to change the frame used for the picon. If you want to save time, make sure you select the frame for the picon before you name any subclip you make. If you don't, you'll have to name the subclip, retrieve it, set the frame, and resave it.

Summary

The ability to isolate a shot, to spot the tip of the top of the iceberg, comes with experience. As you log and review footage, use the standard abbreviations to describe the shots. The keyboard shortcut to make a subclip is one of the first ones you should learn.

Important Points to Remember

- Don't get carried away with naming subclips. Call them what they are.
- Any name you use is more descriptive than the name your editing system will assign by default. Too much typing impedes creativity.

- Subclips are short, nondestructive copies of your original clips.

- Always leave your original clip as is.

- Always make new subclips from the original clip. In some systems, modifying IN and OUT points on the original clips can make it confusing and difficult to reset them to their original lengths.

- Deleting the original clip deletes all the copies and subclips you make in most editing systems.

- Remember that subclips are pointers to the media files, not the media files.

The Frosting

Effects are like the frosting on a cake. Bakers add the frosting after the cake is baked. The most efficient approach in a digital environment is to add the effects after you've told the story.

Desktop Special Effects

It once took millions of dollars of equipment to create the simplest video effect. Today, almost anything can be created on a home computer. The only difference between what you can do at home and what a professional does in a postproduction facility comes down to speed and experience. Professionals can manipulate images, move layers, and create animated wonders in seconds. These identical effects can also be done on a desktop system; however, it will take considerably longer to do because professionals work with more horsepower in their high-end systems. Although this chapter won't turn you into an experienced special effects wizard, it can help you understand how to use special effects in the editing process.

Most editing systems present a clear picture of any effects in the timeline. You can see all the video clips, any effects placed on adjacent clips, or any effects stacked vertically. The ability to see the overall structure of the effects in your show is invaluable. Digital editing has made building effects a visual rather than conceptual process.

Editors take some special effects for granted. Digital editing makes it possible to play a clip in reverse at speeds that are faster or slower than normal, or freeze the clip and transform full-motion video into a still image. Transitions are easy to apply and modify. You can add titles and graphics in a few simple steps. Most editing systems even let you manipulate the individual pixels in a frame of digital video. You can move, shrink, expand, tumble, and flip your footage. You are only limited by your imagination and the flexibility of your editing system.

Special effects can be used to entertain, explain, or impress the audience. They help keep audiences interested. However, they're not the story. Professionals understand that no amount of special effects can save a show that doesn't tell a decent story. Effects, which are affectionately called *bells and whistles*, have often been misused or overused. As a result, they have gained a bad reputation. Regardless, there are more shows with effects than without them. Special effects are prominently used in commercials and television promos. They add sizzle and pizzazz.

One important use of effects is that they fix problems so the audience never sees them. Luckily, the near limitless capacity that people have for making mistakes is matched by the vast array of repair tools included in a digital editing system. The tools consist of the same special effects that are capable of creating magical manipulations of the image. The best reason for an editor to study and understand effects comes down to the prosaic—digital special effects are the best tools for fixing problems when they arise.

A Digital Approach to the Effects Workflow

An editor's primary focus is to assemble a show that tells a story. The editor makes choices about the pictures and sounds that will be used to tell that story. It's counterproductive to focus on the intricacies involved with effects when you're doing the rough cut. Keep it simple. Use the cut as your basic transition from shot to shot. Unadorned transitions reveal how your show flows in its rawest form.

If you create effects as you progressively build the show, there's always the chance that you'll add an effect prematurely. When you're shaping the story during the rough cut, clips are being rearranged, deleted, and swapped in and out. It would be a waste of time to build an effect using a clip that's temporarily in your show. By adding effects after the story is completed, you enhance the material that's made the final cut.

Desktop space is always at a premium when you're editing. There are open bins, toolbars, and viewers. The additional windows and toolbars needed to make an effect only add to the clutter. If you concentrate on one task at a time, you can reduce the number of open windows on the desktop.

Types of Effects

Effects fall into two categories—clip effects, which are applied to a single clip or subclip, and timeline effects, which are applied to multiple clips. Clip effects can be made at any point during editing. These effects are stored as subclips in a bin. Timeline effects can only be made on the timeline. Wait until after the rough cut is completed to begin working on timeline effects.

Clip Effects

Clip effects are changes to the properties of an existing clip. Professionals often experiment with effects before they choose the one they want. The standard procedure is to make a duplicate of the existing clip and save it. Use the duplicate clip for your experiments. If you make a permanent change to the original clip, it can be time consuming to undo some clip effects.

Timeline-Based Effects

Timeline effects are those that combine multiple sources. A transition is a typical timeline effect that combines two adjacent clips. A dissolve or wipe would be an example of this type of timeline effect. A different kind of timeline effect involves combining clips that are stacked above each other. These effects are called *layered effects*. Superimposing a title graphic over video is an example of this effect. Stacking multiple layers on a clip or clips in a unified sequence is called *compositing*. Compositing involves complex layering, which is covered in Chapter 9, "Gilding the Lily." Occasionally, a timeline effect might involve only one clip. The other source is often generated by the effect itself—for example, when a patterned mask is applied to a clip.

Typical Clip Effects

The following section presents a few of the common clip effects.

Playback Speed

The normal frame rate for video is 29.97 *frames per second* (fps) in North America (NTSC standard[1]) or 25 fps in Europe (PAL standard[2]). In most systems, the editor can change the frame rate or modify the speed as a percentage of normal. You can create fast or slow motion. Reversing the motion may involve changing the frame rate or using a negative number. The

---

[1]National Television Standards Committee.
[2]Phase Alternating Line.

minus sign (–) is often used for reverse and the plus (≤) is used for forward. Every editing system seems to come up with a new wrinkle on how to modify speed. Sometimes speed is listed as part of the clip's properties. *Fit to fill* is a special type of speed effect. This effect is used to expand or contract the duration of clip to fill a gap in the timeline. The clip slows down if it's too short and speeds up if it's too long.

Strobe

A strobe creates a stuttered effect. Motion that is normally smooth looks staccato. The strobe effect works by freezing a frame in the clip, holding the freeze, and then releasing the freeze a few frames later before the cycle begins again. In some editing systems, a quick succession of still frames is called a *strobe effect*.

Freeze

This effect turns a field or frame in a video clip into a still image. Whenever a clip is paused, the editing system displays a still image or freeze. Most editing systems let you save this image as a clip in a bin. Some editing systems give the editor discretion to choose between a field or frame freeze. It's important to know the difference between the two types. Each video frame has two distinct fields. When you freeze a clip, the picture may flutter. This happens because the fields are displaying slightly different pictures of the action. When the two fields are combined, the image on the screen appears to flutter back and forth. It's inappropriate for a still picture, unless the sub-

A Shooting Tip

Shoot action at a high shutter speeds if you plan to use slow motion. A higher shutter speed, such as 1/125th, 1/250th, or 1/500th of a second, will capture a very sharp picture. When you slow the footage down in your editing system, the individual frames will be much sharper than if you shoot at the normal shutter speed, which is a 1/60th (or 1/50th in PAL) of a second.

ject is a hummingbird. If you use the field freeze setting, the problem will be solved. Our rule of thumb is to use a frame freeze unless there's rapid motion that causes a flutter.

Whether the freeze is one field or one frame, it must be processed as normal video for display and output to tape. To do this, your editing system must create a media file. If the freeze is a field freeze, the editing system has to duplicate your chosen field or create a second field to make a complete frame. Usually, you can choose to use duplication or interpolation. Sometimes you can produce a better looking freeze if you choose interpolation instead of duplication. With some editing systems, you have no choice; it's all done automatically.

Color

Color correction—manipulating the red, green, and blue channels in video —is a clip effect. The amount of control you have over the video image will depend on the sophistication of your editing system.

Editing systems modify color by adjusting the *hue, saturation, and luminance* (HSL) or the *red, green, and blue* (RGB) components. If you have the choice, use the controls with which you're most comfortable.

Most editing systems include some basic color correction tools. These are usually enough for simple tasks like correcting the white balance of a clip. For example, if the footage was shot outdoors with the color correction filter set to indoors, the resulting images will have an overall blue cast. This problem can be fixed using the color tools that are available in most editing systems to remove the blue.

Color correction tools can also be used to match color, brightness, and tone from one shot to the next. After the editing is completed, you can go through your show shot by shot and adjust the color to achieve a uniform look. This gives your show an integrity that is sure to be noticed by the audience.

You can create special image treatments by tinting clips; this is one of the most useful clip effects. For example, applying a brown sepia tone tint can give the footage an antique or period look. On many systems, tints are applied as filters. The editor usually has control over color and opacity. It's a good idea to save any filter settings you modify for reuse later. If your editing system can't save these settings for use with other projects, write down the settings in a notebook. That way you won't have to start from scratch every time.

What Is White Balance?

Most digital camcorders have a setting for indoor and outdoor lighting. Why? Legendary WCAU-TV broadcaster Gene Crane, who's been on the air since the day the station opened in 1948, explains it this way: "You've got to teach the camera what white is."

Think about it this way. If you open a book in a candlelit room, the pages appear white. If you go outside and open the book, the pages are still white. However, candlelight is yellow and the light outdoors has a blue cast because of the sky. Our brains automatically compensate for the differences because we expect the pages to be white. To compensate for the differences in the color of the light, camcorders have a white balance setting.

Some camcorders let you set a manual white balance. The method is simple. Aim the camera, fill the frame with a white object, and press the button to set the white balance. The camera makes that object look pure white. You can fool the camera to make a warmer (redder) or colder (bluer) picture by aiming the camera at an object that isn't white. A light blue piece of paper makes the picture warmer and a light red piece of paper makes the picture colder. This should make sense because red and blue are opposites. Diminishing one increases the other.

How to Tint Clips The first step in the process is to duplicate the clip if possible. Then get rid of the color on the duplicate clip by adjusting the saturation to zero. This should leave you with a black and white image. Next, manipulate the red, green, or blue controls to tint the clip. Save the tinted version of the clip.

The following are a few more of the common clip effects.

Negative

Reverses the color values and creates what appears to be a photographic negative.

Solarization

Reverses the highlight and shadow values. This effect makes the white values dark and silvery, and makes the black values bright and shiny.

Posterization

Reduces the color values in the image from millions to a relative handful. Limiting the number of colors creates banding in areas of graduated color. The image often looks like a 1980s music video.

Flip (flop)

Results in an upside-down image if the image is rotated on its horizontal or x axis (width). If the image is rotated on its vertical or y axis (height), the image will be a backwards or mirror image. A backwards shot comes in handy every now and then. As long as there are no visible indicators of direction, such as the steering wheel of a car or lettering on a sign, a backwards or mirror image can correct a shot taken from the wrong angle. You can also flip a shot to use it twice. For example, a shot of an airplane flying left to right could be used to represent taking a trip from Los Angeles to New York and when flipped, the shot can be used for the New York to Los Angeles return. It's not part of the production planning process, but flipping a shot demonstrates how you can solve a problem inexpensively. When producers say we'll fix it in post, this is one of things they mean.

The Workflow for Clip Effects

The way you create effects varies from editing system to editing system. However, the workflow remains the same. Select the clip you want to use. Duplicate the clip. Select an effect and apply it to the duplicate clip. Adjust the settings using the tools in your editing system. There might be a drop-down menu, tool palette, or dialog box for adjustments. Preview the effect and make further adjustments, if necessary. When you're satisfied, save the clip with the effect in a bin. Edit this clip onto the timeline. Then play the timeline to see how the effect works in your show. If you're satisfied, you

The Basics of Video Color

Digital editing systems manipulate color using either the Hue, Saturation, and Luminance (HSL) or Red, Green, Blue (RGB) models. If you'll be adjusting values and changing colors, you should understand how each model works. It is equally important to understand that video color space is smaller than the color space displayable on a computer monitor. This means you can create or modify colors that cannot be reproduced in video. Digital video describes the values for each color channel on a scale from 0 (black) to 255 (white). The legal limits are 16 to 235 for video in a broadcast environment. Anything above or below these values will be clipped. This might not make much sense unless you are in front of your editing system. You can click on a color and display its numeric values to check whether it's within the limit. Highly saturated colors are the ones that can cause the problems.

Hue, Saturation, and Luminance

Video signals contain information about color: the chroma and hue, and luminance or brightness. *Chroma* is an abbreviation of chrominance, which refers to the amount of color or saturation in the image. Hue is the specific point on a color wheel or the value on the color spectrum that indicates the actual color we see. Luminance is the black and white portion of the signal.

Saturation, unless your show must meet broadcast standards, is like salt. Adjust to taste. Create rich colors, pale pastels, or lower the saturation to zero for a black and white image.

Luminance describes the black and white information in the image. Video has brightness and contrast values regardless of the color information. Brightness adjusts the overall level of the image from black to white. Contrast changes the gray values. As you lower the contrast, you will see more midtones (gray values) and the image will appear flatter. As you raise the contrast, you will see fewer midtones. Eventually, the image becomes all black and all white.

Red, Green, and Blue

Video cameras record color as components of the primary colors red, green, and blue.

The green channel provides the luminance information for the image. Typically, each channel is independently adjustable using *color gain*.

(continues)

(*continued*)

Gamma adjusts the midtones or gray values in the image without affecting the extreme black or extreme white values.

The *Black Level* adjusts the black or shadow areas of the picture. The *Black Point* is a black level in the picture that the editor uses for reference black. For example, if a dark gray value is used for the Black Point instead of a black value, any graduations between dark gray and true black will become pure black. The *White Level* adjusts the white or highlight areas of the picture. The *White Point* sets a white portion of the picture to pure white and any values above it are clipped to white. These set points are used when the editor makes color adjustments.

Secondaries and Vectorscopes

A secondary color is a mixture of two primary colors. Cyan is a combination of blue and green. Magenta is a combination of red and blue. Yellow is a combination of green and red. Both primary and secondary colors are represented in the SMPTE[3] color bar test signal. If your editing system has a *vectorscope*, you can display a color bar signal as a circular graphic. Check it out. It looks cool, but it has no purpose if you're transferring video in and out of your editing system via Firewire or another digital transport standard.

---

[3]Society of Motion Picture and Television Engineers.

can move on to the next effect you want to add. If you're not, readjust the effects settings until you achieve the look you want.

On some editing systems, you can make those adjustments directly on the timeline. Other systems force you to go back to the beginning and start over. If you find yourself doing this, prepare alternate versions when you're building effects. For example, experiment with slow motion and store clips with different speeds in a bin. Later, when you're editing the slow-motion clip on the timeline, you'll be able to select from a variety of speeds.

Integrating Effects with Match Frame

Cutting from a normal speed to slow motion can be jarring. Slow-motion effects are fine when a shot is seen in isolation. If you cut to an off-speed shot, the audience may feel disoriented. Editors soften the blow by dissolving from off-speed to normal-speed shots. However, if you want to change the speed in the middle of a shot, a different approach is required.

Imagine that you want a shot of a bicycle rider to transition from normal to slow motion fluidly. The method of doing this is to match cut from a frame in the clip to which you've applied a slow-motion effect to the identical frame in the original (normal-speed) clip. Many editing systems have a button or feature that lets you find the frame of a clip on the timeline and the same frame on the clip that's in a bin. If you don't have a match frame feature, you'll need to use the time code number for the frame you want to match. The time code is for the source clip on the timeline. Write down the time code address on a piece of paper. Then find the clip to which you've applied the slow-motion effect. Find the frame that matches the point at which you want to transition from normal to slow motion. Finding the correct frame is easy, but it takes time. This frame will be the IN point (where you switch from normal to slow motion) for the slow-motion clip and the OUT point for the normal-speed clip. Edit the two shots together on the timeline to make the transition from a normal to slow-motion action.

Display

In order to see an effect as you're building it, your editing system must be able to display the results on your desktop and/or video monitor. There might be a dedicated viewer window that displays effects. In single-viewer editing systems, the effects will appear in the multipurpose viewer window. Remember to close any unnecessary windows when you build effects. Creating effects uses up a lot of memory and processing power. Your computer must be running efficiently when you work with effects.

Previews

Most editing systems can create a *snapshot*—a one-frame representation of what an effect will look like or a scrub preview that lets you see one frame at a time as you advance through the effect. If an effect involves movement from one point to another, you might only see points plotted on a simple line drawing with arrows or other indicators for direction, speed, and position. This is called a *wireframe preview*.

Real-Time Previews Versus Real-Time Playback

Faster computers with more memory allow system manufacturers to tout what they call *Areal-time effects* for digital editing. In fact, most are real-time previews, not real-time effects. When you combine two DV sources, a new media file must be created. The data has to be uncompressed and recompressed in the DV format before it can be output to the Firewire port. Real-time playback is only possible when you have specialized hardware. The capabilities of the hardware determine what can be played back in real time (the number of video layers or streams) and the image quality of that material. Video channels are called *streams*. Two video streams are required to create a dissolve in real time. If you're working on effects that require more streams than those available on your editing system, you must render the effect to see full-motion playback.

Rendering

Rendering means creating a media file for the effect you've built. After you create the media file, the effect will behave like any clip and play normally. Rendering takes time. Depending on the speed of your system, you can take a nice break when rendering. Once an effect has been rendered, it can be used as an element in another effect. That composite can be rendered. Another effect can be added to it and so on. One disadvantage is that if you want to change any aspect of a rendered effect, you'll have to rerender it before it will play normally.

Rendering and Video Streams

In the context of cooking, rendering means boiling off the fat. Of course, this is not what happens in your editing system. Baking is a better analogy for effects rendering. You create effects in the same way as you bake a cake. First, you mix together all of the ingredients to make a batter. Unless you bake the batter for the proper amount time at the correct temperature, you don't have a cake. A cake takes as long as it takes to bake. You can't bake it any faster.

Rendering is a fact of life unless you have unlimited amounts of processing power. In high-end postproduction facilities, no rendering is required. Time is money. Advertising agency and broadcast clients don't have time to wait for effects to be rendered. In fact, most pay handsomely for the privilege of avoiding rendering. These customers expect to be able see and change complex effects instantly.

Anyone with talent can replicate effects produced on a high-end system. The only difference is the amount of time it will take to create and render the effect. The results are the same because the process is the same. The good news is that processing power is increasing rapidly, and faster, cheaper hardware is moving us toward a day when multilayered effects will be as fast and easy to do on the desktop as they are on million-dollar systems.

Rendering Strategies

Rendering takes time, which can affect an editor's creative process. Once you've built up a rhythm and are working steadily, you might not want to stop and take a break. If you've previewed the effect and feel comfortable with its appearance, you can postpone rendering until you are ready to stop and take a break. Every editing system we've seen has a *render all* feature that will render any effects that need to be rendered as a group. Professionals use this time to take the client to lunch or catch a break. Afterwards, all of the effects are ready to be played in real time. If all goes well, the editing proceeds.

Types of Timeline Effects

As in life, timing is everything in editing. The transition from one shot to the next should be seamless so that continuity is maintained, or, in the case of montage, the theme is reinforced and kept intact. Cuts are the cleanest transitions if placed correctly. When a cut doesn't work, other types of transitions can take the viewer from one shot to the next. Transitions must be done on the timeline. These effects are added after the clips are in the correct order. Dissolves and wipes are the next most common transitions after the cut.

Fades and Dissolves

A fade is the gradual appearance of a new picture from black or the gradual disappearance of the picture to black. A dissolve is two fades that occur at the same time. The outgoing clip fades to black while the incoming clip fades up from black at the same time. As a result, the two shots blend together. A dissolve from a clip to black is called a *fade to black*. The dissolve is commonly used to signal the passage of time or space in a seamless way. Dissolves can create a poetry of motion by blending together disparate shots. Dissolves are also used to soften visual transitions in effects. For example, if you want a series of playing cards to magically appear in the dealer's hand, you could start with the first shot that depicts the dealer holding a single playing card. Then, you'd edit a second shot from the identical perspective that depicts the dealer with two cards. Follow that shot with another that depicts the dealer holding three cards. If you use cuts, the cards will pop into his hands. If you dissolve between the shots, the cards will flow into his hand.

Dissolves are almost always used to add titles or graphics to a show. Most start out completely transparent and over time become opaque. Most shows begin with a dissolve up from black and end with a dissolve to black. If you watch television, you see hundreds of dissolves everyday without realizing it. A dissolve is like white bread in the world of effects.

Wipe

A wipe is a transition between two adjacent clips where one image replaces the other using a geometric pattern. For example, one image is revealed under the other as the vertical edge of the *top* image moves across the screen from left to right in a *wiping* motion. This classic film transition was called *The Wipe* and now every patterned transition is known as a wipe. It's important to note that all wipe effects, such as a circle, heart shaped, box shaped, clock wipe, and so on, are masking patterns on full-sized images.

Displaying Transitions on a Timeline

Two methods are used to display and apply transitions to a timeline. The most common view is the single-track approach. Transitions are affixed to adjoining clips on a single video track by dragging, dropping, or editing them on the dividing line between the two shots. The transition effect overlaps both from and to the clip. Some systems call this a *single-layered effect*.

The other method uses a diagrammatic display with two video tracks that are labeled A and B. The A track holds the outgoing (or from) clip and the B track shows the incoming (or to) clip. The A track is placed above the B track. The effect applies to the portion of the A and B tracks that overlap.

The straight-line, single-track display is the more common. It's simpler and requires less desktop space. The A/B display has an advantage, especially for beginners, because it shows each clip's frames. The usual highlighting of these extra frames (handles) acts as a visual guide for determining the extent and position of the overlapping shots and the duration of the transition effect. After you're comfortable with the concept of overlapping clips, the A/B model loses its appeal.

Handles for Successful Transitions

To make a successful transition, the clips on the timeline must be long enough to complete the effect. Each clip needs *handles*, which are the extra frames necessary to overlap the adjacent clip. If no handles are available or

Figure 8-1
A and B track display indicates the overlapping contents of a transition on the timeline.

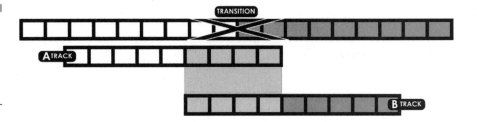

if there are fewer frames than the desired duration of the transition, it will be impossible to create the effect. Typically, this occurs when an IN or OUT point of the clip on the timeline is at, or very near, the beginning or end of the clip in the bin.

Solving Transition Problems

If you have trouble with a transition effect, you should be able to solve the problem by changing the properties of the effect. The following are three tactics you should try (in order of priority):

- *Shorten the duration.* This sounds simple, but it works. If there's not enough media, try a shorter dissolve. For example, if you want 40 frames, try a 30-frame dissolve and you might just have enough media to do the dissolve.

- *Change the point on the timeline where the transition takes place.* Ordinarily, transitions take place at the edit point between the outgoing and incoming

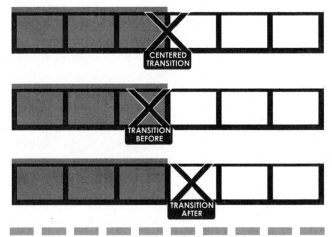

Figure 8-2
Three possible placements of transitions.

clips. If one clip has an insufficient number of frames, move the effect earlier so the transition is completed before the clip runs out of frames (see Figure 8-2).

- *Adjust the clips involved in the transition.* Move the OUT point of the outgoing clip earlier or move the IN point of the incoming clip forward. The trim tools are often integrated into the tools used to edit transitions.

Workflow for Timeline Effects

The following are the steps for creating timeline effects.

Select the Area of the Timeline

Begin by selecting the area on the timeline where you plan to apply an effect. This could be a single clip, multiple clips, a section, or the entire timeline. Remember to only include the tracks to which the effect should be applied.

Select the Effect and Apply It

Next decide on the effect you'd like to use. Experiment with the settings using the preview feature. When you're satisfied with the results, apply the effect to the timeline.

Adjust the Effect

Once the effect has been applied to the selected area, you might need to finish building the effect on the timeline. You'll need to modify and adjust the settings to fit the effect seamlessly into your show.

Building effects can be painstaking work. There are so many choices and possible combinations of timing, color, motion, and style to choose from that just selecting the appropriate effect can be time consuming. If you're working with a partner or client, this time factor increases exponentially. This is why we don't recommend working in groups to do effects.

Review the Effect

Effects that involve transitions and movement change the flow of the show and should be reviewed at normal speed. Play the timeline. Notice how the rhythm of the show is altered by the effect. If the effect won't play, you must render it. Previewing effects frame by frame is only helpful to a point. Because it takes time to render effects, make sure you get it right before you render.

Summary

First, learn how to change clip properties. Then become familiar with your editing system's timeline effects. After you have a firm understanding of these fundamentals, move on to layering and keying, which are covered Chapter 9, "Gilding the Lily."

Important Points to Remember

- Effects are the frosting on the cake and should be applied at the end of the project.
- Effects can be applied to individual clips or to multiple clips on the timeline.
- Some editing systems can preview effects in real time. Others require effects to be rendered.
- For efficiency, render effects as a group.
- Store effects parameters, in a folder or bin if possible, for reuse later.

Gilding
the Lily

In Chapter 8, "The Frosting," we explained how to add effects to a single clip and how to combine two clips in a transitional effect on the timeline. In this chapter, we'll take effects to the next level—literally.

What's Compositing?

Composites are images that are combinations of shots and other elements. This term has its roots in film production. Originally, composites were made in the camera or with special equipment at a film laboratory. With digital video, you can make composites on your editing system. For Steve Owen of Quantel, the difference between editing and compositing is simple. "Stringing frames next to each other is called editing. Stacking them one on top of the other is called compositing." This is the most concise definition we've ever heard.

Composites are constructed on the timeline. A composite is made from two or more elements. In digital video, an element is a layer on the timeline. Layering and compositing are two words with identical meanings. Shots and other elements on the timeline are placed in vertically stacked layers, one on top of the other, which are then combined.

Your editing system has tools that enable you to adjust the transparency of any of these layers. The layers can become like sheets of transparent plastic. Any sections of the layers above the background that are transparent will allow the background to show through. This is how a title graphic can appear to float in the foreground above a video background. We consider titles to be special effects, whether they're white text over a black background or part of a colorful, animated, dazzling sequence. Learning the fundamentals of title placement, movement, and manipulation is a good way to understand compositing. Once you master titles, you can expand your repertoire with more sophisticated effects.

Why Titles?

Titles serve many purposes. They're used at the beginning for the show title and at the end for the credits. Titles are used to reinforce concepts in the body of the show. They're used to paraphrase narration, display sports scores, and provide instructions. The titles that identify an individual are often called *lower thirds* because that's where the title appears in the lower third of the picture. Titles are also used to identify time and place (see Figure 9-1).

The Basics of Title Design

Every editing system has a tool or application that can generate text files for use in digital editing. These title utilities have different capabilities and features. However, all of them are capable of basic text creation. When you create a title, you have to make style choices. The sum of all the choices you make represents the *look* (appearance) of the title. The creation of that look is called a *text treatment*.

Type Fonts

Fonts are different styles of type. Fonts are differentiated by the thickness of the strokes that form the letters and the way the letters are drawn. Many

Figure 9-1
A lower third title treatment.

editing systems use the hundreds of TrueType fonts already loaded on the computer. Type font managers are available that display a line of type in each font's style as you move through the list on your computer. Some title tools also provide this feature. This makes it easy to see the choices so you can make an appropriate selection quickly. Otherwise, you will have to recall the appearance of the font from memory.

Thin wispy letters don't show up well on the screen. Bold and medium fonts are always highly legible. It's simply a matter of how monitors function. Ideally, the fonts you select should have smooth letters. The rectangular pixels in digital video can make curves, circles, or diagonal lines appear to have stair-stepped edges. This is known as *aliasing*. Many programs have an anti-aliasing feature that makes those stair steps appear smooth.

Type Size

Type size is measured in points or scan lines. Bigger and bolder is better for titles (and interfaces). If the font is too small, it will be difficult to read. You can also adjust the kerning (the space between characters) and leading (the space between the lines) to improve readability.

From our experience, a font size of 24 points or 20 scan lines is about as low as most editors will go except perhaps for the fine print in a car commercial. A reliable way to check the type size for a title is to view the monitor at a distance of 10 to 15 feet. If you can't read the title, it's probably too small.

Choose Type Colors

You can fill type with any color, which can be solid or blended. The amount of color saturation that digital video can handle successfully is limited. This is generally not a problem with your internal text generator, which is designed for digital video. However, image-editing applications, such as Adobe Photoshop or JASC Paint Shop Pro, can create titles that have colors outside the color space boundaries of digital video and won't display properly on a monitor.

Always evaluate the colors you're considering over the background. Choose contrasting colors for legibility. For example, yellow text over a blue sky is highly readable.

Add an Edge

Adding an edge (a border or shadow) to the type will improve the legibility of a title (see Figure 9-2). The shadow can be a depth or drop shadow. You can add color to the edges in most systems. Some editing systems give you control over the thickness and softness of the edge (see Figure 9-3).

Figure 9-2
A title with a drop shadow edge treatment.

Figure 9-3
A title with a glow edge treatment.

Add a Text Object

Some title tools let you create simple objects, such as boxes and circles, which can be filled with color or a blend of colors. If a busy background would make it difficult to read the text, you can use these objects to create a background. Thin narrow boxes are used to create an underlined rule. Usually, a wide range of patterns is available to fill text or text objects with which you can experiment.

Set Transparency

Titles are usually opaque. However, you can adjust the transparency of the letters or objects if you want the background to show through. The transparency is usually adjusted to blend a text object with the background (see Figure 9-4).

Figure 9-4
A title over a
transparent box.

Types of Titles

Full Screen

Titles can be created as full-screen artwork. You can create a still image with text and an interesting background to use as a full-frame graphic. If the image isn't live action, it falls under the category of graphics. A text title over a color background is the simplest form of graphic (see Figure 9-5).

Over Video

Titles are usually over video backgrounds. This is standard for most title tools. When you make a title, the letters you type are filled with the colors you selected. At the same time, an alpha channel mask is created. At the technical level, an outline of each letter is created that defines which areas will be opaque or transparent. The outline is a mask called an *alpha channel*. The mask enables the colored letters to be combined with the video background.

Figure 9-5
A full screen graphic.

Rolls

Rolls are titles that move up or down and disappear off screen. This type of title is often used for the credits at the end of a show. Rolling titles add movement to long lists of information.

Crawls

Crawls are titles that move across the screen from left to right. They are used primarily in television. Crawls work best when the movement corresponds to the direction in which the language is read. In English, crawls should appear from the right and move left.

Type-on Titles

Titles can arrive onscreen any number of ways. You can *type on* a title so a letter, word, or line appears onscreen one at a time. Type-on titles are also called *reveals* because the text characters are revealed over time. If a reveal is used for a text list or other full-screen graphic, it's called a *graphic build*.

Editors create graphic builds in reverse. First, the full title (the final image) that the audience sees is created and saved. Then the editor deletes a line and saves this version as a new title. The process is repeated for each step (build). Each step is saved as a separate title. When the titles are placed in the opposite order they were created, the audience will see the lines of text build to the full title. If you use dissolves between each graphic, each line will appear to fade up. It's a simple trick.

Adding Motion

Most digital editing systems let you move text and/or objects across the screen on the x (horizontal) and y (vertical) axes with scale and rotation. Some systems can also move text and objects on the z axis closer or farther away from the surface plane of the monitor. Movement adds production value with relatively little effort (see Figure 9-6). Television promos (the commercials for the shows airing on television) rely on moving titles, graphics, and effects. Don't forget to add a bit more gloss by dissolving these combinations on and off the screen.

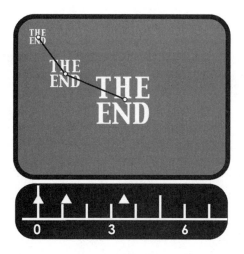

Figure 9-6
A moving title with keyframes (the triangle points).

Workflow for Title Creation

The capabilities of a title tools range from turning out basic text on a background to creating sophisticated graphic animations. Your editing system manual will have details about your title tool. This list specifies the steps most editors follow to create a title:

1. Launch the title tool or application.
2. Type the text. The default font is probably fine for turning out a quick title.
3. After you've typed the text, select the text.
4. Change the font, size, color, border, and shadow.
5. Position the title onscreen.
6. Save the title. A title clip will be created. Place the clip in the appropriate bin. Remember to name the clip. Some editing systems ask for a name before saving the title. Others use a weird default name, which is usually a cryptic number. If this is the case, rename the title so you can find it.
7. Edit the title into your show. If you want the title to be a full-frame graphic, edit the title onto an existing video track. If you want the title to appear over video, you'll probably have to place the title on its own track, which may be labeled as a graphics track, above that section of the video track. This is called *layering*, which we'll discuss in a moment.

Tips for Titles

Here are some tips to remember whenever you're creating titles:

- Check your spelling by reading the text backwards. This always works.

- When you make adjustments to the text, work from left to right using the tool palette and/or the drop-down menu bar so you don't forget any parameters you might want to change. This works especially well at first when you're unfamiliar with all the options that your title tool has to offer.

- Don't bother with auto kerning. It rarely works. Kern the letters manually to get the look you want.

- Save your title settings. Some systems call them *styles*. Others call them *title treatments*. Saving the attributes lets you to make great looking titles quickly.

The Time Anomaly

When a title is faded in or out, the convention is to use the identical duration for the incoming and outgoing fades. Even though the fades are equal in length, the fade in will appear to be faster than the fade out. This anomaly is because when we see a title fade in, we don't recognize it immediately. It's new information that's hidden. As the title becomes visible (as its transparency lessens), we notice its presence and begin to make out familiar words. Of course, because it's text, we have to grasp the words and read it. Hence, for a fade in, the first frames are not always recognizable or even understandable.

In contrast, our eyes are drawn to objects in motion and the brighter parts of the screen. When a title fades out, it appears to linger. Our eyes stay focused on it and we continue to read it. Even when it has lost almost all opacity, the title is still recognizable. We perceive that it is onscreen longer than it actually is.

Due to the physiology of how we see, in order to have a title appear to fade in and out at the same rate, you'll need to make the duration of the fade out shorter than the fade in. For example, if you use a 30-frame duration (1 second) for the fade in, a 20-frame fade out will appear to have the same duration.

Layering

A digital editing system that stacks multiple layers on the timeline resembles a wedding cake. We like this analogy because creating a show is similar to baking a wedding cake. Bakers start with ingredients, mix them together to make a batter, and bake a cake for each layer. The editor starts with a number of elements and mixes them together to create a coherent arrangement. After the cakes are baked, the baker stacks the layers for the wedding cake and applies the frosting. Frosting is a part of the cake, not the cake itself. Effects are like frosting—they are added later and are included to create an impression.

Types of Layered Effects

Superimposition is the equivalent of double exposure in photography; two images are mixed together. The term superimposition has different meanings to different manufacturers. In most systems, the term means to mix one shot over another, which results in a blend or mixture of the two shots over time. In the early days of silent movies, images were superimposed over one another by exposing the film twice—hence, the relation to double exposure. As with many film effects, this effect was recreated for use in television and the term took on new meaning. Today, a superimposition, or *super*, can also mean that a graphic is over the top of a picture. The graphic is overlaid on a fully visible background. This type of super is also called a *key* or *matte*. As you can see, this is another instance in the endless saga of confusing terms that plague the film and video industry.

Keys and Mattes

A key, or matte key, is a hole cut into the video image. The hole will be filled with another video source. There are different types of keys based on the way in which the hole or pattern is developed. In each case, the key source video is superimposed over a second video image through a pattern. The transparent portion of the key source video, which is defined by the pattern, enables the second video image to be seen.

The Origins of Compositing Terms

If you go back to the early days of silent films, you can see where the terms we use come from. Early filmmakers got the idea to mask a portion of the lens so they could have more control over double exposures. They were experimenting with new ways of storytelling.

One of their first ideas was the split screen, where two scenes appear onscreen simultaneously separated by a vertical line down the center of the frame. To accomplish this, the cameraman placed a black card in front of the lens to mask one side. After shooting the first scene, the film was rewound and reloaded into the camera. The mask was moved to the other side so the film could be exposed again. This time the side where the second scene would appear was shot and the side with the first scene was behind the mask.

As a result, the audience would see two scenes on the film image. Experimentation with different masking frames, which were called *mattes*, provided more interesting ways to film a scene. The binocular matte is arguably the most famous. Incidentally, the device that holds the matte in place was incorporated into the camera's lens shade and later became known as the *matte box*.

A typical silent film convention that best illustrates the use of a matte is the Victorian hallway scene. When a character, often a maid, wanted to spy on characters who were in another room, he or she would look through the keyhole in the door. Thus, the keyhole matte was born.

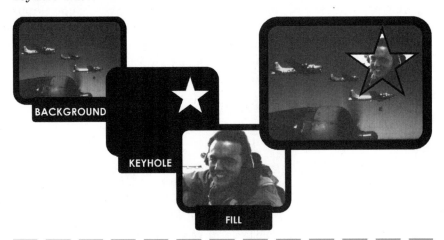

Figure 9-7
A basic key contains three elements.

Luminance Key

In this type of key, the pattern is determined by the difference between the black and white portions of the signal. The difference in contrast creates the key source—the pattern. The luminance key can be adjusted for sensitivity. It's important to adjust a luminance key to obtain a pattern with a very clean edge. This adjustment is called *clipping*. One option for a luminance key is to invert (reverse) the whites and blacks. Luminance keys were used for graphics in the early days of television. Better choices are available in the digital environment.

Chroma Key

This key is similar to the luminance key. However, the key source is created using a particular color in the source image. The idea is to create a hole using a solid color. Chroma keys are used in broadcast television to place the weather forecaster over maps and other visuals.

The forecaster is shot against a solid color wall. Any portion of the image that reveals the wall will be filled with a second video source—a weather map or whatever. When this type of key is used outside of a television studio, the subject is shot against a screen of blue or green fabric—hence, the name *blue* or *green screen work*. Blue or green screen effects can be used to cut out any object, person, or graphic in order to superimpose them over a background source. The illusion of Spiderman swinging around the city is created using this technique.

A chroma key effect can be affixed to any clip in a timeline. There are clip and color controls available for setting and adjusting the key edge. The first step is to select the hue that will be the designated chroma key color. Next, adjust the clip values for a perfect edge. Save the values for later reuse.

Matte Key

A key source with exacting dimensions can be created using a graphic image and alpha channel. Photoshop, Paint Shop Pro, and other image-editing applications can create a mask as an alpha channel. An alpha channel mask works in the same way as the other keys. A specific area defined by the alpha channel creates the keyhole. Any clip that has an alpha channel can be used as a matte. The masked area of the graphic becomes transparent when it is used over video. Because these types of mattes don't

A Shooting Tip

The color blue is most often used to key a person over a background. This is because blue does not appear in flesh tones. It's the opposite color on the color wheel and a clean hole can be cut from a blue source. Green is also used because blue is a popular color for clothing. You should always avoid using red because red appears in flesh tones and the resulting keyhole will be poorly defined.

To make the effect believable, the lighting on the subject has to match the lighting in the background footage. If you want a person to appear as if he or she is standing outdoors, use a green screen. Daylight has a blue cast because of the sky. To match the look of the outdoors, you'll need to shoot the person in the studio with a touch of blue gel on the lights. If you use a green screen, you won't have any problems with partially blue lighting.

For example, if the subject is supposed to be outdoors on a sunny day, you'll need to shoot the person so the direction of the light and shadows matches the sun in the background scene. The person needs to be lit evenly for a clean chroma key. Also make sure his or her wardrobe does not have any green colors. You will lose the effect if the background shows through the person's clothing.

depend on luminance or color, it's easy to get a clean sharp edge. A graphic with an alpha channel can be adjusted by inverting (or reversing) the alpha channel, giving you the flexibility to make what was transparent opaque.

The most common use for an alpha matte key is to position a colorful logo over video. The foreground or fill is the graphic source clip (the logo) and the background is any video clip on your timeline. The shape of the logo defines the shape of the alpha channel pattern.

Animated Mattes

An animated matte is used when moving graphics or titles are keyed over video. Compositing applications, such as After Effects, Boris Effects, or Combustion can create the necessary sequence of frames. Each frame has a corresponding alpha channel to accomplish this effect.

Elements of a Keyed Effect

All key effects consist of three elements: a background layer, which may be black, a color background, or a video source; a key source or alpha channel, which is the element that contains the pattern; and the fill or foreground layer. In the case of a chroma key or a title key, the fill layer is also the key source. The key source clip cuts a hole and, in effect, fills its own hole. This is also true for a matte key based on a graphic with an alpha channel. The fill and pattern for the graphic come from the same source. You just have to select a source for the background layer in order to complete the composite effect.

The Order of Layers

Some editing systems stack the tracks up and others stack them down. If your editing system stacks the layers up, a key will always reside on the track above its background. The background layer in a digital editing system can be one video track or multiple video tracks. Every track with a video clip positioned directly below the key source will be part of the composite effect.

Applying Effects

Editing systems apply effects on a layer or section of the timeline in a variety of ways. A typical approach is to drag and drop the effect over the appropriate section. Once the effect is placed, play or preview the results. Adjust and change the settings until you're satisfied.

Working with Layers

You should make a separate timeline for effects work. The compositing timeline can be incorporated into your show after you finish creating the effect. This approach will serve you well if you decide to do advanced effects work in another application and import the results into your editing system. If multiple timelines can be open at once in your editing system, make a scratch or garbage timeline for the effect. Copy the section of the timeline you want to use for the composite. In the new timeline, paste that section and begin working. After you've finished building the composite effect, you can cut and paste the section back into your show, replacing the original section. The advantage is that all of the individual layers are intact and available for future modification. Sometimes you must make a rendered composite to play the effect. In that case, cut and paste the rendered composite into the show timeline and save the effect timeline with the layers intact for future reference.

Nesting

Nesting is a term used in some editing systems to describe the grouping of effects layers. Nesting several layers makes it easier to move a composite effect around because it's a single container that acts like a clip. Some editing systems have unlimited video tracks and don't bother with nesting. Other systems use nesting to increase the number of video layers that can be composited because they limit the number of video tracks. Some editors use nesting as a management tool; others don't bother.

The Other DVE (Digital Video Effects)

This term is a misnomer. All the effects on your editing system are, of course, digital effects. The use of the acronym DVE reflects the point of view of video professionals who use digital equipment alongside their analog video systems. The transformation to digital video editing is nearly complete, but DVE persists. It refers loosely to the video effects devices editors once used to manipulate the video images. These proprietary devices, such as Ampex's ADO, have long since been retired to the museum of video technology. We fondly remember those outrageously expensive black boxes (think hundreds of thousands of dollars) that let us rearrange, transform, manipulate, and distort analog video. Today the same capabilities are available on your desktop for $100.

Picture in Picture

This term, which is used by editing system manufacturers, appears to be derived from marketing campaigns for television sets capable of displaying two channels at once—a small picture of a second channel overlaid on a corner of the first. This effect usually controls the scale, rotation, opacity, position, and shape of the full-frame video image. How and what you control depends on your editing system. These types of effects can offer two- or three-dimensional control over the image.

Size

The editor can manipulate the size of the image by expanding or shrinking it. The aspect ratio of an image can be maintained or changed. The technical terms for this are *scaling* and *resizing* the image (see Figure 9-8). If you want to control the height or width separately, then you'll need to manipulate the horizontal and vertical dimensions of the image, respectively. It's easy to get confused since the terms *horizontal* and *vertical* have multiple meanings. Horizontal can mean direction, as in left to right or up and down if you think in terms of raising or lowering a horizontal bar. Many editing systems treat horizontal and vertical as directions instead of following the technically correct approach—the way video images are scanned. For most editors, it makes more sense to think of vertical as the up-to-down direction and horizontal as the left-to-right direction. Another way of expressing these directions is to describe the vertical direction as the *y* axis and the horizontal direction as the *x* axis.

Figure 9-8
Resizing or scaling the picture.

Crop

This tool lets you cut the image, changing its height or width, without squeezing or expanding the image. Crop is useful for cleaning up the lines at the edges of the frame.

Perspective

A three-dimensional perspective isn't possible if your editing system can only manipulate the horizontal (x axis) and vertical (y axis) dimensions because that only adds up to two dimensions. The surface of the screen forms another plane (the z axis), which is the third dimension. If your editing system can manipulate the x, y, and z axes of the image, you can create three-dimensional effects. In a two-dimensional system, an editor can create the illusion of depth by skewing the corners of the frame. This distortion of perspective under the right circumstances can fool the audience into thinking you've manipulated the image in three dimensions. (See Figure 9-9.) Other factors can help you add to the magic.

Position

Along with expansion and contraction, the image can be placed anywhere onscreen along the horizontal (x) or vertical (y) axes. The image can also be placed outside the visible screen area in the virtual space surrounding the

Figure 9-9
Manipulating the picture to create the illusion of perspective.

video frame. This space is useful for positioning images *off stage* and smoothing the beginning and/or end of a movement.

Motion and Rotation

Images can be rotated on the horizontal (x), vertical (y), or the front-to-back (z) axis in an editing system with three-dimensional capabilities. The rotation points can be moved (the default is dead center) and repositioned to produce spins, tumbles, orbits, flips, pinwheels, cartwheels, and dozens of other interesting movements. (See Figure 9-10.) For example, the effect, which turns a flat video image into a cylinder, involves manipulating the axis of rotation on the front-to-back (z) axis.

Images, text, graphics, and video can be moved fluidly across the screen using the motion tools in your editing system. When motion is combined with rotation to skew the image, it's possible to create effects that imitate a piece of paper floating or flying through the air.

To create movement, a screen object must have a starting point, finishing point, and a duration for the movement from beginning to end. The perceived motion occurs during the time it takes to travel from the starting point to the finish point (see Figure 9-11a through 9-11c). If you want the

Figure 9-10
X, Y, and Z axes.

Figure 9-11a
Rotating the image
on the X axis.

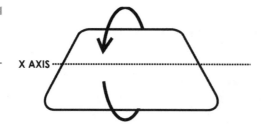

Figure 9-11b
Rotating the image
on the Y axis.

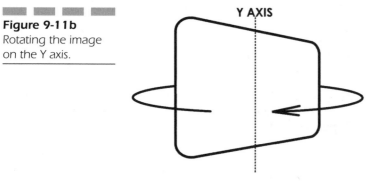

Figure 9-11c
Rotating the image
on the Z axis.

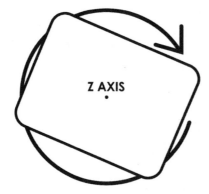

movement to appear faster, the duration of the trip must be shortened because the distance traveled will remain the same. This is a simple concept. However, it takes a bit of practice before you get a feel for moving images over time.

Keyframe

In a digital environment, the most important tool for controlling actions involving the timing of movements is the keyframe. The keyframe is a point along the effects timeline where actions can be changed. Every action must have at least two keyframes: a starting point and ending point. Whenever a change is required in the movement of an image or any parameter associated with an image, such as a pause, angle, rotation, and so on, a keyframe must be added to trigger these changes. When the effect is played back, the movement will change at those keyframe or trigger points (see Figure 9-12).

Some of the parameters that can be changed as an effect moves through time include its shape, rotation, color, borders, size, direction, speed, position, angle, softness, sharpness, and much more. In short, just about anything that can be adjusted can be readjusted at periodic intervals during

Figure 9-12
An effects timeline with keyframes (the triangle points) at each point of change.

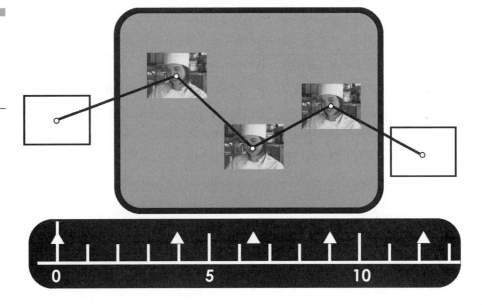

the time span an effect is onscreen. The keyframes represent these mile-stones along the path.

When the path of the movement is diagramed, the path takes on the appearance of a game of connect the dots. Each dot is a keyframe. This is called the effect's *motion path*. The motion path can begin outside the boundaries of the screen and move anywhere onscreen in x, y, and z space.

Movement along this path can be linear and abrupt or smooth. It's a cre-ative decision whether the effect moves in crisp movements or flows smoothly. The list of creative possibilities is nearly endless. Here are a few of the factors that determine the smoothness of the effects path.

Start/Stop

The amount of acceleration determines whether an effect starts with a jolt or eases off. Acceleration determines whether the effect comes to an abrupt stop or eases in. Depending on the amount of acceleration, the movement of an effect from point A to point B can appear to be constant or gradually speed up or slow down.

Straight Line or Curved Path

The motion path of the effect can move in a direct linear fashion from point to point or in smooth arcs that flow from point to point. Smooth motion is more polished and gracious. An editor learning to move effects around the screen is similar to someone learning to ride a bicycle. At first, the turns seem difficult and scary. However, after practice, the bicycle rider's hard right and left turns become graceful sweeping arcs. Eventually, the rider achieves complete control and can make any turn possible. An editor learn-ing effects should have the same goal: to achieve full control and be able to accomplish whatever he or she is asked to do.

Interpolation

Interpolation is the manner of adjustment to the motion made over time. If the motion path for a digital picture-in-picture effect involves multiple keyframes so the object can change direction, a decision has to be made about the qualities of the route the object takes. A linear route with no brak-ing for changes in direction will appear abrupt. A curved route with braking at each change in direction will appear smooth. The amount of braking and speed is controlled by the amount of interpolation taking place between the keyframes. If a lot of interpolation is taking place, the corners are more rounded because all of the points between the keyframes are estimated and averaged. With practice, exploration, and experimentation, you'll learn to easily control motion paths.

Organize Your Effects

Create bins for your effects and clips with effects applied. The elements you produce in the course of building effects can and should be saved. The rules are the same for any clip. Use unique names for each subclip. The ability to find titles, effects, keys, layers, and a dozen different treatments of the same shot depends on how accurately you named them.

Digital systems permit an unlimited amount of duplicate clips. When you're experimenting with various looks and treatments, you'll want to save the parameters or preferences for the effect. Editing system manufacturers have varied approaches to saving this useful information. Refer to your editing system manual to see how it works in your system. .

Here are some suggestions for bins to organize your work:

Graphics	Titles	Motion effected clips
Effects backgrounds	Mattes	Tinted clips
Imported effects	Animated mattes	

We're sure you'll figure out dozens of bins once you get started.

Summary

We have learned some fundamental lessons about working with keyframes over the years:

- *Fewer keyframes are better*.   Effects need two keyframes to start, as mentioned previously. However, add more keyframes sparingly. Experiment with one. Pay attention to how just one interruption in the motion path of an effect can have a significant impact. Change it, add another, and watch again. Beware of trying to overcontrol the events along the path. The editing system will transform the path into a curve without you trying to force changes. Beginners have a tendency to add multiple points along the path in order to get the flow they want. Not only is this unnecessary, but more keyframes will give you less control because you will have more interference.

- *Keyframes can be copied and pasted.*   There's no better technique for getting the results you want than copying and pasting the parameters of a keyframe from one spot to another. Why should you create everything from scratch? Work smarter, not harder.

- *Use the Wire-Frame Preview.*   A wire-frame preview can usually display the motion path of the effect accurately. Use it to avoid rendering. Remember that if you're trying to check the motion path and make adjustments, the wire-frame view is fine.

- *Use the Single-Frame Preview.*   Step through the effect by jogging frame by frame or by skipping ahead 10 frames at a time for longer effects. Step through each keyframe to verify any changes. Only render the effect when you have everything the way you want it.

- *Resize and blur are huge memory hogs.*   These two effects take the longest time to preview and render. Rebuilding all those pixels takes a tremendous amount of interpolation and processing power. If you want to resize or blur a graphic, don't put in the maximum number value for the effect. Put in the values that the effect requires—no more, no less. If you put more, you just give your editing system more to think about. If you put in less, you compromise the integrity of the effect.

- *Learn how your editing system handles rendering.*   There could be some tricks you could learn to improve the speed and efficiency of the system. For example, render every other effect on the timeline. Pay attention to what effects, if any, can be played back in real time. Then calculate the amount of time required to render similar-looking effects. One version may be considerably faster than another.

- *A little movement goes a long way.*   Static pictures on the screen can be enhanced with small position changes. If the clip is on the screen for a few seconds, then its movement can be short and subtle. Professionals know that small changes are often more interesting.

Getting It In and Out

We Waited as Long as We Could

This is the most technical chapter in this book. If technical information isn't your forte, only read the sections such as monitoring that are important for setting up your system. Then, wait until you're about to do a procedure, such as importing a graphic or making a DVD, to read those sections. Use this chapter as a reference to supplement what appears in your editing system manual. Most manuals explain the process of getting things in and out of a digital editing system in great detail. We don't want or need to get that specific. Instead, this chapter provides the basics so you can understand the big picture and avoid any pitfalls.

Most of the progress being made in digital editing involves turning procedures that were once difficult, complicated, and highly technical into simple actions such as pressing play and record. Hopefully, some of the procedures mentioned in this chapter will be even easier to do when you get ready to do them.

What Goes In?

A digital editing system is useless unless you can move material in and out of the system. The vast majority of what you edit *digitial video* enters and exits the editing system through a Firewire, *serial digital interface* (SDI), or *high-definition SDI* (HD-SDI) cable. Unfortunately, different formats and variations within the formats often make the process of getting video in and out more complicated than it should be. Writing this book would be easier if only one format was available.

Other materials (for example, photographs, illustrations, music, and sound effects) also need to move in and out of your system. You could shoot the still images or record the music and sound effects with a digital camcorder and transfer that recording into your system along with all of your other footage. However, most of the time that's not practical. If those materials already exist in a digital format, it should be easy to get them into your editing system. We wish it were as simple as it sounds.

What Goes Out?

After you've finished editing, you'll need to get your show out of the editing system—unless, of course, you plan to invite people over to see your show and sit them down in front of the editing system to watch it. In that case, your show is finished. Otherwise, you'll need to output your show in a form that can be played elsewhere.

You may decide to record and store the show on an object you can hold in your hand, such as a CD, DVD, or videotape. You might also let people see your show on the Internet where it can reside as a file for download or as a streaming video.

Some shows might not be finished. You might need better compositing, audio-sweetening, or finishing tools than the ones available on your system. In this case, you'll need to export the information in your timeline for someone else to use. Whether you're going to a sophisticated audio editing system down the hall or to a postproduction facility in another city, your finished timeline and/or media files must be saved in a format that another system can use. This is yet another way of getting what you've done out. We'll try to cover all these topics as simply as we can.

Why Is Monitoring Important?

One of the challenges of digital video editing is consistency. It's absolutely necessary that what you see and hear on your editing system matches what anyone will see and hear elsewhere. Imagine the havoc that would ensue if you created a color effect that looks blue on your system, but appears pink when played elsewhere. You're probably saying to yourself, "Hey, everything is digital. There's no way this could happen." You'd be wrong. Let's find out why.

Digital information remains consistent when you duplicate it. Copy a digital media file 100 times. Each copy contains the identical information. Unfortunately, this has nothing to do with how you see or hear the contents of the media file. Editors don't look at the ones and zeros in a file; they evaluate material on video monitors and speakers.

The images displayed on your editing system's computer monitor are only approximations and should not be used to judge the quality of the video picture. This is why your editing system should include a video monitor. The same rule applies for audio. The tiny speaker found in most computers is only there to provide some audio feedback (beeps and clicks) while you work. Audio should be evaluated using quality speakers or headphones since the audio in your editing suite must match the audio when the show is played elsewhere.

Other issues make monitoring difficult. No two people see color identically. We rely on our eyes and brains, which are unique. Thankfully, the differences in how people see color are very subtle unless the person happens to be colorblind (8 percent of men and 1 percent of women have some form of colorblindness). Our eyes aren't the principal problem. What gets everyone into trouble is that monitors, for computers or television, have controls. The *if-there's-a-knob-they'll-turn-it* rule predominates. It's easy to adjust or misadjust the picture. Monitors typically have controls for brightness, contrast, hue, and saturation. With four control knobs, there is a slim possibility that the monitor is set correctly and a nearly infinite possibility that it's set incorrectly.

Monitoring Video

A video evaluation monitor is an essential tool in professional editing suites. These monitors have special controls, reproduce colors more accurately, and display more detail than ordinary monitors or television sets. These higher-quality monitors are more expensive. However, an evaluation monitor is the only way to be sure that the picture you see matches what others will see elsewhere. A high-quality television set is an adequate substitute for home use. The challenge is that television sets are designed to show a pleasing rendition rather than an accurate picture.

Every monitor should be adjusted using a standardized signal. The SMPTE color bar signal is the standardized signal used for standard definition video signals. (See Figure 10-1.) This signal can be output by professional cameras and some prosumer cameras. Editing systems that are designed for professional use can generate SMPTE color bars and other test signals. Home users with cable or satellite television access should be able

Figure 10-1
SMPTE color bars.

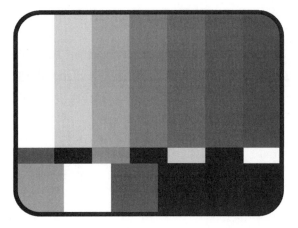

to find a channel that displays a color bar signal for at least part of the day. The CD included in this book has a 5-second clip of SMPTE color bars with a 1 kHz audio signal in case your editing system doesn't generate these test signals. Web sites, such as www.whizkidtech.net/monitor, offer a graphic representation of the color bar signal that you can use to set up a computer monitor.

How to Set Up a Video Monitor

The process of setting up a video monitor should take under 5 minutes. If you find yourself staring at the screen and adjusting the colors for longer than that, you'll need to clear your eyes before you continue. You're probably aware that if you continually smell a strong scent, after several minutes you can't smell it at all. The same is true for our eyes. After a few minutes of looking at strong colors, no one can accurately judge color. The solution is to look at a white or gray wall for a few minutes or go and take a break.

Here are several methods that can be used to set up a video monitor. The quick-and-dirty approaches work well enough and produce good results. They even work with all the television sets in your house. However, for accurate results that you can rely on, follow the professional approach.

Five-Step Quick-and-Dirty Approach

1. Let the monitor or television warm up for 10 minutes.
2. Turn all the color (chroma) off. Turn the sound off.
3. Use the brightness and contrast controls to make the blacks black and the whites white.
4. Turn the color (chroma) back on. Turn up the level of saturation to suit your taste.
5. Adjust the flesh tones with the hue (tint) control. A shot of a network news anchor is the best quick-and-dirty reference for accurate flesh tones.

Two-Step Quick-and-Dirty Approach If Your Camcorder Can Generate Color Bars

1. Connect the monitor to the camera and let it warm up for 10 minutes.
2. Use the hue (tint) control to make the yellow bar as yellow as possible.

The Professional Approach

These steps involve adjusting the brightness, contrast, hue (phase), and color (chroma) controls on your monitor. If you have a consumer television, you'll need a deep blue filter or gel to accurately adjust the hue and color. Professional monitors can turn off the blue gun to adjust these controls. The least expensive way to get a blue filter is to pick up a free sample swatch book of lighting gels at a professional film, photography, or video supply store. A deep pure blue (such as Roscolux 83 or Rosco CalColor 90 Blue #a4290 or Lee #a713 Winter Blue or Kodak Wratten 39 or 47) will do fine. Follow these steps:

1. Allow the monitor to warm up for about 10 minutes before you begin making any adjustments.
2. Display an SMPTE color bar signal on the monitor. You'll see three bands of colors. The top band is composed of seven vertical bars, which are (going from left to right) light gray, yellow, cyan, green, magenta, red, and blue. The middle band contains the same colors, but they are

Figure 10-2
SMPTE color bars
seen through a
blue filter.

reversed with every other bar set to black. The bottom band has a white (the *I*) bar, a black (the *Q*) bar, and a PLUGE signal. The PLUGE (Picture Line Up Generation Equipment) consists of three thin black bars that are used to set monitor brightness: a superblack bar, which is blacker than black, a black bar, and a whiter than black bar, which is very dark gray (see Figure 10-3).

3. Adjust the color or chroma control so the picture is almost black and white.

4. The PLUGE is on the bottom band at the far right. Adjust the brightness control until there's no visible difference between the superblack and black bars. If it's correctly adjusted, there will be a barely visible difference between those two bars and the whiter than black bar.

5. Adjust the contrast so the white bar on the bottom band appears bright white.

   A *technical note:* If the gray bars on your monitor have a blue, green, or pink tint when the color is turned completely off, your monitor is in need of service.

6. Look at the monitor through the blue filter or press the blue-only switch.

7. Adjust the color or chroma control to its midpoint.

8. Adjust the hue (tint) or phase control until you see four blue bars separated by three black bars.

Figure 10-3
Lower right corner of
the SMPTE color bar
signal enlarged to
show the PLUGE.

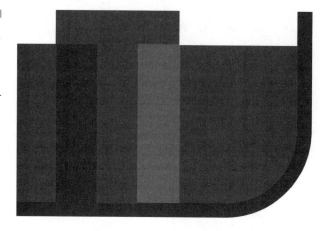

9. Adjust the color or chroma control until the two outer blue bars in the top and middle bands match.

10. Fine tune the hue (tint) or phase control by making a slight adjustment so the middle two blue bars in the top and middle bands match.

11. Your monitor or television set is now properly adjusted. Turn off the blue-only switch.

Monitoring Audio

What's necessary for judging audio quality is tough to find in an edit suite. Ideally, you'll have the highest-fidelity speakers (ones that are capable of reproducing the entire audio spectrum) and a perfectly quiet room. Most editing systems aren't located in rooms designed for audio. In fact, most editing suites are filled with the worst kind of noise (such as whirring fans, hard-drive noises, and other ambient sounds from editing systems and video recorders) at a volume just loud enough to hide the subtleties of your show's audio tracks. In contrast, audio suites are carefully designed with sound-absorbing and sound reflecting materials to create an environment in which audio quality can be accurately judged. The sound quality is evaluated by listening in close proximity to expensive reference speakers designed especially for this purpose.

So what can you do? The simplest solution is to buy the most expensive closed headphones you can afford. Closed headphones block out any outside sounds. If you plan to buy good-quality powered speakers to use with your editing system, select ones that have a front-mounted headphone jack. That way you can easily connect headphones whenever you need to critically listen to the audio. Headphones also solve another problem for home users. To hear every nuance, you need to increase the volume. With headphones, you can make it as loud as necessary without disturbing others.

As much of the noisy equipment as possible should be moved into an adjacent room for a professional editing suite. If that will not work, the equipment should be surrounded by sound-absorbing materials to soak up as much machine noise as possible. Purchase excellent reference speakers. A good amplifier, mixer, and headphones are also necessities. Be aware of how the room colors the audio and use headphones for critical evaluations.

Ins and Outs

The first rule of getting material in or out of your editing system—the rule that will save you an enormous amount of time—is that you must understand what is needed at the destination. If your editing system only accepts DV video using Firewire, then you need a recorder with a Firewire connection. If you're trying to import a graphic, you need to know which file formats are supported. Use the Help feature or look in your manual to figure out which ones will work on your editing system. Check before you create and save the image. It's very frustrating and a waste of time to try to import a file format that your editing system cannot handle.

If the final audio mix will be done at a separate facility, find out what they'll need to do the job. Write down the exact requirements so you can determine whether your editing system can export files in the format that meets their needs. If it doesn't, you may need to figure out a solution. This could include finding a different facility that's more compatible with what your system can deliver or perhaps buying software that can convert your format.

Does this sounds like simple common sense? Absolutely correct. However, with dozens of formats, aspect ratios, sample rates, resolutions, file types, codecs, and standards, it's easy to get confused. Therefore, the first thing you should do whether you're attempting to get materials into your editing system or out of your editing system is to figure out what is required on the other end. Look for the formats that match what your editing system can output and what the other system is capable of inputting or vice versa.

The devil is in the details. Importing and exporting, transferring video, and outputting the show are complex operations. You might have to set a dozen parameters. When in doubt, use the default settings. Unless you have a reason to change, leave the settings alone. Don't make life more complicated than necessary.

The distinction between output and export is blurry. Editing systems designed to digitize analog video use the word *output* to describe printing a completed show to tape and use the word *export* to describe the process of copying or converting media files for use on another editing system. In an all-digital environment, the editing system is always copying or converting files. In the context of this chapter, if a data stream is available on your editing system when you play the timeline, the word *output* should be used. For example, DV is available via the Firewire cable whenever you play the timeline. If you do not have a spigot putting out a streaming video format, obtaining one falls into the export category.

Compression and Digital Formats

What's a Codec?

The term *codec* appears whenever DV is discussed. Codec is a contraction of the words *compression* and *decompression*. It is used to describe the software extensions that manufacturers develop for the standards used in digital editing and for Internet applications. These extensions are developed to support the transfer, viewing, and output of digital video with their hardware or software products. Most DV editing systems wrap the data from the DV tape into a QuickTime or AVI file to store, display, and edit DV on a computer. A codec makes this possible.

Video capture boards that transform analog video into digital files use a codec to digitize and/or compress the audio and video signals. Codecs are evaluated for quality by comparing the image quality at various levels of compression. Highly compressed video requires less storage space. The tradeoff is that image quality goes down as it becomes more highly compressed.

Timesavers for Exporting Digital Media

- Every clip in your timeline must be available. The media files for each clip must be stored on your editing system's drives otherwise, the export will fail.

- Anything that must be rendered in a timeline should be rendered before you export the timeline.

- Check to make sure every clip in the timeline has the same audio sample rate and video resolution. Mixed sample rates or resolutions will halt the export process.

- The pan and volume levels on the audio tracks should be set as you want them for the export. For example, if you want the export to have a mono, split, stereo mix, 5.1 surround, or any other arrangement, the timeline must be set to play that type of mix. If you're exporting audio files for further mixing on a digital audio workstation, all the tracks you want to include in the mix should be active.

- Review your editing system manual for tips on how to speed up the export process. For example, recapturing the clips in the timeline reduces the size of the associated media files because only the portion of the media in use is recaptured. In some systems, this makes exports significantly faster.

- Always perform a test first. Export a small section of your timeline before attempting to export the entire show. Check the test to make sure it works as expected. If you can, double-check the test by copying it to another computer to make sure it works everywhere.

- Exporting an entire show can be a lengthy process. Conversions from one video or audio format to another format (such as DV to MPEG or DV to AIFF-C audio) take an enormous amount of time.

- Think ahead. Schedule or start an export before you go to lunch, dinner, or home for the night. The process takes time, often uses all the available resources of your editing system, and prevents you from doing anything else. Once the export is launched, you're locked out.

What's DV?

The DV tape format is an international standard developed jointly by a group of 10 companies. The tape is ¼ inch in width. Pictures and sounds are recorded in a digital format that has been compressed at a 5:1 ratio. The image size is 720×480 pixels. The picture information is sampled at 720 pixels per scanline. This sample rate is also used in professional video formats such as D-1, D-5, and Digital Betacam. The luminance is sampled four times as often as the color difference signals. In technical terms, DV uses 4:1:1 color sampling in North America (NTSC). In Europe (PAL), DV uses 4:2:0 color sampling.

What's IEEE-1394 and OHCI?

IEEE-1394, which is also called Apple Firewire or Sony iLink, is a hardware and software standard for transporting data at 100, 200, 300, or 400 megabits per second (Mbps). This is a digital interface so nothing gets lost when the data is transferred from one place to another. Apple developed the original standard.

Today, most IEEE-1394 interface cards use the *Open Host Controller Interface* (OHCI). The OHCI specification standardizes how the Windows operating system interacts with the 1394 bus. The 1394 bus moves digital information into the computer.

What's the DV Codec?

The Mac and Windows operating systems provide DV codecs for their respective operating systems. Despite the presence of generic versions, editing system manufacturers provide their own proprietary DV codec. If your editing system is connected to a DV camcorder or recorder through an IEEE-1394 cable, the codec is unimportant. No compression or decompression happens. You're just doing a data transfer; nothing goes through the codec.

However, the codec has other purposes. The appearance of DV on your computer (both the image quality and motion reproduction) depends on the codec. The codec is involved whenever transitions, titles, or effects have to be rendered. Visible quality differences do exist. The differences are most noticeable when a previously rendered file is used as a video source in an effect and is then rerendered and output back to DV tape. Most people can't see any differences between the codecs until the video image is projected on a large screen. Then even the untrained eye can spot the differences between a poor codec and an excellent one.

What's an Encoder?

Encoding is the process of converting information from one format to another. Encoding happens in your camcorder when the pictures and sounds are recorded in the DV format. The camcorder has a hardware encoder that converts the information captured by the CCDs[1] and microphone into the compressed (5:1) DV format that is recorded on the tape.

An encoder is any hardware or software that converts video or audio signals or digital files into a specific format. Encoders use algorithms to compress the data. Some hardware encoders can input analog video and output it as DV so you can edit with a digital editing system. These *bridges* between analog sources and DV or between analog and SDI use an encoder to convert the information. An encoder is involved when you convert the media files stored on your editing system to MPEG-2 or export a timeline in a streaming video format. Digital editing systems typically use a software encoder to convert from the editing system's native format (typically QuickTime or AVI files) to the formats used on CDs, DVDs, and the Internet.

Videotape for Input and Output

You should check the following things before you try to get material into or out of your editing system using videotape.

---

[1]CCD is a light-sensitive device (charge-coupled device) that converts light passing through the camera's lens into digital data.

Is the Editing System Capable of Handling the Videotape Format You Want to Edit?

You must have a recorder that can play the tape. The recorder must be connected via Firewire, SDI, or HD-SDI to the digital video editing system. If the tape was originally recorded with a NTSC camcorder (the standard used in North America), the recorder must be able to play an NTSC tape. Conversely, a PAL (the standard used in Europe) tape must be played back on a PAL recorder. If the tape and recorder have analog connections, you might need a bridge to convert analog signals to a digital format that the system can accept. See Appendix B, "Resources," for companies that make these devices.

Do the Project or Timeline Settings Match the Material You Plan to Edit?

Most digital editing systems can be set to edit in NTSC or PAL. The setting must match the standard used to record the tape. The frame size and pixel aspect ratio (nonsquare except for HD) of the source must match the settings in your project or timeline. Some systems are resolution independent. This means that they can edit any frame size of video from 640×480 analog to the largest HD format 1,920×1,080. Others are capable of handling only a single format, such as, the 720×480 DV format.

Be sure the aspect ratio matches how the video was recorded. There are three possibilities: 4:3, 16:9, or 16:9 electronically squeezed DV.

Make sure the frame rate of the videotape matches the project settings for the timeline's time database. NTSC is 29.97 *frames per second* (fps). PAL is 25 fps. HD video can be 23.98, 24, 25, 29.97, 30, 59.97, or 60 fps. This is very important if you plan to export an *edit decision list* (EDL) in order to conform a film or finish a video project at another post facility.

The sample rate used to record the audio should match your project or timeline settings. Most systems automatically resample audio if it differs from the preset sample rate. Converting from a 32 kHz sample rate to a 48 kHz sample rate may dramatically distort the sound. See the Ins and Outs of Audio section for more information.

Getting the Finished Show on Tape

The process of getting your finished show back on videotape will be straightforward if you use the same tape format that you originally used to input the material. If you're using a different format, you may need to check the output settings in your editing system. Here are two methods you can use to output your show to tape.

The Quick-and-Dirty Method

1. Every show should fade up from black. If your show does not do this, insert a few seconds of black and add a fade up.

2. Make sure your timeline will play without any hesitations or pauses. If anything needs to be rendered, render it. If you still have trouble getting the timeline to play smoothly, you might need to move some media files to a different drive or defrag your editing system's storage drives. Check the troubleshooting section of your manual.

3. Make sure the timeline cursor is parked at the start of your show.

4. Place a blank or blacked tape in the recorder. A blacked tape is better for the reasons outlined in the print-to-tape method.

5. Make sure the recorder is properly connected to the editing system.

6. Press Play and Record on the videotape recorder or camcorder to begin recording.

7. Wait 10 seconds and then press Play on your editing system so the timeline begins to play.

8. Stop the recorder 30 seconds after the timeline has finished playing.

The Print-to-Tape Method

1. Prepare a blacked (also called *prestriped*) tape by recording a black signal (on a camcorder, leave the lens cap on and disconnect or turn off the microphone) and time code on the tape.

2. Every show should fade up from black. Insert a few seconds of black and add a fade up if it isn't already in your show.

3. Make sure your timeline will play without any hesitations or pauses. If anything needs to be rendered, render it. If you still have trouble getting the timeline to play smoothly, you might need to move some media files to a different drive or defrag your editing system's storage drives. Check the troubleshooting section of your manual.

4. Place the blacked tape in the recorder.

5. Make sure the recorder is properly connected to the editing system and that the deck control settings are correct. If the connection is via IEEE-1394, the deck control settings should indicate IEEE-1394.

6. Set up a leader. Some editing systems automate the process of creating a leader or header that appears on the tape before your finished show. If your system doesn't have this feature, use your editing system's text or title tool to make a slate. Edit the slate into the timeline before your finished show.

The purpose of the slate is twofold: to identify the contents and move the show (the valuable information) farther away from the head of the tape. The head and tail of a videotape have the highest dropout rates. These sections of the tape are also prone to damage from the recorder in the natural course of playing the tape.

We suggest:

- The first time you record on a new tape, record 30 seconds of SMPTE color bars and tone at the head. If you're adding another show to a master that has the bars and tone at the head, this is not necessary.

Figure 10-4
A slate recorded at the head of the tape before the show.

Date:
Title:
TRT:
Audio: Ch1&Ch 2 mixed
Director:
Editor:

- Follow the bars and tone with 30 seconds of black. Use 20 seconds if you're just separating shows on a master tape.

- Create a slate with the Production Date, Title, *Total Running Time* (TRT), Audio track (track 1 and 2, 1, 2, 3, 4, and so on), Mix information (mono on 1 and 2, mono on 1, music and effects on 2, stereo on 1 and 2, 5.1 surround, and so on), and any authorship information you want to include (the director, editor, or production company).

- Include an address and phone number on the slate if you're sending the tape out for duplication or broadcast. This way if problems do arise, it's easy to get in contact with you or someone at the facility that edited the show. This also helps if the label falls off or the box is lost.

7. Preview the leader and double-check to make sure the recorder is getting a signal. Editing systems that can create a leader usually have a preview function so you can see it before you record it.

8. Do a test recording. Press Print to Tape and Record for a few minutes. Play back the recording to make sure everything works correctly. If you're working with a professional recorder, check to make sure all the levels are set correctly.

9. Print to tape. Label the videotape with the title of the show and indicate that the tape is a MASTER.

10. Make protection masters. You should always make a backup copy of any valuable master. This is especially true if you send one to a client or duplication facility. People lose things. You don't want to have to recreate all the work that went into a show.

Ins and Outs of Audio

Audiences will not accept poor quality sound. This section is a guide to moving audio in and out of your editing system.

Single or Double?

Analog and digital video production usually follows a single-system approach to sound. This is when audio is recorded along with video on the

Labeling and Protecting Masters

Digital editing has changed the concept of a master. Every master is the same. No generation loss occurs because a copy of a digital tape is an exact duplicate as long as you use a digital connection. However, it's still useful to label tapes.

The videotape master of your show should be labeled *ASHOW* MASTER@ or A*EDIT* MASTER@. Any copies of that master should be labeled accordingly such as—EDIT MASTER COPY (or CLONE). The master you send to a duplication facility should be labeled *ADUB* MASTER. Dub is short for *dubbing*, which means to duplicate a videotape. The master you send to the client should be labeled *ACLIENT* MASTER. Use the MASTER stickers that come with the videotape. That's what they're there for. Never use the MASTER sticker on original source footage tapes—you don't want to confuse what some people call *camera masters* with a finished SHOW MASTER.

It also helps to date the tapes in case changes are required later. Nothing is more frustrating than having three masters with the same title and no dates as you try to determine which one is the latest version of the show your client wants to duplicate.

Make sure the tab is set to prevent erasure on your master tapes! Accidents happen when you don't pay attention.

videotape. The audio tracks are always in sync with the video. Audio is sampled at different rates than video and the data is stored uncompressed. The amount of audio information is small in comparison to video so you don't need to compress it. Audio and video are transferred together into a digital editing system if a digital connection such as Firewire, SDI, or HD-SDI is used.

Audio Sample Rates

The sample rate at which the audio is recorded is one of the major factors that determine sound quality. The higher the sample rate, the more potential there is for an accurate reproduction of the full audio spectrum. When we refer to the *full spectrum*, we're talking about everything within the range of human hearing. The sound that dogs and cats can hear is unimportant to an editor. The sample rates common in digital video production

Double-System Sound

At times, a double-system approach makes sense. It's the standard approach when shooting film or HD at 24 fps. The double-system refers to the fact that the audio is recorded separately using an audio recorder that runs at a constant speed. The audio recording is synced to the picture by the editor. This is also known as *resolving the sound*. This works because a visual and audio cue is recorded simultaneously by the camera and audio recorder. The clapper or time code slate makes it easy for the editor to resolve the sound to the picture.

Figure 10-5
Time code slate.

The advantage of the double-system approach is that the sound recordist doesn't have to be tethered to the camera. Audio recorders offer better control and higher-quality sound reproduction than what's found on most video recorders. In addition, the recording is on a separate tape, which means that if one or the other is damaged, you'll still have either picture or sound. The disadvantage is that it requires a lot of extra work just to get the sound back in sync with the picture. You have to manage twice as many tapes. You also need extra equipment and personnel during production.

The argument about which approach is better has been going on for years. We won't settle this argument, but will say that the single-system approach is fine for most people. More important is to use a professional microphone instead of the one that comes with the camcorder if you want excellent sound quality.

are 32, 44, 48, and 96 kHz. The bit depth (8, 12, or 16 bits) is indicated alongside of the sample rate.

The DV tape format can record 2 tracks of audio at the 48 kHz (16-bit) rate or 4 tracks of audio at the 32 kHz (12-bit) rate. Most consumer DV camcorders can only record 2 tracks at 48 kHz. A few can record two or four tracks.

Production Tip

Shoot everything for a project at one audio sample rate. You can't mix material with different audio sample rates on the same timeline in many editing systems. Resampling the audio from 48 to 32 kHz or 32 to 48 kHz can introduce distortion. Pick a rate and stick with it.

The 44 kHz rate is used for audio CDs. Professional *digital audiotape* (DAT) recorders use either the 44 or 48 kHz sample rate. Multitrack audio recorders that are used in professional studios for mastering music albums use the 96 kHz sample rate. You probably think that everything has been sorted out on the audio recording side since it's been around nearly twice as long as video recording. Think again. It's just as arcane and has almost as much potential for confusion.

The Gist of It . . .

Audio quality is better when sampled at a higher rate. However, human speech falls into a very narrow band of the audio spectrum. It's easy to record, and any of the sample rates we've mentioned are more than adequate to accomplish the task. The wider the gap between sample rates, the more likely distortion will occur when you down- or up-sample audio.

Exchanging Audio Files

There are many reasons to move audio files in and out of your editing system. It's rare for all of the sound elements in a show to arrive on videotape. Music and sound effects come on CDs or DAT tape. Stock music and sound-effect libraries sell CDs and digital audio clips on the Internet. Sound studios are also connected to the Internet. The voice-over narration for a show can be done wherever the voice actor resides. Digital audio files from a recording session are small enough to be sent via e-mail or downloaded from the studio's web site using FTP (*file transfer protocol*) software.

After you finish editing, you may need to send the audio tracks to an audio-sweetening facility for additional sound work. If the music for the show will be composed after editing is completed, the composer will need all the tracks (picture and sound) to create music that fits the show. After the composer writes and records the music, it will come back to you in the form of a digital audio file that you'll need to insert into the timeline.

Several file formats are commonly used to exchange digital audio data: the *Audio Interchange File Format* (AIFF-C) developed by Apple Computer, the WAVE format developed by IBM and Microsoft Corporation, the *Open Media Framework™ Interchange* format (OMFI) format developed by Avid Technology, and the MP3 (MPEG-1 Audio Layer-3) format developed by the Motion Picture Experts Group.

AIFF-C

AIFF-C stores uncompressed or compressed digital audio data. AIFF-C supports a variety of bit resolutions, sample rates, and one or two channels. It is widely used on Mac platforms to exchange files. Apple originally designed the format for that purpose. However, files with an .aif extension are also used on the Windows platform.

The AIFF-C format doesn't support time code. If you export the audio on a timeline as an AIFF-C file, the information is stored in a single file. All of the edit points are lost. This file format doesn't support handles so only the audio on the timeline is included in the exported file.

The lack of extra media on both sides of an audio clip can make it difficult or impossible for an audio-sweetening facility to do dissolves or cross fades. You can work around this by adding handles to the audio clips on the timeline before you export the file. Of course, you'll also need to send a copy of the show as it stands so the facility can differentiate between handles and show audio.

WAVE

The WAVE file format has become a standard on the Windows platform. The .wav extension identifies these files. This is an uncompressed format so the file sizes are often quite large. Beyond the digitally sampled waveform, these files contain information about the number of channels (mono or stereo), sample rate, and bit depth of the recording. WAVE files provide high-quality sound.

MP3

The MP3 format compresses files in WAVE format to approximately one-twelfth of their original size and preserves the original sound quality. The Motion Picture Experts Group developed an algorithm that applies more compression to the sounds most people cannot hear. Creating MP3 files from audio CDs is easy. MP3s have near-CD sound quality and have become the most preferred file exchange format on the Internet.

OFMI

The OMFI format was developed by Avid Technology for digital video production purposes. An OMFI audio file contains the audio media, time code for each clip's in and out points, track separations, transitions, motion effects, sample rate, bit depth, video frame rate, and pan and level information. The file contains all this information, but what actually carries over to another system depends on the capabilities of that digital audio workstation or digital video editing system.

Tips for Exporting Audio Tracks for Sweetening

- Determine which file format will work before you export.
- Place each voice or sound element (such as the music, effects, room tone, or ambience) on its own track.
- Remove any filters or equalization.
- Make sure all the timeline tracks to be exported are active.
- Set all volume levels to 0 *decibels* (dB).
- Set the pan controls in the middle.
- Set the appropriate sample rate and bit depth.
- If plan to do cross fades and dissolves, make sure you have enough handles (extra media).
- If you are using AIFF-C, insert a one-frame sync beep at the beginning and end of every track.
- If you are using OMFI, embedded audio can be in the WAVE or AIFF-C format. Make the appropriate choice.

Exporting Media Files

OMFI

OMFI is a platform-independent format that can store the information contained in a timeline and the digital media associated with that timeline. It doesn't matter if an OMFI file is exported on a Windows platform or imported into an application running on a Mac platform. Any application that supports OFMI will be able to import an OMFI file.

You have the choice to embed or link to digital media files during an OMFI export. The media should be embedded (stored in the file) whenever you export files for use elsewhere. You have the choice to embed audio only, video only, or both audio and video media. The link to selection (composition-only export) is useful if you only need to export the information about the timeline. Or, when the person receiving the OMFI file has the same access to the digital media files as you do. This might be true if you're working in a networked environment. An OFMI composition-only export is a much smaller file; no digital media is attached.

QuickTime and AVI

Most editing systems use either the QuickTime or AVI format for editing video. Professional programs can export in either format. Consumer products are often more limited. A QuickTime-based editing system typically exports only QuickTime files, and AVI-based editing systems typically only export AVI files.

QuickTime is available for the Mac and Windows platforms. The AVI format is used on the Windows platform. However, the general options are the same when you export. The first consideration is how big can the file be? The higher the video quality, the larger the file size will be.

The factors that determine the overall quality include the frame size, frame rate, image quality, audio format, and compression codec. Typically, you can decide to export audio only, video only, or audio and video. The frame size can be full or a percentage of full. The frame rate can be anywhere from 29.97 fps on down. The image quality depends on whether you decide to compress the file and how much it is compressed. Your choice of compression codec also has an impact. Every manufacturer provides its own codecs and most include others such as the Cinepak and Sorenson codecs. Specialized applications, such as Discreet's Cleaner or Canopus' ProCoder, can export multiple file formats using a variety of codecs.

Exchanging Information with Other Systems

Every editing system gathers information and builds a database. Some systems make it quite easy to import information from other applications and to exchange information with other applications. Consumer editing systems often have limited capabilities in this regard. However, most consumers don't need these professional features.

You might want to import information such as a log or timeline. Log files are used to create a batch transfer list. A timeline file is useful in three situations: if you need to reedit a show you made, if you need to change or enhance a show that someone did elsewhere on the same type of system, or if you need to change or enhance a show made on another type of editing system.

Logs

The automatic scene detection function found in some digital editing systems is not a substitute for a good log. On the other hand, paper logs don't save time if you have to type in time code numbers to transfer footage into your editing system. Specialized logging applications let you view your footage, mark time code INs and OUTs, and output a list of selected scenes, takes, or shots for batch transfer into your editing system. A typical log file may include the clip name, IN and OUT points, video and audio track information, audio sample rates, and, most important, your notes about each scene, take, or shot. Some editing systems can import a properly prepared spreadsheet or word processing file and build a batch transfer list.

Check your editing system manual for information about importing log files. Some editing systems provide logging applications that will run on any computer. Some editing system manuals provide instructions on how to create log files that are compatible with the system using a word processing application. Some logging applications can output log files in a variety of formats.

Edit Decision Lists (EDLs)

An EDL is a list (in table form) of instructions that are used to create a show in a linear video editing environment. The EDL is the oldest method of information exchange in the video realm. The list includes time code in and out points for the source and record machines. It can also include cuts, wipes, dissolves, and fades. CMX Corporation developed the EDL about 30 years ago as a way of saving the decisions an editor made in case he or she wanted to roll back the master and redo an earlier edit.

EDLs were designed for edit controllers that operated videotape machines. Over the years, different formats were developed by edit controller manufacturers including the Grass Valley Group and Sony Corporation. However, years after the company's demise, the CMX_3600 version of the EDL format is still the mostly widely used format.

The list begins with a header that indicates the title and type of time code (drop or nondrop) to be used in the list of events. Every entry in the list is considered to be an event and has an event number. Because this is linear video editing, each event must be performed in the order in which it appears in the list.

The reel name of the videotape that should be in the source player for a particular event appears in the second column from the left. The reel name in CMX format can be three numbers or letters. *AX* is used to signify an auxiliary source such as a switcher or character generator. *BL* is used for black.

The next column over indicates which tracks are to be active on the recorder. *V* is used to indicate that video will be inserted on the recorder. If the audio will be inserted on track 1, a letter *A* will appear beside the *V*. The following are some possible options for a recorder with two audio tracks:

V—   Video only

VA-   Video, audio 1

VAA   Video, audio 1 and 2

-A-   Audio 1 only

—A   Audio 2 only

-AA   Audio 1 and 2 only

```
TITLE:    BL KIDS VIEW SEQ
FCM: NON-DROP FRAME
001      AX      AA/V  C        00:00:00:00 00:00:30:00 01:00:00:00 01:00:30:00
* FROM CLIP NAME:  SMPTE_BARS.PCT  2:1
002      BL       V    K B      00:00:00:00 00:00:20:00 01:00:30:00 01:00:50:00
002      AX       V    K    000 00:00:39:14 00:00:59:14 01:00:30:00 01:00:50:00
* EFF_BLEND_GRAPHIC
* KEY CLIP NAME:  2/15 ROUGH CUT SLATE.04
003      BL       V    C        00:00:00:00 00:00:00:00 01:01:00:00 01:01:00:00
003      AX       V    D    030 00:00:07:15 00:00:14:00 01:01:00:00 01:01:06:15
* BLEND, DISSOLVE
* TO CLIP NAME:  BLLOGO ALPHA.PCT
004      AX       V    C        00:00:14:00 00:00:14:00 01:01:06:15 01:01:06:15
004      BL       V    D    030 00:00:00:00 00:00:01:00 01:01:06:15 01:01:07:15
* BLEND, DISSOLVE
* FROM CLIP NAME:  BLLOGO ALPHA.PCT
005 KIDS_VIE AA        C        01:00:00:00 01:02:24:04 01:01:09:00 01:03:33:04
* FROM CLIP NAME:  KIDS VIEW SHORT
006      BL       V    K B      00:00:00:00 00:02:25:17 01:01:09:00 01:03:34:17
006 KIDS_VIE V         K    000 01:00:00:00 01:02:25:17 01:01:09:00 01:03:34:17
* EFF_SBLEND
* KEY CLIP NAME:  KIDS VIEW SHORT
007 KIDS_VIE AA        C        01:02:24:04 01:02:24:04 01:03:33:04 01:03:33:04
007      BL       AA   D    040 00:00:00:00 00:00:01:10 01:03:33:04 01:03:34:14
* BLEND, AUDIO DISSOLVE
* FROM CLIP NAME:  KIDS VIEW SHORT
008      BL       V    K B      00:00:00:00 00:00:04:18 01:03:34:17 01:03:39:05
008      AX       V    K    012 00:00:33:14 00:00:38:02 01:03:34:17 01:03:39:05
* EFF_SBLEND
* EFF_BLEND_GRAPHIC
* BACKGROUND EVENT ON KEY EVENT AT SEQUENCE TIME 01:03:34:17 CONVERTED TO A CU
* T.
* KEY CLIP NAME:  SAVE MORE.01
009      BL       V    K B      00:00:00:00 00:00:00:13 01:03:39:05 01:03:39:18
009      AX       V    K O  013 00:00:38:02 00:00:38:15 01:03:39:05 01:03:39:18
* EFF_SBLEND
* EFF_BLEND_GRAPHIC
* BACKGROUND EVENT ON KEY EVENT AT SEQUENCE TIME 01:03:39:05 CONVERTED TO A CU
* T.
* KEY CLIP NAME:  SAVE MORE.01
010      BL       V    K B      00:00:00:00 00:00:02:00 01:03:39:18 01:03:41:18
010 KIDS_VIE V         K    000 01:02:30:18 01:02:32:18 01:03:39:18 01:03:41:18
* EFF_SBLEND
* KEY CLIP NAME:  KIDS VIEW SHORT
011 KIDS_VIE AA        C        01:02:31:15 01:02:47:11 01:03:40:15 01:03:56:11
* FROM CLIP NAME:  KIDS VIEW SHORT
012      BL       V    K B      00:00:00:00 00:00:03:18 01:03:41:18 01:03:45:06
012      AX       V    K    012 00:00:26:09 00:00:29:27 01:03:41:18 01:03:45:06
* EFF_SBLEND
* EFF_BLEND_GRAPHIC
* BACKGROUND EVENT ON KEY EVENT AT SEQUENCE TIME 01:03:41:18 CONVERTED TO A CU
* T.
* KEY CLIP NAME:  1997 2002
013      BL       V    K B      00:00:00:00 00:00:00:13 01:03:45:06 01:03:45:19
```

The fourth column indicates transitions using *C* for cuts, *D* for dissolves, and *W* for wipes.

The next two columns are for the source time code in and the source time code out. The far right columns are for the master record time code in and time code out.

A CMX_3600 EDL has no audio level, color correction, or effects information. It's a simple text file designed for a different era in which the idea that digital video editing would be available for anyone to use was an unimaginable dream and the Internet was still a concept buried deep within the U.S. Department of Defense.

Tips for Exporting an EDL for Use in an Online Edit

■ Ask which EDL format the facility's edit controller can read before you export the EDL.

■ If you're not sure, save the EDL in several formats.

■ Make sure the edit controller can read high-density 3.5-inch diskettes.

■ Find out if you'll need to generate a dupe reel list. This list tells an editor which of the tapes will need to be duplicated prior to the online edit.

■ Save the EDL on a 3.5-inch diskette. Name the EDL file using six or fewer alphanumeric characters, all in uppercase, with a file name extension of .EDL.

■ Print out a copy of the EDL in *A*-mode sort (shots listed in reel number order) to use as a reference.

Finally, a New Type of EDL Arrives

In 1996, a group of digital editing manufacturers decided it was time to create a new type of EDL. Their goal was to develop some way of preserving all the information stored in the show created on one manufacturer's editing system so it could be recreated at a later date on another manufacturer's editing system. Because video editing was only a facet of the growing multimedia environment that includes games, interactive television, the Internet, streaming, and broadcast, they expanded their goals.

This new cross-platform multimedia file format had to make it easier to reuse or repurpose content. *Content* in this context refers to television programs, films, video games, interactive CD-ROMs, DVDs, and anything else you can think in the world of entertainment. Everyone felt it should be much easier to take a television program and turn it into video game or perhaps turn video games into interactive television shows. After all, everyone was working with digital media files.

The trouble was that everyone used proprietary formats. Most formats were written to take advantage of software running on a specific hardware platform and operating system. The information about how to sequence or modify the media files and turn them into a finished show wasn't transferable.

This group decided that creating multimedia content—what we've been calling *editing* digital video—should be called *authoring*. Authoring included developing the content and all the information about how you turned that digital media into content.

The Advanced Authoring Format (AAF) Association

The group called itself the Advanced Authoring Format (AAF) Association. After years of discussion, they developed a new approach that would enable two types of data—*essence* and *metadata*—to be interchanged using an AAF file. Essence data refers to audio, video, still images, graphics, text, animation, music, and other forms of multimedia. The group called it this because it is the essential data perceived by the audience. Metadata refers to the information about how to combine or modify the essence data or supplementary information about it. Closed captioning is a form of metadata that is included in an AAF file.

In simple terms, metadata is data about other data. The metadata in an AAF file provides the information that an editing system needs to know to combine and modify the essence data in the file to produce a finished show. A long list of information is stored in metadata such as how to find the essence data and other parts of the metadata, the rules for controlling how audiences access the content, technical parameters such as sampling rates and streaming formats, and a detailed description of how to assemble (edit) the essence.

What Does Metadata Mean to an Editor?

Metadata is the record of not only the creative decisions you made, but also the steps you followed to reach the final output, the sources and equipment you used to create the output, and all of the alternatives you might decide to choose at some point in the future.

So what does this mean? If everything in your timeline (all the settings for audio equalization, color correction, layered effects, digital media file locations, and other information that lets you output a finished show) could be transferred to any editing system anywhere in the world without losing any information, you could work with the best person instead of the one with the most compatible system.

Is It AAF Compliant?

AAF files cannot be played or streamed. AAF compliance simply lets you transfer complex edits from one production department to another or from one facility to another without recreating the project every time you transfer it to a new system. The AAF file enables a show to be automatically assembled on other equipment with appropriate capabilities and it can track the history of the material in the finished show directly back to the original source recordings.

The original intent to make it easy for everyone to repurpose content has been fulfilled. You can track every source and application used to modify the media. Best of all, this new type of EDL brings us one step closer to a time when every digital editing system is compatible with every other system. Instead of including this chapter, which has dozens of confusing technical terms, we'd have a footnote in the back of this book that would say, "If your editing system is AAF compliant, you don't have to worry about getting it in or out of anyone else's system. It's easy and seamless." Thankfully, that day isn't far off.

Using AAF

Your editing system must be AAF compliant to import or export AAF files. The list of compliant systems is constantly growing. An AAF file has two types of data. You can select whether to export the media (essence) with the metadata or only export the metadata. If you decide to export an AAF file with embedded media, you'll also have the choice of whether to include video, audio, or both. Audio media can be embedded in either the WAVE or AIFF-C format.

Recording DVDs

As we write this, multiple incompatible DVD standards are competing for dominance in the marketplace. The list includes DVD-Recordable (DVD-R), DVD-ReWriteable (DVD-RW), DVD-ROM, DVD+R, and DVD+RW. Different standard sizes of DVDs are also available including DVD-5 (4.7GB), DVD-9 (8.54GB, dual-layer), DVD-10 (9.4GB, double-sided, single-layer), and DVD-18 (17GB, dual layer, double-sided). This entire mess is only going to get worse before it gets better. A new format based on blue laser technology rather than red will reach the market in 2003.

The issue of country permissions must also be considered. At the behest of Hollywood, the world was divided into six regions: the United States and Canada; Europe, Japan, South Africa, Egypt, and the Middle East; Australia and New Zealand; Southeast Asia; China; and Africa and the former Soviet Union is in one region and Europe is in another. Every DVD player has a hardware encoder for one of those six designated regions. The publisher (which is you if you're the one making the recording) can decide where to allow a DVD to be played. So don't plan on expanding your DVD collection or bringing DVDs from the United States to Europe or anywhere else.

The only consistency in all of this is that DVDs are recorded in the MPEG-2 format. DVD players and recorders are getting cheaper by the minute. The format has been accepted by consumers at a faster rate than any technology in history, including audio CDs. Therefore, it's clear that DVDs will replace VHS tapes as the home video format. This is why every editing system manufacturer includes the capability to record a DVD.

Most editing systems provide a separate application to create a basic DVD menu and convert a QuickTime or AVI file into an MPEG-2 file to record on a DVD. It is a big pain to export a show as a QuickTime file, import it into another application, or export MPEG-2 to record on your computer's DVD recorder approach. The only people who should be doing this are professionals who are getting paid for it. Seriously, you should only take this approach if you need to create a complex DVD. Authoring applications let you build interactive menu structures that could, for example, permit a user to watch a series of short video segments stored on the DVD in the order he or she desires instead of a preset order.

We side with consumers on this one. We prefer simpler technology. DVD recorders that look like a VHS VCR with an IEEE-1394 port are coming on the market. If you want to make your own DVDs, buy one of these machines.

You'll have to use the quick-and-dirty method we described for recording a show on DV tape. A DVD recorder isn't a camcorder or a DV deck. Your editing system won't be able to control the functions of the DVD recorder. To solve this problem, hook the recorder up to your editing system via Firewire, put it in record, and press Play on the timeline. We wish we could say that the DVD you just recorded will play in any DVD player. Maybe that will be true one day.

Web Formats

QuickTime, Windows Media, and Real are the major video formats used on the Internet. Real files are streamed and heavily compressed. QuickTime files can be uncompressed, compressed at various rates, or streamed. Windows Media files can be compressed at various rates or streamed.

Compressing video for the Internet is part art and part science. Cleaner EZ is a popular software application included with a lot of editing systems. It's designed to convert and/or compress QuickTime and AVI files for use on the Web. Books have been written about the ins and outs of compression. We suggest you read them or take a class if you're serious about streaming video on the Internet.

Importing and Exporting Graphics

Importing graphics into an editing system should be an easy process considering how often people do it. Most editing systems appear to make it easy. There's usually drop-down menu choice to import graphics. After that, it goes downhill fast. You must select a graphic file format to import that matches the format in which the image was stored. The size and resolution of the graphic must match the size of the digital video format you're editing. The image should match the aspect ratio of the video format.

We're not done yet. The shape of the pixels that form the image must match. Last but not least, the color space (the range of colors that can be displayed, which is much smaller in video than the available range on a computer) must be adjusted to match the color space of video. Why things are this way is beyond all reason.

Graphics created with computer software use square pixels because computer monitors use square pixels. Graphics created with digital video editing software use rectangular (nonsquare) pixels because video monitors have rectangular pixels. Standard definition digital video formats use nonsquare pixels. HD video formats use square pixels. Perhaps there's light at the end of the tunnel.

Graphic File Formats

Graphic file formats have proliferated with the same rapidity as video formats. The four most commonly used file formats are JPEG, PICT, Targa, and TIFF. The latter three formats can store an alpha channel mask. The alpha channel determines which parts of the picture will be transparent when keyed over a background.

The JPEG format was developed by the Joint Photographic Experts Group. The acronym for the group gave the file format its name. JPEGs can be highly compressed and retain image quality. However, this format doesn't support an alpha channel. The default extension is .JPEG or .JPG.

The PICT format was developed as a common image format for use on the Mac by Apple Computer. The format supports multiple color depth. The default extension is .PICT or .PIC.

The Targa file format was originally developed by Truevision (now part of Pinnacle Systems) to be used with its video capture cards. This is an uncompressed format. The image quality is outstanding, but the file sizes are very large. The default extension is .TGA.

The TIFF file format (Tagged Image File Format), was developed by Aldus (now part of Adobe Systems) and Microsoft Corporation. It's one of the most commonly used file formats and has the widest possible array of color depths. The maximum supported on professional editing systems is 48-bit color with a 16-bit alpha channel.

Turning Squares into Rectangles So Circles Look Like Circles

This section explains what you need to know to make sure circles remain circles when importing graphics into your editing system. It doesn't matter whether the graphic is a still image from a camera, a scanned negative, a transparency or print, or something you created in a drawing program. If it was created on a computer, it has square pixels.

Standard-definition video monitors use nonsquare pixels. The squares in a computer graphic are automatically transformed into nonsquare pixels whenever you import a graphic. If you don't do anything about it, a perfect circle on your computer-generated graphic will end up looking like an oval in your video. If you follow these steps, your circles will stay circles:

1. What is the standard of the video you are editing?

   The answer determines the frame size in pixels.

Video Standard	Timeline Frame Size
NTSC (North American television standard) SMPTE 601	−720×486
DV-NTSC (miniDV, DVCPro, DVCAM)	−720×480
PAL (European television standard) 601	−720×576
DV-PAL (miniDV, DVCAM, and DVCPro)	−720×576
720p ATSC* HD standard	−1,280×720 (square)
1080i/p ATSC HD standard	−1,920×1,080 (square)

   *Advanced Television Systems Committee

2. Determine whether you're editing standard-definition video in the 4:3 aspect ratio or the 16:9 widescreen aspect ratio. If you're using the 16:9 aspect ratio for video, the graphics must be sized for 16:9.

3. Open your graphics application.

4. Set the image size based on the following timeline frame size table:

Timeline Frame Size	Graphic Image Size at Creation
720×486 (4:3)	720×540
720×486 (16:9)	864×540
720×480 (4:3)	720×534
720×480 (16:9)	960×534
720×576 (4:3)	768×576
720×576 (16:9)	1,024×576
1,280×720	1,280×720
1,920×1,080	1,920×1,080

5. Create a graphic at the appropriate size and save it. Make sure the essential information appears within the title safe area. The image resolution should be 72 pixels per inch (*dots per inch* [dpi]) unless you plan to zoom in on a section of the image. Crop the previously created images to the appropriate size. Save the new version as a copy of the original. This is just good professional practice.

   Ask yourself if t his graphic will be full screen or larger? Images that will fill the frame or appear smaller within the frame only need an image resolution of 72 dpi, which is the resolution of a video monitor. However, if you plan to use a small section of the image to fill the frame, you'll need a higher image resolution. Determine the maximum percent to which you'll enlarge the image. Multiply by 72 to calculate the maximum image resolution you'll need. For example, if you plan to enlarge the image 200 percent, you'll need to save with an image resolution of 144 dpi. This ensures that you will have enough resolution to enlarge the image, not the pixels.

6. Resize the graphic to the appropriate timeline frame size unless you're working in HD. Make sure to uncheck the maintain aspect ratio option in your image-editing application. The idea is to change the aspect ratio. Any circle in the graphic should now appear to be an oval.

For professionals only:

6a. Video has a narrower color space than other graphic environments. Color correct images in your graphics application. Highly saturated colors may be outside the limits of the video color space. Professional digital-editing systems will indicate the presence of illegal colors and adjust them to legal levels. You may need to adjust the black and white level settings in your graphic application to avoid clipping. Check your manual for more details.

7. Select a file format in which to save the graphic. Pick one that your editing system can import.

8. Save the resized graphic in a directory that's easy to find from within your editing system. If possible, use a descriptive name to make it easier to select the correct image. Many editing systems don't have a preview that lets you see the contents of the file before you select it sfor import.

9. Launch your editing system application and import the graphic into a bin.

▬ ▬ ▬ Summary

The technical aspects of digital editing are simpler than ever. Basic skills, such as setting up a monitor, will serve you well. However, you don't have to understand how to fix an editing system to operate one.

Important Points to Remember

▪ Don't let technical information overwhelm you.

▪ A reliable reference monitor is important because it assures you that what you see on your screen is what the audience will see on theirs.

▪ Use high-quality headphones to accurately monitor audio.

▪ Once you've successful transferred material into your editing system, avoid changing the system settings.

What Are They Talking About?

After 50 years, you'd think everyone would use the same words to describe the same things. You'd be wrong. Digital video editing embraces concepts and words from film editing, television production, and computer technology. Throw in the desire of manufacturers to reinvent the wheel and you have the mess that confronts anyone who just wants to make a a movie.

Editing Terminology Cross Reference

System	Timeline	Timeline Cursor	Organization	Bins
Affinity	Tracksheet	Playhead	Project Window	Folders
After Effects	Timeline	Current Time Marker	Project Window	Folders
Avid	Timeline	Position Indicator	Project Window	Bins
Avio	Storyboard	Pointer	Projects	Scene Bin
Blade	Composition	Pointer	Project Window	Bins
Boris FX	Timeline	Current Time Indicator	N/A	N/A
Cinestream	Composition/ Sequencer	Timeline Cursor	Project Window	Bins
CWS 100	Timeline	Timeline Cursor	Materials Area	Bins/ Folders
DV Edit	Sequence Editor	Current Time Bar	Bin Manager	Bins
Edit*	Timeline	Timeline Cursor	Job	Bins

Table 11-1

Picons	# of Viewers	Insert	Overwrite	Source	Master
Posters	Single	Ripple	Overwrite		Clip Editors
N/A	Single	N/A	N/A		Composition
Representative Frame	Multiple	Splice	Overwrite	Source Monitor	Record Monitor
	Multiple	Insert	Replace	Workbox	Record
Thumbnail	Multiple	Ripple	Nonripple	Source	Result
N/A	Multiple	N/A	N/A	Preview	Composite
Poster Frame	Multiple	Insert	Overwrite	Source	Program
Thumbnail	Multiple	Insert	Overwrite	Source Preview	Timeline Preview
Clip Icon	Multiple	Insert	Replace	Source Window	Sequence Window
Picons	Multiple	Insert	Overrecord	Source Viewer	Record Viewer

continues

System	Timeline	Timeline Cursor	Organization	Bins
Editbox	Event Line	Current Frame Marker	Job	Libraries
Edition	Timeline	Timeline Cursor	Project Window	Racks
Final Cut Pro	Timeline	Playhead	Browser	Bins
Fire (Smoke)	Timeline	Positioner	Projects	Clip Library
Flash 5	Timeline	Playhead	Library Window	Folders
Hy-Brow	Timeline	Progress Indicator Bar	Filer-Fax Window	Categories
iFinish (PC)	Program Window	Current Time Indicator	Project Window	Bins
IMovie	Clip Viewer/ Timeline	Playhead	Project	Scrolling Shelf
Incite	Storyboard	Position Bar	Project Window	Collections
IQ	Timeline/ Storyboard	Timeline Cursor	Library	Clip Bins
Kron	Storyboard	Pointer	Project	Scene Bin
Lightworks	Stripview	Current Frame Marker	Project	Galleries/ Racks
Liquid Blue	Master Viewer	Playline	Project Window	Racks
Media 100xr IFinish Mac	Program Window	Current Time Indicator	Project Window	Bins
Media Studio Pro	Timeline Window	Cursor	Production Library	Galleries/ Folders

Table 11-1 (*continued*)

Picons	# of Viewers	Insert	Overwrite	Source	Master
Miniatures	Multiple	Insert	Replace	Viewer	Viewer
Picons	Multiple	Film Style	Overwrite	Source Viewer/ Inlay	Master Viewer/ Inlay
Poster Frame	Multiple	Insert	Overwrite	Viewer	Canvas
Proxy Frame	Multiple	Ripple	Nonripple	Proxies	Big Player
N/A	Single	N/A	N/A		Stage
Mini-Pic	Multiple	Insert	Add	Source Screen	Edit Screen
Clip Keyframe	Single	Insert	Overlay		Edit Suite Window
Thumbnail	Single	Normal	Paste over		Monitor Window
Thumbnail	Multiple	Film Mode	TV Mode	Clip Monitor	Edit Window
Clip Miniature/ Thumbnail	Multiple	Insert	Replace	Floating Clips	Edit Window
	Multiple	Normal	Insert	Workbox	Preview Window
Tiles	Multiple	Insert	Overwrite	Viewer	Viewer
Picons	Multiple	Filmstyle	Overwrite	Source	Viewer
Clip Keyframe	Single	Insert	Overlay		Edit Suite Window
Thumbnail	Multiple	Ripple	Overwrite	Source Window	Preview Window

continues

System	Timeline	Timeline Cursor	Organization	Bins
MoviePack	Timeline	Timeslider	Browser	Albums
Mule	Timeline	Locator	Library Window	Silos
Premiere	Timeline	Edit Line	Project Window	Bins
Raptor Edit	Film Timeline	Timeline cursor	N/A	DV BIN
Rex Edit	Film Timeline	Timeline Cursor	N/A	DV BIN
Screenplay	Storyboard	Cursor Bar	Materials Bin	Clip Drawer
Speed Razor	Composition	Pointer	Project Window	Bins/ Subbins
Studio 8	Storyboard/ Timeline	Timeline Scrubber	Movie Window	Album
Vegas Video	Trackview	Cursor	Project/Media explorer	Media Pool
Video Factory	Trackview	Cursor	Project/Media Explorer	Media Pool
Video Studio	Storyboard/ Timeline	Scroll Bar	Project	Library/ Folders
Xpri	Timeline	Playline	Project	Folder/ Bins

Table 11-1 (*continued*)

Picons	# of Viewers	Insert	Overwrite	Source	Master
Thumbnail	Multiple	Insert	N/A	Source Viewer	Video Control
Icons	Multiple	Insert	Overwrite	Source Viewer	Timeline Viewer
Poster Frame	Multiple	Insert	Overlay	Source Viewer	Program Viewer
N/A	Single	Ripple	Insert		Preview Video
N/A	Single	Ripple	Insert		Preview Video
Thumbnail	Single	Normal Mode	Insert		Viewing Screen
Thumbnail	Multiple	Ripple	Nonripple	Source	Result
Thumbnail	Single	Normal	Insert		Preview Window
Thumbnail	Single	Ripple Edit	Nonripple		Video Preview
Thumbnail	Single	Ripple Edit	Nonripple		Video Preview
Thumbnail	Single	Normal	N/A		Preview Window
Index Picture	Multiple	Splice-In	Overwrite	Source Viewer	Master Viewer

Keyboard Shortcut Cross Reference

System	Play	Stop	Mark In
Affinity	Spacebar, ` L	Spacebar, K	I
After Effects	Spacebar	Spacebar	[
Avid	Spacebar, L, `, 5,	Spacebar, K	I, E
Blade	Spacebar, F1, F10, Alt D P	Spacebar, F2, Alt D S,	I
Boris FX	Spacebar	Spacebar	N/A
Cinestream	D, Spacebar	D, Spacebar	I
CWS 100	0, Enter, Up Arrow	Esc	Cntrl I, 1, 40
DV Edit	Spacebar, L, P	Spacebar	Cntrl 4, 4NP, I, F3
Edit*	P, Spacebar, JL, J4NP	Spacebar	I
Edition	Spacebar, L	Spacebar, K	A
Final Cut Pro	Spacebar, L	Spacebar, K	I
Fire (Smoke)	V	Spacebar	Right Alt
Flash	Enter	Enter	N/A
Hy-Brow	Down Arrow	Spacebar	Mouse
Ifinish	F5, Cntrl., Cntrl+Alt +P, Cntrl ' ,5NP	Cntrl., 0NP	F9, -NP
Imovie	Spacebar	Spacebar	Mouse
Incite	V, Down Arrow, Spacebar	C, Spacebar	Q

Table 11-2

Mark Out	Split Clip	Undo	Prev Edit	Next Edit
O	[	Cmd Z	A	S
]	Cntrl Shift D	Cntrl Z	J	K
O, R	P	Cntrl Z	A	S
O	Insert	Cntrl Z	Cntrl Left Arrow, Shift M	Cntrl Right Arrow, Alt M
N/A	N/A	Cntrl Z	Alt Left Arrow	Alt Right Arrow
O	Cntrl /	History Window	Option Left Arrow, 4	Option Rght Arrow, 5
Cntrl O, 2, 5	Cntrl D	Cntrl Z	Home, Shift Home	End, Shift End
Cntrl 6, 6NP, O, F4	/	Cntrl Z	Mouse	Mouse
O	/	U	Tab, Cntrl Left	Shift Tab, Cntrl Right
S	. (period)	Cntrl Z	Page Up	Page Down
O	Cntrl V	Cmd Z	Option E, Up Arrow	Shift E, Down Arrow
Right Cntrl	Delete	Backspace	Z	X
N/A	N/A	Cntrl Z	Page Up	Page Down
Mouse	Mouse	Mouse	Shift tab	Tab
F10, +NP	Ctrl /	Cntrl Z	Cntrl Tab	Tab
Mouse	Cmd T	Cntrl Z	Mouse	Mouse
W	F6	Cntrl Z	-	+

continues

System	Play	Stop	Mark In
IQ	Spacebar	Spacebar	Dedicated Key
Kron/Avio	F11	H, F10, F12,	I
Liquid Blue, Silver, Purple	Spacebar, L	Spacebar, K	A, I
Media 100 xr	Cmd., Esc, Cmd P, Spacebar, F5	Cmd., Esc, Spacebar	F1
Media Studio Pro	Enter	Enter	F3
MoviePack	Spacebar	Spacebar	Mouse
Mule	Spacebar, L	Spacebar, K	I
Premiere	Spacebar, L	Spacebar, K	I
Raptor Edit	Enter, F2	Escape, F1, F3	Cntrl I
Rex Edit	Enter, F2, Spacebar	Escape, F1, F3	Cntrl I, Shift Up
Screenplay	6NP	5NP, 8NP	-NP
Speed Razor	Spacebar, Cntrl F9	Spacebar	I
Studio 8	Mouse	Mouse	Mouse
Vegas Video/ Video Factory	Spacebar, Cntrl Spacebar, F12, J	Spacebar Escape, Enter, K	I, [,
Video Studio	Enter	Enter	F3
Xpri	5, L	K, Spacebar	E, I, P

Table 11-2 (*continued*)

Mark Out	Split Clip	Undo	Prev Edit	Next Edit
Dedicated Key	Pen	Cntrl Z	Dedicated Key	Dedicated Key
O	SS	Cntrl Insert	Left Arrow	Right Arrow
S, O	. (period)	Cntrl Z	Page Up	Page Down
F2	Cmd/	Cmd Z	Control Tab	Tab
F4	S	Cntrl Z	Page Up	Page Down
Mouse	Mouse	Cntrl Z	Mouse	Mouse
O		Z	Down Arrow	Up Arrow
O	Mouse	Cntrl Z	Cntrl Shift Left Arrow or Page Up	Cntrl Shift Right Arrow or Page Down
Cntrl O	Cntrl D	Cntrl Z Alt Backspace	Shift Home	Shift End
Cntrl O, Shift Down	Cntrl D	Cntrl Z Alt Backspace	Shift Home	Shift End
+NP	2NP	Page Down Key	N/A	N/A
O	Insert	Cntrl Z	Cntrl Left Arrow, Shift M	Cntrl Right Arrow, Alt M
Mouse	Mouse	Cntrl Z	Mouse	Mouse
O,]	S	Cntrl Z, Alt Backspace	Cntrl Alt Left Arrow	Cntrl Alt Right Arrow
F4	N/A	Cntrl Z	Mouse	Mouse
R, O, [	P	Cntrl Z	A	S

continues

System	Select Clip	Insert Edit	Overwrite Edit
Affinity	C	V	B
After Effects	Mouse	N/A	N/A
Avid	T	V	B
Blade	Mouse	Alt R (toggle)	Alt R (toggle)
Boris FX	Mouse	N/A	N/A
Cinestream	Mouse	Q	W
CWS 100	Mouse	Alt R	Insert
DV Edit	Up/Down Arrow, T	Y	H
Edit*	Z	Insert	Insert (toggles)
Edition	Assignable	\ (toggles)	\ (toggles)
Final Cut Pro	Option A, X	F9	F10
Fire (Smoke)	Mouse	G, Cntrl B	H
Flash	Mouse	N/A	N/A
Hy-Brow	Mouse	Mouse	Mouse
Ifinish	Mouse	Alt F12, Alt F11	F12, F11
Imovie	Mouse	Mouse	Shift Cmd V
Incite	S	F8, '	F8 (toggle)
IQ	TBD	TBD	TBD
Kron/Avio	Mouse	Windows Key Insert	Windows Key I
Liquid Blue, Silver, Purple	Assignable	\ (toggles)	\ (toggles)

Table 11-2 (*continued*)

Remove w/ Gap	Remove No Gap	Cut	Copy	Paste
Delete, P,]	Delete P,] (ripple on)	Cmd X	Cmd C	Cmd V
N/A	N/A	Cntrl X	Cntrl C	Cntrl V
Z	X	Cntrl X	Cntrl C	Cntrl V
Cntrl X, Delete	Cntrl Shift C, Cntrl Delete	Cntrl X	Cntrl C	Cntrl D, Cntrl V
Delete	Delete	Cntrl X	Cntrl C	Cntrl V
/	Period	Cntrl X	Cntrl C	Cntrl V
Delete	Delete	Cntrl X	Cntrl C	Cntrl V
Shift Delete	Delete	Cntrl X	Cntrl C	Cntrl V
Delete	Delete	Cntrl X	Cntrl C	Cntrl V
Cntrl, Delete	Cntrl ,Delete	Cntrl X	Cntrl C	Cntrl V
Delete	Shift Delete	Cmd X	Cmd C	Cmd V
(Lift) Shift Period	(Extract) period	[	O	P
N/A	N/A	Cntrl X	Cntrl C	Cntrl V
Mouse	Mouse	Mouse	Mouse	Mouse
Delete, Cntrl Shift Delete	Alt Delete, Cntrl Alt X	Cntrl X	Cntrl C	Cntrl V
N/A	Delete	Cmd X	Cmd C	Cmd V
Delete, F7	Delete, F7	Cntrl X	Cntrl C	Cntrl V
Pen	Pen	N/A	Pen	N/A
Windows Key Delete	Cntrl Delete	Cntrl X	Cntrl C	Cntrl V
Delete	Delete	Cntrl X	Cntrl C	Cntrl V

continues

System	Select Clip	Insert Edit	Overwrite Edit
Media 100 xr	Mouse	Option F12, Option F11	F12, F11
Media Studio Pro	Mouse	R (cycles)	R (cycles)
MoviePack	Mouse	Mouse	Mouse
Mule			
Premiere	Mouse	, (comma)	. (period)
Raptor Edit	Mouse	Alt R (toggle)	Alt R (toggle)
Rex Edit	Mouse	Alt R (toggle)	Alt R (toggle)
Screenplay	Mouse	Mouse	Mouse
Speed Razor	Mouse	R (toggle)	R (toggle)
Studio 8	Mouse	Mouse	Mouse
Vegas Video/ Video Factory	T	Cntrl L	Cntrl D
Video Studio	Mouse	Mouse	N/A
Xpri	T	V	B

Table 11-2 (*continued*)

Remove w/ Gap	Remove No Gap	Cut	Copy	Paste
Cmd X	Option Cmd X	Cmd X	Cmd C	Cmd V
Delete	Delete	Cntrl X	Cntrl C	Cntrl V
Delete	Delete	Cntrl X	Cntrl C	Cntrl V
Delete				
Backspace	Alt Backspace	Cntrl X	Cntrl C	Cntrl V
Delete	Delete	Cntrl X	Cntrl C	Cntrl V
Delete	Delete	Cntrl X	Cntrl C	Cntrl V
Delete	Delete	F1	F2	F3
Cntrl X, Delete	Cntrl Shift C, Cntrl Delete	Cntrl X	Cntrl C	Cntrl D, Cntrl V
Mouse	Mouse	Cntrl X	Cntrl C	Cntrl V
Delete	Delete	Cntrl X, Shift Delete	Cntrl C, Cntrl Insert	Cntrl V, Shift Insert, Cntrl Shift V
N/A	Delete	Cntrl X	Cntrl C	Cntrl V
Z	X	Cntrl X	Cntrl C	Cntrl V

continues

System	Clears Marks	Make Keyframe	Playback Loop
Affinity	G	Mouse	Dedicated Key
After Effects	N/A	Mouse	N/A
Avid	G	N	Alt 6
Blade	N/A	Mouse	/
Boris FX	N/A	Cntrl N, Alt Click	
Cinestream	[	Mouse	F
CWS 100	9	Mouse	Alt S R
DV Edit	F9		F11
Edit*	Ctrl Shift I, Cntrl Shift O	Alt K, A,	Shift P
Edition	G	K	Shift Spacebar
Final Cut Pro	Option X, Option Click	Mouse	Control L
Fire (Smoke)	Shift *(NP)	I	Cntrl Y
Flash	N/A	F6	Alt CL
Hy-Brow	Mouse	N/A	Mouse
Ifinish	Mouse	Cntrl K	Mouse
Imovie	Cmd D	N/A	Menu
Incite	N/A	Left click	N
IQ	TBD	Pen	Spacebar

Table 11-2 (*continued*)

Play in Reverse	Audio Scrub	Audio Waveform	Scale Timeline	Render
J	Always on	Always on	F11, F12, +, -	N/A
Cntrl Alt R	Cntrl Drag	N/A	=, -, ;	Mouse
J	Cap Locks, Shift Cursor	Assignable	Up/Down Arrows	Assignable
Down Arrow, Alt D J L, F9	N/A	Cntrl W	Cntrl Home, +-	Menu
	N/A	N/A		
N/A	Cmd Cntrl+Alt	Mouse	+, -	Menu
Down Arrow	Alt G	N/A	Cntrl E	N/A
J	F12		F7, F8	Shift Cntrl R
JJ	Cntrl	Mouse	+, -, W	F4
J	Scroll Lock	Mouse	Up or Down Arrow	N/A
J	Shift S	Cmd Option W	Option -, Option +	Option R
C	Cntrl Shift V, Cntrl, Ctrl Shift			N/A
N/A	N/A	N/A	Cntrl=, Cntrl -	Menu
N/A	N/A	N/A	Mouse	N/A
N/A	Cntrl ` (prime)	Menu	Cntrl+, Cntrl-, Shift >, Shift <, F2	Mouse
Cmd [	N/A	N/A	Mouse	Menu
X	Mouse	Menu	F3, F4	Mouse
Pen	TBD	Pen	Pen	N/A

continues

System	Clears Marks	Make Keyframe	Playback Loop
Kron/Avio	N/A	N/A	N/A
Liquid Blue	G	K	Shift Spacebar
Media 100 xr	Cmd H	Mouse	Cmd \
Media Studio Pro	N/A	Mouse	Shift Spacebar
MoviePack	Mouse	Mouse	Mouse
Mule			
Premiere	G	Mouse	Mouse
Raptor Edit	N/A	N/A	Menu
Rex Edit	Menu	N/A	Alt Enter
Screenplay	N/A	N/A	N/A
Speed Razor	N/A	Mouse	/
Studio 8	Mouse	N/A	Mouse
Vegas Video/ Video Factory	N/A	Mouse	Q
Video Studio	N/A	N/A	Mouse
Xpri	G	[	6

Table 11-2 (*continued*)

Play in Reverse	Audio Scrub	Audio Waveform	Scale Timeline	Render
N/A	N/A	w	Windows Key Page Up/ Page Down	F9
J	Scroll Lock	Mouse	Up/Down Arrows	N/A
N/A	Cmd ` (prime)	Menu	Cmd =, Cmd), Cmd+, Cmd-, Shift <, Shift >	Mouse
menu	N/A	N/A	+ -, Z, Shift Z	Enter
N/AS	Menu	Always on	F3, F4	Cntrl R
J	Menu			Cntrl R
Cntrl Alt Spacebar or Cmd Option Spacebar	N/A	Mouse	\ or Mouse	Enter
Shift<- Shift Space	Shift Drag	N/A	Mouse	Menu
N/A	Alt G	N/A	Mouse	Menu
N/A	N/A	N/A	N/A	N/A
N/A	N/A	Cntrl W	Cntrl Home, +-	Menu
N/A	N/A	N/A	Mouse	Menu
J	Always on	Menu	Up/Down Arrow, Cntrl Up/Down Arrow, /	Menu
N/A	N/A	N/A	Cntrl Mouse Scroll	Menu
J	Assignable	Assignable	Cntrl +, Cntrl -	Assignable

Films to Watch

Films to Watch

You can learn a lot about editing by watching any film that appeals to you. Just watch closely and try to analyze why you like it. From an editor's perspective, the reason some scenes are preferable to others relates to timing. Timing and motion are the two keys to shot selection. Either the shot has great timing (due to the performance or action) or the editor has to create timing with the placement of the cuts. Each shot has either motion within the frame or camera movement that creates motion or the editor must create motion outside the frame using a cut. Ideally, a cut occurs when you want to refocus the audience's attention. This is a way to make them turn their bodies or heads. In an interview, John Huston explained,

> To me, the perfect film is as though it were unwinding behind your eyes and your eyes were projecting it themselves, so that you were seeing what you wished to see. Film is like thought. It the closest to thought processes of any art. Look at that lamp across the room. Now, look back at me. Look back at the lamp. Now look back at me again. Did you see what you did? You blinked. Those are the cuts.[1]

To concentrate on the editing, watch our recommendations with the sound off. Next, watch the film a second time with the sound on and pay attention to the sound editing. Alan Splet, one of the most influential sound editors of the past 30 years, when asked what his contribution to a film was, simply said, "Sound is a heart thing."[2] Watch some of your favorite films with and without the sound. Ask yourself, "Do I still like it without the sound?"

---

[1]Louise Sweeney. Christian Science Monitor (August 11, 1973).
[2]From a radio interview conducted by Randy Thom in 1980 that was recalled by Thom in *Mix Magazine* (February 1995): 141.

If You Only Watch One . . .

Raging Bull   A masterpiece of storytelling and editing from Marty
Scorsese and Thelma Schoonmaker, editor. There's so much to
learn from this film. Roger Ebert does a three-hour seminar at
Film Festivals that only begins to scratch the surface.

Editing 101

Amadeus, edited by Nena Danavic and Michael Chandler.
Watch the scene where Mozart's wife meets with Salieri. Music,
narration, live action, and flashback are intercut. Note also the
scene in which Salieri describes the Requiem.

The Apartment, edited by Daniel Mandell.   Watch for dialogue and
scene setup.

Apocalypse Now, edited by Lisa Fruchtman, Gerald B. Greenberg,
Richard Marks, and Walter Murch.   Watch the helicopter
sequence set to Wagner in which the Vietnamese village is
bombed. Note how the music score and the rhythm of editing
build to a climax. Watch also for the moment of silence that's part
of this soundscape.

The Birds, edited by George Tomasino.   Watch the gas station
attack for an example of rhythm in editing.

Bullitt, edited by Frank P. Keller.   The chase sequence in San
Francisco is remarkable for its simplicity and length.

Chinatown, edited by Sam O'Steen.   Every scene has a clear
beginning, middle, and end. Jack Nicholson's character always
exits and enters the frame unraveling the story as we move with
him. A Roman Polanski masterpiece.

Day of the Jackal, edited by Ralph Kemplan. Watch the attempted assassination of President DeGaulle for editing that builds suspense through perfect timing.

Deer Hunter, edited by Peter Zinner. Watch the Russian roulette scene.

Easy Rider, edited by Don Cambern and directed by Dennis Hopper. Watch the montage sequences cut to rock music that evoke independence and freedom. The acid trip sequence among the graves of New Orleans is a classic.

The Exorcist, edited by Norman Gay, Evan Lottman, and Bud S. Smith. Watch the opening scenes of what is a classic horror film.

The Godfather, edited by William H. Reynolds and Peter Zinner. Coppola's three-part masterpiece. Watch the baptism scene for a classic example of montage American-style in which Michael Corleone takes revenge on his enemies while his child is being baptized.

The Good, The Bad, and The Ugly, edited by Eugenio Alabiso and Nino Baragli. Watch the final showdown for a classic lesson in how to build a scene.

Groundhog Day, edited by Pembroke J. Herring. Watch the meticulous construction of the scenes as the same day is repeated over and over throughout the film. The editing pace changes from sequence to sequence, reflecting the character's point of view.

Harold & Maude, edited by William A. Sawyer and Edward A. Warschilka. Watch for a great example of parallel editing in the funeral scene and the sixties era music montage sequence that shows their budding relationship.

Home Alone, edited by Raja Gosnell. Watch the sequence that opens the film—a child is advertently left at home that builds to the point when his mother remembers that he is not on the airplane with the rest of the family.

Indiana Jones and the Temple of Doom, edited by Michael Kahn. The opening sequence starts in China with a nightclub number and titles, and ends in India.

The Insider, edited by William Goldberg, David Rosenbloom, and Paul Rubell. Another great example of parallel editing throughout the film. Watch the sequence that climaxes with the first time the whistleblower testifies at a court hearing.

It Happened One Night, edited by Gene Havlick.   Dozens of cheats such as cuts on lens changes no one would do today.

Jaws, edited by Verna Fields.   A course in how to make something out of nothing.

The Longest Day, edited by Samuel Beetley.   Watch the landing sequence and Omaha beach assault.

The Matrix, edited by Zach Staenberg.   Watch the fight sequences that broke new ground, especially for use of motion effects.

Miller's Crossing, edited by Michael Miller.   Brilliant pacing in this Coen Brothers' crime drama. Watch the assassination attempt on Leo, Albert Finney's character, in his burning house, set to the great Irish tenor, Frank Patterson, singing "Oh Danny Boy."

The Natural, edited Stu Linder.   Watch the closing scene for a textbook example of building to a climax.

On the Waterfront, edited by Gene Milford.   Watch the opening scenes, the scene in the back of a taxicab, and Brando's confrontation with the dock bosses at the end.

The Professional, edited by Michelle David.   Watch the action editing in the final scenes when the hit man meets the renegade detective.

Pulp Fiction, edited by Sally Menke.   Watch how the chronological order of scenes are rearranged to maximum effect.

Purple Rose of Cairo, edited by Susan E. Morse.   Watch how the two realities—the characters interacting with the characters in the movie within the movie—play out.

Psycho, edited by George Tomasino.   Watch the shower scene.

Raiders of the Lost Ark, edited by Michael Kahn.   Watch the opening scene—classic storytelling.

Rocky, edited by Scott Conrad and Richard Halsey.   Watch Rocky's training routine, the training montage leading up to the climatic fight, and the fight itself for classic storytelling. Shot in Philadelphia so we had to include it.

Ronin, edited by Tony Gibbs.   A great, more recent lengthy car chase through Paris directed by John Frankenheimer who shot chases the old-fashioned way.

Singin' in the Rain, edited by Adrienne Fazan.   All the blinks in the right places.

The Shining, edited by Ray Lovejoy.   The suspense and horror in this Kubrick masterpiece comes from the editing.

Speed, edited by John Wright.   Watch the action cutting as the runaway bus moves through traffic and as Sandra Bullock's character takes control of the bus.

The Sting, edited by William Reynolds.   A Hollywood classic where timing, continuity editing, and editing create smooth suspense.

The Thirty-Nine Steps, directed by Alfred Hitchcock.   Note the overlapping sound of the train whistle as a maid discovers a corpse in an empty flat. A moment that has been imitated for sixty years.

This is Spinal Tap, edited by Robert Leighton.   Documentary-style editing with nearly no cutaways, which makes the film feel over the top. Watch the scene under the rock concert arena in Cleveland, Ohio.

Traffic, edited by Stephen Mirrione.   Raw editing complemented the other design elements to give the film a gritty, hard reality.

Unforgiven, edited by Joel Cox.   Pauses amid action add to the remarkable timing in every scene.

Usual Suspects, edited by John Ottman.   Careful editing throughout guarantees the secret identity remains intact.

Wall Street, edited by Claire Simpson.   Watch the scenes where stocks are bought and sold in a frenzy. Great action editing of what is essentially an office scene.

The Wild Bunch, edited by Lou Lombardo.   Editing makes the film's opening—the gang is assaulted in an ambush following a failed bank robbery in a Texas border town and the climatic end when they are cut to ribbons after being double-crossed by a Mexican warlord. Two of the most violent shoot-ups ever filmed. At the time, the film set a record for highest number of edits in a feature film.

Winter Sleepers, edited by Katya Dringenberg.   Watch the auto accident scene, which is particularly well edited.

Witness, edited by Thom Noble Watch these scenes—the murder, the young boy recognizing the killer's photograph, and the love scenes. Compare the barn-raising scene to the same scene in Oklahoma!

Avanced Editing Techniques

Bonnie and Clyde, edited by Dede Allen.   Watch the bank robbery montage sequence set to Flat and Scruggs' "Foggy Mountain Breakdown."

The Candidate, edited by Robert Estrin and Richard A. Harris. Watch the scene in which Robert Redford's character, Bill McKay, watches Don Porter's character, Senator Crocker Jarmon, give a speech. You'll notice quiet shots, reaction shots, that draw the audience in and move the story along.

The Conversation, edited by Walter Murch.   Watch the party scene in the loft office for a wonderful illustration of Walter Murch's ideas about editing.

The French Connection, edited by Jerry Greenberg.   Watch the car chase under the elevated train with the sound off so you can see all the tricks and then watch it with the sound to see how the sound makes the chase work. Bullit, also has a great chase sequence, an earlier effort from the same filmmaking team.

Goodfellas.   Another masterpiece from Marty Scorsese and Thelma Schoonmaker, editor.

Maltese Falcon.   Great timing within the scenes, which is the director's doing, but the editor knows that and uses it to great advantage.

Mean Streets, edited by Sidney Levine.   Marty Scorsese's first film with his expedient and original editing.

Medium Cool, edited by Verna Fields.   Watch for the integration of documentary and dramatic scenes. Filmed during the Democratic National Convention in Chicago in 1968.

The Oxbow Incident, edited by Allen McNeil, and *12 Angry Men,* edited by Carl Lerner.   Watch either film for advanced techniques on how to sustain audience interest and handle big groups. Stories that handle big groups of people are rarely attempted in film.

Run Lola Run, edited by Mathilde Bonnefoy.   Circular construction based on the unity of time. The events are reedited with minor adjustments of time and space to show various possible conclusions as a woman runs to save her boyfriend.

For Comedy Editing

Annie Hall, edited by Wendy Greene Bricmont and Ralph Rosenblum.   The editing makes the film.

His Girl Friday, edited by Gene Havlick.   There's no action in the film so the editor creates all the speed and action.

M*A*S*H, edited by Danford B. Greene.   The comic timing comes from the editing

For Sound Editing

Apollo 13, edited by Daniel Hanley and Michael Hill.

Das Boot, edited by Hannes Nikel.   Watch of the carefully built sound scape of precise sounds and suspenseful silence.

Eraserhead, The Black Stallion, Never Cry Wolf, Dune, Sound Editing by Alan Splet.

Hunt for the Red October, edited by Dennis Verkler and John Wright. Sound as a reality. Note the underwater scenes where sound editing and reaction shots create an intense reality.

The Matrix or other special-effects-driven films are also good to watch for sound editing.

Pearl Harbor is a recent example of a film that doesn't work well without the sound.

For Documentary Editing

Day After Trinity by Jon Else.

Harlan County by Barbara Koppel.

Hoop Dreams, Bill Haugse, Steve James, Frederick Marx.

Law and Order by Frederick Wiseman.

Let It Be, Michael Lindsay-Hogg.

Night and Fog, Alain Resnais.

Roger and Me, Michael Moore.

Salesman by Albert Maysles and Charlotte Zwerin.

Silverlake Life, The View from Here by Peter Friedman.

Thin Blue Line by Errol Morris.

The Wonderful, Horrible Life of Leni Riefenstahl, Ray Muller III.

Woodstock, by Thelma Schoonmaker.

Award Winners

American Cinema Editors is an honorary society of motion picture editors founded in 1950 that gives out Eddie Awards in two categories: Drama Feature and Comedy or Musical Feature. The Eddie Award nominees are listed from 1970 to the present. The winners are in bold. The same indication is used for the nominees and winners of the Academy Award for film editing that follow the list of Eddies. The Academy Award list goes back to 1934. Where appropriate we've made notes about the films and suggested scenes to watch. Not every award winner is a great film. In a close-knit industry sometimes reasons other than quality intercede. The Academy Awards were started and have been dominated by the Hollywood studios. Some classic films on many top 100 lists have been ignored by the Academy. However, it's a good starting point for any student of the art of motion pictures.

Eddie Award Nominees

2001

A Beautiful Mind, Dan Hanley, Mike Hill.   Watch the scenes leading up to the discovery of his mental illness.

Black Hawk Down, Pietro Scalia.   Watch the battle sequence.

Harry Potter and the Philosopher's Stone, Richard Francis-Bruce. Special Effects extravangza.

The Lord of the Rings: The Fellowship of the Ring, John Gilbert. Watch the scene where the decision is made to send Frodo with the Ring and the battle between the members of the Fellowship and the Orcs at the end.

Memento, Dody Dorn.   Storytelling in reverse done well, though not as well as in *Winter Sleepers,* which preceded this film.

Comedy/Musical Film:

Amelie, Herve Schneid

Gosford Park, Tim Squyres

Monsters, Inc., Jim Stewart.   Animation.

Moulin Rouge, Jill Bilcock.   Musical redux.

The Royal Tenenbaums, Dylan Tichenor.   Comedy.

Shrek, Sim Evan Jones.   Animation

2000

Billy Elliot, John Wilson.   Watch the dance sequence when Billy discovers his abilities.

Cast Away, Arthur Schmidt.   Watch how tension is created with only one character and one location.

Crouching Tiger, Hidden Dragon, Tim Squyres.   Watch the balletic fight sequence in the courtyard and across the roofs.

Gladiator, Pietro Scalia.   Watch the opening 20 minutes.

Traffic, Stephen Mirrione.   Watch each story individually and then compare the editing from one story to the next.

Comedy/Musical Film:

Almost Famous, Joe Hutshing and Saar Klein.   Watch the scene with the groupies in the hotel.

Best In Show, Robert Leighton.   Watch the dog show sequence that's the climax of the film.

Chocolat, Andrew Mondshein.   Romantic comedy.

O Brother, Where Art Thou? Roderick Jaynes and Tricia Cooke. Watch the scene in which George Clooney confronts his wife and her new husband.

Shanghai Noon, Richard Chew.   Watch this or any Jackie Chan movie for the editing in the fight scenes that makes the action work.

1999

American Beauty, Tariq Anwar, Christopher Greenbury.   Watch the sequence in which Lester transforms himself in the garage and the dinner table scene when he announces he's lost his job.

The Insider, William Goldenberg, David Rosenbloom, Paul Rubell.

The Matrix, Zach Staenberg.   Watch the fight scenes for the use of motion effects.

The Sixth Sense, Andrew Mondshein.   Look for the clues the editor left that all is not what it seems.

The Talented Mr. Ripley, Walter Murch.   Watch the boating sequence.

Comedy/Musical Film:

Analyze This, Christopher Tellefsen.   Pay attention to how the subplots are handled or not handled in this film.

Being John Malkovich, Eric Zumbrunnen.   Watch the scene when Malkovich discovers there's someone inside his head and the scene with dozens of John Malkoviches.

Election, Kevin Tent.

Man On The Moon, Christopher Tellefsen, Lynzee Klingman, Adam Boome.

Run Lola Run, Mathilde Bonnefoy.

1998

The Horse Whisperer, Hank Corwin, Freeman A. Davies, Tom Rolf. Watch the accident scene.

Out Of Sight, Anne V. Coates.

Saving Private Ryan, Michael Kahn.   Watch the first 20 minutes and compare to other WWII battle scenes, including *The Thin Red Line*.

Shakespeare In Love, David Gamble.   Watch the performance for the Queen and the love scenes.

The Thin Red Line, Leslie Jones, Saar Klein, Billy Weber.   Watch the battle scenes and compare to *Saving Private Ryan*.

1997

Air Force One, Richard Francis-Bruce.   Airplane disaster movie. Pay attention to the sound design and the rousing climax when Ford defeats the terrorists.

As Good As It Gets, Richard Marks.   Watch the scenes in the diner.

Good Will Hunting, Pietro Scalia.   Watch the scene in the bar as Matt Damon tries to pick-up Minnie Driver.

L. A. Confidential, Peter Honess.   Watch the climatic gun battle.

Titanic, Conrad Buff, James Cameron, Richard A. Harris.   Watch the ballroom sequence followed by the party below decks.

1996

The English Patient, Walter Murch.   Watch the scene in the church with the nurse.

Evita, Gerry Hambling.   Watch the scene in the bar that introduces Antonio Banderas.

Fargo, Ethan Coen, Joel Coen.   Watch the two scenes in which Marge asks Jerry about the murders and his car.

The Rock, Richard Francis-Bruce.   Watch the sequence in which Sean Connery escapes from his handlers and the assault sequence that leads to the team being slaughtered.

Shine, Pip Karmel.   Watch the scene in which Helfgott plays the piano in a restaurant and pay attention to the sound design.

1995

Apollo 13, Daniel P. Hanley, Michael Hill.   A great film for its sound design.

Braveheart, Steven Rosenblum.   Watch the battle scenes and compare to *Gladiator*.

Casino, Thelma Schoonmaker

Crimson Tide, Chris Lebenzon.   Another great film for sound editing.

The Usual Suspects, John Ottman.   Thriller with a twist.

1994

Forrest Gump, Arthur Schmidt.   Noted for placing Tom Hanks in historic events and making it look seamless.

Pulp Fiction, Sally Menke.

The Shawshank Redemption, Richard Francis-Bruce.   Prison drama.

Speed, John Wright.

True Lies, Conrad Buff, Mark Goldblatt, Richard A. Harris.

1993

The Fugitive, Don Brochu, David Finfer, Dean Goodhill, Dov Hoenig, Richard Nord, Dennis Virkler.   Watch the train wreck sequence for action editing.

In the Line of Fire, Anne V. Coates.   Watch the sequence in which Eastwood recalls the assassination.

In the Name of the Father, Gerry Hambling.

The Piano, Veronika Jenet.

Schindler's List, Michael Kahn.

1992

A Few Good Men, Robert Leighton.   Taut courtroom drama.

The Last of the Mohicans, Dov Hoenig, Arthur Schmidt.   Watch the battle scenes.

The Player, Geraldine Peroni.   Watch the opening 30 minutes.

Scent of a Woman, Harvey Rosenstock, William Steinkamp, Michael Tronick

Unforgiven, Joel Cox. Watch the opening sequence and the climactic gun battle.

1991

JFK, Joe Hutshing, Pietro Scalia.

The Silence of the Lambs, Craig Mckay.

Terminator 2: Judgment Day, Conrad Buff, Mark Goldblatt, Richard A. Harris.

1990

Dances with Wolves, Neil Travis.   Watch the sequence in which Costner arrives at his lonely outpost.

Ghost, Walter Murch.   Watch the love scenes between Patrick Swayze and Demi Moore.

Goodfellas, Thelma Schoonmaker.   Watch the scene in the Copacabana nightclub and the scene in which Joe Pesci reveals his violent nature.

1989

Born on the Fourth of July, edited by David Brenner, Joe Hutshing.

Field of Dreams, edited by Ian Crafford.   Watch how the scene is built as the spectators arrive to watch the ballgame.

Glory, edited by Steven Rosenblum.   Watch the battle scene on the beach and compare to *Saving Private Ryan* or the *Longest Day.*

1988

Mississippi Burning, edited by Gerry Hambling.

Rain Man, edited by Stewart Linder.

Who Framed Roger Rabbit, edited by Arthur Schmidt.

1987

Broadcast News, edited by Richard Marks.   Watch the scene that establishes the interplay between Albert Brooks, William Hurt, and Holly Hunter as Brooks relays questions from Hunter to Hurt.

Fatal Attraction, edited by Peter E. Berger, Michael Kahn.   Watch the climatic scene in which Douglas kills Glenn Close.

The Last Emperor, edited by Gabriella Cristiani.   Wonderful editing of an epic story.

1986

Hoosiers, edited by C. Timothy O'Meara.   Watch the basketball games and the scene's that establish Hackman's lonely existence.

The Mission, edited by Jim Clark.

Platoon, edited by Claire Simpson.   Watch how the editing shifts the story from character to character.

1985

Out of Africa, edited by Pembroke J. Herring, Sheldon Kahn, Fredric Steinkamp, William Steinkamp.

Runaway Train, edited by Henry Richardson.

Witness, edited by Thom Noble.

1984

Amadeus, edited by Michael Chandler, Nena Danevic.

The Killing Fields, edited by Jim Clark.   Watch the trek to escape sequence.

Romancing the Stone, edited by Donn Cambern, Frank Morriss. Watch the opening scene that reveals Joan's character traits, which follows immediately after the first action sequence.

1983

Flashdance, edited by Walt Mulconery, Bud Smith.   Watch the dance sequences.

The Right Stuff, edited by Glenn Farr, Lisa Fruchtman, Tom Rolf, Stephen A. Rotter.

Wargames, edited by Tom Rolf .

1982

E. T.: The Extra-Terrestrial, edited by Carol Littleton.

Gandhi, edited by John Bloom.

Tootsie, edited by Fredric Steinkamp, William Steinkamp.   Watch the opening scene that establishes Dustin Hoffman's character clearly in just a few minutes.

1981

On Golden Pond, edited by Robert L. Wolfe.

Raiders of the Lost Ark, edited by Michael Kahn.

Reds, edited by Dede Allen, Craig Mckay.   Watch the Russian revolution sequence and pay attention to the placement of the witnesses that are intercut with the drama.

1980

Coal Miner's Daughter, edited by Arthur Schmidt

Fame, edited by Gerry Hambling. Watch the dance sequences.

Raging Bull, edited by Thelma Schoonmaker

1979

All That Jazz, edited by Alan Heim. Watch the dance sequences.

Apocalypse Now, edited by Lisa Fruchtman, Gerald B. Greenberg, Richard Marks, Walter Murch

The Black Stallion, edited by Robert Dalva. Watch the storm at sea sequence.

1978

The Deer Hunter, edited by Peter Zinner. Watch the Russian roulette sequence.

Hooper, edited by Donn Cambern

Superman, edited by Stuart Baird.

1977

Close Encounters of the Third Kind, edited by Michael Kahn

Star Wars, edited by Richard Chew, Paul Hirsch, Marcia Lucas

The Turning Point, edited by William H. Reynolds. Watch how the dance sequences are used to point out the contrasts between the characters.

1976

All the President's Men, edited by Robert L. Wolfe

Network, edited by Alan Heim

Rocky, edited by Scott Conrad, Richard Halsey. Watch the boxing sequences.

1975

Jaws, edited by Verna Fields

The Hindenburg, edited by Donn Cambern

One Flew Over the Cuckoo's Nest, edited by Richard Chew, Sheldon Kahn, Lynzee Klingman

1974

Earthquake, edited by Dorothy Spencer

The Longest Yard, edited by Michael Luciano

The Towering Inferno, edited by Carl Kress, Harold F. Kress

1973

The Day of the Jackal, edited by Ralph Kemplen

Jonathan Livingston Seagull, edited by James Galloway, Frank P. Keller

The Sting, edited by William H. Reynolds

1972

Cabaret, edited by David Bretherton

The Godfather, edited by William H. Reynolds, Peter Zinner

The Poseidon Adventure, edited by Harold F. Kress

1971

The African Elephant, edited by Alan L. Jaggs

Fiddler on the Roof, edited by Antony Gibbs, Robert Lawrence

The French Connection, edited by Gerald B. Greenberg

Kotch, edited by Ralph E. Winters

Summer of '42, edited by Folmar Blangsted

Willard, edited by Warren Low

1970

Airport, edited by Stuart Gilmore

The Great White Hope, edited by William Reynolds

M*A*S*H, edited by Danford B. Greene

Patton, edited by Hugh S. Fowler

Tora! Tora! Tora! edited by Inoue Chikaya, Pembroke J. Herring, James E. Newcom

Oscar Nominees for Achievement in Film Editing

2001

A Beautiful Mind Mike Hill, Dan Hanley.

Black Hawk Down, Pietro Scalia.

The Lord of the Rings: The Fellowship of the Ring, John Gilbert.

Memento, Dody Dorn.

Moulin Rouge, Jill Bilcock.

2000

Almost Famous, Joe Hutshing, Saar Klein.

Crouching Tiger, Hidden Dragon, Tim Squyres.

Gladiator, Pietro Scalia.

Traffic, Stephen Mirrione.

Wonder Boys, Dede Allen.

1999

American Beauty, Tariq Anwar.

The Cider House Rules, Lisa Zeno Churgin.

The Insider, William Goldenberg, Paul Rubell, David Rosenbloom.

The Matrix, Zach Staenberg.

The Thin Red Line, Bill Webber, Leslie Jones.

1998

Life Is Beautiful, Simona Paggi.
Out of Sight, Anne V. Coates.
Saving Private Ryan, Michael Kahn.
Shakespeare in Love, David Gamble.
The Thin Red Line, Bill Webber, Leslie Jones.

1997

Air Force One, Richard Francis-Bruce.
As Good As It Gets, Richard Marks.
Good Will Hunting, Pietro Scalia.
L.A. Confidential, Peter Honess.
Titanic, Conrad Buff, James Cameron, Richard A. Harris.

1996

The English Patient, Walter Murch.
Evita, Gerry Hambling.
Fargo, Roderick Jaynes.
Jerry Maguire, Joe Hutshing.
Shine, Pip Karmel.

1995

Apollo 13, Dan Hanley, Mike Hill.
Babe, Marcus D'Arcy, Jay Friedkin.
Braveheart, Steven Rosenblum.
Crimson Tide, Chris Lebenzon.
Seven, Richard Francis-Bruce.

1994

Forrest Gump, Arthur Schmidt.

Hoop Dreams, Bill Haugse, Steve James, Frederick Marx.

Pulp Fiction, Sally Menke.

The Shawshank Redemption, Richard Francis-Bruce.

Speed, John Wright.

1993

The Fugitive, Don Brochu, David Finfer, Dean Goodhill, Dov Hoenig, Richard Nord, Dennis Virkler.

In the Line of Fire, Anne V. Coates.

In the Name of the Father, Gerry Hambling.

The Piano, Veronika Jenet.

Schindler's List, Michael Kahn.

1992

Basic Instinct, Frank J. Urioste.

The Crying Game, Kant Pan.

A Few Good Men, Robert Leighton.

The Player, Geraldine Peroni.

Unforgiven, Joel Cox.

1991

The Committments, Gerry Hambling.

JFK, Joe Hutshing, Pietro Scalia.

The Silence of the Lambs, Craig McKay.

Terminator 2: Judgment Day, Conrad Buff, Mark Goldblatt, Richard A. Harris.

Thelma & Louise, Thom Noble.

1990

Dances with Wolves, Neil Travis.

Ghost, Walter Murch.

The Godfather, Part III, Lisa Fruchtman, Barry Malkin, Walter Murch.

Goodfellas, Thelma Schoonmaker.

The Hunt for Red October, Dennis Virkler, John Wright.

1989

The Bear, Noelle Boisson.

Born on the Fourth of July, David Brenner, Joe Hutshing.

Driving Miss Daisy, Mark Warner.

The Fabulous Baker Boys, William Steinkamp.

Glory, Steven Rosenblum.

1988

Die Hard, John F. Link, Frank J. Urioste.

Gorillas in the Mist, Stuart Baird.

Mississippi Burning, Gerry Hambling.

Rain Man, Stu Linder.

Who Framed Roger Rabbit, Arthur Schmidt.

1987

Broadcast News, Richard Marks.

Empire of the Sun, Michael Kahn.

Fatal Attraction, Peter E. Berger, Michael Kahn.

The Last Emperor, Gabriella Cristiani.

Robocop, Frank J. Urioste.

1986

Aliens, Ray Lovejoy.

Hannah and Her Sisters, Susan E. Morse.

The Mission, Jim Clark.

Platoon, Claire Simpson.

Top Gun, Chris Lebenzon, Billy Weber.

1985

A Chorus Line, John Bloom.

Out of Africa, Pembroke Herring, Sheldon Kahn, Fredric Steinkamp, William Steinkamp.

Prizzi's Honor, Kaja Fehr, Rudi Fehr.

Runaway Train, Henry Richardson.

Witness, Thom Noble.

1984

Amadeus, Michael Chandler, Nena Danevic.

The Cotton Club, Robert Q. Lovett, Barry Malkin.

The Killing Fields, Jim Clark.

A Passage to India, David Lean.

Romancing the Stone, Donn Cambern, Frank Morriss.

1983

Blue Thunder, Edward Abroms, Frank Morriss.

Flashdance, Walt Mulconery, Bud Smith.

The Right Stuff, Glenn Farr, Lisa Fruchtman, Tom Rolf, Stephen A. Rotter, Douglas Stewart.

Silkwood, Sam O'Steen.

Terms of Endearment, Richard Marks.

1982

Das Boot, Hannes Nikel.

E.T.: The Extra-Terrestrial, Carol Littleton.

Gandhi, John Bloom.

An Officer and a Gentleman Peter Zinner.   Watch Richard Gere's boxing scenes.

Tootsie, Fredric Steinkamp, William Steinkamp.   Watch the opening scene that establishes the character of the role Dustin Hoffman played.

1981

Chariots of Fire, Terry Rawlings.   Watch the racing scene in the courtyard.

The French Lieutenant's Woman, John Bloom.   Drama.

On Golden Pond, Robert L. Wolfe.   Drama.

Raiders of the Lost Ark, Michael Kahn.

Reds, Dede Allen, Craig McKay.

1980

Coal Miner's Daughter, Arthur Schmidt.   Watch the performance scene editing.

The Competition, David Blewitt.   Romance.

The Elephant Man, Anne V. Coates.   Watch the scene in which the doctor discovers the Elephant Man.

Fame, Gerry Hambling.   Watch how the dance performances are edited.

Raging Bull, Thelma Schoonmaker.

1979

All That Jazz, Alan Heim.   Watch the dance sequences for editing.

Apocalypse Now, Lisa Fruchtman, Gerald B. Greenberg, Richard Marks, Walter Murch.

The Black Stallion, Robert Dalva.   Watch the storm sequence for classic editing.

Kramer vs. Kramer, Jerry Greenberg.   Watch how the breakup scene is edited.

The Rose, C. Timothy O'Meara, Robert L. Wolfe.   Watch the editing of the performance scenes.

1978

The Boys from Brazil, Robert E. Swink.

Coming Home, Don Zimmerman.   Watch the love scene.

The Deer Hunter, Peter Zinner.

Midnight Express, Gerry Hambling.

Superman, Stuart Baird.

1977

Close Encounters of the Third Kind, Michael Kahn.

Julia, Walter Murch.   Watch the sequence of Julia traveling to Germany to see how tension and suspense is created.

Smokey and the Bandit, Walter Hannemann, Angelo Ross. Compare these car chases to *Bullitt* or *French Connection*.

Star Wars, Richard Chew, Paul Hirsch, Marcia Lucas.

The Turning Point, William Reynolds.   Watch how the dance sequences are edited.

1976

All the President's Men, Robert L. Wolfe.   Newspaper suspense story.

Bound for Glory, Pembroke J. Herring, Robert Jones.   Watch David Carradine's arrival at the Okie camp and compare to the *Grapes of Wrath*.

Network, Alan Heim.   Watch the editing in the sequence in which Peter Finch's character goes mad.

Rocky, Scott Conrad, Richard Halsey.   Watch the boxing scenes and compare to *Raging Bull*, *Champion*, and other boxing films.

Two-Minute Warning, Walter Hannemann, Eve Newman.   Skip it.

1975

Dog Day Afternoon, Dede Allen.   Robbery film with no action.

Jaws, Verna Fields.

The Man Who Would Be King, Russell Lloyd.   Adventure.

One Flew Over the Cuckoo's Nest, Richard Chew, Sheldon Kahn, Lynzee Klingman.

Three Days of the Condor, Don Guidice, Fredric Steinkamp.   Watch the opening sequence from when Redford goes to lunch and returns.

1974

Blazing Saddles, Danford Greene, John C. Howard.   Comedy.

Chinatown, Sam O'Steen.

Earthquake, Dorothy Spencer.

The Longest Yard, Michael Luciano.   Watch how the football game is edited.

The Towering Inferno, Carl Kress, Harold F. Kress.   Watch how the editing of the party scene builds into the scene of panic.

1973

American Graffiti, Verna Fields, Marcia Lucas

The Day of the Jackal, Ralph Kemplen.   Watch how the sequence of the assassin prepping for his job.

The Exorcist, Norman Gay, Jordan Leondopoulos, Evan Lottman, Bud Smith.   Watch the exorcism scene.

Jonathan Livingston Seagull, James Galloway, Frank P. Keller

The Sting, William Reynolds.

1972

Cabaret, David Bretherton.   Musical combined with drama.

Deliverance, Tom Priestley.   Watch the classic Dueling Banjos sequence.

The Godfather, William Reynolds, Peter Zinner.

The Hot Rock, Fred W. Berger, Frank P. Keller.   Watch the raid on the police station—edited for hilarity.

The Poseidon Adventure, Harold F. Kress.   The airplane disaster on a boat film.

1971

The Andromeda Strain, Stuart Gilmore, John W. Holmes.

A Clockwork Orange, Bill Butler.   Watch Alex's retraining sequence.

The French Connection, Jerry Greenberg

Kotch, Ralph E. Winters.   Comedy.

Summer of '42, Folmar Blangsted.   Coming of age drama.

1970

Airport, Stuart Gilmore.   Watch the last 30 minutes as the editor builds the climax.

M*A*S*H, Danford B. Greene

Patton, Hugh S. Fowler.   Watch the scene in the hospital when Patton hits a soldier.

Tora! Tora! Tora!, Inoue Chikaya, Pembroke J. Herring, James E. Newcom.   Watch the attack on Pearl Harbor sequence and compare to *Pearl Harbor.*

Woodstock, Thelma Schoonmaker.   Watch how Joe Cocker and Jimi Hendrix's performances are edited.

1969

Hello, Dolly!, William Reynolds.   Musical.

Midnight Cowboy, Hugh A. Robertson.   Watch the editing in the sequence as Voight attempts to earn his living as a gigilo.

The Secret of Santa Vittoria, Earle Herdan, William Lyon.   Comedy.

They Shoot Horses, Don't They?, Fredric Steinkamp.   Watch how the dance marathon is edited to convey the exhaustion of the dancers.

Z, FranJoise Bonnot.   Costa-Gravas' masterpiece of a political thriller.

1968

Bullitt, Frank P. Keller

Funny Girl, William Sands, Robert Swink, Maury Winetrobe. Musical.

The Odd Couple, Frank Bracht.   Comedy

Oliver!, Ralph Kemplen.   Musical.

Wild in the Streets, Fred Feitshans, Eve Newman.   Comedy.

1967

The Dirty Dozen, Michael Luciano.   Watch the action editing.

Doctor Dolittle, Samuel E. Beetley, Marjorie Fowler

Guess Who's Coming to Dinner, Robert C. Jones.   Skip.

In the Heat of the Night, Hal Ashby.   Mystery.

1966

Fantastic Voyage, William B. Murphy.   Special effects submarine film.

Grand Prix, Henry Berman, Stewart Linder, Frank Santillo, Fredric Steinkamp.   Watch the auto racing sequences for action editing. Compare this to *Ronin* also directed by John Frankenheimer.

The Russians Are Coming The Russians Are Coming, Hal Ashby, J. Terry Williams.   Comedy.

The Sand Pebbles, William Reynolds.   Watch the sequence when Petty Officer Holman arrives to take over control of the ship's engines from the chinese workers.

Who's Afraid of Virginia Woolf?, Sam O'Steen.   Watch how the editor heightens the tension in this closed room drama.

1965

Cat Ballou, Charles Nelson.   Comedy.

Doctor Zhivago, Norman Savage.   Watch the exodus sequence that takes place on trains.

The Flight of the Phoenix, Michael Luciano.   Watch how the characters are developed in this "stranded in the desert film." How does it compare to *12 Angry Men* or *A Few Good Men.*

The Great Race, Ralph E. Winters.   Watch the duel and barroom brawl sequences for action editing.

The Sound of Music, William Reynolds.   Musical.

1964

Becket, Anne Coates.   Excellent drama and dialogue editing.

Father Goose, Ted J. Kent.   Comedy.

Hush...Hush, Sweet Charlotte, Michael Luciano   Horror.

Mary Poppins, Cotton Warburton.   Won for special effects integration with live action.

My Fair Lady, William Ziegler.   Musical.

1963

The Cardinal, Louis R. Loeffler.   Skip this.

Cleopatra, Dorothy Spencer.   Watch first hour if you must.

The Great Escape, Ferris Webster.   Watch the tunneling sequence and the breakout for action editing.

How the West Was Won, Harold F. Kress.   Watch the running the rapids sequence and imagine it as IMAX film, which it was in its day.

It's a Mad, Mad, Mad, Mad World, Gene Fowler Jr., Robert C. Jones, Frederic Knudtson.   Comedy. Significant because the editor juggles at least eight parallel stories.

1962

Lawrence of Arabia, Anne Coates.   Watch the first half for superb editing.

The Longest Day, Samuel E. Beetley.

The Manchurian Candidate, Ferris Webster.   Watch the sequence in which Sinatra is in captivity.

Meredith Wilson's The Music Man, William Ziegler.

Mutiny on the Bounty, John McSweeney Jr..   Skip this and watch the 1935 version instead.

1961

Fanny, William H. Reynolds.   Drama

The Guns of Navarone, Alan Osbiston.   Watch the assault sequence for action editing.

Judgment at Nuremberg, Frederic Knudtson.   Courtroom drama.

The Parent Trap, Philip W. Anderson.   Hayley Mills plays a double role made possible by editing.

West Side Story, Thomas Stanford.   Musical. Watch how the dance sequences are edited.

1960

The Alamo, Stuart Gilmore.   Watch the final attack sequence.

The Apartment, Daniel Mandell.   Comedy.

Inherit the Wind, Frederic Knudtson.   Courtroom drama. Compare the editing to *Judgement at Nuremberg.*

Spartacus, Robert Lawrence.   Watch the gladiator battle scenes and the revolution. Compare the editing approach to *Gladiator.*

1959

Anatomy of a Murder, Louis R. Loeffler.   Courtroom drama.

Ben-Hur, John D. Dunning, Ralph E. Winters.   Watch the chariot race and the sequence in the slave galley.

North by Northwest George Tomasini.   Watch the crop dusting and Mount Rushmore sequences for classic Hitchcock storytelling.

The Nun's Story, Walter Thompson.   Drama.

On the Beach, Frederic Knudtson.   Drama

1958

Auntie Mame, William Ziegler.

Cowboy, Al Clark, William A. Lyon.   Watch the cattle round up sequence and compare to *City Slickers.*

The Defiant Ones, Frederic Knudtson.   Sidney Poiter and Tony Curtis chained together. Compare how their escape is edited to the escape in *O Brother, Where Art Thou?*

Gigi, Adrienne Fazan.   Minnelli Musical.

I Want to Live!, William Hornbeck.   Crime drama directed by Robert Wise, a first-rate editor.

1957

The Bridge on the River Kwai, Peter Taylor.   Watch how the editing reinforces character and the action sequences.

Gunfight at the O.K. Corral, Warren Low.   Watch the gunfight for action editing.

Pal Joey, Viola Lawrence, Jerome Thoms.   Musical.

Sayonara, Philip W. Anderson, Arthur P. Schmidt.   Skip this.

Witness for the Prosecution, Daniel Mandell.   Courtroom drama.

1956

Around the World in 80 Days, Gene Ruggiero, Paul Weatherwax. Watch how the pace reflects the hero's progress.

The Brave One, Merrill G. White.   A boy and a bull drama.

Giant, Philip W. Anderson, Fred Bohanan, William Hornbeck.   Two generations of Texans face off.

Somebody Up There Likes Me, Albert Akst.   Watch the boxing sequences in this biopic of Rocky Graziano. Compare to the boxing sequences in *Raging Bull, Rocky, Body and Soul,* or *Champion.*

The Ten Commandments, Anne Bauchens. Cecile B. DeMille's. Moses biopic.

1955

Blackboard Jungle, Ferris Webster.   A classroom drama.

The Bridges at Toko-Ri, Alma Macrorie.   Watch the flying sequences for editing.

Oklahoma!, George Boemler, Gene Ruggiero.   Watch the Oklahoma song sequence.

Picnic, William A. Lyon, Charles Nelson.   Watch the editing in the picnic scene that introduces Holden and Novak.

The Rose Tattoo, Warren Low.   A romance.

1954

20,000 Leagues Under the Sea, Elmo Williams.   Watch the editing in the action sequences.

The Caine Mutiny, Henry Batista, William A. Lyon.   Watch the mutiny sequence that takes place in a typhoon.

The High and the Mighty, Ralph Dawson.   The first airplane disaster movie. Great close quarters editing. Compare this to *Stagecoach.*

On the Waterfront, Gene Milford.   Watch the editing in the back of the taxicab scene with Brando and Rod Steiger and the climatic sequence when Brando confronts the bosses on the docks.

Seven Brides for Seven Brothers, Ralph E. Winters.   Watch the magnificent barn-raising dance sequence.

1953

From Here to Eternity, William Lyon.   Watch the attack on Pearl Harbor that combines actual footage and the beach scene with Burt Lancaster and Deborah Kerr for brilliant editing.

The Moon Is Blue, Otto Ludwig.   Dated.

Roman Holiday, Robert Swink.   A romantic comedy with Audrey Hepburn.

The War of the Worlds, Everett Douglas.   Watch George Pal's special effects sequences for the editing.

1952

Come Back, Little Sheba, Warren Low.   A drama.

Flat Top, William Austin.   A World War II flight-training story.

The Greatest Show on Earth, Anne Bauchens.   Watch the train wreck sequence.

High Noon, Harry Gerstad, Elmo Williams.   A classic that focuses on the clock to create tension and dissect the characters.

Moulin Rouge, Ralph Kemplen.   A Toulouse-Lautrec biopic.

1951

An American in Paris, Adrienne Fazan.   Watch the editing in the musical sequences.

Decision Before Dawn, Dorothy Spencer.   A World War II spy thriller.

A Place in the Sun, William Hornbeck.   Watch the scenes that establish the wealth of the characters.

Quo-Vadis, Ralph E. Winters.   A drama about ancient Rome.

The Well, Chester Schaeffer.   Psycho-drama about a black child stuck in a well.

1950

All About Eve, Barbara McLean.   Watch the way the dialogue is edited in this witty classic.

Annie Get Your Gun, James E. Newcom.   Musical.

King Solomon's Mines, Conrad A. Nervig, Ralph E. Winters. Hollywood searches for diamond mines in this spectacle.

Sunset Blvd., Doane Harrison, Arthur Schmidt.   A classic of flashback storytelling. The main character floats dead in a swimming pool in the opening minute and it gets better from there. Pay attention to the editing approach in the final scene with Gloria Swanson and Joseph Von Sternberg.

The Third Man, Oswald Hafenrichter   Joseph Cotton hunts Orson Welles in this classic spy thriller. Watch the sequence in which Cotton finds Welles' secret crossing near the latter half of the film.

1949

All the King's Men, Al Clark, Robert Parrish.   Watch Broderick Crawford's drunken scene and compare how the film is paced before and after in this rise-to-power film.

Battleground, John Dunning.   A Hollywood version of the Battle of the Bulge.

Champion, Harry Gerstad.   Watch the boxing sequences. Compare to the boxing sequences in *Raging Bull*, *Rocky*, or *Somebody Up There likes Me*.

Sands of Iwo Jima, Richard L. Van Enger.   Watch the combat sequences.

The Window, Frederic Knudtson.   Watch the scene in which the boy witnesses the murder.

1948

Joan of Arc, Frank Sullivan

Johnny Belinda, David Weisbart.   Watch to see how the setting is established in the film.

The Naked City, Paul Weatherwax.   A trendsetter at the time. A step-by-step murder investigation carefully edited.

Red River, Christian Nyby.   Watch the cattle drive sequences and then watch *City Slickers*.

The Red Shoes, Reginald Mills.   Watch to see how the dancing sequences are integrated into the drama. A classic dance film.

1947

The Bishop's Wife, Monica Collingwood.   A Christmas fantasy.

Body and Soul, Francis Lyon, Robert Parrish.   Watch the boxing sequences. Compare to the boxing sequences in *Raging Bull, Rocky, Champion*, or *Somebody Up There Likes Me.*

Gentleman's Agreement, Harmon Jones.   A drama.

Green Dolphin Street, George White.   Watch the special effects scenes only.

Odd Man Out, Fergus McDonnell.   A great suspense film of an Irish rebel being hunted down. Watch the pacing of the editing to see how it's done.

1946

The Best Years of Our Lives, Daniel Mandell.   Watch the homecoming scenes in the opening section for superb editing that intercuts and contrasts each character's story.

It's a Wonderful Life, William Hornbeck.   The Capra classic. Seamless.

The Jolson Story, William Lyon.   A biopic.

The Killers, Arthur Hilton.   Crime drama.

The Yearling, Harold Kress.   Watch the 128-minute version of this boy and deer drama.

1945

The Bells of St. Mary's, Harry Marker.   The sequel to *Going My Way* with Bing Crosby.

The Lost Weekend, Doane Harrison.   A drama about alcoholism. The editing enhances the unrelenting nature of the film.

National Velvet, Robert J. Kern.   Watch the steeplechases for editing.

Objective, Burma!, George Amy.   Watch the action sequences in the 142-minute version.

A Song to Remember, Charles Nelson.   Chopin Biopic. Well-edited but silly.

1944

Going My Way, Leroy Stone.   A Bing Crosby and Barry Fitzgerald drama.

Janie, Owen Marks. A comedy.

None But the Lonely Heart, Roland Gross.   Dated comedy.

Since You Went Away, Hal C. Kern, James E. Newcom.   A tear jerker.

Wilson, Barbara McLean.   A biopic of Woodrow Wilson that flopped despite multiple awards.

1943

Air Force, George Amy.   World War II bomber movie with virulent wartime era dialogue.

Casablanca, Owen Marks.   Watch the sequence which begins and ends in the café that includes a flashback to Paris.

For Whom the Bell Tolls, John Link, Sherman Todd.   Watch the action scenes for editing.

The Song of Bernadette, Barbara McLean.   Won five awards.

1942

Mrs. Miniver, Harold F. Kress.   Drama

The Pride of the Yankees, Daniel Mandell.   Watch the last 10 minutes.

The Talk of the Town, Otto Meyer.   A comedy.

This Above All, Walter Thompson.   A romance.

Yankee Doodle Dandy, George Amy.   Michael Curtiz musical with Jimmy Cagney.

1941

Citizen Kane, Robert Wise. Flashback storytelling.   Watch the marriage dissolution sequence for economy of storytelling.

Dr. Jekyll and Mr. Hyde, Harold F. Kress.   This version is a character study of Hyde.

How Green Was My Valley, James B. Clark.   John Ford classic about coal miners. Watch the work scenes.

The Little Foxes, Daniel Mandell.   William Wyler directs Bette Davis in a Lillian Hellman play about a Southern family.

Sergeant York, William Holmes.   Watch the battle scenes.

1940

The Grapes of Wrath, Robert E. Simpson. John Ford does Steinbeck. Watch the scenes of the Okies moving to California to escape the dustbowl.

The Letter, Warren Low.   A drama set in Malaysia.

The Long Voyage Home, Sherman Todd.   John Ford tells a character study of men at sea.

Rebecca, Hal C. Kern.   Hitchcock builds suspense and tension through the editing.

1939

Gone With the Wind, Hal C. Kern, James E. Newcom.   The first half of the film is tightly edited. Watch the sequence leading up to the party at Twin Oaks that introduces all the characters.

Goodbye, Mr. Chips, Charles Frend.   Overstays its welcome.

Mr. Smith Goes to Washington, Al Clark, Gene Havlick.   Watch the scene where Jimmy Stewart filibusters in Congress.

The Rains Came, Barbara McLean.   Watch the earthquake and flood scenes.

Stagecoach, Otho Lovering, Dorothy Spencer.   One of John Ford's best with newcomer John Wayne. The editing in the stagecoach is superb.

1938

The Adventures of Robin Hood, Ralph Dawson.   The definite swashbuckler. Watch Flynn's action sequences for the editing.

Alexander's Ragtime Band, Barbara McLean.   Corny musical fare.

The Great Waltz, Tom Held.   The waltz sequences are worth watching.

Test Pilot, Tom Held.   Watch this one to see why it no longer works.

You Can't Take It With You, Gene Havlick.   Entertaining corn.

1937

The Awful Truth, Al Clark.   An excellent screwball comedy with Cary Grant.

Captains Courageous, Elmo Vernon.   Watch the action sequences.

The Good Earth, Basil Wrangell.   Spencer Tracey in an adaptation of a Pearl Buck novel.

Lost Horizon, Gene Havlick, Gene Milford.   Watch the final sequences.

One Hundred Men and a Girl, Bernard W. Burton.   Watch for the blend of comedy and music. The real significance of this film featuring the Philadelphia Orchestra and Deanna Durbin is the sound recording and editing which was remarkable for the time.

1936

Anthony Adverse, Ralph Dawson

Come and Get It, Edward Curtiss.   This film has also been called *Roaring Timber.*

The Great Ziegfeld, William S. Gray.   Watch Luise Rainer's classic telephone scene.

Lloyds of London, Barbara McLean.   Standard Hollywood fare with a love triangle set against the story of an insurance company.

A Tale of Two Cities, Conrad A. Nervig.   Features Ronald Coleman. Intercut storytelling.

Theodora Goes Wild, Otto Meyer.   A fun farce.

1935

David Copperfield, Robert J. Kern.   Well-told George Cukor film of the Dickens novel.

The Informer, George Hively.   A dated film but it has its moments.

Les Miserables, Barbara McLean.   A classic of storytelling through continuity editing.

The Lives of a Bengal Lancer, Ellsworth Hoagland.   Watch the snake charming scene.

A Midsummer Night's Dream, Ralph Dawson.   A stagey adaptation of Shakespeare with stunning B&W photography from Hal Mohr who won the Oscar for best cinematography in a write-in vote campaign, the only time in history that's happened.

Mutiny on the Bounty, Margaret Booth.   Best version of the story starring Clark Gable and Charles Laughton.

1934

Cleopatra, Anne Bauchens, editor.   Cecile B. DeMille directs Claudette Colbert.

One Night of Love, Gene Milford.   A musical that continues to delight audiences.

APPENDIX **B**

Resources

Magazines

AV Video Multimedia Producer

Cinemeditor

The Independent Film and Video Monthly

Millimeter

Post Magazine

Res Magazine

Videomaker

Videography

Video Systems Magazine

Suggested Reading

Aristotle. *Poetics*. Translated by S. H. Butcher. New York: Hill and Wang Publishers, 1989.

Barnouw, Erik. *Documentary: A History of the Non-Fiction Film*. 3rd edition. New York: Oxford University Press, 1993.

Block, Bruce. *The Visual Story: Seeing the Structure of Film, TV, and New Media*. Boston: Focal Press, 2001.

Bordwell, Douglas and Kristin Thompson. *Film Art: An Introduction*. 5th edition. New York: McGraw-Hill, 1996.

Brenneis, Lisa. *Final Cut Pro 3 for Macintosh*. Berkeley: Peachpit Press, 2002.

Burder, John. *16mm Film Cutting*. Boston: Focal Press, 1976.

Campbell, Joseph. *The Hero with a Thousand Faces*. 2nd edition. Princeton, N.J.: Princeton University Press, 1990.

Caputo, Tony C. *The Art of Visual Storytelling*. New York: Watson-Guptill Publishers, 2002.

Coles, Robert. *Doing Documentary Work*. New York: Oxford University Press, 1998.

Douglass, John S. and Glenn P. Hardnen. *The Art of Technique: An Aesthetic Approach to Film and Video Production*. Boston: Allyn and Bacon, 1996.

Dmytryk, Edward. *On Film Editing*. Boston: Focal Press, 1988.

Egri, Lajos. *The Art of Dramatic Writing*. New York: Simon and Schuster, 1977.

Eisenstein, Sergei. *Film Sense*. New York: Harcourt Brace Jovanovich, 1989.

———. *Film Form*. New York: Harcourt Brace Jovanovich, 1972.

Kauffmann, Sam. *Avid Editing: A Guide for Beginning and Intermediate Users*. Boston: Focal Press, 2000.

LoBrutto, Vincent. *Sound on Film: Interviews with Creators of Film Sound*. New York: Praeger Publishers, 1994.

Murch, Walter. *In the Blink of an Eye: A Perspective on Film Editing*, 2nd edition, Los Angeles: Silman-James Press, 2001.

Monaco, James. *How to Read a Film*. New York: Oxford University Press, 1981.

Pogue, David. *iMovie2: The Missing Manual*. Boston: O'Reilly and Associates, 2001.

Rabiger, Michael. *Directing the Documentary*. 3rd edition. Boston: Focal Press, 1998.

Reisz, Karel and Gavin Millar. *The Technique of Film Editing*. Boston: Focal Press, 1995.

Rose, Jay. *Producing Great Sound for Digital Video*. New York: Miller Freeman Books, 2001.

Rosenblum, Ralph. *When the Shooting Stops . . . the Cutting Begins*. New York: Penguin, 1980.

Vogler, Christopher. *The Writer's Journey: Mythic Structure for Writers*. Los Angeles: Michael Weise Publications, 1998.

Internet Resources

Editing & Filmmaking

www.aafassociation.org

www.ace-filmeditors.org

www.aivf.org

www.creativecow.net/cgi-bin/select_forum.cgi?forum=communications

www.digitalvideoediting.com/Htm/DVEditHomeSet1.htm

www.editors.net

www.editorsguild.com

www.editorsnet.com

www.editsuite.com

www.filmsite.org

www.Filmsound.org

www.gen.umn.edu/faculty_staff/yahnke/filmteach/teach.htm

www.ifp.org

Information about Compression and Codecs

www.codeccentral.com

www.microsoft.com/windows/windowsmedia/default.asp

www.onerivermedia.com/codecs

www.recipe4dvd.com/index.html

www.siggraph.org/education/materials/HyperGraph/video/codecs/Default.htm

www.streamingmedia.com

www.streamingmediaworld.com/video/tutor/streambasics2

Nonfiction Filmmaking Resources

journalism.berkeley.edu/program/courses/dv/cookbook.html

www.d-word.com

www.docos.com/distributors.html

www.documentary.org/resources/funding.html

www.edn.dk/action.lasso?-database=artikel&-layout=1&response=
index2.html&nr=210&-search

www.indiebin.com/resources/funding.shtml

www.mediarights.org

System-Specific Sites

www.avidarchives.itg.uiuc.edu/avid

www.avideditor.com

www.kenstone.net/fcp_homepage/fcp_homepage_index.html

www.lafcpug.com

Online Equipment Buying Guides

www.SYPHAonline.com

Manufacturers

5D

1 Boundary Row, London SE1 8HP, United Kingdom
Office: 44-20-7620-4810   Fax: 44-20-7620-4815
E-mail: info@five-d.com   Web site: www.five-d.com
This company manufactures high-end visual effects and digital cinema tools. Its products include Cyborg, a resolution-independent effects system; Colossus, a digital grading and finishing system; Monsters, a visual effects plug-in package; and Masher, an offline effects system for Quantel systems.

Accom, Inc.

1490 O'Brien Drive, Menlo Park, CA 94025
Office: (650) 328-3818   Fax: (650) 327-2511
E-mail: info@accom.com   Web site: www.accom.com
Accom, Inc. manufactures digital video editing tools including Dveous/HD, Abekas 6000, Affinity, WSD/HD, Dveous, and Axial 3000.

Adamation, Inc.

1940 Webster Street, Suite 250, Oakland, CA 94612
Fax: (510) 452-5033
E-mail: info@adamation.com   Web site: www.adamation.com
PersonalStudio offers real-time, full-screen, nonlinear digital video editing and compositing without the need for hardware acceleration.

Adaptec, Inc.

691 South Milpitas Blvd., Milpitas, CA 95035
Office: (408) 945-8600   Fax: (408) 262-2533
Web site: www.adaptec.com
DVpics Plus packages Adaptec's three-port Firewire card called FireConnect 4300 with Windows software: MGI VideoWave 4 SE and Sonic MyDVD.

Adobe Systems Incorporated

345 Park Avenue, W16, San Jose, CA 95110
Office: (408) 536-6000   Fax: (408) 537-6000
Web site: www.adobe.com
This company produces software solutions for the Web, print, and video. Its products include After Effects, Photoshop, and Premiere.

ADS Technologies, Inc.

12627 Hidden Creek Way, Cerritos, CA 90703
Office: (562) 926-1928   Fax: (562) 926-0518   Toll free: (800) 888-5244
E-mail: productinfo@adstech.com   Web site: www.adstech.com
This company makes the PYRO line of 1394 Firewire cards. These *Pulse Code Modulation* (PCM) or card bus adapters for Windows and Mac platforms may come with Adobe Premiere or Ulead Video Studio software.

AIST

715 West Orchard Drive, Suite 7, Bellingham, WA 98225
Office: (360) 527-1489   Fax: (360) 527-1619   Toll free: (866) 924-2478
E-mail: sales@aistinc.com   Web site: www.aistinc.com or www.aist.com/cinegy/
AIST develops animation, digital editing, and graphics software. Its products include the MovieX line—MovieXone, MovieXonePlus, MovieDV, MoviePack, eXtreme, and Cinegy.

AJA Video

443 Crown Point Circle, P.O. Box 1033, Grass Valley, CA 95945
Office: (530) 274-2048   Fax: (530) 274-9442   Toll free: (800) 251-4224
E-mail: sales@aja.com   Web site: www.aja.com
AJA Video manufactures digital video conversion products and cards for *serial digital interface* (SDI) and *high-definition SDI* (HD-SDI) video capture on the Mac platform.

All-Vision, Inc.

9A Tianxiang Building, Tian`an Cyber Park Shenzhen 518040, China
Office/fax: 86-755 356 2936
E-mail: marketing@all-vision.com   Web site: www.all-vision.com
This company develops turnkey systems and software that use Matrox
cards. Its products include AVE 2000LG, AV2000LE, SPARK2000, DV2000,
Vivid 3000, and Focus 2000.

Applied Digital Technology

3622 Northeast 4th Street, Gainesville, FL 32609
Office: (352) 338-0516   Fax: (352) 338-1108
E-mail: amerideth@applied-digital.com
Web site: www.applieddigital.com
This company makes Windows software for editing MPEG-2 video, includ-
ing the ADedit MPEG-2 Segmenter and ShearMPEG MPEG-2 Cuts Editor.

Applied Magic

2120 Las Palmas, Suite D, Carlsbad, CA 92009
Office: (760) 931-6417   Fax: (760) 931-6440   Toll free: (888) 625-9404
E-mail: marketing@applied-magic.com   Web site: www.applied-magic.com
This company develops standalone editing appliances for professionals, pro-
sumers, and broadcasters. Its products include the ScreenPlay 60GB NLE.
Optional features include Luma Key, Chroma Key, and A/B Roll.

Array Microsystems, Inc.

3520 North Prospect, Colorado Springs, CO 80907
Office: (719) 471-7141 or (866) 471-7142
E-mail: sales@array.com   Web site: www.array.com
This company makes the VideoONE Recorder, which is an MPEG-1 capture
card, and the VideoONE Producer, which is a hardware and software solution for digital compression and authoring that includes the Cinax
iFilmEdit MPEG-1 editor and Asymetrix's Digital Video Producer.

Artbeats Digital Film

1405 North Myrtle Road, Unit 5, Myrtle Creek, OR 97457
Office: (541) 863-4429   Fax: (541) 863-4547   Toll free: (800) 444-9392
E-mail: info@artbeats.com   Web site: www.artbeats.com
This company provides royalty-free stock footage for broadcast, desktop video, and multimedia usage.

Aurora Video Systems, Inc.

7633 Nineteen-Mile Road, Sterling Heights, MI 48314
Office: (586) 726-5320   Fax: (586) 726-5815
E-mail: sales@auroravideosys.com   Web site: www.auroravideosys.com
This company manufactures capture cards for the Mac platform including the Fuse001, IgniterLT, Igniter001, Igniter101, IgniterRT, IgniterRT011, IgniterRT111, IgniterRT211, and IgniterRT311. All are compatible with QuickTime applications, such as Final Cut Pro and Premiere.

Authoringware Co.

21514 Talisman Street, Torrance, CA 90503
Office: (310) 540-5248   Fax: (310) 316-5804
E-mail: vtung@authoringware.com   Web site: www.authoringware.com
This company produces DVD authoring and premastering software. Its products include DVD Junior and DVD Wise.

Automatic Duck, Inc.

13331 25th Avenue Northeast, Seattle, WA 98125
Office: (206) 618-0228   Fax: (425) 988-8723
E-mail: wes@automaticduck.com   Web site: www.automaticduck.com
Automatic Duck, Inc. is a plug-in product that moves metadata from Final Cut Pro and Avid editing systems into Adobe After Effects.

Avid Technology, Inc.

Avid Technology Park, One Park West, Tewksbury, MA 01876
Office: (800) 859-2843   Fax: (978) 851-0418
Web site: www.avid.com
Avid Technology provides digital media creation, storage, management, and distribution solutions for film and video postproduction, audio, three-dimensional animation, and broadcast news.

Boris FX

381 Congress Street, Boston, MA 02210
Office: (617) 451-9900   Fax: (617) 451-9916   Toll free: (888) 77-BORIS
E-mail: sales@borisfx.com   Web site: www.BorisFX.com
This company supplies effects and titling software and plug-ins. Its products include Boris FX, which provides 3D compositing, keying, advanced color manipulation, *Digital Video Effects* (DVEs), and particles; Boris GRAFFITI, which provides 2D and 3D title animation; Boris RED, which provides all the features of Boris FX and Boris GRAFFITI plus vector paint, rotoscoping, motion tracking, image stabilization, and more; Boris CONTINUUM, which provides plug-in filters for Final Cut Pro and After Effects; and Boris FACTORY, which provides special effects plug-ins for Adobe Premiere, Canopus, and Ulead Media Studio Pro.

BOXX Technologies

9390 Research Blvd., Kaleido II, Suite 300, Austin, TX 78759
Office: (512) 835-0400   Fax: (512) 835-0434   Toll free: (877) 877-2699
E-mail: sales@boxxtech.com   Web site: www.boxxtech.com
BOXX manufacturers high-performance, high-bandwidth Windows 2000 and Linux hardware for digital content creation, including HDTV, digital film, and visual effects.

BSP

2789 Chrysler Road, Cheyenne, WY 82009
Office: (307) 778-8888 Fax: (307) 778-8387
E-mail: lori@bspus.com Web site: www.BSPus.com or www.LogicKeyboard.com
BSP manufactures custom keyboards for video- and audio-editing systems.

Canopus Corporation

711 Charcot Avenue, San Jose, CA 95131-2208
Office: (408) 954-4500 Fax: (408) 954-4504
Web site: www.canopuscorp.com
This company makes hardware and software for digital editing, including the DVRaptor card, the StormRack system with Premiere and Canopus Storm Edit, Procoder transcoding software, and the CWS-100 turnkey editing system based on Canopus Rextor software.

Cavena Image Products AB

Nytorpsvägen 26, P.O. Box 47, S-183 21, Taby, Sweden
Office: 46-8-544-709-80 Fax: 46-8-473-02-15
E-mail: info@cavena.com Web site: www.cavena.com
This company provides software for subtitle editing and preparation that reads time code without special hardware.

Chrome Imaging

Rue Hugo-de-Senger 3, Geneva CH-1205, Switzerland
Office: 41-22-807-2360 Fax: 41-22-807-2370
E-mail: info@chrome-imaging.com Web site: www.chrome-imaging.com
Chrome Imaging develops high-performance special effects software for digital content creation. Its products include Matrix Compositing, which provides paint, motion tracking, and compositing software, as well as Matrix 3D Particle, which creates complex particle effects in a 3D environment.

Computer Prompting and Captioning Co.

1010 Rockville Pike, Suite 306, Rockville, MD 20852-1419
Office: (301) 738-8487   Fax: (301) 738-8488   Toll free: (800) 977-6678
E-mail: info@cpcweb.com   Web site: www.cpcweb.com
This company provides closed captioning, teleprompting, and subtitling software and services for video, DVDs, and the Internet.

Contour Design, Inc.

10 Industrial Drive, Windham, NH 03087
Office: (603) 893-4556   Fax: (603) 893-4558   Toll free: (800) 462-6678
E-mail: info@contourdesign.com   Web site: www.contourdesign.com
This company makes ShuttlePRO, an inexpensive jog wheel with programmable buttons for editing systems.

Creative Support Services

1948 Riverside Drive, Los Angeles, CA 90039
Office: (323) 666-7968   Fax: (323) 660-2070   Toll free: (800) 468-6874
E-mail: info@cssmusic.com   Web site: www.cssmusic.com
This company supplies royalty-free music and video CD and DVD collections.

Curious Software

1118 Paseo Barranca, Santa Fe, NM 87501
Office: (505) 988-7243   Fax: (505) 988-1654
E-mail: info@curious-software.com   Web site: www.curious-software.com
Curious Software offers still and animated map graphics for broadcast and Internet use.

Darim Vision Co., Ltd.

3F Visual Tech Building, Expo Venture Town, 3-1 Doryong-Dong, Yusung-Gu, Daejeon 305-340, Republic of Korea
Office: 82-42-601-1330   Fax: 82-42-861-2484
E-mail: sales@darim.com   Web site: www.darvision.com
This company provides MPEG encoder cards and MPEG digital editing systems. Its products include the MPEGator Pro, MG 100, MPEGator 2, DVMPEG, and WebGator.

DataCal Enterprises

531 East Elliot Road, Chandler, AZ 85225
Office: (480) 813-3108   Fax: (480) 813-3280
E-mail: info@datacal.com   Web site: www.docustom.com
DataCal Enterprises makes customized keyboard templates, key overlays (stickers), and dedicated video-editing keyboards for Discreet, Final Cut Pro, Media 100, Adobe Premiere, and others.

Data Translation, Inc.

100 Locke Drive, Marlboro, MA 01752-1192
Office: (800) 249-1000   Fax: (508) 460-1372
E-mail: broadway@datx.com   Web site: www.b-way.com
Broadway Pro is a video capture card bundled with Ulead Media Studio software.

Dayang Technology Development, Inc.

F3, 22 Zhongguancun Street, Beijing 100080, China
Office: 86-10-62569111-1843   Fax: 86-10-62628469
Web site: www.dayang-image.com
Dayang develops digital editing software for professionals and broadcasters.

Desktop Images

2603 West Magnolia Blvd., Burbank, CA 91505
Office: (818) 841-8980   Fax: (818) 841-8023   Toll free: (800) 377-1039
E-mail: info@desktopimages.com   Web site: www.desktopimages.com
Desktop Images produces training programs for products such as NewTek's
LightWave 3D and Aura, Adobe Photoshop, and Adobe After Effects.

DigiEffects

1806 Congressional Circle, Austin, TX 78746
Office: (512) 306-0779   Fax: (512) 306-1310   Toll free: (888) 344-4339
E-mail: info@digieffects.com   Web site: www.digieffects.com
DigiEffects develops digital effects tools for video and film professionals,
professional artists, web designers, and hobbyists.

Digital Anarchy

120 Pierce Street, Suite 10, San Francisco, CA 94117
Office: (415) 621-0991   Fax: (208) 330-1620
E-mail: info@digitalanarchy.com   Web site: www.digitalanarchy.com
Digital Anarchy develops plug-in software that makes it easier to create
and animate text and graphics for After Effects, Final Cut Pro, Discreet
Fire/Flame/Inferno, and Macromedia Flash.

Digital Juice

1736 Northeast 25th Avenue, Ocala, FL 34470
Office: (352) 369-0930   Fax: (352) 368-6091   Toll free: (800) 525-2203
E-mail: info@digitaljuice.com   Web site: www.digitaljuice.com
This company supplies high-quality, royalty-free graphics and animations
for video editing. Its products include loopable animations, still graphics,
photos, textures, and music.

Digital Video Innovation

4F Onse Telecom Building, 192-2 Goomi, Bundang, Sungnam, Korea 463-810
Office: 82-31-728-1394   Fax: 82-31-717-8980
E-mail: sales@dvico.com   Web site: www.dvico.com
This company's products include the Firebird line of DV capture cards bundled with DocuCap software (some of which include Premiere) and Fusion MPEG (an MPEG encoder card).

Digital Voodoo

17B Market Street, South Melbourne, Victoria, 3205, Australia
Office: 61-(3)-9682-9477   Fax: 61-(3)-9682-9466
E-mail: simon.h@digitalvoodoo.net   Web site: www.digitalvoodoo.net
Digital Voodoo manufactures hardware for broadcast design, composition, and editing in standard definition and high-definition formats for After Effects, Combustion, and Final Cut Pro.

Discreet

10 Duke Street, Montreal, Quebec, H3C 2L7, Canada
Office: (514) 393-1616   Fax: (514) 393-0110   Toll free: (800) 869-3504
E-mail: lyne.arseneault@discreet.com   Web site: www.discreet.com
Discreet develops systems and software for visual effects, animation, non-linear editing, infrastructure, and streaming media markets. Its products include Fire/Smoke, Flint/Flame, Combustion, and 3D Studio Max.

Eagle Research S.A.

272 Vouliagmenis Avenue, Ag. Dimitrios, 173 43, Athens, Greece
Office: 301-9769-280   Fax: 301-9769-289
E-mail: info@eagle.gr   Web site: www.eagle.gr
This company manufactures mobile and rack-mounted hardware systems for digital editing.

Edirol Corporation

425 Sequoia Drive, Suite 114, Bellingham, WA 98226
Office: (360) 594-4273   Fax: (360) 594-4271
E-mail: sales@edirol.com   Web site: www.edirol.com
This company makes the DV-7 Digital Video Workstation, which is a stand-alone editing appliance.

Editware

200 Litton Drive, Suite 308, Grass Valley, CA 95945
Office: (530) 477-4300   Fax: (530) 477-4304
E-mail: jerryl@editware.com   Web site: www.editware.com
This company makes the Fastrack VS hybrid editing system.

The Electronic Farm

Sturegatan 64, SE-114 36, Stockholm, Sweden
Office: 46-8-528-09-990   Fax: 46-8-528-09-991
E-mail: christer@electronicfarm.com   Web site: www.electronicfarm.com
The Electronic Farm manufactures Mule digital editing software for the Silicon Graphics O2, Octane2, and Onyx2 platforms.

Eskape Labs (A Hauppauge Company)

91 Cabot Court, Hauppauge, NY 11788
Office: (631) 434-1600   Fax: (631) 434-3198
E-mail: sales@eskapelabs.com   Web site: www.eskapelabs.com
MyVideo and MyCaptureII are *universal serial bus* (USB) plug-and-play breakout boxes bundled with Strata VideoShop software for the Mac OS platform.

EVS Broadcast Equipment, Inc.

9 Law Drive, Suite 200, Fairfield, NJ 07004
Office: (973) 575-7811   Fax: (973) 575-7812
E-mail: sales@evs-broadcast.com   Web site: www.evs.tv
CleanEdit is an offline news editing system for use in a broadcast
server environment. EVS makes a variety of server products for broadcast
applications.

Eyeon Software Incorporated

2181 Queen Street East, Suite 201, Toronto, Ontario, M4E 1E5, Canada
Office: (416) 686-8411   Fax: (416) 698-9315
E-mail: marketing@eyeonline.com   Web site: www.eyeonline.com
This company produces Digital Fusion 3.1 compositing software with
advanced text-generation tools.

Focus Enhancements

1370 Dell Avenue, Campbell, CA 95008
Office: (408) 866-8300   Fax: (408) 866-8659   Toll free: (800) 338-3348
E-mail: info@FOCUSinfo.com   Web site: www.FOCUSinfo.com
FOCUS Enhancements designs digital video production equipment and
PC-to-TV video conversion technology. Its products include consumer and
professional scan converters, scalers, mixers, special-effect generators,
recording solutions, and character generators.

Global Streams

25 North Brentwood Blvd., St. Louis, MO 63105
Office: (800) 788-7205
E-mail: info@globalstreams.com   Web site: www.globalstreams.com
This company manufactures the GlobeCaster line of hybrid digital editing
video systems designed for streaming and OnQ, which is a presentation
product.

Inscriber Technology Corporation

26 Peppler Street, Waterloo, Ontario, N2J 3C4, Canada
Office: (519) 570-9111   Fax: (519) 570-9140   Toll free: (800) 363-3400
E-mail: douglas@inscriber.com   Web site: www.inscriber.com
This company produces character-generator and video-titling software and
hardware.

Interactive Effects

17351 West Sunset Blvd., Suite 404, Los Angeles, CA 90272
Office: (310) 998-8364   Fax: (310) 998-8364
E-mail: info@ifx.com   Web site: www.ifx.com
This company makes Piranha HD, which is a full-featured compositing,
effects, paint, and editing system for film and HD video, and Amazon Paint
3D, which is a 64-bit paint system for the SGI and Linux platforms.

IS Distribution

Home Farm, Shere Road, Albury, Guildford Surrey GU59RL, United
Kingdom
Office: 44-1483-205825   Fax: 44-1483-203078
E-mail: info@mokey.net   Web site: www.mokey.net
This company distributes Mokey, which is a software tool that separates
foreground and background elements without traditional keying tech-
niques. This software automatically produces a clean background clip and
a matte of the separated foreground element.

KDDI R&D Laboratories, Inc.

2-1-15 Ohara, Kamifukuoka-shi, Saitama 356-8502, Japan
Office: 81-492-78-7397   Fax: 81-492-78-7510
E-mail: sales@kddilabs.com   Web site: www.kddilabs.com
This company develops authoring software for mobile (MPEG-4) and fast
SDTV/HDTV MPEG nonlinear editing software.

Laird Telemedia

2000 Sterling Road, P.O. Box 720, Mount Marion, NY 12456
Office: (845) 339-9555   Fax: (845) 339-0231   Toll free: (800) 898-0759
E-mail: sales@lairdtelemedia.com   Web site: www.lairdtelemedia.com
This company supplies turnkey solutions for editing DV using Avid XpressDV. It is targeted toward broadcasters.

Leitch Incorporated

920 Corporate Lane, Chesapeake, VA 23320
Office: (757) 548-2300   Fax: (757) 548-0019   Toll free: (800) 231-9673
E-mail: leitch@leitch.com   Web site: www.leitch.com
Leitch manufactures postproduction equipment, including the dpsVelocityQ editing system (a multistream editor featuring real-time playback of four video streams), the dpsVelocityJ v8.0 editing system, the dpsRealityHD editing system, and the VR475 NEWSFlash-II FXJ that integrates DV- and MPEG-2-based editing in one system.

Lightworks, Inc.

2050 Bleury Street, Montreal, Quebec, H3A 2J5, Canada
Office: (514) 844-8555   Fax: (514) 844-3777
E-mail: sales@lwks.com   Web site: www.lwks.com
Lightworks manufactures the Lightworks Touch system.

Ligos Technology

55 Stockton Street, Suite 450, San Francisco, CA 94108
Office: (415) 249-0100   Fax: (415) 249-0150
E-mail: marcom@ligos.com   Web site: www.ligos.com
Ligos is the world's leading provider of real-time software media technology for consumer, enterprise, and postproduction applications. Ligos codec systems for MPEG-1, MPEG-2, and MPEG-4 provide software developers and video professionals the ability to encode, edit, and play back broadcast-quality video on standard PCs, and distribute streams across any network.

Linux Media Arts

10442A Rockport Circle, Reno, NV 89511
Office: (775) 852-7159   Fax: (775) 852-5053
E-mail: lmacorp@linuxmediaarts.com   Web site: www.linuxmediaarts.com
This company makes the Cineterra system that runs Linux and Broadcast
2000 open-source editing software.

Linux Media Labs

3190 Squaw Valley Drive, Colorado Springs, CO 80918
Office: (719) 231-3173   Fax: (719) 593-9452
E-mail: vleo@linuxmedialabs.com   Web site: www.linuxmedialabs.com
This company makes capture cards for the Linux platform.

MacroSystem US

5485 Conestoga Court, Boulder, CO 80301
Office: (303) 440-5311   Fax: (303) 440-5322
E-mail: rick@casablanca.tv   Web site: www.casablanca.tv
This company makes Casablanca Kron, Avio, and AvioDVPro standalone
editing appliances.

MainConcept AG

Elisabethstraße 1, 52062 Aachen, Germany
Office: 49-241-40 10 8-0   Fax: 49-241-40 10 810
E-mail: info@mainconcept.de   Web site: www.mainconcept.com
This company produces MainActor editing software for the Windows and
Linux platforms.

Mathematical Technologies, Inc.

209 Angell Street, Providence, RI 02906
Office: (401) 831-1315   Fax: (401) 831-1318
E-mail: info@mathtech.com   Web site: www.mathtech.com
IntelliDeck® 2002 is digital image and audio-processing software for Windows and SGI platforms that provides dust, dirt, and scratch removal, disk-to-disk color correction tools and audio resampling, pitch correction, and mixing.

Matrox

1055 St-Regis, Dorval, Quebec, H9P 2T4, Canada
Office: (514) 685-7230   Fax: (514) 685-2853
Web site: www.matrox.com
Matrox manufactures hardware for graphics and digital video editing. Its products include the Digisuite line of video capture cards for Premiere, Incite, and the RTMac for Final Cut Pro.

Medea Corp.

5701 Lindero Cyn Road, Building 3-100, Westlake Village, CA 91362
Office: (818) 597-7645   Fax: (818) 597-7643   Toll free: (888) BY-MEDEA
E-mail: sales@medeacorp.com   Web site: www.medea.com
Medea manufactures hard disk arrays for digital content creation featuring either the Ultra160 *Small Computer Systems Interface* (SCSI) or Fibre Channel interfaces at a reasonable cost.

Media 100

290 Donald Lynch Blvd., Marlboro, MA 01752-4748
Office: (508) 460-1600   Fax: (508) 481-8627
Web site: www.media100.com
This company manufactures turnkey editing systems. Its products include iFinish (Mac or Windows) and the 844/X system.

MediaWare Solutions

GPO Box 1985, Canberra ACT, 2601, Australia
Office: 61-2-6247-4438   Fax: 61-2-6247-4557
E-mail: info@MediawareSolutions.com
Web site:www.MediawareSolutions.com
This company produces MPEG asset management and editing software. Its
products include M2-edit Pro, M1-edit Pro, M2-edit CL, and dbFlix.

Miglia Technology Limited

Graphic House, Higham Mead, Chesham HP5 2AH, United Kingdom
Office: 44-(0)-870-7472988   Fax: 44-(0)-870-7472989
E-mail: info@miglia.com   Web site: www.miglia.com
This company makes external DV converters—Director's Cut Take 2 and
Director's Cut Take 1, and the Director's Cut PCI card—that are compati-
ble with DV editing software.

Miranda Technologies, Inc.

3499 Douglas-B, Floreani, Montreal, Quebec, H4S 2C6, Canada
Office: (514) 333-1772   Fax: (514) 333-9828
E-mail: ussales@miranda.com   Web site: www.miranda.com
This company produces hardware and software products for editing. Its
products include DV-Bridge Pro for DV encode/decode from RGB/YUV and
composite analog; DV-Bridge+, which adds conversion between DV on
IEEE-1394 to and from SDI; and Miranda MediaWorks, which is an asset
management solution.

Monal Systems

Rue Jean Baptiste Clément 135, Boulogne, F-92100, France
Office: 33-1-55-38-02-10   Fax: 33-1-55-38-02-11
E-mail: info@monalsystems.com   Web site: www.monalsystems.com
Monal Systems provides subtitling software for off- and online editing and
laser-subtitling film engravers.

Natural Tools

Gran via 86, Edif. España, Grupo 5, 240, Madrid, 28013, Spain
Office: 34-91-542-7976   Fax: 34-91-542-7028
E-mail: contact@naturaltools.tv   Web site: www.naturaltools.tv
Natural Tools develops software for the television and video industries. Natural New is a news editing and creation tool for stations.

NewTek

5131 Beckwith Blvd., San Antonio, TX 78249
Office: (210) 370-8000   Fax: (210) 370-8001   Toll free: (800) 847-6111
Web site: www.newtek.com
This company produces the Video Toaster 2 digital editing system.

Optibase, Inc.

1250 Space Park Way, Mountain View, CA 94040
Office: (650) 903-4900   Fax: (650) 969-6388   Toll free: (800) 451-5101
E-mail: sales_usa@optibase.com   Web site: www.optibase.com
This company makes MPEG MovieMaker encoders, VideoPump standard- and high-definition capture cards, and Clipper software.

Origin Systems

15 Station Road, Madeley, Telford TF7 5AY, United Kingdom
Office: 44-0701-0701-443   Fax: 44-0701-0701-453
E-mail: sales@origin-systems.co.uk   Web site: www.origin-systems.co.uk
This company makes the Optima turnkey digital editing system.

Panasonic Broadcast and Television Systems Company

1 Panasonic Way, Secacus, NJ 07094
Office: (201) 348-7621
Web site: www.panasonic.com/broadcast
Panasonic makes the DVedit, QuickCutter50, and NewsByte50 editing systems and other products for video production.

Pinnacle Systems

280 North Bernardo Avenue, Mountain View, CA 94043
Office: (650) 526-1600   Fax: (650) 526-1601
Web site: www.pinnaclesys.com
This company develops digital media creation, storage, management, and distribution systems. Its products include Pinnacle Studio 7, Vortex News, Targa Cinewave, and Targa 3000.

Pixel Power Ltd.

College Business Park, Coldhams Lane, Cambridge CB1 3HD, United Kingdom
Office: 44-1223-721000   Fax: 44-1223-721111
E-mail: jgilbert@pixelpower.com   Web site:www.pixelpower.com
This company supplies character generators, still/clip stores, and paint/animation workstations based on proprietary hardware (Collage2 and Graphite2) or on the Windows platform (Clarity2) in standard- and high-definition configurations.

Profound Effects

3900 Meridian Circle, Verona, WI 53593
Office: (608) 573-5775   Fax: (608) 829-1094
E-mail: sales@profoundeffects.com   Web site: www.profoundeffects.com
This company supplies After Effects and Avid AVX plug-ins, including Elastic Gasket, which runs After Effects plug-ins on Avid systems; Move, which is a pan and zoom high-resolution plug-in for Avid editing systems; and Useful Things, which is a user-programmable plug-in factory.

Quantel

Turnpike Road, Newbury, Berkshire RG14 2NX, United Kingdom
Office: 44-(0)-1635-48222   Fax: 44-(0)-1635-31776
Web site: www.quantel.com
This company manufactures graphics and digital editing systems for professionals. Its products include eQ, which is a slower version of the iQ for standard and high definition at half the price of the iQ; Qeffects, which is a Windows software version of iQ with the identical toolset for editing and compositing at PC prices; and Qpaintbox, which is a Windows version of Quantel's proprietary Paintbox system. All are *Advanced Authoring Format* (AAF) compliant.

Roxio, Inc.

455 El Camino Real, Santa Clara, CA 95050
Office: (408) 367-3100   Fax: (408) 367-3101
E-mail: sales@roxio.com   Web site: www.roxio.com
This company provides Cinematic and VideoWave 5 editing software, and VideoPack DVD authoring software for the Windows platform.

SCM Microsystems

47211 Bayside Parkway, Fremont, CA 94538
Office: (510) 360-2300   Fax: (510) 360-0211   Toll free: (888) 212-8045
E-mail: scmmicro5@custhelp.com   Web site: www.dazzle.com
This company produces the Dazzle Digital Video Creator, Dazzle DV-Editor, and Dazzle DV-Bridge lines of products for digital video applications.

SGO Holding Company

Gran via 86, Edif España, Group 5, Floor 2428013, Madrid, Spain
Office: 34-91-542-79-76   Fax: 34-91-542-70-28
E-mail: cdiaz@sgo.es   Web site: www.sgo.es
SGO Holding Company supplies Jaleo and Jaleo HD editing and compositing software for SGI O2, Octane, and Onyx2 Irix platforms.

Skymicro, Inc.

2060D Avenue Los Arboles PMB344, Thousand Oaks, CA 91362-1361
Office: (805) 590-0188   Fax: (805) 590-0187
E-mail: sales@skymicro.com   Web site: www.skymicro.com
This company makes the Merlin DV and MPEG-2 capture card with SDI
and composite inputs, and analog-to-SDI converter boxes.

Snell and Wilcox

2225-I Martin Ave. Santa Clara, CA 95050
Office: (408) 260-1000   Fax: (408) 260-2800   Toll free: (800) 827-4544
E-mail: info@snellamerica.com   Web site: www.snellwilcox.com
Snell and Wilcox manufactures digital imaging products for television, postproduction, and digital cinema applications, including Splicer, a Java application used to conform standard- and high-definition programs that runs on
the Windows and Irix platforms.

SoftLab-NSK Ltd.

Universitetskii pr. 1, Novosibirsk 630090, Russia
Office: 7-(3832)-399220   Fax: 7-(3832)-332173
E-mail: multimedia@softlab-nsk.com   Web site: www.softlab-nsk.com
This company develops multimedia software and hardware. Its products
include DDClip Pro (SE and LE editing software) and Forward (a hardware
and editing software bundle).

Sonic Desktop Software

9836 White Oak Avenue, Suite 209, Northridge, CA 91325
Office: (818) 718-9999   Fax: (818) 718-9990   Toll free: (800) 454-1900
E-mail: info@sonicdesktop.com   Web site: www.smartsound.com
SmartSound Sonicfire Pro is soundtrack creation software based on
patented SmartSound technology, which enables users to generate concise,
professional soundtracks of any length in minutes.

Sonic Foundry

1617 Sherman Avenue, Madison, WI 53704
Office: (608) 256-3133   Fax: (608) 256-7300   Toll free: (800) 577-6642
Web site: www.sonicfoundry.com
Sonic Foundry develops tools for the creation, editing, and publishing of digital multimedia.

Sony Electronics, Inc.

1 Sony Drive, Park Ridge, NJ 07656
Office: (201) 930-1000   Fax: (201) 930-4752
Web site: www.sony.com/professional
Sony makes the Xpri digital video editing system and thousands of other products for video production.

Strata Software

567 South Valley View Drive, Suite 202, St. George, Utah 84770
Office: (435) 628-5218   Fax: (435) 628-9756   Toll free: (800) 678-7282
E-mail: sales@strata.com   Web site: www.strata.com
This company produces Strata DVplus and Strata DVpro editing software for Mac and Windows platforms.

Synthetic Aperture

31011 Via Errecarte, San Juan Capistrano, CA 92675
Office: (949) 493-3444   Fax: (949) 203-2108
E-mail: sales@synthetic.ap.com   Web site: www.synthetic-ap.com
Synthetic Aperture creates plug-in tools for video editing and production, including Color Finesse, which is an advanced resolution-independent telecine-style color corrector for After Effects and Final Cut Pro, and Echo Fire, which is a real-time *National Television Systems Committee* (NTSC)/*Phase Alternating Line* (PAL) video preview tool for After Effects and Photoshop.

Synthetik Software

Seven Waterfront Plaza, 500 Ala Moana Blvd., Suite 400, Honolulu,
HI 96813
Office: (866) 511-9971   Fax: (808) 261-1837
E-mail: info@synthetik.com   Web site: www.synthetik.com
This company produces Studio Artist 2.0, the only software that automatically rotoscopes video with over 2,000 editable intelligent painting tools.

SysMedia Limited

Gatwick House, Peeks Brook Lane, Horley, Surrey RH6 9ST, United
Kingdom
Office: 44-1293-814-200   Fax: 44-1293-814-300
E-mail: sales@sysmedia.com   Web site: www.sysmedia.com
SysMedia develops solutions for DVD, closed caption, open caption, and
DVB subtitling. Their family of subtitling products offers the latest nonlinear video technology with combined offline-live subtitling preparation tools.

Technical Animations and Video

640 Pearson, Suite 302, Des Plaines, IL 60016
Office: (847) 297-1000   Fax: (847) 297-4820   Toll free: (888) 447-4935
E-mail: sales@techanim.com   Web site: www.techanim.com
Technical Animations and Video specializes in 3D animation and video editing software and training materials for Discreet 3D Studio Max, Combustion 2, Character Studio 3, and Adobe products.

TerraTec ProAudio, Inc. (Fostex Corporation of America)

15431 Blackburn Avenue, Norwalk, CA 90650
Office: (562) 921-1112   Fax: (562) 802-1964
E-mail: info-us@terratec.net   Web site: www.terratec-us.com
This company makes the Cameo line of IEEE-1394 cards. The Cameo 200
DV includes a Cameo 200 DV card and Cyberlink PowerDirector Pro 2.0 DE
software. The Cameo 400 and 600 are bundled with Media StudioPro.

Thomson Multimedia

17 Rue du Petit Albi, B.P. 8244 Cergy-Pontoise, F-95801, France
Office: 33-134-20-70-00   Fax: 33-134-20-70-47
E-mail: marketing@thomsonbroadcast.com   Web site: www.thomson-broadcast.com
This company manufactures hundreds of products, including Surf Proxy editor and EditStream, a news editing solution for broadcasters based on a *storage area network* (SAN).

Trapcode

Ihres v 13, 75263, Uppsala, Sweden
Office: 46-7-030-38-855   Fax: 46-7-184-61-864
E-mail: peder@trapcode.com   Web site: www.trapcode.com
Trapcode develops graphics and audio plug-ins. Its products include Shine for After Effects, which makes fast light rays.

Ulead Systems

20000 Mariner Avenue, Suite 200, Torrance, CA 90503
Office: (310) 896-6388   Fax: (310) 896-6389   Toll free: (800) 858-5323
E-mail: info@ulead.com   Web site: www.ulead.com
This company supplies video, imaging, DVD authoring, and Internet graphics software for the PC. Ulead's products are technically advanced yet intuitive in design and give users intelligently creative tools to accomplish design objectives.

United Media, Inc.

4771 East Hunter, Anaheim, CA 92807
Office: (714) 777-4510   Fax: (714) 777-2434
E-mail: sales@unitedmediainc.com   Web site: www.unitedmediainc.com
Multicam and On-Line Express digital editing software supports Matrox hardware running on the Windows platform.

Video3

6385 Old Shady Oak Road, Suite 290, Eden Prairie, MN 55344
Office: (952) 925-8858   Fax: (952) 915-1198
E-mail: sales@webAdTV.com   Web site: www.videocubed.com
Video3 is a developer of digital asset management solutions and offers an online suite of tools focused on leveraging an organization's rich-media assets. Video3's current products offer users a cost-effective solution for video archiving, retrieval, editing, and streaming.

Visual Infinity, Inc.

455 Spadina Avenue, Suite 208, Toronto, Ontario, M5S 2G8, Canada
Office: (416) 596-0931   Fax: (416) 596-2377   Toll free: (877) 596-0931
E-mail: mail@visInf.com   Web site: www.visinf.com or www.grain-surgery.com
This company manufactures Grain Surgery, an intelligent noise manipulation plug-in for After Effects, FCP, Commotion, and Avid. This product removes film grain, video noise, and compression artifacts while preserving detail. It can be used to match the noise between two scenes or add realistic grain to your HD or DV project.

VITEC Multimedia

556 Weddell Drive, Suite 3, Sunnyvale, CA 94089
Office: (408) 752-8483   Fax: (408) 752-8486
E-mail: usa_info@vitecmm.com   Web site: www.vitecmm.com
This company's products include Video CLIP MPEG-2 Pro, DVD Toolbox, *DVD Cut Machine* (DCM), and MPEGProfiler for the Windows platform.

Script for Exercise: The Dicey Question

by Adam Gooder

FADE IN:

INT. STEEL RESTAURANT KITCHEN - DAY

A young man and woman, both in their early 20s, JEFF and MOLLY, stand side by side at a waist-high counter, peeling and chopping vegetables in preparation for a big stew. They wear white smocks and paper chef's hats. The raw vegetables are piled between them. She chops carrots. It's quiet, as the restaurant is not yet open. The steel kitchen, with its giant freezers, ovens, mixers, bowls, pots, and utensils, is behind them.

Molly chops vigorously, having found a rhythm. Jack is distracted. He glances at her hands, her neck. Her close proximity makes him nervous. He's been trying to think of something casual to say for the last 10 minutes.

> JEFF
> Hey. Where did you learn to
> chop so fast?

> MOLLY
> (distracted)
> Same place as you, here,
> remember?

She turns to look at the soup kettle.

> Come on, soup's on in half
> an hour.

> JEFF
> Oh. I mean, you've got
> really nice hands.

She blows the hair out of her eyes. She's not really listening.

                      MOLLY
              Nice hands?

He's stopped peeling. He's about to say more.
Beat. She thinks for a moment, stops chopping, and
notices that he's stopped. He snaps out of it and
resumes peeling.

                      MOLLY
                  (Grinning)
            Are you asking me out?

                      JEFF
            No....Not really.

                      MOLLY
                  (pauses)
            Well, cuz if you did,
            I might say yes.

                      JEFF
        Aggh!

He drops the knife and carrot. He's cut himself on
the finger. He's bleeding.

                      MOLLY
                (Grimmacing)
        Oh no!

She quickly drops her knife, grabs the clean white
towel on the table, and covers his hand with hers,
gently applying pressure. Beat. She looks at him.
He looks at her. He looks at his hand in hers.

                      JEFF
        So, you want to go grab
        dinner sometime?

                    MOLLY
                 (laughs)
        No food, okay? How about a
        movie?

                    JEFF
        Yeah, but not one with too
        much blood and gore in it,
        okay?

They laugh together.

FADE OUT.

INDEX

ABOUT THE AUTHORS

Robert M. Goodman is an Emmy-nominated director and an award-winning writer/producer whose work has appeared on PBS and in dozens of countries around the world. He's a contributing editor for *The Independent Film & Video Monthly* and an acknowledged expert in digital production who has reviewed every major editing system introduced since 1994. Goodman has presented workshops at the major film festivals in Los Angeles, New York, San Francisco, Atlanta, and for AIVF, IFP, SMPTE, Women in Film, and the Sony Corporation. He's been profiled on Bravo's *Split Screen* and is the co-producer of *Stone Reader*, which won the top awards—the Audience Award for Best Feature Film and a Grand Jury Special Honor—at the 2002 Slamdance Film Festival.

Patrick J. McGrath is a faculty member at the Art Institute of Philadelphia and an Avid-certified instructor who has taught the art of editing to thousands of students over the past decade. As an independent producer, his recent projects have included commercials, documentaries, and over 70 live concert performances. During his long careers as Executive Producer of Bell Atlantic Corporate Television, McGrath produced nearly one thousand programs and has won business, industry and teaching awards for his work. He has been a professional video editor since 1974.

Both authors live in Philadelphia.